COMPUTERS

WILEY

COMPUTERS

INTRODUCTION TO COMPUTERS AND APPLIED COMPUTING CONCEPTS

Charles H. Davidson

Eldo C. Koenig

University of Wisconsin

JOHN WILEY AND SONS, Inc.   New York London Sydney

Library of Congress Catalog Card Number: 67-19447
Printed in the United States of America

Preface

The computer exercises such an important and widespread influence on our society today that any educated person needs to understand something about it. With this thesis, the authors undertook in 1962 to establish a broad but intensive survey course for the general nontechnical college student, aimed at showing him what a computer is, how to talk to it and use it, and what its principal uses and their social and economic implications are in the world around us. Although such a student may never use a computer again, he will encounter a computer every week of his life in an ever increasing variety of ways.

For the continuing college student, the text should prepare him for the use of computers in later problem-solving courses, and should help to inspire him to take more advanced courses in the computer sciences. For the student who approaches the subject only for its cultural value, or because of a general interest or curiosity, the text should bring an understanding of the field that will be useful in any other field of endeavor, and an appreciation of the role of the computer in the world around him. It can serve as an excellent introduction for selected high school students, with ample freedom for the teacher to select those aspects of the subject he wishes to emphasize. For the more mature undergraduate or graduate student with a minimum of mathematical training, the book can be the basis for a more advanced course in computing in which a greater amount of the text material and a larger number of problems are worked than in an earlier computing course for less experienced students.

Finally, for the mature layman in whatever field, use of the book as a self study text can help him acquire an awareness and an understanding of what the computer is all about and the effects it is having in today's society.

All the experience gained in teaching computers since 1950 has reinforced our conviction that the use of computers cannot be taught in a vacuum—there must be a real computer to write for and actually run programs on. Consequently the course is built around the do-it-yourself principle. Students are taught early the rudiments of FORTRAN programming, and thereafter as each new area of application is taken up, they actually do simplified, watered down, illustrative examples on the computer showing the problems and the advantages of the use of the computer in such applications. During the course of the semester students write and run programs in such assorted areas as roots of polynomials, sorting and table look-up, business data processing, inventory control, tracking a satellite, library information retrieval, game playing, and many others.

FORTRAN was chosen as the principal language because it is the most nearly universal programming language available today, and because the use of a high-level language enables the student (or anyone else) to bridge the gap more quickly between formulating and specifying his problem, and writing out instructions for a computer to produce answers to that problem. We see no reason why the general student, who will be at best only a sometime programmer, should be forced to wade through the far more detailed intricacies of machine language before being handed the much easier symbolic and algebraic languages, just so he will "understand better what is going on inside the computer." It is not necessary for him to understand at that level of detail in order to understand what a computer can do and cannot do, and how it can be made to do it. We suspect that some of the motivation behind this from-the-ground-up pedagogical approach is the fact that *we* had to learn it that way, and we want today's generation to suffer too.

Many years of professional experience have guided the development and teaching of this text over a four year period to over 1000 students in many different teaching situations. It is intended to give a gradual and logical approach to the explanation of the fascinating subject of computing, to develop and illustrate some of the underlying concepts clearly but without mathematical rigor, and to afford a working knowledge of programming. The methods of presentation are those that have been found most successful during the teaching experience with individuals having a wide variety of backgrounds and a minimum of mathematics. Although the primary objective has been clarity, accomplished by the liberal use of examples and applications, the question of fundamentals has been kept constantly in mind and introduced whenever possible and in a way that is consistent with the mathematical prerequisite. It is hoped that some appreciation of the fundamentals will be developed in students of the book, particularly those who will be inspired to take more advanced courses in computer sciences and computational methods.

The first part of the book constitutes a presentation of the elementary FORTRAN language. It has been written with complete awareness that many students have little aptitude for programming, although the illustrative uses of the language do assume a level of intelligence that may reasonably be expected of above average high school seniors, and of college or university freshmen.

The latter part of the book covers mainly topics important to the understanding of the general field of computing. These are treated with progressively more conciseness in keeping with the increased comprehension of the motivated student. This policy has been followed also in the illustrative flow charts and programs and in the problems. Sections in these later chapters may be reasonably omitted and the simpler problems assigned when the text is used for an early course for high school seniors or for college freshmen.

In the authors' use of the text for a one semester, three credit liberal arts course, approximately 80% of the material is covered in thirty 50-minute lectures, meeting twice a week, and the material is supplemented, discussed, and practiced in a 2-hour discussion/laboratory meeting once a week. Material most often omitted includes parts of Sections 5.5 and 5.6, Section 8.5, parts of Sections 9.3, 9.4, and 10.4, most of Section 12.3, and portions of Chapter 15.

Many more problems are included than can hope to be programmed in this time period, but our experience has found that, given good access to a computer system with fast turnaround and good diagnostics, most students can complete between 20 and 30 programming problems (where parts (a) and (b) of a problem count as separate programs). The instructor is encouraged to experiment freely with these and other excellent problems such as those found in *Programs for Computer Solution* by Gruenberger and Jaffray, Wiley, 1965.

It might be noted, finally, as an illustration of the wide range of computer applications discussed in the book, that the index to the book itself was prepared using a computer program on the IBM 1620 written by Barton G. Prieve.

The authors appreciate the valuable suggestions and experience received from college and high school teachers who took advanced introductory courses in summer institutes using this text. Appreciation is also expressed to the teaching assistants who have participated over the past four years, in particular Joyce Fodor, Rochelle Wilson, Thomas Talbot, Ray Hamel, and Robert Wilson, who assisted in the programming of many of the problems and in the writing of first versions of several of the chapters, and to Tom Kroncke and Robert Claeson who developed NOPE and SADSIM respectively. Valuable criticism and comments have been made by several of our colleagues, particularly Richard McCoy and Donald Dietmeyer. To Patricia Rardin, Gloria Koenig, Bert Wilson, and many others, go our thanks for the accurate typing and retyping of the manuscript, to the point where any residual mistakes are the authors' own fault.

CHARLES H. DAVIDSON
ELDO C. KOENIG

April, 1967

Contents

CHAPTER 1.

The Information Machine

1.1 WHY IS IT IMPORTANT?

NEW COMPUTER TO SPEED OPERATIONS
AT MAIN NATIONAL BANK

said the headline in this morning's paper.

"The IBM 7094 Computer," said the television announcer bringing us the latest election returns, "predicts Smith will be elected with a 53% majority."

When we watched the last astronaut blast off, it was the computer that decided swiftly and unhesitatingly whether the proper orbit had been achieved, and therefore whether to continue the flight.

The last time we paid an insurance premium, registered for a class, made a reservation for an airline flight, or received a paycheck, it was very likely an IBM card or a computer-printed document that we handled.

Whenever there is information to be sent, recorded, remembered, dug up, worked on, worked over, taken apart, put together, put back, sorted, merged, compared, compiled, presented, or thrown away—then we are likely to find an automatic computer. Processing information—doing in fact almost everything imaginable to it except ignoring it—is the peculiar capability of this electronic creation. Let us think of it for a while as an "information machine."

We want to look at some of the kinds of information our information machine processes, some of the kinds of processing it does, and to what end it works. We shall try to get a picture of what kinds of things go on inside computers, what their capabilities are, and how these capabilities have led to their use in various kinds of applications.

We do not intend to study these applications solely by hearing about them. This is a "do it yourself" course in computer appreciation. *There is no better way to appreciate what computers can be made to accomplish, and how they are told what to accomplish, than to learn how to tell them yourself.* We will start by learning enough of one language for talking to a computer (FORTRAN) so that we can give it simple instructions and make it do simple problems. Then, each time we learn about a new capability of the computer, and look at some of the corresponding areas of application that have grown up, we shall actually work out and run on the computer some sample problems of the type we are talking about.

One of the best computers for learning on is the IBM 1620 Data Processing System, better known as a 1620 Computer (Figure 1.1-1). Although not the most recent computer on the market, it is of the modern generation of computers in that it is a solid-state machine. By

Figure 1.1-1

that we mean merely that its memory or storage element is made of solid-state devices (magnetic cores instead of moving mechanical parts), and that its main logic and control circuitry is likewise of solid-state transistors and diodes instead of vacuum tubes.

The 1620 is not particularly fast; to add two 8-digit decimal numbers, for instance, keeping complete track of the decimal point, takes it almost $\frac{1}{1000}$ of a second. But even though that is pretty slow compared with some of its bigger brothers, the modern high-speed computing giants, this computer is still fast enough and powerful enough so that we can learn to employ on it just about all the techniques of programming and problem solving that have made automatic computers such a fundamental and indispensable part of the world around us today.

In the ensuing treatment we shall assume that there is available at least an IBM 1620 on which to try out the ideas that we shall be talking about. We do not mean, of course, that this is the only computer which can be used; any computer with a reasonably powerful and easy-to-use FORTRAN processor will work fine. But the 1620 is a good choice for two reasons: it is in extremely wide use in schools and colleges all over the country (and indeed the world), and there has been developed for the 1620 a processing system called FORGO which is extremely well adapted to teaching FORTRAN to inexperienced programmers.

1.2   WHAT CAN IT DO?

The automatic computer is a new, and to many people, a mysterious thing. What can we compare it with to get an idea of its capabilities?

One of the most ancient devices that has been used to help people manipulate numbers is the Chinese abacus (Figure 1.2-1). Although in the hands of a skilled operator this makes possible extremely rapid arithmetic operations, it should not properly be called a computer or even a calculator. It does no processing of information itself, but merely keeps score of the results of the operations performed by the human operator.

The engineering slide rule shown in Figure 1.2-2 comes closer to satisfying the definition of a computer, for, by the way it is constructed, it converts the simple operations of adding and subtracting lengths on a stick to higher mathematical operations like multiplying and finding logarithms. With proper care a slide rule may be of considerable assistance in complicated scientific and engineering calculations, and in many situations where you would hate to grind out all the arithmetic calculations by hand, it is a real lifesaver.

Figure 1.2-1   Abacus

Unfortunately, as its users well know, a slide rule won't do everything. It is of no help at all in addition, for instance. Nor can it be used if a precision of more than 3 figures is needed; one-half of 1% is approximately the limit of its useful accuracy.

For such a problem—say an atomic physics calculation to 5 significant figures, or even a bank balance accurate to the exact number of dollars and cents—another kind of mechanical aid to computation, the desk calculator, comes in very handy.

Now, these desk calculators (the Friden, shown in Figure 1.2-3, the

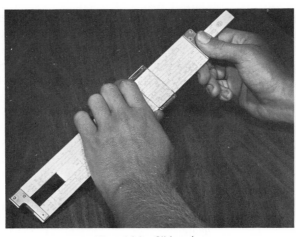

Figure 1.2-2   Slide rule.

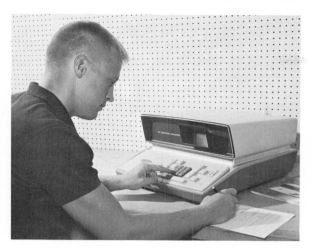

Figure 1.2-3   Desk calculator.

Marchand, or the Monroe) have been pretty well refined so that they will perform any of the four basic arithmetic operations—add, subtract, multiply, or divide—upon the touch of a single button. Furthermore, they will perform them so fast that by the time you have entered 1 number, entered another number, pushed "divide," picked up your pencil, and found your place on the page, the answer will be sitting on the dials looking at you. In other words, the calculator can handle the arithmetic about as fast as the operator can feed the data and the instructions to it.

If this is true, if the desk calculator can keep up with the operator now, why should we want a faster computer? Why should we want a high-speed computer that can do arithmetic hundreds or thousands of times faster than this? How would we ever keep it busy?

The answer, of course, lies in the repetitive nature of so much of modern computation. If you had to give the high-speed computer a new instruction for every operation it performed, of course its great speed would be wasted. But if we apply it to a problem where the same set of operations needs to be carried out many, many times, then we can afford to build a computer with a very high rate of internal operations.

Look at a simple example. Suppose somebody asked you to evaluate an algebraic expression that looked like this:

$$y = 4x - \sqrt{7 + x^3} \qquad (1.1\text{-}1)$$

for, say, $x = 2.3$, but you want the answer to 5 significant figures. How would you go about it?

You would probably have to sit down with pencil and paper and start figuring. You would multiply x by x, and that by x again, then add 7. The square root might slow you down a bit, and maybe you would want to go to a set of tables if you did not remember how to take it yourself. Or, if you knew a little about a desk calculator and had one handy, you might use that to help. One way or another, you get the square root, then subtract it from the result of multiplying 4 by x. Behold, the answer is y. Whatever the method you use, you would have the answer much faster than if you were to try writing a program to have the computer calculate it for you. It would be ridiculous to use the computer for such a problem.

But now suppose we change the statement of the problem a little. Suppose we want to find

$$y = 4x - \sqrt{7 + x^3} \qquad \text{where } x = 0 \ (0.1) \ 20 \qquad (1.2\text{-}1)$$

as before, but now we are asked for a table of values from x equaling the initial value, 0, increasing in steps of 0.1, until it reaches a maximum of 20. In other words, we want y for $x = 0$, then y for $x = 0.1$, then for $x = 0.2$, and so on out to y for $x = 20$. Now, how would you go about doing the problem?

Do you want to sit down to do the job by hand calculation? You could probably finish it, but perhaps not on the same day you started. Even with a desk calculator, the job would be long, tedious, and distasteful. Doing the same thing 201 times! What a stupid, crank-grinding type of assignment!

Please note that this is exactly the kind of situation in which the human performs very poorly—a lot of repetitive routine calculations, that quickly get boring and tedious. And not only does the human resent the waste of time, he soon starts to make mistakes. The longer it goes on, the worse he gets. What an ideal spot for an automatic computer!

Let us take a closer look at this mysterious creation, the information machine. What sort of creature is it? The Sunday supplements, and the popular writers, have for years liked to call computers "giant brains," or "machines that think." We shall see that a much better name would be "giant moron." Nevertheless, even a giant moron, once you learn how to use it, can be a very useful slave.

What can this moron do? Basically, nothing but arithmetic. Figure 1.2-4 shows a functional block diagram of a generalized digital computer. At the heart of *any* automatic digital computer is a device for performing arithmetic operations accurately, reliably, and at high speed. As we have indicated, however, its high speed capability would be wasted here if, for each of its operations, it had to come back and get its numbers

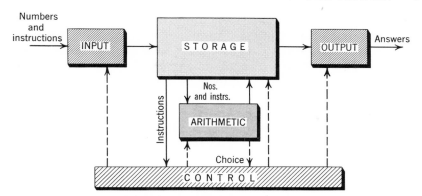

Figure 1.2-4   Any automatic digital computer.

and instructions directly from us, the users. It can operate much more efficiently if we provide an electronic storage or memory, with which the arithmetic unit can communicate at electronic speeds.

Stored in this memory are three kinds of information: data, numbers to be sent to the arithmetic unit to work with; results received from the arithmetic unit; and the list of instructions for what to do next, called a "program." Having this list of instructions stored in the high-speed memory not only makes it possible to read out this list at high speed as each instruction is needed, it also makes it possible to read out the list over and over again, when the calculations are to be repeated. Furthermore, having the instructions stored in the memory, just like the numbers themselves, makes it possible for the computer to modify the instructions themselves as the calculation progresses. The power gained from this method of operation—of storing the program in the high-speed memory itself—is tremendous, and we shall see several examples later on of operations that are possible only because of this.

To regulate the flow of information among the various parts of the computer, we have an elaborate network called a control section. Its job is to interpret the coded instructions and translate them into the proper set of voltages and timing signals in order to get all the other units to dig out the right pieces of information, perform the right manipulations on them, and put them away in the right places. These control functions are shown as dotted lines in Figure 1.2-4. You will note that the control gets to stick its fingers into everything else that is going on.

The last two units, the input and output, serve as buffering devices between the computer and the outside world. Specifically, the input unit can take in information at the slow rate the human can say it, either directly or through a mechanical contraption such as a typewriter or card reader, and spit it out again at a rate fast enough to keep up with the high-speed memory itself. The output unit works the other way around; the control unit can have some answers transferred at high speed from the memory to the output unit, and then the processing unit can go ahead with more computations while the output unit chugs away at the slow job of putting out those answers in a form humans can make use of them.

At doing arithmetic, then, this computer can run rings around humans. It has three uncontested areas of superiority:

(1) *speed.* Modern transistor circuitry can carry out entire arithmetic operations in microseconds that the human mind needs tenths of seconds or seconds to complete. Furthermore, it never pauses. Operation follows right upon operation. The computer is at least 1000 times faster, and sometimes millions of times faster;

(2) *accuracy* or, more accurately, precision. The computer can work with several digits at a time, as easily as with one;

(3) *reliability.* A modern computer demands a performance figure of less than 1 error in 10 billion operations. It is not affected by boredom, fatigue, or complicated numbers to work with.

In speed, accuracy, and reliability, then, the computer has it all over the poor human. What are the shortcomings of the computer? Why should it be called a moron?

(1) It has an extremely *low intelligence.* It cannot figure out anything for itself. It must be told exactly what to do, in complete detail down to the *n*th degree. You cannot expect a computer to exercise the slightest bit of judgment or common sense. The one instruction nobody has built into a computer yet is, "You know what I mean!"

(2) It has a very *limited language*-handling capacity. Its vocabulary is tiny—some 50 or 100 words. Its grammar and syntax are primitive, and it insists that you use its own medium—holes punched in tapes or cards—when you have something to say to it. This small vocabulary means, for instance, that it can understand and carry out only the most basic arithmetic operations, together with a few simple control functions like compare and stop. All of the mathematical operations must be broken down into a carefully spelled out step-by-step procedure of just these basic operations.

(3) It has a complete *inability to learn.* No matter how many times you tell it the same thing, you must always tell it all over again, in just as much detail as the very first time. This is perhaps the shortcoming hardest to forgive, and the one in which a great deal of brilliant research is being concentrated today. If we could find out how to build a com-

puter that could learn, we could overcome most of the rest of these deficiencies.

So, there you have it—a giant moron. All in all, not a bad nickname to keep in mind as you learn how to program for a digital computer. Imagine you had available a complete but willing moron, who is nevertheless a skillful and efficient desk-calculator operator. If you keep in mind how you would have to explain to *him* the steps he must do to solve your problem, you have gone a long way toward learning to program an automatic computer to do your problem.

1.3 HOW DO YOU TELL IT WHAT TO DO?

Let us write out in detail all the explanations you would have to give this moron to solve one simple little problem. We will take the equation we were looking at awhile ago:

$$y = 4x - \sqrt{7 + x^3} \tag{1.3-1}$$

over the range of x from 0 in steps of 0.1 to a maximum of 20. How do we start?

Well, the most important thing to get across to our moron is the exact nature of the function we are going to ask him to evaluate. Now, to a computer, the nature of a function means what arithmetic operations, carried out in what sequence of steps, does it imply? So the language of algebra for computers lays particular stress on stating those operations very clearly within the framework of what can be typed on one line or punched on a card. We would probably state the function something like this:

$$y = 4 \cdot x - \sqrt{7 + x \cdot x \cdot x}$$

In this case it is just a single equation. In other problems it might take many lines.

We will symbolize this statement of the calculations to be done—this set of step-by-step instructions to our desk calculater operator for calculating y from x—this way, in a block called a calculation block, and represent it as in Figure 1.3-1*a*.

Calculate
$y = f(x)$

Figure 1.3-1*a*   Calculate block.

If this set of instructions is given to our moron now with the command to go ahead and calculate, we shall encounter some frustrating responses. On the one hand, Moron will readily admit the instructions for calculating y from x are completely clear, but at the same time will insist it is impossible to start. Why? Because we have not said what number to use for x.

Trying hard to be completely explicit, we say to start with $x = 0$, and when that is finished to go back and do the same calculation again for all the rest of the values of x. We even draw a picture—Figure 1.3-1b.

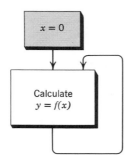

Figure 1.3-1b   Initialization block.

Unfortunately, when we come back a while later to see how it is doing, we find it still working on $x = 0$. Not that it has not finished even once, but it is just doing the same calculation over and over again. Why? Because we did not tell it explicitly to change x, or how to change x. What is needed is an additional box like the one shown in Figure 1.3-1c.

If we call x_{now} the value of x we are working with at any particular time, and x_{next} the next value of x, then

$$x_{next} = x_{now} + \Delta x$$

which says: x_{next}, the new x, is obtained by taking the old value x_{now} and increasing it by the increment in x, called delta x. More specifically, as we see in Figure 1.3-1c, all we need to do is add a box which says:

$$x = x + 0.1$$

or, "add one-tenth to x and put it back." Now when Moron finishes calculating for one value of x, it will step x to the next value before repeating the calculation.

This time we set it to do the calculations with high hopes that at last the moron has it through its thick skull what to do. When we return, we find it is indeed working on an x fairly far down the line.

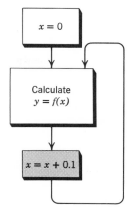

Figure 1.3-1c   Substitution block.

"Fine," we say. "Let us look at your list of answers."

"Answers? What answers? You did not say anything about answers."

The moron is right. We didn't.

Back to the drawing board goes our set of instructions to add another statement. This time we insert a block calling for the moron to list an answer for each time around, before it throws away the old one and starts calculating a new one.

Now, in Figure 1.3-1d, at last we have a program that will produce a

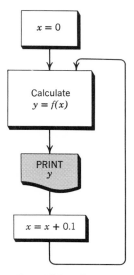

Figure 1.3-1d   Output.

complete set of the calculations we want. There are still, however, two more changes that it is desirable for us to make.

For one thing, when we look at the long list of answers shown in Figure 1.3-2a, 201 of them, we find it a bit confusing to extract any given answer from the list. How do we find the value of y for $x = 6.3$, for instance? The only way here is to carefully count our way down from the beginning until we come to the 64th one, and triumphantly seize upon that number as the answer we are looking for. A tedious procedure, and one full of possibilities for mistakes. After a moment's reflection on the manner in which tables are usually printed, we realize that the result of our calculations would be much more useful if we asked Moron to list both the current value of x, and the associated value of y, side by side, as in Figure 1.3-2b. Now our answer will look like this, making it a simple matter to read off y for any given value of x.

One more feature, however, had better be included to compensate for Moron's extreme literal-mindedness. It has to be told to stop when the problem is done. This, in turn, means it has to be told how to tell when the problem *is* done. Since in this problem we have a definite range of x over which we want the calculation made, we can instruct Moron to compare the new value of x every time it increases x to see whether it is still within the desired range: if so, go back through the loop again; if not, stop.

Our symbolic set of program steps for the process of comparing and choosing between two alternatives looks like Figure 1.3-1e. All automatic computers have simple comparison or testing procedures like this built

	X	Y
−2.6458	0.0000	−2.6458
−2.2459	.1000	−2.2459
−1.8473	.2000	−1.8473
−1.4508	.3000	−1.4508
−1.0578	.4000	−1.0578
−.6693	.5000	−.6693
−.2863	.6000	−.2863
.0902	.7000	.0902
.4592	.8000	.4592
.8199	.9000	.8199
1.1716	1.0000	1.1716
1.5137	1.1000	1.5137
1.8457	1.2000	1.8457
2.1673	1.3000	2.1673
2.4785	1.4000	2.4785
2.7790	1.5000	2.7790
3.0689	1.6000	3.0689

(a) Unidentified answers   (b) Answers with identification

Figure 1.3-2   Results of problem of Figure 1.3-1.

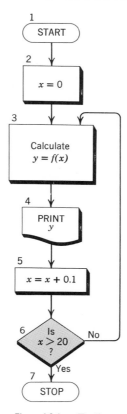

Figure 1.3-1e   Testing.

into them, and the necessary instructions for making the test are included in their vocabulary. In fact, it is exactly this ability to make a simple decision, limited though it is, that gives the computer what claim it does have to be able to think. Computers can be programmed to do some pretty complicated analyses of some very complex situations, but the complicated procedures are all made up of nothing but sequences and combinations of just such simple binary choices as this one.

Let us review this procedure for instructing our giant moron how to do a problem. The set of step-by-step instructions we have to write is called a program. The diagram, which symbolizes the operations, is called a flow chart or flow diagram. A flow diagram helps in two ways:

(1) Flow diagrams often summarize the effects of whole groups of operations in terms of final accomplishments of these groups. For example, look at Block 3.

(2) It gives a pictorial chart of the pattern or sequence of calculations, indicating at a glance what follows what.

As the problem gets more and more complicated, the flow chart becomes more and more necessary. Even in the most complicated cases, however, we find that the building blocks are essentially the 5 types we have been considering here, as shown in Figure 1.3-3.

(1) The set-up or *initialization* block. In this problem, it consists merely of specifying the initial value of x, namely, $x_0 = 0$.

(2) The operation or *calculation* block. This is the first block we worked out, No. 3 in Figure 1.3-1e, consisting of the steps to calculate y for a given x. Note also that there may be more than one step to this operation, and we may use more than one block to illustrate this part of the flow path.

(3) The *substitution* block—getting ready for the next step. The only operation necessary here is to step x by Δx. Notice the way the statement is written in this block, No. 5 in Figure 1.3-1e. It says $x = x + 0.1$. Now this is obviously not an equation in which one is supposed to solve for x. There *is* no value of x which would make it an equality. Instead, it is an instruction that says: "take the current value of x, increase it by 0.1, and put it back to be the new value of x." In general,

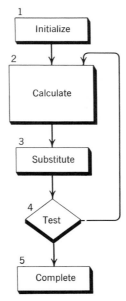

Figure 1.3-3   Generalized flow chart.

these statements mean: "calculate the quantity described on the right-hand side, and store it away as the quantity on the left."

(4) The alternative or *testing* block. It always asks a question, usually in a yes-or-no form. There are, then, two possible exits from the block: one if the answer is yes, one if it is no. Sometimes there may be more than two possible choices, as when we ask if one variable is less than, equal to, or greater than another.

(5) The fifth type is a conclusion or *completion* block. In this particular example, the conclusion block is particularly simple—an instruction to stop. In other situations, however, there will be some final details to take care of before leaving this phase of the problem and going to the next.

One variation might be pointed out in the organization of the fundamental flow diagram for doing a repetitive type of calculation. The substitution block is shown here in the main stream of calculation. The substitution is made first, before testing, so that we are ready to go back and calculate the next value if the testing block tells us we should. Now, there may be situations in which we find it easier to make the test first, and, if the test tells us to go back, include the substitution block in the feedback path. Situations will vary and help you choose which is the most efficient program.

Now let us see what the instructions for this problem look like when we write out the complete program. Well, they look a great deal like the list of operating steps we made a while ago, for telling Moron how to do the same problem on the desk calculator. Shown in Figure 1.3-4 is the program written in what is called FORTRAN language for the 1620. In the next chapter we will learn a lot about FORTRAN and how to talk in FORTRAN language. For now, we find that we already know a great deal about the language, as we can see by looking at the program. We have already been through most of the steps, so all we have to do is get used to the symbols and signs this language uses, and we can read it right off.

We can come close to doing that right now. Quite obviously, the first instruction

$$X = 0.$$

merely sets the initial value of x to be 0. The decimal point that must be used in places like this is merely a convenient way of telling the computer that this is a floating-point number, or is going to be used in floating-point calculations later on. But once again, more about that in the next chapter.

The next statement

$$Y = 4. * X - SQRT(7. + X * X * X)$$

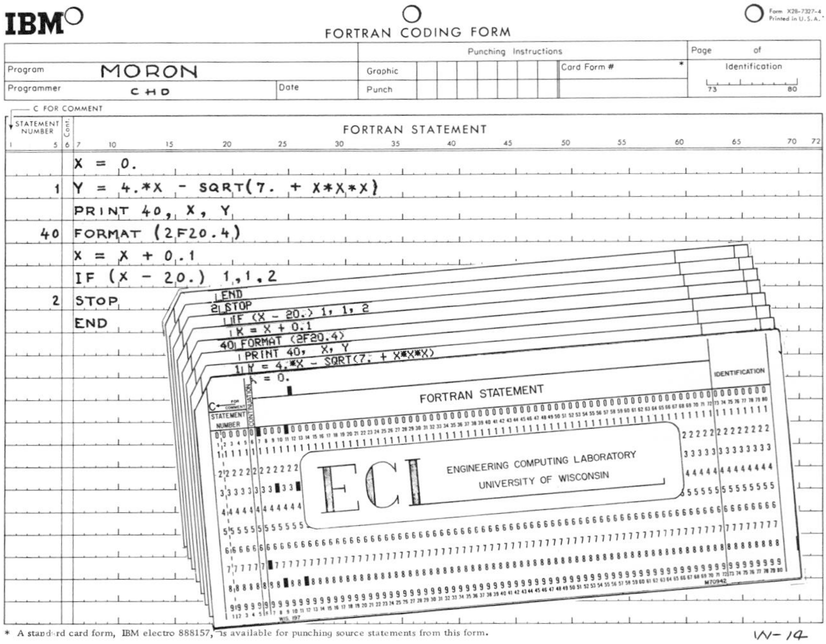

Figure 1.3-4   Program.

is written almost identically to the way we wrote out the list of arithmetic operations we said anybody would have to perform to calculate this function. Note the use of the * to indicate a multiplication operation. This is a convenient compromise to enable us to use a symbol available on an ordinary typewriter that is much less likely to get confused with something else than either a period or an *x* would be. You will find that you get used to it very quickly.

As soon as *y* has been calculated for a given *x*, we cause the computer to list the current values of both *x* and *y* by printing them out, using what we call a PRINT statement. The FORMAT statement which follows is merely to describe the form of the numbers as they are to appear on the final printed page. We then step *x*, increasing it by Δx, and put it back to be the new value:

$$\begin{aligned} &\text{PRINT 40, X, Y} \\ 40\quad &\text{FORMAT (2F20.4)} \\ &\text{X} = \text{X} + 0.1 \end{aligned}$$

The next instruction

$$\text{IF (X} - 20.) \ 1, 1, 2$$

makes the test to see whether or not x is still in the desired range, and tells the computer what to do in either case. We form the difference between the *current* value of x, whatever that is, and the *final* value of x, which is 20, and then say: "If this difference is negative or zero, x has not yet exceeded 20, and we should go back to statement 1 and do it again. If this difference is positive, x has passed 20, so go on to statement 2. Statement 2, of course, just stops the computer.

Complicated? No, not particularly. In fact, there is a surprising similarity between the FORTRAN statements that make up the program for the 1620 computer and the list of steps we would have to make for ourselves in organizing just how we were going to do the problem.

1.4   WHAT LANGUAGES ARE AVAILABLE?

FORTRAN, we are going to find out, is a very easy language for us to learn and to use. But we ought to realize that FORTRAN is not the native language of the computer. It is an intermediate language that has been developed by computer experts to make the computer look a lot smarter than it really is. It has to be taught to the computer, and then the computer is ready to converse with us in a language that makes for much greater fluency and ease of communication.

It is worth taking a few minutes to understand how these languages work, how much has been done for us by the men who build and work with computers, and how much simpler our job is because of the language work they have done. It will also help us understand some of the limitations of these languages.

Programs for accomplishing this language-translating operation are variously called assemblers, compilers, and translators. They have to be written in the computer's own language and read into the computer. We can then give the computer instructions in a more elaborate language, using bigger words than the computer would understand by itself, and operations it does not normally know how to perform. The computer, under control of the translator, translates these complex instructions into a sequence of basic machine language instructions that will actually accomplish the result wanted. This procedure, of getting the computer to help write its own program, is often called, somewhat optimistically, automatic programming.

Of the many such systems, we will confine our attention at present to the two principal systems that are currently available for use with the 1620: FORTRAN, and FORGO.

The first of these, FORTRAN (short for "formula translator"), gets its name from the fact that the source language, the language the user can use to write his own program, is very similar to the language in which one expresses ordinary algebraic relations and formulas. When this source language program is presented to the computer, as in Figure 1.3-5a, with the FORTRAN processor already loaded, it translates these algebraic statements into a machine language program, does not execute them, but writes out the results of this translation as a tape or a punched deck of cards. Now you can take this object program and feed it into the computer again, and this time it will execute those machine language instructions, run your problem, and give you, you hope, the answers that you asked for.

Notice that in this system you, the user, have to present the problem to the computer twice, the first time in your own language, and the second time in its language. The fact that the machine does the translating between the two is the saving feature that makes the whole process so attractive. Nevertheless, (on a small computer the size of the basic 1620) you do have to handle the information twice.

Now this may be either an advantage or a disadvantage. If you are an engineer in an industrial laboratory, you are likely to have spent considerable time on the program for the problem you are bringing to the computer, and anticipate that, when you get it working, it will be a very valuable money and time saver indeed. When you finally get it debugged and working, you are likely to want to use it over and over again, with many different sets of data. Here, there is considerable advantage in saving the object program deck, which is all compiled and ready to run, for day-to-day use.

On the other hand, if you are a student learning to use the computer, you will have many relatively short and simple problems which have no great lasting value once they have been solved. Then, another approach is much more valuable.

The big bottleneck in the FORTRAN approach is not the compiling time, which must be gone through anyway, but the intermediate output and input process, both because input and output are always the slowest part of any computer, and because of the extra card handling involved. By making some compromises we can eliminate the intermediate punch-out process entirely, as shown in Figure 1.3-5b. We will now let the computer compile a machine language program, but instead of punching it out, the computer stores it away in its own memory as it goes. Then, when it is finished making out the object program, it can transfer to that immediately and start executing it. This mode of operation is called "load-and-go." The most useful programming system that operates this way on the 1620—that translates FORTRAN statements and goes

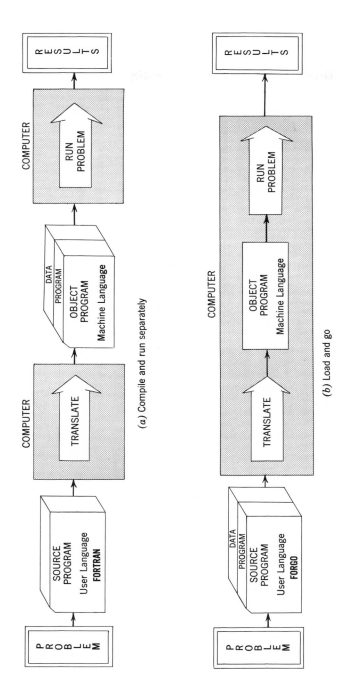

(a) Compile and run separately

(b) Load and go

Figure 1.3-5 Two systems of "automatic programming."

19

ahead and executes them—is called FORGO, for load-and-go FOR-TRAN.

We mentioned some compromises. The difficulty here is storage, or memory space, in the computer. Most dictionaries, you know, are bulky if they are complete enough to be any good, and the compilers and translators for the data-processing languages are no exception. In fact, the processor for a language as flexible and convenient as FORTRAN takes up so much space in the computer that, unless some special arrangements are made, there is no room to store the object program it generates. The object program has to be punched out word by word as it goes along. In order to make room to keep the object program in memory as it is compiled, something has to give.

We could follow either of two approaches: cut down on the space requirement, or add another wing to the house.

The first approach has been used for some languages. The space requirement could be cut down in two ways:

(1) The processor could be simplified, which means backing down on the flexibility of the user's language. In such a language many operations that are simple in FORTRAN would be much more awkward, however, and some others just could not be done at all.

(2) The size of the problem that can be handled could be restricted.

Such processing languages have been written. They are not designed to handle big, complicated problems, but simple, short ones when answers are wanted in a hurry. If the size of the computer available is such as to restrict us to this approach, there are still a fair number of problems encountered in various fields of work that can be done fairly conveniently in such a language, and it can serve as an excellent introduction to the computing process.

If, however, you are not willing to pay the price of these restrictions, the only alternative is to shell out the price to get some more memory, because, once you do have expanded storage on the 1620, you can keep the full power of the FORTRAN processing language and still have room to compile the whole object program inside the computer and run it immediately upon completion of compilation.

The most useful such system for instructional purposes is the FORGO* system, which not only offers load-and-go operation, but also has several powerful language features built in, some very valuable checking operations to help catch mistakes in your program, and some debugging abilities to help you get the program working right. If you have access

---

* Developed at the University of Wisconsin Engineering Computing Laboratory, by a group under the direction of Charles W. McClure.

to a 1620 with FORGO available on it, you should read Appendix A-2 along with Chapter 2 to take advantage of the simplified treatment possible for some of the topics.

An alternate approach available on some 1620's as well as some other computers is to add, not more high-speed memory, but an auxiliary disk file. This enables a type of load-and-go operation in which the object program is written out on the disk by the computer as it is compiled, and if the program is found to be satisfactory it can be called back into the computer and executed, still under automatic control. There are several FORTRAN compilers which operate in this way, although they do not share the other advantages of FORGO as mentioned above.

In the next chapter we will present some of the features of both the FORTRAN language and the operating system that goes with it. You will not find all of it there, but enough to get you started and on your own. Get some operating experience in how to talk to a computer, and a bit of feeling for what kinds of things our information machine can do. Then we will be in a much better position to start talking about how it is used in so many different fields in the world around us.

Later on, as you become more proficient, you will be in a better position to go ahead and learn more about the FORTRAN language and even other languages, so that you can make even more powerful use of our giant moron.

Remember that it is much more of a giant moron than a giant brain. Nevertheless, we have seen that even a giant moron can be a useful slave if we learn to speak its language and always talk down to it, patiently, and with complete detail. It will not do any of your thinking for you.

So much for generalities about computers, programming systems, and data-processing languages. In the next chapter we will open the FORTRAN manual and take a closer look at the language itself—its vocabulary and structure—and we will learn how to write FORTRAN programs for the solution of a few simple problems.

CHAPTER 2.

The Fortran Language

2.1 PERSPECTIVE

Now that we have a clearer picture of the intelligence and comprehension level of our useful slave, the giant moron, and know some of the problems to keep in mind when we try to communicate with it, let us get down to the business of learning its language. We will start out by taking a close look at the different parts of speech in this FORTRAN language so that we will learn what words we can use and what they mean. Then we will try putting them together in a few simple phrases, and finally whole sentences. Before long we will be writing whole essays (and complete instructions for how to solve a problem) in FORTRAN.

2.2 VOCABULARY OF FORTRAN

Figure 2.2-1 gives a simplified outline of the FORTRAN vocabulary, showing that we have, effectively, four parts of speech: data words, operations, control statements, and specifications. The *data* words serve very effectively as nouns in this language, and the *operations* are the verbs, telling what actions the nouns can perform on each other. The *control statements* function most of the time like conjunctions in show-

Data Words
  Constants
    Integer   0 — 99999   no decimal point
    Real   .99999999E — 50 to   must have a decimal point
                           .99999999E + 49

  Variables
    Integer   must start with I — N
    Real   must start with A — H, or O — Z

Operations
  Arithmetic Operations (two operands)
    =   Set equal to
    +   Addition
    —   Subtraction
    *   Multiplication
    /   Division
    ** Exponentiation
  Functions (one operand)
    SIN   Sine   (angle in radians)
    COS   Cosine   (angle in radians)
    ATAN   Arctangent   (angle in radians)
    LOG   Logarithm   (natural, or base *e*)
    EXP   Exponential   (*e* to the power)
    SQRT   Square Root

    ABS   Absolute value
  Input-Output
    READ
    ACCEPT*
    PUNCH*
    TYPE*
    PRINT

Control Statements
    GO TO
    Computed GO TO
    IF
    IF (SENSE SWITCH)*
    DO
    PAUSE*
    CONTINUE
    STOP

Specifications
    END
    DIMENSION
    FORMAT

Figure 2.2-1 Basic vocabulary of FORTRAN. Statements marked with an asterisk should be avoided by inexperienced programmers.

ing which parts of the sentence are related to which, and how, and sometimes like adverbs, by modifying both these relationships and the operating statements or verbs as well. The *specifications*—well, they are more like a glossary that belongs in the appendix. They do not do anything themselves, but they help to define what some of the other words mean.

Data Words

The data words in FORTRAN are of two kinds: constants and variables. The *constants* are just what they claim to be, numbers that stay constant through the course of the calculation, like 2 or π. On the other hand, algebra is useful exactly because it permits us to work with quantities which do not always have to stay the same, nor be completely specified in advance. Their values are sometimes determined by the course of the calculations; other times they will be left free to be assigned as parameters, varying from calculation to calculation. These are the *variables,* and the ability to make up names for these quantities and work with the names themselves is one of the most valuable aspects of an algebraic language.

Constants. Constants are further broken down into two classes: integer and real. The *integer* constants are of course always whole numbers or integers. They were formerly called fixed-point numbers, but today that name is being reserved for a special format of real numbers. You can think of them as having an assumed decimal point at the extreme right end. Examples of integer constants are

$$1 \quad -28 \quad 6800$$

Integer numbers are mainly used for counting, as in keeping track of the number of pieces of data, or the number of times an operation has been performed, and for subscripts, indices, and the like. The range of integers that can be handled in a given FORTRAN dialect depends primarily on the computing machine it is designed for: in 1620 FORTRAN and in USA Standard Basic FORTRAN it can be any 4-digit decimal number from 0 to 9999; in FORGO, in 1620 FORTRAN II, and in several others, 5 digits are permitted, from 0 to 99999; in most binary machines the limit depends on the maximum number of bits or binary digits available to store the constant as a binary number, as for example the limit of $2^{17} = 131,072$ for the IBM 7090 and its family, and the $2^{47} - 1$ limit allowed by the CDC 1604.

The integers are, of course, but a subset of the set of *real* numbers. For a real number whose magnitude is greater than the maximum permissible integer, or for a real number which may have a fractional part, *floating point* notation must be used. This scheme of representation, developed by scientists and engineers who must work with large ranges of real numbers that rarely come out even, involves using only a given number of significant digits, and keeping track of the decimal point on the side. For example, the significant digits of

$$271. \qquad 271,000. \qquad \text{and} \qquad .00271$$

are all the same. But the proper position of the decimal point is obviously quite different in the three cases, and can be indicated by a separate number carried along with those digits. We convert any number to scientific notation by first moving the decimal point from wherever it may be to the standard position, immediately to the right of the first nonzero digit, and then multiplying by whatever factor is necessary to show how many places we moved it. This way the true magnitude of the number ends up unchanged. The decimal-point factor of course is always a multiple of 10, so it can be expressed very simply as 10 raised to that power. If, for instance, we move the decimal point x places to the left to get it in the standard position, then we multiply by 10^x. For example:

271. would become 2.71×10^2 which in FORTRAN is 2.71E2
271,000. would become 2.71×10^5 which in FORTRAN is 2.71E5
.00271 would become 2.71×10^{-3} which in FORTRAN is $2.71\text{E}-3$

If the decimal point is in its proper place already, then the exponent is zero, and need not be written at all:

2.71 would become 2.71×10^0 which in FORTRAN is 2.71

Now for the purpose of writing numbers in FORTRAN, it is not always necessary to have floating-point numbers in exactly this form. In most FORTRANs

46. .46E2 46000.00E $-$ 3 and 4.6E1

would all be read in properly and treated as the same number, which they are.

The range of values a real number can assume will similarly vary among dialects of FORTRAN. Almost any FORTRAN will accept up to 8 digits and a sign for the significant-figure part, but there is a variation in the range of exponents that can be handled. Some FORTRANs for the 1620 permit a range from 10^{-100} to 10^{+100}, but others permit only $10^{\pm 50}$, and some machines (why?) have limits like 10^{-38} to 10^{38}. FORGO actually allows the exponent to range between 10^{-50} and 10^{+49}, but these limits are well beyond anything we will have to do with in this book.

One of the limitations of dealing with a helper of such limited intelligence is that we always have to specify for each constant we use whether it is an integer or real number—essentially, whether to treat it in fixed- or floating-point form. How do we tell FORTRAN this? By a very simple trick: in real constants a decimal point always appears somewhere between its two ends; integer constants do not have a decimal point.

Variables. How about variables? Do they have to be divided into integer and real classes also? They certainly do. There is, however, a difference in the way we specify which class a variable belongs in, as we shall see in a moment.

To begin with, we can make up names for our variables by choosing almost any combination of from 1 to 5 characters, subject to the following restrictions:

(1) The first character must be a letter of the alphabet.
(2) Subsequent characters can be any letter or decimal digit.
(3) No special characters like $, ', or . may be used.

This allows literally millions of possible combinations. We can use X for x, YP for y prime, SUM, K14, MONEY, and many, many more. You will often find it helps a great deal to use a name for a FORTRAN variable which suggests the actual name or function by which we think of the variable.

Now restriction No. 3 above raises a problem. If we cannot use special characters like a decimal point in a variable name, how are we going to distinguish between integer and real variables? The answer is that a different trick is used here: we will use the *initial letter* of a name to indicate the difference. Because letters in the middle of the alphabet are often used for subscripts, indices, and the like, the rule in FORTRAN is: an integer-variable name must start with one of the letters I, J, K, L, M, N. A real-variable name must start with one of the other 20 letters of the alphabet. Thus

> N
> MONEY
> K14

are all integer-variable names;

> X
> YP
> SUM
> A2

are all real-variable names.

These rules for distinguishing between integer and real constants and variables are particularly important because of one more restriction, and this will get you a reckless driving ticket in FORTRAN every time: *You must not mix integer and real numbers in the same calculation!*

This is easy to say, and seems simple enough to accept, but turns out to be maddeningly hard to remember. Be warned right now: unless you are highly exceptional, one of your most common mistakes in learning to write in FORTRAN will be forgetting to use the decimal point that must be included in all real constants. Whenever you want to increase X by two, for instance, or multiply it by ten, you cannot write: X + 2, or 10 * X; it must be X + 2., 10. * X, and so forth. You must not mix the two kinds of numbers!

In the same way, the different kinds of variable names cannot be used in the same expression. For instance, if you knew that the price of a certain item was so much, then to get the total cost of buying a certain number of these items it would seem quite logical to try to write in FORTRAN something like

COST = PRICE * NUM

Unfortunately, that sentence is bad grammar, and FORTRAN gets confused. You must make up a name for NUM which does not start with one of the six letters I through N. A simple thing to do here, for instance, would be to call it XNUM, and then we could write

COST = PRICE * XNUM

A tiny change like this will make all the difference between a FORTRAN program being accepted and not being accepted by the computer, and is typical of the exact attention to detail that has to be followed in dealing with a moron.

In ALGOL* and in several of the newer versions of FORTRAN, additional classes of data words are included in the vocabulary such as complex, double-precision, and Boolean. For the work we will be doing here, integer and real will be plenty.

Arrays and Subscripts. Suppose we give a little thought to how we name variables when we have a whole string of them, related to each other. When you were learning how to use algebra you often found situations in which you were working with a series or an array of quantities that had a definite order or sequence. It would be misleading as well as awkward to have to use completely different symbols to represent them. You probably started out, for instance, calling the coefficients of x in a polynomial a, b, c, d, etc., thus

$$ax^2 + bx + c.$$

* See Section 15.1.

Later on you found it more advantageous to call them

$$a_1 x^2 + a_2 x + a_3$$

and still later a_i where $i = 1, 2, 3, \ldots, n$.

The FORTRAN notation permits us to use subscripts exactly like this to identify the different members of such a list. We call the collection of variables, either integer or real, that have the same name but different subscripts an *array,* and we can use for the identifying subscript either an integer-constant or an integer-variable name. The only difference is that since writing subscripts below the line calls for awkward manipulating of a typewriter carriage, and cannot be done at all on a keypunch, we say that an integer-constant or variable name enclosed in parentheses automatically means a subscript. Thus B(J) is read B_J. In the same way we can have X(KROW), Y(7), and IMAGE(N2).

Furthermore, it often happens when using subscripts that we would like to compare two different elements in the array. For instance, if we are trying to sort a list of numbers we may want to compare any given element with the preceding one to see whether it is larger or smaller. In such a case, we might want to refer both to element A(J) and to element A(J − 1). In the FORTRAN language, this is perfectly permissible, and in fact a subscript expression can be anything up to

$$c_1 * v \pm c_2$$

where c_1 and c_2 are constants and v a variable name.

Be careful, though, that you do not let subscripts become negative, or even zero; they must always be positive integers. This is an unfortunate and actually unnecessary restriction in almost all present FORTRANs; ALGOL and some of the newer processing languages are removing it (see Chapter 15).

Furthermore, two-dimensional arrays are perfectly in order, and, in some FORTRANs, three. A(I, J) can easily be pictured as a two-dimensional array laid out in rows and columns, thus:

A(1, 1) A(1, 2) A(1, 3)
A(2, 1) A(2, 2) A(2, 3)
A(3, 1) A(3, 2) A(3, 3)

It might be noted in passing that whenever we use an array of variables, we always have to warn the parking lot attendant inside the FORTRAN processor by telling him, in a DIMENSION statement, how many elements there are going to be, so that he will know how many consecutive spaces in memory to save. For the above 3 by 3 array called A, for instance, the statement

DIMENSION A(3, 3)

would be enough. However,

DIMENSION A(50, 50)

would also work. The two restrictions on the use of the DIMENSION statement are:

(1) The DIMENSION statement specifying the size of an array must *precede* the first use of that array. In some FORTRANs it must always be at the very beginning of the program; this is actually a good habit to get into.

(2) The size specified for the array in a DIMENSION statement is a *maximum* size; it must be equal to or greater than the largest subscript the program is ever called upon to handle.

There is strong temptation to play safe here and always specify a size much greater than we expect to need, but it should be realized that such practice is extremely wasteful of memory space, and, to a lesser extent, of time.

This is the first instance we have encountered of a *specification* statement; we will be seeing more of them later on.

So much for the nouns—the data words—in our FORTRAN vocabulary. Now let us look at some of the things we can do with them.

Operations

There are 6 basic kinds of operations we can perform on the nouns, as shown in Figure 2.2-1.

Arithmetic Operations. The 4 common arithmetic operations—addition, subtraction, multiplication, and division—are all too familiar to need further explanation here, once you get used to the choice of an * (a rather logical choice, when you come to think of it) to symbolize multiplication, rather than an X (which may be wanted to mean itself) or a · (which is not available on an ordinary typewriter, or keypunch either). Even exponentiation is not a new process (A ** B merely means A raised to the B power, or A^B), but merely a new symbol made up of two of the others. Only the first one, the equality operator, really needs a word of comment.

The equal sign is not a passive verb in FORTRAN, nor is it a form of the verb "to be," merely recognizing a state of equality that may exist between two quantities. It is an active verb, and A = B causes a very specific action to take place. It can be looked at in either of two ways, which are actually equivalent: the old value of the variable A is replaced by the current value of the variable B; or, calculate the quantity B on the right-hand side, which may be any expression involving arithmetic and other operations and not just a single variable name, and store it away as the quantity A on the left-hand side.

The significance of this operation is so great, and so easily confused with a conventional indication of equality, that in some FORTRAN-like languages (ALGOL, for instance) it is actually called the "replacement operation," and instead of an $=$ a different symbol $\leftarrow$ called a "replacement operator," is used. In FORTRAN we will stick with the $=$, but it is a good idea to get in the habit of thinking of it as you read it as "is set equal to" or "is replaced by." Try it.

As you see in Figure 2.2-2, an arithmetic statement can be a very simple or a very complex thing. On the one hand, the expression on the right may be merely a single constant or variable; it may say to set the quantity called SUM $=$ X1 $+$ X2; or that "efficiency" is to be calculated by dividing "work out" by "work in." It may even get completely carried away with itself and say that something called WAVE NUMBER is to be calculated by that entire longwinded expression shown at the bottom.

Now all of these expressions, you notice, consist just of a succession of the simple arithmetic operations listed in Figure 2.2-1. The expression must, of course, clearly indicate the order in which the various operations are to be carried out, for it sometimes makes a very great difference. What do you mean, for instance, when you say "6 divided by 3 divided by 2"? The result depends upon which operation is performed first. Look at Figure 2.2-3, and actually carry out the operations indicated there. If you divide 6 by 3 first and then that result by 2, you get 1. Starting with 3 divided by 2 first, you get 4.

There is fortunately in FORTRAN a complete set of rules and conventions to determine just exactly what the computer will calculate when presented with any given expression. The device which enables you to specify the exact *sequence* of operations you desire is the parenthesis. Figure 2.2-3 indicates how parentheses can be used to group operations, and to specify which ones are to be carried out before others.

To be sure, you do not have to use parentheses. If you want to live dangerously, you can get from the manuals the information that in the absence of other instructions, FORTRAN will always operate according

$$X = 0.$$
$$I = J$$
$$SUM = X1 + X2$$
$$EFF = WOUT/WIN$$
$$WAVNO = R * (1./(XN + A) ** 2 - 1./(XM + B) ** 2)$$

Figure 2.2-2 Arithmetic statements.

$$\boxed{6/3/2 = ?}$$

X = (6./ 3.)/2.	ANSWER = 1.
X = 6./(3. /2.)	ANSWER = 4.
X = 6 /(3 /2)	ANSWER = 6! (*why?*)

Figure 2.2-3   Indicating order of operations.

to a fixed hierarchy: exponentiations take first precedence; then multiplications and divisions; and finally additions and subtractions. Furthermore, within a given rank of the hierarchy it will execute operations in the sequence encountered in scanning from left to right. In this way you can frequently get by without so many parentheses, though not without any. But if you want to be a careful programmer, and are more interested in successful programs than in cute ones, you will use parentheses fairly liberally in getting started, and certainly whenever there seems to be any question about *what* is to be calculated.

One reason we have to resort more to parentheses in FORTRAN than in ordinary algebra is the lack of a long horizontal bar dividing an entire numerator effectively from the denominator. A single slanting slash of course cannot do the same thing at all, for it appears only as a single character between two other characters when writing everything on one line. Here is one particular place where parentheses are often absolutely necessary to indicate precisely the exact extent of the division operands.

Applying the left-to-right rule, for instance, would the two following expressions give the same thing?

$$B/2. * A$$
$$B/(2. * A)$$

Functions. In addition to the 5 arithmetic operations which operate on *two* operands there are many commonly used functions of *one* variable that are available as single operations in most versions of FORTRAN. The 6 shown in the first part of Figure 2.2-1 are part of the vocabulary of almost all FORTRANs, including 1620 FORTRAN. In FORGO, USASI Basic FORTRAN, and many others the ABS (absolute value) function has been added, and in some the list has been extended to include 20 or 30 different functions.

In most FORTRANs the argument of the function is restricted to being a real constant or variable; watch this.

In all of these functions the definition has been built into the language of the FORTRAN, so that all the user need do is write the name of the function as an operator whenever he needs it. In Chapter 6 we will see that in many FORTRANs there is an additional procedure which permits the user to define new functions as he needs them, assigning names to them as he goes along. This greatly increases the flexibility and convenience of the language, but is beyond what we will need here.

In many of the older FORTRANs it is necessary to distinguish between ordinary variable names and names of functions by adding the letter F at the end of all function names, so that for instance SIN(X) would become SINF (X). (You can think of this as being read "sine function of x," if you wish.) The trend, however, is away from such restrictions on notation, and in particular, USA Standard FORTRAN has dropped it completely. In FORGO its use is optional; you can leave out the F for simplicity, or if you need to have a program which will run on one of the other machines as well, you may include the F if you wish. Function names with and without the terminal F produce the same effect.

There is a small precaution to watch out for here, however. You had better not make up a name for a new variable that looks exactly like one of the existing function names. You can see how confusing it would be to anybody trying to translate your program, be it person or compiler, if you tried to call a variable SIN, particularly if you attached a subscript, and tried to multiply X * SIN (J).

The arithmetic operations and the functions are very polite to each other; each will allow the other to appear in one of its own expressions. As you can see in Figure 2.2-4, you can multiply the sine by something in a single statement, or you can take the square root of the sum of two things. In fact, there is hardly any limit to the formula you can ask the computer to handle. The last equation in Figure 2.2-4 comes from electric circuit theory, but do not let that bother you. It happens to be an expression for the characteristic impedance of a certain four-wire transmission line, but it is inserted here just to show how formidable a formula can be, and yet still be capable of complete expression in an in-line FORTRAN statement.

The only real limit to the size of the expression you can write is that

V = VMAX * SIN(THETA)
C = SQRT(A2 + B2)

$$\left(Z = \frac{AK}{\sqrt{e}} \log \frac{2D_2}{D\sqrt{1 + \left(\frac{D_2}{D_1}\right)^2}} \right)$$

Z = (AK/SQRT(EPS)) * LOG((2. * D2)/(D * SQRT(1. + (D2/D1) * (D2/D1))))

Figure 2.2-4   Expressions involving functions.

set by the amount you can get on one card, 72 characters. Although in some FORTRANs there are procedures for continuing a statement from one card to another, for our purposes we will find that if we really do run into an expression that will not fit on one card it is a simple matter to break the operation up into two or more steps, write one statement for each, and then fit them all together.

Please note once again, however, the very strict rule against mixing integer and real numbers in the same expression. There are only two exceptions to this rule:

(1) Subscripts must be in the integer mode, regardless of whether the array name is integer or real. They may be either constants or variables or both.

(2) Exponents of real quantities may be in either integer or real mode. There is a very real difference in the calculating procedure called forth here, though not (theoretically) in the final result:

$$\text{(a) } 2.**3 \text{ is compiled into } 2.*2.*2.$$
$$\text{(b) } 2.**3. \text{ is compiled into EXP } (3.*LOG(2.))$$

Mathematically, for numbers of infinite precision and without regard to calculating time, these two are equivalent. Practically, in a computer working with finite numbers of digits in real time, the former will be calculated much faster for small values of exponent, and may actually produce a different answer. In FORGO the break-even point is surprisingly about 25: that is, for an exponent ≤ 25, version (a) is faster; for exponents above 25, use version (b).

Note that this rule applies to mixing within an expression but does *not* prohibit mixing across the equal sign. That is, you may write

$$I = (A*B)/R$$

which will cause the quantity on the right-hand side to be computed in the floating-point mode, converted to an integer (which means truncated to the 5 digits immediately to the left of the decimal point), and stored away as the quantity I. Similarly

$$B = I + M$$

will cause an integer sum to be formed, converted to floating-point form, and stored away. In other words, the rule says: it is permissible to mix modes across the equal sign, but the entire expression on the right-hand side must be in a single mode.

Two important words have been used fairly freely here; let us be sure we have them straight. An *expression* consists of anything from a single constant or variable up to the most complicated combination of arithmetic and function operations that can be fitted into one line on a card, but does *not* include an equal sign; an *arithmetic statement* results when this is set equal to something. That something, however, can be only a single name: an integer-variable name, a real-variable name, or an array element name. It is the name under which the result of the arithmetic expression on the right-hand side is stored away. The arithmetic statement, then, takes the general form:

Arithmetic statement:

VARIABLE = EXPRESSION

Input-Output. Input and output are also operations or verbs in our FORTRAN vocabulary, because they cause actual manipulation of data. Information can either be brought into the computer from the outside environment, through a punched card reader, the console typewriter, magnetic-tape storage units, or other devices; or can be put out from the computer into the outside world, using a card punch, the console typewriter again, high-speed printers, magnetic-tape or disk units, or a host of other mechanical, magnetic, or optical devices.

On the 1620, however, the magnetic-tape devices are not standard equipment, and the computer is usually limited to a single input and a single output device for standard operation. The most efficient use of this and indeed most computer systems can be made if normal input is from punched cards, and normal output is by means of an associated printer. For our use, therefore, we will condense the long list of input-output operations to just two: READ and PRINT.*

Input-output statements:

General Form	Examples
READ *n*, List	READ 40, A, MONTH
PRINT *n*, List	PRINT 42, N, X, Y

In the former as many items are read in from punched cards as are called for in the READ statement list, and in the latter all the information named in the PRINT statement list is printed out on a printed page. Any other input or output statement will complicate, or hang up, operations, and should be avoided at this time.

---

* Many installations do not have an on-line printer to achieve this speed-up and simplicity of the output process. In most such systems the FORTRAN instruction PRINT will usually cause output to appear on the console typewriter. If the volume of work handled by this computer is at all great, however, it is probably preferable to have the output punched onto cards and then listed separately using an off-line printer, like a 407. If this is the case, the word "PUNCH" can be substituted for the word "PRINT" in all the rest of this material with almost no other changes.

Now what about that small *n* that appears so ubiquitously in all these input and output statements? It is called a "format statement number," and is actually the entry point to a great deal of confusion. We are going to postpone just as many of the details about FORMAT statements as we can until Chapter 6, and reduce what we have to learn at this time to the bare minimum. If you are using FORGO or one of the other systems that permit a "free" format, that minimum actually becomes zero; skip to p. 38 and read Appendix 2A instead.

The FORMAT statement is not in itself an executable statement; it is found instead among the specifications statements listed in Figure 2.2-1. It always appears in conjunction with either an input or an output statement, and tells the FORTRAN processor in the first case what the FORMAT of the data to be found on the input card will be, and, in the second case, in what FORMAT to output the results for printing. There are several types of FORMAT specifications available, and a flexible set of additional capabilities which are particularly useful for dressing up the output and printing it in attractive, well-documented, and easy-to-use form. Most of this material, however, will be omitted here and presented in Chapter 6. Instead, we will memorize two standard FORMAT specifications, learn how to use each and when, and go ahead to get some actual experience in writing and running programs on a computer.

As stated above, every input or output statement must always have a FORMAT statement associated with it, with a description for every variable name in the I-O statement list. Specifically, every input or output statement must contain the number of another statement, a FORMAT statement, and there must be such a FORMAT statement somewhere in the program. One good practice is always to follow a READ or PRINT statement immediately with its associated FORMAT statement, so that the two actually occur in pairs, thus:

```
      READ 40,  N
40 FORMAT (    )
```

Now what goes in the parentheses? It will be one of two specifications, depending on whether the variable name in the input-output list is integer or real. For the present, use one of the following two specifications

If the Variable Name Is	Use FORMAT Specification
Integer	I12
Real	1PE12.4*

* 1620 users limited to one of the IBM-supplied FORTRAN processors for this machine will be forced to substitute the still more awkward 1XE11.4 for real variables, because of the highly unconventional operation of their E specification.

If it is desired to read in a single integer variable, the input pair above would then become

```
        READ 40,  N
     40 FORMAT (I12)
```

But if the variable to be read in is of type real,

```
        READ 40,  X
     40 FORMAT (1PE12.4)
```

If there is more than one item in the list, the specification must be repeated:

```
        READ 41,  N, KOST, LIMIT
     41 FORMAT (I12, I12, I12)
```

Note particularly that in the case of a mixture of integer- and real-variable names, it is necessary to see to it that the list of specifications in the format statement agrees item by item with the input-output list, as follows:

```
        READ 42,  K, X, N1, N2
     42 FORMAT (I12, 1PE12.4, I12, I12)
```

Let us consider for a bit the form of the data numbers which are going to be read in by these statements. If we give the computer a program to compile and execute, and in the program we tell it to **READ** in certain data, we had better be sure that at the end of our program we supply those data, also punched on cards. The number 12 that appears in all of those FORMAT specifications means that the computer will be expecting each data item to occupy its own 12-column-wide field on the data card. If the item is an integer, it must furthermore be *right-justified* in that field, so that for instance a 3-digit integer like 497 would have to be punched in columns 10, 11, and 12 of the appropriate 12-digit field on the card. In the case of a real data item this restriction can be relaxed somewhat, for so long as the number is punched completely within its proper 12-digit field, the presence of the decimal point which should always be present will cause the item to be read in correctly, provided there is no exponent! Some FORTRANs still give erroneous response if an exponent is not completely right-justified. There is, however, quite a bit of leeway in the form in which the real constant and its exponent can be punched. Examples of lists of numbers that could be read in by the input pair

```
        READ 43,  N, A, B
     43 FORMAT (I12, 1PE12.4, 1PE12.4)
```

are the following:

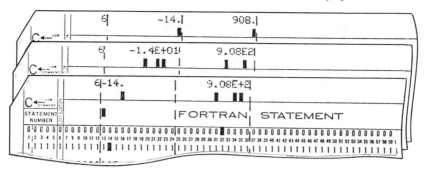

But note that *none* of the three numbers below would be read in correctly. Why?

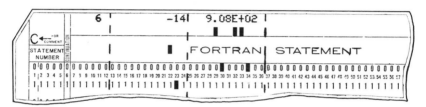

In output operations the behavior of the FORMAT statement is very much the same. Here the format specification is telling the FORTRAN processor, not in what form within a given 12-column field on the card to *look* for the data item to be read in, but in what form within the proper 12-digit field as we go across the line on the printed page to *put* it. If the name in an output list is that of an integer variable, the value of that variable at the time of executing the PRINT statement will be printed out as an integer, right-justified in a field of 12 columns; if the name is that of a real variable, the number stored in the computer under that name will be printed out in standard scientific notation, with 1 digit to the left of the decimal point and 4 to the right, followed by an appropriate exponent (if nonzero) in E notation. For example, if the data read in, in the example above, were printed out using the statement pair

```
      PRINT 44,  N, A, B
   44 FORMAT (I12, 1PE12.4, 1PE12.4)
```

it would appear as

```
    6 -1.4000E+01  9.0800E+02
```

With that brief simplification of the input-output class of operations, we have now discussed three kinds of things that can be done with numbers: we can do arithmetic with them, we can calculate a few higher functions, and we can read them in and print them out.

Control Statements

We are ready to pass on to the third class of FORTRAN words, the control statements. These tie the various pieces of the program together and tell the computer where to go, and sometimes when to go there.

GO TO. Some of these statements are so simple that they are best explained sufficiently by illustration. For instance, if we wanted to perform such a simple (and relatively useless) operation as taking the square root of a series of numbers supplied, we could write a program like the one shown in Figure 2.2-5 to do it. There are three steps to be performed for each number: READ in the number, take the square root, and PRINT the answer. Having done these three, the program is directed to GO TO statement number 1, which repeats the sequence. If you have ever done coding in machine or symbolic language on other machines, you will recognize GO TO as merely a jump or unconditional transfer.

IF. Sometimes, however, such a jump is to be conditional upon the progress of the calculation. *If* the calculation has progressed to a certain point, go *here; if not,* go *there.* This is a situation we often encounter when a preassigned range of numbers is to be calculated, as in the variation of the preceding problem shown in Figure 2.2-6. Here the problem is: take the square root of all integers from 1 to 20. Now, instead of having

Figure 2.2-5   Program illustrating GO TO statement.

```
 ┌── C FOR COMMENT
 ┌─STATEMENT─┐ │
 │ NUMBER    │ │                               FORTRAN STATEMENT
 1         5 6 7    10      15      20      25      30      35      40      45
 C            TO TAKE THE SQUARE ROOT OF ALL
 C            INTEGERS FROM 1 TO 20

              X = 1.
        1     Y = SQRT(X)
              PRINT 40, X, Y
       40     FORMAT (1PE12.4, 1PE12.4)
              X = X + 0.1
              IF (20. - X) 2, 1, 1
        2     STOP
              END
```

Figure 2.2-6   Program illustrating IF statement.

to READ in a new X each time, we generate it from the old one by the simple expedient of incrementing by 1. Here an unconditional GO TO would leave us feeling very much like the sorceror's apprentice. The computer would never stop until we pushed the panic button. But a conditional jump, or an IF statement, turns out to be just what we need.

After we calculate each square root, punch X and Y, and step X, we ask the question: "Are there any more X's to be done?" The difference between the final value of X (20) and the current value of X (whatever that is), is formed and tested for sign. If this difference is negative, there is no more to be done; go to 2 and stop. If it is not negative, but zero or positive, go to 1 and repeat.

The general form of the IF statement looks like this:

IF statement:

$$\text{IF (E) } n_1, n_2, n_3$$

Here n_1, n_2, and n_3 must be statement numbers, and represent where to go if the expression E is $-$, 0, or $+$, respectively. E can be any expression, integer or real, within the limits described in the section on operations. We use an IF statement if we want to let the course of the program be contingent upon the numbers encountered or upon results of the calculation.

Computed GO TO. In our example, we used an IF statement merely to make a 2-way choice: do it again, or stop. Since there are three possible exits from an IF, it can be used as a 3-way branch. Occasionally, however, there is a situation that calls for an *n*-way branch with several different exits, depending on some parameter to be set, or choice to be made. The Computed GO TO helps out here. You can specify a large number of different exits from the Computed GO TO, along with an integer variable to be tested. The program will go to the first statement in your list if the value of the variable at that point is 1, the second statement if 2, and so on down the line.

To illustrate the use of the Computed GO TO, consider the following: a computer program checking student registration cards reads one variable off a card (called NYEAR) which tells whether the student is a freshman, sophomore, junior, or senior, by whether the variable has the value 1, 2, 3, or 4. Depending on his classification, there are four completely different sets of requirements against which his program must be checked; these begin at statements 25, 27, 30, and 36, respectively. A statement to transfer control to the appropriate spot in the program would be:

GO TO (25, 27, 30, 36), NYEAR

DO. Often we know exactly how many times we want to repeat a given sequence, and may use an IF statement for nothing more than counting how many times we go around. In this case a DO statement can be used just as well as an IF. Figure 2.2-7 shows the same problem rewritten to use a DO statement to perform the counting. It says: "DO the next three operations repeatedly, while a counter called K goes from 1 to 20, increasing in steps of 1. When K finally passes 20, quit."

If this were all there were to the DO statement, it would offer only questionable advantage over the IF. Actually, however, the DO statement is considerably more powerful than that. In addition to counting,

```
C       TO TAKE THE SQUARE ROOT OF ALL
C       INTEGERS FROM 1 TO 20,
C       USING A DO STATEMENT

        X = 1.
        DO 3 K = 1, 20
        Y = SQRT(X)
        PRINT 40, X, Y
    40  FORMAT (1PE12.4, 1PE12.4)
     3  X = X + 1.
        STOP
        END
```

Figure 2.2-7   Program illustrating DO statement.

it can make certain changes in the program each time it goes through. Let us look at a slightly more complicated example to illustrate the power of the DO.

Suppose we want to evaluate a fourth-degree polynomial in X for a given value of X:

$$Y = A_1X^4 + A_2X^3 + A_3X^2 + A_4X + A_5. \tag{2.2-1}$$

Pre-analysis will tell us that we will have fewer arithmetic steps if we first factor this polynomial in the form

$$Y = (((A_1X + A_2)X + A_3)X + A_4)X + A_5. \tag{2.2-2}$$

This is a procedure called "nesting." Before you go further, convince yourself of two things:

(1) Equation (2.2-2), the factored form for Y, is exactly the equivalent of Equation (2.2-1) the original polynomial form, and

(2) the number of arithmetic operations (multiplications and additions) is considerably greater in the first case than in the second.

Now let us assume we have been given a numerical value of X, and want to substitute it into Equation (2.2-2) to calculate the corresponding value of Y. What steps do we go through? Starting at the left end, this expression tells us to do the following:

(1) Multiply A_1 by X, and call it some intermediate value, say F.
(2) Add A_2 to that.
(3) Multiply that result by X.
(4) Add A_3 to that.
(5) Multiply that by X.
(6) Add A_4 to that.
(7) Multiply that by X.
(8) Add A_5 to that, yielding Y.

Monotonous, isn't it? Multiply and add. Multiply and add. Doing the same pair of operations over and over again, in this case four times. Well, that is exactly what the moron is designed to handle for us: repetitive, routine operations. Let us set up a DO loop to go through this pair of operations four times. Figure 2.2-8 lists the 8 operations to be done, showing how they consist of repetitions of the same pair of steps.

But wait a minute. It is *not* exactly the same set of operations, is it? To be sure, we multiply by X every time, right enough. But what is it we add to F in step 2? It is A_2, isn't it? And what do we add in step 4? A_3! And in step 6, A_4. And eventually, A_5.

$$F = A_1 * X$$

$$F = F + A_2$$

$$F = F * X$$

$$F = F + A_3$$

$$F = F * X$$

$$F = F + A_4$$

$$F = F * X$$

$$Y = F + A_5$$

Figure 2.2-8   Steps in evaluating a polynomial.

Now what do we do? Can we use a DO loop to go through the same pair of operations four times, when one of the coefficients actually changes each time through? Well, as you might have suspected, the answer is yes. This is, as a matter of fact, the most powerful property of the DO statement—that it enables you to use the same variable that is keeping track of the iteration count either as an independent variable or as a subscript in any other statement within the range of the DO loop. This way, the first time through we can have the program pick up A_1; the second time, A_2; and so on right down to A_5. Here is how it works.

Figure 2.2-9 shows the program to accomplish the evaluation of our fourth-degree polynomial in X. The first thing to note is that we read in and store the coefficients as an array, called logically enough A(I), where I goes from 1 to 5. The first DO loop accomplishes this reading-in operation:

```
        DO 1 I = 1, 5
    1   READ 40, A(I)
   40   FORMAT (1PE12.4)
```

This merely says: DO everything from here down to statement 1, five times, with I going from 1 to 5. The first time, I will have the value 1, so the first number found in the data list waiting at the card reader is read in and stored away as A(1); the second time through the loop I will equal 2, so the second data item will be stored as A(2); and so on down to the fifth one which will be called A(5). When the index I is incremented once more, it will have the value 6, exceeding the final value it is supposed to take on, 5, so the DO loop is said to be satisfied, and the program then, but not until then, goes on to the next statement, and reads in the value of X for which the polynomial is to be evaluated.

```
┌─ C FOR COMMENT
│┌STATEMENT    ┌                                    FORTRAN STATEMENT
││ NUMBER      │Cont.
│1          5│6│7    10      15      20      25      30      35      40      45
C                         ** POLY **
C
C             TO EVALUATE A POLYNOMIAL IN  X

              DIMENSION  A(5)
              DO 1  I = 1, 5
     1        READ 40, A(I)
    40        FORMAT  (1PE12.4)
              READ 40, X
              F = 0.
              DO 2  I = 1, 5
     2        F = F*X + A(I)
              PRINT 41, X, F
    41        FORMAT  (1PE12.4,  1PE12.4)
              STOP
              END
              1.
              2.
              3.
              4.
              5.
                  2.5
```

Figure 2.2-9   Program to evaluate a fourth-degree polynomial.

Note that the FORMAT statement for the READ X operation would be identical to the one for reading A(I), so we can actually use the same FORMAT statement (number 40), and let both READ statements refer to it. This is perfectly legal.

Are we ready to start the cycle? Not quite, for as usual there is a set-up step or two required, and here it consists of the odd-seeming act of setting F = 0. We will see why in just a moment.

Our second DO loop is also composed of only two statements. The first is the DO statement itself, initializing the index, and specifying the range and the number of repetitions. The second statement constitutes the body of the loop and carries out the operation whose repetitions are needed. Let us follow its operation step by step.

As we enter the loop the first time, I is set equal to 1, and control is passed to statement 2. Now we see why we wanted F initially set equal to 0. The first time statement 2 is executed, with I having the value 1, its effect will be to multiply 0 by X, and add A(1). In other words, at the end of one pass through the loop F will have the value A(1).

At this point I is incremented by 1 and the new value 2 is compared against the iteration limit, which in this case is 5. Since I has not yet exceeded the limit, control is passed back to the beginning of the DO loop to execute it again.

This time I has the value 2 and F is equal to A(1). After executing statement 2 the second time F will have the value

$$F = A(1) * X + A(2)$$

You can see that we are beginning to build up the parenthetical expressions in Equation 2.2-2.

After stepping I from 2 to 3 and finding that it still has not passed the limit the loop is executed a third time producing

$$F = \Big(A(1) * X + A(2)\Big) * X + A(3)$$

The fourth time it will give

$$F = \Big((A(1) * X + A(2)) * X + A(3)\Big) * X + A(4)$$

and finally

$$F = \Big(((A(1) * X + A(2)) * X + A(3)) * X + A(4)\Big) * X + A(5)$$

This time when I is increased from 5 to 6 and compared against 5 it is at last found to have exceeded the limit, so further repetitions are dispensed with, the loop is said to be "satisfied," and control passes on out of the loop.

The remaining steps, of course, merely put out the results and stop the program. Note the arrangement of the data that follow the program itself; they must be in exactly the same sequence that the program is going to call for them at execution time: first the 5 coefficients A(I) and then a single value of X. There is nothing magical about which columns the data are punched in. The only restrictions are that each number be completely contained in the first 12 columns, and that there is nothing in column 1 (this will be explained in Chapter 6).

What the DO statement does for us here, then, is to cause the iterative execution of a specified set of statements (here only 1) precisely 5 times, but changing one of the subscripts each time through. Here is the general form of the DO statement:

DO statement:

General Form	Examples
DO n $I = m_1, m_2, m_3$	DO 30 I = 1, 12, 3
DO n $I = m_1, m_2$	DO 2 NUM = 2, K

The statement says: DO everything from here down to statement n (the *object* of the DO), with the *index* I going from m_1 to m_2 in steps of

m_3. As you repeat this loop, I will not only act as a counter but may be used as an integer variable in its own right. At any time I will have the value last given it by the counting mechanism of the DO loop itself. The most common use of the index variable within the DO loop is as a subscript, but many other uses are valid.

The quantity n must be the statement number of a statement that physically follows the DO; I may be any unsubscripted integer-variable name; and m_1, m_2, and m_3 (called the *parameters*) are positive integer constants or unsubscripted integer-variable names. m_1 is the initial value to which the index I is set; m_2 the final value against which I is tested at the conclusion of each pass; and m_3 is the increment to be added to m_1 each time. Since m_3 is most often wanted to be 1, the option exists of omitting m_3; if this is done it is merely taken to have the value 1.

The sequence of events, then, is as depicted in Figure 2.2-10, and can be described as follows:

(1) When control reaches the DO statement, the index I is assigned the value m_1.

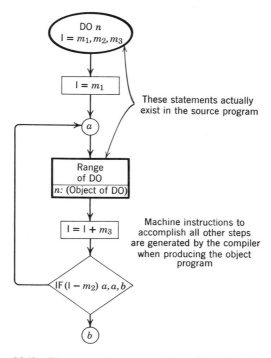

Figure 2.2-10   Diagrammatic representation of the DO statement.

(2) Control passes to the first executable statement following the DO.

(3) The entire set of statements from the first executable statement following the DO, down to and including its object, is executed. This set is called the *range* of the DO.

(4) After the object is executed, the index I is incremented by the amount m_3.

(5) The new value of the index I is tested against the value of the final parameter m_2.

(6) If the index I is less than or equal to m_2, control is passed back to the beginning of the loop (step 2 above).

(7) If the index I is greater than m_2, the DO is said to be *satisfied,* the index I becomes undefined, and control passes to the next executable statement following the object of the DO.

A few rules and restrictions are noted:

(1) Note that the parameters (m's) may not be expressions involving any operations.

(2) Although in both examples shown here the object is the very next statement, there is no such restriction. DO loops are often many statements long.

(3) Although the parameters m_1, m_2, and m_3 may be variables and change during execution of the main part of the program, *within the range of the DO no statement may change the value of either the index or any of the parameters.*

(4) None of the parameters may have zero or negative values at the time a DO loop is entered. Furthermore, m_1 should not exceed m_2 or erroneous operation may result. As can be seen from Figure 2.2-10, the range of the loop is executed first, and then the index is tested. This says that the loop will always be executed at least once.

(5) Never transfer into the range of a DO loop, for its index may be undefined. Always enter through the DO statement itself.

(6) You may transfer out of a DO loop at any time. Its index value will be preserved as the value last assigned it.

(7) A DO loop may be completely inside another DO loop, and they may even share the same object, but one DO loop may not be partially inside and partially outside another. In other words, loops must be completely nested or not at all. Nested loops must not have the same index, since this would violate rule 3.

(8) If nested loops use the same object, the innermost loop which has not been satisfied, will always be in control of the stepping and testing operations. This says that control will iterate around the innermost loop until it is satisfied, then the index of the next loop will be stepped and tested, and control transferred accordingly.

(9) The object of a DO must not be a transfer-of-control type of statement: a GO TO, a Computed GO TO, an IF, or a DO (this last is prohibited anyway, by rule 7).

A DO statement in general does three things for us: it counts how many times we have gone through the loop, it tests to see whether we have satisfied the specification, and, if not, it returns control to the starting point.

Specifications

Of the three specifications statements listed in our version of the FORTRAN vocabulary, one (FORMAT) has been briefly introduced, with a more complete discussion postponed until Chapter 6, and the other two (DIMENSION and END) have already been made use of. We will discuss these last two briefly here.

END. The END statement is particularly simple to use once its purpose is realized. It is not equivalent to a STOP statement (although in some FORTRAN compilers it can perform this function also), but marks the physical end of the list of FORTRAN statements that make up your program. It is equivalent to telling the FORTRAN compiler: this is all there is to this program; wrap up the compilation process and go on to the next job. Depending on the operating system, that next job may be any of several possibilities: (1) In FORGO, the compiler looks back to see if any errors have been found; if not it transfers control to the beginning of the object program it has just compiled and starts executing it; if errors have been found it puts out the appropriate error comments and waits for the next program to be presented to it. (2) In 1620 FORTRAN, it finishes punching out the object deck for the program just compiled, and stops. This deck will now have to be read into the computer along with a subroutine deck and any data desired in order for execution to take place. (3) In 1620 FORTRAN II, it finishes punching out the intermediate deck for this program. This deck will have to be read in again with Pass 2 of the compiler in order to get the final output deck, which when eventually loaded with a subroutine deck and data causes execution of the program. (4) In Monitor systems with larger machines, or under Monitor control on the 1620 with a disk file attached, it can cause the compiled object program, which has been placed in intermediate storage on magnetic tape or the disk file, to be called back into the memory of the computer and execution accomplished, without further operator attention.

In any case, the END statement is the last statement of any program. The only information that can meaningfully follow it is data, to be called for by means of READ statements when the program is executed.

There must be one and (until we get to more complex program structure in Chapter 6) only one END statement in every program.

DIMENSION. The DIMENSION statement has two purposes, both associated with arrays: to help the processor identify all array names as arrays, and to inform the processor how many consecutive storage locations to save for each array. Before any references are made to any array in a program, that array name must appear in the list of a DIMENSION statement, together with the maximum number of elements that will ever be encountered in that array. If it is a 2-dimensional array, each subscript range must be separately dimensioned:

DIMENSION A(10), NLOG(6), PRICE(5, 20)

Points to note in writing DIMENSION statements:

(1) There is no comma between the word DIMENSION and the first item in the list.

(2) Commas are used to separate successive elements in the list, and the different subscripts in a multi-dimensional array.

(3) The size specification may not be left as a variable, to be assigned later, but must be a simple numeric constant.

(4) As many items may be included in the list of one DIMENSION statement as will fit on one card, or several different DIMENSION statements may be used.

Since the detailed operation of the FORMAT statement is being postponed to Chapter 6, all that will be said here is that, like the END and the DIMENSION statements, FORMAT is not executable in its own right. It must always occur in connection with an input or output statement, and its purpose is to provide the processor with enough information to know how to set up machine instructions to carry out the input or output operation called for.

This emphasizes the common characteristic of the three statements grouped together in the "specifications" category: they are not executable statements; they are not instructions to the computer about how to do your problem; they are instructions to the compiler about how to compile your program so it can be properly executed by computer.

We are now in possession of just about the complete vocabulary of FORTRAN. We have discussed two kinds of data words: constants and variables; 3 classes of operations: arithmetic statements, functions, and input-output operations; most of the forms of control statements; and the three specifications statements. Two of the control statements listed in Figure 2.2-1—PAUSE and IF (SENSE SWITCH)—we have deliberately omitted, and intend to leave out for a while. Both of these, it turns out, involve a degree of manual intervention with the computer operation at run time that can slow it down wastefully. So, until you can demonstrate why you need those features, most operating systems (including FORGO) are designed not to permit their use.

Of those statements that are included in the basic FORTRAN operating vocabulary, only the CONTINUE statement, whatever that is, remains to be discussed. Even that we are going to postpone until the next section, and work it into one of the examples we will be going through there.

2.3 CASE STUDIES

We have now built up a fairly complete picture of the various parts of speech that make up the FORTRAN language: data words for nouns, operations for verbs, control statements to play the role of adverbs and conjunctions, and specifications to be a glossary to help define the others. But the only real test of mastery of any language is to have to speak it, and to try to get across important ideas in it, such as "How much does this cost?" or "What is the best way to get there from here?"

So now we will try applying our FORTRAN knowledge by writing some programs for a few simple examples. We will carry those examples from a statement of the physical problem, through the laying out of the flow diagram and the writing of the program in FORTRAN language. Then, in the next section, we will go ahead and punch one of these programs out on cards, load it into the 1620, and actually run it on the computer.

The physical situation we are going to consider is real enough, although the mathematical nature of the problem to be solved is actually far too trivial to bother a computer with. For our purposes that is fine, because it allows us to concentrate on the programming part of the problem, without having to worry about the mathematics, too.

Let us assume we are designing a television tower, and need some figures on the type of material, amount, and cost of the thousands of feet of guy wires that help support it. From Figure 2.3-1, it is obvious that the cost can be calculated as the length of the wire times the cost per foot, and it is almost as obvious that the length L is merely

$$L = \sqrt{A^2 + B^2}$$

where A = altitude to the point where the wire is attached,

B = distance along the ground from the foot of the tower to the anchor point of the wire

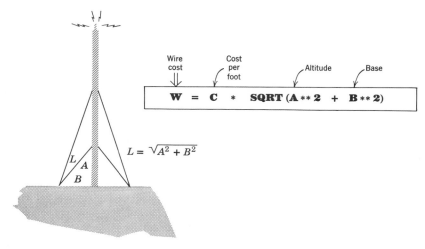

Figure 2.3-1   *Guy wire*.

according to a formula originally derived by Pythagoras. So our working equation for all the considerations that follow is just

$$W = C \sqrt{A^2 + B^2}$$

or in FORTRAN language

$$W = C * SQRT(A ** 2 + B ** 2)$$

Four versions of the problem will be considered, as tabulated in Figure 2.3-2. For the first case we limit ourselves to a single given value of both C and A, and tabulate the variations of W with B, the base of the triangle. These results might be left merely as a list of answers, or they might be used to plot a curve from which the value of W corresponding to any value of B could be read off. In cases 2 and 3, we plot a whole family of curves, each showing the variation of W with B for a different value of A, still with C remaining constant. The difference between case 2 and case 3 is that in case 2 the next value of B is obtained from the preceding one by a simple incrementing process, using an IF test to see whether the range of B has been covered; in case 3 the entire set of values for B is read into the computer as an array, and then repeatedly stepped through using a DO statement. In both cases 2 and 3, the new value of A is obtained when the old one is finished with, merely by going back to read in a new value to supersede the old. Not until case 4, where C also is to cover a range of values, do we find the need for keeping two different arrays in storage, so that we can go back and use each set of values repeatedly. Here both A and B are

GUY WIRE

$$W = C * SQRT(A ** 2 + B ** 2)$$

GUY 1   C = 1
        A = 100
        B = 20 (20) 200

GUY 2   C = 1
        A = 25, 50, 100, 250, 500
        B = A/5 (A/5) 2A

GUY 3   C = 1
        A = 25, 50, 100, 250, 500
        B = 5, 10, 20, 50, 100, 200, 500

GUY 4   C = .70, 1.00, 1.20
        A = 25, 50, 100, 250, 500
        B = 5, 10, 20, 50, 100, 200, 500

Figure 2.3-2   Four versions of *GUY WIRE*.

stored as arrays, and two different DO loops are used to go through them, one loop inside the other. The variable C is now the one that is read in one value at a time, calculated with, and then thrown away by reading in a new one on top of the old.

Let us consider these cases one by one, paying particular attention to how the iteration is accomplished for each variable in each case.

GUY 1 is very similar to the Moron problem worked with in Chapter 1. As is seen from the flow chart, Figure 2.3-3*a*, a calculation is made for a certain value of the independent variable and the results are printed out. A specified amount is added to the independent variable, and then the new value is tested against the final value in an IF test. If it is still within the range, control is returned to box 6 to do it again; if not, it goes to box 10 and stops.

Now look at the program that actually calculates W for the specified set of conditions, Figure 2.3-3*b*. Since both C and A are constants, we merely set each of them equal to its given value and immediately print it out to help identify the set of answers that the program produces. Next, we initialize B to be 20 and start calculating. The FORTRAN statement that actually accomplishes the calculating is not a highly complex expression, but a relatively simple arithmetic statement. You can see how it itemizes the arithmetic operations to be done: W equals C times Square Root Function left parenthesis A star star 2 plus B star star 2 right parenthesis.

Note the step B statement—another of those so-called equations

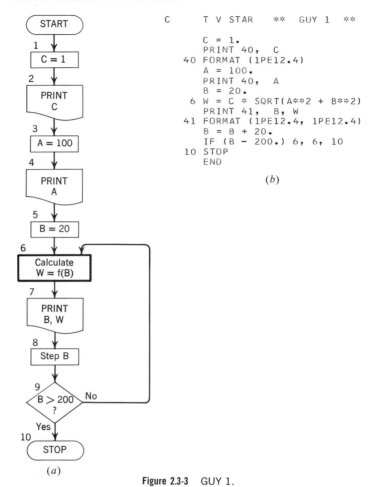

```
C      T V STAR    **  GUY 1  **

       C = 1.
       PRINT 40,  C
40 FORMAT (1PE12.4)
       A = 100.
       PRINT 40,  A
       B = 20.
6  W = C * SQRT(A**2 + B**2)
       PRINT 41,  B, W
41 FORMAT (1PE12.4, 1PE12.4)
       B = B + 20.
       IF (B - 200.) 6, 6, 10
10 STOP
       END
```

(b)

Figure 2.3-3   GUY 1.

which really means: add 20 to the old value of B and store the new value in place of the old one.

Then we test for completion of the desired range using an IF statement. We compare the current value of B against the limit 200, by forming B − 200. If this difference is negative, we tell the program to go back to statement 6 and go through the calculation again for another value of B. If this difference is positive, then we have covered the specified range, and instead we tell the program to go to statement 10, which is a stop.

GUY 2, the flow chart for which is shown in Figure 2.3-4a, is a little

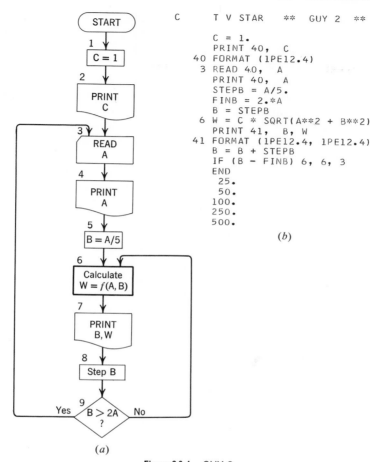

```
C       T V STAR    **   GUY 2   **
        C = 1.
        PRINT 40,  C
    40  FORMAT (1PE12.4)
     3  READ 40,  A
        PRINT 40,  A
        STEPB = A/5.
        FINB = 2.*A
        B = STEPB
     6  W = C * SQRT(A**2 + B**2)
        PRINT 41,  B, W
    41  FORMAT (1PE12.4, 1PE12.4)
        B = B + STEPB
        IF (B - FINB) 6, 6, 3
        END
        25.
        50.
        100.
        250.
        500.
```

(b)

(a)

Figure 2.3-4   GUY 2.

more elaborate in that it goes through the same series of calculations several times, each time with a different value of A, the altitude of the triangle. We would like a table showing how W varies with B for A = 25, another table for A = 50, and so forth over quite a wide range of A. As far as the inner loop is concerned we can handle it exactly as we did before: calculate with a given value of B, step B, and then test it in an IF statement. If there is more to do, go back to statement 6 to calculate again; if it has completed its range go way back to statement 3 to get a new value of A, and start the series of calculations for different values of B all over again.

The program for GUY 2 follows in a quite straightforward fashion from the flow chart, as can be seen in Figure 2.3-4b. Make sure you understand what is accomplished by each statement, and how it derives from the corresponding operation in the flow chart. Note that unlike GUY 1, this program is not terminated by executing a STOP statement; it never encounters any. This program will terminate by running out of data. There will come a time when the program is sent back to statement 3 to read in another value of A, and there are no more cards waiting to be read. At this point, in one way or another processing will stop, and the program will be terminated. Note however that the END statement must still appear, as always.

In this connection it is well to plan at this point the proper arrangement of the data we will be presenting for the program to work with at execution time. Every time our program passes through the READ statement, it will try to read in a number from a card. It will work better if we have seen to it that it reads in the right number. Since in this system no object deck is produced for us to have to handle, all we need to do is follow the END statement which marks the end of our list of instructions with the series of values of A for which we want the calculations performed, as shown at the end of Figure 2.3-4b. These should be punched one to a card, for each time the A loop is executed the next card is passed through the reader, and its contents read in.

In retrospect, what GUY 2 accomplishes is a calculation of W for a series of values of A, each for a series of values of B. The several values of B are obtained by stepping through the specified range, first adding the given increment and then iterating using an IF statement to test and branch.

Suppose we try an alternate way of doing almost the same thing. Let us use a DO loop instead of an IF loop. This means that instead of generating the next B from the preceding one we specify in advance a set of values, as listed in Figure 2.3-2, then use our subscripting power to step through them. Seven values of B are shown, covering about the same range as before.

One of the first things noticed in the flow diagram for GUY 3, Figure 2.3-5a, is that there are two DO loops, not one. The first is used merely to get the 7 values of B read in and stored as an array; the other is used inside the A loop to step through the 7 values of the B array in the calculation block. In this diagrammatic representation, note that two different symbols are used together to represent a DO loop: one to mark the beginning and point of return; the other, the end of the range and the index test performed. When this is compared with the actual program in Figure 2.3-5b, however, it will be seen that the second of these blocks, the diamond symbolizing the test-for-completion part

```
C       T V STAR    **   GUY 3   **
C       THIS IS GUY 3 TO TABULATE THE FUNCTION   W = C * SQRT(A**2 + B(J)**2)
C       OVER THE RANGES  B(J)=  5, 10,  20,  50, 100, 200, 500
C               AND     A = 25, 50, 100, 250, 500
C
        DIMENSION B(7)
        C = 1.
        PRINT 40,  C
   40 FORMAT (1PE12.4)
        DO 4  J = 1, 7
    4 READ 40, B(J)
    6 READ 40,  A
        PRINT 40,  A
        DO 10  J = 1, 7
        W = C * SQRT(A**2 + B(J)**2)
   10 PRINT 41,  B(J), W
   41 FORMAT (1PE12.4, 1PE12.4)
        GO TO 6
        END
         5.
        10.
        20.
        50.
       100.
       200.
       500.
        25.
        50.
       100.
       250.
       500.
```

(b)

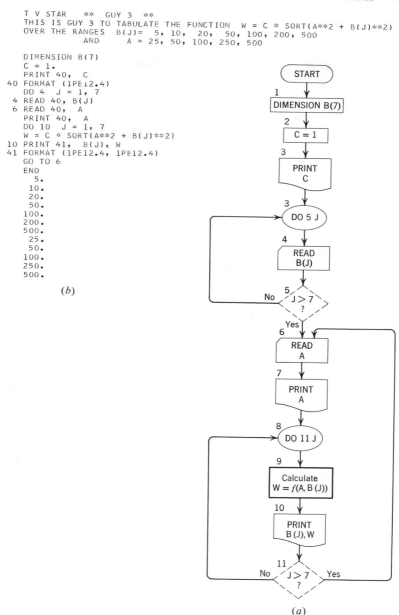

(a)

Figure 2.3-5   GUY 3.

of the operation, does not have to be included in the program as any specific statement. Its function is completely included in the DO statement itself. This means, furthermore, that the numbered statement to which the DO statement refers—its "object," as we call it—can be the last statement *preceding* the diamond-shaped test block. As an example, look at the lower DO loop here in Figure 2.3-5*a*, and keep it in mind as you look at the actual program written from this diagram, Figure 2.3-5*b*.

The second DO statement says. "DO everything down to statement 10 with J ranging from 1 to 7." Each time through we calculate a new W, using the current B(J), otherwise proceeding exactly as in GUY 2. The only two places the subscript J is used in this loop are here, in squaring B(J) and adding it to A squared, and in the PRINT statement to put out the current value of B(J) for identification. Notice that this DO loop includes a PRINT statement so that the 7 values of W are calculated *and printed* before going on to the next statement, which in turn sends control back to read in the new value of A.

As was mentioned above, although the object of the DO statement in the flow diagram of Figure 2.3-5*a* seems to be the test "Is J greater than 7?" which is block 11 in the diagram, we find in the program proper, Figure 2.3-5*b*, that there is no such statement. The solution, it was said, is to hang the statement number we want to use as a target on the last executable statement which precedes block No. 11. Accordingly, we find in Figure 2.3-5*b* that the second DO statement indeed says

$$DO\ 10\ J = 1, 7$$

This is why blocks 5 and 11 are drawn dashed in the flow chart, part *a*. Although valid logic operations, they do not give rise to any actual FORTRAN statements in the program of part *b*.

Take a quick look over the earlier part of the program, too. A very extensive set of initial comments has deliberately been included to show the variety in type of heading that can be produced. Any card that starts with a C in column 1 will be ignored by the processor, so this procedure may be used to cause comments to be printed in our listing which will make it easier for other people, and for us, to follow our program. The price paid for this convenience is the slight extra effort of punching a few extra cards, plus a small amount of extra time at "read in" and in the listing procedure, but the time saved in most cases through greater readability and increased understanding is almost always well worth the price.

In the program proper, a DIMENSION statement comes first to reserve consecutive storage locations for the array B( ), then the DO loop to read in B( ), and then the main loop as discussed above.

Note the complete set of data which must accompany the instructions to make up the complete program. The sequence of presentation of the numerical values is not arbitrary, but is carefully arranged so that the numbers will be presented to the computer in exactly the same sequence that the instructions will call for them as the program is executed.

Consider yourself a computer for a moment and scan the instructions of the program GUY 3 as though you were actually executing the program, looking particularly for READ statements. What is the first one you come to? It is statement

4 READ 40, B(J)

So the first numerical value in the data list below the END statement should be the first value of B, B(1), which indeed it is [B(1) = 5]. In the course of executing the program, what is the next READ statement encountered? Statement 6? Not at all. Statement 4 is embedded in a DO loop, which will require that it be executed seven times before being satisfied. Each time statement 4 is passed through, the computer will try to read a card, calling the number it finds punched there the next element in the array B(J). Then and only then does control finally reach statement 6 which calls for reading in another number and calling it A. The number 25 is found, and read in. Now the second DO loop is entered and calculation with that A and with each of the seven values of B is carried out. When all seven have been done and the DO loop satisfied, control finally passes on to the GO TO statement, which of course returns it to statement 6 where the next value of A is read. Since all calculations with the old value of A have been completed, we do not need that value any longer, and each time the new value of A can be read in on top of, destroying and superseding the old.

In this fashion execution of the program continues until 5 values of A have been read in and used. The sixth time it tries to execute statement 6, no further cards are found waiting in the data deck, and computation stops.

While on the subject of assigning values to variables, it may have been noticed that we first defined C as a variable and then immediately specified a constant value for it each time. Why not merely use the constant 1 in the first place, or even omit it all together, since it is a multiplicative constant at that? The reason this has been done in all versions of GUY WIRE to date shows up when we look at the specifications of the last of the four versions, GUY 4, in Figure 2.3-2. In this version we have at last a true 3-variable problem: we specify not only a series of values for B, and another series for A, but also 3 different numbers for C which we want the computer to step through automatically. This turns out to require two DO loops, one inside the other.

The first part of the flow diagram shown in Figure 2.3-6a merely handles the initialization process, dimensioning, reading in, and so forth. Note that there are now 2 arrays which have to be completely read in and stored before we can start calculating.

We do not bother to write a DO loop for the various values of C, but merely treat this variable as we have been treating A, reading in a new value each time we finish all the calculations on the old. However, A is stepped by a DO loop, using I as the index, and for each value of A(I), B is stepped by another, this time using J. This is perfectly legal and we can nest any number of DO's we like so long as each is completely inside the next with no overlapping.

One odd point should perhaps be commented on here. It was pointed out in the discussion of GUY 3 that the object of a DO loop can be made the last statement preceding the point at which one would insert the test for completion. How does this work out in GUY 4, where one DO is inside another? The last operation in the outer DO loop is block No. 11, the test for completion on I, but the operation immediately preceding that pseudo-statement is the test in the inner DO loop, block No. 10. The flow charts show the DO statements numbered according to the fictitious operations, one saying DO 10 and the other DO 11. How do we write actual FORTRAN statements to do this?

Since it has been said that the statement to be associated with the object-statement number must be the last executable statement inside the loop, it seems right enough that the object of the No. 10 loop should be the PRINT statement, block No. 9, so the DO statement, block No. 7, should read

$$DO \ 9 \ J = 1, 7$$

However the last actual operation inside the outer loop, the operation which terminates the I loop for A(I), is the PRINT statement also. Do we number the PRINT statement both 9 and 11, or will we have to have two different statements here?

The answer is neither. Quite apparently we cannot have two different statement numbers for the same statement, but it turns out we can use the same statement with the same number as the object of two different DOs. Since this feature automatically guarantees that one DO loop will be completely within the range of the other, it is perfectly proper for them to have a common last statement. So the first DO statement corresponding to block No. 5 can also say

$$DO \ 9 \ I = 1, 5$$

In the actual program listing, Figure 2.3-6b, it can be seen how this works out: the J loop for B(J) goes down to the PRINT statement each

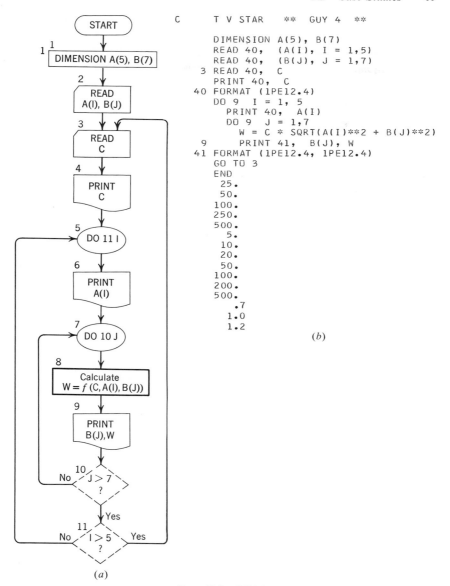

```
C     T V STAR   **  GUY 4  **

      DIMENSION A(5), B(7)
      READ 40,  (A(I), I = 1,5)
      READ 40,  (B(J), J = 1,7)
   3  READ 40,  C
      PRINT 40,  C
  40  FORMAT (1PE12.4)
      DO 9  I = 1, 5
         PRINT 40,  A(I)
         DO 9  J = 1,7
            W = C * SQRT(A(I)**2 + B(J)**2)
   9        PRINT 41,  B(J), W
  41  FORMAT (1PE12.4, 1PE12.4)
      GO TO 3
      END
       25.
       50.
      100.
      250.
      500.
        5.
       10.
       20.
       50.
      100.
      200.
      500.
       .7
      1.0
      1.2
```
(*b*)

(*a*)

Figure 2.3-6   GUY 4.

time, and, after executing the PRINT operation, tests for completion of
this DO. So long as it is incomplete, it returns to the *nearest* DO and
calculates again. When this DO loop is finally satisfied, the program is
able to keep track of the fact that it is still in the process of working on

another DO from farther back, so it increments this index I and tests to see whether this DO is satisfied. If not, it goes back to the DO statement that initiated the I loop and starts calculating with the next A(I). This actually means reentering the inner DO loop, reinitializing it, and going around on this one 7 more times, this time with a new value of A(I). Not until the outer loop is finally satisfied does control finally pass on to the GO TO statement, which in turn sends it back to statement 3 to read in another C.

One bit of shorthand has been employed in this program that has not been presented before. Look at the form of the first two READ statements, corresponding to block 2 in the flow chart, which read in the two arrays A( ) and B( ). This notation is called "implied DO," or "indexing in an input-output list." The similarity to the index and parameter part of a DO statement is quite apparent. The first of these statements means, for instance, READ in all values of A(I), with I going from 1 to 5. Note that the *range* of the implied DO loop is specified by enclosing in parentheses that part of the operation which is to be repeated.

In fact the pair of statements

$$\text{DO } 1 \text{ I} = 1, 5$$
$$1 \quad \text{READ } 40, \text{A(I)}$$

would perform exactly the same function as the single statement

$$\text{READ } 40, (\text{A(I)}, \text{I} = 1, 5)$$

although at the expense of appreciably more writing and one extra card to be punched and read in.

In fact we can go still further than is shown here. Just as we can follow one DO loop with another, so we can combine these two "implied DO" READ statements into a single list belonging to one READ statement, thus:

$$\text{READ } 40, (\text{A(I)}, \text{I} = 1, 5), (\text{B(J)}, \text{J} = 1, 7)$$

In section 2.2 one item of business was left unfinished—the explanation of what a CONTINUE statement is, what it does, and how it is used. What it is, is simple: a statement that causes no operation to take place but merely passes control on to the next statement. Why it is, is a bit harder to understand. We will study the why by studying an example of a program that makes use of it, for there is no better way to appreciate the CONTINUE statement than to try to write, without it, a program that has to have it.

The following problem can be stated quite simply and comprehended relatively easily, and a procedure for arriving at the answer can be sketched out without much difficulty. Only when we try to write that procedure in FORTRAN do we hit an unseen snag, forcing us to invent a new type of statement if we want to continue.

Problem. What is the largest integer N for which the expression "sum of the squares of integers from 1 to N" does not exceed a specified limit L? For example, if L = 100, then N = 6, thus:

$$1 + 4 + 9 + 16 + 25 + 36 \qquad = 91$$
$$1 + 4 + 9 + 16 + 25 + 36 + 49 = 140$$

Figure 2.3-7*a* shows the flow chart for a calculating procedure that will produce the N asked for. Note that the technique of accumulating a sum always requires that we clear the tally register first, by setting NSUM = 0. Once that has been done we can use a DO loop and the index N itself to add successive terms to this sum. Each time we increase it, however, we must test the new value of the sum against the specified limit L, as in block No. 5, using an IF statement of the form

$$\text{IF (NSUM} - \text{L)} \; a, b, c$$

Block No. 6 we should be familiar with by now, being the implied IF test that is set up by the machinery of the DO itself. We have learned that we do not use the test in block 6 itself as the object of the DO, but can use the last preceding executable statement as the object. Unfortunately, if we tried that here, and wrote for block 3

$$\text{DO 5 N} = 1, \text{L}$$
$$\text{NSUM} = \text{NSUM} + \text{N} * \text{N}$$
$$5 \quad \text{IF (NSUM} - \text{L)} \; ?, ?, ?$$

we would run into two very real and unsurmountable problems.

(1) Back in the material on the DO statement in section 2.2, rule 9 says that the last statement in a DO must not be a transfer-of-control type of statement. A consideration of the diagrammatic representation of the DO, Figure 2.2-10, and a little speculation on how it would work in the present situation, tells us why. The machine language instructions to step the index and test it against m_2 are inserted into the machine language program immediately following the object statement, so that only *after* the object is executed does control pass on to the incrementing and testing operations. If the object, however, were a transfer of control, and it sent control on or back to some place else, the incrementing and testing operations would constantly be bypassed and the DO machinery would never work.

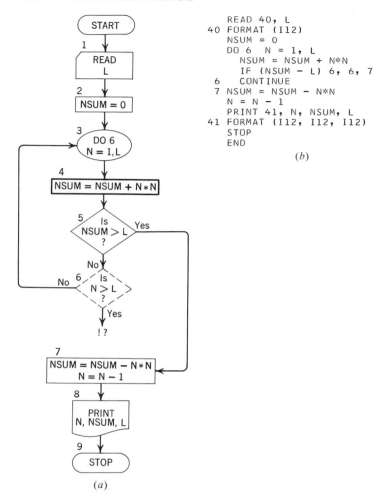

```
        READ 40, L
    40  FORMAT (I12)
        NSUM = 0
        DO 6   N = 1, L
            NSUM = NSUM + N*N
            IF (NSUM - L) 6, 6, 7
     6      CONTINUE
     7  NSUM = NSUM - N*N
        N = N - 1
        PRINT 41, N, NSUM, L
    41  FORMAT (I12, I12, I12)
        STOP
        END
```

(b)

Figure 2.3-7   Example to illustrate use of CONTINUE statement.

(2) In this particular case, the fact that we are in trouble shows up even sooner than that. The *c* exit for the IF test of block No. 5 is clear enough; it should go on to block No. 7 to back up one term and print the answer. But if quantity NSUM − L is less than or equal to zero, where do we want the program to go? We cannot direct control back to the DO statement, for that would re-initialize the DO and start over every time. We cannot have the IF send control back to block No. 4, the calculate block, for that would by-pass the incrementing and testing operations of the DO. And if we try to go on to the next statement

(remember there is no FORTRAN statement corresponding to block No. 6), we are at block No. 7, and we never iterate at all.

Figure 2.3-7*b* shows the way out of the jungle. The solution is achieved by inserting a statement 6, and making it a CONTINUE statement.

What is a CONTINUE? What does it do, and what is it doing here? Oddly enough, the answer is that it does not "do" anything. It causes no movement of data into or out of the computer, or from one part of the computer to another; it causes no operations to be performed. All it says is: "Go on to the next." But, by just being here, it serves as an excellent hatrack. It is a place for us to hang the statement number that marks the end of the range of the DO loop. As such, it performs a very valuable function indeed.

There are two situations in which you will find you need a CONTINUE statement as the object of a DO: if the last executable statement would otherwise be a transfer of control, or if the flow path is split within the DO loop but comes together again at the end of the range. In either case, it furnishes a very necessary reference point on which to hang the statement number marking the end of that range.

By now, enough sample programs and case studies have been presented to give a fairly comprehensive picture of the various ingredients of the FORTRAN language, and how to talk and write in it. In the following section one of these case studies, GUY 2, will be followed through the procedure of punching that program on cards, listing it, checking it, correcting it, and finally running it on the computer and getting some answers.

2.4   OPERATING PROCEDURE

Having spent some time in learning the vocabulary of the FORTRAN language, we must now apply the acid test. Can we really make ourselves understood in this language? How bad is our accent? In particular, can we use instructions that a moron can follow correctly?

To see what the remainder of the communication problem really consists of, let us punch out GUY 2 and put it on the computer. In this section we will repair to the Computing Laboratory and carry through the complete procedure to be followed in preparing a problem, checking it, trying it out, correcting it, and finally running it on the computer.

Operating procedures vary widely, and no procedure that we describe here could be general enough to cover exactly all the steps in the procedure followed at any other computing installation, let alone yours. For that reason we will pick one and describe all its steps in detail, trusting to the staff operating the computer at your installation to issue the revisions and corrections necessary to bring it into conformity with the procedure *you* should follow. The procedure we will describe is operation under the FORGO system on the 1620, both because it is fairly common and because it is one of the simplest to describe.

Did we say we wanted to punch some cards? Then a handy device would be a card punch, shown in Figure 2.4-1. Although technically named the IBM 026 Printing Card Punch, it is commonly called a keypunch. *You* press a key, *it* punches a corresponding column of holes in a card. Each key produces the holes that correspond to one character. Each FORTRAN statement goes on one card.

There is a layout card or drum control card, mounted on a program drum at the rear of the 26. Its function is to set the tab stops and otherwise get the card layout you want. Sometimes these program drum cards get changed, so before you start punching, check to make sure that showing through the window at the top of your machine is the word FORGO as you can see in Figure 2.4-2. If not, call the staff member on duty in the laboratory. While you are at it, make sure that all three switches on top of the keyboard are thrown up, or to the ON position, too.

The machine should have been left with some cards in the hopper, and a blank card already fed into the punching station. If so this card will appear in the right-hand space of the three open spaces at the front

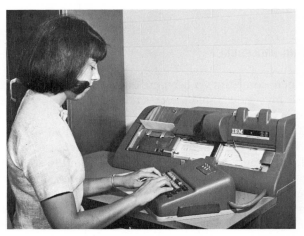

Figure 2.4-1   Keypunch.

Figure 2.4-2 Close-up of keypunch.

of the machine. If no card shows, press FEED (see Figure 2.4-3). A card will come down from the hopper into this space. Press FEED again. The first card will move to the left into position at the punches— this operation is called registering—and a second card will come down. Now we are ready to punch.

Punch what? We said, GUY 2. But where is it? This is not the time to

Figure 2.4-3 Keyboard of keypunch.

fumble around getting out our copy of the program we are going to punch. It should be all laid out beside us on the 26, ready to copy line by line, exactly as spelled out in Figure 2.3-4.

No reference has been made so far to the identification card that precedes every program deck into the 1620 in the FORGO system. The first card of every program must be a control card, laid out according to Figure 2.4-4. It must have the following information punched in it:

(1) At the extreme left, in columns 1 and 4, C   C. This identifies it as a control card and initiates the processing of a new program.

(2) Skip columns 5 and 6.

(3) Starting in column 7 FORGO expects a 6-digit identification number. This number will be reproduced on all output documents for positive identification.

(4) After the identification number, space twice more and add your name. This helps to identify you and your program.

(5) In addition to the above required punching, you may at this point, following your name, skip at least two more spaces and then put any other information you wish. You may want to have a name for your program, you may want to identify the course and assignment number, or you may have some other comments you want to use as a

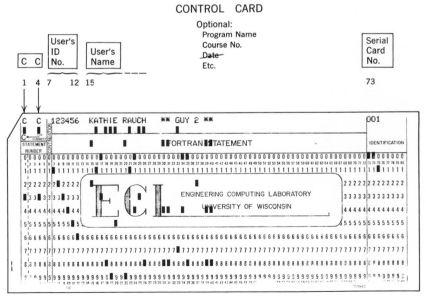

Figure 2.4-4   FORGO control card.

heading. The entire contents of the control card will be printed across the top of the page when you make the listing of your program, and you may use all the rest of the card up through column 72 for this information. If the information you would like to see printed is more than will go into that space, you may add any number of additional comment cards following the control card, or for that matter anywhere in the program.

To make a comment card, punch a C in column 1, after which you may punch any combination of meaningful (or meaningless) letters and characters anywhere else in the card. The C in column 1 will cause the rest of the card to be completely ignored by the FORTRAN processor. Recommended practice is to skip, after the initial C, to column 7, which is the beginning of FORTRAN statements themselves.

It would appear offhand that the date might be a useful piece of information to put on a control card, yet we see in Figure 2.4-4 that this item has been crossed off. Why? Because it is such valuable information that the 407 printer has been instructed to supply it at the top of every page you print. It is therefore not necessary to punch it in your heading —it is supplied free.

Having completed the desired heading in the remaining columns of the control card, there is one last bit of punching that is highly desirable. Using the 8 columns from 73 to 80, it is strongly recommended that you serially number the cards of your program. Not only does this bit of identification help when checking and correcting your program, the first time you neglect to serially number your cards and then drop them, you will wish you had.

In this example we will use columns 73, 74, and 75 for a 3-digit identification number. It is well to leave a spare column or two at the right of your serial punching for insertion of additions or corrections later. If you find you need to add 2 cards between 13 and 14, for instance, you can call them 13.1 and 13.2, or if you prefer, 13A and 13B. This *card number,* by the way, is completely ignored by the computer. It is not to be confused with the *statement number* which you place to the left of certain statements to identify that point in your program to the computer. These card numbers are for your identification only.

This completes the information you should include on a control card. Now back to the keypunch and let us punch it all in.

Starting in column 1 hit: C space space C; this takes us up through column 4. Now you could space twice, passing 5 and 6, and you would be ready to punch in 7, where the next item goes. Alternatively, you could, after punching the second C in column 4, just use the tab stop setting in the program drum card to skip to column 7. To do this just push SKIP. From anywhere west of column 6, this will land you right at 7 ready to go. It might be noted in Figure 2.4-3 that there are 2 keys with the word SKIP, but only the one at the right actually performs this operation. The upper key is associated with certain accounting procedures for a "skip-on-minus" operation, which does not concern us here.

Note that the information keys are light grey and the control keys, in most cases, are dark. Our main use of the latter will be with DUPLICATE, RELEASE, FEED, SKIP, NUM, and occasionally REGISTER. Now we are about to encounter the upper case shift key for numerals. In columns 7 to 12 is to go our 6-digit identification student number, but before we start punching, a careful look at that keyboard is in order. It is arranged like an ordinary typewriter keyboard as far as letters are concerned, but not with respect to numbers. They are not only arranged in three rows of three over at the right, but they are all in upper-case positions. This means that we must always shift to upper case before striking a numeral, and furthermore, we must hold the shift key down for every numeral key we punch. There is no shift lock. The shift key is called NUM for numerals, and in Figure 2.4-5 we show the procedure for actually punching the first digit of our sample student identification number, a 1. Note that this must be the digit 1 and not a lower case L, as is often used in straight typing. After the student identification number, hit the space bar twice and type your name. After that move over two more spaces and add any other information

Figure 2.4-5   Upper case for numerals on the 026.

you want. Hit SKIP again and the card will stop at column 73 where you may insert your serial card number. When you have completed punching all the information to be entered on any one card, merely press release, REL. This will cause three things to happen:

(1) The card you have just punched will be released and moved over to the reading station where you can see it in the middle window.

(2) The card waiting behind the card you are punching will be moved over to the punching station and registered with column 1 under the punches.

(3) Another blank card will feed in and stay in the waiting position.

Now, you are ready to start on your second card, the first line of your program. This is an arithmetic statement, which says C = 1., and, like all unnumbered statements, it should start in column 7. The first thing to press then is SKIP, which will automatically line you up in column 7. There is nothing, by the way, which says you cannot start farther to the right than column 7; in fact, providing that you do not put anything to the left of column 7, you may use spaces just about anywhere you wish in your statements. The spacing will not affect the operation and it can sometimes be used to make a more pleasing arrangement and one that is more easily followed by the eye. So, go ahead and punch the C, with or without a space after it, then the equals sign, and then space, the digit 1, and finally a decimal point. There are a couple of problems here. The equal sign and the decimal point, like certain other punctuation marks and special characters, are both in the upper-case position. So, it is necessary to hold down the numerals key while punching those, too. It is a cross-handed operation which makes any true typist wince, as there is only one numerals key, at the left side of the keyboard, but eventually it will seem almost natural. In this case, having no good habits to break is actually an advantage.

After the last digit and the decimal point, skip to column 73, enter your card number, and release.

Card No. 3—PRINT 40, C. The process here is very similar to that used for card 2: skip, punch the statement, skip, punch the card number, release. No problems here.

What happens when you look up for a moment and lose your place in the line? Or, if you are not quite sure what you actually struck for the last character and want to look at it to see? This is one of the most annoying features in the design of this particular piece of equipment. The last two or three columns punched are hidden under the punch head and will not come into view until you move on. The way to get around this is to use the back space button, which appears in Figure 2.4-5 just about in the center of the picture. It is the fairly good-size, squarish, grey button, right above the three toggle switches on the top of the keyboard in this picture. Press it once and it backs up one column. Hold it down and it continues to back space until what you want to see comes into view. Having determined what you want to know, be sure to restore the card to the proper column for the next punch, simply by using the space bar as many times as needed. Of additional assistance at times like this is the column indicator which points to the column number ready to be punched. In Figure 2.4-6 this indicator reads 13, which says that apparently we just punched the comma in 12 and are now ready to hit the space bar for column 13 and go on to put the C in 14.

If you find that you have made a mistake, one of the beauties of working with punched cards is that you can throw away just that one card and re-do it without having to go over all the rest of the program. The best procedure here is to release, take a black marker or pen, and make a very obvious X on the offending card, which should now be in the middle window in front of you. This way you can go ahead and punch the correct version now without stopping to try to get the bad card out of the punch while in the middle of the punching operation; it can be removed later when all the cards are out.

When you have finally finished punching your program (which should end with an END card of course—the statement END punched starting in column 7, just like any other statement), you should go ahead to punch any data the program will call for.

The data arrangement, since all these data items are real numbers and

Figure 2.4-6   Column indicator on the 026.

must have decimal points, is quite flexible, provided we observe two restrictions: (1) all the characters (digits, sign, decimal point, exponent-field, etc.) pertaining to any one item must be entirely within the first 12 columns—we shall see in Chapter 6 why none of them should be in column 1; (2) no spaces should be inserted in the middle of any number. There may be as many as desired before and after, such as might be wanted to line up decimal points, but once a number is started there should be no spaces until it is finished. This means, for instance, that minus signs should be punched immediately to the left of the first digit or the decimal point; plus signs may be included or omitted as desired.

When you have punched the last card of your data, how do you get the last card out? Just press REL as many times as necessary until your last card has been moved over to the left window and stacked up with the rest of your deck. True, this moves an extra blank card across the punch behind your program, but the next user can merely set aside the first card he gets out. The second card out will be his control card.

Now that you have your program deck completely punched, are you ready to run it on the computer? Far from it. There are two things you must do with your program yet before you are ready to go on the computer: list it, and check it.

To make the listing we go over to the 407, shown in Figure 2.4-7. Its official designation is an IBM 407 Accounting Machine, but for our purposes it is just a printer. Its input is punched cards; its output is a copy of what is punched on those cards, printed on a page. To list your cards, joggle them on the joggle plate on the top of the machine so that

Figure 2.4-7 IBM 407 printer.

Figure 2.4-8   Placing cards in the 407 read hopper.

the edges of the deck are smooth, and then place your cards face down, cut corner out, in the read hopper located toward the left (see Figure 2.4-8). Place the cover plate back on the cards and then press START. You will have to hold the start button down until the first card prints; then the cards will keep feeding by themselves. As each card feeds, its contents are printed on one line across the page.

The 407 will stop when it reads in your last card, but when it stops it will probably not have printed the last line. Press START again and hold

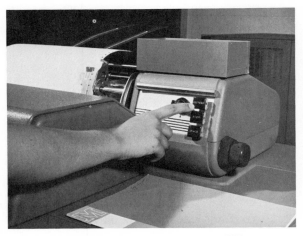

Figure 2.4-9   Restore button on the 407.

it until the last card has fed through the machine and has been stacked up with the rest of your deck.

Now remove your program deck from the stacker. When the last card was printed the 407 advanced the paper to the beginning of a new sheet. You should look at what it has printed at this point to make sure it has indeed printed your last line. If so, advance it one more page by pressing the RESTORE button (Figure 2.4-9) *once,* and when the paper stops, tear off the sheet or sheets with your program. There is a waste-basket handy for printed pages that are no good or not wanted. There is also a pile for blank pages that are torn off. The listing of your program produced by the 407 is shown in Figure 2.4-10. Now you are ready for the second of those two remaining steps: check your program through. This checking can *only* be done by two people working together. If you try to read it over by yourself, we *guarantee* that you will miss something. The only reliable method we have found is shown in Figure 2.4-11: get someone to help you check it over, sitting down side-by-side with your original coding sheet and the printed listing you made on the 407. As one person reads aloud from one copy, the other follows with his eye the other copy all the way through.

What is the value of all this? Simply that in our experience you can read through your program by yourself as many times as you wish, and still pass right over such obvious mistakes as the one shown in Figure 2.4-12. It is amazing how stupid our fingers can be.

More important than worrying about how it happened, let us correct the mistake. First, finish checking the rest of the list to see whether there are any more mistakes. If not, remove the offending card from the deck. Punch out a correctly spelled one and insert the good one in the

```
C   C   123456   KATHIE RAUCH    ** GUY 2 **                    001
        C = 1.                                                  002
        PRINT 40,  C                                            003
      3 READ 40,   A                                            004
        PRINT 40,  A                                            005
     40 FORMAT (1PE12.4)                                        006
        STEPB = A/5.                                            007
        FINB = 2*A                                              008
        B = STEPB                                               009
      6 W = C * SQRT(A**2 + B**2)                               010
        PRIMT 41,  B, W                                         011
     41 FORMAT (1PE12.4, 1PE12.4)                               012
        B = B + STEPB                                           013
        IF (B - FINB) 6, 6, 3                                   014
        END                                                     015
        25.                                                     016
        50.                                                     017
        100.                                                    018
        250.                                                    019
        500.                                                    020
```

Figure 2.4-10   407 listing of program.

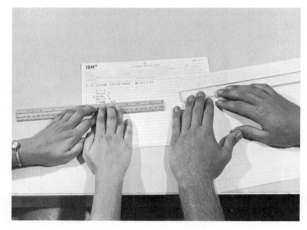

Figure 2.4-11   Checking program.

proper place in the deck. Better put the bad card in the salvage box right now to make sure it does not get picked up and used by mistake.

At last you are ready to match wits with the moron. You have the three prerequisites: your deck of punched cards, your 407 listing, and at least the first couple of answers you expect to get out of the program. Please do not waste valuable computer time by showing up with any of these three missing. You will not be permitted to use the computer. If you do have a deck, a listing from that deck, and some check answers, then when the time allotted you arrives, you can at last move over to do battle with the machine.

The 1620 computer shown in Figure 2.4-13 actually consists of 3 units: the main console and central processing unit, the 1623 auxiliary memory, holding an extra 20 or 40 thousand storage positions, and the 1622 card reader and punch unit. There may in addition be a 1443 on-line printer (we shall assume one for the following discussion), a 1311 disk file, or even a 1621 paper-tape reader. On the main console is an electric type-writer, which is wired directly into the computer and is used for certain testing operations, occasionally for inserting corrections and control statements, and for typing messages to the user.

Having signed in on the log book or deposited your time card, go over to the 1622, shown in Figure 2.4-14. First load your program deck,

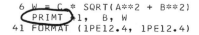

```
  6 W = C * SQRT(A**2 + B**2)
    PRIMT 1,  B, W
 41 FORMAT (1PE12.4, 1PE12.4)
```

Figure 2.4-12   Finding mistake.

Figure 2.4-13 IBM 1620 data-processing system.

Figure 2.4-14 Placing program in the 1622 read hopper.

with your control card at the beginning, into the read hopper of the 1622 located at the right end of this machine. Joggle the deck first to be sure the edges are even, and follow the instructions indicated on the hopper as to the direction and orientation of the cards. Once they are in place, there are only two buttons to press, one on this machine and one on the main console. The right-hand green button on the card read-punch says READER START. Press it. The words READER READY will light up. Then turn to the main console, press the START button there, and step back. The computer is reading in your program cards—you can see them piling up in the reader stacker just under the READER START button—and under control of FORGO, it is looking carefully at each statement, testing it and, only after the statement passes all tests, compiling it. A few seconds of intermittent light blinking and then the typewriter starts clacking. What does it say? "PROGRAM NOT ACCEPTED."

Now why do you suppose it said that? We will find out in just a minute, but first, since FORGO has rejected your program, we should get out of the way so someone else can use it. We sign out on the log, and turn to the 1622. First, pick up the program cards from the right-hand stacker bin. Because you had some data cards behind the program cards, however, some of your cards are still inside the machine. To get them out, lift up anything that is left in the read hopper, cover plate and all, and hold down the white button that says NON PROCESS RUN OUT. Any cards still in the machine will be run on out and deposited in the next stacker bin—the second from the right. Now put all three parts together, being careful to keep them in exactly the same sequence: first, the deck that had been run completely through, from the first stacker bin; second, the cards that were still in the machine, from the second bin; and, third, the cards not yet read into the machine still left in the read hopper.

Is that all? Not quite. It seems that FORGO has not only been checking your program very carefully before trying to compile and run it, it has kept track of what it found at every step along the way, and its findings are summarized in error comments it was making as it went along. Depending on the system, these may be printed on the console typewriter or on the on-line printer, or punched onto cards for off-line printing on the 407. Whatever the process, collect your copy and let us examine them (Figure 2.4-15).

```
FINB = 2*A
ERROR   AR-4  IN STATEMENT  0003   +   03 LINES

PROGRAM NOT ACCEPTED
```

Figure 2.4-15   Error comments.

Your control card is listed at the top for easy reference, next comes a message that error AR-4 has been detected in statement 3 plus 3 lines, with a copy of the offending statement right above it, and lastly the information we already knew, that the program was not accepted.

What is wrong with the statement in Figure 2.4-15? The statement says very simply

$$\text{FINB} \quad = \quad 2*A$$

To be sure, you have extra spaces around the equal sign, but that is not supposed to matter, and indeed, it does not. What is error AR-4? To find out what it means we refer to Figure 2.4-16. Note that part (*a*) is for error messages at compile time and part (*b*) for error messages at run time.

Running down the particular code cited on this occasion, we find that $AR-4$ indicates mixed mode in an arithmetic statement. Mixed mode, of course, refers to mixing integer and real quantities in the same expression. As you see from Figure 2.4-15, and can verify further from your original listing shown in Figure 2.4-10, you have indeed tried to do just that—mix modes. What is needed, of course, is a decimal point after the 2, so that the statement reads

$$\text{FINB} \quad = \quad 2.*A$$

As soon as you punch up a new card, making this statement in the proper form, you can ask for a chance to try it again. When you do, you go through the same procedure as before: cards in the read hopper, press READER START on the 1622 and the START button on the 1620. This time you get a much more encouraging message on the console typewriter: "PROGRAM ACCEPTED."

The program has not been run yet, but this is the signal that compilation has been completed, and the computer is now starting to execute the object program. If all goes well, your answers are probably just starting to come out.

It has been a struggle, but at last you have succeeded. The computer is busy calculating and printing away on your problem. You check the first answers that are put out by comparing them with the answers you had prepared in advance. In a very short time the computer finishes the data you gave it and says it is through with the problem by typing out a message indicating that it has finished with your program. When you look at the entire set of answers it gives you—and in Figure 2.4-17 we have listed the program and answers all on one sheet for simplicity—the final set of answers looks like this. Notice at the start of the answers the single value of C; at the head of each group, the value of A corresponding to that group; then 10 pairs of values of B and W.

(a) Compilation errors

Arithmetic	AR — 0	Undefined variable
	AR — 1	Improper sequence of operators
	AR — 2	Improper use of hierarchy
	AR — 3	Missing operator
	AR — 4	Mixed mode
	AR — 5	Argument of a function is fixed point
	AR — 6	Statement too complex
Control card	CC — 1	Second control card in program
Constants	CO — 1	Improper character in constant
	CO — 2	Improper fixed-point constant
	CO — 3	Improper floating-point constant
Dimension	DI — 1	Improperly formed dimension statement
	DI — 2	Improper size in dimensioning information
DO	DO — 1	No statement number given
	DO — 2	Object of DO is a transfer statement
	DO — 3	Object of DO has already appeared
	DO — 4	Improperly formed index
	DO — 5	Improperly formed parameters
Format	FT — 1	Unnumbered format statement
	FT — 2	Contradictory format reference
Computed GO TO	GO — 1	More than 11 statement numbers
	GO — 2	Improperly formed Computed GO TO
	GO — 3	Improperly formed index
IF	IF — 1	Improperly formed IF statement
	IF — 2	IF (SENSE SWITCH) without permission
	IF — 3	Sense switch not identified properly
Input-output	IO — 0	Undefined variable in output list
	IO — 1	Typewriter reference without permission
	IO — 2	Comma missing
Last card	LC — 1	No END statement in program
Overflow	OV — 1	Program too large for memory
	OV — 2	Symbol table too large for memory
Pause	PA — 1	PAUSE without permission
Subscripts	SS — 0	Undefined variable in subscript
	SS — 1	No DIMENSION statement for subscripted variable
	SS — 2	Improper subscript expression
Statement number	SN — 0	Undefined statement number
	SN — 1	Multiply defined statement number
	SN — 2	Improperly formed statement number
Subroutines	SR — 0	Undefined subroutine
	SR — 1	Multiply defined subroutine
Statements	ST — 1	Column 6 misused; statement missing altogether
	ST — 2	Too many or unpaired parentheses; illegal character
	ST — 3	Undecodeable statement
Symbols	SY — 1	Name of variable not correct
	SY — 2	Name of variable starts with numeral
	SY — 3	Variable already dimensioned

Arithmetic	AD	Addition	(It should be noted that square
	SB	Subtraction	root is handled as **.5)
	MP	Multiplication	
	DV	Division	−0 Undefined numerical quantity
	XX	Exponentiation(**)	−1 Fixed-point overflow
	EX	Exponentiation(EXP)	−2 Floating-point overflow
	LG	Logarithm	−3 Division by zero
	SI	Sine	−4 Negative number
	CS	Cosine	−5 Zero
	AT	Arctangent	
	SQ	Square root	
	FF	Fixing or floating	
	VA	Storing a variable	

Subroutine	CL − 1	A RETURN before a CALL, or two CALLS without a RETURN
DO	DN − 0	Undefined parameter or index
	DN − 1	Some parameter is not positive
	DN − 2	Nested DO loops have same index, or range of DO has been entered improperly
Format	FM − 1	Some error in using a format statement
Computed GO TO	GO − 0	Index is undefined
	GO − 4	Index is outside range of branches
IF	IF − 0	Argument of IF statement is undefined
Input	IN − 1	Some error in input data
Last card	LC − 2	Ran out of data cards
Output	OR − 0	Undefined numerical quantity
	OR − 2	Mixed mode between number and format statement
	OR − 3	Data exceeded width given in format statement
	OR − 4	Exceeded maximum line image of 120 characters (This may destroy part of processor, but if so the processor will not operate.)
Subscripts	SC − 0	Subscript is undefined
	SC − 1	Subscript is outside range of DIMENSION statement

(c) General

Each error message consists of an error code and the number of the offending statement. The error code consists of two letters and a numeral, which together indicate the type of error detected. The error codes given above are divided into those produced during compilation and those produced during execution of the object program.

It should be noted that the compiler may give an error comment on an acceptable statement if some previous error has given the compiler incorrect information. For example, statement 1 below will produce an AR − 4 error message, and because of this, statement 2 will produce an AR − 0 message.

$$\begin{array}{ll} 1. & X = 1. + 2 \\ 2. & Y = X \end{array}$$

Figure 2.4-16 Error messages.

```
C   C   123456   KATHIE RAUCH    ** GUY 2 **

    C = 1.
    PRINT 40,  C
 40 FORMAT (1PE12.4)
  3 READ 40,  A
    PRINT 40,  A
    STEPB = A/5.
    FINB = 2.*A
    B = STEPB
  6 W = C * SQRT(A**2 + B**2)
    PRINT 41,  B, W
 41 FORMAT (1PE12.4, 1PE12.4)
    B = B + STEPB
    IF (B - FINB) 6, 6, 3
    END
     25.
     50.
    100.
    250.
    500.
```

(a) Program

```
1.0000
2.5000E+01
5.0000        2.5495E+01
1.0000E+01    2.6926E+01
1.5000E+01    2.9155E+01
2.0000E+01    3.2016E+01
2.5000E+01    3.5355E+01
3.0000E+01    3.9051E+01
3.5000E+01    4.3012E+01
4.0000E+01    4.7170E+01
4.5000E+01    5.1478E+01
5.0000E+01    5.5902E+01
5.0000E+01
1.0000E+01    5.0990E+01
2.0000E+01    5.3852E+01
3.0000E+01    5.8310E+01
4.0000E+01    6.4031E+01
5.0000E+01    7.0711E+01
6.0000E+01    7.8103E+01
7.0000E+01    8.6023E+01
8.0000E+01    9.4340E+01
9.0000E+01    1.0296E+02
1.0000E+02    1.1180E+02
1.0000E+02
2.0000E+01    1.0198E+02
4.0000E+01    1.0770E+02
6.0000E+01    1.1662E+02
8.0000E+01    1.2806E+02
1.0000E+02    1.4142E+02
1.2000E+02    1.5620E+02
1.4000E+02    1.7205E+02
1.6000E+02    1.8868E+02
1.8000E+02    2.0591E+02
2.0000E+02    2.2361E+02
2.5000E+02
5.0000E+01    2.5495E+02
1.0000E+02    2.6926E+02
1.5000E+02    2.9155E+02
2.0000E+02    3.2016E+02
2.5000E+02    3.5355E+02
3.0000E+02    3.9051E+02
3.5000E+02    4.3012E+02
4.0000E+02    4.7170E+02
4.5000E+02    5.1478E+02
5.0000E+02    5.5902E+02
5.0000E+02
1.0000E+02    5.0990E+02
2.0000E+02    5.3852E+02
3.0000E+02    5.8310E+02
4.0000E+02    6.4031E+02
5.0000E+02    7.0711E+02
6.0000E+02    7.8102E+02
7.0000E+02    8.6023E+02
8.0000E+02    9.4340E+02
9.0000E+02    1.0296E+03
1.0000E+03    1.1180E+03
```

(b) Answers

Figure 2.4-17 Program with answers.

OPERATING PROCEDURE

(To punch program and data)

(26) 1. Check that FORGO layout card shows and that all switches are on.
2. Punch Control Card (follow sample).
3. Punch program, one statement per card. For keyboard layout, control switches, see diagram. Use NUM for upper case, SKIP to tab to 7 or 73, REL to release.

(To list what has been punched)

(407) 1. Turn ON.
2. Joggle cards; load in read hopper, bottom first, face down.
3. Press START, hold for two cycles. When it stops, press again till last card.
4. Check that listing is complete; press RESTORE and tear off.
5. Turn OFF.

> **CHECK PROGRAMS!**
> **OBTAIN CHECK ANSWERS!**

(1620) (To run program)

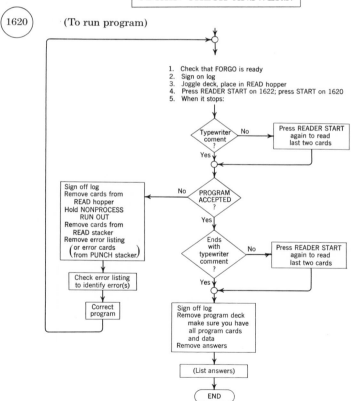

Figure 2.4-18 How to run a FORGO problem on the 1620.

The format used here is the standard floating-point form, 1 digit to the left of the decimal point, the whole thing rounded to 5 significant figures. That looks good, and off you go to plot those results.

Now, can you remember all those steps? Could you walk into the laboratory and do your next program alone, without any coaching? No? That is not too surprising. Even reduced to this degree of simplicity, the world of computers is a confusing, even though fascinating, new environment. To help sort out the details of these operations in your mind, and to serve as a useful reference for future operations, Figure 2.4-18 presents a summary of FORGO operating procedures.

At any rate, your first communication test has been successfully passed. You were able to say it in FORTRAN, and say it clearly enough (on the second try, anyway) so that the moron knew what you meant. It will take a lot more experience, of course, to become really fluent, but with the confidence that you do know how to make it work, you are in a good position to go ahead in the next chapter and acquire that experience, fluency, and a knowledgeable awareness of just what the information machine is good for.

PROBLEM 2.2-2   "Parens Know Best"

In the following expressions, assume that the variables have the values

$$A = 1$$
$$B = 2$$
$$C = 3$$
$$D = 4$$

Fill in the blanks with the value that would be calculated. After you have finished, go back over the list and notice in which cases the parentheses changed the meaning.

(A)   C * B/A
       (C * B)/A
       C/A * B
       (C/A) * B

(B)   B * C ** 2
       B * C ** 2.
       B * (C ** 2.)
       C ** 2. * B
       C ** (2. * B)

(C)   A + B * C
       (A + B) * C
       A + (B * C)

(D)   B + C/A + D
       (B + C)/(A + D)

CHAPTER 3.

Things Worth Computing:
[A] THE SAME THING OVER AND OVER

3.1 PERSPECTIVE

Now that we have learned a little about the vocabulary and grammar of the language of our giant moron—this language called FORTRAN—let us find out how good our accent is. The real test of mastery of a new language, of course, is to have to use it, to get across important ideas, like, "How much does this cost?" or "Can you direct me to the place I am looking for?"

In the rest of the book we are going to be making a survey of some of the things our moron can do. We will look separately at several of the capabilities of high-speed computers, and in each case discover a few of the areas of application that this particular capability has led to. We will try to get a feeling for the types of problems to be solved, and the ways the computer can help, by actually using the language to program some simple examples in each case. Some of the problems will be extremely easy, so much so that you may wonder why on earth anybody would use a computer to do such a simple job. But after we have added a few complicating factors, and then a few more, the problem will begin to take on enough meaning so that it is not hard to extrapolate the rest of the way to the kind of situation existing in real life, and have a fairly good picture of just how computers are really put to work.

In this chapter we will look at some of the routine, repetitive calculations that the computer can do for us so well. These are jobs that require doing the same thing over and over again, for hundreds and even thousands of times, each time with one or more of the numerical factors slightly different.

If the computer is supposed to work with slightly (or even grossly) different numbers each time it repeats, a good question to ask is, "Where does the next set of data come from?" There are two answers to that.

3.2 EXTERNAL DATA

In one whole class of problems, the next number or set of numbers comes from outside the machine; they are *external* data. That is, the person who writes the program does not include the data in the program, but expects at least some of it to be *read* in (that means using a READ statement, of course) at the time the program is actually run. In a typical situation, a program will carry out one set of calculations, do something with the result, and then go back to (GO TO) a READ statement earlier in the program to *read* in the next piece or set of data.

As an example, let us get the computer to help us do a very simple problem: convert an altitude from feet to miles.

It is common today to talk of a jet plane cruising at 37,000 feet, or of another having a ceiling of, say, 70,000 feet. It sometimes helps to visualize this altitude if we express it in miles; however, for most of us this conversion (dividing by the number of feet in a mile, or 5280) is not a simple operation to be done rapidly in the head.

We shall assume that we are going to ask a computer to make these conversions for us. We approach the computer, therefore, with a set of cards, each of which has punched in it 1 number, a height expressed as a real number between 0 and 100,000. What is required is a computer program that will read a card, take the number punched in it to be a height in feet, calculate the corresponding height in miles, print it out, and repeat until it runs out of cards.

Figure 3.2-1*a* shows the flow chart of a program, and (*b*) the program itself.

If this program is punched up and data attached as shown in Figure 3.2-1*c*, the result is as shown in (*d*) of the same figure.

The important characteristic of this program to note here is that when the calculation is finished for one set of data, we go back to a READ statement and read in a new value. The data for the calculation come from outside the program.

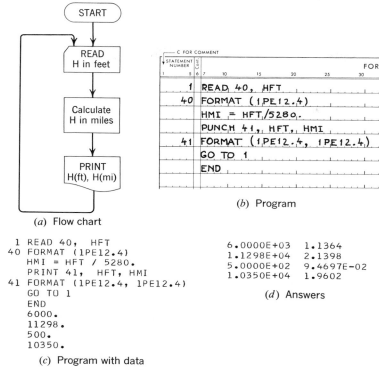

(a) Flow chart

(b) Program

(c) Program with data

(d) Answers

Figure 3.2-1a, b, c, d   Altitude conversion.

3.3   INTERNAL DATA

A fundamentally different type of program is called for if we decide that, instead of feeding the computer a series of unrelated values of height to work with, one at a time, we will ask it to make up a conversion table. Now we will ask it to step uniformly through the range of values of height we expect to be interested in, and print out two columns of numbers: an altitude in feet and the equivalent altitude in miles. One of the lists of numbers (usually the one to the left) should be arranged in ascending order, and progress by uniform steps of nice round numbers through the desired range.

This now means that all of the data that determine the desired values of the independent variable can be included in the program itself, and the program can *generate* its own next data.

If we decide, for instance, that we would like a table giving an entry for each value from 0 to 100,000 feet, in steps of 5000 feet, the program could look like the one in Figure 3.3-1.

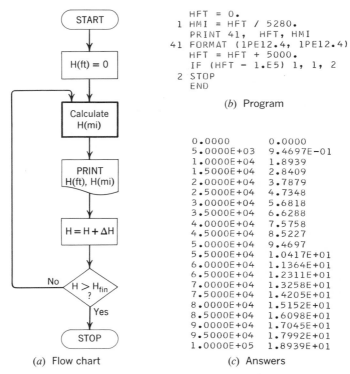

```
             HFT = 0.
         1   HMI = HFT / 5280.
             PRINT 41,   HFT, HMI
        41   FORMAT (1PE12.4, 1PE12.4)
             HFT = HFT + 5000.
             IF (HFT - 1.E5) 1, 1, 2
         2   STOP
             END
```

(*b*) Program

```
0.0000          0.0000
5.0000E+03      9.4697E-01
1.0000E+04      1.8939
1.5000E+04      2.8409
2.0000E+04      3.7879
2.5000E+04      4.7348
3.0000E+04      5.6818
3.5000E+04      6.6288
4.0000E+04      7.5758
4.5000E+04      8.5227
5.0000E+04      9.4697
5.5000E+04      1.0417E+01
6.0000E+04      1.1364E+01
6.5000E+04      1.2311E+01
7.0000E+04      1.3258E+01
7.5000E+04      1.4205E+01
8.0000E+04      1.5152E+01
8.5000E+04      1.6098E+01
9.0000E+04      1.7045E+01
9.5000E+04      1.7992E+01
1.0000E+05      1.8939E+01
```

(*a*) Flow chart   (*c*) Answers

Figure 3.3-1   Altitude conversion table.

A few points can be noted about this program:

(1) The most important thing is that when one calculation is finished (and printed out), the program itself generates the next value to be used for the computation. The data come from within the program itself; they are *internal* data.

(2) Since we cannot rely on merely running out of data cards to stop the program (it does not READ any), another way must be found to terminate the program. In this case the specification of the problem itself includes the range of the independent variable which the table should cover; we need merely insert this upper limit into a test that determines whether or not HFT is still within the desired range (the IF statement).

(3) Why is the set of alternate exits to the IF statement 1, 1, 2? Don't we want to quit at 100,000? The best way to answer this question is to try to write it 1, 2, 2, and then consider carefully what would be punched, and what exit would be taken, as HFT reached 90,000, 95,000, 100,000, and 105,000. Try it.

3.4 FUNCTION EVALUATION

A very important special case of this table-making type of operation occurs frequently in mathematics—the evaluation of functions. This frequently involves the making of just such a table of values of the independent and the dependent variable, usually so that we can plot the values and get a better picture of the behavior of the function.

For very simple equations, very simple procedures suffice to give us a picture. If

$$y = 5 \qquad (3.4\text{-}1)$$

for instance, it does not take a lot of calculating to be able to draw a picture of how y varies with x. It doesn't.

The equation

$$y = 2x + 3 \qquad (3.4\text{-}2)$$

is not a lot harder. Even if you do not recognize the type of equation, even if you do not remember that a *linear* relationship gives a *straight line,* in this case one that crosses the y axis at 3 and climbs twice as fast as x, calculation of just a few points would soon point out that the shape is as shown in Figure 3.4-1.

However, as the complexity of the function increases, our need for computational aid grows rapidly. Even a quadratic would slow most of us down a bit, and by the time we were asked to sketch out a graph of the function

$$y = x^6 - 5x^5 + 14x^4 - x^3 + 2x^2 - 9x + 17 \qquad (3.4\text{-}3)$$

a call for help is clearly in order. This is unquestionably a job for the computer.

What do we want the computer to do? Obviously we would like to be able to say, "Plot a curve of the interesting range of this function, and determine all the real roots." Well, leaving aside the fact that the word "plot" is not in our FORTRAN vocabulary (some computers do have curve drawing equipment directly attached), what is *most* wrong with this job statement is the phrase "the interesting range." How is a moron going to tell what range of the independent variable contains the behavior of interest? And are we going to be necessarily interested in the same things a moron is?

We will obviously have to be more specific. The best we can ask for at this stage is: "Tabulate the value of this function for all values of x from here to there, increasing in steps of so much."

What are the words in this instruction that will have to be replaced by numbers before the computer can do the work? They are: *this function, here, there,* and *so much.*

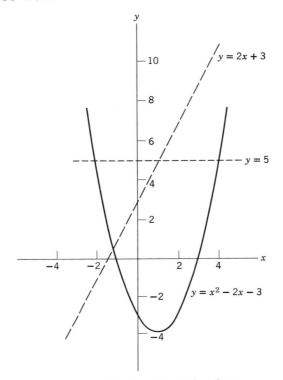

Figure 3.4-1   Graphs of simple functions.

Let us take the last three first. These are merely the familiar specifications of the range of the independent variable, and obviously require that we will have to supply to the program an initial value of x, a final value of x, and an increment by which x is to be increased between calculations.

The first one, *this function*, is easy for some types of functions, but can get much more complicated for others. To keep things simple, let us assume we are working on one class of functions only: polynomials in x. This means, for one thing, that we can use the polynomial evaluating scheme that we worked out in Chapter 2, when we first started looking at the DO statement. Let us see how we might construct such a program.

This program, *Polyplot*, shown in Figure 3.4-2a, is little more than a combination of the internal data-stepping program, discussed in the preceding section, with the polynomial evaluating program *Poly* from Chapter 2. Two small changes have been introduced in the process.

```
          DIMENSION A(30)
          READ 40, N
       40 FORMAT (I12)
          NP1 = N + 1
          READ 41, (A(J), J = 1, NP1)
       41 FORMAT (1PE12.4)
          READ 42, XINIT, DELX, XFIN
       42 FORMAT (3(1PE12.4))
          X = XINIT
        3 F = 0.
          DO 1 J = 1, NP1
        1 F = F*X + A(J)
          PRINT 43, X, F
       43 FORMAT (2(1PE12.4))
          X = X + DELX
          IF (X - XFIN) 3, 3, 2
        2 STOP
          END
               3
               1.
             -12.
              29.
             -16.
             -10.           1.           10.
```

(*a*) Program

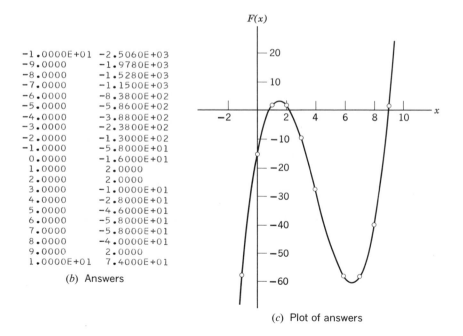

```
-1.0000E+01  -2.5060E+03
-9.0000      -1.9780E+03
-8.0000      -1.5280E+03
-7.0000      -1.1500E+03
-6.0000      -8.3800E+02
-5.0000      -5.8600E+02
-4.0000      -3.8800E+02
-3.0000      -2.3800E+02
-2.0000      -1.3000E+02
-1.0000      -5.8000E+01
 0.0000      -1.6000E+01
 1.0000       2.0000
 2.0000       2.0000
 3.0000      -1.0000E+01
 4.0000      -2.8000E+01
 5.0000      -4.6000E+01
 6.0000      -5.8000E+01
 7.0000      -5.8000E+01
 8.0000      -4.0000E+01
 9.0000       2.0000
 1.0000E+01   7.4000E+01
```

(*b*) Answers

(*c*) Plot of answers

Figure 3.4-2   *Polyplot*.

(1) *Poly* has been generalized to make it work for any *n*th-degree polynomial instead of merely a fourth-degree polynomial. This is accomplished by replacing the constant 4 by a variable N wherever it occurs, and requiring that before reading in the coefficients we will read in the value of N. We would then *like* to say, at S 0040 + 02 L,*

$$\text{READ } 41, (A(J), J = 1, N + 1)$$

but the parameters in a DO statement (see Section 2.2) are not permitted to be expressions, only constants or variables. We get around this by inserting an extra step to calculate N plus 1, and assign a new variable name to this quantity, NP1, in S 0040 + 01 L. Now S 0040 + 02 L can use this quantity to set up the implied DO loop to read in the coefficients, and so can the DO statement S 0003 + 01 L.

(2) It begins to get tiresome repeating format specifications as many times as there are items in the list. There is a shorter way, which is to supply a "repeater" in front of any specification to indicate how many times it is to be repeated. With this scheme

	I12, I12, I12	becomes 3I12
but		
	1PE12.4, 1PE12.4	becomes 2(1PE12.4)

and the FORMAT statement to read in the list called for in S 0041 + 01 L takes the form shown in S 0042 + 00 L.

Study how the 6 lines of data, which are punched one line to a card, are read in by the 3 READ statements. The first READ statement gets N first, for NP1 must be calculated in a separate statement. The second reads the next 4 lines, one at a time, to be the 4 coefficients. The last READ statement reads the 3 parameters, which are punched all on one card to show how it can be done.

The results of applying *Polyplot* to the equation

$$y = x^3 - 12x^2 + 29x - 16 \tag{3.4-4}$$

including a plot of the data so obtained, are illustrated in Figure 3.4-2*b* and *c*.

3.5   ROOT FINDING

One rather useful extension of *Polyplot* will be described before leaving this discussion. From Figure 3.4-2*b* it is apparent that there are

---

* S 0040 + 02 L is an abbreviation for Statement 0040 + 02 Lines, and refers here to the second READ statement.

roots of the equation (values of x that make the function zero) at *about* $+1^-$, $+2^+$, and $+9^-$ (1^+ means a value slightly greater than 1).

How could we get these values more accurately? To be precise, let us say to 5 significant figures?

Obviously a finer interval size is going to be needed. But it is certainly to be hoped that it will not be necessary to tabulate the entire range shown here in steps of 10^{-5} in x! For that matter, even now that we know the approximate range, if we ask the computer to use the finer step size to tabulate only the three intervals we know contain the roots (0–1, 2–3, 8–9), we are still asking for 300,000 iterations. Surely there must be a better way!

The clue comes from this last suggestion, that as soon as we know that a root lies within any given interval, we can increase the fineness of the scan for *that interval,* without wasting more than at most seven of the nine additional calculations. Now, if we can arrange to iterate on this process, whereby we track down the root to finer and finer intervals, we will have a reasonably efficient scheme.

There are two points to this scheme that help to make it efficient. One is that we use the smaller step size only in the interval where we have determined the root to lie. The other is that, whatever the level we are working, *as soon as* we discover we have passed a root, we back up and reduce the step size only in that interval just passed, so that we make no further evaluations of the function for the remaining tenths of the preceding interval.

For instance, if we are working from 2.2 to 2.3 in steps of .01 (Figure 3.4-2), we need evaluate only 2.21 (we already have 2.20), 2.22, 2.23, and 2.24, before we find we have passed the root. There is therefore no need to do any of the values from 2.25 to 2.29, but we start immediately on the 2.23 to 2.24 interval in steps of .001.

The flow chart of Figure 3.5-1*a* is worth studying, not only to see how the above principle applies, but to pick up a few points we have not mentioned.

For one thing, although we have spoken blithely about "noticing that we have passed a root," how do we explain to Moron how to watch for and detect this condition? Is there not a more automatic way than punching out all the answers, plotting them up, and requiring that we look at the results of every step and tell Moron what to do?

Of course there is. It requires analyzing a little more carefully the procedures we are so used to going through that we do not bother to think about the details any more.

How do *we* know when we have passed a root? Isn't it when we discover that the curve has crossed the x axis? And how do we know it has crossed the axis? Because the preceding value of the function was positive and this new one is negative, or vice versa. In other words, the sign of F has changed since the last value calculated.

IF (Sign Change) is quite easy to write in the FORTRAN language. It can be done in three IF statements if the sign tests are made one at a time, but it can be done in a single one if we remember that the rule for the sign of a product of two algebraic quantities is exactly the same

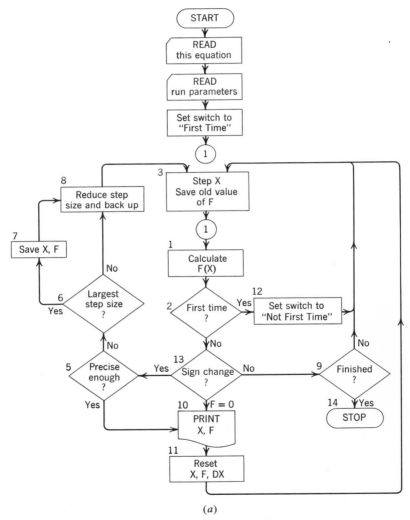

(a)

Figure 3.5-1   Roots by decimal tabulation.

```
C          ************************************
C          **   ROOTS BY DECIMAL TABULATION   **
C          ************************************
C       DIMENSION A(10)
                                    READ IN THIS EQUATION
        READ 40,  N
     40 FORMAT (I12)
        NP1 = N + 1
        READ 41,  (A(J), J = 1, NP1)
     41 FORMAT (1PE12.4)
C                                   READ PARAMETERS FOR THIS RUN
        READ 42,  XINIT, DELX, XFIN
     42 FORMAT (3(1PE12.4))
C                                   SET SWITCH TO *FIRST TIME*
        SW = 0.
        F  = 0.
        X = XINIT
        DX = DELX
        GO TO 1
C                                   SUBSTITUTE FOR NEXT PASS
      3 X = X + DX
        FOLD = F
C                                   CALCULATE F(X)
      1 F = 0.
        DO 4  J = 1, NP1
      4 F = F*X + A(J)
C                                   TEST FOR *FIRST TIME*
        IF (SW) 12, 12, 13
C                                   YES. SET SWITCH TO *NOT FIRST TIME*
     12 SW = 1.
        GO TO 3
C                                   NO. TEST FOR SIGN CHANGE
     13 IF (F*FOLD) 5, 10, 9
C                                    NO. TEST FOR XFIN, REPEAT
      9    IF (X - XFIN) 3, 14, 14
C                                   YES. IS THIS PRECISE ENOUGH
      5    IF(ABS(DX/DELX)-1.E-5)10,10,6
C                                    NO. WAS THIS A FIRST STEP
      6      IF (DX - DELX) 8, 7, 8
C                                      YES. SAVE X, F
      7        XSAVE = X
               FSAVE = F
C                                    IN ANY CASE, DECREASE DX
      8        DX = DX * (-.1)
               GO TO 3
C                                   YES. PRINT ROOT, RESET
     10      PRINT 43, X, F
     43 FORMAT (2(1PE12.4))
     11 X = XSAVE
        F = FSAVE
        DX = DELX
        GO TO 3
     14 STOP
        END
          3
          1.
        -12.
         29.
        -16.
          0.          1.         10.

 7.9727E-01 -6.7000E-05
 2.2388      5.9000E-05
 8.9639     -4.5300E-04
```

(b)

Figure 3.5-1*b*

as the rule we want to apply: If the two are different, the sign is negative; if the same, positive. So we can branch on the sign of the product of (the current value of F) and (the preceding value of F).

This means, of course, that we must always have the preceding value of F available for comparison. We see from the flow chart and the program of Figure 3.5-1, that each time we enter the central loop, before we calculate a new value of F we save the old value by copying it down: FOLD = F.

There is one problem: what to use for the old value of F the first time through? We cannot ignore the problem by arbitrarily setting F to something easy like zero; erroneous operation might occur, or a root missed, or both. It could be handled by always requiring that the value of F corresponding to XINIT be calculated by the user and read in along with the other data. But why make the user go through this? Instead, what we do is put a special switch in the program to bypass the test for sign change the first time. We name a variable SW for "switch," and test the sign of it in an IF statement (block 2). SW is set to zero by block number 0, which is executed only once, as the program is first entered. This first time control is sent directly to the calculate block and value of F corresponding to XINIT is calculated. Block 2, however, prevents the program from getting to block 13, for a sign change test at this point would be meaningless. Instead it sends it to block 12, where SW is set to 1, and then back to block 3. From now on block 2 always passes control on to block 13, and block 12 is never seen again.

Notice, furthermore, that it is never necessary to do resetting or starting over while tracking down any one root. To re-cover the interval using the next smaller step size, the only operation necessary is to multiply the last increment used by $-.1$, and return to the X = X + DX loop. A resetting operation is necessary, however, after a root has been found, to get back to the intervals specified in the input. For this reason the last values of X and F obtained on the original interval scan are saved, and later restored.

One very important final precaution should be stressed in the use of a program such as this. Without some knowledge of the behavior of the function, it is impossible to know what limits to set for the search, or indeed how fine the step size needs to be. The *only* way to be sure of finding all real roots is to have a reasonably accurate picture of the shape of the graph of the function first, and to pick the limits and step size so as to investigate all known and suspected real roots. It is therefore strongly recommended that, unless the information is known without going through the process, a tabulating program like *Polyplot* be used first, to enable a root-finding program like the *Roots by Decimal Tabulation* to be used intelligently.

PROBLEM 3.2-1   "Conversions"

WANTED

Programs that will accept data items, one at a time, calculate from each a converted or derived quantity, output both the given and the calculated values, and repeat. Prepare 5 data items to be used as input in each case.

	Input	Calculate
(A)	x (degrees)	sin (x)
(B)	x (degrees)	cos (x)
(C)	x (radians)	tan (x)
(D)	x (degrees)	tan (x)
(E)	x	arc sin (x) (radians)
(F)	x	arc sin (x) (degrees)
(G)	x	arc cos (x) (radians)
(H)	x	arc cos (x) (degrees)
(I)	C (degrees Centigrade)	F (degrees Fahrenheit)
(J)	F (degrees Fahrenheit)	C (degrees Centigrade)

PROBLEM 3.2-2   "Pythagoras Jones"

GIVEN

A series of cards each of which has two numbers punched in it, representing the two sides of a right triangle.

WANTED

Read a card, calculate the hypotenuse of the right triangle, print all three sides, and repeat until you run out of cards.

PROBLEM 3.2-3   "Score"

GIVEN

One card for each student in a class, each containing three exam grades (each is an integer between 0 and 100).

WANTED

Each student's average. Read a card, calculate the average of the three grades, and print the three grades and the average, for each. Repeat for the next student.

VERSION A. Show the answer as the nearest integer that does not exceed the average.

VERSION B. Show the answer as accurately as you can. Is it exact?

VERSION C. Show the answer rounded to the nearest integer.

VERSION D. Show the answer rounded to one decimal place.

VERSION E. Repeat A, except that the cards come in batches, one batch per student. In each batch, the first card contains a student identification number (one to four digits); each following card contains one exam grade only, but there may be from none to five exams for any student; a last card contains some identification to show that it is the last card in the batch. You determine how you would like to see such a card identified, and write your program accordingly. Print out the student identification number, the number of exam grades for him, and his average.

VERSION F. How could E be simplified if all identification numbers were exactly four digits, with the leftmost digit nonzero? Program it.

VERSION G. Modify E by requiring each exam grade to be accompanied by the student identification number punched in the same card.

PROBLEM 3.2-4   "Elapsed time"

GIVEN

Two time entries per card, each in hours and minutes, the second always later than the first (example: 745 850).

WANTED

The elapsed time between the two entries, in minutes (in the example, 65).

PROBLEM 3.2-5   "Here's Your Change"

GIVEN

Two cards, each containing a floating-point number. The first represents the cash register total of your weekly purchases at the local super-market; the second, the amount of money you offer the clerk to pay for them. Assume that both the cash register total and the amount of money offered are less than or equal to $100.00.

WANTED

Write a program to calculate the number of bills and coins of each denomination (common U.S. currency) you should receive in change.

PROBLEM 3.2-6   "Quad"

GIVEN

A series of cards, each punched with three real numbers; call them A, B, and C.

ASSUME

These are the 3 coefficients of the quadratic equation:

$$Ax^2 + Bx + C = 0$$

WANTED

Using the quadratic formula, calculate the 2 roots of the equation for each set of coefficients; call them X1 and X2. Print out A, B, C, X1, and X2.

VERSION A. Assume all roots are real, and that no identification is necessary.

VERSION B. Test for all possible conditions: real, complex, double, not quadratic but linear, etc. Try to figure a way to print out each type of answer set so that it can be identified.

VERSION C. Repeat B using FORMAT statements to dress up your output.

PROBLEM 3.2-7   "Lots for Sale"

A man wishes to buy a lot. At the local realtor's office, data are available (on punched cards, of course) on several lots. There is a card for each lot, punched with the following information:

Lot identification number	Length of lot (feet)	Width of lot (feet)	Land value (dollars per square foot)

The customer has only $2,500 to spend.
   Write a program which will:

   (1) Read in the data for one lot.
   (2) Calculate the area of that lot. (Assume that all lots are rectangular.)
   (3) Calculate the price of that lot.
   (4) Test whether that price is less than (or equal to) the customer's maximum price.

(5) *If it is,* write out all the input data for that lot, together with its area and total price.

(6) Repeat until all data cards are processed.

A flow chart for the program is shown in Figure P3.2-7. Note that no output is produced for lots the customer cannot afford.

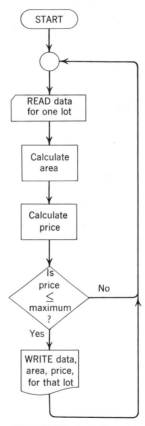

Figure P3.2-7 Lots for sale.

DATA:

ID	Length	Width	Value
101	150	70	$0.12
120	200	65	0.10
137	120	50	0.09
168	400	100	0.11
227	140	100	0.35
230	118	78	0.60
250	100	50	0.50

PROBLEM 3.2-8 "Choice Lots for Sale"

The customer of Problem 3.2-7 now has two restrictions:

(1) He is interested only in lots having an area of at least 10,500 square feet.
(2) He has only $2,500 to spend.

Now write a program which will:

(1) Read in the data for one lot.
(2) Calculate the area of that lot. (Assume all lots are rectangular.)
(3) Test whether that area exceeds (or equals) his minimum value.
(4) *If it does,* calculate the price.
(5) Test whether that price is less than (or equal to) his maximum price.

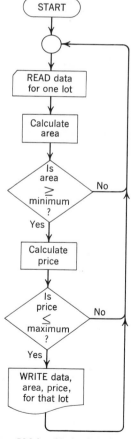

Figure P3.2-8 Choice lots for sale.

(6) *If it is,* write out all the input data for that lot, together with its area and total price.

(7) Repeat until all input cards are processed.

The flow chart now looks like Figure P3.2-8. Note that no output is produced unless *both* conditions are satisfied.

PROBLEM 3.3-1   "Trig Conversion Tables"

WANTED

Tables of trig functions punched out by the computer over the desired range. Be sure to include both end points.

	Function	Starting Value	Increment	Final Value
(A)	sin (x)	0 deg	1 deg	45 deg
(B)	cos (x)	0 deg	1 deg	45 deg
(C)	tan (x)	0 rad	.1 rad	3.2 rad
(D)	tan (x)	0 deg	1 deg	45 deg
(E)	arc sin (x) (rad)	0	.02	.7
(F)	arc cos (x) (rad)	1	−.01	.7

PROBLEM 3.3-2   "Temperature Conversion Tables"

WANTED

Conversion tables between temperature in degrees Fahrenheit and degrees Centigrade, as given by the equation

$$F = \tfrac{9}{5}C + 32$$

These are to be punched out by the computer over the specified range. Be sure to include both end points.

(A)	−5°C	(1°)	30°C
(B)	−30°F	(5°)	100°F
(C)	−20°C	(2°)	45°C
(D)	60°F	(1°)	90°F
(E)	0°C	(100°)	1800°C (melting point of Ti)

PROBLEM 3.3-3   "Temperature Conversion"

Fahrenheit to Centigrade temperature conversions

$$°C = \frac{5(°F - 32)}{9}$$

are most conveniently performed by most people by looking them up in a table. We will try two ways of using the computer to help us.

(A) EXTERNAL DATA. Given a series of cards, each containing a temperature in degrees Fahrenheit. Write a FORTRAN program to read these in, one at a time, convert them to degrees Centigrade, and print out both numbers, side by side:

TEMPERATURE   TEMPERATURE

°F   °C

(B) INTERNAL DATA. Write a FORTRAN program to calculate a conversion table from Fahrenheit to Centigrade for the range

$$°F = -50 \text{ (5) } 100$$

Print the numbers in pairs, as above.

PROBLEM 3.5-1   "Polyrooting"

Use *Polyplot* and *Roots by decimal tabulation* to find all of the real roots. Plot the curve.

(A) $x^2 - 3x + 1 = 0$
(B) $x^3 + 3x^2 - 19x - 22 = 0$
(C) $x^4 + 3x^3 - 4x^2 - 8x + 7 = 0$
(D) $x^4 - 2x^3 + x^2 - 5 = 0$
(E) $-7x^6 - 6x^5 - 5x^4 + 4x^3 + 3x^2 + 2x + 1 = 0$
(F) $x^7 - 5x^4 + x + 2 = 0$

Use the methods of *Polyplot* and *Roots by decimal tabulation* to find all of the real roots. Plot the curve.

(G) $3 \cos (x) + x$
(H) $.1 - xe^{-x}$
(I) $4x - \sqrt{7 + x^3}$

PROBLEM 3.5-2   "Roots by Decimal Tabulation"

Rewrite the program of Fig. 3.5-1, *Roots by Decimal Tabulation*, using a Computed GO TO instead of the IF(SW) statement to bypass the test for sign change the first time F is evaluated.

PROBLEM 3.5-3   "Roots by Decimal Tabulation"—Mod 1

Try the program of Figure 3.5-1, *Roots by Decimal Tabulation*, on the following equations, using the range $x = 0(1)10$. What happens? Fix it.

(A) $x^2 - 3.1x = 0$
(B) $x^2 - 5.2x + 6.4 = 0$
(C) $x^2 - 6.1x + 8.4 = 0$
(D) $x^2 - 7x + 12 = 0$

Be sure to try your fix on all 4 cases.

PROBLEM 3.5-4   "Roots by Decimal Tabulation"—Mod 2

Analyze what happens in the program of Figure 3.5-1, *Roots by Decimal Tabulation*, if, while running a polynomial over the range 0(1)10 with a required precision of 10^{-5}, it encounters any of the following situations:

(A) a root exists at zero.
(B) the first root is an integer > 0.
(C) the first root is not an integer, but the next one is.
(D) roots exist at two consecutive integers.

Does it put out the roots correctly? Does it proceed properly to the next interval? Does it perform the next sign change test correctly?
    If the answer to any of these is no, propose a correction. Be sure to test your correction on all 4 cases.

PROBLEM 3.5-5   "Polyplot and Roots by Decimal Tabulation"

Combine the programs of Figures 3.4-2, *Polyplot*, and 3.5-1, *Roots by Decimal Tabulation*, into a single program which both
(A) puts out the value of the function at specified increments over a specified range, and
(B) puts out (preferably at the end of the program) the precise value of all roots located within this range.

PROBLEM 3.5-6   "Polyplot"

Use *Polyplot* to tabulate the following functions over the range indicated. Plot the result. Do you think all roots have been located? If you think not, extend your search.

		XINIT	DELX	XFIN
(A) $x^2 - 3x + 1$	$x =$	0	(.2)	3
(B) $2x^2 + 5x - 3$	$x =$	-5	(1)	5

(C) $100x^2 - 1$ $x =$ -1 (.1)   1
(D) $x^3 + 3x^2 - 19x - 22$ $x =$ -10 (1)   10
(E) $x^3 + 6x^2 - 7x - 60$ $x =$ -6 (.5)   0
(F) $3x^3 - 38x^2 + 29x + 36$ $x =$ -5 (1)   15
(G) $x^3 - x^2 - x - 2$ $x =$ 0 (.2)   3
(H) $x^4 + 3x^3 - 4x^2 - 8x + 7$ $x =$ -6 (2)   4
(I) $x^4 - 1$ $x =$ -3 (.5)   3

CHAPTER 4.

The Second Industrial Revolution

4.1 MEANING OF THE REVOLUTION

The second industrial revolution, which is now occurring, is rapidly eliminating the repetitive mental tasks in our economic system. The computer is the main factor in this revolution. A small amount of human mental effort exerted in the writing of a program is amplified by a computer to produce results representing enormous amounts of mental effort. A program once developed may be used intermittently over extended periods of time producing an almost unlimited number of calculations without a single undetected error. Many hours of repetitive calculations may be performed by a computer to design a giant high-energy accelerator used to explore atoms; to design, launch and track spacecraft; and to review and update many thousands of items of inventory each day.

The large number of computers installed over the last decade and the increase in their overall capabilities provide evidence that this second revolution is occurring. The number installed in the United States has grown from just a few in the early 1950's to an estimated 5000 in 1961. This growth can be approximately described as a doubling of the number of installed computers each year (at the end of 1964 the number installed was estimated to be 25,000). This same rate of growth has taken place in Europe in more recent years—from approximately two dozen in 1955 to an estimated 1500 in 1961. Moreover, the average computing power per installed computer today is many thousands of times greater than it was in the early 1950's. The largest computer built in 1965 could execute on the average of over three million instructions per second.

It is very fortunate that the second industrial revolution is occurring at this time. When computers first appeared, it was becoming apparent that the impetus of the first industrial revolution, which had maintained the rate of improvement in our economic and social well-being, was soon to be spent, and that our standard of living would reach a plateau. Since physical effort had nearly reached a minimum in our economy as a result of the first industrial revolution, the great potential for maintaining a steady improvement in our economic and social well-being was to reduce the human mental effort. This effort had grown to a large proportion of the total.

4.2   WHERE ARE COMPUTERS USEFUL?

Three areas basic to our economy and in which applications of computers are of great importance are: (1) product design, (2) control of material and product flows, and (3) research. We will discuss these areas of application individually.

Product Design

We may carry out a design of a product by either of two methods, or a combination of both. If we do not know any computational mathematics, we must achieve designs by experimenting with *physical models.* We must build a series of the models and, by continuous improvement, we hope to finally arrive at an acceptable design. Computers are of little or no use in this method.

We may build and experiment with *computational models* as a second method of achieving a design, provided we know the necessary computational mathematics to build the model. First, we must be able to develop equations which describe the desired characteristics of the product we design. Second, we must be able to calculate solutions of the equations. If we are able to do both, we can then build as many models as may be required to arrive at an acceptable design. The computer can be used to obtain solutions of the equations for each computational model we build.

Designs may be of such complexity that no known computational mathematics exists for building complete and accurate computational models, and a combination of the two methods must be employed. For example, both methods were used in the design for the launching and orbiting of satellites.

The method of computational models is not always the best. There are cases, particularly in the design of electronic devices such as a television receiver, where it may be cheaper and require less time to achieve a working design by building physical models. It requires very little time to replace electronic components in a circuit, and the replaced components can be reused many times.

We shall describe the two methods of achieving an acceptable design by an example. Suppose we are required to design roof trusses of a building of the type shown in Figure 4.2-1. The width of the building w and the height h from the horizontal at the eaves to the ridge are given dimensions. The 2 rafter members are to be of equal length and are to be cut from lumber of a predetermined width and thickness and of any practical length. We will neglect, for the moment, problems of stresses and strength, and concern ourselves solely with making the pieces fit. If we did not know the computational mathematics of trigonometry, we would be forced to accomplish the design by experimenting with the physical pieces themselves. The actual wooden members would have to be held in place, marked with a pencil, and sawed. If they did not quite fit, they would have to be refitted and modified until the proper angle and length were obtained.

By contrast, assume that we have sufficient qualifications to establish the computational model, and the equations we develop are

$$\theta = \arctan \frac{h}{w/2}$$

$$l = \frac{h}{\sin \theta}$$

where θ is the angle of cut at the ridge and l is the length of the rafter along its shortest edge. These equations can be readily solved and will serve as a general model in the design of any rafter of this type. A par-

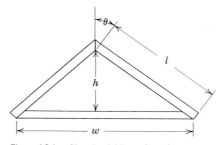

Figure 4.2-1   Simple design of roof truss.

ticular model can be built by substituting the appropriate values of *h* and *w* in the equations and calculating the solutions.

If we had a large business in manufacturing rafters, we might find the design problem a good application of the computer, particularly if we let the computer produce a complete dimensioned drawing which could be sent directly to the shop as instructions on how to saw lumber. This function of our business could be drawn as shown in Figure 4.2-2. Information received on a customer's order such as the customer's identification and the roof truss dimensions *h* and *w*, is presented as input to the computer. The computer makes calculations by using the program of the computational model and the program for plotting the drawing. The output in the form of a drawing is sent to the shop. The complete operation may take only a few minutes compared to perhaps several hours if done manually, and the cost is likely to be reduced.

Because we have a computer, or access to a more capable and cheaper computer, we may find that we can economically design a more complex roof truss that will give equal or better performance at a lower cost. The design shown in Figure 4.2-3 has 2 more members than the first design shown in Figure 4.2-1. The sizes of the other members of the roof truss can be greatly reduced when the 2 members are added, so that the total amount of material used is less. The cost of design plus the added cost of labor required in its construction may be more than offset by the savings in the cost of materials. If this is the case, the flow diagram of this function in our business takes the form shown in Figure 4.2-4. The diagram is similar to 4.2-2 except that the shop function is added. For the same amount of flow of wood materials into the plant, we are able to *increase* the number of roof trusses coming from the plant. If we did not automate the plant to increase the output per man in production, an *increase* in the number of shop people would be necessary because of the increase in the number of pieces to be

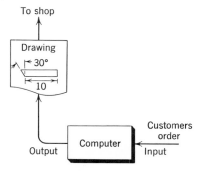

Figure 4.2-2   Computer applied to the design of the roof truss of Figure 4.2-1.

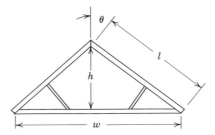

Figure 4.2-3   A design of roof truss which may reduce amount of material.

assembled. Since the economy will continue to favor the use of more accurate and complex models in design, the people who were engaged in the repetitive model calculations may now pursue the building of more accurate computational models for this particular design, or they may build models for designs that will give equal or even better performance at a still lower cost.

Control of Flow of Materials and Products

Inventory Control. Control of flow of materials and products in the economic system is the second significant application of computers. Inventory control is a primary function in the control of flow, and it is of such importance that we can learn a great deal by examining it in detail. If the item of inventory is food, it may spoil. If the items are clothes or automobiles, they will decrease in value because their styles become obsolete, i.e., they lose consumer value. For many other items which hold relatively constant value, the cost of excess inventory is still not small. After considering such factors as the cost of storage space

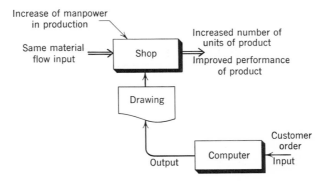

Figure 4.2-4   Relative effect of improving design of a product on manpower and material per unit product.

and facilities, interest on money invested, and property taxes, the total cost of having excess inventory may be as high as 20% of the value of the stock per year. A typical manufacturing company may normally carry inventory of five million dollars. If this can be reduced to four million, and the cost of carrying this excess inventory is 20%, the saving in reducing this inventory to four million is $200,000 per year. Computers have been making such reductions possible.

To see how control is improved through the use of computers, we must investigate the requirements of inventory control. Inventory in a supermarket or manufacturing plant may consist of many thousands of items. A record must be kept on each item, and each record updated at intervals as to the amount removed through sales and the amount restored through shipments received from the supplier or vendor. When inventory drops down to a *minimum order-level,* a new shipment should be ordered from the vendor, requiring a purchase order to be issued. The amount to be ordered, or *order-quantity,* must be established. The minimum order-level and order-quantity depend on such variables as prices, shipping rates, promptness of delivery, predicted demand, and rate of obsolescence. Knowing last year's usage over the same period may be important in predicting the demand for the item.

We see that a large number of records must be kept and many calculations made on every item if wise decisions are to be made in inventory control.

If control of inventory is manual, items are likely to be grouped, and a fixed minimum order-level and order-quantity established for each group over extended periods of time. Figure 4.2-5 describes a manually controlled inventory system and shows the effect on average inventory level (AIL) when average rate of inventory depletion (ARID) changes. The number of units of product in inventory is plotted against time in days. At time zero when we start our study, the number of units in inventory is 20 (point A). Units are removed from inventory until the minimum order-level (MOL) of 10 units is reached (point B). Since we are unable to make a complete check of our records daily, we do not discover immediately that we have reached the minimum order-level. The time required to detect the minimum order-level and to initiate a purchase order (t_d) is 6 days and may be called a *delay* or detection period. Delivery time as determined by our supplier (t_f) is 4 days and may be called the *forecast* period. During this 10 day period, inventory continues to drop, reaching a low at point C. We then receive our shipment of order-quantity equal to 20 units which raises the number of units in inventory to point D.

Figure 4.2-5a shows an average rate of inventory depletion (ARID)

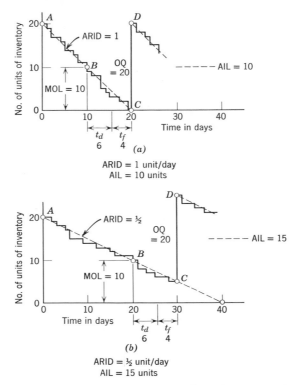

Figure 4.2-5   Manual inventory control, showing effect of average rate of inventory depletion (ARID) on average inventory level (AIL).

Minimum Order-Level (MOL) = 10 units
Order-Quantity (OQ) = 20 units
Time to detect MOL and issue purchase order (t_d) = 6 days
Shipping Time (t_f) = 4 days

for normal business conditions of 1 unit per day. This rate combined with the two delays, results in an average inventory level (AIL) over an extended period of 10 units. If, because of poor business conditions, the average rate of inventory depletion (ARID) drops to $\frac{1}{2}$ unit per day as shown in Figure 4.2-5b, the average inventory level (AIL) rises from 10 to 15 units. On the other hand, it is apparent that, if the depletion rate were greater than 1 unit per day corresponding to improved business conditions, we would find our stock exhausted before shipment arrived. After a few of these experiences in actual practice, steps would be taken to readjust MOL and OQ.

When a computer is applied to inventory control, we have the ability to survey inventory on a daily basis, i.e., update and review inventory daily if we desire. This means we can reduce the time (t_d) required to detect minimum order-level and to initiate a purchase order. An additional advantage is that the necessary calculations can be performed to vary the minimum order-levels and order-quantities to meet the current business conditions. Figure 4.2-6 describes the application of a computer to the control of the example inventory problem of Figure 4.2-5. We will say that $t_d + t_f$ can be reasonably reduced from 10 days for manual control to 5 days for computer control. This permits us to predict inventory conditions at point C more accurately and to

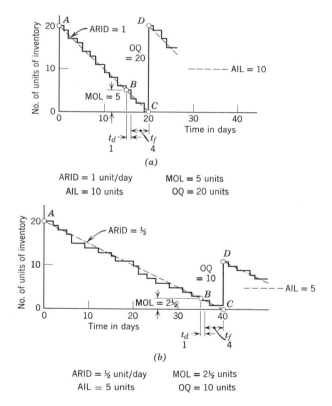

Figure 4.2-6   Computer inventory control, showing effect of average rate of inventory depletion (ARID) on average inventory level (AIL).

Time to detect MOL and issue purchase order (t_d) = 1 day
Shipping Time (t_f) = 4 days

adjust the minimum order-level accordingly. Comparing Figure 4.2-6*a* with Figure 4.2-5*a*, the minimum order-level is shown as 5 units reduced from 10 units and the order-quantity is 20 as before. No change results in the average inventory level for these assumed normal business conditions. Comparing Figure 4.2-6*b* with 4.2-6*a*, we again have the average rate of inventory depletion changed from 1 unit per day to $\frac{1}{2}$ unit per day. Since our system is now under computer surveillance, we can readily detect these changing business conditions and reduce the minimum order-level proportionally from 5 to $2\frac{1}{2}$ and the order-quantity from 20 to 10. The resulting average inventory level actually goes down —from 10 to 5. If business conditions improved relative to normal, MOL and OQ are readjusted to increase the average inventory level, and shortages are avoided. The flow diagram for the operation of inventory control by a computer is shown in Figure 4.2-7.

We will now compare the results of our analysis of the example problem. When the average rate of inventory depletion was reduced from 1 to $\frac{1}{2}$ unit per day corresponding to adverse business conditions, the average inventory level under manual control was *increased* from 10 to 15 units, which is in excess of the requirements. Under computer control, the average level was *reduced* from 10 to 5 units, which is a desirable amount of inventory. If the depletion rate would be increased to more than 1 unit per day corresponding to improved business conditions, manual control would result in a shortage of stock while computer control would adjust the minimum order-level and order-quantity to maintain desirable inventory conditions.

Control of Flow in Process. Control of material and product flows includes, in addition to inventory control, the control of flow through the shop or production facilities. We will only briefly describe this control operation and the need to apply computers to the function. Some important methods will be presented in later chapters for accomplishing control by

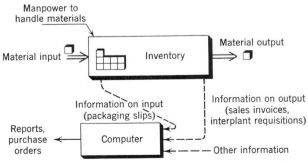

Figure 4.2-7   Flow diagram of inventory control by computer.

computers, and programming problems in various areas of application will be discussed.

Material flow through a shop or production facilities increases in complexity as new and improved products become more complex. Products may contain a large number of component parts each requiring a number of separate processes in their manufacture. Many of the parts may be processed simultaneously before they are mixed or combined in subassemblies. The final product may contain a large number of subassemblies or mixes. For example, an automobile is an assembly of a number of subassemblies, such as the motor, transmission, rear axle, and body, and each of these subassemblies contains many component parts. In the chemical industry, a final product may be a mixture of many compounds and each of these may involve complex processes. Process equipment of a wide variety is required and each piece of equipment is best suited for a particular type of process.

The objectives of control are to determine when and on what facility a required process should be performed. Under normal conditions the criterion is simply to achieve the most efficient use of the production facilities, however, under abnormal or urgent conditions particular products are given higher priorities so that their production may be speeded up to satisfy the demand. The latter condition is achieved, of course, only at the price of decreased efficiency in the use of equipment and delay in delivery of other products, so that the conditions under which function two should be invoked are extremely complex and involve many economic considerations. Furthermore, since customer orders or sales determine the demands for flow of materials, and since those demands are likely to fluctuate so widely as to make accurate prediction almost impossible, frequent readjustment of control, or rescheduling, is necessary if efficient use of the facilities and efficient overall production are to be maintained.

Computers applied to this control operation are performing an equivalent amount of human mental effort many times greater than that previously employed under manual control, and the control is greatly improved. Since computers continue to decrease in cost per unit of calculation, still greater efficiencies in the use of production facilities will be realized in the future without an increase in cost of the control operations.

Research

Computers are increasing the research activities by improving the efficiency of the scientist; i.e., they are making it possible to increase these activities without increasing the human effort. They are also enabling the scientist to obtain knowledge which otherwise could not be acquired. These accomplishments as attributed to computers are being achieved mainly in (1) the data gathering operations, (2) the formulation of facts, and (3) the retrieval of information. We will examine each of these activities as they relate to the use of computers.

Data Gathering. The block diagram of Figure 4.2-8 represents a basic communication system for these first two activities involving computers and man. In the data gathering operations, Computer A, as well as a wide variety of other equipment, aid the scientist in gathering world-wide facts. This equipment is placed between the data source and the scientist to broaden the range and to increase the efficiency of communication.

Before computers and special input devices were developed and applied to data gathering, a vast amount of repetitive mental effort was employed in obtaining data from the sources, and the information that could be obtained was limited. This was particularly true in research and development. If events changed slowly, instruments could be read and data recorded manually in the same manner as you read and record temperatures from a thermometer, or velocity values from a speedometer. Several seconds are required to manually read and record a single value. When events occurred too rapidly for human observers to keep up, it was necessary first to photograph or to rapidly plot their values with special equipment, and then at a later time, manually read and record data from these photographs and charts. Data obtained in this manner during a few seconds—for example, during the firing of a ground missile—took weeks and many man-hours of effort to extract or reduce data from the charts and photographs and to interpret the meaning of the data. Much of the data obtained in this manner was never reduced to information because of the time and cost involved.

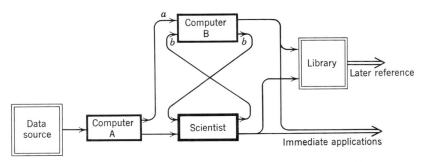

Figure 4.2-8　System showing information flow in the research activities of data gathering and the formulation of facts.

The capability of this method was often exceeded in obtaining data on very rapidly changing events.

With the aid of special input devices computers can read, store, and edit data at rates as high as many thousands of values per second from hundreds of sources without human intervention. As a result, information can be obtained on rapidly changing events now, while it never could before. Also, modifications can frequently be made and experiments terminated without delay, thereby reducing the length of time between experiments and eliminating needless scientific effort. They are being used in increasing numbers, specifically for data-gathering operations. Such machines are usually relatively small in size and frequently contain the required data-input equipment for direct reading of data from many sources. Examples of applications are: neurophysiology in the study of neuron responses to auditory stimuli, rocket engineering in the studies of fuels and aerodynamics, control engineering in the analysis of processes to be controlled, and education in the study of the human mental processes.

Formulation of Facts. The second activity to be examined as an application of computers is the sifting, testing, and combining of countless small items of observations and data into an organized collection of facts from which significant conclusions can be drawn and useful extensions made. We constantly strive to simplify the task of dealing with such data by finding generalizations and formulas—this activity can appropriately be called the formulation of facts.

In this activity, man-computer interactions are required; i.e., man and computer must perform alternately in achieving final results or in reaching conclusions of a research project. The computer used for this purpose takes its place in the communication system of Figure 4.2-8, Computer B, and may be of the *digital* type introduced in the preceding chapters or of either the *analog* or *hybrid* types discussed in Chapter 12. The communication channels *b* between the scientist and the computer carry information to accomplish the interaction. Data obtained from the data-gathering operations enter this communication loop through the media of magnetic tape and punched cards if collected by the data-gathering computer, or through the media of paper tape, cards, and printed material if collected by other equipment. If no special manual preparation of the data is required, it may be communicated directly to the computer shown as channel *a* of the figure.

The formulation of facts accomplished through this man-computer interaction may be an involved procedure in many research efforts. The computer may be required to perform calculations involving any known computational methods and procedures ranging from the simple evaluation of polynomials, probabilities, and simultaneous equations covered in secondary school mathematics, to the most recent and advanced computational procedures. The results of the calculations are reviewed by the planner, checked against his hypothesis, and modified, and then perhaps different computational methods are chosen and a new computation initiated on the computer. The results of the new computation are then reviewed and the cycle repeated, in some cases many times, over an extended period of time, before final results are obtained or conclusions are reached on the research project. The end result is frequently a computational model or formula which describes a biological, social, or economic system, or the performance characteristic of a new type of product. The final result or conclusion—recorded as printed output from the computer, written language, drawings or photographs— may be applied directly to some process or stored in libraries for a permanent record.

Information Retrieval. The application of computers to the third activity in the area of research, namely, retrieval of information, remains to be analyzed. Information retrieval may be defined as the communication of recovered facts established at an earlier time. The three principal work functions involved are abstracting, locating facts of apparent interest, and language translating. The principles and methods of information retrieval by computers will be discussed in Chapter 13. Here we will discuss the importance of the application of computers to this activity.

Information retrieval is highly essential in research in order to avoid duplication and redundance of effort. Before a research effort is pursued, it is desirable to establish whether results have already been obtained on the proposed project and whether related information exists which will aid in the progress and influence the approach to the effort. These decisions are made by reviewing all available published material on the subject. If a review is accomplished solely through manual effort, the task is likely to be formidable, for in many fields of research many hundreds of man-years of reading are produced each year, and the production rate is rapidly increasing. This increase may be considered evidence of the beneficial effects of the use of computers in the first two activities discussed.

Computers aid the scientist in the reviewing effort by performing, at least in part, the functions of abstracting, locating of facts of apparent interest, and language translation. The computers used must have large amounts of low-cost memory, and information stored in memory must be obtained rapidly on request, to achieve practical application to any of these three functions. As computers come closer to meeting these specifications and improved methods of performing these functions are established, further reductions in human mental effort will be achieved and a more rapid and thorough job will be done in information retrieval. As a result, the overall research effort will be more effective in acquiring additional knowledge.

4.3   THE OVERALL EFFECT

All three of the major areas of applications of computers discussed in the preceding section—product design, control of flow of materials and products, and research—exist in an industrial system when it contains the three principal types of operations *Process, Control,* and *Planning*. Such a system for the production of a consumer product is summarized by the block diagram of Figure 4.3-1a, for it represents an important segment of our economy. The three types of operations Process P, Control C, and Planning F cannot be accomplished independently but require constant two-way communication up and down the chain, as well as with the outside world.

The process operations P relate to the physical mixing, shaping, and molding of materials to accomplish useful products. The flow of materials into the process operations is represented by the double line arrow p_{01} of the figure and the flow of finished product to the customer by the double line arrow p_{40}. The 4 distinct operations performed within P, as shown in the more detailed Figure 4.3-1b, are P_1, the storage and handling of incoming materials; P_2, the processing of the materials on the various processing facilities; P_3, the central storage and handling of the finished product; and P_4, the storage and handling of the products at the centers of distribution or at the warehouses.

The control operations C may be divided into *daily operations control* C_1, and *high level control* C_2. C_1 provides control of the daily operations associated with the process, including the component operations of product design and control of flow of materials and products, as well as other associated operations related to money matters. The operations of product design establish how materials are to be processed in P_2 as described by the block diagram of Figure 4.2-4. The operations for control of flow are: inventory control of materials for controlling the operations of P_1, scheduling or control of flow of materials and product components through the processing operations of P_2, control of central product inventory for controlling the P_3 operations, and inventory control of products in warehouses for controlling the operations of P_4.

The communications required to accomplish control are based on

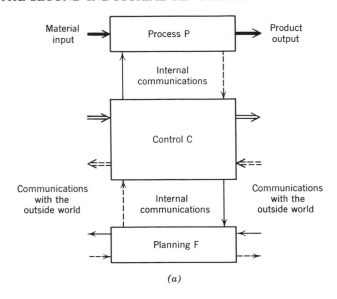

(a)

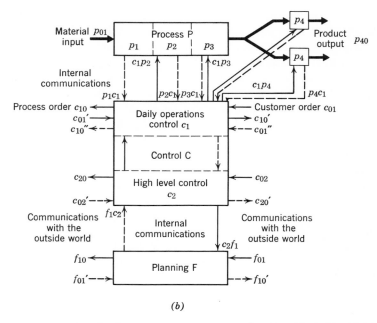

(b)

Figure 4.3-1   An industrial system containing the operations process, control, and planning.

control principles which are discussed in detail in Chapters 9 and 11 under the subjects of real-time systems and simulation. These principles require that for each communication channel carrying instructions or *action requests* in one direction, a second must be provided for carrying the *action results* in the opposite direction. With this communication requirement in mind, we may follow with better understanding the description of the information carried by each of the channels between P and C_1 as shown in the system diagram of Figure 4.3-1. Action requests are carried by the solid line arrows and the action results by broken line arrows.

As a result of action requests in the form of purchase orders sent to the vendor through channel c_{10}, materials are received on Channel p_{01}, and their receipt is reported back to C on channel p_1c_1. Channel c_1p_2 then carries processing instructions to P_2 in the form of material requisitions, drawings, inspection requests, and schedules. p_2c_1 and p_3c_1 convey the results of executing these action requests, and also payroll information as required for determining salaries and wages of shop personnel. Channel c_1p_3 carries instructions for distributing products of central inventory P_3 to points of distribution P_4, and c_1p_4 the instructions for shipping products from there to customers as a result of order requests communicated through c_{01}. Channel p_4c_1 conveys information on materials received from central inventory and the executed shipping instructions.

Materials, products, supplies, equipment, and services are involved in the combined performance of the system. Since money is the medium of exchange for goods and services, operations pertaining to the flow of money are required. These operations of C_1 which include billing, accounts receivable and payable, payroll, and tax and stockholders' reports are all applications of computers, as can be seen from the list in Appendix 4A. They require communication with the outside and will be discussed in greater detail in Chapter 7.

High Level Control C_2 attempts to maintain a best performance of the total system in consideration of the future as well as the present. It communicates with daily operations control through channels c_2c_1 and c_1c_2 to maintain a best performance in the production of current products. It also communicates with Planning F through channels f_1c_2 and c_2f_1 to maintain a best performance in achieving planning objectives which will lead to future expansion and growth in production. Computers are used to solve special problems in these decision-making and policy-forming operations—for example, in making market analyses which are required before decisions can be made to do research on and develop new products. C_2 communicates with the outside through channels $c_{02}{}'$

and c_{20}, as shown in the figure, to obtain market data and other economic information as may be required in performing the control operations. Requests for data are received through channel c_{02} and the data are sent out on channel c_{20}'.

Research, the third major area of applications of computers discussed in the preceding section, is usually the principal part of Planning, although Planning may include such other operations as product development and planning for new and increased processing facilities. Special problems arising from these operations can also receive the benefit of computer attention. Communications with the outside are accomplished through the f channels as shown in Figure 4.3-1, and are of great importance in scientific information retrieval previously described, as one of the activities of research where computers are becoming of great importance.

The operations of Planning are performed in a sequential manner in accomplishing objectives established by high level control. After making a market analysis, C_2 may establish a planning objective for a new type of product. Research is required, for example, to find a high temperature alloy with special characteristics, or to determine certain body chemistries as influenced by a proposed new drug. If the results of these efforts are successful, product development proceeds. A mix of chemicals or an assembly of various shaped components, believed to perform as a whole according to specifications, is made and tested. If C_2 decides that the product model is sufficiently close to the original product objective with respect to cost, quality, and performance, production facilities must be planned. Here a new host of influencing factors enter, including sources of labor and materials, and geographical areas of demand and their effect on shipping costs.

We see that computers have been extensively applied to all major operations in daily operations control. Secondly, we see that daily operations control issues action requests, or gives instructions for performing the process operations that are specific and very well defined. These facts precipitated the *systems concept* in the application of computers to the total system of C_1, which in practice is called *total systems operation*. The definition of a total systems operation is a computer, or a combination of computers, performing all the operations within daily operations control without human intervention. Man is required in monitoring the system operation and may be required to handle unusual conditions.

A total systems operation generally cannot be suddenly implemented, but must be planned and established in stages over a period of time. In the early stages when separate programs to accomplish different parts of the tasks are run individually and the results of each are handled by the human, the best that can be done is to stack the different jobs for the computer together and do them by *Batch Processing*. As experience is gained and more operations are brought under computer control, human intervention can be gradually reduced by letting the computer make more and more of the intervening human decisions until finally a total systems operation is achieved.

A total systems operation, described in Reference 4.3-1 at the end of this section, is shown in Figure 4.3-2. The process operations pertain to the manufacture of electric coils for motors and generators. By 1958 computer programs for many of the operations of C_1 had been established and were being batch processed on the IBM 704 Computer. At that time, the total systems operation was planned and two years later the system as shown was in operation.

Process P can be divided in the same manner as that of Figure 4.3-1, except that operations P_4 do not exist. Insulated copper wire and insulation materials are received from the vendor and put in storage, corresponding to operation P_1. In the first operations of P_2, the wire is taken from storage, wound, and formed into coils. In the operations that follow, insulating materials are taken from storage and the coils wrapped with insulating tape, dipped in insulating varnish, baked in an oven, and the coil insulation tested. The completed coils are put in product storage as operation P_3, and are shipped directly to the customer from this central storage. All the operations of C_1 which provide action requests from Process P are performed by the IBM 704 Computer. The specifications from a customer's order are punched in cards and read into the computer. From this small amount of data, the computer produces in one continuous operation all the instructions required by P_2 to make the set of coils. The instructions are in the form of material requisition tickets; coil drawing; inspection, labor and move tickets; and a production schedule. The output of the computer also includes shipping orders, which are sent to P_3, and purchase orders and pay checks, although the latter two were not used as official documents at this early stage of development. Value analysis and sale summaries are obtained as output on demand by high level control. Inputs to the computer are completed labor tickets giving the results of all actions performed in P_2, and confirmations that materials were received and products shipped.

The electric coil described above is only one component of many that make up a complete motor or generator. The establishment of a total systems operation for control of the processing of products containing many complex components requires a lot of human effort. High

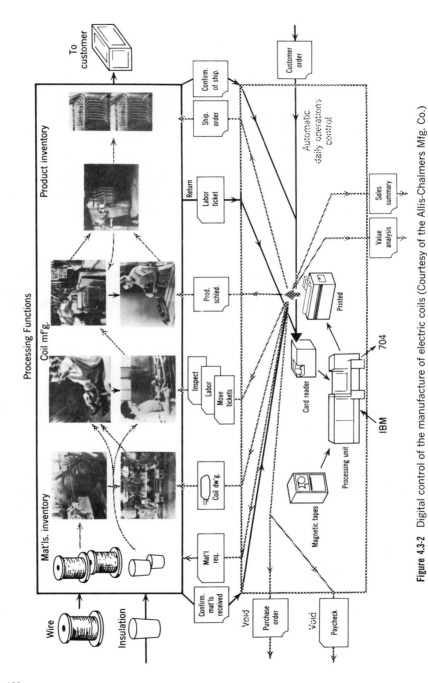

Figure 4.3-2 Digital control of the manufacture of electric coils (Courtesy of the Allis-Chalmers Mfg. Co.)

To customer

Product inventory

Processing Functions

Coil mf'g.

Mat'ls. inventory

Wire

Insulation

Confirm.
of ship.

Ship.
order

Return

Labor
ticket

Prod.
schled.

Inspect

Labor

Move
tickets

Coil dw'g.

Mat'l
req.

Confirm.
mat'ls
received

Automatic
daily operations
control

Customer
order

Sales
summary

Value
analysis

Printed

Card reader

704

IBM

Processing unit

Magnetic tapes

Void

Purchase
order

Void

Paycheck

level control in particular is very difficult to reduce to complete computer control, primarily because it deals less with routine matters and more with those involving many interrelated factors. However, since the action requests generated by daily operations control are specific and usually well-defined, total systems operation can be achieved here, and will evolve from present Batch Processing Systems.

We can summarize our discussion of Process, Control, and Planning and their relationships to the three areas of applications of computers as follows:

PROCESS P

P_1 storage and handling of incoming materials
P_2 processing of the materials on the processing facilities
P_3 central storage and handling of the finished product
P_4 storage and handling of the product at centers of distribution

CONTROL C

C_1 *Daily Operations Control*—can be a total systems operation in the use of computers
   (1) Product design—one of the fundamental areas of application of computers that establishes how materials are to be processed in P_2
   (2) Control of flow of materials and products—a second fundamental area of applications of computers
      (a) inventory control of incoming materials for control of P_1
      (b) control of flow of materials and product components through the processing operations of P_2
      (c) control of central product inventory for control of P_3
      (d) inventory control of products in warehouses for controlling P_4
   (3) Control of flow of money—an area of application of computers not directly related to materials and products

C_2 *High Level Control*
   (1) Control of over-all operations of P—computers applied to special problems of decision-making and policy forming
   (2) Control of Planning Operations—computers applied to special problems in establishing objectives of planning

PLANNING F

F_1 *Research*
   (1) Data gathering—small computers used with special input equipment
   (2) Formulation of facts—analog, digital, and hybrid computers

for individual problem solution; scientist and computer work alternately

(3) Scientific information retrieval—aid in determining what has already been done

F_2 *Other*
(1) New facilities
(2) Special problems
(3) Etc.

All systems operating in our economy may be considered to contain the three types of operations—Process, Control, and Planning—when we view them for computer applications. The size and importance of the component operations of P, C, and F may vary widely among systems, and for many systems some of the component operations are absent. One system will be described as an example applying the terminology used in our discussion of Figure 4.3-1.

The system of an educational institution is seemingly different from that of an industrial system for the production of products, but when properly analyzed in the study of computer applications, its operations may also be described in terms of the diagram of Figure 4.3-1. When an undergraduate university is considered, the input to the Process P consists of high school graduates and transfer students equivalent to raw and preprocessed materials. The P_1 operations are nonexisting, but the instructional operations P_2, in which the mental processing takes place, requires four or more years for entering freshmen. The finished product is the bachelor's graduate who is idle, product in storage, until he becomes either gainfully employed or a graduate student.

Daily operations control C_1 performs all the operations related to the control of the instruction operations. The operations of C_1 include the design of the curriculum which is equivalent to product design; class scheduling and assignment of classrooms and instructors which pertain to control of flow; feedback from P_2, reporting the progress of each component through the fabrication process; and also those operations for handling money matters for the whole system.

If an institution has a graduate school, the research operations of Planning F are important and likely to be a sizeable portion. The graduate student participates in the operations of the system during the time he spends in the research and teaching operations.

High level control performs the over-all control which is similar for all systems.

Computer applications for all these component operations of an educational institution may be classified according to those of an industry for the production of products.

Since each of the many systems in our economy contains the operations of P, C, and F when viewed for computer applications, the complete national economy may be represented by the diagram of Figure 4.3-1, and the general effects of the use of computers on the economy can be established. We will consider for the moment only the operations of Process P and Control C. The input become materials since they occur naturally without any human effort invested, such as mineral deposits. We now prefer to say the output or end result is anything that contributes to the present economic and social well-being, such as consumer products, products of defense, medical insurance. Process P requires a wide variety of facilities and services of people, and the total Control C now includes governmental controls.

Figure 4.3-3 shows a simplified diagram of P and C and the effects of applying computer control as compared with manual control. These relative effects are established from the results of our analysis of Section 4.2. With the same quantity of materials entering the process, there is an improvement in output resulting from the application of computers to design. Improved scheduling, achieved through the application of computers to control of flow, increases the utilization of the process facilities so that the improved output may be accomplished on approximately the same facilities. Although an increase in human effort in P is required because of the increased complexity of the output and the quantity to be handled, there is a decrease of human effort in the control operations.

The increase in human effort in the process operations occurs unless *automation* is applied. The word automation was coined around 1950 to describe process operations performed by machines which could greatly aid man in executing the instructions of C. For example, consider a steel mill operation where C issues instructions to roll sheets of steel to certain thickness specifications. If automatically controlled equipment

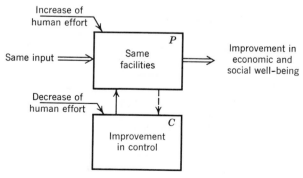

Figure 4.3-3   Effect of computermation in control *C*.

is installed, a man is no longer required to continually watch and make adjustments during the rolling operations in order to maintain thickness specifications. All he has to do is set appropriate dials to these specifications at the beginning of the operation so that the mill, in effect, can watch its own output, and the operator instead of being occupied with only one machine can now operate several. Furthermore, since the machine can watch its own output better, it rolls steel faster and to closer tolerances.

Automation does not depend on computers, and would have grown even if computers had never been invented. Further, the use of computers does not depend on automation. In some process systems, automation cannot be applied. In these systems, the motor skills of the human cannot as yet be duplicated by automatic process machines. The making of electric motor and generator coils described by Figure 4.3-2 is an example of a process which cannot be readily automated, yet computers were applied to the fullest extent in the generation of instructions for performing the process operations.

We might coin a new word, *computermation,* to describe operations performed by computers. Computermation and automation have been occurring in parallel and are both responsible for this second industrial revolution, although computermation is making by far the greater contribution. Computermation adds to automation in that the computer can give the far more precisely detailed instructions required by an automated machine, and if the automated machine can interpret the instructions of the computer, man can sometimes be eliminated entirely from the process operation.

It is well known that automation increases output per man in the process operation. If we consider the combined effects of computermation and automation, the net effect is shown by the diagram of Figure 4.3-4. With the same material input, P as well as C is performed with a decrease in human effort.

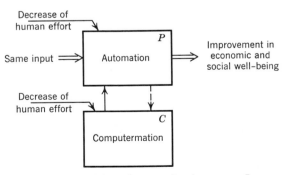

Figure 4.3-4   Effect of automation in process P.

We shall now establish what appear to be the effects of computers and automation on the overall economic system to date, and then determine what effects can be expected in the future. Since we have had nearly full employment, the same human effort has been employed in the combined operations of P and C, and in the operations of F, as would have been employed had automation and computermation never existed. When all the conditions shown in Figure 4.3-4 are adjusted accordingly and the operations of P and C are combined, the conditions for the mid-1960's may be said to be those shown in Figure 4.3-5*a*.

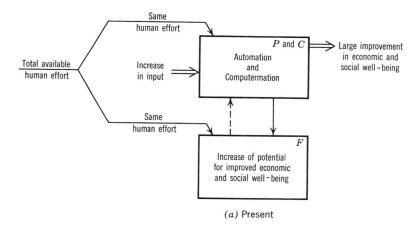

(*a*) Present

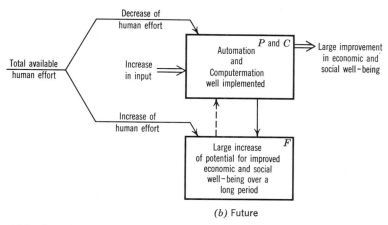

(*b*) Future

Figure 4.3-5   Combined effect of computermation and automation on overall economic system.

Input of materials is increased to where the combined human efforts of P and C are the same as without computermation and automation. The output then adjusts to a large improvement in our economic and social well-being. Upgrading of skills and updating of technical knowledge have been occurring in these operations, and human effort has been required in establishing and implementing automation and computermation.

For Planning F, the same amount of human effort is employed and an increase of potential exists for improvement in the economic and social well-being as a result of the application of computers to these operations.

Since automation and computermation are not fully implemented at this time, it is reasonable to expect that P and C will require a decreasing proportion of the available human effort to maintain the current rate of improvement, and that the human effort spent in operations of planning will gain accordingly. The conditions will then be those of the diagram of Figure 4.3-5b. The continued increase in the planning activities is desirable to assure a continued improvement in our prosperity over a long period of time. Very long-range planning might include research in extended space explorations, health, or economic methods for purification of sea water in preparation for future populations.

There is another very important improvement as a result of computers which cannot be described by the diagrams of Figures 4.3. The important benefit is an increased economic stability as business achieves better control of inventory. Writing in the *Wall Street Journal* early in 1963, economist George Shea says: "The new theory is that computer controls are enabling businessmen to keep stocks of goods from rising to excessive levels, such as have triggered recessions in the past." He adds the cautious prediction of economists: " 'There's reason to hope the days of dangerous excessive inventory buildup may be over'."

It is difficult to conceive of any facet of economic life, large or small, that will not be significantly touched by the second industrial revolution. There is every reason to believe that intelligent application of the basic capabilities of automatic computers to these operations will help to bring continued increase in economic and social well-being to our society, and to all people.

PROBLEM 4.2-1   "Manually Controlled Inventory"

Write a program to simulate manual control of inventory for a single item. The initial inventory level at the beginning of a period is 20 units, fixed minimum order level MOL is 8 units, and fixed order quantity OQ is 20 units. The data to be read in are the number of items requested from our stock each day, which therefore deplete our inventory. Although two columns of data are shown, time in days and requisition quantity, it is recommended that only the requisition quantity be read in and a counter set up in the program to keep track of the days.

When inventory drops down to or below MOL, notice of need of additional units should be put out. We will assume that:

(1) The check of inventory level against MOL is made each day after the requisition quantity for the day is processed.

(2) Automatically t_f' days later ($t_f' = t_d + t_f$ in Figure 4.2-5), the specified OQ is received, and the inventory should therefore be increased by that amount on that day.

(3) For the day an order is placed and for the day an order is received, the requisition quantity is processed before the order is placed and received.

(A) Let $t_f' = 10$ days. We will not be concerned with the quantity t_f.

INPUT DATA

Time (days)	Requisition Quantity (units removed)
1	2
2	0
3	1
4	1
5	2
6	1
7	0
8	2
9	2
10	1
11	0
12	0
13	2
14	1
15	1

OUTPUT WANTED

(1) Inventory level for each day.

(2) The day an order is found to be needed, and the quantity to be ordered.

(3) Make a plot of inventory level against time in days, similar to that of Figure 4.2-5a.

(B) With the aid of the flow chart shown in Figure P4.2-1*b*, carry the inventory program of part (*a*) through two complete cycles—that is, through the process of ordering and receiving shipment twice. Repeat the input data table twice more to cover days 16–45 (now do you see why it is better to have read in only the requisition quantity in part (*a*))?

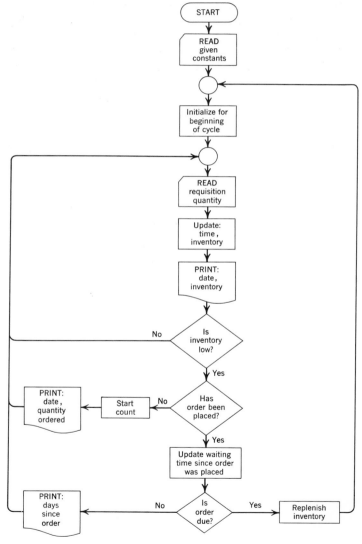

Figure P4.2-1*b*

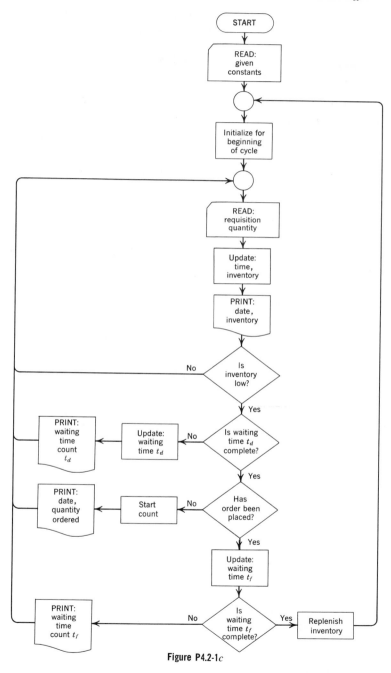

Figure P4.2-1c

If stock runs out, show backed-up requisitions as negative inventory. For the day shipment arrives, show the net inventory at the end of the day.

(C) To make the simulation a little more realistic, assume t_f' is broken down into its separate delays:

$t_d = 6$ (time to detect low inventory and issue a purchase order)
$t_f = 4$ (forecast of shipment)

Now two separate delay counts will have to be used. With the aid of the flow chart of Figure P4.2-1c, have the program issue a detectable indication of the following three events each time they occur:

(1) Inventory level is low (equal to or less than MOL).
(2) Purchase order issued, together with OQ (t_d days after event 1).
(3) Shipment received (t_f days after event 2).

(D) To show the effect of changing business conditions, repeat part (B) or (C) with the input data in Figure P4.2-1d. As before, repeat the data twice more to get 45 days of input.

For each plot calculate ARID and AIL over the 45 day period.

(E) Repeat part (D) above for the set of data in Figure P4.2-1e.

PROBLEM 4.2-2   "Computer Controlled Inventory"

(A) Repeat 4.2-1 (B) to simulate *computer* control of inventory by making the minimum order level MOL and the order quantity OQ

Time (days)	Requisition Quantity (units removed)	Time (days)	Requisition Quantity (units removed)
1	2	1	2
2	0	2	1
3	1	3	2
4	0	4	1
5	0	5	0
6	1	6	2
7	1	7	2
8	0	8	1
9	2	9	3
10	0	10	1
11	0	11	1
12	1	12	2
13	0	13	0
14	1	14	1
15	1	15	2

Figure P4.2-1d   Figure P4.2-1e

variable, and by reducing t_f' from 10 days to 5. This is realistic if we assume the computer control permits t_d to be cut from 6 days to 1.

MOL and OQ are calculated as needed from the equations

$$MOL = MOLS * (I_i - I_c)/t_c$$
$$OQ = OQS * (I_i - I_o)/t_o$$

where:

MOLS and OQS are standard quantities to be read in; make them 8 and 20 for a first try.

I_i is the initial inventory at the beginning of *each cycle;* it needs to be reset after shipment is received. Make $I_i = 20$ initially.

I_c is the inventory after each daily updating.

I_o is the inventory at the time an order is to be placed. Note, however, that this needs to be calculated only once in each cycle, and therefore I_o is merely the I_c for that day.

t_c is the time in days measured from the beginning of the current cycle to the day under consideration.

t_o is the time in days measured from the beginning of the current cycle to the day an order is placed. As in I_o' however, t_o is needed only to calculate OQ, and can therefore be taken as t_c on the day that calculation is needed.

t is the time in days measured from the start of the simulation. It will probably be wanted for output purposes.

Taking all these comments into account, the equations for MOL and OQ above reduce to

$$MOL = MOLS * (I_i - I_c)/t_c$$
$$OQ = OQS * (I_i - I_c)/t_c$$

(B) Repeat 4.2-2(A) for part (D) of 4.2-1. Start with the same initial values, and see if the program is able to adjust. Are there any advantages to computer control of inventory?

(C) Repeat 4.2-2(B) for the data of 4.2-1(E).

PROBLEM 4.3-1   "Discussion of Daily Operations"

Daily operations control may be divided into the four principal control operations shown as w, x, y and z in the diagram. The operation z pertains to accounting and w, x, and y are related to the control of the process operations P_1, P_2, P_3, and P_4.

(1) Discuss the functions of w, x, and y and their communications with the process and the outside.

(2) Describe the applications of the computer to each of these three operations.

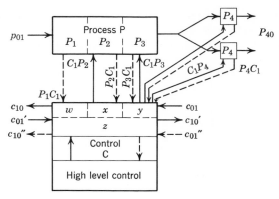

Figure P4.3-1

REFERENCES

4.3-1. Chrystal, Donald P., Thomas G. Guenther, and Eldo C. Koenig. "Applying Control Concepts to an Organization." *Total Systems,* American Data Processing Inc. Detroit, 1962.

CHAPTER 5.

Things Worth Computing:

[B] OVER AND OVER TO GET AN ANSWER

5.1 PERSPECTIVE

In Chapter 3 we looked at two ways in which the numbers the computer was working with could be changed from one calculation to the next. We saw a variety of interesting things the computer could be asked to do, all of which involved repeating the same calculations over and over again. One thing almost all those problems had in common, however, was that each calculation was essentially complete in itself, and resulted in an individual answer.

Another, even larger, class of calculations takes advantage of the computer's ability to repeat an operation many times, by asking it to *try* a given operation many times, expecting that many of the answers will be rejected, until eventually it succeeds in producing one (or several) which are accepted.

An example of this could be the case of trying, one after another, a long but finite list of possible answers until one is found that will fit. This might be compared with the problem of finding the right key to open the door (when it's a little too late to be able to focus sharply enough to pick out the right key any other way). We know one of them will fit, and it is merely a matter of trial and error until we hit upon the right one. In another type of problem, we build upon the answer achieved in the preceding trial, trying to improve, and getting a better answer with each succeeding attempt—much as each turn of the crank of a pencil sharpener takes the result of the preceding operation and refines it a bit further.

Still other types of repetition will come up, but, in each, the consistent difference from the problems of Chapter 3 remains: the result of many trials is one, or one set of, answers.

5.2 CONVERGING ITERATION

Let us try the pencil sharpener type of problem first.

For one thing, it follows naturally from the last application we were looking at in Chapter 3: the finding of roots of equations. The method of decimal tabulation is in a sense a systematic method of locating the answers we want by a process of trial and error, and narrowing the search by examining the results of previous operations. There are, however, even more powerful methods of locating roots, based upon various methods of accelerating the convergence of the iterations.

In many situations this is almost the only method open to us; in others it is one of the best of several alternatives. Recall the *Polyplot* program of Figure 3.4-2, and note that part (c) of that figure shows that the function

$$y = x^3 - 12x^2 + 29x - 16 \qquad (5.2-1)$$

crosses the axis three times, in the approximate neighborhood of 1^-, 2^+, and 9^-. Now the method of decimal tabulation can be employed to refine these to (theoretically) any required degree of precision. But the number of calculations involved, and hence the computing time, could get very large, particularly as the function being calculated gets more and more messy. It would be very nice to find some way of speeding up the process.

If we put an efficiency expert to work analyzing the decimal tabulation process, he would (if he were worth his consulting fee) come up with the following discovery: what is wasteful about this method is that we throw away most of the information we worked so hard to get. Although we keep careful track of the x value at every step, all we do with the F values we so laboriously calculated is look to see whether they are plus or minus. F could be 6.9851×10^{17} or 1.0003×10^{-4}—all we do is test it to see whether it has changed its sign.

As long as we go to all that work (use all that computer time) to calculate the actual value of F corresponding to each x, there ought to be some way to use that information to help us improve our guess for the next value of x, instead of just blindly plowing ahead by tenths.

There is.

Longhair mathematicians like to call this method "Regula Falsi"; those with shorter haircuts are willing to use the translation "Rule of False Position."

Let us assume that we have been plugging along on this equation, and have found that for

$$x = 2, \quad y = \quad 2$$

and for

$$x = 3, \quad y = -10$$

(5.2-2)

Now surely it should be apparent from Figure 5.2-1a (or even without it) that the curve crosses the x axis considerably nearer the x = 2 point than the x = 3 point. How much nearer? Let us see if we can make a good guess.

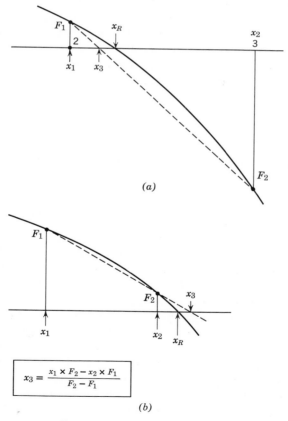

(a)

(b)

$$x_3 = \frac{x_1 \times F_2 - x_2 \times F_1}{F_2 - F_1}$$

Figure 5.2-1 Rule of False Position.

If the curve were a straight line between these two points, it would pass through x_3 on Figure 5.2-1a. All we would have to do would be to calculate the location of x_3 from similar triangles, and we would have our root. Even though we are quite aware of the fact that the curve is not a straight line, and that the true root x_R will be somewhat displaced from x_3, it should be clear that in most normal situations x_3 will be closer to the true root x_R than is either x_1 or x_2.

This then is the origin of the name, and the secret of success of the method. We will go ahead and calculate the location of x_3, knowing it is a false goal and not a true root, because x_3 is closer to x_R than x_1 or x_2. From x_3 we can get an x_4, which is still closer, and from that x_5, and by doing this enough times eventually obtain the value of x_R as accurately as we require.

Let us take a look at Figure 5.2-1b which is a close-up of the region in which a curve like this cubic crosses the axis. Assume that we have points x_1 and x_2 near a crossing, and that we know the values of F_1 and F_2 corresponding to both of these. How could we use this information to calculate the location of x_3? Let us derive an equation.

There are obviously two similar triangles: x_3-x_1-F_1 and x_3-x_2-F_2. By taking advantage of a theorem proved a long time ago, having to do with the ratios of corresponding sides of similar triangles being equal, we can say

$$\frac{x_3 - x_1}{x_3 - x_2} = \frac{F_1}{F_2} \tag{5.2-3}$$

Since in this situation we know x_1 and x_2, and their corresponding F values, and would like to find x_3, we solve Eq. (5.2-3) for x_3, yielding:

$$\boxed{x_3 = \frac{x_1 \times F_2 \quad - \quad x_2 \times F_1}{F_2 \quad - \quad F_1}} \qquad \text{Rule of False Position} \qquad (5.2-4)$$

This is the goal we have been working for: an expression that enables us, given two points reasonably close to a root, to calculate a third point which will be still closer. If we iterate on this procedure, we ought to keep getting closer and closer.

How about this iterating? How do we proceed from here? It seems clear enough that x_3 is closer, and should be used in the next calculation to get still closer, but what do we take for our second point? This rule always requires a *pair* of points in order to calculate a third. What shall we use for our second point, together with x_3? Either x_1 or x_2 could be saved, and the other discarded and replaced by x_3. Now, using that pair of one old value and one new, we would actually be able to calculate an x_4 that will be still better than x_3. But as a matter of practicality —something which people who use computers always have to worry about—it is not hard to show that the iteration converges more rapidly (it takes fewer turns of the pencil sharpener handle) if we find out which old value of x is *closer* to our new one, and always use that one. Figure 5.2-2 shows a flow chart and the corresponding FORTRAN program describing a procedure for persuading our computer to do just that.

In this program we first supply the computer with a description of the function, by reading in the coefficients of the polynomial, and then give it two points that have been found by some other means to be fairly close to a root. The program takes over from there, calculating successively closer approximations to that root. At the end are listed the answers actually obtained at each step in the iteration, showing that once we have begun to approach the root the convergence is very rapid, resulting is an improvement of one or even two more significant figures (an improvement of from 10 to 100 times) in each iteration!

How does this compare with the method of Chapter 3—Roots by Decimal Tabulation? Well, if you recall the procedure there, each time we found a sign change we had to decrease DX by a factor of 10, and commence stepping back through the interval to obtain one more digit in the root. Now, that new digit might be found on the first try, or not until the tenth; on the average it will take five tries. So one can predict that this method will take about five times as many calculations to arrive at a given accuracy as the false position method.

Let us write one more program using the false position before we go on. Figure 5.2-3 shows the *Roots by Decimal Tabulation* program of Figure 3.5-1 modified to find *Roots by False Position*. The first part of the program is shaded to show that it is essentially the same, although one should check carefully the sequence of data being called for. However, once a pair of points bracketing a root has been found (by detecting a sign change), the program uses the method of false position to home in on the precise value of the root, rather than tabulating by tenths. Just like the other program, however, it has to save its last calculated position when it interrupts its orderly march along the function, so that after the root has been tracked down it can reset itself to its original conditions and carry on from there.

Figure 5.2-4 shows the printed output of both of these programs, modified so that they punch out the results of every step. It is informative to compare how many calculations each program requires to pin down a root, once the first sign change has been found. The comparison for all three roots is as follows:

	Decimal Tabulation	False Position
ROOT 1	22	6
ROOT 2	24	5
ROOT 3	32	4

The prosecution rests its case.

Once precaution should be mentioned before we leave with the impression that everything always works perfectly. Will x_3 always be closer to x_R than either x_1 or x_2? The answer, as might be suspected, is no.

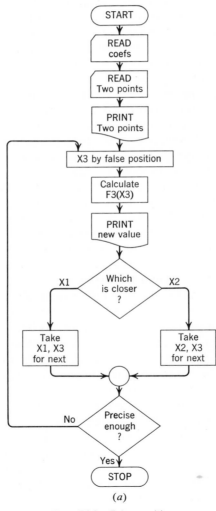

(a)

Figure 5.2-2   False position.

There is, unfortunately, no quarantee that the result of such a process is in general any closer to the correct value than the starting numbers, nor that the process will converge to any number at all. In fact, for a given equation, the process may converge or diverge depending on the numbers we start with. Obviously the closer the starting points are to the correct root the safer we will be, and for the majority of cases

```
C                    ** FALSE POSITION **
C                                         LOAD POLY
         DIMENSION A(10)
         READ 40, N
      40 FORMAT (I12)
         NP1 = N + 1
         READ 41, (A(J), J = 1,NP1)
      41 FORMAT (1PE12.4)
C                                         READ 2 POINTS, PRINT FOR ID
         READ 42, X1, F1, X2, F2
      42 FORMAT (4(1PE12.4))
         PRINT 43, X1, F1
      43 FORMAT ((2(1PE12.4)))
         PRINT 43, X2, F2
C                                         PUT OUT BLANK LINE
         PRINT 44
      44 FORMAT (/)
C                                         CALC X3 BY *FALSE POSITION*
       4 X3 = (X1*F2 - X2*F1)/(F2 - F1)
C                                         CALC F3(X3)
         F3 = 0.
         DO 5 J = 1,NP1
       5 F3 = F3*X3 + A(J)
         PRINT 43, X3, F3
C                                         WHICH IS CLOSER
         IF(ABS(X3-X1)-ABS(X3-X2)) 7,7,8
C                                           X1
       7   X2 = X3
           F2 = F3
           GO TO 9
C                                           X2
       8   X1 = X3
           F1 = F3
C                                         PRECISE ENOUGH OR DO IT AGAIN
       9 IF(ABS(X2-X1)-1.E-5) 10,10,4
      10 STOP
         END
               3
               1.
             -12.
              29.
             -16.
               2.          2.          3.        -10.
ANSWERS

      2.0000        2.0000
      3.0000       -1.0000E+01

      2.1667        6.7129E-01
      2.2509       -1.1792E-01
      2.2383        4.8130E-03
      2.2388        3.5000E-05
      2.2388       -4.0000E-06
```

(*b*)

Figure 5.2-2*b*

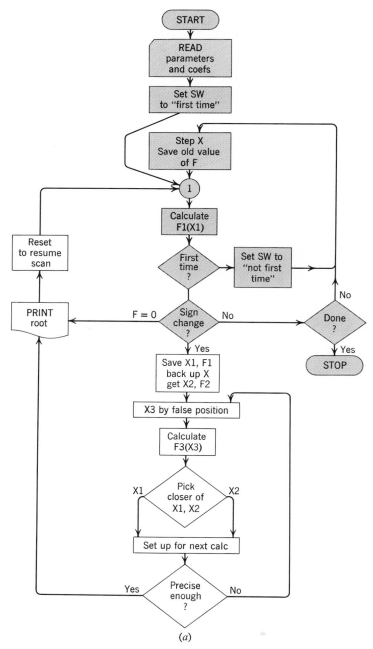

Figure 5.2-3 Roots by false position.

```
C      **  ROOTS BY FALSE POSITION  **
       DIMENSION  A(10)
       READ 40,  N
    40 FORMAT (I12)
       NP1 = N + 1
       READ 41,  (A(J), J = 1, NP1)
    41 FORMAT (6(1PE12.4))
       READ 42,  XINIT, DELX, XFIN
    42 FORMAT (3(1PE12.4))
       SW = 0.
       F1 = 0.
       X1 = XINIT
       GO TO 4
     3 X1 = X1 + DELX
       FOLD = F1
     4 F1 = 0.
       DO 24 J = 1, NP1
    24 F1 = F1*X1 + A(J)
       IF (SW) 6, 6, 7
     6 SW = 1.
       GO TO 3
C                                                      TEST FOR SIGN CHANGE
     7 IF (F1*FOLD) 10, 17, 8
C                                                      NO. TEST FOR XFIN, REPEAT
     8    IF (X1 - XFIN) 3, 9, 9
C                                                      YES. SAVE X1, F1
    10    XSAV = X1
          FSAV = F1
          X2   = X1 - DELX
          F2   = FOLD
C                                                      CALC NEXT X BY FALSE POSITION
    11    X3 = (X1*F2 - X2*F1)/(F2 - F1)
          F3 = 0.
          DO 22 J = 1, NP1
    22    F3 = F3*X3 + A(J)
C                                                      WHICH IS CLOSER
          IF(ABS(X3-X1)-ABS(X3-X2)) 14,15,15
C                                                          X1
    14       X2 = X3
             F2 = F3
             GO TO 16
C                                                          X2
    15       X1 = X3
             F1 = F3
C                                                      PRECISE ENOUGH OR DO IT AGAIN
    16    IF(ABS(X2-X1)-1.E-5) 17,11,11
C                                                      YES. PRINT ROOT, RESET
    17       PRINT 43,  X3, F3
    43       FORMAT (2(1PE12.4))
             X1 = XSAV + DELX
             FOLD = FSAV
             GO TO 4
     9 STOP
       END
             3
       1.        -12.        29.         -16.
      -10.         1.        10.

ANSWERS
   7.9728E-01  0.0000
   2.2388     -4.0000E-06
   8.9639      3.9000E-05
```

(b)

Figure 5.2-3*b*

-1.0000E+01	-2.5060E+03	2.2382	5.6790E-03
-9.0000	-1.9780E+03	2.2383	4.7110E-03
-8.0000	-1.5280E+03	2.2384	3.7430E-03
-7.0000	-1.1500E+03	2.2385	2.7720E-03
-6.0000	-8.3800E+02	2.2386	1.8040E-03
-5.0000	-5.8600E+02	2.2387	8.3500E-04
-4.0000	-3.8800E+02	2.2388	-1.3600E-04
-3.0000	-2.3800E+02	2.2388	-3.7000E-05
-2.0000	-1.3000E+02	2.2388	5.9000E-05
-1.0000	-5.8000E+01		
0.0000	-1.6000E+01	2.2388	5.9000E-05
1.0000	2.0000		
9.0000E-01	1.1090	4.0000	-2.8000E+01
8.0000E-01	3.2000E-02	5.0000	-4.6000E+01
7.0000E-01	-1.2370	6.0000	-5.8000E+01
7.1000E-01	-1.1013	7.0000	-5.8000E+01
7.2000E-01	-9.6755E-01	8.0000	-4.0000E+01
7.3000E-01	-8.3578E-01	9.0000	2.0000
7.4000E-01	-7.0598E-01	8.9000	-3.4510
7.5000E-01	-5.7813E-01	8.9100	-2.9192
7.6000E-01	-4.5222E-01	8.9200	-2.3845
7.7000E-01	-3.2827E-01	8.9300	-1.8468
7.8000E-01	-2.0625E-01	8.9400	-1.3062
7.9000E-01	-8.6161E-02	8.9500	-7.6263E-01
8.0000E-01	3.2000E-02	8.9600	-2.1606E-01
7.9900E-01	2.0270E-02	8.9700	3.3347E-01
7.9800E-01	8.5220E-03	8.9690	2.7839E-01
7.9700E-01	-3.2460E-03	8.9680	2.2333E-01
7.9710E-01	-2.0680E-03	8.9670	1.6830E-01
7.9720E-01	-8.9100E-04	8.9660	1.1330E-01
7.9730E-01	2.8700E-04	8.9650	5.8332E-02
7.9729E-01	1.6900E-04	8.9640	3.3930E-03
7.9728E-01	5.1000E-05	8.9630	-5.1516E-02
7.9727E-01	-6.7000E-05	8.9631	-4.6023E-02
		8.9632	-4.0538E-02
7.9727E-01	-6.7000E-05	8.9633	-3.5045E-02
		8.9634	-2.9552E-02
2.0000	2.0000	8.9635	-2.4067E-02
3.0000	-1.0000E+01	8.9636	-1.8573E-02
2.9000	-8.4310	8.9637	-1.3080E-02
2.8000	-6.9280	8.9638	-7.5950E-03
2.7000	-5.4970	8.9639	-2.1010E-03
2.6000	-4.1440	8.9640	3.3930E-03
2.5000	-2.8750	8.9640	2.8470E-03
2.4000	-1.6960	8.9640	2.2910E-03
2.3000	-6.1300E-01	8.9640	1.7440E-03
2.2000	3.6800E-01	8.9640	1.1970E-03
2.2100	2.7466E-01	8.9640	6.5100E-04
2.2200	1.8025E-01	8.9639	9.5000E-05
2.2300	8.4767E-02	8.9639	-4.5200E-04
2.2400	-1.1776E-02		
2.2390	-2.0740E-03	8.9639	-4.5200E-04
2.2380	7.6170E-03		
2.2381	6.6490E-03	1.0000E+01	7.4000E+01

(*a*)

Figure 5.2-4 Comparison of convergence.

```
C     **  ROOTS BY FALSE POSITION  (MODIFIED)  **

 -1.0000E+01  -2.5060E+03
 -9.0000      -1.9780E+03
 -8.0000      -1.5280E+03
 -7.0000      -1.1500E+03
 -6.0000      -8.3800E+02
 -5.0000      -5.8600E+02
 -4.0000      -3.8800E+02
 -3.0000      -2.3800E+02
 -2.0000      -1.3000E+02
 -1.0000      -5.8000E+01
  0.0000      -1.6000E+01
  1.0000       2.0000

  8.8889E-01   9.9863E-01
  7.7808E-01  -2.2950E-01
  7.9879E-01   1.7788E-02
  7.9730E-01   2.7500E-04
  7.9728E-01  -1.0000E-06
  7.9728E-01   0.0000

  7.9728E-01   0.0000

  2.0000       2.0000
  3.0000      -1.0000E+01

  2.1667       6.7129E-01
  2.2509      -1.1792E-01
  2.2383       4.8130E-03
  2.2388       3.5000E-05
  2.2388      -4.0000E-06

  2.2388      -4.0000E-06

  4.0000      -2.8000E+01
  5.0000      -4.6000E+01
  6.0000      -5.8000E+01
  7.0000      -5.8000E+01
  8.0000      -4.0000E+01
  9.0000       2.0000

  8.9524      -6.3276E-01
  8.9638      -6.2310E-03
  8.9639       3.2000E-05
  8.9639       3.9000E-05

  8.9639       3.9000E-05

  1.0000E+01   7.4000E+01
```

(b)

Figure 5.2-4b

145

of practical interest, the process will give no trouble. However, no high-way, not even the relatively safe and swift modern throughway, has yet been designed that is safe to drive on with your eyes shut.

5.3 SORTING

Quite a different type of problem is presented by the key-ring problem. No longer do we have the profitable situation of building on previous results, of refining our answers a little more with each turn of the crank. Now we are faced with a long list of choices, one of which satisfies our needs, yet we have (usually) no better approach than to examine them all, one at a time, until we find the one we want.

Find Largest

As an example on which to concentrate our attention, suppose we are designing a bookcase around a specific set of books. Consider a single shelf: we have lined up in front of us in Figure 5.3-1a the books that are to go on that shelf, and we wish to know the height of the tallest book so we can know how high to make the shelf. How do we find the tallest book?

To begin with, it is important to recognize a fundamental difference between the way computers and people go about such an operation. The human eye, and the brain it is coupled to, can scan very quickly over such an array, rejecting with little effort most of the books as being "obviously" not worth considering. In only a few cases will it have to pause somewhat before it can reject the smaller and eventually end up with the single tallest book. Even if the heights are converted into numbers printed on a page, the problem is not much different.

Not so the computer. There is no such operation as "scan"; it knows only "examine carefully." It can pick one out of a set only by comparing it one at a time against every other in the set.

Consider for a moment what we mean by "comparing" two numbers. To say one number is larger than another could be thought of as arranging them in an ordered list if you wish, but how do you determine their place in the list? Is it not, essentially, by *subtraction,* by seeing if you can subtract one number from the other? Or stated more precisely, if one number *is* subtracted from the other, is the result positive?

This is essentially the way a computer has to compare, by subtracting one from another and testing the sign of the result. Furthermore it has to make this detailed comparison for *each* number on the list, by actually subtracting it from another. This is one type of operation in which the computer is relatively far less efficient than the human.

However, we said "relatively." Inefficient though the computer is compared with other operations, it can usually still perform such a searching and sorting operation faster than people can, for one thing because it can go right ahead and use the answer as soon as it finds it. It does not have to stop to say it, or write it down, or punch it on a card for a computer. So, it is worth learning how to program a computer to make such a search.

No one, of course, would go about actually designing a bookcase this way. But stated in simple mathematical terms:

> GIVEN: a set of *n* numbers
> WANTED: the largest number

the problem is extremely general. We will go ahead and develop a computer program to do the comparing among these numbers for us, and keep the bookcase picture to help us visualize the situation as we go.

If the computer is going to do the scanning and comparing for us, does this mean it is going to be necessary to subtract every number from every other number in the array? Not at all. Once a number has been rejected as smaller than another, it is not necessary to look at it again. The next comparison can be made against the number that has already been found to be larger, until a still larger one is found. Proceeding in this way, we need look at each element in the array only once, always using for the number to compare it against the largest that we have discovered so far. Then by the time we make the last comparison we know that the larger of these last two is indeed the largest number in the entire array.

Since there is nothing known about the books in advance, and therefore no reason to prefer any one over the others on the basis of size, we make the starting assumption that the first book (the one at the left end), is the tallest and is the one against which the others will be tested, one at a time. In the flow chart, Figure 5.3-1*b*, this is block 2. If, when we get to the end of the shelf, we have not found any that is taller, that first one *is* the tallest. If, however, one of the others turns out to be taller, we can forget about the first book and make all subsequent comparisons against this new "tallest" book.

To put it in mathematical language, the procedure illustrated in Figure 5.3-1*b* starts out by comparing B(1) against B(2). If B(1) is larger, then B(1) is compared with B(3), then with B(4), and so forth down the line. On the other hand, if B(2) were found to be larger than B(1), then B(2) would be the standard of comparison, because it would

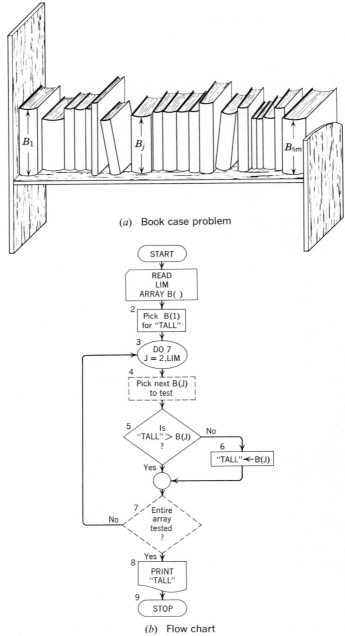

(a) Book case problem

START

READ
LIM
ARRAY B( )

2
Pick B(1)
for "TALL"

3
DO 7
J = 2,LIM

4
Pick next B(J)
to test

5
Is
"TALL" > B(J)
?

No

6
"TALL" ← B(J)

Yes

7
Entire
array
tested
?

No

Yes

8
PRINT
"TALL"

9
STOP

(b) Flow chart

Figure 5.3-1a, b Find largest.

```
DIMENSION  B(30)
   READ 40,  LIM
40 FORMAT (I12)
   READ 41,  (B(J), J = 1, LIM)
41 FORMAT (1PE12.4)
   TALL = B(1)
   DO 7  J = 2, LIM
      IF (TALL - B(J)) 6, 7, 7
 6    TALL = B(J)
 7    CONTINUE
   PRINT 41,  TALL
   STOP
   END
```

(*c*) Program

```
DIMENSION  B(30)
   READ 40,  LIM
40 FORMAT (I12)
   READ 41,  (B(J),  J = 1, LIM)
41 FORMAT (1PE12.4)
   L = 1
   DO 7  J = 2, LIM
      IF (B(L) - B(J)) 6, 7, 7
 6    L = J
 7    CONTINUE
                         OR COULD SAY
   PRINT 41,  B(L)       PRINT 42,  L, B(L)
                      42 FORMAT (I12, 1PE12.4)
   STOP
   END
```

(*d*) Alternate program

Figure 5.3-1c, *d*

be the largest that had been found to date, and B(2) would be compared with B(3). After each test, whatever the result, the next element in the list is the one taken to be tested next. The difference in the two cases is that, depending on the result of the test, the original element is kept as the standard of comparison, or the new one is substituted for it. In either case, by the time the process reaches the end of the list, the element called "tallest," is the tallest.

What does this mean in terms of actual program steps? In Figure 5.3-1c we see that the actual program listing is a lot more compact than the flow chart describing the same problem. But the program is much easier to lay out, or to follow, once it has been determined, in a flow chart, just what the function of each of these operations is supposed to be.

After B( ) is dimensioned, to specify the maximum amount of storage necessary, the array can be read in by two READ statements under the assumption that preceding the actual heights is a single card containing the number of books on the shelf, called "LIM." Then we pick out the first one and set it aside, calling it "TALL," and are ready to start comparing.

How do we actually do the testing? As you might have suspected, the actual comparing is done by an IF statement. An IF actually calculates the expression inside its parentheses, remember, so if we call for two B's to be subtracted, the branching will be done on the sign of the difference of these. Since the first element has been set aside to be the initial "TALL," we need only run our DO loop from 2 to LIM, so that the first comparison is really between B(1) and B(2). If this difference B(1) − B(2) is positive, B(1), or "TALL," is the larger, and we skip to statement 7 and continue. Statement 7, being the object of the DO loop, steps the index J, and after finding that it has not exceeded the limit, returns control to the beginning of the DO loop to test the next one. If, on the other hand, B(2) were found to be larger than B(1), control would be sent to statement 6, where the number called "TALL" would be replaced by the new one that had been found to be larger—in this case by B(2).

So, when the DO loop is satisfied, and we have reached the end of the list, whatever is the latest number to have been stored under the name "TALL" is actually the largest number that has been found in the entire list. Therefore we print it out, and retire.

An alternate method to this scheme for finding the height of the tallest book on the shelf is presented in Figure 5.3-1d. The total number of statements is the same, and the only significant advantage seems to lie in the possibility of identifying more precisely the original position of the tallest book on the shelf. (Could you get that information in Figure 5.3-1c by writing PRINT , J, TALL?) Nevertheless, we shall shortly encounter some situations where this alternate method has some very powerful advantages over the first, and a study of it is recommended.

Find Largest X and Associated Y

The advantages of this alternate method begin to show up in the next problem. We merely make the additional request that the program tell us not only what is the height of the tallest book, but also which one *is* the tallest. We will not try to handle the alphabetic rendition of the actual title and author, but will assume each book is identified by a call number (such as its library classification). The data now consist of pairs of associated numbers, one being the height of each book, and the other the call number of that book.

GIVEN

A set of data cards each containing two numbers: BOOK(J) and CALL(J). There are LIM of these cards, and this number LIM is punched on a card which precedes the others.

WANTED

The largest of these numbers BOOK(J) and its corresponding call number CALL(J).

Figure 5.3-2a shows that the procedure is very similar to that followed in the preceding case, except that we have to dimension for 2 arrays, set initial values for both, and replace 2 numbers every time the comparison indicates that a new maximum has been found.

Now we shall see that the alternate method of Figure 5.3-2b is not only physically shorter (by 2 statements), but that the elimination of the second replacement operation (S 0006 + 01 L in Figure 5.3-2a) will eliminate a considerable amount of needless data shuffling, and significantly speed up the running of the problem.

Table Look-Up

Closely related, is the frequently encountered situation called table look-up. We are all used to referring to printed tabulations of such mathematical relationships as trigonometric functions, and logarithms

```
      DIMENSION  BOOK(30), CALL(30)
      READ 40,  LIM
40 FORMAT (I12)
      READ 41,  (BOOK(J), CALL(J),  J = 1, LIM)
41 FORMAT (2(1PE12.4))
      TALLB = BOOK(1)
      TALLC = CALL(1)
      DO 7  J = 2, LIM
         IF (TALLB - BOOK(J)) 6, 7, 7
  6    TALLB = BOOK(J)
       TALLC = CALL(J)
  7    CONTINUE
      PRINT 41,  TALLB, TALLC
      STOP
      END
```

(a) Program

```
      DIMENSION  BOOK(30), CALL(30)
      READ 40,  LIM
40 FORMAT (I12)
      READ 41,  (BOOK(J), CALL(J),  J = 1, LIM)
41 FORMAT (2(1PE12.4)
      L = 1
      DO 7  J = 2, LIM
         IF (BOOK(L) - BOOK(J)) 6, 7, 7
  6    L = J
  7    CONTINUE
      PRINT 41,  BOOK(L) , CALL(L)
      STOP
      END
```

(b) Alternate program

Figure 5.3-2 Find largest X and associated Y.

when doing hand calculations, but the computer usually finds it easier to calculate the value of the function corresponding to a given argument than to store and look up those values when needed. There are, however, cases in which the values of the dependent variable cannot be conveniently calculated, and we have no other recourse than to store the information in a table, and, when we need a particular number, look it up. Consider an application of computers to inventory control as described in Chapter 4. It must be realized, of course, that for any sizable company the number of different items in inventory is quite large. We will assume that the record of current inventory consists of 2 arrays or lists of numbers: a series of part numbers, called NUM( ), and for each of these the current inventory of that part on hand, called INV( ). In most cases the first of these arrays, NUM( ), will be arranged in ascending (or descending) order, although that feature is not needed for at least the first version of our problem. We do know, however, that we have been given a particular part number, called NN, which is presumably exactly equal to some value of NUM. We would like to know the value of INV corresponding to that value of NUM.

Here is a case (as shown in Figure 5.3-3) where the DO loop is rarely satisfied. Although the parameters of the loop are set to cover the entire array if necessary, it is expected that somewhere in the course of the examination a match will be found, and the program will jump out of the loop. It should be noted that this is perfectly legal, and whatever value the index K had at the time the match was found will be retained until it is specifically changed. It is only when leaving the loop in the normal way, by satisfying it, that the index may become undefined.

Check over this table look-up example shown in Figure 5.3-3—we will be making use of this program in Scheduling, the next section.

Sorting

If these techniques have been reasonably well mastered, we should be in a good position to tackle the principal topic of this section—sorting an array into a prescribed sequence. Sorting can be accomplished by nothing more than a repeated performance of the searching operation we have just been going through, but there are many variations on what is done with the result of any one scan. We will look both at the basic problem and at one elaboration, and in each case consider one or two variations on how the programming might be accomplished.

Let us consider first the simple job of sorting an array A( ) into descending order, assuming there is sufficient storage space available in the computer to completely copy the array into the new set of locations B( ) as we sort it.

First let us see if we can outline in a flow chart the tasks to be

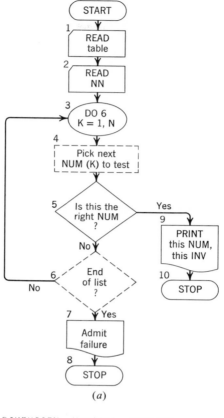

(a)

```
DIMENSION  NUM(30), INV(30)
      READ 40,  N
40 FORMAT (I12)
      READ 41,  (NUM(I), INV(I),  I = 1, N)
41 FORMAT (2I12)
      READ 40,  NN
      DO 6  K = 1, N
        IF (NN - NUM(K)) 6, 9, 6
6     CONTINUE
      PRINT 40,  NN
      STOP
9 PRINT 41, NUM(K), INV(K)
      STOP
      END
```
(b)

Figure 5.3-3 Table look-up.

accomplished at each step, as in Figure 5.3-4*a*. Block 3 in the center is the least of our worries, for we have just worked out several different techniques for doing this. Let us assume that such coding has been written, and turn our attention elsewhere. The commentary on block 2, the first DO loop, is more pertinent, since it lists the functions we are going to have to perform to move on through the list after we have found each "largest." Let us look at each of these functions.

If, as we have assumed, there is enough storage to completely copy the entire list into a new set of locations as we sort it, the first task will be simple: the largest found on the first pass through we store as B(1); we scan the remaining list and put the largest found on the second pass into B(2); and so forth until the entire list has been copied.

Step 2, "eliminate it from the list," is a bit harder to accomplish. There is no way we can leave an empty space in the array, nor can we conveniently program the DO to skip over a particular element in the list. The program will insist on looking at every element every time. But what we can do with the number we want eliminated is to insure that even though it will be picked up and used in a comparison, the

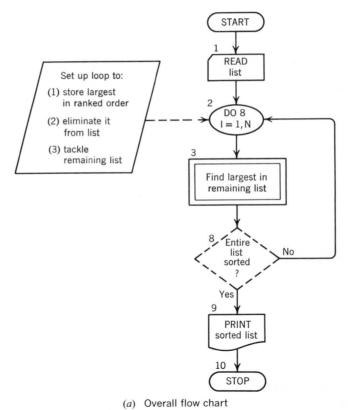

(*a*) Overall flow chart

Figure 5.3-4 Sorting with plenty of room.

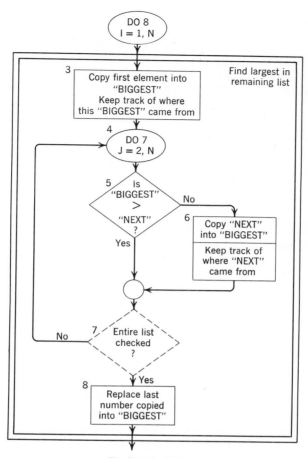

(b) Detail of block 3

```
      DIMENSION  A(30), B(30)
      READ 40,   N
40 FORMAT (I12)
      READ 41,  (A(I),   I = 1, N)
41 FORMAT (1PE12.4)
      DO 8  I = 1, N
        B(I) = A(I)
        L = 1
        DO 7  J = 2, N
          IF (B(I) - A(J)) 6, 7, 7
6         B(I) = A(J)
          L = J
7       CONTINUE
8     A(L) = -9.E48
      DO 9  I = 1, N
9  PRINT 42,  I, B(I)
42 FORMAT (I12, 1PE12.4)
      STOP
      END       (c)  Program
```

Figure 5.3-4*b*, *c*

number in that slot will never be found larger than the number it is being compared against. This in turn means we must make that number smaller than anything else in the list. For some sets of numbers, zero would be a satisfactory number to substitute, for as compared to any positive number, zero would certainly be found smaller and passed over. But if the list were to contain some legitimate zeros, or worse, negative numbers, it would be necessary to substitute something very close to the smallest number that can be stored in the computer being used.

Statement S 0008 + 00 L in Figure 5.3-4c:

$$8 \text{ A(L)} = -9.\text{E}+48$$

accomplishes this operation, replacing the A we want eliminated, A(L), by the very small number -9.0×10^{48}. This means that from now on whenever we pick up that particular A to compare, it will never be found larger than the number being tested and so will be passed over and ignored.

This, then, effectively accomplishes the step 2 we were worried about, and in fact we are in a position to show that all three of the set-up operations outlined in the flow chart are indeed performed by the program shown in Figure 5.3-4c. Between statement S 0041 + 02 L and statement S 0006 + 00 L, we can be sure that by the time the inner loop—DO 7—has been satisfied each time, the number in the corresponding element of the B( ) array is the largest one left in the A( ) list. Statement S 0008 + 00 L then eliminates it as we have seen, and since it is the object of the outer loop—DO 8—it causes advance of the index I and return to the beginning of the loop, thus preparing for a new pass through the array. It is not quite correct to say that the new pass is made only over the "remaining" list; it must cover the full length of the list every time, but it is a list in which a steadily increasing number of the entries have been "eliminated."

The procedure just described, that of Figure 5.3-4, is one of the most straightforward ways of going about the sorting problem, but there are many angles that can be improved upon, one of which is the requirement that a complete double set of storage locations in the memory be available. This requirement is indeed extravagant; we will now examine a method that requires only *one* additional storage location (which we shall call TEMP).

Sorting with Limited Room

The main principle employed here is the *interchange*. If we look at requirements 1 and 2 in the overall flow chart diagram, Figure 5.3-4a, we realize that we can accomplish both at once if, when we find the largest in the list, we put that number in the first position *of the same array,* placing what was originally in position No. 1 into the position vacated by the largest. In other words, we interchange the first and the largest. Then for the next pass, if we consider only elements 2 to N, we have truly eliminated the largest from the list to be scanned.

Furthermore, this process can be repeated. Each time we complete a pass and interchange, we have added 1 to the length of the list already sorted, and subtracted 1 from the "remaining list." Not only does the list to be checked become progressively shorter with each pass, but the process can actually stop one short. For by the time the first $N - 1$ of the elements have been found, it does not take much arguing to convince yourself that the Nth one, the only one remaining, belongs where it is—in last place. So the outside DO loop in Figure 5.3-5a—the first variation—need cover only the range from $J = 1$ to $N - 1$. Such an expression, unfortunately, is not permitted in the DO statement itself, but we can get around the restriction very easily in the manner shown in part (*b*) of the figure by inserting a preceding statement to define a new variable called "N minus one"

$$NM1 = N - 1$$

and then using this variable as the parameter in the DO statement itself:

$$DO\ 7\ J = 1,\ NM1$$

Now, how do we perform this operation called interchange? Remember that defining a new value for a variable, which is equivalent to writing a new number into a location in memory, destroys the previous value of that variable, so we cannot just write

$$A(1) = A(2)$$
$$A(2) = A(1)$$

Both variables would have the value originally held by $A(2)$, if we tried it. However, if we have available even one extra space in memory, to serve as temporary storage, then we can accomplish the interchange of two numbers by the trio of statements:

$$TEMP = A(1)$$
$$A(1)\ \ \ = A(2)$$
$$A(2)\ \ \ = TEMP$$

This is the procedure followed in Figure 5.3-5a and b, in which the inner loop locates the largest remaining element in the list by the following sequence of operations

(1) It starts by assuming that the head of the remaining list is the largest element in that list.

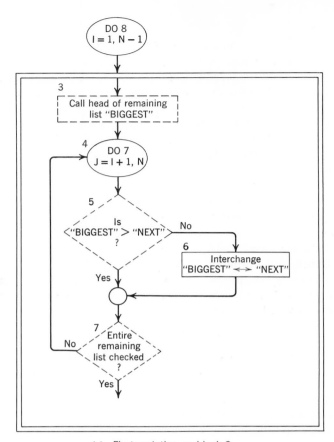

(a) First variation on block 3

```
      DIMENSION  A(30)
      READ 40,  N
40 FORMAT (I12)
      READ 41,  (A(I),   I = 1, N)
41 FORMAT (1PE12.4)
      NM1 = N - 1
      DO 7  I = 1, NM1
        IP1 = I + 1
        DO 7 J = IP1, N
          IF (A(I) - A(J)) 6, 7, 7
6         TEMP = A(I)
          A(I) = A(J)
          A(J) = TEMP
7       CONTINUE
      DO 9  I = 1, N
9 PRINT 42,  I, A(I)
42 FORMAT (I12, 1PE12.4)
      STOP
      END
```

(b) Program—first variation

Figure 5.3-5 Sorting with limited room.

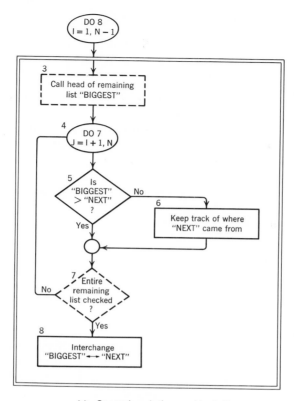

(c) Second variation on block 3

```
      DIMENSION A(30)
      READ 40,   N
40 FORMAT (I12)
      READ 41,   (A(I),   I = 1, N)
41 FORMAT (1PE12.4)
      NM1 = N - 1
      DO 8  I = 1, NM1
         IP1 = I + 1
         L = I
         DO 7  J = IP1, N
            IF (A(L) - A(J)) 6, 7, 7
 6          L = J
 7       CONTINUE
         TEMP = A(I)
         A(I) = A(L)
 8       A(L) = TEMP
      DO 9  I = 1, N
 9 PRINT 42,   I, A(I)
42 FORMAT (I12, 1PE12.4)
      STOP
      END
```

(d) Program—second variation

Figure 5.3-5c, d

(2) It tests all other elements in the list against that one.

(3) Each time it finds a larger one, it interchanges that element with the element in the head position.

Therefore, by the time the end of the list is reached, the largest element in the entire list is in the head position.

Figure 5.3-6 shows a step by step record of what an array might look like at each step in the sorting process. It assumes that the unsorted list shown at the left (1, 7, 2, 9) is sorted by the program and eventually put out as (9, 7, 2, 1). Careful comparison with the actual program of Figure 5.3-5b should go a long way toward making clear exactly what happens at every step.

The method of Figure 5.3-5 has two great advantages over that of 5.3-4.

(1) It requires only one working storage position instead of an entire double set.

(2) It requires only $\dfrac{N(N-1)}{2}$ comparisons instead of $N(N-1)$— exactly half as many.

There is one disadvantage, however, and that is that interchanging takes three times as many operations as merely copying a number from one location into another, as we did in the first method. Here the alternate method of Figure 5.3-5c and d comes to the rescue, allowing us to complete the scan, merely keeping track of the subscript of the largest, and then when the bottom of the list is reached perform only one interchange.

The advantage of this shows up best if we compare the flow charts of the two methods of Figure 5.3-5, noticing that this interchanging operation is transferred from the inner loop in the first version to the outer loop in the alternate. The difference becomes even more striking if we extend the problem to one more (the last) variation: that of

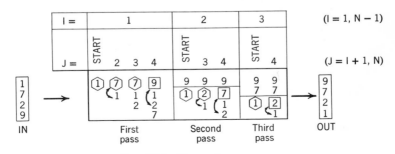

Figure 5.3-6   The sorting process.

sorting a list containing several related columns into a prescribed sequence for one of the columns. To be precise, consider the following problem statement for analyzing the weekly performance of a sales force:

GIVEN

A series of data cards, each containing two numbers:
  (1) the number of units sold by a particular salesman, NSALE(K)
  (2) the identification number of that particular salesman, MAN(K).

```
      DIMENSION  MAN(30), NSALE(30)
      READ 40,  N
   40 FORMAT (I12)
      READ 41,  (NSALE(I), MAN(I),  I = 1, N)
   41 FORMAT (2I12)
      NM1 = N - 1
      DO 7  I = 1, NM1
        IP1 = I + 1
        DO 7  J = IP1, N
          IF (NSALE(I) - NSALE(J)) 6, 7, 7
    6       ITEMP    = NSALE(I)
            NSALE(I) = NSALE(J)
            NSALE(J) = ITEMP
            ITEMP    = MAN(I)
            MAN(I)   = MAN(J)
            MAN(J)   = ITEMP
    7     CONTINUE
      DO 9  I = 1, N
    9 PRINT 42,  I, NSALE(I), MAN(I)
   42 FORMAT (3I12)
      STOP
      END
```

(a) Program

```
      DIMENSION  MAN(30), NSALE(30)
      READ 40,  N
   40 FORMAT (I12)
      READ 41,  (NSALE(I), MAN(I),  I = 1, N)
   41 FORMAT (2I12)
      NM1 = N - 1
      DO 8  I = 1, NM1
        L = I
        IP1 = I + 1
        DO 7  J = IP1, N
        DO 7  J = IP1, N
          IF (NSALE(L) - NSALE(J)) 6, 7, 7
    6       L = J
    7     CONTINUE
          ITEMP    = NSALE(I)
          NSALE(I) = NSALE(L)
          NSALE(L) = ITEMP
          ITEMP    = MAN(I)
          MAN(I)   = MAN(L)
    8     MAN(L)   = ITEMP
      DO 9  I = 1, N
    9 PRINT 42,  I, NSALE(I), MAN(I)
   42 FORMAT (3I12)
      STOP
      END
```

(b) Alternate program

Figure 5.3-7 Sorting A and B on A.

An ordered sales record for the entire sales force, arranged with the output of the most successful salesman (largest NSALE) at the top.

If there is any doubt of the superiority of the alternate method, a comparison of flow charts drawn for the two programs of Figure 5.3-7 should dispel them.

5.4 SCHEDULING

Student scheduling, or sectioning, is one of the very promising areas in which it is hoped that computers can relieve the almost unmanageable torrents of documents that periodically inundate us. At registration time in a school of any size we are regularly faced with an increasingly complex series of operations that must be performed either by people or by machines for a sharply increasing number of people, all within a relatively short time. These operations include reading, scanning, identifying, testing, comparing, selecting, and deciding—all operations that fit precisely under the heading of this chapter, and involve particularly many of the classes of operations we have just been examining in Section 5.3.

What Can I Take

Let us look in some detail at Problem 5.4-1 at the end of this chapter, *What Can I Take*. Take time to read through the statement of the problem before proceeding further, paying particular attention to version (A).

We will carry through, in this section, an analysis of the tasks involved in version (A), and develop a solution for that much of the problem. This solution will serve as a basis for the expanded versions of the program called for in the other parts of the problem.

The first task is to determine a workable means of storing the timetable information in the memory of the computer, so that it can be referred to when processing the student's selections, thereby eliminating the need for him to punch the meeting time information. It should not be necessary for him to do more than punch the coded identification of each of the courses he selects, as shown in Figure 5.4-1.

At the same time, we must plan a means of taking each student's selections and filling them in on some internal representation like a schedule card, entering the meeting times of each course he selects, so that any schedule conflicts can be detected.

Dept.	Course No.	Meets	NC
1 ENG	1	9 MWF	101
5 MATH	60	1 MWF	560
6 NA	32	11 TΘ; 1Θ	632
8 BIOL	1	12 TΘ; 2Θ	801

(*a*) As written by student   (*b*) As punched on cards

Figure 5.4-1   Sample student's selection.

Although the conventional form of such a schedule card is a 2-dimensional array, with columns for days of the week and rows for hours of the day, it is slightly simpler to let the computer representation be a 1-dimensional list running consecutively from 1 to 35, as shown in Figure 5.4-2. This code will be used for both of the above representations: the timetable information will be stored in this code, and a 1-dimensional array called IMAGE( ) will be built up for each student with all meetings of each class entered at the appropriate places in this array. In this way, if any two courses have the same meeting time, the attempt to enter an element in IMAGE where there already is an entry can be immediately detected, and a conflict message issued.

The machine representation of the timetable will be as shown in Figure 5.4-3*b*, each row being identified by an entry number I, with I running from 1 up to the total number of courses offered NTOT. The entries in each row of the timetable are then: NCO, the coded identification of the Number of Course Offered, including a department number as well as the particular course number; and MT1, MT2, and MT3, the three meeting times of that course, identified by the index number of the IMAGE( ) array. Compare entries for the same course in Figure 5.4-3*a* and *b*, referring to Figure 5.4-2, the IMAGE index code. Note that in this first version each column of the timetable has a

Hour	DAY M	T	W	Θ	F
9	1	2	3	4	5
10	6	7	8	9	10
11	11	12	13	14	15
12	16	17	18	19	20
1	21	22	23	24	25
2	26	27	28	29	30
3	31	32	33	34	35

Figure 5.4-2   Meeting Time Codes (IMAGE Index).

Field	Dept.	Course No.	Meets	(I)	NCO	MT1	MT2	MT3
Humanities	1 ENG	1	9 MWF	(1)	101	1	3	5
	2 HIST	4	10 MWF	(2)	204	6	8	10
....	3 RUSS	1	9 MTΘ	(3)	301	1	2	4
Math	5 MATH	60	1 MWF	(4)	560	21	23	25
	6 NA	32	11 TΘ; 1 Θ	(5)	632	12	14	24
....	8 BIOL	1	12 TΘ; 2 T	(6)	801	17	19	27
Science	9 CHEM	2	10 TΘ; 1 Θ	(7)	902	7	9	24

NTOT

(a) As printed in catalog   (b) As punched on cards and stored in computer

Figure 5.4-3   Time table representation.

completely separate name—MT1, MT2, and MT3—rather than using subscripts like MT(1). In later versions where different courses have different numbers of meeting times it may be desirable to use a 2-dimensional array here, MT(I,K), with K going from 1 to the total number of meeting times for that course, and I going from 1 to NTOT.

Having the timetable stored as data makes the program independent of the particular timetable being used, and the same program can be used term after term with different timetables. The timetable can be read in simply by the program statements

```
        DIMENSION NCO(20), MT1(20), MT2(20), MT3(20)
        READ 41, NTOT
41      FORMAT (I12)
        READ 40, (NCO(I), MT1(I), MT2(I), MT3(I), I = 1, NTOT)
40      FORMAT (4I12)
```

With the meeting time of each course stored as part of the timetable inside the machine, it now becomes possible to simplify greatly the information that has to be entered for each student. All he needs to punch is the identification of each course, NC in Figure 5.4-1b, corresponding to the identification number NCO shown in Figure 5.4-3.

We are now in a position to lay out, in a flow chart, the steps the program must accomplish. As Figure 5.4-4a shows, it should read in each student's course selections, one at a time; identify the course number and look up the meeting time information stored in the timetable (this process begins to sound familiar—it is a table look-up procedure); enter the meeting times of each class in his IMAGE array,

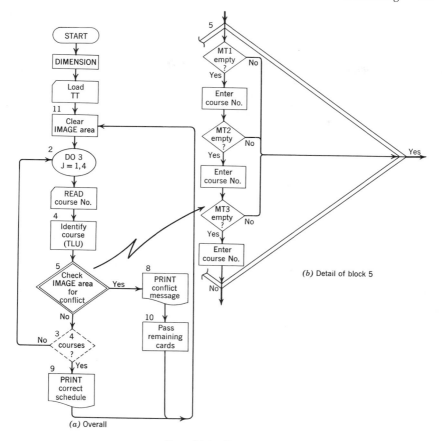

Figure 5.4-4 Flow chart.

checking for conflict as it goes; and then issue either a conflict message or a copy of his correct schedule. Iteration over his four course selections can be handled by a DO loop; we must be sure to clear out the IMAGE array (set all entries to zero) before starting to work on each student's schedule; and we must not overlook the requirement that, since detection of any conflict voids the entire schedule, and further processing of that student's selections is terminated, we must be sure to pass over all remaining cards belonging to that student before starting the next.

Having identified the course number selected by a student, the detailed operations that must be gone through to check for possible conflicts are shown in part (*b*) of Figure 5.4-4. This should be studied simultaneously with the listing of the actual program written from this flow chart, Figure 5.4-5. The operation we have just completed, identifying the course number, has meant finding which row contains that course number, identified by the subscript K for entry number. When the program jumps out of the table look-up loop, block 4, the value of the index K will be the number of the row we want. So in block 5 we can pick up, one at a time, the IMAGE index M corresponding to each of the three meeting times of that course. We first dig out the

```
C          ** WHAT CAN I TAKE **
           DIMENSION  IMAGE(35), NCO(20), MT1(20), MT2(20), MT3(20)
C
C                                      * LOAD TIME TABLE *
C
           READ 41,  NTOT
       41 FORMAT (I7)
           READ 40,  (NCO(I), MT1(I), MT2(I), MT3(I), I = 1, NTOT)
       40 FORMAT (4I12)
C
C                                      * CLEAR IMAGE AREA *
C
       11 DO 1   M = 1, 35
        1    IMAGE(M) = 0
C
C                                      * READ CARD AND IDENTIFY COURSE NUMBER *
C
        2 DO 3   J = 1, 4
             READ 41,  NC
             DO 4   K = 1, NTOT
             IF (NC - NCO(K)) 4, 5, 4
        4    CONTINUE
C                                      * K = I OF COURSE CHOSEN
C                                      * CHECK FOR CONFLICT--ENTER COURSE NO. IF FREE
        5    M = MT1(K)
             IF (IMAGE(M)) 8, 6, 8
        6    IMAGE(M) = NC
C
             M = MT2(K)
             IF (IMAGE(M)) 8, 7, 8
        7    IMAGE(M) = NC
C
             M = MT3(K)
             IF (IMAGE(M)) 8, 3, 8
        3    IMAGE(M) = NC
C                                      * SCHEDULE OK--PRINT IT OUT *
        9    PRINT 21
       21 FORMAT (//6X12HSCHEDULE   OK//)
             DO 20   K = 1, 35, 5
             MM = K + 4
       20    PRINT 22, (IMAGE(M), M = K,MM)
       22 FORMAT (5I5)
             GO TO 11
C
C                                      * CONFLICT *
C
        8    PRINT 23, IMAGE(M), NC
       23 FORMAT (//21H      CONFLICT BETWEEN I5,5H   AND I5)
C
C                                      * SKIP OVER REMAINING CARDS *
       10    NR = 4 - J
             IF (NR) 11, 11, 12
       12 DO 13   KK = 1, NR
       13    READ 41, NC
             GO TO 11
             END
```

(a)

Figure 5.4-5a   Program.

IMAGE index of MT1(K), calling it M. Then using M itself as a sub-script, we check to see whether that space in the IMAGE array, IMAGE(M), is blank, meaning still zero.

If it is still zero, we enter in that space in the IMAGE array the number of this course, and go on to look at the next meeting time. Note that we *could* use as the course number NCO(K) from the stored timetable; it is simpler just to use NC, the course number just read in from the student's card. They have been found to be the same, remember.

If this space in the IMAGE array is *not* zero, it means that one of the courses already processed has a class at this same meeting time, and the program exits to block 8, to print a conflict message.

Only two boxes remain. If all three meeting times for all four classes

```
DATA
                7
              101          1          3          5
              204          6          8         10
              301          1          2          4
              560         21         23         25
              632         12         14         24
              801         17         19         27
              902          7          9         24
              101
              204
              560
              801
              101
              301
              632
              902
              204
              301
              632
              801

ANSWERS

            SCHEDULE   OK

     101      0   101      0   101
     204      0   204      0   204
       0      0     0      0     0
       0    801      0    801     0
     560      0   560      0   560
       0    801      0      0     0
       0      0     0      0     0

            CONFLICT  BETWEEN   101   AND   301

            SCHEDULE   OK

     301    301      0   301      0
     204      0   204      0   204
       0    632      0   632      0
       0    801      0   801      0
       0      0     0   632      0
       0    801      0      0     0
       0      0     0      0     0
```

(b)

Figure 5.4-5*b*

are successfully entered into the IMAGE area, the schedule is satisfied, and we proceed to print it out. You will note that the two PRINT statements corresponding to block 9 each uses a special FORMAT statement. Although not until the next chapter will we look into how to write these FORMAT statements, it is nice to see how they can greatly improve the appearance of the output. The last box is No. 10, which performs the operation, referred to above, of passing all remaining cards belonging to a student whose program has been found to contain a conflict, before clearing the IMAGE area and proceeding to process the next student's schedule.

5.5 THIS WORKS BEST

There are conditions which work best in achieving almost any objective, and the largest computers are often required to determine what these conditions are. There are other times when we find conditions which work best for many simple problems in our everyday life without the aid of computers. For some of them we obtain rather crude approximations and would find the use of computers to our advantage. Some examples of these simple problems and the way in which they are solved will help us to appreciate the role of computers in solving the highly complex problems and to realize that a large number of them exist.

At a very early age we learned to tune a radio to a station. We find a position on the tuning dial which makes the radio work best in receiving a particular station. How do we accomplish this tuning?

Figure 5.5-1 shows loudness of reception plotted against distance

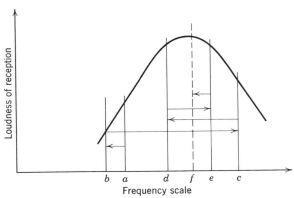

Figure 5.5-1   Tuning characteristics of a radio.

along the radio tuning or frequency scale. The volume control remains unchanged. Suppose the dial indicator was initially at position *a* on the scale when we first turned on the radio. We heard the program we wished to hear but did not know if it was tuned properly. Suppose we repositioned the indicator to the left to position *b*. We noted a decrease in volume which indicated that the proper direction to move the indicator was to the right. Then, while we moved the indicator to the right, the program became increasingly louder until we neared position *c* where we noted a decrease in volume indicating that we had passed the position of maximum volume. Using the same technique in moving from position *b* to *c* we went from *c* to *d*, from *d* to *e*, and from *e* to *f* which is a position near the peak of the loudness curve and our desired tuned position. With each move, we came closer to the condition which worked best or which gave *optimum* performance. At this dial position corresponding to the peak of the curve, we noted there was essentially no change in loudness for a small change in position of the indicator.

Another simple example where we find a condition which works best is the adjusting of the fuel-air mixture of an internal combustion engine, such as an outboard motor of a boat. There is a particular setting of the carburator dial which will give maximum boat speed, and this dial position is obtained using the same technique as that used in tuning a radio.

There may be influences beyond our control that change conditions which have worked best to give optimum performance and require us to solve problems repeatedly. This may be demonstrated by going back to the problem of tuning the radio. The curve t_1 of Figure 5.5-2 is the same curve shown in Figure 5.5-1. Curve t_2 is the characteristic curve of the radio obtained some time after curve t_1 was obtained. This

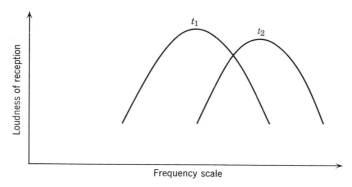

Figure 5.5-2   Change in characteristics with time.

change in characteristics may be the effect of changing temperature or humidity or aging of the electronic tubes. We could not rely on a fixed marking on the dial for positioning the indicator, but tuning must be repeated.

The characteristic curves of optimizing problems such as that of Figure 5.5-1 have a variety of shapes. If they are sharply peaked, adjusting for the optimum performance is critical, whereas if they have relatively flat tops, adjustment is much easier. When the curves have flat tops, changes in the uncontrolled conditions have much smaller effects on performance, and the knobs or the controlled conditions need not be readjusted as often.

In the case of the television receiver, there are usually two dials to adjust for picture clarity instead of one as in the tuning of a radio. Figure 5.5-3 shows a characteristic curve in three dimensions where picture clarity is plotted against indicator position of two dials. Adjusting two knobs to get to the top of the mountain of three-dimensional curves is not nearly as simple as adjusting single knobs to get to the top of a two-dimensional curve.

Numerous optimizing problems in economic systems require the adjustment of many knobs, particularly in daily operations control and to some extent in high-level control. Two of the most important and frequently used methods for determining conditions which work best for these complex problems are *linear programming** and *critical path.* Some government agencies consider the critical path method so important in the saving of time and money that bidders are required to use it.

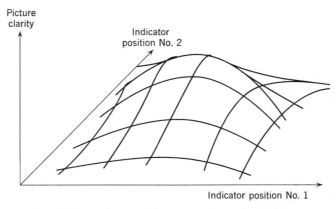

Figure 5.5-3   A characteristic curve in three dimensions.

* Linear programming is the name of a mathematical method and is not to be confused with computer programming, although the utility of the method depends on the computer.

These methods will increase in importance as more of their applications are recognized and they become more generally known. They eliminate the need to make many of the repeated trial adjustments of conditions as we are required to do in tuning a radio or in adjusting a television picture for clarity. But manual calculation of solutions using these methods is still too costly and time consuming for most problems, and computers must be used. The methods have been programmed for most of the computers in use today, including the largest, such as the IBM 7094 and the Control Data 1604, and the programs are readily available. Many man-years of effort have been required in the program development. It is desirable that we become familiar with these important methods and with the types of problems they can solve.

Linear Programming

It is in the design operations of any system that the method of linear programming has its greatest applications. In some cases, the method may be applied and the optimum design obtained directly without any trial adjustments, or, it may be applied in combination with other methods requiring some trial adjustments to obtain designs which are nearly optimum. In still other cases, there may be no apparent application of the method of linear programming and various trial methods must be used. Even if the crudest of trial methods must be applied, many more trials can be profitably made by a computer than by man, and we can come closer to having the conditions which work best. In these cases, as computers become cheaper and more capable, the strictly trial method will bring us even closer to the best or optimum designs.

We will give a few examples of design objectives in industrial systems where conditions must be adjusted so that the combined cost of materials and processing are at a minimum and the performance specifications are met. One example, discussed in Chapter 4, is the design of roof trusses where the number of members, their size and position is each a condition which must be adjusted during the design operations so that the combined costs of materials and processing are at a minimum and the truss will still withstand the snow and wind loads. In chemical and petroleum industries there are sometimes hundreds of conditions to adjust during design, such as heat rates and the amounts and flow rates of component materials. There are many knobs to adjust in the design of electric motors in proportioning the copper and various types of iron to minimize the combined costs of materials and processing and at the same time meet the performance specifications.

We will apply the method of linear programming to the design of a breakfast and will use a graphical approach to finding a solution. The similarity of this simple problem to more complex industrial problems will be apparent.

Assume that we are overweight and wish to limit our calorie intake. At the same time, we must meet certain minimum vitamin requirements. We wish to eat, if possible, the foods we like best and, also, to hold living expenses to a minimum. The specific problem is: Find the minimum total cost of milk and eggs for breakfast to supply a maximum of 500 calories and a minimum of 1000 units of vitamin B_2. An ounce of milk contains 200 units of vitamin B_2 and 10 calories and costs $\frac{1}{2}$ cent. An ounce of whole egg contains 25 units of vitamin B_2 and 50 calories and costs 2 cents.

We must first express our problem in mathematical language, or establish a mathematical model of our system. Since the quantities of milk and eggs are unknown, we let:

$$M = \text{the unknown amount of milk in ounces}$$
$$E = \text{the unknown amount of whole egg in ounces}$$

It is required that M and E be equal to or greater than $(\geq)$ 0; i.e., we cannot have negative amounts of eggs and milk. Then:

$10M$ is the number of calories to be obtained from milk.
$50E$ is the number of calories to be obtained from the whole egg.
$200M$ is the number of units of B_2 to be obtained from milk.
$25E$ is the number of units of B_2 to be obtained from whole egg.
$\frac{1}{2}M$ is the cost of the milk.
$2E$ is the cost of the eggs.

The mathematical expression describing our calorie requirement is

$$10M + 50E \text{ must be less than or equal to } (\leq) \text{ 500 calories.} \quad (5.5\text{-}1)$$

The mathematical expression describing our vitamin requirement is

$$200M + 25E \text{ must be greater than or equal to } (\geq) \text{ 1000 units of } B_2 \quad (5.5\text{-}2)$$

Our total cost is expressed as

$$\tfrac{1}{2}M + 2E = \text{minimum cost} \quad (5.5\text{-}3)$$

Figure 5.5-4 shows a graphical representation of expression (5.5-1). The amount of whole egg, E, is plotted against the amount of milk, M. The solid curve is for the particular equation

$$10M + 50E = 500 \text{ calories}$$

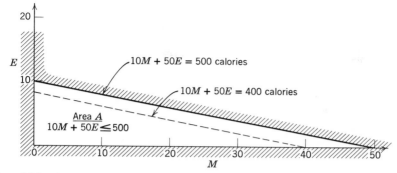

Figure 5.5-4   Graphical representation of expression (5.5-1) describing calorie requirements. Points in area *a* and on boundaries acceptable.

For all other calorie amounts less than 500, the curves of the equations fall below this solid curve as is shown by the dashed curve for the particular equation

$$10M + 50E = 400 \text{ calories}$$

Since M and E cannot be negative, all points which can satisfy the expression (5.5-1),

$$10M + 50E \leq 500,$$

must lie within area A enclosed by the shaded area and on its boundaries as shown in the figure. This area is bounded by the M and E axes and the solid curve for 500 calories.

Figure 5.5-5 shows a graphical representation of the expression (5.5-2) describing vitamin requirements and is similar to Figure 5.5-4 in construction. The solid curve is for the particular equation

$$200M + 25E = 1000 \text{ units of } B_2$$

For all other vitamin amounts greater than 1000, the curves of the equations fall to the right of this solid curve as is shown by the dashed curve for the particular equation

$$200M + 25E = 1200 \text{ units of } B_2$$

Again, since M and E cannot be negative, all points which can satisfy the expression (5.5-2),

$$200M + 25E \geq 1000,$$

must lie within area B and on its boundaries as shown in the figure. This area includes the complete upper right-hand quadrant except for the shaded area in the lower left-hand corner.

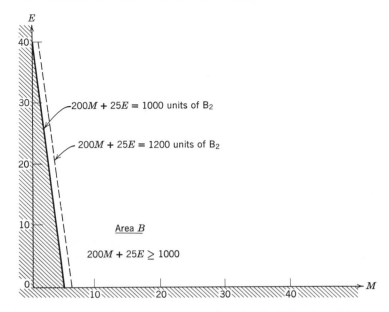

Figure 5.5-5 Graphical representation of expression (5.5-2) describing vitamin requirements. Points in area *b* and on boundaries acceptable.

When Figures 5.5-4 and 5.5-5 are superimposed, there is an area common to areas *A* and *B*. This is shown as area *C* in Figure 5.5-6. All points within this area satisfy both expressions (5.5-1) and (5.5-2) and are bounded by the *M* axis and the solid curves

$$10M + 50E = 500 \text{ calories}$$

and

$$200M + 25E = 1000 \text{ units of } B_2$$

We must still determine the unknown minimum cost defined by equation (5.5-3). It is associated with the area *C* of Figure 5.5-6 which, as we have said, is the area where all points including those on the boundaries satisfy the diet requirements. In determining the minimum cost, we proceed to find particular cost equations which pass through the corner points of area *C*. The particular equation whose curve passes through the corner point *a* of the figure ($M = 50$, $E = 0$) is

$$\tfrac{1}{2}M + 2E = 25 \text{ cents}$$

The particular equation whose curve passes through the corner point *b* ($M = 5$, $E = 0$) is

$$\tfrac{1}{2}M + 2E = 2\tfrac{1}{2} \text{ cents}$$

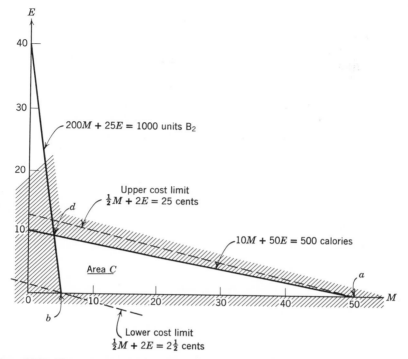

Figure 5.5-6 Plots of upper and lower cost limits. Points in area c and on boundaries satisfy diet requirements.

The curves for these two equations are plotted in Figure 5.5-6 as dashed curves. Since the cost curves for all other particular equations involving points of area C fall between these two curves, an upper limit cost of 25 cents and a lower limit cost of $2\frac{1}{2}$ cents, the latter is the lowest-cost breakfast and is the breakfast we wanted to determine. It has the following specifications:

> 5 ounces of milk, approximately $\frac{1}{2}$ glass ($M = 5$)
> no eggs ($E = 0$)
> $2\frac{1}{2}$ cents, total cost
> 1000 units of B_2 (5×200)
> 50 calories (5×10)

As a check on our diet requirements, we see that we have just met our vitamin requirements of 1000 units and we have less than 500 calories.

As a matter of interest, the highest-cost breakfast of eggs and milk which has 500 calories or less has the following specifications:

50 ounces of milk, approximately 6 glasses ($M = 50$)
no eggs ($E = 0$)
25 cents, total cost
10,000 units of B_2 (50×200)
500 calories (50×10)

Other useful information can be obtained from Figure 5.5-6. If we were not interested in the lowest cost but only in meeting the diet requirements, we could adjust the mix of eggs and milk as desired as long as we choose points within area C. If we preferred the maximum amount of eggs, for example, the point at the upper left-hand corner of the area (point d) would be selected. This point gives approximately 9 ounces of eggs and 4 ounces of milk.

For this simple diet problem, there were but two quantities, M and E, to adjust to obtain a minimum cost, and the graphical approach was adequate. When there are hundreds to adjust, only the most capable computers can find the answers.

Critical Path

After a design is complete, there remains the task of achieving what is designed. The critical path method has great applications in daily operations control for determining a best plan of flow of materials through the processing facilities. The best plan utilizes manpower and equipment in such a way that in meeting specified conditions the overall cost related to processing is minimized.

Finding the time to complete a task is very important in establishing any best plan. The time influences cost and frequently is a given specified maximum or is to be minimized along with costs. It is varied by adjusting assigned manpower and process equipment to the many jobs to be performed simultaneously and sequentially in combinations in accomplishing the complete task.

Finding the few jobs which most critically influence the time to perform the complete task from the total number is the first part of the problem solved by the critical path method. The second part involves the adjustment of conditions of manpower and facilities of these critical jobs and between these jobs and others to achieve improvement in the plan. This procedure may be repeated a large number of times before the best plan is established.

The critical path method has applications in almost any industrial system. The method may be applied to any task for achieving what is designed, such as the preparation of a family meal, construction of expressways and buildings, and accomplishment of large social events.

In all cases, the time to complete the total task is an important factor in establishing the best plan objectives.

We will first present three very simple example problems to illustrate the wide application of critical path analysis and to clarify a scientific method of organizing problems for the analysis. The computer application will be investigated only in the third example problem.

First Example. The first example arises in course scheduling and is described as follows: An entering college freshman is very interested in taking a course called C and wishes to plan his program so that he can finish the course in the shortest time possible. The university bulletin gives him the following information:

Course name	Duration of course (semesters)	Prerequisite courses
C	1	B, E
E	1	D, A
B	2	For entering freshmen
D	1	For entering freshmen
A	2	For entering freshmen

If all courses are offered every semester (including the first semester of the two-semester courses), what is the shortest time to complete C and what courses determine this time?

No doubt you have solved many problems similar to this one in your own way and have been quite successful. What is your answer to this problem?

Let us use a scientific approach in organizing the problem. Beginning with the objective to finish course C, we proceed down the list of information as it was taken from the bulletin and establish the diagrams (a), (b), (c), and (d) shown in Figure 5.5-7. Each of the courses is represented by an arrow which either terminates or originates at a point. The courses represented by terminating arrows (by arrows drawn to a point) are prerequisite courses for those represented by originating arrows (by arrows drawn from the point). Courses B, D, and A are listed for entering freshmen and their arrows are drawn from a single point as shown in diagram (d). The single terminating arrow then represents high school as an educational background requirement (a prerequisite).

A complete description of the schedule of courses may now be established from diagrams (a) through (d). This is done in two steps:

(1) Redraw the diagrams on a single horizontal line in the order (a) through (d) from right to left.

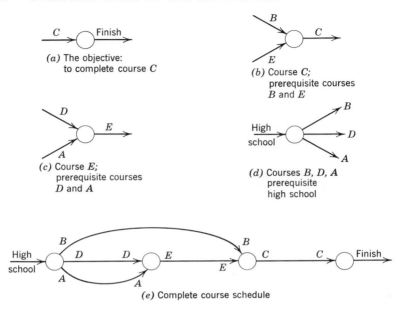

(a) The objective:
to complete course C

(b) Course C;
prerequisite courses
B and E

(c) Course E;
prerequisite courses
D and A

(d) Courses B, D, A
prerequisite
high school

(e) Complete course schedule

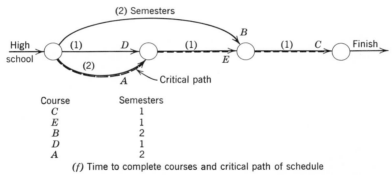

Course	Semesters
C	1
E	1
B	2
D	1
A	2

(f) Time to complete courses and critical path of schedule

Figure 5.5-7   Construction of diagram describing schedule of courses and critical path analysis.

(2) Connect originating and terminating arrows of the same course identification.

Diagram (e) of Figure 5.5-7 results when these two steps are performed. If the courses are taken in the series-parallel combination shown, the requirements as specified by the college bulletin are satisfied.

With the problem organized, we are ready for the second and final step in the solution of the problem. This final step requires diagram (*f*) of the figure, which is diagram (*e*) with the times of the courses identified with the arrows. We will now follow through the diagram from left to right and list the courses for each of the different paths and the time to complete them:

Path	Courses	Time (semesters)
1	B, C	$2 + 1 = 3$
2	D, E, C	$1 + 1 + 1 = 3$
3	A, E, C	$2 + 1 + 1 = 4$

The series of courses *A*, *E*, and *C* of path 3 requires the longest time to complete course *C*. They are the *critical* courses and the path is the *critical* path through the system, as shown by the dashed line in diagram (*f*). Unless the university changes the requirements, there is no way the student can shorten the time of four semesters.

The student must give careful attention to the critical courses. He must try hard not to fail in any of them and must take them on schedule. On the other hand, he is permitted a certain amount of flexibility with courses *D* and *B*. If he takes *D* the first semester upon entering college and fails, he can repeat the course the second semester without upsetting the time schedule. He has similar flexibility with course *B*.

Second Example. Let us calculate a numerical value for *Y* as given by the equation $Y = AX + Z$. In the first example, a job or operation to be performed was a course to be taken by a student; in this case, a job is an operation involving one or more mathematical calculations. We will assume each of the quantities *A*, *X*, and *Z* can be calculated independently.

What are the jobs to be performed in obtaining a numerical value for *Y*, and what are the prerequisite jobs of each? In the previous example, this information was given in the bulletin, but in this case it must be determined from the given equation. This is very simple to do. In fact, we can draw the diagrams directly. We will use the quantities of the equation to identify the jobs. The job $(AX + Z)$ is required in calculating the sum of the quantities *AX* and *Z* and is the prerequisite job for achieving the objective, which is obtaining a value for *Y*, as shown by diagram (*a*) of Figure 5.5-8. The job $(AX + Z)$ requires the values of the quantities *AX* and *Z* and the prerequisite jobs are *AX* and *Z* (diagram (*b*)). The job *AX* is the calculation of the product of the values of *A* and *X* and its prerequisite jobs are *A* and *X* (diagram (*c*)). The beginning jobs are *A*, *X*, and *Z*, and involve the calculation of the numerical values of the quantities *A*, *X*, and *Z* as shown in diagram (*d*).

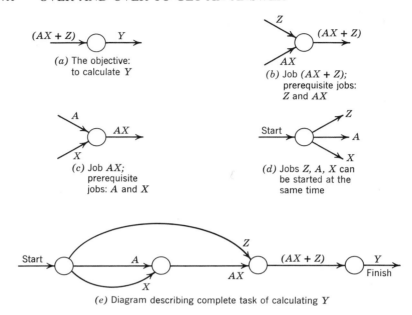

(a) The objective:
to calculate Y

(b) Job $(AX + Z)$;
prerequisite jobs:
Z and AX

(c) Job AX;
prerequisite
jobs: A and X

(d) Jobs Z, A, X can
be started at the
same time

(e) Diagram describing complete task of calculating Y

Figure 5.5-8   Construction of diagram describing task of calculating $Y = AX + Z$.

The description of the complete task of calculating Y is obtained as before, by redrawing the diagrams on a single horizontal line in the order (a) through (d) from right to left and by connecting pairs of originating and terminating arrows of the same job description. The resulting diagram is diagram (e), which closely resembles that of Figure 5.5-7. We intentionally chose an equation which would give the same job arrangement as that of the course schedule problem.

What is the value of this diagram (e)? First, it describes an arrangement of the jobs to be performed which will complete the task in a minimum of time. To see why this is true, we review (a) through (d), from which (e) was constructed. For each of the diagrams, a given job, represented by an originating arrow, is assumed to start as soon as its prerequisite jobs, represented by terminating arrows, are completed. After they are combined into the single diagram (e), all these jobs may still begin as soon as the prerequisite jobs are completed, and the complete task is performed in a minimum of time.

As we have seen, diagram (e) is also important in finding the critical jobs and the time to complete the task. The analysis performed is called the critical path analysis and requires that the times to perform the jobs be known.

A Second Way of Expressing the Relationship of Jobs. For many tasks to be performed, the relationship of jobs is expressed in a different way. In the preceding examples, single jobs and their prerequisite jobs were listed. For the case of the course scheduling problem, we had:

Course name	Prerequisite courses
C	B, E
E	D, A
B	For entering freshmen
D	For entering freshmen
A	For entering freshmen

For many tasks, it is normal to think in terms of the jobs that can be started upon completion of a given job, called a leading job, and to list them accordingly. This is equivalent to listing all jobs having common prerequisite jobs. Such a listing for the course scheduling problem may be prepared from the preceding one and is given below:

Leading jobs (prerequisite courses)	Starting jobs (courses having common prerequisite courses)
High school	A, D, B
A	E
D	E
B	C
E	C

The diagrams that we may draw from this list are the same as the diagrams (*a*) through (*d*) of Figure 5.5-7 when the arrows of leading jobs *A* and *D* with common starting course *E* and those of *B* and *E* with common starting course *C* are terminated on single points and when the diagrams are identified in reverse order. The diagram for the complete schedule is diagram (*e*) of Figure 5.5-7.

In describing the list, we may say, for example, that course *E* cannot be started before both its leading courses *A* and *D* are completed and that *E* can be started as soon as these two are completed. All starting jobs meet two conditions; (*a*) they cannot be started before their leading jobs are completed and (*b*) they can be started as soon as all their leading jobs are completed. Job *C*, for example, satisfies the first condition as a starting job of *D*, but it does not satisfy the second with respect to *D* and cannot be so listed.

This second way of expressing the relationship of jobs is frequently used in analyzing large tasks in industry where the jobs involve specific operations of man and machines. Since computers are currently playing an important role in the critical path analysis of these tasks, the third example problem has been chosen from this area.

Third Example. We choose the task of building a residential dwelling to demonstrate how the relationship of jobs is expressed this second way. To simplify the problem, many small jobs will be combined; for example, excavating for the foundations, pouring of the footings, building of the concrete forms, and pouring of the foundation walls will all be combined into a single job which we will call building of the foundation. The basic jobs for the total task and the *normal* time in days required to complete each job are listed in Figure 5.5-9. These normal times have been established from data obtained on assignments of manpower and equipment to similar jobs previously performed.

For the first part of the problem, we will find the few jobs which determine the total time it takes to accomplish the task on the basis of these initial assignments of manpower and equipment. We proceed by preparing a list of all the jobs shown in Figure 5.5-9 as leading jobs, and, for each, list all others given in the figure that (*a*) *cannot* be started *until* the leading job is completed, and (*b*) *can* be started as soon as the leading job is completed. For example, when we list job 1, start of task, as a leading job, all other jobs meet the requirement (*a*) but only jobs 2 through 5 meet requirement (*b*). It is obvious that painting, for example, could not begin at this time and cannot be listed. If we have sufficient knowledge of the building industry, we can establish the job starting list for all leading jobs, as shown in Figure 5.5-10.

Number and name of job	Normal time (days)
1. Start of task	–
2. Building foundation	10
3. Awarding of electrical contract	8
4. Awarding of plumbing contract	8
5. Awarding of plaster contract	6
6. Installing plumbing to street	4
7. Installing house plumbing	5
8. Erecting frame and roof	8
9. Installing electrical wiring	4
10. Plastering	3
11. Installing trim and doors	3
12. Painting	4
13. Paving	2
14. Finish of task	–

Figure 5.5-9

Leading jobs LJ	Starting jobs SJ
1	5, 3, 2, 4
2	8, 9, 7
3	9, 8, 7
4	7, 8, 9
5	10, 11, 6
6	14
7	6, 11, 10
8	6, 10, 11
9	10, 11, 6
10	12, 13
11	12, 13
12	14
13	14

Figure 5.5-10

The information contained in the starting list may be presented in the form of *tree graphs*. In such graphs the start of the task is represented by an arrow, and at the head of the arrow a *node* (circle) is drawn and labeled as job 1, as shown in Figure 5.5-11. From this node, arrows of convenient lengths are drawn to represent the starting jobs for the leading job 1 and nodes are drawn at the heads of these arrows to identify starting jobs 5, 3, 2, and 4. Continuing with the starting list of Figure 5.5-10, we proceed to find the starting jobs for each of the now leading jobs, 5, 3, 2, and 4 and then construct additional branches of our tree to represent the new starting jobs. By repeated use of this procedure, we finally reach the terminating branches or the finish of task, 14.

Such tree graphs can be used to find the sequence of jobs which determine the time to complete the project. To do this, we must trace every path from the start to the finish. The dashed line in the figure represents a typical path. The sequence of jobs from the start to finish of the task is 3, 9, 11, and 12. From Figure 5.5-9, we find the normal time in days to be 8, 4, 3, and 4, respectively, and the total time to perform this sequence of jobs is then 19 days. If this is the longest time for any of the many job sequences, it is the time required to complete the task and the path is called the *critical path*. We will not know if this is the longest time unless we trace through all the paths. How many paths are there?

Our simplified project of building a residential dwelling produced the rather complex graph of Figure 5.5-11. Other tasks, and even our example task handled in detail, involve hundreds of jobs. Is there a way to simplify the problem? The answer is yes. We notice there are

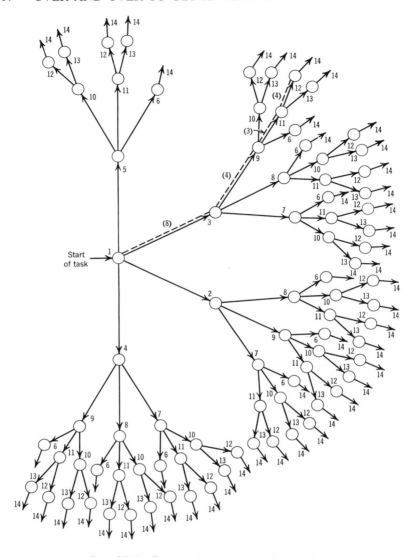

Figure 5.5-11   Tree graph for critical path analysis.

many identical branches in Figure 5.5-11 and this would be true of graphs drawn directly from a job starting list for any other task. We can much more easily determine the critical path when identical branches of the graph are eliminated. For our simple example, we can very easily scan the list of starting jobs, SJ, of Figure 5.5-10 and locate the identical groups of starting jobs. Only the leading job 1, the start of the task, can have its arrow terminating on the first node, and the corresponding starting jobs 5, 3, 2, 4 are represented by arrows originating from the first node as shown in Figure 5.5-12a.

Next, treating starting jobs 5, 3, 2, and 4 as leading jobs, we find from Figure 5.5-10 that the starting jobs, i.e., the jobs that can be started at the completion of these now leading jobs, are 10, 11, 6; 9, 8, 7; 8, 9, 7; and 7, 8, 9. Since the starting jobs of 3, 2, and 4 are identical, we may terminate their arrows on a common node as shown in Figure 5.5-12b.

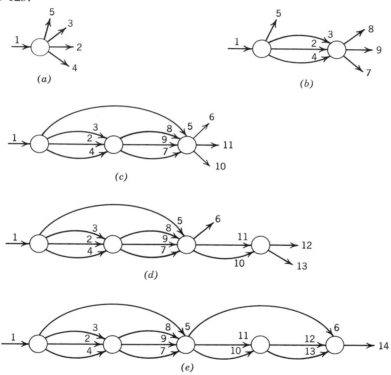

Reduced job starting list

Leading jobs, RLJ	Starting jobs, RSJ
1	5, 3, 2, 4
3, 2, 4	8, 9, 7
5, 8, 9, 7	6, 11, 10
11, 10	12, 13
(f) 6, 12, 13	14

Figure 5.5-12 Construction of reduced graph.

The next set of leading jobs are those whose arrows originate at the last node and also those jobs previously analyzed whose arrows have not yet terminated on a node. The new leading jobs are then 8, 9, 7, and 5. The jobs that can be started when these leading jobs are completed, according to Figure 5.5-10, are 6, 10, 11; 10, 11, 6; 6, 11, 10 and 10, 11, 6. Since these groups are all identical, the arrows of all the leading jobs 8, 9, 7, and 5 terminate on a single node as shown in Figure 5.5-12c.

If we proceed in a similar manner, we obtain Figure 5.5-12d and finally (e) which may be called the reduced graph of Figure 5.5-11. This diagram corresponds to the diagrams of Figures 5.5-7f and 5.5-8e of the preceding examples and also represents the arrangement of jobs that will complete the task in a minimum of time.

A reduced graph may be described in tabular form as shown in Figure 5.5-12f for the graph of 5.5-12e. For each line taken in sequence, another node is added and construction follows that shown from (a) to (e) of Figure 5.5-12.

Now that the graph for our example problem has been greatly simplified, we are able to readily determine the critical path and the time required to build the residential dwelling. Figure 5.5-13 shows the graph of Figure 5.5-12e with the addition of normal time in days for each job (numbers in parentheses). The path through the system giving the longest total time or the time to complete the task can be obtained by inspection and is identified by the broken line. The job sequence is 2, 8, 11, and 12. The times in days to accomplish the jobs are (10), (8), (3), and (4), respectively. A total time of 25 days to complete the project is thus established.

Now that we know the jobs which determine the time to complete the task, we may proceed to change the conditions related to those jobs

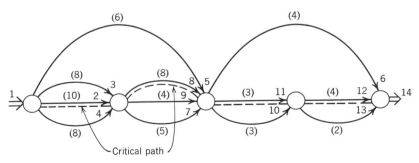

Figure 5.5-13   Graph of Figure 5.5-12e showing normal time in days to complete jobs and the critical path.

in an effort to improve the plan by reducing costs. Suppose, for example, the builder is required to pay $75 per day penalty to the customer for each day exceeding 22 days which is the contract time for completion. The builder can hire larger earth-moving equipment, and for $50, $75, and $100 he can reduce the time of building the foundation (job 2) by 1, 2, and 3 days, respectively. He finds that his *possible* savings are then $25, $75, and $125 for the 1-, 2-, and 3-day reduction of time, or for 9, 8, and 7 days' time to build the foundation. When these changes are made in Figure 5.5-13, we find that a 2-day reduction in time for the job is satisfactory and desirable and the saving is $75. Any reduction in time of more than 2 days for job 2 does not reduce the total time of the project, because the critical path moves from job 2 to jobs 3 and 4. When we plot the savings for these different conditions against the days to complete job 2, we obtain the familiar curve of Figure 5.5-14.

There may be other ways of improving this particular plan by adjusting of manpower and equipment between the critical jobs and other jobs of the system. When the best plan is achieved, it will establish the controls necessary to actually accomplish the task.

Programming Procedure. If a task is detailed, made up of many jobs, the graph reduction problem for finding the critical path is a very worthy application of a computer, and involves an extension of the sorting methods discussed in Section 5.3. A procedure will be described which will aid in the writing of a program.

In outlining a procedure for the program, we will draw tables in the form of arrays which we may visualize to be present in the computer memory. Data of the job starting list of Figure 5.5-10, which is the

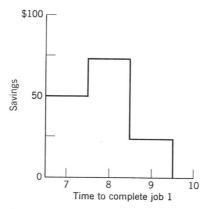

Figure 5.5-14   Plot of savings accomplished through modification of equipment assignment.

input data, may be written in the form of arrays as shown in Figure 5.5-15a. For the data as input, we will require that no matched jobs exist between any two or more groups of starting jobs unless all jobs are matched. The jobs of matched groups need not be in the same sequence. For our example problem, leading jobs 2 and 3 have identical or matched starting jobs 8, 9, 7 and 9, 8, 7, respectively, and satisfy the data requirements. If the starting jobs were 8, 9, 7 and 10, 9, 7, the require-

LJ(J)

J	
1	1
2	2
3	3
4	4
5	5
6	6
7	7
8	8
9	9
10	10
11	11
12	12
13	13
14	0
15	0

SJ(J, K)

J	1	2	3	4	5
1	5	3	2	4	0
2	8	9	7	0	0
3	9	8	7	0	0
4	7	8	9	0	0
5	10	11	6	0	0
6	14	0	0	0	0
7	6	11	10	0	0
8	6	10	11	0	0
9	10	11	6	0	0
10	12	13	0	0	0
11	12	13	0	0	0
12	14	0	0	0	0
13	14	0	0	0	0
14	0	0	0	0	0
15	0	0	0	0	0

(a)

RLJ(J, K)

J	1	2	3	4	5
1	1	0	0	0	0
2	3	2	4	0	0
3	5	8	9	7	0
4	11	10	0	0	0
5	6	12	13	0	0

RSJ(J, K)

J	1	2	3	4	5
1	5	3	2	4	0
2	7	8	9	0	0
3	6	11	10	0	0
4	12	13	0	0	0
5	14	0	0	0	0

(b)

Figure 5.5-15

ments would not be met and the data would not be acceptable as input for our procedure.

The required output which is the reduced job starting list of Figure 5.5-12*f* may also be presented in the form of arrays as shown in Figure 5.5-15*b*.

We see that the LJ(J) array in Figure 5.5-15*a* is a one-dimensional array, or list. We have learned how to program such an array for input and output operations. Two-dimensional arrays, however, whose elements are variables with double subscripts, are new to us. Let us pause a moment to investigate the handling of the input and output of these arrays.

Figure 5.5-16 shows the general symbols to identify the elements in a two-dimensional array or matrix (*a*), with the first subscript corresponding to the row and the second to the column, and two sets of numerical values that might serve as data (*b*) and (*c*). Note the conventions used here to aid in tracking data through the input and output operations: the elements of array A7 all have a 7 for their units digit; those of array A8 have an 8. The digits in the first two decimal places correspond to the subscripts used to identify the position of the element in the array. For example, 7.23 is the value of the element A7 (2,3).

Figure 5.5-16*d* shows a program for reading and printing one such array, followed by the data punched in the form shown in (*b*). Note that the data are read in by means of a DO loop, consisting of a DO statement to count the row subscript J, and a READ statement, the object of the DO, which steps the column subscript K by means of indexing within the READ statement itself.

The array is then printed out three times, as shown in part (*e*), using three different techniques. Study them.

It appears that indexing in the input or output statement will do everything that separate DO statements can do. This is not quite true because of the limitations of some of the FORMAT statements. Note

		K				K					K	
J	1	2	3	J	1	2	3	J	1	2	3	
1	A(1, 1)	A(1, 2)	A(1, 3)	1	7.11	7.12	7.13	1	8.11	8.12	8.13	
2	A(2, 1)	A(2, 2)	A(2, 3)	2	7.21	7.22	7.23	2	8.21	8.22	8.23	
3	A(3, 1)	A(3, 2)	A(3, 3)	3	7.31	7.32	7.33	3	8.31	8.32	8.33	

(*a*) General array A(J, K)   (*b*) Array A7(J, K)   (*c*) Array A8(J, K)

Figure 5.5-16*a, b, c.*

```
C *** PROGRAM  ARRAY 1 ***
      DIMENSION  A7(4,4)
C
C      READ IN ARRAY
C
      READ 41, M, N
   41 FORMAT (2I12)
      DO 1  J = 1,M
    1 READ 42, (A7(J,K), K = 1,N)
   42 FORMAT (3(1PE12.4))
C
C      NESTED DO LOOPS PRODUCES A SINGLE COLUMN
C
      DO 2  J = 1,M
      DO 2  K = 1,N
    2 PRINT 43, A7(J,K)
   43 FORMAT (1PE12.4)
C
C      INDEXING IN OUTPUT STATEMENT PUTS ALL OF ONE ROW ON A LINE
C
      DO 3  J = 1,M
    3 PRINT 42, (A7(J,K), K = 1,N)
C
C      DOUBLE INDEXING CAN DO THE SAME THING IN A SINGLE STATEMENT
C
    4 PRINT 42, ((A7(J,K), K = 1,N), J = 1,M)
      STOP
      END
            4             3
         7.11          7.12          7.13
         7.21          7.22          7.23
         7.31          7.32          7.33
         7.41          7.42          7.43
```

(d)

```
ANSWERS    *** ARRAY 1 ***

   7.1100
   7.1200
   7.1300
   7.2100
   7.2200
   7.2300
   7.3100
   7.3200
   7.3300
   7.4100
   7.4200
   7.4300

   7.1100        7.1200        7.1300
   7.2100        7.2200        7.2300
   7.3100        7.3200        7.3300
   7.4100        7.4200        7.4300

   7.1100        7.1200        7.1300
   7.2100        7.2200        7.2300
   7.3100        7.3200        7.3300
   7.4100        7.4200        7.4300
```

(e)

Figure 5.5-16d, e

that the numeric value of N (here N = 3) appears as a constant in FORMAT statement 42. If N is not known in advance, or varies with different arrays, to make the method of statement 3 work, the repeater must be made equal to or larger than the largest N, thus:

$$\text{DO 3 J} = 1, \text{M}$$
$$3 \quad \text{PRINT 42, (A7(J,K), K} = 1, \text{N)}$$
$$42 \quad \text{FORMAT (6(1PE12.4))}$$

This sequence will now produce the desired output of one row to a line for N ≤ 6. There is, however, no way (except in special FORTRANs) of doing this for the general case using the double indexing method of statement 4. It is therefore recommended that the combined method of statement 3 be used for both the input and output of arrays when arrangement by rows and columns is desired.

Figure 5.5-17 shows several ways of handling 2 arrays. Notice that once they are read in and stored in the computer with the proper names and subscripts, they can be called on for computation or output in just about any way desired.

The manner in which the computer may be instructed to manipulate the data with the use of these arrays is described as follows:

Step 1—Initial preparation: Since the start of task is the only leading job that can terminate on the first node, we may transfer this leading job (1) directly from LJ(1) of Figure 5.5-15*a* to the output array RLJ(1, 1) of Figure 5.5-15*b* and the corresponding starting jobs from SJ(1, K) to RSJ(1, K).

For our example problem, leading job 1 and starting jobs 5, 3, 2, and 4 are transferred from the input arrays and appear in RLJ(1, 1) and RSJ(1, K), respectively, as shown in Figure 5.5-15. The graph of the first node shown in Figure 5.5-12*a* can then be drawn from this information contained in the output arrays for J = 1.

Step 2—Setting up arrays of current leading and starting jobs: We will establish working arrays in the computer for storing leading jobs of current consideration and their corresponding starting jobs. These arrays will be used to accomplish the search for identical starting jobs. The array CLJ(J) in Figure 5.5-18*a* contains the current leading jobs which were the starting jobs related to the last node analyzed and all previous jobs whose arrows did not terminate on nodes.

In the case of the second node of our example problem, current leading jobs for consideration are 5, 3, 2, and 4 as shown in Figure 5.5-18*a*.

The array CSJ(J, K) in Figure 5.5-18*b* contains the current starting jobs for those leading jobs of CLJ(J). They are readily obtained from

SJ(J, K) by first matching the leading jobs of CLJ(J) with the leading jobs of LJ(J).

In consideration of the second node, the jobs 5, 3, 2, and 4 are matched with LJ(L), and their corresponding starting jobs in SJ(J, K) are then transferred to CSJ(J, K).

Step 3—Setting up arrays for performing the search for identical starting jobs: It is desirable to establish 3 temporary arrays to accomplish the search of identical starting jobs in CSJ(J, K). One of these arrays CSJT(J) of Figure 5.5-18c is established to contain the jobs of the first column of CSJ(J, K). Searches are made to find matches between each of the jobs in CSJT(J) and the jobs in CSJ(J, K).

```
C *** PROGRAM  ARRAY 2 ***
      DIMENSION  A7(4,4),  A8(4,4)
C
C     READ IN TWO ARRAYS, ONE AFTER THE OTHER
C
      READ 44, M, N
   44 FORMAT (2I12)
      DO 5  J = 1, M
    5 READ 45, (A7(J,K), K = 1,N)
   45 FORMAT (6(1PE12.4))
      DO 51  J = 1,M
   51 READ 45, (A8(J,K), K = 1,N)
C
C     OUTPUT SAME AS INPUT
C
      DO 6  J = 1,M
    6 PRINT 45,  (A7(J,K), K = 1,N)
      DO 61  J = 1,M
   61 PRINT 45, (A8(J,K), K = 1,N)
C
C     PRINT THE TWO ARRAYS SIDE BY SIDE
C
      DO 7  J = 1,M
    7 PRINT 46, (A7(J,K), K = 1,N), (A8(J,K), K = 1,N)
   46 FORMAT (6(1PE12.4))
C
C     PRINT THE ELEMENTS OF THE TWO ARRAYS IN PAIRS
C
    8 PRINT 47, ((A7(J,K), A8(J,K), K = 1,N), J = 1,M)
   47 FORMAT (2(1PE12.4))
      STOP
      END
            4              3
         7.11           7.12          7.13
         7.21           7.22          7.23
         7.31           7.32          7.33
         7.41           7.42          7.43
         8.11           8.12          8.13
         8.21           8.22          8.23
         8.31           8.32          8.33
         8.41           8.42          8.43
```

Figure 5.5-17a

ANSWERS   *** ARRAY 2 ***

7.1100	7.1200	7.1300
7.2100	7.2200	7.2300
7.3100	7.3200	7.3300
7.4100	7.4200	7.4300
8.1100	8.1200	8.1300
8.2100	8.2200	8.2300
8.3100	8.3200	8.3300
8.4100	8.4200	8.4300

7.1100	7.1200	7.1300	8.1100	8.1200	8.1300
7.2100	7.2200	7.2300	8.2100	8.2200	8.2300
7.3100	7.3200	7.3300	8.3100	8.3200	8.3300
7.4100	7.4200	7.4300	8.4100	8.4200	8.4300

7.1100	8.1100
7.1200	8.1200
7.1300	8.1300
7.2100	8.2100
7.2200	8.2200
7.2300	8.2300
7.3100	8.3100
7.3200	8.3200
7.3300	8.3300
7.4100	8.4100
7.4200	8.4200
7.4300	8.4300

Figure 5.5-17*b*

The other two arrays LJT(J) and MJT(J) of Figure 5.5-18*d* and *e* are desirable to keep records of the results of searches for identical jobs. Whenever a match is obtained, the leading job of CLJ(J) corresponding to the matched starting job is placed in MJT(J). The search is then continued through all remaining rows of CSJ(J, K). If a complete search is made of CSJ(J, K) and no matching jobs are found, the leading job CLJ(J) for that starting job in CSJT(J) is placed in LJT(J).

CLJ(J)		CSJ(J, K) K						CSJT(J)		LJT(J)		MJT(J)	
J		J	1	2	3	4	5	J		J		J	
1	5	1	10	11	6	0	0	1	10	1	5	1	0
2	3	2	9	8	7	0	0	2	9	2	0	2	3
3	2	3	8	9	7	0	0	3	8	3	0	3	2
4	4	4	7	8	9	0	0	4	7	4	0	4	4
5	0	5	0	0	0	0	0	5	0	5	0	5	0
(*a*)		(*b*)						(*c*)		(*d*)		(*e*)	

Figure 5.5-18

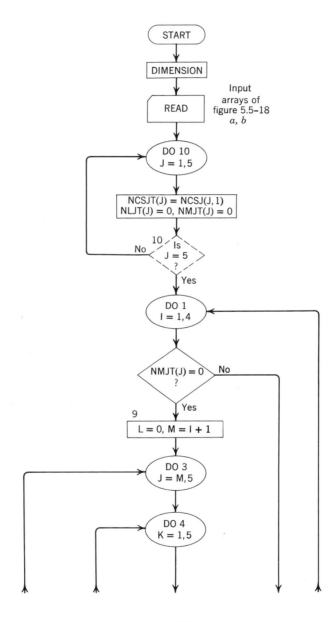

Figure 5.5-19

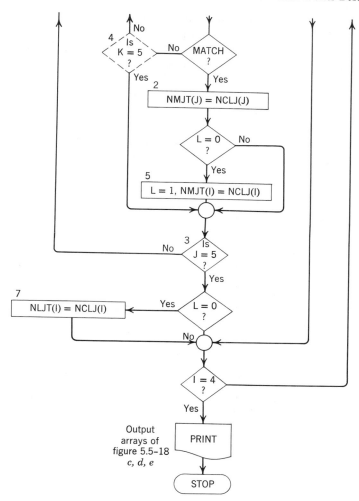

Figure 5.5-19 Flow chart for performing step 3.

The use of these three arrays may be demonstrated in the second node analysis of our example problem. CSJT(J) contains the jobs 10, 9, 8, and 7 which were transferred from CSJ(J, 1) as shown in Figure 5.5-18. A complete search for matches between the first job 10 in CSJT(1) and all jobs in rows J = 2, 3, and 4 of CSJ(J, K) reveals no matching jobs. The leading job 5 in CLJ(1) corresponding to the starting job 10 is placed in LJT(1). Job 9 in CSJT(2) is then selected, and a search for a match is made between this job and the jobs in rows

J = 3 and 4 of CSJ(J, K). Matches are found in positions (3, 2) and (4, 3) of CSJ(J, K). And leading jobs 2 and 4 in positions J = 3 and 4 of CLJ(J) are placed in positions J = 3 and 4 of MJT(J). Leading job 3 corresponding to the matching job is also placed in MJT. For this second node analysis, no further searching is required.

Figure 5.5-19 shows the flow chart for performing step 3, and Figure 5.5-20 shows the program. The data of the arrays of Figure 5.5-18*a* and *b* are read as input, and the data of the three remaining arrays are produced as output. Note: the elements of LJT(J) and MJT(J) are set equal to zero at the beginning of the program. Why?

```
C       PROGRAM STEP3
        DIMENSION NCLJ(5),NCSJ(5,5),NCSJT(5),NLJT(5),NMJT(5)
        READ 20,(NCLJ(J), (NCSJ(J,K), K=1,5), J=1,5)
 20 FORMAT(6I3)
        DO 10 J=1,5
        NCSJT(J)=NCSJ(J,1)
        NLJT(J)=0
 10 NMJT(J)=0
        DO 1 I=1,4
        IF(NMJT(I))8,9,8
 8  GO TO 1
 9  L=0
        M=I+1
        DO 3 J=M,5
        DO 4 K=1,5
        IF(NCSJT(I)-NCSJ(J,K))4,2,4
 4  CONTINUE
        GO TO 3
 2  NMJT(J)=NCLJ(J)
        IF(L)3,5,3
 5  L=1
        NMJT(I)=NCLJ(I)
 3  CONTINUE
        IF(L)1,7,1
 7  NLJT(I)=NCLJ(I)
 1  CONTINUE
        DO 11 I=1,5
 11 PRINT 21, NCSJT(I),NLJT(I),NMJT(I)
 21 FORMAT(3I10)
        STOP
        END
  5 10 11  6  0  0
  3  9  8  7  0  0
  2  8  9  7  0  0
  4  7  8  9  0  0
  0  0  0  0  0  0

ANSWERS
        10        5        0
         9        0        3
         8        0        2
         7        0        4
         0        0        0
```

Figure 5.5-20

Step 4—Organizing output: The information contained in the 2 temporary arrays LJT(J) and MJT(J) provides the information required for the output arrays of Figure 5.5-15. Since the leading jobs in MJT(J) have identical starting jobs, i.e., their arrows terminate on a common node, they are transferred to RLJ(J, K) of Figure 5.5-15. The corresponding starting jobs of any one of these leading jobs are obtained from CSJ(J, K) and placed in RSJ(J, K).

Since the starting jobs in LJT(J) did not terminate on the current node, they are transferred to CLJ(J) in any desired sequence in preparation for the next node analysis. Steps 2 through 4 are repeated for each additional node.

For our second node analysis, the leading jobs 3, 2, and 4 in RLJ(2, K) are transferred from MJT(J) and the starting jobs 7, 8 and 9 in RSJ (2, K) transferred from CSJ(4,K). The graph described by the information in these output arrays is shown in Figure 5.5-12*b*.

A Need for Frequent Recalculation of Optimum Performance

We have said that there are influences beyond our control that change conditions which have worked best to give optimum performance and require us to solve problems repeatedly. This was demonstrated by the change in position of a curve with time in Figure 5.5-2. The problem of building a residential dwelling and the diet problem are not exceptions. In the case of building the dwelling, there is the common influence of weather that changes conditions which have worked best, and for the diet problem, prices of food are subject to change. We must then recalculate solutions at intervals with these changes incorporated. We can recalculate too often or too seldom in achieving a maximum *net* savings over a period of time, for there are costs involved in performing the recalculations which must be subtracted from the gross savings. Here is a second optimizing problem which is common in *all* daily operations controls. We will continue with the diet problem as an example and consider it to be a general one arising in restaurants, hospitals, or in industries making mixed foods for humans, pets, or cattle.

Figure 5.5-21*a* shows gross saving per day plotted against days. At the beginning of the first day, a gross saving of $100 per day was achieved through improved design by using linear programming to minimize the costs in producing a food mix. The vitamin and calorie content and prices of the food components changed over the 10 days that followed and decreased the gross saving at an assumed constant rate of $10 per day. At the end of the tenth day, a recalculation was made, and by readjusting the diet mix the gross saving is returned to the original value of $100 per day. The average saving per day, AS, over the 10-day period is $50 and the average loss of saving, AL, is also $50 per day.

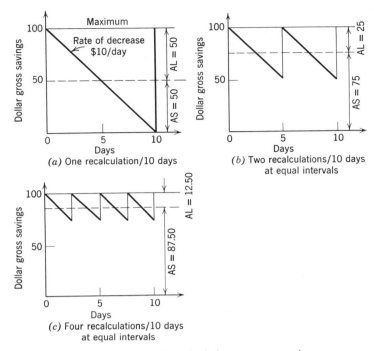

Figure 5.5-21   Effect of recalculations on gross savings.

In Figure 5.5-21*b*, the rate of decrease in gross saving is the same as that of (*a*) but after 5 days and again after 10 days, recalculations were performed and the food mixes readjusted to return the gross saving to the original value. The average gross saving per day, AS, by recalculating a solution two times during the 10-day period, is $75 and the average loss in saving, AL, is $25 per day.

The effect of four recalculations at equal intervals every 10 days is shown in Figure 5.5-21*c*. AS is $87.50 and AL is $12.50 per day.

For this assumed constant rate of decrease in savings, each time we double the number of recalculations, we halve the value of *AL*. Then, for 8 equally spaced recalculations, AL is $6.25 and AS is $93.75 per day.

We now must determine the net saving and the best frequency for recalculations. Figure 5.2-22*a* shows a plot of the data of Figure 5.5-21 of total gross saving over the 10-day period plotted against the number of recalculations. Also shown is a straight-line curve of the costs of performing the recalculations at the rate of $125 per calculated solution. The net saving (gross saving minus cost of recalculating the solutions) is shown by the dashed curve and clearly shows that *two* equally spaced

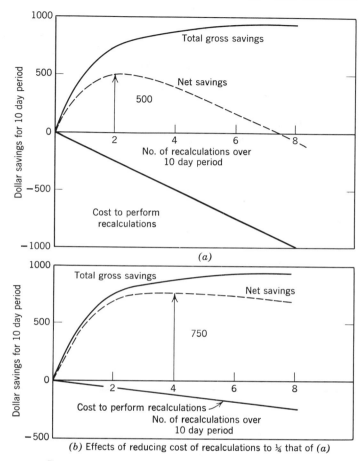

Figure 5.5-22   Determining best frequency of recalculation.

recalculations for the 10-day period will give the *maximum* net saving of approximately $500 for the period.

Figure 5.5-22*b* shows a plot of the same total gross saving, but the cost of performing the calculations is reduced to one-fourth. We may say that the costs described by Figure 5.5-22*a* represent the costs of manual calculations, and the plot of costs reduced to one-fourth represents the costs of performing the calculations by computer as shown in (*b*). The net savings described by the dashed curve shows a maximum net savings of $750 when the recalculations are performed approximately 4 times during the 10-day period as compared to a maximum of $500 for 2 recalculations when the calculating costs are 4 times greater.

5.6 IN THE LONG RUN

Many mathematical models or equations require the use of random numbers to obtain numerical solutions. The Monte Carlo method requires very large amounts of computing time but shows great promise for the future when computers are expected to be faster and cheaper per unit calculation.

Generating Random Numbers.

There are several simple examples of the need for random numbers. First, let's see how we can obtain such a set of numbers to help establish the meaning of random as it applies to numbers. Suppose you had a container in which you placed a set of numbers 0 through 9, written on identical squares of cardboard. You shake the container to mix the pieces of cardboard thoroughly, and by reaching in you draw a number without intended preference. You read and record the number and return the piece of cardboard to the container. You repeat the process until you have obtained as large a set as you may wish to acquire.

Figure 5.6-1 shows a listing of 100 numbers actually obtained by this method. This list may be called a set of *random numbers*, but we do not know if the numbers are truly random. If our process for obtaining them or our sampling is not truly random, a bias may have been introduced and the numbers are *pseudo-random*, i.e., they are a false set of random numbers. A bias may be introduced in a number of ways; for example, if the pieces of cardboard on which the numbers are written are dissimilar in size or in surface condition, they will not mix properly and you may be partial in your drawing of the numbers from the container. Bias is introduced to some degree by any method of sampling we may choose, so that, strictly speaking, all intended random numbers are pseudo-random.

2	6	5	4	9	2	5	8	5	5
6	8	6	0	9	1	2	6	5	9
0	7	0	6	9	2	2	4	8	7
7	3	9	1	9	5	1	6	1	0
2	5	9	9	0	6	4	2	1	7
8	3	2	0	1	5	2	7	8	9
6	0	3	5	9	3	1	1	3	5
5	4	1	6	4	5	0	3	0	1
0	1	9	7	5	1	7	0	5	4
4	1	1	2	0	4	6	1	0	8

Figure 5.6-1

How can we determine how good a process is in obtaining or generating random numbers? One direct method may be demonstrated by analyzing the set we obtained in Figure 5.6-1. The *probability, P,* that any given number will be drawn in any *one* of the samplings is the ratio of the number of pieces of cardboard, h, containing the number to the total number of pieces that can be drawn, $(h + f)$. Since each of the 10 numbers appeared on only one cardboard, the probability of drawing any one of the numbers in any *one* drawing is:

$$P = h/(h + f) = 1/10 = 0.10$$

If we have made more than one sample, the relative frequency, P', of drawing a number is the ratio of the number of successes in drawing that number, h', to the sum of the successes and failures, $(h' + f')$, or the total number of samples or drawings. For example, if we consider the first five columns of numbers of Figure 5.6-1, there are 50 numbers corresponding to 50 samples and the number of successes in drawing the number 2 is four. Then:

$$P' = h'/(h' + f') = 4/50 = 0.08$$

In the same manner, we can calculate the relative frequencies of the remaining numbers. These values may then be plotted as shown in Figure 5.6-2a. The probability, P, being equal to 0.1 for all the numbers, forms a straight-line curve which is also shown in the figure.

We note that the curves of P' and P of Figure 5.6-2a are much different. We would hope that as we make more samples, the curve P would come closer to being the same as P. For if we had truly random sampling, P' would equal P for a very large number of samples and the numbers would be truly random. If sampling is not random, P' will never equal P regardless of the number of samples taken, and the numbers in our set would be pseudo-random. There is some hope that the numbers in Figure 5.6-1 are somewhat random, for we see that the curve of P' for the complete set of 100 samples as shown in Figure 5.6-2b comes closer to the curve of P than the curve for 50 samples (Figure 5.6-2a). Because of the labor involved in enlarging the table, we will assume without further testing that the numbers are not greatly different from random numbers.

It is apparent that our method of drawing numbers, say, from 0 to 10,000 from a container would be very impractical, and storing them all in a computer when our computer programs required them, would consume valuable memory space. How can we let the computer generate numbers of many digits as we need them in a computer calculation? There have been a variety of mathematical methods developed for this

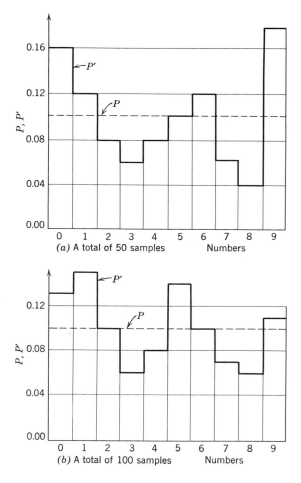

(a) A total of 50 samples

(b) A total of 100 samples

Figure 5.6-2   Test for randomness.

purpose. The general approach used in many of these methods might be demonstrated by the mid-square method established by Von Neumann and Metropolis. It is described as follows: take a number such as 2061 as the first number of a series to be generated. Square this number to obtain 04247721. Take the middle 4 digits, 2477, as the second random number. Square this number to obtain 06135529 and the third random number is 1355. This process can be repeated by the computer each time our program calls for a random number. Some of the mathematical methods give better approximations to random numbers than others. None are known to produce pure random numbers. Some eventually produce zeros; still others repeat long strings of generated numbers. Tests have shown that the mid-square method, using 3142 as a starting number, ceases to give good approximations to random numbers after about 50 are generated. Other starting numbers may yield better results.

What types of problems require random numbers? We shall investigate some examples.

Selecting Values of Parameters

Many complex models require random numbers to obtain numerical solutions. Selecting values of parameters for solutions is often required when specific values must be obtained from statistical data. These values may be selected from statistical data in the form of frequency distributions by the Monte Carlo method.

In the preceding section, the critical path method was discussed and required the values for the number of days to accomplish the 12 jobs. Figure 5.6-3 shows the frequency distribution of a number of similar residential dwellings requiring different number of days to build the foundation. Unpredictable conditions, such as weather, occurred to produce the variation in the required time. We will assume that we have similar data for the other 11 jobs. What values of time should we use in calculating a critical path? Should we use the number of days required by the largest number of residential dwellings; for example, from Figure

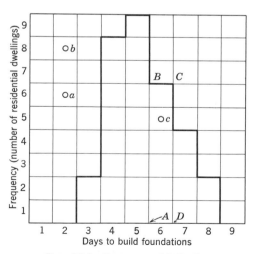

Figure 5.6-3   Frequency distribution.

5.6-3, should we take 5 days as the time to build the foundation? If we did, our solution to the problem would not be realistic.

We will proceed to demonstrate a method of selecting values with the use of Figure 5.6-3 and our table of random numbers, Figure 5.6-1. We will let the number of days to build the foundation $= x$ and the frequency $= y$. The random numbers in Figure 5.6-1 will be used in pairs. Let the first random number (2) be the value of x and the second random number of this first pair (6) be the value of y. This point when plotted in Figure 5.6-3 as point a lies outside the frequency distribution curve and gives us no information. We choose the second pair, 0 and 7, for the values of x and y, and find that this point also lies outside our graph. We have a similar experience with the next pair, 2 and 8, plotted as point b. However, the plotted point c for the next pair of random numbers, 6 and 5, lies under the frequency distribution curve and establishes a value of 6 days to build the foundation. It is a proper value to use in calculating the critical path. The same procedure would be used in obtaining values for the other jobs if we had similar statistical data.

Why is this an acceptable procedure? From our statistical data for this example, the probability of building a foundation requiring 6 days is

$$P = 6/31 = 0.19$$

where 6 is the number of dwellings requiring 6 days to build the foundations and 31 is the total number of dwellings built. In our sampling procedure for determining a value of time in days, the relative frequency

$$P' = h'/(h' + f')$$

should also equal, 0.19 for a very large number of samples if our procedure is acceptable. If we continued our procedure using random numbers and plotted, say 31 points, under the frequency distribution curve, 6 of these would be likely to fall under the individual curve for 6 dwellings requiring 6 days to build the foundations (shown as curve $ABCD$ in Figure 5.6-3). That is, the number of successes, h' would most likely equal 6 and the number of failures, f', to obtain points under this individual curve would be 25. As more points are plotted, there would approach an even distribution of points under the frequency distribution curve and P' could approach the value of $P = 0.19$. Our sampling procedure is then a model of the actual building of foundations.

An extension of the procedure just described for selecting values from statistical data gives a method for calculating areas with boundaries of any shape. The unknown area must lie within a known area which may be called a reference area.

Calculating Areas

Suppose we wished to find the area under the frequency distribution curve of Figure 5.6-3. We will call this area B. The dimensions of the axes, frequency, and the number of days are changed to distances in inches. The area of the square 9 inches on each side will be the reference area A.

Let us use pairs of random numbers of Figure 5.6-1 to plot points. Those points falling within area B will be called successes, and the number of successes will be called h'. Those points falling outside area B but within the boundaries of area A will be called failures, and the number of failures will be called f'. Those points falling outside area A will be disregarded. Then, the relative frequency is:

$$P' = h'/(f' + h')$$

If we randomly selected points from a total of $9 \times 9 = 81$ representing one for each square inch of area A, the probability P of obtaining a point within area B would be

$$P = B/A$$

If we accepted the random selection procedure used in establishing the random numbers in Figure 5.6-1, we would place the 81 pieces of cardboard in a container, each containing a point in area A. The probability, P, of drawing a cardboard with a point for area B would be B/A.

Since

$$P = B/A$$

we would hope that P' for the number of points plotted in Figure 5.6-4 would nearly equal P, and we would be able to determine a fairly accurate value for area B.

For the points plotted in Figure 5.6-4, we find

$$h' = 17$$
$$f' = 20$$

Then

$$P' = h'/(h' + f') = 17/37 = 0.46$$

If P' is a good approximation to B/A,

$$B = P' \times A$$

and

$$B = 0.46 \times 81 = 37 \text{ sq. in.}$$

For the simple boundaries of area B in our example problem, we calcu-

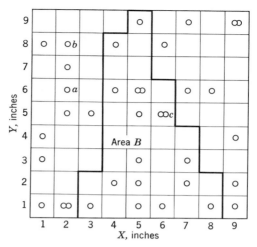

Figure 5.6-4   Plot of points from random numbers for finding area b.

late the area by the standard method to be $B = 31$ sq. in. as compared to 37 sq. in. by the procedure using random numbers. The probability

$$P = B/A = 0.38$$

compares with 0.46 for our procedure using random numbers.

If our table of random numbers were extended and the numbers were truly random numbers, as more points are plotted, the value of P' would approach the value of P, or our Monte Carlo method would be an acceptable method of calculating areas.

It is apparent that we can expand our method for calculating areas to the calculation of volumes. This is done by selecting numbers in groups of three rather than by pairs.

Now that we have established a method of finding areas using random numbers, we may proceed to use the method to investigate an interesting problem of finding the value of π. We will first determine the equations describing a circle in rectangular coordinates. Figure 5.6-5 shows a plot of a quadrant of a circle of radius R with its center at the origin. We see that R is defined by the equation

$$R = \text{SQRT} (Y ** 2 + X ** 2) \tag{5.6-1}$$

The area under the curve of the circle of Figure 5.6-5 is

$$AC/4 = \pi * (R ** 2)/4 \tag{5.6-2}$$

Figure 5.6-6 describes the manner in which we will use random number pairs to determine π. The quadrant of a circle with the center

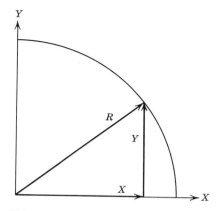

Figure 5.6-5 Quadrant of a circle with center at origin.

at the origin is contained in a square whose sides are equal to $R = 1.0$. The ratio of the area under the curve to the area of the square is

$$(AC/4)/AS = (\pi * (R ** 2)/4)/R ** 2 = \pi/4 \qquad (5.6\text{-}3)$$

From our established method of finding areas by random number pairs, this area ratio is also defined as

$$(AC/4)/AS = h^1/(f^1 + h^1) \qquad (5.6\text{-}4)$$

where h^1 is the number of successes in obtaining points for random number pairs under the curve of Figure 5.6-6 and f^1 is the number of

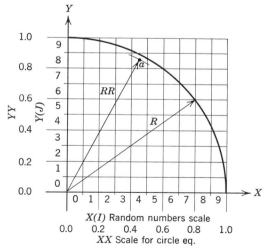

Figure 5.6-6 Plot describing method of calculating pi.

failures or the number of points obtained above the curve but within the square. Then from equations (5.6-3) and (5.6-4), we have

$$\pi = 4 * h^1/(h^1 + f^1) \tag{5.6-5}$$

The equations (5.6-1) and (5.6-5) are required for our problem.

An outline of a flow chart for a program is shown in Figure 5.6-7. Input data includes random number pairs $X(I)$ and $Y(J)$ unless they are generated or calculated internally as they are needed. The plot of Figure 5.6-6 shows random numbers from 0 to 9, inclusive, assigned to 10 equal spaces along 2 sides of the unit square.

The radius R for the circle is also read and may be given the value of unity as is the case for the circle described in Figure 5.6-6.

An important function performed by Block 4 of the flow chart is scale changing. Before we can determine if the points for the random number pairs fall below or above the circle curve, we must change from the random number scale to the scale used in plotting the circle equation. We can illustrate the procedure by referring to Figure 5.6-6. Point a is a plot of the random number pair $X_1(I) = 4$ and $Y_1(J) = 8$ as shown on the random number scale. The location of the same point when read on the scale used in plotting the circle equation is $XX_1 = 0.45$, $YY_1 = 0.85$. XX or YY is related to $X(I)$ or $Y(J)$ by the equation

$$XX = cX(I) + d \quad \text{or} \quad YY = cY(J) + d \tag{5.6-6}$$

It is easy to determine the constants c and d by inspection if we have similar values on a second point such as the point for a random number $X_2(I) = 6$, $Y_2(J) = 5$ which is located at $XX_2 = 0.65$, $YY_2 = 0.55$ on the other scale. We see 0.05 is a constant common to all XX and YY values and is the value of d. When we subtract this value, it is easy to see that $c = 0.1$. The values of c and d may also be determined by the following equations

$$c = (XX_1 - XX_2)/X_1(I) - X_2(I) \tag{5.6-7}$$
$$d = XX_2 - cX_2(I) \tag{5.6-8}$$

where the numbered subscripts refer to values on the scales for two different point locations.

After the values of XX and YY are determined by equation (5.6-6) in Block 4, the value of RR is determined in Block 5 and compared with the given circle radius R. RR is given by the equation

$$RR = \text{SQRT} (XX ** 2 + YY ** 2)$$

and is the radius of a circle which passes through the random selected point. Since it is calculated using values determined from the same

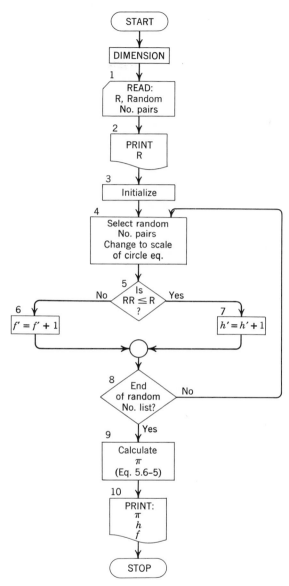

Figure 5.6-7   Flow chart for calculating pi.

scale as that used in determining the given circle curve, the values of R and RR may be compared to establish whether we have successes h' or failures f' in the random location of points. There are three main factors which influence the accuracy of our results:

(1) The grid size or the number of divisions of the area.
(2) The number of games played equal to $h^1 + f^1$.
(3) The pureness of the random numbers.

Random Walks

We shall investigate still another interesting way of solving certain types of problems with the use of random numbers. It is sometimes called "nature's" way and requires insight of the physical problem.

We will use a grid system as before but instead of the grid defining areas to be randomly selected, we will use them for defining paths. *Random walks* will follow these grid paths or lines through the system where the direction of each walk beginning at a grid path intersection will be determined by random numbers.

A physical system which may be studied by the method of random walks consists of a mouse in a maze as shown in Figure 5.6-8. The maze contains places of entry and exit for the mouse as shown. After the mouse enters the maze, the place of entry is closed. If we assume he is constantly motivated to leave the maze, with each re-entry and rediscovery of the exit, the mouse's learning of the maze increases and the number of maze sections required to find the exit decreases.

The maze as a grid system is described in rectangular coordinates in Figure 5.6-9 where the grid lines represent the paths through the maze. The entrance is at location 0, 1 and the exit at 2, 2.

We will make use of random numbers to establish the different routes the mouse may take through the system beginning at point of entry 0, 1 and terminating at the exit 2, 2. For his first time through the system,

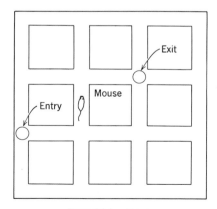

Figure 5.6-8   Maze.

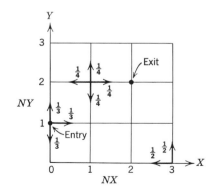

Figure 5.6-9   Grid system for maze in rectangular coordinates.

we will assign two random digits to each of the four possible directions of travel as follows:

0 or 1	positive X direction
2 or 3	negative X direction
4 or 5	positive Y direction
6 or 7	negative Y direction
8 or 9	no action

At the terminal of a walk, which is at the intersection of grid paths, a random number is used to determine the direction of the next walk. Since there are only two possible directions at grid path intersections at the four corners of the maze, we must disregard any random numbers we obtain that would take the route beyond the boundaries of the maze. The probability of selecting either of the two acceptable directions for this special condition is then $\frac{1}{2}$ as shown for the example grid point 3, 0 of Figure 5.6-9. A second special condition occurs at other grid path intersections on the periphery of the maze where three directions are acceptable and the probability of selecting any one of the three is $\frac{1}{3}$ as shown, for example, at grid point 0, 1 of the figure. For all other points of intersection not on the periphery, as for point 1, 2, the probability of going in any of the four directions is $\frac{1}{4}$.

Figure 5.6-10 shows the shortest route, which involves three grid or maze sections, and the probability of taking each of the three walks. The theoretical probability P of taking the route marked is equal to the products of the probabilities of these three dependent events:

$$P = P(1) * P(2) * P(3) = 1/3 * 1/3 * 1/4 = 1/36.$$

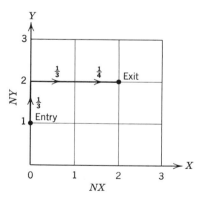

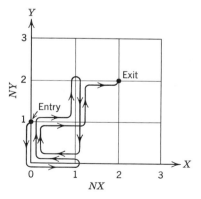

Figure   5.6-10   Maximum   probability route.

Figure 5.6-11   Random route determined by random numbers of Figure 5.6-1.

The route we have just analyzed was the shortest route which was 3 grid sections in length. We could map out a route from entry to exit of any length we may choose, and the longer the route, the less the probability of the route being taken. We expect then that in actual practice of the mouse walking the maze or in the process of solving the problem with random numbers, a very long route could be experienced.

Figure 5.6-11 shows the route established by using the random numbers of Figure 5.6-1 and our established assignment of the number from 0 through 7 to the four directions. Starting at the point of entry, a direction of the route must be decided. The first random number, 2, requests a walk in the $-X$ direction beyond the boundary of the maze and must be disregarded. The second number, 6, requests a walk in the $-Y$ direction, which can be accomplished. The request is executed by taking a walk of 1 grid section in length to point 0, 0 where a direction of the next walk must be decided. The third number, 0, of the random number list, requests a walk in the $+X$ direction which when executed extends the route to 1, 0. A continuation of the process establishes a complete route from entry to exit of 13 grid sections in length and requires the first 19 random numbers of Figure 5.6-1.

We will establish a program to help us solve the maze problem using the method of random numbers. We will make studies of the routes taken by a number of different mice. A first study will be made for the condition of the mice walking the maze for the first time and a second for the condition of the mice walking the maze after they have partially learned the maze from previous experiences.

Since the study will require a large number of random numbers, we will generate the numbers by the computer as we need them using the mid-square method described earlier in this section.

To facilitate the checkout of large complete programs, it is desirable to write and test component programs. Figure 5.6-12a shows the program for generating random numbers, which is a component of the complete program for solving the maze problem. The chosen starting number FN is the value of pi times 1000. Each digit NR(I) of the 4-digit number generated becomes a random number for deciding the direction of a walk in the maze.

Figure 5.6-12b shows the calculations performed by the computer in generating the first number NFN = 8721 and the calculations of the DO loop for I = 1 in obtaining the leftmost digit NR(1) = 8 from that number. The remaining three single digits NR(2) = 7, NR(3) = 2, and NR(4) = 1 are obtained by repeating the calculations of the DO loop. Figure 5.6-13 shows 100 single-digit numbers by columns obtained by specifying NT = 100 in the program.

```
C        PROGRAM RANGEN
         DIMENSION NR(4)
         READ 1, NT
    1    FORMAT (I4)
         FN=3142
         INT=0
   10    FNN=FN**2/100.
         INM=FNN/10000.
         FNM=INM
         NFN=FNN-FNM*10000.
         FN=NFN
         IB1=0
         DO 9 I=1,4
         K=4-I
         IB2=FN/10.**K
         NR(I)=IB2-10*IB1
         PRINT 1,   NR(I)
    9    IB1=IB2
         INT=INT+1
         IF(INT-NT/4)8,7,7
    8    GO TO 10
    7    STOP
         END
100
```

(*a*)

Corresponding
numerical calculation
for first random digit

$$FNN = 98721.64$$
$$INM = 9$$
$$FNM = 9.$$
$$NFN = 8721$$
$$FN = 8721.$$
$$IB\ 1 = 0$$
$$I = 1$$
$$K = 3$$
$$IB\ 2 = 8$$
$$NR(I) = 8$$
$$PRINT \quad 8$$
$$IB\ 1 = 8$$

(*b*)

Figure 5.6-12

Mid-square random nos., Starting no. = 3142

8	9	5	6	2
7	2	3	5	9
2	8	5	5	6
1	3	6	6	2
0	1	6	9	7
5	7	8	8	7
5	4	6	1	3
8	0	7	1	4
3	0	1	2	8
1	2	5	5	1
1	7	5	5	4
3	6	6	7	7
6	0	4	5	3
9	7	2	3	7
0	6	1	8	3
7	1	1	2	6
7	5	7	9	9
0	7	3	6	5
6	9	2	5	7
6	1	5	9	6

Figure 5.6-13

Now that the component program or subroutine for generating random numbers is checked out, it may be incorporated in the maze program. Figure 5.6-14 shows the flow chart of the complete program in which all statements of the number generator beginning with statement 10 and ending with 9 are contained in Block 10. Output of the generator which is NR(I) is not punched but used directly by the main program.

Input to the complete program must provide maze information and

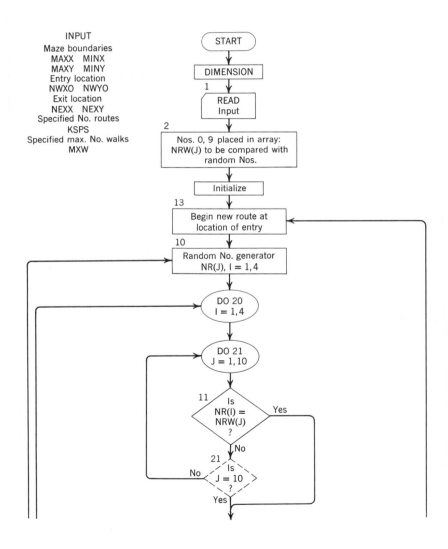

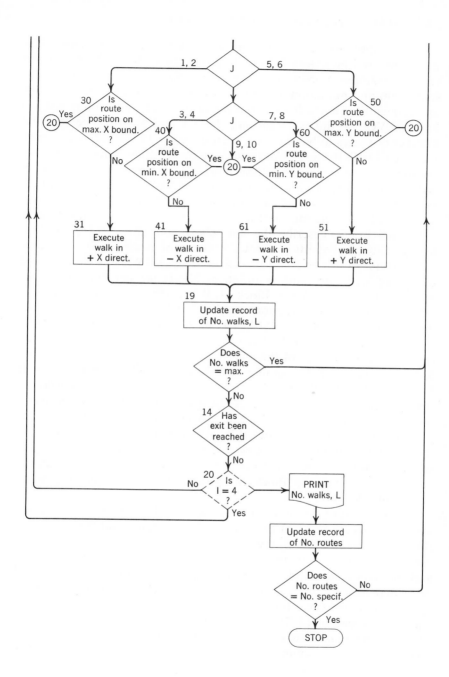

Figure 5.6-14 Flow chart of maze problem.

necessary specifications for solving a problem on a given maze. The maximum and minimum X boundaries are MAXX and MINX which for our example problem of Figure 5.6-8 are equal to 3 and 0. The maximum and minimum Y boundaries are MAXY and MINY which are also equal to 3 and 0 for our example. The entry location is NWXO and NWYO and the exit location is NEXX and NEXY. The specified number of routes to be obtained, corresponding to the number of mice that are to walk the maze from entry to exit, is KSPS. Since a very large number of walks may be experienced before the exit is reached, it is desirable to specify a maximum number, MXW, that will be permitted. When this number is reached the route is terminated, which is equivalent to removing the mouse from the maze before he reaches the exit.

We will briefly describe the flow chart of Figure 5.6-14, which is designed for the condition of mice walking the maze for the first time.

Numbers 0 through 9 are placed in array NRW(J) in Block 2 and compared with the random numbers NR(I) for deciding directions at grid path intersections in Block 11. Whenever one of the numbers of NRW(J) is equal to the random number NR(I), that value of J switches the operations to Block 30, 40, 50 or 60, and the direction of the walk has been established. If the walk can be executed without going beyond the boundaries of the maze as determined by Block 31, 41, 51, or 61, the record of the number of walks, L, is updated in Block 19. If L has not exceeded the specified maximum number of walks MXW, the new location for the mouse is checked against the exit location in Block 14. If the locations agree, the exit has been found, and the number of walks L is punched (Block 17). When a new route is found, the record of the number of routes is updated and checked against the specified number to be found KSPS. If more routes are to be found, the computer goes back to Block 13 to seek out a new route beginning at the entry location.

The program for the flow chart is shown in Figure 5.6-15. The maze specifications are those of the maze of Figure 5.6-8, and the values are shown by the listing of the last card. The data also show that 7 mice (KSPS) are to walk the maze from entrance to exit for the first time and the maximum number of walks per route (MXW) allowed is 100. Note that to get 7 integers conveniently on one line, our FORMAT specification describes the numbers as each occupying a field of 5 columns, instead of 12. The results of the program are shown in Figure 5.6-16a. The minimum number of walks per route is 3 for the 7th mouse and the maximum is 67 for the 4th mouse. The average number of walks per route is $16\frac{5}{7}$.

The program is easily modified to consider the condition of the mice

```
C       PROGRAM MAZE
        DIMENSION NRW(10), NR(4)
   1    READ 3,MAXX,MINX,MAXY,MINY,NWXO,NWYO,NEXX,NEXY,KSPS,MXW
   3    FORMAT(10I4)
        M=-1
        DO 2 J=1,10
        M=M+1
   2    NRW(J)=M
        KTS=0
        FN=3142
  13    L=0
        NWX=NWXO
        NWY=NWYO
  10    FNN=FN**2/100.
        INM=FNN/10000.
        FNM=INM
        NFN=FNN-FNM*10000.
        FN=NFN
        IB1=0
        DO 9 I=1,4
        K=4-I
        IB2=FN/10.**K
        NR(I)=IB2-10*IB1
   9    IB1=IB2
        DO 20 I=1,4
        DO 21 J=1,10
        IF(NR(I)-NRW(J))21,22,21
  21    CONTINUE
  22    GO TO (30,30,40,40,50,50,60,60,20,20),J
  30    IF(MAXX-NWX)20,20,31
  31    NWX=NWX+1
        GO TO 19
  40    IF(MINX-NWX)41,20,20
  41    NWX=NWX-1
        GO TO 19
  50    IF(MAXY-NWY)20,20,51
  51    NWY=NWY+1
        GO TO 19
  60    IF(MINY-NWY)61,20,20
  61    NWY=NWY-1
  19    L=L+1
        IF(L-MXW)14,13,13
  14    IF(NWX-NEXX)20,18,20
  18    IF(NWY-NEXY)20,17,20
  17    PRINT 4, L
   4    FORMAT (I4)
        KTS=KTS+1
        IF(KTS-KSPS)13,12,12
  20    CONTINUE
        GO TO 10
  12    PRINT 5, MAXX,MINX,MAXY,MINY
   5    FORMAT (4I4)
        PRINT 5, NWXO,NWYO,NEXX,NEXY
        PRINT 6, KSPS,MXW
   6    FORMAT (2I4)
        STOP
        END
   3    0   3   0   0   1   2   2   7 100
```

Figure 5.6-15

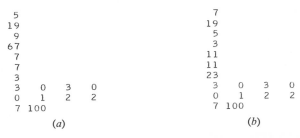

Figure 5.6-16 Results of Maze Problem. (*a*) Results of seven mice walking maze for first time; average no. walks/route = 16⅞. (*b*) Results of seven mice walking maze after previous experiences; average no. walks/route = 11⅞.

walking the maze after a number of previous experiences. We will say that we can represent the learning by assigning three of the 0, 9 numbers to the $+X$ direction instead of two and include the number 8 with the previous numbers 0 and 1. At grid path intersections within the boundaries, the probability of deciding to go in the $+X$ direction becomes ⅓ and the probability of deciding to go in any of the other three directions is ⅔. The only change to be made in the program is in statement 22, which now should read GO TO (30, 30, 40, 40, 50, 50, 60, 60, 30, 20), J where 30 replaces 20 when J = 9.

When this change is made in the program the results are those shown in Figure 5.6-16*b*. The minimum number of walks per route is 3 and the maximum, 23. The average number of walks per route is 11⅔ as compared to 16⅞ for the condition of the mice walking the maze for the first time.

A number of different conditions may be studied or additional information may be obtained with relatively minor changes in the program. Two or more exits may be made in the maze, or the right wall of the maze may be removed. Additional information may be obtained from the program; for example, records may be kept of the number of walks made in each of the two directions in the maze sections.

Many other types of problems may be studied in a similar manner—the spread of disease, flow of heat, magnetic fields, fluid flow, and nuclear and molecular diffusion.

PROBLEM 5.3-1   "Log Data"

GIVEN†

A log sheet recording the actual time used on a computer. Each entry contains the student identification number (use 5-digit numbers—why?),

---

† Assume given. Actually, to test your program, make up your own data.

and the time on and time off for that particular run (two 4-digit numbers in 24-hour time).

WANTED

(A) The log sorted by student number in ascending order, giving the amount of time run by each student. Assume no number appears more than once.

(B) Assume some numbers do appear more than once. Combine all entries for the same student, and prepare a sorted output list as before, but now the list will give the total time used by each student.

PROBLEM 5.3-2   "Inventory Sorting"

GIVEN

A record of parts sold in an auto supply store on a given day. Each entry in the record consists of an inventory number (a 4-digit number), and the number of items of that part sold.

WANTED

The inventory numbers arranged in ascending order, each with its record of the number of items sold next to it.

(A) The data consists of one day's sales.

(B) The data consist of six days' sales. Assume each day's data contain the same number of entries, and that each inventory number appears every day with its number of items sold for that day. If none are sold, the column contains a zero.

   (1) Sort the inventory numbers for each day in ascending order with the number of each item sold next to the inventory number. Print out a daily record.

   (2) Combine the lists into a master list for the week. Combine sales of the same item by totalling the daily sales of each item. Print out the weekly totals.

(C) The data consist of six days' sales. Assume each day's data consist only of the record of items actually sold that day. It will therefore be of variable length, and an inventory number may or may not have appeared before. In the entire set, some inventory numbers may appear only once, some twice, some several times.

   (1) Sort the inventory numbers for each day in ascending order with the number of each item sold next to the inventory number. Print out a daily record.

   (2) Merge the lists into a master list for the week. Combine sales of the same item by checking the inventory numbers, and adding sales

when the same part appears more than once. Print out the master list for the week.

PROBLEM 5.3-3   "Hall of Fame"

In this problem you are to write a program for computing baseball batting averages and arranging them into a table. This resembles the work done to prepare the table found in daily papers. Data decks will be supplied with the following integers prepunched 5 to a card:

   player no.   times at bat   hits   runs batted in   home runs

There will be fewer than 100 cards in this deck, and the last card will have 000 punched as the player number. Note that this is the only way that you can tell when all cards have been read.

Conventionally the "batting average" is taken to be

$$\frac{1000 * \text{no. of hits}}{\text{no. times at bat}}$$

VERSION A. Sort the data into a table where the following appears on each line:

   player no.   times at bat   hits   runs batted in   home runs

The table should be arranged by *increasing player number.*

VERSION B. Read the data, calculate the batting average for each player, and produce a table giving:

   player no.   batting average   runs batted in   home runs

This table should be arranged by *decreasing batting average.* You may assume that no two players have the same average.

VERSION C. Same as (B) except that players may have the same average. You should list players having the same average in order of increasing player number.

VERSION D. Same as (C) except that you should also

   (1) Pick out and list separately the five leading batters in terms of runs batted in.

   (2) Pick out and list separately the five leading home run hitters.

   (3) Check for the illegal conditions: number of home runs greater than number of times at bat, and number of hits greater than number of times at bat.

VERSION E. Same as (D) but also calculate and punch the cumulative average for the team (all batters in the list).

PROBLEM 5.4-1   "What Can I Take"

The timetable of Eezee College (which offers a limited curriculum) is displayed in Figure P5.4-1. At registration time each student will elect four courses, and write them one to a card. Prior to registration time you (the Assistant Registrar) are to (1) determine how to codify the timetable information and store it in your computer; (2) codify the student's selections to require a reasonably small amount of on-the-spot keypunching; (3) develop a program which will (4) allow each student's selections to be presented to the computer in batches of four cards; (5) determine whether or not any conflicts exist either in schedule or other requirements; and (6), if not, print out a final copy of his schedule.

VERSION A. It is assumed that each student's chosen program of courses has been checked for suitability, and only direct schedule conflict is to be checked (two classes meeting at the same time). For simplicity, it is assumed that all courses meet exactly three times a week, and are three credits.

VERSION B. In addition to checking for schedule conflict as in (A), the

Time table

Field	Dept.	Course no.	Meets
Humanities	1 Eng	1	9 MWF
	2 Hist	4	10 MWF
	3 Russ	1	9 MTΘ
Math	5 Math	60	1 MWF
	6 NA	32	11 TΘ; 1 Θ
Science	8 Biol	1	12 TΘ; 2 T
	9 Chem	2	10 TΘ; 1 Θ

(a)

Sample student's selection

Dept.	Course no.	Meets
1 Eng	1	9 MWF
5 Math	60	1 MWF
6 NA	32	11 TΘ; 1 Θ
8 Biol	1	12 TΘ; 2 T

(b)

Figure P5.4-1*a,b*

program is now to check that Rule 16, "Each student must elect at least one course from each of the three fields: humanities, mathematics, and science," is satisfied. Furthermore, it should catch and point out selection of courses not being offered (no such course number in timetable).

VERSION C. Use the timetable from versions (A) and (B) with the changes shown in Figure P5.4-1c.

Math	5 Math	60	1 MTΘF
	6 NA	32	11 TΘ; 1 TΘ
Science	8 Biol	1	L 12 TΘ; Q 2 T; Lab 1-3 M
	9 Chem	2	L 10 TΘ; Q 1 Θ; Lab 9-11 M

Figure P5.4-1c

Please note the changes that have been made from version (B): the humanities courses still meet three periods per week while the math courses now meet four periods per week and the science courses now meet five periods per week.

Input: Each deck of cards will now be given in batches of five with the first card in each deck a 5-digit student identification number and the remaining cards the four course selections as before.

Output: Each student's identification number is followed by either: a completed schedule if one exists, or a statement of conflict or error in course selection.

VERSION D. Use the timetable from version (C) with the changes shown in Figure P5.4-1d.

Please note the changes that have been made from version (C): each science course has two alternate lab periods. Since a student attends one or the other lab section, there are now two possible ways to schedule each science course. The student does not choose one of these lab sections at registration time but only chooses his four courses as before. Your program now has the additional task of *finding* a nonconflicting program if one exists.

Input: As in version (C).

Output: As in version (C).

Science	8 Biol	1	L 12 TΘ; Q 2 T; Lab (1) 1-3 M
			Lab (2) 1-3 W
	9 Chem	2	L 10 TΘ; Q 1 Θ; Lab (1) 9-11 M
			Lab (2) 2-4 W

Figure P5.4-1d

PROBLEM 5.4-2 "Now What Can I Take?"

The expanded timetable of Eezee College is displayed in Figure P5.4-2. The timetable is now a bit more realistic on several points: (1) different courses meet different numbers of times a week and (2) carry different numbers of credits; (3) more than one course is offered by most departments; and (4) more than one section is listed for some courses or parts of courses.

Time table

	Dept.	Course No.	Cr.	Meets Lect.	Quiz or lab
Humanities	1 Eng	1	3	L1 9 MWF	
				L2 2 MWF	
	1 Eng	2	3	10 MWF	
	1 Eng	10	3	11 MWF	
	2 Hist	4	3	L 9 TΘ	Q1 9 W
					Q2 9 F
					Q3 1 Θ
	2 Hist	5	3	L 11 TΘ	Q1 11 M
					Q2 11 W
					Q3 1 T
	3 Russ	1	4	L 10 MWF	Q1 10 T
					Q2 10 Θ
					Q3 12 T
	3 Russ	2	4	L 1 MWF	Q1 1 T
					Q2 1 Θ
Math	5 Math	60	5	L1 9 MTWΘF	
				L2 12 MTWΘF	
	5 Math	61	5	L1 10 MTWΘF	
				L2 2 MTWΘF	
	6 NA	32	3	L 11 TΘ	Lab1 2-4 M
					Lab2 2-4 T
					Lab3 2-4 Θ
Science	8 Biol	1	4	L 11 MWF	Lab1 1-3 M
					Lab2 1-3 W
					Lab3 9-11 Θ
	9 Chem	2	4	L 12 MWF	Lab1 9-11 T
					Lab2 2-4 W
					Lab3 2-4 F

Figure P5.4-2

VERSION A. It is assumed that each student's chosen program has been checked for nonexistent courses as well as for suitable field selections. The problem for the computer is now: given a selection of four courses, find a schedule.

VERSION B. As in (A), with the additional constraints:
  (1) At least one course from each field.
  (2) No two courses from the same department.
  (3) Total number of credits must not exceed 15.
  (4) Indication is given of an attempt to elect a nonexistent course.

FINAL NOTE: ignored even in this final program are such real-life considerations as the following: a timetable may contain as many as several thousand courses; twenty or thirty thousand students may be registering at one time, for from one to seven courses; the computer program should have access to each student's record to determine his eligibility to take the indicated courses in terms of such factors as standing, load permitted, prerequisites; regulations vary from field to field within a college; and finally, the different sections of each course should be kept reasonably balanced and within maximum limits.

If you develop a working program to handle this situation, please contact your instructor about a position on the staff.

PROBLEM 5.5-1   "Sleep"

A student is interested in determining the number of hours of sleep that will give him his best in performance. For the extremes of very little sleep and a large amount approaching 24 hours per day, his performance would be very low. A number of hours somewhere in between will give him this best performance. He has found that the equation:

$$P = -S^2/72 + S/4$$

describes his performance for the number of hours sleep ranging from 6 to 12 hours where P is the performance and S is the number of hours of sleep. In establishing a unit of measure of performance, he has chosen to let performance equal unity for 6 hours of sleep, i.e., when S is given the value of 6 in the equation, P equals 1. Establish a method similar to that given in Section 3.4 for finding roots of polynomials and write a program for determining the number of hours he should sleep to give him maximum performance. Determine also the corresponding value of performance. Since he can set his alarm clock with an accuracy of plus or minus one minute, he must know the value of S to that accuracy.

PROBLEM 5.5-2   "Diet"

For the diet problem discussed, obtain a graphical solution for the case where the calorie requirements for breakfast must be greater or equal to 500 calories. All other conditions remain the same. Give the complete specifications for the minimum-cost breakfast.

PROBLEM 5.5-3   "The Best Course Schedule"

A college student has just completed course F. He is interested in taking course E and wishes to finish the course in the shortest time possible. The university bulletin gives him the following information:

Course name	Duration of course (semesters)	Prerequisite courses
E	2	C, B, D
B	2	A
C	1	A
A	1	F
D	2	F

(A) Organize the problem in the form of a diagram that describes the schedule for completing the course in a minimum of time. Show the steps required in the construction of the diagram.

(B) For each path through the diagram list the courses, the time required for each course, and the total time. Identify the critical path. Does the student have any flexibility?

(C) The department offering course B has decided to change the course from a two-semester, two-hour course to a one-semester, four-hour course. Determine the critical path (or paths). What can you say of the flexibility in the student's schedule?

PROBLEM 5.5-4   "Critical Path"

(A) The arrays of Figure 5.5-18 contain data used in the analysis for the second graph node of the building problem. Show the contents of these arrays for the third and fourth node analyses for the same problem. This is to be accomplished by manually following the procedures outlined in the text.

(B) Write a program for step 1 given in the text as part of the procedure for reducing graphs. Program as input the complete array data of

Figure 5.5-15a. Print out data of RLJ(1, 1) and RSJ(1, K) for the first node.

(C) Write a program for step 2 as outlined in the text, and incorporate the program of step 1 written for part (B) of this problem. Print out the data shown in CLJ(J) and CSJ(J, K) of Figure 5.5-18a and b.

(D) Write a program for step 3 as given in the text and incorporate the program of step 2 written for part (C) of this problem. Print out only the data shown in the arrays of Figure 5.5-18d and e and the first node results of Figure 5.5-15b.

(E) Write a program for step 4 given in the text and incorporate the program of part (D). Print out only the results for the first and second nodes of the output array of Figure 5.5-15b.

(F) With the program of part (E), establish a complete program for reducing a tree graph and obtain results for the building problem.

PROBLEM 5.6-1   "How Long Will it Take"

Write a program to determine the number of days it takes to receive shipment of an item for inventory by the random number method. The historical data are in the form of a frequency distribution curve given in Figure 5.6-3. Use the random numbers in Table 5.6-1 to determine a time. Repeat each time a value of shipping time is needed.

PROBLEM 5.6-2   "Test for Randomness"

Manually calculate the relative frequency of occurrence of the numbers 0 through 9 for the 100 numbers in Figure 5.6-13 obtained by the mid-square method of generating random numbers. Prepare a plot similar to that of Figure 5.6-2b. Does this set of numbers appear more random than those of Figure 5.6-1?

PROBLEM 5.6-3   "Pi"

(A) Write a program for calculating pi by the random number method as described by Figures 5.6-6 and 5.6-7. Let $R = 0.5$ for the radius of the given circle and use the random numbers in Table 5.6-1. Calculate pi using 25 and 50 pairs of random numbers. Note any difference in accuracy. Can you improve on the method of programming suggested in Figure 5.6-7?

(B) Repeat (A), except generate the random numbers internally using the mid-square method. Divide each 4-digit random number into 2 random pairs.

(C) If a random number generating program is available at the computer installation where your problems are run, repeat (A) using the generating function available. This will probably be more accurate and much less susceptible to degeneration than our simple method, and may well run much faster, too. Try 100 pairs, 500 pairs (1000 pairs? 10,000 pairs?).

PROBLEM 5.6-4   "Two-Exit Maze"

Modify the maze program of Figure 5.6-15 to solve a two-exit problem. The second exit is at location 1, 2. All other maze specifications are the same as those given by the listing of the last card. Ten mice walk the maze for the first time from entry to exit.

Include as output

(A) The number of mice that find each exit.

(B) The average number of walks per route for each exit.

PROBLEM 5.6-5   "Crashland"

Twenty people aboard a plane crash on an island unharmed during severe fog conditions. The island is in the general form of a square and has a heavy growth of trees and vegetation. The conditions are such that it is equally as easy to travel in any of the four directions on the island. There is a gradual sloping beach on one side of the island where passing ships can be readily signaled and temporary shelter can be found. The captain knows of these conditions and tells the passengers to separate and seek this desirable side of the island independently.

Modify the program of 5.6-15 to analyze the routes of the 20 people. Divide the island into 4×4 grid system. The location of the crash is at location 2, 2 and the beach is along the side of the Y axis ($X = 0$).

Include as output:

(A) The number of walks per route required of the 20 people to find the beach.

(B) The number of people that end the route at each of the 5 possible points along the shore.

PROBLEM 5.6-6   "Best Conditions"

Finding conditions which work best was discussed in Section 5.5. Sometimes problems arise which require that the best conditions be determined by trial and error. Approximations for the best values of x and y for the problem described below can be obtained by trial and

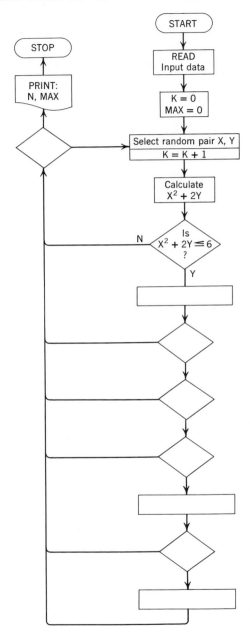

Figure P5.6-6 Best conditions.

error using random numbers. Note that the first condition is nonlinear in x and that the problem would be a linear programming problem if all the conditions were linear.

GIVEN

Conditions
(1) $x^2 + 2y \leq 6$
(2) $x - 2y \leq 2$
(3) $x \geq 1$
(4) $y \geq 0$
(5) $(2x + y) \rightarrow$ to be a maximum

REQUIRED

(A) On a plot of y versus x, shade the area where values of x and y satisfy the given conditions (1) through (4).

(B) Show the point that also satisfies condition (5).

(C) Complete the flow chart which describes a method of using random number pairs to solve the problem.

(D) Write a program and obtain an approximate solution for x and y using 100 pairs of random numbers. Generate the random numbers as part of the program using the mid-square method.

CHAPTER 6.

Further Fortran

6.1 PERSPECTIVE

In Chapter 2 we stated that our goal was to acquire as quickly as possible a working elementary knowledge of FORTRAN—enough at least to get us from the hotel to the store in this strange country, and to accomplish successfully, if haltingly, those simple economic transactions that were our immediate need. Elementary FORTRAN serves this need quite well, for it is a language quite close to that combination of mathematics and English in which we are used to stating many of our problems. The use of FORTRAN therefore enables us to bridge, with a minimum delay, the gap between being able to recognize our problem, and being able to get the computer to solve it for us.

That brief exposure, of course, falls far short of making expert programmers out of us, although it should be encouraging to look back and see how much we *have* accomplished already. Since what we have accomplished has enabled us to acquire some operating experience on the computer, including actually running several problems, we are now in a good position to dig a little deeper into FORTRAN, and find out what else we can do with it.

We will look particularly at two additional features available to us in the FORTRAN language: *FORMAT* and *Subroutines,* and then glance quickly over the rest of the list of topics.

6.2   FORMAT

We will find times when there is almost no way to get the computer to do what we want except by using FORMAT statements. There are two things we can do only with FORMAT:

(1) At input time, we can control the exact analysis of input data. We can cause the program to skip over certain columns that have been punched on the cards, and can select various items from what has been punched, even when no spaces or separators have been left.

(2) At output time, we can greatly dress up the appearance of a final output (usually the printed page). We can:

(a) Cause alphabetic information such as column headings, remarks, names of quantities, or units, to be printed.

(b) Control the number of figures, location of the decimal point, and style of output numbers.

(c) Control the spacing and arrangement of the output on the page.

Just to appreciate what FORMAT can really do for us, let us take a preliminary look at a couple of examples of its use. We will take Problem 3.2-6 (QUAD) dealing with the solution of a quadratic equation, as a situation in which the problem itself is well understood, the solution is fairly readily attained, but presenting the output in a clear and unambiguous manner is quite a problem. After getting the general idea from this preliminary examination, we will get down to examining the exact structure of the FORMAT statement and the precise rules for its use.

"QUAD"

First Part of QUAD. In part (A) of the problem we are told we can assume that the coefficients are such that only real roots exist. That is, when we try to find the roots by the quadratic formula

$$x_{1,2} = \frac{-b \pm \sqrt{b^2 - 4ac}}{2a}$$

we have a solemn promise that the quantity under the radical sign (the discriminant) will always be positive. The solution is straightforward, and the program, data, and results obtained are shown in Figure 6.2-1. The circled numbers highlight the following points regarding the use of FORMAT statements:

① The use of an E11.4 specification produced the so-called "adapted" scientific notation with the decimal point at the left of the first digit.

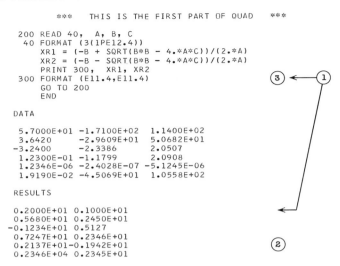

```
        ***   THIS IS THE FIRST PART OF QUAD   ***

  200 READ 40,   A, B, C
   40 FORMAT (3(1PE12.4))
      XR1 = (-B + SQRT(B*B - 4.*A*C))/(2.*A)
      XR2 = (-B - SQRT(B*B - 4.*A*C))/(2.*A)
      PRINT 300,  XR1, XR2
  300 FORMAT (E11.4,E11.4)
      GO TO 200
      END

DATA

   5.7000E+01 -1.7100E+02  1.1400E+02
   3.6420     -2.9609E+01  5.0682E+01
  -3.2400     -2.3386      2.0507
   1.2300E-01 -1.1799      2.0908
   1.2346E-06 -2.4028E-07 -5.1245E-06
   1.9190E-02 -4.5069E+01  1.0558E+02

RESULTS

   0.2000E+01 0.1000E+01
   0.5680E+01 0.2450E+01
  -0.1234E+01 0.5127
   0.7247E+01 0.2346E+01
   0.2137E+01-0.1942E+01
   0.2346E+04 0.2345E+01
```

Figure 6.2-1   First part of QUAD.

This is contrary to scientific usage, and should be avoided. This is why we have been using that 1P so carefully. It is called the P scale factor, and we will learn how it works shortly.

② The spacing of the output is poor, with the two results crowded together in line 5.

③ Furthermore, although the specification E11.4 was given twice to emphasize the correlation between the specifications in the FORMAT statement and the items in the list of the PUNCH statement, we have seen that this is not necessary. A "repeater" before the letter E allows the single specification 2E11.4 to do the same thing.

While this program does produce results from the input data, the output FORMAT could be improved by adding more spaces to facilitate reading of the answers, and by somehow shifting the decimal point.

Second Part of QUAD. For the second part of our example, let us consider the additional part of the program necessary to handle the complex roots referred to in part (B). In Figure 6.2-2 we assume that in this case *all* sets of coefficients lead to a negative discriminant, and proceed accordingly. Some additional comments can be made on this program.

④ By the use of the 4X specifications, we have spread out the results in a much more readable form.

⑤ Mathematicians write complex numbers in the form $a \pm bi$, where

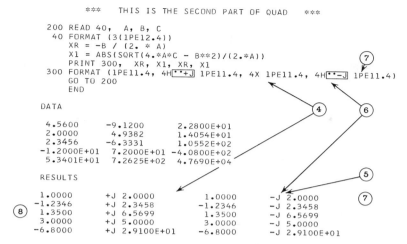

```
        ***   THIS IS THE SECOND PART OF QUAD   ***

  200 READ 40,   A, B, C
   40 FORMAT (3(1PE12.4))
      XR = -B / (2. * A)
      X1 = ABS(SQRT(4.*A*C - B**2)/(2.*A))
      PRINT 300,   XR, X1, XR, X1
  300 FORMAT (1PE11.4, 4H ••+J  1PE11.4, 4X 1PE11.4, 4H ••-J  1PE11.4)
      GO TO 200
      END

  DATA

    4.5600      -9.1200       2.2800E+01
    2.0000       4.9382       1.4054E+01
    2.3456      -6.3331       1.0552E+02
   -1.2000E+01   7.2000E+01  -4.0800E+02
    5.3401E+01   7.2625E+02   4.7690E+04

  RESULTS

    1.0000    +J 2.0000        1.0000    -J 2.0000
   -1.2346    +J 2.3458       -1.2346    -J 2.3458
    1.3500    +J 6.5699        1.3500    -J 6.5699
    3.0000    +J 5.0000        3.0000    -J 5.0000
   -6.8000    +J 2.9100E+01   -6.8000    -J 2.9100E+01
```

Figure 6.2-2 Second part of QUAD.

i is the symbol for $\sqrt{-1}$. Engineers, because the letter i appears in so many of their equations as a symbol for electric current, almost always use the notation $a \pm jb$ to mean the same thing. Suit yourself.

⑥ The 4H specification allowed us to insert $+J$ and $-J$ before the imaginary portions of the root. Since the convention is always to treat the magnitude of the imaginary root itself as positive, the one column blank spacing after the letter J is adequate separation.

⑦ Use of the P scale factor has caused the position of the decimal point to be shifted right 1 place in the significant figure portion of the number, and the exponent to be decreased accordingly. This produces standard scientific notation, and is much more acceptable. It should almost always be used with the E specification. Actually, although the 1P is shown as part of *each* E specification, most FORTRAN processors retain the most recently specified value of P for the remainder of that same FORMAT statement, so it does not have to be repeated. In other words, the FORMAT specification

```
      (1PE11.4, 4H  +J E11.4, 4X E11.4, 4H  -J E11.4)
```

would do exactly the same thing as the one shown in statement 300.

⑧ Column 1 on either the punched card or the printer is used by most FORTRANs to control line spacing and page advance on the 407 or other printing device. Information punched in column 1 may either be lost completely, or cause erratic behavior, wasted paper, and a bizarre final appearance. Unfortunately, in this case no extra space was left at the left margin, since the field width of 11 which was specified is just barely wide enough to hold all the information asked for. As a result, the two minus signs which belong in column 1 in rows 2 and 5 of the output are in danger. We made sure the controls were set to allow these signs to print this time, but without special attention they might have just disappeared without a trace. Moral: arrange both input and output to *stay out of column 1!*

Final Version of QUAD. The final version of QUAD, which is shown in Figure 6.2-3, is a combination of the first two parts with some testing to decide which part to use. The following points should be studied carefully, as they illustrate several new features of FORMAT statements:

⑨ Column headings were produced by a FORMAT statement which contains only X and H specifications, used in conjunction with an output statement that has no list.

⑩ One FORMAT statement produced two different lines of output by the use of a slash in the middle of the FORMAT statement.

⑪ Note that to cause double spacing (a completely blank line) after an output record, a double slash at the end of the FORMAT statement is used. Warning, however: one slash at the *beginning* of a FORMAT

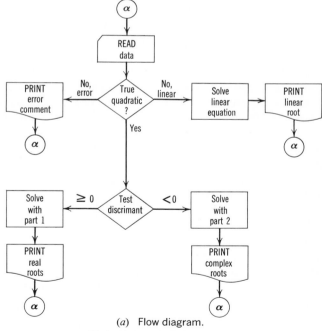

(*a*) Flow diagram.

Figure 6.2-3 Final part of QUAD.

```
        ***   THIS IS THE FINAL PART OF QUAD   ***
        PRINT 10
10 FORMAT (6X 1H⬚A 8X 1H⬚B 8X 1H⬚C/27H⬚ ⬚⬚⬚⬚⬚⬚ ⬚⬚⬚⬚⬚⬚ ⬚⬚⬚⬚⬚⬚)     ⑨⑩
 3 READ 40, A, B, C
40 FORMAT (3(1PE12.4))
   IF (A) 2, 6, 2
 6 IF (B) 1, 7, 1
C==== THE EQUATION IS LINEAR ====
 1    ROOT = -C/B
      PRINT 11, A, B, C, ROOT
11 FORMAT(3F9.2, 22H**IS A LINEAR EQUATION/36X 9HROOT**=**1PE11.4//)
   GO TO 3
 7 PRINT 16, A, B, C
16 FORMAT (3F9.2,13H**NO EQUATION)
   GO TO 3
C==== TEST DISCRIMINANT =====
 2    D   = B*B - 4.*A*C
      IF (D) 4, 5, 5
C==== EQUATION HAS TWO REAL ROOTS ====
 5    ROOT1 = (-B + SQRT(D))/(2.*A)
      ROOT2 = (-B - SQRT(D))/(2.*A)
      PRINT 12, A, B, C
12 FORMAT (3F9.2, 20H**HAS TWO REAL ROOTS)
      PRINT 13, ROOT1, ROOT2
13 FORMAT (38X 7HR1**=**1PE11.4/38X 7HR2**=**1PE11.4//)     ⑪
   GO TO 3
C==== EQUATION HAS TWO COMPLEX ROOTS ====
 4    R1  = SQRT(-D)/(2.*A)
      RR  = -B/(2.*A)
      PRINT 14, A, B, C
14 FORMAT (3F9.2, 23H**HAS TWO COMPLEX ROOTS)
      PRINT 15, RR, R1
15 FORMAT (36X 9HREAL**=**1PE11.4/31X 14HIMAGINARY**=**1PE11.4//)     ⑬
   GO TO 3
   END
```

(b) Program.

```
        1.        -5.         6.
        1.        -5.         7.
        2.         4.         1.
        2.E1       4.E+1      3.00E+01          ⑫
        0.         9.71     -24.68
          0.         0.        9.
```

(c) Data.

```
     A         B         C
   ------    ------    ------
     1.00     -5.00      6.00   HAS TWO REAL ROOTS
                                        R1  =    3.0000
                                        R2  =    2.0000

     1.00     -5.00      7.00   HAS TWO COMPLEX ROOTS
                                      REAL  =    2.5000
                                 IMAGINARY  =    8.6603E-01

     2.00      4.00      1.00   HAS TWO REAL ROOTS
                                        R1  =   -2.9289E-01
                                        R2  =   -1.7071

    20.00     40.00     30.00   HAS TWO COMPLEX ROOTS
                                      REAL  =   -1.0000
                                 IMAGINARY  =    7.0711E-01

     0.00      9.71    -24.68   IS A LINEAR EQUATION
                                      ROOT  =    2.5417

     0.00      0.00      9.00   NO EQUATION
```

(d) Results.

Figure 6.2-3*b, c, d*

statement will cause a line to be skipped *before* that particular line of output. Each FORTRAN has its own (sometimes weird) conventions with regard to the effect of slashes.

⑫ The input data (see Figure 6.2-3c) should be examined because they are not so "pretty" as those for some previous programs. In E specification input of a real variable, the presence of a decimal point in the data itself insures the number being read in properly regardless of its position in the field, *provided there is no exponent*! If an exponent is supplied, then the entire number, including the exponent, must be right justified in the field. A few variations in the form of the exponent are permitted, however, and some of these are shown.

⑬ FORMAT statement No. 11 occupies the full 72 columns on a card, which is the maximum length for any statement contained on one card. If a few more spaces are needed, two blank spaces in this FORMAT statement could be omitted without changing the effect (which ones?). If more than two are needed, two pairs of PRINT and FORMAT statements can be used, as is done in statements 14 and 15, or continuation cards, which are allowed in some FORTRANs, can be very handy devices at such times.

Output FORMAT

FORMAT is most valuable when used with output statements, in controlling the output form of numbers processed by the machine. The programmer is able by means of FORMAT statements to present the results of his computations in a style which will be pleasing, informative, and useful.

A FORMAT statement and an output statement always work together in the preparation of output from a program. The output statement supplies the list of items to be put out, and the FORMAT statement determines the exact form for each item in the list. In addition, the FORMAT statement supplies information about spacing, general arrangement, and comments to accompany the numerical information.

A FORMAT statement is made up of three parts: a statement number; the word FORMAT; and a set of one or more specifications, the entire set enclosed in parentheses. There are three general classes of FORMAT specifications, as shown in Figure 6.2-4.

List Specifications. Each of the list specifications describes the form of output of one element in an output list, and each item in a list must have a corresponding FORMAT list specification. The I is an *integer* format; the E and F are both real, the E being a floating-point form with an *exponent,* and the F a *fixed*-point form without; and the A describes a much more complicated process of reading in mixed alpha-

1. List specifications

> I
> F
> E
> (A)

2. Self-contained specifications

> X
> H

3. Control specifications
   Separators:

> ,
> /
> (
>)

Repeaters

P scale factor

Figure 6.2-4   Classes of FORMAT specifications.

meric information, treating it as floating-point numbers, and eventually putting it out again. The A specification is much less commonly used, and can profitably be postponed for a while.

An *I specification* consists of two items: the letter **I**, followed by a 1- or 2-digit number, **w**, specifying the number of columns (in the card or on the page) the number is to occupy (called the *field width*). The number will always be right-justified in the field. For example, if the variable NO has the value 12, then the output pair

```
      PRINT 50,  NO
   50 FORMAT (I5)
```

would put out the number 12 in columns 4 and 5. Remember that you should always allow one column to the left of the leftmost digit for a sign, even though it will not be printed if +, so make **w** *at least* one greater than the number of digits in the largest number you expect. Usually **w** is made even larger, for this is the simplest way to achieve

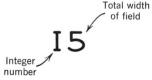

Figure 6.2-5   I Format specification.

spacing between fields. For example, if J K L M have the values 5 12 7 609, then below is shown the appearance of the output produced by printing them out with the statement

```
PRINT 40,  J, K, L, M
```

and the five different FORMAT statements:

```
40 FORMAT (4I2)        (should give error comment)
40 FORMAT (4I3)        5 12  7609
40 FORMAT (4I4)          5  12   7 609
40 FORMAT (4I5)           5   12    7   609
40 FORMAT (4I6)            5    12      7     609
```

An *F Specification* consists of four items as is shown in Figure 6.2-6: the letter **F**; a field width **w**; a decimal point **.** ; and another integer **d** which is the number of decimal places—digits to the right of the

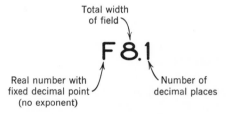

Figure 6.2-6   F Format specification.

decimal point. For example, if the variable Y has the value 12.345678 within the computer, then the output pair

```
PRINT 51,  Y
51 FORMAT  (F8.1)      would produce      ••••12.3
```

where the dot above the line is used to indicate a blank space. To show the effect of changing **w** and **d** separately, observe:

```
51 FORMAT  (F8.3)                 ••12.346
51 FORMAT  (F10.1)               ••••••12.3
51 FORMAT  (F10.3)               ••••12.346
```

Note that if **d** is less than the number of digits existing in the number, most FORMAT routines produce a *rounded,* not a truncated, result.

Provided we know for sure the range of numbers we are dealing with, so that we can predict exactly how many digits will be needed to express the integer portion of the number and how many for the fraction, the F specification produces the nicest looking form for real (floating-point) numbers. Not only the decimal points but corresponding decimal places always line up with one another, making it easy to follow variations in the range of listed quantities.

Total width
of field

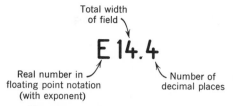

Real number in
floating point notation
(with exponent)

Number of
decimal places

Figure 6.2-7   E Format specification.

```
INTERNAL                F10.2                    1PE14.4*
.087204114        •••••••.09            ••••8.7204E-02
.11046293         ••••••••.11           ••••1.1046E-01
9.8870246         ••••••9.89            ••••9.8870
12.349807         •••••12.35            ••••1.2350E+01
81.780906         •••••81.78            ••••8.1781E+01
987.01964         ••••987.02            ••••9.8702E+02
1234.5614         •••1234.56            ••••1.2346E+03
```

Figure 6.2-8   Comparison of E and F Format specifications.

The trouble with the F specification, however, is that the number may become either too big, causing it to run off the left end, or too small, resulting in a loss of precision down to, possibly, a loss of all significant figures. These conditions may arise either because we are too careless in laying out the fields, or because the number turned out much bigger or smaller than we expected. This condition, in turn, is not too uncommon, for after all when tackling a new problem for the first time we may not have any idea what the range of values taken on by a particular variable may be. It may go from 10^{-6} to 10^5 for all we know.

For this reason the commonest output FORMAT specification for scientific and technical work, at least, is the *E specification,* which gives the output in true floating-point form complete with exponent. The same four elements comprise an E specification as an F: the letter **E**; a field width **W**; a decimal point **.**; and the number of decimal places **d**. The biggest difference in the makeup of this specification is that the field width **w** contains the four additional columns that are needed for the exponent element, too.

Suppose, for example, our variable Y took on the succession of values shown in the first column of Figure 6.2-8. Then the result of putting it out with both an F10.2 and an E14.4 is shown in remainder of the same figure. For the single number Y = 12.345678 the effect of varying w and d within the E specification is shown below:*

```
FORMAT (1PE10.2)          ••1.23E+01
FORMAT (1PE10.4)          1.2346E+01
FORMAT (1PE12.2)          ••••1.23E+01
FORMAT (1PE12.4)          ••1.2346E+01
```

* We will explain the P part shortly.

To dissect the bottom line, for instance, our 1PE12.4 counts out *from right to left* as follows: 4 for the exponent, comprised of the letter E, sign, and 2 digits; 4 more for the significant figures called for to the right of the decimal point; 1 for the decimal point itself; and 1 for the leading digit to its left. In addition, 1 should always be allowed for the sign, bringing the total up to 11 used spaces, which means that at least one blank space (two if the number is positive) will always be left at the left edge of this field, to separate it in appearance from the field to its left. It is because this is the minimum E specification which will guarantee such separation that we recommended back in Chapter 2 that you use this format to put out real numbers: 1PE12.4.

Now what about that mysterious P that was thrown in in front of the E itself? What is that for? Probably the best way to explain what it does is to see what the output would look like without it. Suppose we tried the same listing shown in Figure 6.2-8, but without the P, just using the FORMAT specification E14.4. Figure 6.2-9 shows what we get.

In other words, if we merely specify E-type FORMAT, which supposedly gives a true floating form with exponent, the FORMAT control puts the decimal point at the extreme left, just *before* the first digit, and then supplies the number of digits specified by d and the proper power of 10 by which the number must be multiplied to give the true value. Each number is thus normalized to lie in the range $\geq .1$ but < 1!

Now this, it turns out, is exactly how the numbers are represented inside the computing machine, but it is not the way we would like to see them put out for our own use. "Standard Scientific Notation," for more years than computing machines have been around, has meant: the first, the most significant, digit is written to the left of the decimal point, then the decimal point, and then as many more figures to the right of the point as are significant. All handbooks, 99 out of 100 other technical books, and almost complete universal practice follows this convention; only FORTRAN is out of step. What was apparently a preoccupation with the internal form of numbers was unfortunate in 1957, when IBM published the first FORTRAN; that it has been perpetuated in almost every American FORTRAN since is deplorable.

INTERNAL	E14.4	1PE14.4
.087204114	••••••.8720E−01	••••8.7204E−02
.11046293	••••••.1105	••••1.1046E−01
9.8870246	••••••.9887E+01	••••9.8870••••
12.349807	••••••.1235E+02	••••1.2350E+01
81.780906	••••••.8178E+02	••••8.1781E+01
987.01964	••••••.9870E+03	••••9.8702E+02
1234.5614	••••••.1235E+04	••••1.2346E+03

Figure 6.2-9   Effect of P scale factor.

Only Control Data Corporation, as in their FORTRAN 63 for the 1604 and 3000 series, gives a true scientific notation in their E specification output.

Fortunately, with the P scale factor available, this deficiency becomes merely an inconvenience. The control element P means nothing more than "scale factor," and the digit in front of the P merely tells the FORMAT control how many places to the right to move the decimal point before putting out the number. Correspondingly, of course, the exponent must be reduced by the same factor to keep the true value of the number correct. Therefore, even though the E specification alone gives a hybrid and completely unsatisfactory type of output, the combination 1PE does give a true scientific floating-point notation, and is therefore the form most recommended.

Some FORTRANs such as the IBM-supplied FORTRAN for the 1620, do not contain a P scale factor. They give something of the same capability by putting a variable number of figures to the left of the decimal point, depending on the difference between **w** and **d**. This, however, has the disadvantage that a separate X specification must be used to create spaces between numbers.

Self-Contained Specifications. Two classes of information may be specified and put out directly by the FORMAT statement itself, without the necessity for correlating with any list or list element. These two are blanks and alphameric information, controlled by the X and H FORMAT specifications, respectively.

The *X specification* is particularly simple; writing a **wX** causes the generation of **w** blank spaces in the corresponding output record. Although this is frequently handy for inserting spacing between columns of numerical values, it is even more valuable when used in conjunction with the H specification.

The *H specification* also comprises two elements: **wH** tells the FORMAT control that the next **w** characters in that *FORMAT statement itself* (be they punched, typed, or stored) are to be put out exactly as they appear, digits, letters, blanks, special characters, and all. Note that this is the one exception to the statement in Section 2.4—blank spaces may be inserted freely with no effect. Within an H field, blanks are counted and treated exactly like any other character.

Two examples of the use of H specification:

(1) Suppose we were going to put out three columns of information with the output statement:

```
PRINT 51,  N, Y, Z
```

and that furthermore we wished to have the separate columns identified by separate column headings:

$$N \qquad Y \qquad Z$$

This can be achieved by inserting an additional pair of statements: one, another PRINT statement, must occur somewhere in the sequence of executable instructions prior to entering the loop that calculates Y and Z; the other, the corresponding FORMAT statement, may appear anywhere. This pair might say:

```
     PRINT 50
  50 FORMAT (19H[ᐧᐧN·······Y········Z])
```

Note that at execution time there is no necessity for the FORMAT control to have to match up a list specification with the corresponding element in the output list; there is no output list. The entire FORMAT statement is self-contained.

(2) This same heading could have been produced by a mixture of H and X specifications. Prove to yourself that the following output pair produces exactly the same effect:

```
     PRINT 50
  50 FORMAT (3H[ᐧᐧN] 6X 1H[Y] 8X 1H[Z])
```

Control Specifications. Certain punctuation marks have very specific use as *separators* in FORMAT statements. If you recall (and you had better) that items in an input or output list must always be separated by commas, then it is easy to remember that the corresponding list specification in a FORMAT statement must be treated the same way. More specifically, each list specification must always be followed by a comma (or other separator) to mark the end of the specification. Not so the self-contained specifications. Here the comma separator is optional; it may be terminated with a comma, or the specification may be followed immediately by the next specification.

In both of these cases, additional spaces may be inserted at will to improve the readability—except of course within the field of H specification—and such practice is recommended.

The comma separates one item in a list (and its corresponding list specification) from the next; the slash in general separates one line in the output from the next. Specifically, a slash in a FORMAT statement tells FORMAT control: "end this line, and start a new one."

Suppose we want to put out two lines of alphameric information with a single FORMAT statement. This is accomplished by inserting a slash at the point where we want the first line to end. You can think of it as equivalent to executing a "carriage return" on a typewriter at that spot. For example, if we want to underline the column headings we were writing in the section just above, we could write

```
     PRINT 50
  50 FORMAT (3H·· N  6X 1H Y  8X 1H Z /22H·--- ·· -------- ·· -------)
```

which would produce the output:

```
         N        Y          Z
        ---    -------    -------
```

A couple of points need rather close attention in using the slash:

(1) Since a slash terminates the line that has been produced to date, and starts a new one, a slash at the beginning of a FORMAT statement produces a completely blank line (double space before starting the record).

(2) For the same reason in many FORTRANs a single slash at the end of the FORMAT statement has no effect; the closing parenthesis terminates the record anyway. To get double spacing *after* an output record, *two* slashes at the end of the FORMAT statement are needed.

Note that in the sense used in the last paragraph, the closing parenthesis at the right end of a FORMAT statement is itself a separator. It is not necessary to place a comma after the last specification in a FORMAT statement; the parenthesis serves this function as well.

There is one additional feature of FORMAT control that often comes in handy, and that is the ability to have a single specification or set of specifications repeated as many times as desired without having to write them all over again. As was pointed out in one of the examples in Section 3-4, if we wish in one output statement to put out two succesive numbers with the same FORMAT specification, a *repeater* digit before the specification accomplishes exactly that.

```
          FORMAT (E11.4, E11.4)
```

is exactly equivalent, for instance, to

```
          FORMAT (2E11.4)
```

Furthermore, if we would like a set of specifications to be repeated in sequence, we can enclose the set we want repeated in a pair of parentheses and place a repeater in front of the parenthesized set.

```
          FORMAT (I3, E11.4, I3, E11.4, F10.2)
```

is therefore exactly equivalent in effect to

```
          FORMAT (2(I3, E11.4), F10.2)
```

It should be noted here that although the first right parenthesis replaces the comma which would otherwise be needed after the E11.4, a comma is still called for after the parenthesis, since the parenthesized set now acts like a single list specification.

The *P scale factor* is a control specification that belongs in this list, but its use with the E specification has already been discussed. In some FORTRANs the P scale factor may also be applied to F specifications, although it must be realized that when so used it actually *changes* the value of the number being put out. The rule here is:

$$\text{Output number} = \text{internal number} \times 10^P$$

In this connection either $+$ or $-$ values of P may be meaningfully used. Other FORTRANs, however, reflecting the fact that this type of conversion may be adequately performed by additional statements within the program, exclude this usage, and define a meaningful P only when used with the E specification.

As a final note, the user should be cautioned that there is considerable variation among different FORTRANs as to the exact effect of some of the more complicated combinations of specifications, separators, and repeaters, and that careful study of the FORTRAN manual for the particular system being used, together with some judicious experimenting, is called for when true elegance is desired.

How to write FORMAT statements

The best advice on the construction of proper FORMAT statements is to proceed backwards—start with the result you want, and then figure out how to tell the computer how to produce it.

The first step in writing an output FORMAT statement, then, is to consider the associated output statement and determine the exact form of the output desired. The easiest way of doing this is to spell out an exact line image of the information as you want it to appear, space by space, digit by digit, character by character. In this line image, all numeric and alphabetic information should be laid out, being certain to allow a sign to the left of the first digit of each numeric output, and to show a decimal point in the desired location in all floating point quantities. Make certain that the line does not exceed the allowed limit of 72 characters for card output (80 columns in some FORTRANs, 120 in others).

Now proceed from left to right through the line image, considering each element or field one at a time, and writing the specification necessary to produce that element. Within each field, however, the FORMAT specification should be made up by counting character positions from the *right* edge of the field, since all list items are put out by FORMAT control right-justified within the field width specified. This process of counting character by character through the field from right to left was illustrated in one of the examples earlier, under the discussion of E FORMAT, and should be reviewed at this point.

It will further help us to write correct FORMAT statements if we have as full an understanding as possible of the exact process gone through by the compiler to cause execution of output under FORMAT control. The procedure is rather complicated, since it involves frequent transfer of control back and forth between the output statement and the FORMAT statement, but it follows a few simple rules, and can be quite straightforwardly described.

When an output statement is first encountered at execution time, the first step is to search out the associated FORMAT statement identified in the output statement and transfer to it. This FORMAT statement is then scanned from left to right, and each specification executed item by item. Execution consists of causing to be built up in an output area, usually in a designated location within the high-speed memory itself, a line image of what is to be put out from the computer. As each specification is executed, as many characters as are called for in that specification (its field width) are transferred to the output area; when enough are finally accumulated, that information is physically put out of the Central Processing Unit of the computer, either by direct printing or punching on a card, or by writing on a magnetic device for later printing.

When the specification encountered is self-contained, the information specifying the characters to be transferred to the output area is contained in the FORMAT statement itself; either the characters are all blanks in the case of an X specification, or the characters themselves are contained in the FORMAT statement in the case of an H specification. When, on the other hand, that specification encountered is a list specification, control is transferred back to the output statement to seek the next element in the output list. The value of the variable so named is ascertained from memory, edited into the format described by the specification being executed in the FORMAT statement, and the appropriate digits and characters are written into the output record. In either case, when one specification has been executed, control returns to the FORMAT statement, not the output statement, to determine what information should be added to the record next. The only time control goes to the output statement, after once starting on the FORMAT operation, is when the next specification encountered in working through the FORMAT statement is a list specification; control then goes to the output statement to find out *what* list element should be put out.

Note that each list specification is associated with a particular item in the output list; when one list element has been put out, the next list element is associated with the next list specification encountered in the FORMAT statement. Hopefully the mode of the list specification agrees with the mode of the variable name comprising the next list element. If not, some FORTRANs will convert, and others balk. This is one of the nuisance details that must be kept completely straight when writing FORMAT statements.

This then is how the image of the output line gets built up in the output area. What determines when the output line is dumped? The information in the output area will be transferred to the appropriate external device when one of the following events happens.

(1) The line in the output area becomes full—72 columns for some FORTRANs, 80 for others, 120 for still others.

(2) A slash is encountered.

(3) The output operation is completed.

In the case of either 1 or 2, the execution of the same FORMAT statement continues, starting a new line in the same place in the output area; if the record is terminated by event No. 3, then control is transferred to the next executable statement in the sequence following the output statement.

What determines when an output operation is completed? Is it when scanning reaches the right-hand parenthesis of the FORMAT statement? Not necessarily. If there are still items in the output list remaining, execution does not stop here, but scanning of the FORMAT statement resumes at the beginning of the FORMAT statement again (or goes back to the rightmost left parenthesis, or even some other point—FORTRANs differ). On the other hand, if the output list is exhausted while list specifications still remain in the FORMAT statement, execution will terminate. To be specific, all specifications in the FORMAT statement will be executed until a list specification is encountered for which there is no corresponding entry in the output list. Then the execution terminates, and that unfulfilled list specification, and anything left after (to the right of) it is also passed over.

Input Format

Although much could be written in great detail about input FORMAT as well as output, only two things will be said here.

(1) If you do have to use FORMAT for input, almost all the descriptions and details of the output FORMAT apply.

(2) Do not use input FORMAT if you do not have to. If free FORMAT is available, the only time it is desirable to use input FOR-MAT is if you are stuck with the necessity of reading in prepunched (someone else's) data, and he did not leave blanks between variables. Under those conditions only FORMAT will separate the fields.

6.3 SUBPROGRAMS

We have seen several instances so far of certain small programs having extensive and varied use, sometimes within the same larger program. Having worked out a program to evaluate a polynomial, for instance, or sort an array, we would not like to have to compose it all over again every time we encountered a situation calling for its use.

Consider the hypothetical program sketched in Figure 6.3-1, for instance. Notice that in four different places in this brief fragment we have occasion to call on a sorting program. How can we conveniently arrange it to be able to use the same sorting program in each place, without physically copying the whole set of sorting instructions into the program at each of the four places? The way to accomplish this is to make the sorting program into a subroutine.

SUBROUTINE Subprograms

Suppose we had a set of instructions for accomplishing some fre-quently encountered task made into a package that we could call in whenever we had that task to accomplish. What are the pieces of infor-mation we would have to give the subroutine?

(1) We would have to tell it where to get the data to work on.
(2) We would have to tell it where to put its result.
(3) We would have to tell it where to go when done.

In this situation telling it where to get the data is equivalent to telling it the names of the variables it is supposed to use, and in the same way where to put results means under what names to file them away, so that we could make use of them in the rest of the program. These first two could be accomplished, although somewhat awkwardly, by estab-lishing some naming conventions and sticking to them. The third, however—how to establish return communication—would be quite a bit more difficult.

There is, in fact, no convenient technique available to us in the FORTRAN procedures we have learned so far that would enable us to

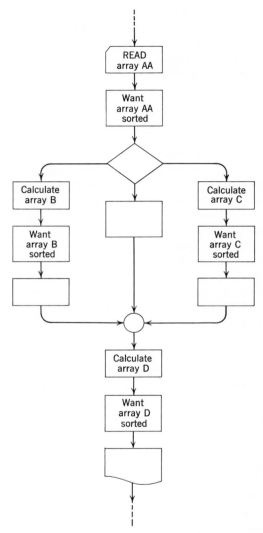

Figure 6.3-1 Needing a subroutine.

leave the subroutine after execution and return to the main program at any arbitrary spot from which we might have called in the subroutine. It is for this reason that we find it desirable to introduce into the FORTRAN vocabulary three new statements: SUBROUTINE, CALL, and RETURN.

The first, SUBROUTINE, is the mechanism by which we identify to the FORTRAN compiler any set of FORTRAN statements which we want to have so treated. Among the properties with which such a subroutine is endowed are those which enable us to CALL it in when needed and RETURN when through.

We call in a subroutine when we need its help by using the CALL statement. In the process we convey to the subroutine the first two pieces of information we talked about a few lines back: the names of the data and the names to call the answers; we will see how in just a bit. RETURN is a statement that is incorporated in the subroutine itself; it exists for the sole purpose of accomplishing the third of those requirements. Whenever in the course of executing a subroutine a RETURN statement is encountered, control is transferred back to that statement in the main part of the program which immediately follows the CALL statement that called in the subroutine. This is a completely new type of control statement, but one which proves to be invaluable in these operations.

Along with these new statements we find a new symbol to represent this process on a flow chart. Figure 6.3-2 illustrates the same program situation shown in Figure 6.3-1, with the idea of a subroutine incorporated.

Let us be more specific on just how we write and use this sorting subroutine. We have already seen in Chapter 5 quite a few ways to accomplish sorting; let us pick one of them (Figure 5.3-5*b*), and arrange it for use as a sorting subroutine.

It is important to keep in mind in this process that although a subroutine may be written by one person at one time, if it is written with sufficient generality it can be used by many other people in many other situations. Therefore, the means of exchanging the information described under points 1 and 2 above must be very explicitly understood.

The first statement in a subroutine accomplishes three things: it tells the compiler that what follows *is* a subroutine; it *names* the subroutine; and it tells what input *arguments* are called for and what output *arguments* are provided. It is written

SUBROUTINE SORT (N, A)

In this case the written description which always accompanies the subroutine, providing instructions for its use, would explain that the first argument N is the number of elements in the array, and that A is the name of the array. Note that, except for certain input-output operations allowed in some FORTRANs, this is the only place an array name may appear without being followed by parentheses. It does have

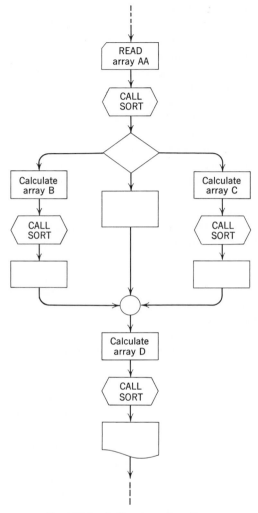

Figure 6.3-2 Calling for subroutine.

to be followed, preferably immediately, by a DIMENSION statement specifying the maximum size of any arrays used:

DIMENSION A(100)

Now what if the user has not used N in his program to denote the size of the array, but has called it something like K47? And if you answer that he can change the name in his program to agree with the name used in the subroutine, what if he wants to use the subroutine in several different places in his program, where his different arrays are described by different integer-variable names? This has been allowed for in the way the CALL statement is organized. When the user wants to call in the subroutine he may write:

CALL SORT (K47, COST)

Thus in the CALL statement he gives the name of the subroutine he wants (there may be several different subroutines on call), after which he must supply a list of arguments that tells the subroutine by what names these quantities are known in his program. His argument list must therefore match the one in the subroutine definition statement on two counts: for every entry in the subroutine argument list there must be a corresponding entry in the CALL list, so there must be the same number of names; and each name must be of the same type as the corresponding name in the subroutine list. This means that if the first name in the subroutine list is that of an integer variable, telling, for instance, the size of the array the subroutine will sort, the first name in the CALL list must be the name of an integer variable, telling the size of the array to be sorted. The names do not have to be the same, although they may be if desired; they must correspond, in the same sequence. If the second name in the subroutine list is that of an array, indicated by being dimensioned in a DIMENSION statement within the subroutine, and that DIMENSION statement describes it as a one-dimensional array (it has only a single subscript), the second name supplied by the user in the CALL argument list must also be that of a one-dimensional array, and it must be so dimensioned in a DIMENSION statement in the main program itself.*

For the type of sorting operation we propose to do there is no output-variable name to be specified, for the sorted array ends up in the same set of locations under the same name as the input array. In other cases, however, the argument list will need to tell not only the names of the input variables, and the names (or numerical values) of certain parameters like the number of elements, but also the names under which the output variables are to be put away. Note that the user may at any time use a constant instead of a variable name if he wishes. If he knows, for instance, that the array to be sorted at a certain point in his program always has exactly 7 elements in it, he could write

---

* In some FORTRANs there is an additional requirement that the arrays be dimensioned to the same *size*!

CALL SORT (7, X)

Figure 6.3-3 illustrates how all this might actually be used. The top part of the figure shows part of what is called a main-line program, the program situation in which a user encounters the need for a subroutine. At the point in his program where he has completed the calculation of an array which he has called ARRAY, he writes his CALL statement, calling in the subroutine called SORT to sort his array, with name ARRAY and size LIM. He then goes on to do whatever further calculation he needs with the (now sorted) array. Note that both the main program and the subroutine are complete program entities and that they contain their own DIMENSION statements and END statements. The subroutine, however, does not have a STOP, but a RETURN. It may in fact have more than one RETURN if the situation calls for it; a subroutine to find the roots of a quadratic equation, for instance, might have a RETURN in place of each of the four GO TO 3 statements as they occur in Figure 6.2-3, the final version of QUAD. Note that as used here, the subroutine uses no predefined quantities except

```
        DIMENSION   ARRAY(20)
            •
            •
            •
        DO 28   K = 1, LIM
            •
            •
            •
28      ARRAY(K) = .  .  .
        CALL SORT(LIM, ARRAY)
        DO 35   L27 = 1, LIM
            •
            •
            •
        STOP
        END
        SUBROUTINE SORT(N, X)
          DIMENSION   X(50)
          NM1 = N - 1
          DO 8   I = 1,NM1
            L = I
            IP1 = I + 1
            DO 7   J = IP1, N
              IF (X(L) - X(J)) 7,7,6
6           L = J
7           CONTINUE
            TEMP = X(L)
            X(L) = X(I)
8           X(I) = TEMP
          RETURN
          END
```

Figure 6.3-3

those appearing in its argument list; it is up to the user to see to it that each variable in the argument list used by the subroutine has been previously defined in his main-line program.

Correlating Names

We have said that a name in a subroutine has no connection with a name in the main program. Suppose there is an accidental duplication of names? Suppose in this example of Figure 6.3-3 the user had been using the name N for something entirely different—a part number, a parameter in another DO loop, or something like that. Have we not said that the compiler catches all references to a variable, and always associates a particular address in memory with that name? Does this not mean that there will be a confusion between the N in the main program and the N in the subroutine? Will a subroutine writer have to be constantly trying to pick names that will not coincide with names selected by the users?

The answer is no. By some ingenious bookkeeping and separate tables of reference, the compiler will always treat these two N's as completely different names. It is as though each name used in a subroutine had a separate subscript attached to it, so it could always be identified as belonging to that subroutine, but nothing else. This makes life a lot easier for everybody.

This picture is, of course, significantly oversimplified on several counts. As a programmer becomes more and more adept at taking full advantage of the flexibilities available to him in whatever language he is using, he begins to want still more powers, to wish that certain restrictions, which he was very glad to accept when first learning, could now be removed. This name independence is just such a restriction, and, without going further into it here, it should be noted that when so wanted it is possible to declare that two different programs share certain variables in COMMON, or even that certain variable names are EQUIVALENT. As the programmer reaches the stage of working often with subroutines and other subprogram units, he should read further about these two statements COMMON and EQUIVALENCE. See, for example, Organick, *A FORTRAN Primer,* or McCracken and Dorn, *Numerical Methods and FORTRAN Programming.*

Other Types of Subprograms

In the same vein, the reader should be aware of the existence of several other ways of extending the vocabulary of FORTRAN besides SUBROUTINES. There are several varieties of functions, ranging from built-in functions we have been using all along, like SIN, SQRT, and ABS, through the FUNCTION statement, to the FUNCTION subprogram. None of these, however, will be referred to any more here, and the interested programmer is referred once again to either Organick, or McCracken and Dorn. The SUBROUTINE subprogram which we *have* looked at in this chapter (and which is the most general and powerful of these additional features) is enough to illustrate the concept and to point out something of what can be done by such devices.

Libraries

It is also worth pointing out, before dropping the subject, that the generalized subroutine offers an excellent way to preserve the programming efforts of one person at one time, and make them available again at a later time to other people. Most computing installations, in fact, maintain a fairly large library of both whole programs and subroutines, storing them in various ways, from mere written descriptions and listings, through punched source decks, or already compiled object decks, to ready-to-use object programs stored on magnetic tape or disk, available for immediate use when called by a program being executed.

These library programs usually represent not only the work of members of that computing installation, but the pooled effort of organizations of computing machine users called Users Groups. For the IBM 1620, for instance, there is a 1620 Users Group (now called COMMON, since it also includes users of the 1130 and 1800 Computers, as well as users of the smaller size IBM 360 computing systems), having over a thousand members who exchange information, experience, problems, and solutions. A 1620 Program Library is maintained jointly by COMMON and IBM, containing over 700 programs and their documentation, available free to any user.

Similar organizations and libraries exist for almost all commercial computers in use today, since successful programs and people's experience with them represent far too much time, money, and effort not to take full advantage of experience already gained.

6.4 OPERATING SYSTEMS

For any complex process to be run efficiently, there must be a minimum of wasted time. If the process has a large number of different possible operations, with very little that is routine and predictable about the succession of jobs to be carried out, it can become exceedingly difficult for even very skilled operators to keep the whole process going smoothly without delays, waste, and mistakes ranging from minor to catastrophic. This is precisely the problem presented by running a computer installation.

As the computer becomes faster and more expensive, it becomes increasingly important that the computer not be allowed to come to a halt at the end of one user's job and wait until the next user moves in and starts it on his job. When computer time costs many dollars a minute, even 30 seconds between jobs (and this calls for some pretty fast maneuvering by the operators), can quickly add up to exorbitant costs and gross inefficiencies.

How can we get around this? Can we get the computer itself to take over some of the responsibility of moving control from one job to the next, and all the associated chores? Let us first see what the job consists of when a human does it.

Without such automatic control, when it is time for a new job the operator must get from the user, either directly or from a file where he has left it, not only the program deck but also some necessary information about the run. He must find out whether it is a FORTRAN, Symbolic, or Machine Language program, or whether it is merely data for some special-purpose program. If it is FORTRAN, which FORTRAN: even for the 1620 it might be 1620 FORTRAN with Format, FORGO, AFIT FORTRAN, PDQ FORTRAN, FORTRAN II, or KINGSTRAN, to mention only a few of the processors in common use! The operator must then dig out the proper processor and see that it is loaded into the computer ahead of the user's program. This is sometimes a two- or three-pass process, involving alternation between the processor or a part of it and the source program, or some intermediate result of operating upon it. Even for a large installation where the processors as well as the intermediate product being put out and read in are on magnetic tape, the operator may be kept pretty busy mounting tapes and throwing switches.

In addition, the user may have presented the operator with data cards and information about special switch settings, and has probably been asked to give a rough figure for the running time of his program and the quantity of output he expects.

When, at the end of a lively session of loading, switching, and dashing here and there, the operator observes that the computer has finally finished the problem (hopefully successfully), and has blinked to a sudden halt, another frenzy of activity erupts, as the operator tries to get this set of results out of the way and the current job off the computer, so it can be started on the next job with a minimum of delay. In between, of course, either the user or the operator should fill out appropriate entries in the log, listing accurately the starting and finishing time, together with the name and project number, so that reasonably accurate accounts can be kept and proper bills sent out.

How much of this could be automated? Quite a bit, it turns out.

Let us start with the assumption that an automatic clerk can be developed. How can we improve the efficiency of our operation?

First of all, we will still further buffer our input-output operations so that the high-speed computer need never wait for those horribly slow mechanical contraptions, the card reader and the card punch. We shall insist that the user's source program decks be transcribed from cards to magnetic tape on some other device (often a small, relatively slow-speed computer) off-line, and that the input to the computer itself be a tape containing a whole batch of programs, ready to be gulped at high speed directly into the memory of the computer. Output will, of course, be treated in the same way; output called for by the program will be written onto magnetic tape, and then removed from the computer to be subsequently processed by slower, lower-cost machines and converted into either printed pages, punched cards, or occasionally, plotted graphs.

Second, we will insist that each user precede his actual program with some documentary material, identifying himself, his project, and the type of program he is submitting, so that our automatic clerk will know what to do with it. This information is usually punched on what are called "Job Cards," which are placed at the beginning of each user's deck.

Third, we will place all our processors such as the various FORTRAN compilers, the assembly programs, and various diagnostic and utility programs on magnetic tape, disk, or drum. These devices can be considered for these purposes either high-speed input, or intermediate-speed storage. The important characteristic is that sizable programs can be kept stored on them, capable of being called in automatically by the computer itself at nearly electronic speeds, without manual intervention. In addition to complete processor programs, part of this file will contain a sizable collection of the most commonly used library subroutines.

Fourth, we will reserve a section on this intermediate storage device for accounting purposes, so that the computer itself can keep the log data records, updating them automatically as a part of each run.

Now we are in a position to describe the operations which our automatic clerk will have to perform. It turns out to be a combination receptionist, file clerk, dispatcher, executive secretary, and bookkeeper.

(1) A small section of a high-speed memory itself will be reserved for a key portion of the supervisory program, which will reside in memory at all times.

(2) At the completion of one job, this supervisor program will scan the Job Cards that appear at the beginning of the next job, decide what process they call for, and call in the appropriate program to handle the job from the intermediate tape or disk storage.

(3) If the job is a compilation or assembly, the processor, once it is in memory, will in turn read in the rest of the user's program and go to work on it. If the processor encounters a need for additional subroutines or other subprograms from the library file, it notifies the supervisor, which prepares the necessary instructions to have them read into the memory when the time comes.

(4) Although use is made of the high-speed memory in the compilation process, the object program is usually built up in the intermediate storage element as it is compiled. The supervisor keeps track of its location and the name by which it may be called. At the completion of compilation the processor returns control to the supervisor.

(5) If the job calls for both compilation and execution of a program, the supervisor calls in the object program from the intermediate storage device and turns control over to it for execution. The object program now controls the reading in of data and putting out of results in the usual fashion.

(6) If, on the other hand, the job calls only for the program to be compiled and stored for later execution, the supervisor now assigns reserved space in the intermediate storage element, and files the object program away under whatever name the user specifies for his program.

(7) Note that this means the supervisor must keep an accurate record of what is stored in the file, where it is located, and under what name it can be called. It must also, of course, keep a constantly updated record of available as well as assigned space in the file, so that it can determine where to put the next item.

(8) It may even be that the user merely wants his program checked out for mistakes, in which case the compiler produces diagnostic comments as it scans the source program, but never actually creates an object program.

(9) It may be that the job does not involve a compilation, but merely asks for the execution of a program previously compiled and stored in the file, perhaps with new data. In this case no processor is needed, but the supervisor must still determine what supporting programs are needed from the file and call them in along with the program to be executed.

(10) Almost no object program, whether generated by a FORTRAN compiler, a symbolic assembler, or whatever, is ever complete in itself, but requires the assistance of several supporting programs at execution time. For example, the processing of input and output data according to FORMAT statements has to be done at execution time, and is usually referred to certain built-in FORMAT subroutines. The compiler inserts into the object program at the appropriate places the necessary calling sequences which, when they are encountered, cause the FORMAT subroutines to take over the process of handling the input and output FORMAT operations. Sometimes these subroutines can all be called into high-speed memory along with the object program and remain there during execution; other times, if storage is limited, each subroutine is called in whenever it is needed, and overlaid with the next portion when it is through. The first method is obviously faster, but of course requires much more storage space. Once again we find an instance where time can be traded for space.

(11) At the completion of a job, whether it be compilation, assembly, execution, or a combination of several, control is turned back to the supervisor, which enters the necessary bookkeeping information, such as running time of the job, in its internal accounting record, and without pausing starts scanning the instructions for the next job.

(12) Note that since there is no pause between jobs, only in emergency situations will the computer ever actually come to a halt. Obviously, such an automatically controlled operation will be far more efficient of both computer time and human operations, and will result in a tremendous increase of what has come to be called "throughput" through the computer.

Such automatic operating systems are called monitors, auto-monitors, supervisors, or residents. A monitor system is a very complex program, which must take into account the various capabilities of different pieces of hardware that make up a computer system, each representing many man-months of programming effort to develop. Nevertheless, they have been found so valuable that all large-scale computers and most intermediate computers now have monitor systems available, developed either by the manufacturer or by a single user or group of users in a cooperative effort. In either case, it is then made available to all users of that type of computing system. Batch processing under monitor system operation today accounts for the great bulk of both scientific computing and business data processing the world over.

To make this very general discussion more concrete, procedures for actually running jobs under two typical monitor systems will be described.

Similar procedure descriptions for other systems, and local details peculiar to the particular computing installation available, can always be obtained from the computing installation concerned.

COOP Monitor (CDC 1604, and with modifications CDC 3600)

```
          JOB Card
Column    | 1 | 2...                                                              |
Contents  | 7 |COOP, | 7008, | WILSON, | I/50/O/51/S/56/57, | 4, | 3000, | 5, | SAMPLE. |
          | 9 |                                                                  |
Field     | ① ② |  ③  |   ④    |         ⑤          | ⑥ |  ⑦  | ⑧ |   ⑨     |
```

(1) The 7 and 9, both punched in column 1, identify this as a control card.

(2) COOP calls into memory from the library the supervisor portion of the COOP Monitor Program.

(3) 7008 is an account number, identifying who is to be billed for the time used by this program.

(4) WILSON is the programmer's name.

(5) This field assigns device (tape unit) 50 to input; unit 51 to output; and 56 and 57 to "scratch" or intermediate storage.

(6) The program is allowed four minutes to run; if it has not ended by that time the monitor will terminate it.

(7) It is allowed a maximum of 3000 lines of printed (or punched) output.

(8) The 5 is a key which instructs that if anything goes wrong (for example, the time limit is exceeded) the monitor is to provide a "dump" of everything in the memory.

(9) The last field is available for comments and/or messages to the machine operator. Here, SAMPLE is the name of the program.

If the program is a FORTRAN program, another control card is needed:

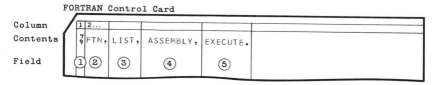

```
          FORTRAN Control Card
Column    | 1 | 2...                                              |
Contents  | 7 |FTN, | LIST, | ASSEMBLY, | EXECUTE.                |
          | 9 |                                                   |
Field     | ① ② |  ③  |    ④     |    ⑤                          |
```

(1) The 7 and 9 in the same column again indicate a control card.

(2) FTN calls the FORTRAN compiler from the library tape.

(3) LIST tells the compiler to list the source program along with the output.

(4) ASSEMBLY causes the program to be compiled in a relocatable form of the symbolic assembly language called CODAP.

(5) EXECUTE causes the monitor to prepare the object program in a condition ready to be executed (not merely to check it for errors, for instance).

For a monitor of this capability and versatility there is a large list of other types of control statements available, but these are enough to see how such a program would work. As an example, Figure 6.4-3 lists the complete set of job cards, control statements, main program, and sub-routines as they would be needed to run a program making use of the simple sorting routine of Figure 6.3-3 on the CDC 1604 under the COOP Monitor.

Monitor I (IBM 1620 with disk file)

Although the purpose and general accomplishment of this monitor are the same, there are several differences, both superficial and funda-mental, stemming primarily from the following system differences:

(1) The 1620 is a much less powerful machine, slower, and more limited in repertoire, input-output facilities, and interrupt capabilities, but it is, of course, much cheaper.

```
7
9 COOP, 7008, WILSON, I/50/0/51/S/56/57, 4, 3000, 5, SAMPLE.
7
9 FTN, LIST, ASSEMBLY, EXECUTE.
```

```
PROGRAM MAIN
   DIMENSION ...
      • • •
   CALL SORT(...)
      • • •
END
```

```
SUBROUTINE SORT(...)
      • • •
   RETURN
      • • •
END
```

```
   END
```

```
   FINIS
```

```
7
9 EXECUTE
```

```
Data
```

Figure 6.4-3   A job to be run under the COOP (1604) Monitor.

(2) The intermediate storage mechanism is a magnetic-disk file rather than magnetic tapes.

(3) Program decks are input directly to the computer, rather than prepared in batches on tape off line.

(4) The monitor system was written and supplied by the manufacturer (IBM) rather than by the Users Group (COOP).

Figure 6.4-4 shows the sequence of cards and decks for running the sample job shown in Figure 6.4-3 under the 1620 Monitor I.

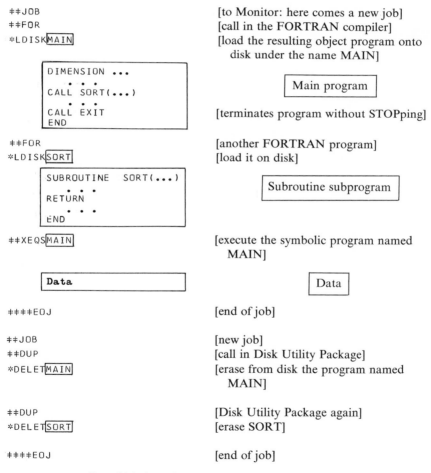

```
‡‡JOB                     [to Monitor: here comes a new job]
‡‡FOR                     [call in the FORTRAN compiler]
*LDISK MAIN               [load the resulting object program onto
                              disk under the name MAIN]

    DIMENSION ...
       • • •              Main program
    CALL SORT(...)
       • • •
    CALL EXIT             [terminates program without STOPping]
    END

‡‡FOR                     [another FORTRAN program]
*LDISK SORT               [load it on disk]

    SUBROUTINE  SORT(...)
       • • •              Subroutine subprogram
    RETURN
       • • •
    END

‡‡XEQS MAIN               [execute the symbolic program named
                              MAIN]

    Data                  Data

‡‡‡‡EOJ                   [end of job]

‡‡JOB                     [new job]
‡‡DUP                     [call in Disk Utility Package]
*DELET MAIN               [erase from disk the program named
                              MAIN]

‡‡DUP                     [Disk Utility Package again]
*DELET SORT               [erase SORT]

‡‡‡‡EOJ                   [end of job]
```

Figure 6.4-4   Same job to be run under 1620 Monitor I.

PROBLEM 6.4-1   "SUBROUTINE SORT"

(A) Write a general sorting subroutine to sort N associated arrays of length L on column N1 in ascending sequence, leaving the arrays in their original storage locations.

(B) Write a FORTRAN program which uses the subroutine from (A) above to solve Problem 5.3-3(A) (Hall of Fame).

(C) Write a FORTRAN program which uses the subroutine from (A) above to solve Problem 5.3-2(C) (Inventory Sort).

CHAPTER 7.

Things Worth Computing:
[C] PROCESSING BUSINESS DATA

7.1 KEEPING TRACK OF DETAILS

In this chapter, we shall describe the commercial and business uses of computers, and determine the necessary features of computers and their language to accomplish data processing in this area. The early applications of computers were classified either as scientific, or as commercial and business, and computers with different features were built for use in both areas. We shall see that the trend is toward a single type of computer system, with the combined features of the two earlier types.

What are some of the commercial and business applications of computers and the data processing features of the applications? For industrial systems most of the applications of computers in the operations of CONTROL are classified as commercial and business. We shall review and expand on the discussion of the control operations of an industrial system given in Chapter 4, to learn of these operations.

The block diagram of Control C of Figure 4.3-1 is redrawn with greater detail in Figure 7.1-1. Control C, as before, is divided into daily operations control C_1 and high-level control C_2. For our current study, the operations of C_1 are broken down into the control operations of accounting, material input, process, and product output. The arrows, as before, represent communication channels and the direction of flows of

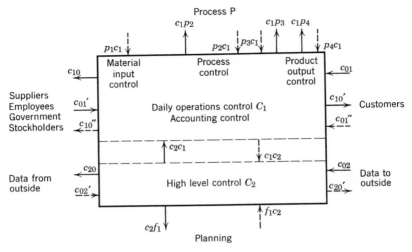

Figure 7.1-1 Operations for control C.

information. The arrows drawn in solid lines carry action requests and those in dashed lines carry the results of actions. The vertical arrows at the top and bottom of the diagram and those between C_1 and C_2 represent internal communications. Those at the top and bottom provide communications with the Process and the Planning operations, respectively. Those on each side represent communications with the outside world.

Accounting

All operations of accounting in daily operations control C_1 are potential applications of computers and, without question, come under the heading of business and commercial applications. These operations are involved in the handling of money and the associated activities of record keeping, and are shown in Figure 7.1-2. The operations of billing send action requests for payment of shipped products to the customers which are communicated by channel c_{10}' in the form of invoices. The operations of accounts receivable receive and record the payments that are sent by the customers as the result of actions.

The operations of accounts payable, payroll, and tax, shown on the left of the diagram, relate to the distribution of money. Requests for action by the supplier in the form of invoices are communicated over channel c_{01}' and accounts payable takes action to issue payments which are sent over channel c_{10}''. Payroll calculates net salaries and issues paychecks, which are sent to employees over c_{10}''. Payments must also

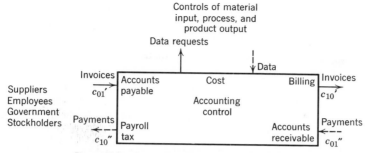

Figure 7.1-2 Operations for accounting control.

be made to the government in meeting tax obligations, and to stockholders and banks.

Still another important operation shown in the diagram is cost accounting, which does not require direct communication with the outside. Its function is to determine all the items of expense and to calculate a total cost of making a product.

Nearly all of the vast amount of data required to perform the accounting operations are generated internally to the industry. Many of the internal data are supplied by request from other control operations of material input, process, and product output as shown at the top of the diagram. Data for each operation of accounting are also obtained from other accounting operations.

These operations of accounting for an average-size industry require a large number of records which must be frequently reviewed and updated. They also require a large number of simple calculations to be performed repetitively. For example, in the payroll operations, an employee's record contains many items of information for calculating deductions, such as, taxes, retirement, medical insurance, bonds, and contributions. In all, there may be two dozen or more record items that must be maintained, searched and used for calculating each paycheck. If the employee is paid hourly or on a piecework basis, large amounts of data must be obtained from the operations of process control to calculate the paycheck.

The computational methods used in obtaining results by the computer are the same as manual methods of performing the operations of accounting. For example, the amount of a paycheck calculated from a given set of data must agree to the penny, regardless of what means is used to calculate the amount. The justification of the cost of a computer in these accounting operations must then be only on the basis of the savings in clerical costs and the elimination of human error, and not on the basis that the computer calculates more accurately.

Other important commercial uses of computers similar to those of accounting are insurance operations in the updating of policies and billing for premiums, and in banking operations. It has been determined that if the hiring rate of banks during the 1950's had continued, by the year 2000 all the available working force in our economy would likely have been employed in these clerical operations. Computers applied to the banking industry since the early 1960's have decreased the hiring rate, while the banking industry and the economy have continued to grow at a substantially constant rate.

Since these operations of accounting are natural for a computer to perform, it is understandable that they should have been some of the first commercial and business applications, and that they should not have been classified as scientific. We shall explore operations other than accounting in the control operations of Figure 7.1-1 which, although properly classified as commercial or business before or when computers were first applied, have become, to some degree, scientific.

The remaining operations of C_1, Figure 7.1-1, control of material input, process, and product output, were discussed in Chapter 4, in order to determine the effect of the use of computers on product and material flows in the system. Our current consideration is the data-processing features of the operations.

Material Input Control

The principal operations of material input control are shown in the diagram of Figure 7.1-3a. They are receiving, purchasing, and material inventory control. Orders are placed by purchasing at the request of the operations of material inventory control and sent to the suppliers over channel c_{10}. Packing slips are enclosed with shipments of materials from the suppliers, and enter the receiving operations by way of channel p_1c_1. Requisitions for materials removed from inventory are also sent by way of this channel. Material inventory control then updates the records accordingly. Information such as abnormal quantities and new material specifications required for inventory must come from the other operations of process and product output control, as shown at the bottom of the diagram.

These operations are highly repetitive, involve a large number of records, and require the handling of large amounts of data. Similar operations of large magnitude exist in retail and wholesale marketing. Computers perform well in these operations.

Process Control

The main operations of process control are shown in the diagram of Figure 7.1-3b. These operations have little direct contact with the out-

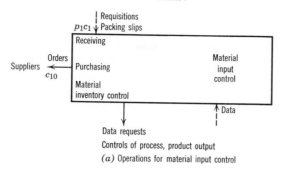

(a) Operations for material input control

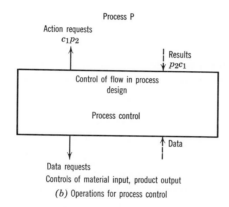

(b) Operations for process control

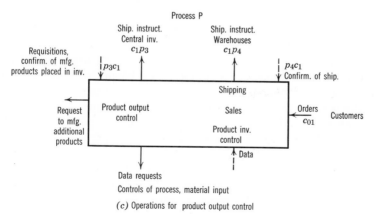

(c) Operations for product output control

Figure 7.1-3   Operations for control C_1—increasingly scientific.

side world. Most of the required data come from within the system, in particular, from the controls of material input and product output, and from Process P, as shown in the figure. Available materials and material costs influence design in minimizing the cost of the products, and this information must come from material input control. Other data required by both design and control of flow are related to customer satisfaction and must come from product output control. Action requests in the form of drawings, material requisitions, and schedules are sent to P by way of channel c_1p_2, and data on the results are sent by return channel p_2c_1. Information such as costs of processing and capabilities of man and machines in P, must be communicated among the operations within process control.

The operations of control of flow in process have been classified as commercial and business applications of computers. Design may be considered to be of this classification when these operations are highly repetitive, as for standard types of products. The design of roof trusses described in Chapter 4 may be considered a commercial and business application after the computational model is established and a computer program is developed for designing trusses of any given dimension.

Product Output Control

The principal operations of product output control are shown in the diagram of Figure 7.1-3c. The sales operations are responsible for obtaining orders from customers entering channel c_{01}. Shipping instructions are issued to warehouses through channel c_1p_4, and confirmations of shipments are sent by return channel p_4c_1. Product inventory control initiates replenishment of warehouse inventory from central inventory by issuing shipping instructions by way of c_1p_3. Requests are sent to Process Control to manufacture additional products, and confirmations that the products are made and placed in product inventory are sent to inventory control on channel p_3c_1. Requisitions for products for shipment are also sent to product inventory control to confirm that the products were removed. The operations of product output control must receive data from the controls of process and material input to establish schedules of shipments, and to be aware of circumstances that may develop in these operations.

These control operations of product output are classified as commercial and business application of computers. They, as well as material input operations, are of large magnitude in retail and wholesale marketing. Since the process operations are minor or nonexisting, material and product inventory appear as one inventory.

The Difference in Data Processing of Accounting and of the Other Three

We have discussed the four major control operations of daily operations control C_1, namely, accounting, material input, process, and product output. There is an important difference between accounting and the other three. The results of the operations of accounting must always be the same regardless of the means used to obtain them, while for the other three the results can be improved upon and better answers obtained through the use of improved methods and computational models.

High-Level Control

High-level control C_2 of Figure 7.1-1 remains to be analyzed for commercial and business applications of computers. Figure 7.1-4 shows these principal operations to be overall control of C_1. The best performance of the overall industrial system is not necessarily achieved when each of the four principal operations of C_1 are performing at their best from day to day. Overall control attempts to find conditions which work best in these operations to achieve the overall best performance. For example, an impending labor strike at a supplier's plant may make it desirable to acquire abnormally large quantities of materials or, because of competitive situations, it may be desirable to lower prices of a product and increase production to an amount above normal. There are many situations, some of them far more complex than these, that require the operations of overall control to issue action requests to the operations of C_1. The figure shows these requests to be sent by way of

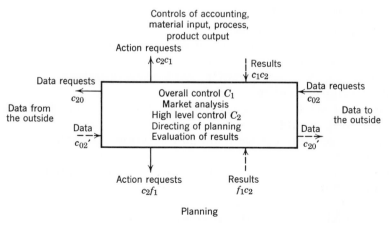

Figure 7.1-4   Operations for control C_2—increasingly scientific.

channel c_2c_1. The large amount of data required to determine what the action requests should be for the best overall performance is obtained from the outside, and from C_1 by way of channels c_{02}' and c_1c_2.

Data from the same sources, and those received from planning by way of f_1c_2, are required in the directing of planning and in making market analyses before new products are introduced, or in determining the best advertising medium. These same data may be searched and organized, and selected data sent out over c_{20}' in response to action requests from the outside which are received by way of c_{02}.

The applications of computers in these decision-making operations of high-level control may all be classified as business and commercial, but the features of data processing differ from those of the other applications in that the processing is nonrepetitive, i.e., different types of problems may be solved each day. The computational methods and models in decision making have improved to the extent that management has become a science, called *management science,* and computers used in these business operations require some of the features of scientific data processing.

Comparison of Data Processing in All Major Control Operations

What do all the operations we have studied as business and commercial applications of computers have in common? They (1) deal with large amounts of data and (2) communicate with many other operations. What have we found to be the data-processing features that differ? The operations may be categorized as follows:

Data Processing Features.

A. Repetitive, nonscientific
(1) accounting control—(a) accounts payable, (b) payroll, (c) tax, (d) billing, (e) accounts receivable, (f) cost
(2) other—(a) insurance operations, (b) banking operations
  B. Repetitive, becoming scientific.
(1) material input control—(a) receiving, (b) purchasing, (c) material inventory control
(2) process control—(a) control of flow in process, (b) design standard products
(3) material output control —(a) shipping, (b) sales, (c) product inventory control
  C. Nonrepetitive, scientific
(1) high level control—(a) overall control of daily operations, (b) market analysis, (c) directing of planning, (d) evaluation of results of planning

Programming Languages for Business Operations

We shall now explore a common business language developed in 1959 especially for use in these operations. One of the main objectives for developing this computer language called COBOL (*CO*mmon *B*usiness *O*riented *L*anguage) was to solve the communications problem between man and computer. There was the difficulty of the nonscientific personnel in these operations writing programs in algebraic and machine symbolic language. There was also the difficulty of obtaining output from the computer which could be easily understood and would be accepted by the many nonscientific people who received the information. For as we have learned, any one of these business and commercial operations must provide information to people in many of the other operations, such as managers of operations who receive periodic reports, and the many employees, stockholders, and policy holders who receive paychecks, dividend checks, and/or premium notices.

The solution of the communications problem was the development of COBOL as a word language. A part of a program written in this language is shown in Figure 7.1-5 and serves to demonstrate statement structure. It is called the **PROCEDURE DIVISION**, and is one of four divisions required of a complete program. This program is for inventory control and uses the method of manual control of inventory discussed in Chapter 4. If you have worked problem 4.2-1, you have already written similar statements in the FORTRAN language. The first line of the program identifies the division, and all following statements are in that division. The word UPDATE, on the second line, identifies the

Sequence (Page) (Serial)	Cont.	A	B								
1 3 4 6	7 8		12	16	20	24	28	32	36	40	44
010		PROCEDURE DIVISION.									
020		UPDATE. SUBTRACT QUANTITY IN REQUIS FROM									
030		QOH IN NI IF QOH IN NI IS NOT LESS									
040		THAN MOL. GO TO REQUIS-EXIT;									
050		OTHERWISE GO TO REORDER-ROUTINE.									
060		REORDER-ROUTINE. IF OQ IN ORDER-RECORD									
070		IS NOT ZERO. GO TO REQUIS-EXIT;									
080		OTHERWISE MOVE OQ IN NI TO OQ IN									
090		ORDER-RECORD. WRITE ORDER-RECORD									
100		REQUIS-EXIT. EXIT									

Figure 7.1-5   Statement structure of COBOL

QOH—the quantity on hand the last time the file NI was processed
  OQ—order-quantity
MOL—minimum-order level

subroutine for updating inventory. The first sentence of this subroutine calls for a subtraction of the quantity taken from stock, which is in the requisition file REQUIS, from the quantity on hand, QOH, in file NI. For the second statement, if the new value of QOH is not less than the minimum order level, MOL, the requisition-exit routine is entered to terminate the processing for that item; otherwise QOH is less than MOL and the reorder routine is entered. In the reorder routine, if an order quantity OQ appears in the order-record file, an order has already been placed. If OQ does not appear, an order has not been placed and OQ is moved from the NI file to the order-record file. The last sentence calls for the writing of the order. The requisition-exit routine is then entered to terminate the processing of that item.

The COBOL language, as we see, requires the writing of many words which, of course, must then be keypunched. COBOL programs in some respects can be considered written descriptions of FORTRAN programs. They can be read and modified without great difficulty, and other operations wishing to use them can easily determine their contents. The output of the computer can also be written in a report form for nontechnical managers which may not differ greatly from reports received before the computer appeared on the scene.

It is not an objective of this book to present the information required to program in COBOL. The subject is covered in the references listed at the end of the chapter.

Desirable Features of the Computers

We shall now explore the desirable features of computers that perform in these operations. Obviously, one of the desirable features is input-output capabilities to handle the large amounts of data flow required in the communications with other operations. The entering data may be in the form of punched cards; handwritten or typed data that must first be punched into cards; magnetic tape if the supplying operation has a computer; and teletype or punched paper tape. Output may also be requested in these forms. Unless input-output facilities are adequate, the computer is input-output bound, i.e., the data-processing facilities are idle waiting for the input-output facilities.

A second desirable feature is data storage capabilities to store the large amounts of data of a number of classifications in data files. A combination of speeds in memory access is required for a balanced system. Core- and disk-memory are required for rapid access to instructions and frequently referenced data. In many large operations, two dozen or more magnetic-tape units may be used to store the many files of data. These files may be transferred to disk when they are frequently referenced.

A third desirable feature is variable-word-length. Most computers used in scientific applications have fixed-word-length, and word-lengths of 48, 36, 24, and 12 bits have been used. In variable-word-length computers, such as the IBM 1460 and 1410, a word may be from 1 bit up to a length equal to the memory size. Variable-word-length machines provide a very desirable flexibility in data processing of alphanumeric characters, and they more fully utilize memory storage.

7.2   INTEGRATED RECORDS AND OPERATIONS

In Section 7.1, we discussed the control operations of C as individual applications of computers, and the corresponding communication between man and computer in accomplishing communications between the control operations. We shall see, that as more operations within an industrial or business system apply computers and become more scientific, how natural it is that the requirements of communications and data processing should change.

The First Phase of Implementation of Electronic Processing

Let us follow the likely sequence of events in development of electronic data processing in a group of operations of C_1, such as material input control. In the first phase of implementation of electronic data processing, the manager of the group of operations applies the computer to the operations one by one over a period of time, and follows closely the manual method of operation in the design of the programs, i.e., very little, if any, improvement in results is achieved at this time. The manner in which the processing would be accomplished on the computer may be described with the aid of Figure 7.2-1a. When data processing for any one of the operations is to be performed on the computer, there are three sets of magnetic tapes to be mounted on tape drives: (1) tapes P which contain record files used in processing including the program, (2) the input tapes I containing input data prepared by associated operations under the manager's supervision, and (3) the output tapes O which are to be written with data requested by associated operations. Other input is required in the form of cards shown as cards I which may contain data from the outside; internal source data, that is, data originating in process P; and data from other operations of C_1 which may not have applied computers and cannot supply data written on magnetic tape. Output may also be required in the form of punched cards to satisfy the requests for data of other operations of C_1 that have not applied computers, and to supply data to the outside and to the operations of process P. Printed output is also required for the outside,

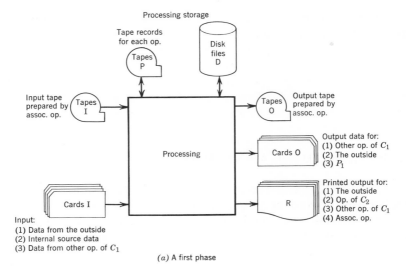

(a) A first phase

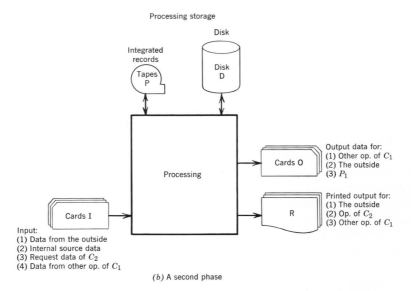

(b) A second phase

Figure 7.2-1 Sequences in the development of electronic data processing.

the operations of C_2, other operations of C_1, and to associated operations. Tape records to be frequently accessed may be transferred to the disk files D during the processing operations.

After processing of an operation is completed, the three sets of tapes are changed to those required in processing for another operation. Processing for each operation frequently occurs once each day.

The Second Phase of Implementation

Usually, in anticipation of a larger, more advanced computer system, preparation is made for a second phase. This results from the discovery that by system design all these associated operations, say, of material input control can be combined, eliminating the need to change tapes and providing for nearly immediate processing of incoming data. For example, in the material input operations, requisition data are read into the computer when items are removed from stock; the inventory records are updated; and a purchase order, if required, may be issued immediately as output.

Figure 7.2-1b shows the requirements of communications and the record file system for data processing for this second phase. Since the records of the associated operations have been integrated, tapes P for record files for processing are the only tapes required. Card input and output must still include data associated with other operations of C_1 if they still use mechanical card equipment. The quantity of printed output in the form of internal reports is reduced for two reasons: (1) fewer people now require reports and (2) only that data of current interest is obtained at the individual's request.

Integrated records and operations require careful systems design. The design is achieved through the use of flow charts similar to those we have drawn in the text in preparation for the writing of FORTRAN programs. Final detailed flow charts may contain hundreds of blocks. The system design may incorporate improved mathematical methods and models to improve results. Provisions are also incorporated for handling exceptional cases to reduce human intervention in the computer operations.

The Changing Requirements of Computers

As more operations of C_1 apply computers and accomplish phase 1, further integration of records and operations can be accomplished. Communications originally involving man occur within the computer or between two or more computers over electronic circuits. We may conclude that the amount of communication between man and computers is continually being reduced.

We have seen that the business and commercial applications of computers are also scientific. The operations of C_1, excluding those of accounting, are becoming more scientific. Those of C_2, in general, involve special problem solutions which are considered scientific.

Scientific data processing in the areas of planning and design, on the other hand, are requiring more of the features of business data processing. Computers are applied in areas of research that require the handling of large amounts of source data. For increasingly complex computational models, communications between man and computer are also increasing.

We have learned the features of the algebraic language of FORTRAN and have become familiar with those of COBOL, the word language. Since there is a merging of the features of data processing in the two areas of science and business and commerce, we see a need for a language not as "wordy" as COBOL and including some features of FORTRAN. In scientific applications we see that it would be desirable for FORTRAN to be more like COBOL, in order to improve communications and have greater flexibility in word length for changing accuracy of calculations at will. Perhaps a single language can be established that will fulfill the needs of both areas. In 1965 a new language was announced, developed by the SHARE* Advanced Language Development Committee and the IBM Corporation, which is designed to be more general and is hopefully applicable to both business and scientific programming.

General-purpose computers are also appearing that have the features required to meet the needs of data processing in all areas. The IBM 360 series of computers are examples.

REFERENCES

7.1-1. McCracken, Daniel D. *A Guide to COBOL Programming,* John Wiley and Sons, New York, 1963.

PROBLEM 7.7-1

Write the COBOL statements of Figure 7.1-5 in the language of FORTRAN. Identify the symbols you use for the variables.

PROBLEM 7.2-1   "Payroll"

An organization has designed an employee record system containing the items of information it requires in its accounting operations as shown in Figure P7.2-1. This information is normally stored on one of the record tapes P of Figure 7.2-1 and processing is accomplished in the COBOL language on a business-and-commercial-type computer. You will use the scientific-type computer and accomplish processing in the FORTRAN language.

* SHARE is an organization of users of large IBM computers.

Employee ID	Sex	Year employed	Year birth	No. depend.	Gov. bonds	Comm. Chest	Salary rate/hr.	Hours worked	Accum. salary	Accum. taxes
1064	1	1956	1925	2	25	3	3.00	80	3000	250
946	2	1960	1930	1	15	2	5.00	84	5500	500
826	1	1945	1920	3	30	5	7.50	86	7000	600
432	1	1950	1931	4	25	5	4.00	81	4500	400
921	2	1962	1940	3	0	3	5.00	75	4000	300

Figure P7.2-1

(A) Payroll is one of the functions of accounting requiring employee records. In the first phase of electronic data processing, the updating of records is accomplished by batch processing. Input of updating data is in the form of cards which are read into the computer in batches prior to the calculation of payroll, as shown in Figure 7.2-1*a*.

In the second phase, when records are integrated and a total system operation has been implemented, updating information, such as the number of working hours of the employees, may be accumulated on one of the tapes P as it becomes available from the costing operations performed on that same computer. Updating of the employee record tape occurs without human intervention in the flow of updating data. Other updating data, such as a change in the number of dependents, is read into the computer in the form of cards as the employee reports the change.

Write a program to update the employee records of Figure P7.2-1 by the batch processing method in preparation for the calculation of payroll. Store the table in the computer as a 2-dimensional array and update these records at the close of the two-week pay period with the data shown in Figure P7.2-1*a*. Produce as output the updated records. (B) Write a program for calculating the hourly payroll for the two-week period. The net salary equals the gross salary minus the amounts for bonds, Community Chest, and taxes. Taxes are calculated on the basis of 10% of the gross salary minus 1% for each dependent. Adjust the records for accumulated salary and taxes. Use the updated records of part (A).

Employee ID	Hours worked	No. depend.
1064	69	
432	80	3
921	82	
826	78	
946	85	2

Figure P7.2-1*a*

Produce as output the employee's identification number, gross salary, amount deducted for bonds, Community Chest, and taxes, and the net salary.

(C) Management requests data on the average employee. Obtain this information with a program for calculating and producing as output the averages for:

(1) year employed
(2) year of birth
(3) number of dependents
(4) investment in bonds
(5) contributions
(6) salary rate per hour
(7) number of hours worked

Dress up your output so that management will understand and will be pleased with your report.

PROBLEM 7.2-2   "Matching Partners"

An organization provides a service for matching couples for marriage, using a computer designed for solving engineering and scientific problems. Numbers 1 to 99 are assigned to the characteristics that are considered important in describing an individual for this purpose. These numbers permit storage and processing of the data on the computer.

A lady desiring marriage is given a standard questionnaire and marks the characteristics that best describe herself. The questionnaire, illustrated in Figure P7.2-2, shows two of the ten characteristic groups. The marked characteristics are for a blond, 5 feet, 3 inches in height, and

Color of hair
    (1) black __
    (2) brown __
    (3) blond $\times$
Height
    (4) 4 feet, 9 inches to 5 feet   __
    (5) 5 feet, $\frac{1}{2}$ inch to 5 feet, 3 inches $\times$
    (6) 5 feet, $3\frac{1}{2}$ inches to 5 feet, 6 inches __
    (7) 5 feet, $6\frac{1}{2}$ inches to 5 feet, 9 inches __
    (8) 5 feet, $9\frac{1}{2}$ inches to 6 feet   __
    (9) 6 feet, $\frac{1}{2}$ inch to 6 feet, 3 inches   __
    etc.

Figure P7.2-2

the characteristic numbers are 3 and 5. Each lady completing a questionnaire is assigned an identification number which is punched on a card followed by her characteristic numbers, LS, as shown in Figure P7.2-2a. Note that the numbers are not punched in the order given on the questionnaire.

A gentleman wishing to find a mate is given the same standard questionnaire and marks those characteristics which he desires in a mate. His identification, followed by the characteristic numbers GL, are also punched on a card and read into the computer. The computer compares the GL numbers with the LS numbers to find the lady with the most characteristics desired by the gentleman.

(A) Write a program to find a best matched couple. Punch cards with the data given in Figure P7.2-2a with a single line of data per card, and store the characteristic numbers, LS, as a 2-dimensional array. Also, for input, assume the gentleman's identification number is 200 and the characteristic numbers, GL, for the mate he would like are

$$87, 76, 49, 28, 2, 7, 51, 16, 33, 69$$

Punch out the identification and characteristic numbers of the best matched pair. Note the similarity of this problem and the problem of step 3 for obtaining a reduced list for a critical path analysis described by the program of Figure 5.5-20.

(B) Since a successful marriage is usually based on mutual satisfaction, a lady's likes and dislikes in a husband must also be considered in the matching operations. This can be arranged by providing the ladies with a second questionnaire for marking the characteristics they desire a husband to have. The characteristics selected by the five ladies of Figure P7.2-2a are identified by the numbers, LG, of Figure P7.2-2b.

It is also required that a gentleman complete a second questionnaire on which he marks the characteristics that best describe himself. We will assume that the gentleman identified by the number 200 in part (A) is described by the characteristic numbers, GS,

$$20, 66, 79, 6, 53, 1, 35, 41, 84, 17$$

Ladies' ID	Characteristic nos., LS
106	3, 5, 15, 21, 36, 41, 56, 69, 78, 92
109	21, 47, 33, 4, 3, 16, 88, 76, 64, 51
104	2, 57, 28, 31, 49, 68, 76, 91, 87, 7
121	96, 84, 62, 79, 52, 1, 9, 41, 39, 19
163	64, 21, 3, 48, 7, 30, 50, 71, 86, 62

Figure P7.2-2a

Ladies' ID	Characteristic nos., LG
106	3, 8, 22, 39, 48, 62, 71, 89, 94, 16
109	20, 41, 38, 6, 1, 17, 84, 65, 78, 53
104	2, 29, 54, 33, 49, 67, 95, 74, 9, 86
121	30, 41, 86, 72, 1, 61, 96, 8, 17, 29
163	26, 38, 49, 81, 54, 3, 68, 9, 79, 12

Figure P7.2-2b

Extend the program of part (A) to include this second search for a match to suit the lady's likes in a husband. A measure of mutual satisfaction is considered to be the sum of the number of matched characteristics resulting from both these searches of the same couples. The pair with the largest number of matched characteristics is best suited. Punch out the identification and characteristic numbers of the best matched pair.

(C) There are certain hereditary diseases that should be considered in matching operations in the interest of health of the next generation. It is very likely that children will have certain diseases if both parties in marriage have ancestors who have had these diseases. To consider these factors, a second type of questionnaire is introduced on which each of the two sexes mark the diseases of this type if they are known to exist in their ancestral records. The table of Figure P7.2-2c gives the identi-

Ladies' ID	Disease identification nos., LD
106	102, 105, 108
109	101, 107
104	103, 109
121	102, 104, 109, 107
163	103, 108

Figure P7.2-2c

fying numbers of the diseases for the five ladies of parts (A) and (B). The gentleman under consideration, No. 200, has marked the diseases numbered 103, 104

Extend the program of part (B) to include this third search. If there is a match of the diseases for a couple, marriage cannot be accepted. Obtain as output the best matched pair as a result of these three searches.

CHAPTER 8.

What Goes on Inside Computers

8.1 PERSPECTIVE

Chapter 1, in which the Information Machine was introduced, showed several diagrams about operations that go on inside the computer, and, in particular, discussed the operation of translating from a FORTRAN language source program into a machine language or object program. Since then, however, we have been treating the computer as though it were a FORTRAN machine, and except for occasional phrases like "error comments at execution time" have almost completely ignored its inner working.

It is quite possible to become a good programmer or other user of computing machines with no more detailed knowledge of its internal operations than this. Nevertheless, to understand just what a computer is, how it can possibly do the things it does, and what its best role is, there is some value in learning a bit more of how it works and what it is made of.

On the subject of how it works, many people already know that a computer works with binary numbers, and even in primary school many presentations of the "new mathematics" make reference to this fact. In this chapter we are going to see in somewhat more detail what the binary number system is, how the computer makes use of it, and just what are some of the internal operations that go on inside the computer. Not only will this help our understanding and appreciation of computers; we will find the investigation intriguing, fascinating, and even fun.

8.2 NUMBER REPRESENTATION

We shall start with a point that should be thoroughly clarified before getting any further into either binary numbers or Boolean algebra: why do computers use binary numbers in the first place?

Why binary?

It should probably be stated at the outset that computers could be built to perform arithmetic operations directly with ordinary decimal numbers. We could design and build circuits that range between 0 and 9, that could be made to distinguish between, for instance, a 4 and a 5, without having to encode the 4 or the 5 or represent them in terms of any more basic set of numbers. But because a computer fundamentally does not have ten fingers to count on, such a number base is artificial to the electronic device, and would be inherently far less reliable.

Consider for a moment the general relation between the input and the output of a large class of electronic amplifier devices, as shown in Figure 8.2-1. Such a relationship, often called by the engineer the "transfer function," is representative of either a vacuum tube or a transistor. It shows in general that, if the input is very small (or negative) there is no output at all—the device is "cut off." As the input increases, the output begins to rise slowly, then more rapidly. Over a considerable range the input-output curve can be made to be quite a straight line, but then eventually conditions are reached such that further increase in input results in very little more output, and finally the curve levels off completely. The device is then said to be "saturated."

Now a great deal of attention has been paid to building circuits that exploit this straight-line region. High-fidelity amplifiers, for instance, are valuable only in so far as they are "linear," to within hundredths or even thousandths of 1%. A VTVM (vacuum tube voltmeter) consists of circuits whereby an electric voltage applied to its input terminals causes a pointer to move across its output scale in direct and linear proportion to the magnitude of the input voltage. On such a scale the difference between 6.7 and 8.2 volts is clearly distinguished; not only units but tenths and sometimes hundredths can be accurately read.

Surely it would be possible to design computer circuits that would operate this accurately, eliminating the necessity for counting by ones and zeros. True. But not for long.

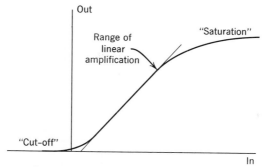

Figure 8.2-1 General input-output relation.

An overlooked item on the VTVM is the "zero adjust" knob, or "calibrate" knob, or whatever it may be called. Such a calibrating adjustment is necessary because these circuits, although producing accurately repeatable results over a short period of time, drift very noticeably over longer periods of time, varying with age, temperature, humidity, and other factors, and often perform very differently when one tube or transistor is replaced by another. Similar fluctuations in audio amplifiers are masked by the operation of the well-known "volume control," which performs these adjustments while providing the user with an even more important measure of control to compensate for variations in type of program, noise level, and desired loudness.

Consider what would happen if a computer circuit, initially properly calibrated to produce an output of, say, 8.2 in response to a certain input, were to drift by as little as 15%. Its "gain" would be reduced as shown in Figure 8.2-3*a*. The same input would produce an output which would be read as 6.7. Even if we were expecting this circuit to provide us with only a single digit of the answer, if that digit is part of a decimal number we would still be reading it as a 7 instead of an 8. Since com-

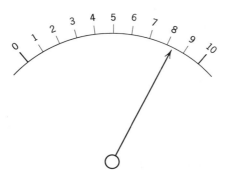

Figure 8.2-2 Linear voltage scale.

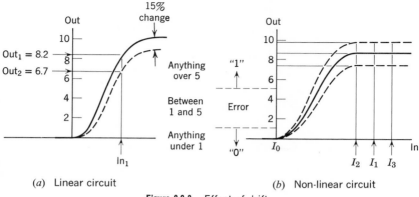

(a) Linear circuit   (b) Non-linear circuit

Figure 8.2-3   Effect of drift.

puters are supposed to be able to perform calculations accurately to 8 (and often more) significant figures, an error of 1 in the *most significant digit* is certainly far too great to tolerate.

Within a computer, there may be many *thousands* of such amplifying circuits, each of which is required to perform accurately for operation after operation, reaching up into the billions, and spanning many hours and even days of uninterrupted calculations. In operating this computer, it is obviously impossible to stop the machine to adjust the calibration of each of these thousands of circuits every several minutes to maintain linear response. What is needed is a type of circuit that will go on giving the same output to a given input *regardless of change in gain!*

Figure 8.2-3b shows how this seemingly impossible performance can be achieved. We shall stop trying to ask the circuit to distinguish among the ten different values which 1 digit may take on, and ask it instead to distinguish only between two possible conditions: either the input is sufficiently large, say I_1, to drive the circuit into saturation, producing an output called "On"; or it is essentially zero, as at I_0, producing an output called "Off." In this way we need merely build the circuit to classify anything over say 5 as an "On" response, and call it "1"; and anything under say 1 as "Off," and call it "0." This is easy to do, electronically. It permits, furthermore, not only an even greater fluctuation in the gain of the circuit, as shown by the three curves of Figure 8.2-3b, but even a considerable variation in the magnitude of the input itself, such as from I_2 to I_3, to be still recorded as a "1," and transmitted to the following stage of operations as such.

What happens if the circuit does change so greatly, or the input signal is so far off, that the output falls below the threshold we have chosen as the minimum necessary to produce a "1"? In this case the circuit can very easily be rigged to give a warning, to indicate that some unit in the computer is not operating reliably, and computation can then be halted while the maintenance crew tracks down the grossly defective circuit and replaces it with a good one.

In this way we can design circuits that will produce a consistent, reliable response over astonishingly large ranges of variation not only in the behavior of the circuit, but in the input signals that come into the circuit as well. We can therefore expect that once checked out and adjusted, the thousands of circuits inside the computer will go on giving reliable results for hundreds and thousands of hours, confident in the knowledge that if a circuit does begin to fail, automatic checking circuits will warn us and stop the machine.

All this, of course, is predicated on the assumption that binary behavior is enough, that it can express all we need to know, and do the manipulating and operating we need to accomplish, in terms of "Ons" and "Offs," of ones and zeros. Is this true? Are binary numbers enough to handle the entire range of numerical information processing? The answer is an unqualified "yes."

What Is Binary?

The conventional decimal number system with which we are so familiar has a base or radix of 10, by which we mean that there are 10 different and distinct symbols. We can count from 0 to 9, as in the first column of Figure 8.2-4, using a different symbol to represent each total value of the count along the way. What happens when we run out of symbols? When we add 1 to 9, we represent the resulting number by putting a 1 in the next position to the left, which means that we have one *full set* of digits, and a 0 in the units position. Although we have no single symbol for this number, we do have a name for it, for it equals the value of the radix itself—"ten." One more added to this produces the number represented by 11—meaning, 1 full set of digits plus 1 over. By the same token, when we add 1 to 19, we have to represent the resulting number by 20—2 full sets and none left over. Not until we have counted 9 full sets and 9 over do we fill the information-representing capacity of these 2 positions; then when we want to count 1 more, we must show the number as a 1 in the third position over, standing *for 1 full set of sets.*

This use of the different positions in which a digit may appear to mean different things is in general called "positional notation"; its special use here to denote sets of the preceding position, and hence increasing powers of the radix, has contributed substantially to the power of mathematics both as a concept and as a tool.

	Decimal	Unary	Binary
Base (radix)	1 0	1	2
No. of different symbols	1 0	1	2
Value represented by digit in that position	1000 100 10 1		64 32 16 8 4 2 1
Power of radix represented by digit in that position	3 2 1 0		6 5 4 3 2 1 0

Numbers	Decimal	Unary	Binary
	0		0
	1	'	1
	2	''	1 0
	3	'''	1 1
	4	''''	1 0 0
	5	'''''	1 0 1
	6	''''' '	1 1 0
	7	''''' ''	1 1 1
	8	''''' '''	1 0 0 0
	9	''''' ''''	1 0 0 1
	1 0	''''' '''''	1 0 1 0
	1 1	''''' ''''' '	1 0 1 1
	.		.
	1 5	''''' ''''' '''''	1 1 1 1
	1 6	''''' ''''' ''''' '	1 0 0 0 0
	.		.
	1 9		1 0 0 1 1
	2 0		1 0 1 0 0
	.		.
	9 9		1 1 0 0 0 1 1
	1 0 0		1 1 0 0 1 0 0

Figure 8.2-4   Positional notation (with significance of digit in each position for different radices).

Now let us compare this counting process as we have reviewed it for the familiar decimal numbers, with the exactly similar procedure to be followed if we are counting in another number system. Specifically, let us learn to count in binary.

The binary number system is so named, of course, because its radix is 2; it has just two distinct symbols. With these symbols we can indicate the complete absence of anything, the null set, which is called "zero," and the presence of a single unit, the quantity called "one." It is therefore convenient to use for the two symbols the same symbols that represent these quantities in decimal or other systems: 0 and 1. As the right-hand column of Figure 8.2-4 shows, however, when we wish to add one more to 1, we have already exhausted our set of symbols, so this quantity must be represented with a 1 in the second position, denoting exactly as before *1 full set*. The 0 in the first position merely shows that there are no other units remaining.

This quantity 10 is called "two" in the binary system, being the name of the radix. In fact, it is worth convincing yourself that in *any* radix system, the quantity 10 represents the number of different symbols employed, and hence the radix itself!

Let us continue our counting. We can add one more to 10 with no difficulty, getting 11, the binary representation of 3. However, at the very next step we need another position, since when one more is added to 11, we need a 0 in the right position, denoting a full set, and to increase the count in the second position, the number of sets, also requires a 0 plus a 1 in the third position. Therefore the number 4 must be written 100, which can be read "1 full set of sets of binary symbols, with none over."

The same procedure can be followed indefinitely, and any total count that can be recorded with decimal numbers can also be expressed with binary. It is quite true that we use up positions at a much faster rate, for since each digit contains less information, more of them are required to express a given amount of information. It can be shown that the ratio of the number of binary digits required to express a given number to the number of decimal digits for the same number is given by the ratio of the logarithms of their radices:

$$R = \frac{\log 10}{\log 2} = 3.3219$$

However, for our purposes it is perhaps worth remembering simply that it takes about $\frac{1}{3}$ as many decimal digits as binary ones.

The binary digit is given a special name, taken from the first two and last letters (or first and last two?): the *bit*. It is the fundamental unit of information; it distinguishes between the two smallest numbers of known quantities; it represents the most primitive logical choice, the dichotomy.

Before leaving Figure 8.2-4, notice carefully the two rows of headings that indicate the significance of the various digit positions. In both the decimal and the binary cases it can be seen that they represent successive powers of the radix. With decimal numbers we speak of the units-digit, the tens-digit, the hundreds, thousands, and so forth. In the binary case we see that, since the significance of the positions goes up by powers of 2, a 1 in successive columns has the value: 1, 2, 4, 8, 16, 32 . . . . This is our clue to simple conversion from one number system to the other.

Conversion

Converting from binary to decimal follows directly from the principle of positional notation. Just as the decimal number

$$627_{10} \text{ means } \quad 6 \times 10^2 + 2 \times 10^1 + 7 \times 10^0$$
$$= 6 \times 100 + 2 \times 10 + 7 \times 1$$

a binary number like

$$10110_2 \text{ means } \quad 1 \times 2^4 + 0 \times 2^3 + 1 \times 2^2 + 1 \times 2^1 + 0 \times 2^0$$
$$= 1 \times 16 + 0 \times 8 + 1 \times 4 + 1 \times 2 + 0 \times 1$$
$$= \quad 16 \quad + \quad 4 + \quad 2$$
$$= 22_{10}$$

For the reverse conversion, a different scheme is conceptually just about as clear, and much simpler to carry out (at least manually). Since we have to keep in mind the decimal equivalent of the first several powers of 2 in order to go from binary to decimal by the method illustrated above, we can use those same powers of 2 to go backward for the reverse conversion from decimal to binary.

To convert, for instance, 27_{10} to binary, we first examine the given number and determine the largest power of 2 contained in it. Since this is $2^4 = 16$, we carry out the following steps

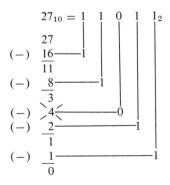

Other methods usually turn out to be more efficient for actual machine conversion (calculation of the conversion by the computing

machine itself), but the two shown here are straightforward enough for manual conversion of small numbers, and are quite close to the meanings inherent in the number representations themselves.

Codes

There is one compromise between decimal and binary representation that should be mentioned. No, we do not mean base 6, but a compromise in the sense that binary numbers are sometimes used to represent separately each decimal digit in a number. For instance, whereas we have seen that the binary representation of 27_{10} is 11011_2, the BCD (which stands for binary-coded decimal) representation of 27_{10} would be 0010 0111. Since it takes 4 bits to represent some decimal digits (which ones?), the BCD scheme always allows 4 bits for each digit, filling in zeros when necessary. In this example, the binary code for the 2 is 0010, and for the 7, 0111. Hence

$$27_{10} = 0010\ 0111_{BCD} = 11011_2$$

Note that the BCD scheme takes more bits than the pure binary representation. This is because it is more wasteful; it throws away a significant portion of its information-representing capacity. With 4 bits we could, of course, count up to 15; when used in this way we never count beyond 9. Therefore $\frac{6}{16}$ of the information capacity of each group of 4 bits is never used. This disadvantage is often felt to be outweighed, however, by the advantage of being able to perform decimal arithmetic directly. This is particularly important when performing many classes of financial operations, such as accounting, payroll, and tax calculations, especially when quantities are rounded off to the nearest cent.

A further advantage to the programmer of working with decimal machines, (binary machines which use binary-coded decimal representations of decimal numbers) is the fact that at every intermediate step all numbers are in decimal digit form, and when the programmer is trying to debug or trace a program that is still not operating as he wishes, there is tremendous advantage to him in being able to recognize the numbers which are the intermediate results, as well as the final answers.

In addition to the extra bits used for this representation of decimal digits, still other bits are sometimes employed beyond the number which would be necessary for pure binary representation of numerical values. On one hand, additional information of a binary nature is sometimes appended to the value of the number: the starting and ending point of the string of bits representing the number; the sign of the number; the sign (in a floating-point number) of the exponent; and so forth. In machines which work with true binary representation of numbers, registers and storage devices are designed to hold strings of bits of a fixed length (two common lengths are 36 and 48 in the IBM and CDC computers, respectively). This string of bits which may represent either a number or an instruction is commonly called a "word." In fixed-word-length machines, at least one of the bits is usually designated to be its sign (two are needed when the word represents a floating-point number). For operations that are mostly numerical, and floating-point numerical at that, such use of a fixed word length can lead to very efficient operation.

On the other hand, many of the data-processing type of operations frequently deal with a wide variety of kinds of information: alphabetic information such as names, short integer records such as date or class, longer integer records such as policy number or social security number, and noninteger numbers with wide ranges such as prices, percentages, and total costs. For the efficient storage and manipulation of such information, it is convenient to be able to store words of various lengths, and to mark the end of such a word by a special "flag" or "record mark." In variable-word-length machines, it is common to allow an extra bit to be associated with each decimal digit, which can do double (and sometimes multiple) duty to indicate either a sign or a flag.

In both classes of machines, the fixed and the variable word length, engineers sometimes employ still more bits for yet another function—checking the accuracy of the storage, transmission, and read-out of information. Just as in human language redundancy is constantly used to help insure the reliability of what is said or written, so in the binary coding of information, extra or redundant bits can be included which carry no new information themselves, but are dependent upon the rest of the message being sent in such a way that if a transmission error occurs, the redundant or check bits will no longer agree with the rest of the information. This condition can be detected, and suitable warning or precautionary measures taken.

Such check bits are often called "parity" bits, because they check the odd- or evenness of the number of 1's in the number. We will not go into detail here as to how this is done. For those interested, Caldwell* has a very readable treatment which discusses the design of codes that not only check but even correct for errors that may have occurred. For our purposes we will merely note that if such checking is going to be done, it will cost additional bits. Whether enough additional bits are included to check each decimal digit, each group of digits, each entire word, or not at all, varies widely with the design of the machine. CDC machines

* Samuel H. Caldwell, *Switching Circuits and Logical Design,* John Wiley and Sons, New York, 1958, Chapter 10.

and the older binary IBM machines preserve no extra spaces. Most variable-word-length machines (which are often business oriented) employ a scheme like that of the IBM 1620, which uses 6 bits for every decimal digit: 4 for the BCD representation of the digit itself, 1 for a flag or sign bit, and 1 for a check bit as described above. It is hard to see any particular trend in the use of check bits winning out; in fact many of the newer class of machines are designed to be so versatile that the internal coding can be varied from problem to problem.

8.3   NUMBER MANIPULATION IN BINARY

Having established the rule for the representation of integer values in the binary number system, and at least one reliable method for converting from decimal to binary and back again, let us now establish the rules that govern operations within the binary system itself. To be specific, let us learn how to do simple binary arithmetic.

Addition

The addition table in binary arithmetic is very simple (Figure 8.3-1a).

Note that two or more 1's produce a carry, but that when 2 numbers are being added, the maximum number of 1's that ever needs to be combined is 3—2 digits and a carry.

Multiplication

The multiplication table (Figure 8.3-2a) is still simpler—anything times 0 is 0; anything times 1 is itself.

Subtraction

The subtraction table (Figure 8.3-3a) shows that the same "units" result obtains as in addition, and also that, like the carry in addition, a "borrow" is required for only one combination of the inputs.

To subtract 1 from zero in any one column, it is necessary to borrow from the next column to the left, and add to the minuend in the

+	0	1
0	0	1
1	1	10

$$\begin{array}{rcl} {}^{\prime}1\ {}^{\prime}1\ 1\ 0 &=& 14_{10} \\ (+)\quad 1\ 0\ 1\ 1 &=& 11_{10} \\ \hline 1\ 1\ 0\ 0\ 1 &=& 25_{10} \end{array}$$

(a) Addition table   (b) Addition example

Figure 8.3-1   Binary addition.

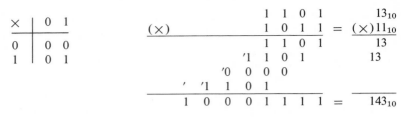

×	0	1
0	0	0
1	0	1

$$
\begin{array}{r}
1\ \ 1\ \ 0\ \ 1 \quad\quad 13_{10} \\
(\times) \quad\quad 1\ \ 0\ \ 1\ \ 1 = (\times)11_{10} \\
\hline
1\ \ 1\ \ 0\ \ 1 \quad\quad 13 \\
'1\ \ 1\ \ 0\ \ 1 \quad\quad 13 \\
'0\ \ 0\ \ 0\ \ 0 \\
'\quad '1\ \ 1\ \ 0\ \ 1 \\
\hline
1\ \ 0\ \ 0\ \ 0\ \ 1\ \ 1\ \ 1\ \ 1 = \quad 143_{10}
\end{array}
$$

(*a*) Multiplication table   (*b*) Multiplication example

Figure 8.3-2   Binary multiplication.

original column. The subtraction can then be performed. However, the transaction must be kept "honest" by paying back the borrow. This can be done in either of two ways. The minuend bit in the left column can be decreased by 1, or the corresponding subtrahend bit increased by 1. Bookeeping, mechanical operations, and carry propagation appear to be simpler in the latter scheme; a typical subtraction with this borrow operation indicated is shown in Figure 8.3-3*b*.

−	0	1	(Minuend)
0	0	1	
1	*1	0	

(Subtrahend)

$$
\begin{array}{r}
1\ \ 1\ \ 0\ \ 1 = 13_{10} \\
(-)\ \ 1\ \ '0\ \ 1\ \ 1 = 11_{10} \\
\hline
0\ \ 0\ \ 1\ \ 0 = 2_{10}
\end{array}
$$

* Means 1 with a borrow

(*a*) Subtraction table   (*b*) Subtraction example with borrow

Figure 8.3-3   Binary subtraction.

If the subtrahend is actually larger than the minuend, the last borrow operation will be incomplete, and will show as a 1 in the next position to the left. If we are working with *n*-bit numbers, we will get a 1 in the $(n + 1)$ st position. This is actually the first of an indefinite string of 1's and is to be interpreted as a signal that the result is really the complement of the number we want, and must be recomplemented to be in the proper form. This is accomplished by taking the number 2^n and subtracting our subtraction result (without the last borrow) from this number, thus:

$$
\begin{array}{r}
1\ \ 0\ \ 1\ \ 1 \\
(-)\ \ '\ \ '1\ \ 1\ \ 0\ \ 1 \\
\hline
1\ \ 1\ \ 1\ \ 1\ \ 0 = \ -
\end{array}
\qquad
\begin{array}{r}
1\ \ \ 0\ \ 0\ \ 0\ \ 0 \\
1\ \ 1\ \ 1\ \ 0\ \ (-) \\
\hline
0\ \ 0\ \ 1\ \ 0
\end{array}
$$

The fact that this subtraction had to be carried out is an indication that the magnitude of the minuend was too small, and the result should have the opposite sign.

On the other hand, subtracting 2 numbers of initially different signs results in a number of larger absolute magnitude than either, and may yield a carry bit:

$$
\begin{array}{rcccccc}
+ & ' & '1 & '1 & '0 & 1 \\
(-) & - & & 1 & 0 & 1 & 1 \\
\hline
+ & 1 & & 1 & 0 & 0 & 0 \\
\end{array}
$$

In this case, the presence of a 1 in the $(n + 1)$ st position has a very different meaning. How do we tell which it means? Analysis shows that, of the eight possible cases of the algebraic addition-subtraction operation

$$\pm A(\pm) \pm B$$

we actually do arithmetic addition in 4 and subtraction in 4. The rule for interpreting the overflow-underflow bit turns out to be:

If actual addition takes place, the presence of a 1 means a carry beyond the capacity of the result register—often called "overflow." In the absence of a 1 the number is correct. In any case, the sign of A is the sign of the result.

If actual subtraction takes place, the presence of a 1 means a borrow beyond the capacity of the numbers involved—sometimes called "underflow." The sign of operand A is the *incorrect* sign for the result; take the complement of the result and change sign. The absence of a 1 means the assumed sign and the difference obtained are both correct.

Complements

An alternate approach to handling minus signs, both as applied to operations and to numbers, is to use complementation whenever a minus sign occurs.

Even in decimal arithmetic, cases occur in which it is easier to convert a negative number into a complement and add than to perform subtraction directly. For instance, a negative logarithm $(-.10236)$ is usually handled by adding and subtracting 10, thus

$$
\begin{array}{rccccccccc}
1 & 0. & 0 & 0 & 0 & 0 & 0 & - & 1 & 0 \\
(+) & -. & 1 & 0 & 2 & 3 & 6 & & & \\
\hline
9. & 8 & 9 & 7 & 6 & 4 & - & 1 & 0 \\
\end{array}
$$

In binary arithmetic, subtraction can similarly be performed by a method which converts the subtrahend into its complement and then adds; thus to find

$$
\begin{array}{rcccc}
& 1 & 1 & 0 & 1 \\
(-) & 1 & 0 & 1 & 1 \\
\end{array}
$$

we complement the subtrahend

$$
\begin{array}{rcccc}
 & 1 & 0 & 0 & 0 & 0 \\
(-) & & 1 & 0 & 1 & 1 \\
\hline
 & & 0 & 1 & 0 & 1
\end{array}
$$

and add

$$
\begin{array}{rcccc}
' & '1 & 1 & '0 & 1 \\
(+) & 0 & 1 & 0 & 1 \\
\hline
1 & 0 & 0 & 1 & 0
\end{array}
$$

But since $A + (2^n - B) = A - B + 2^n$, it is necessary to subtract that extra 1 in the (2^n)th column from the result to get the correct difference

$$
\begin{array}{rccccc}
 & 1 & 0 & 0 & 1 & 0 \\
(-) & 1 & & & & \\
\hline
 & & 0 & 0 & 1 & 0
\end{array}
$$

The entire process is summarized in Figure 8.3-4, showing in parallel columns corresponding operations in the decimal and the binary system.

Division

Division is customarily performed on desk calculators by subtracting the divisor successively from the dividend until a negative difference develops, adding it back in once, and shifting the divisor. To illustrate with binary numbers, an example might take the form shown in Figure 8.3-5. The quotient is correct to 6 binary digits (2 decimal digits), but 11 steps have been required to generate these 6 bits. This is undesirable in any high-speed machine, and particularly unacceptable in synchronized operations.

		Binary					*Decimal*	
	1 1 0 1		Minuend				1 3	
(−)	1 0 1 1		Subtrahend		(−)		1 1	
1	0 0 0 0	2^n		10^n	1	0 0		
(−)	1 0 1 1				(−)	1 1		
	0 1 0 1	Complement of subtrahend				8 9		
	1 1 0 1	Original minuend				1 3		
(+)	0 1 0 1	Complement of subtrahend		(+)	8 9			
1	0 0 1 0				1	0 2		
(−) 1		2^n		10^n	(−) 1			
	0 0 1 0	Correct difference				0 2		

Figure 8.3-4   Subtraction by complements.

Quotient
bits

Problem: $\dfrac{1101}{1011} = ?$

	1101				
	1011	—			Start by subtracting
1.	+0010				Once
	1011				Try again (subtract minuend from subtrahend)
	−1001				Not twice (in binary, never twice)
	1011	+			Add it back in again
	+0010				
	0101	1	—		Shift the subtrahend, subtract
.0	−0011	1			Not even once
	0101	1	+		Back up again
	+0010	0			
	0010	11	—		Shift again, subtract
.00	−0000	11			Still no
	0010	11			Back up
	+0010	00			
	0001	011	—		Shift once more, subtract
.001	+0000	101			Yes
	0000	1011	—		Shift, subtract
.0000	−0000	0001			No
	0000	1011	+		Back up
	+0000	1010			
	0000	0101	1	—	Shift, subtract
.00001	+0000	0100	1		Yes

$\dfrac{.00001}{1.00101} = 1.16$

Figure 8.3-5 Binary division—the hard way.

The unproductive operations can be avoided by the following scheme. Define the dividend as R_0 (the remainder after zero operations), and the divisor as D. After subtracting once, the remainder is R_1, etc. The recursion formula for these quantities is

$$R_1 = R_0 \quad - \qquad D \quad \text{(subtract)}$$
$$R_2 = R_1 \quad - 2^{-1} \; D \quad \text{(shift, subtract)}$$
$$R_n = R_{n-1} - 2^{-(n-1)}D \quad \text{(shift, subtract)}$$

In this notation, the procedure just illustrated can be written

If R_n is $+$, go ahead: $\quad R_{n+1} = R_n \quad - 2^{-n} \quad D$ (8.3-1)

If R_n is $-$, back up: $\quad R_{n-1} = R_n \quad + 2^{-(n-1)} \; D$ (8.3-2)

$$R_{n+1} = R_{n-1} - 2^{-n} \quad D \qquad (8.3\text{-}3)$$
$$= R_n \quad + 2^{-(n-1)} \; D - 2^{-n}D \qquad (8.3\text{-}4)$$
$$= R_n \quad + 2^{-n}(2D - D = D) \qquad (8.3\text{-}5)$$
$$= R_n \quad + 2^{-n} \quad D \qquad (8.3\text{-}6)$$

By comparing equations (8.3-1) and (8.3-6), the following rule can be formulated

Depending on whether R_n is $\pm$, form: $R_{n+1} = R_n \mp 2^{-n}D$

In this method, called "nonrestoring division," only one step is needed to generate each bit.

To illustrate, the same example now looks like Figure 8.3-6. Six steps, 6 bits. To get n bits, n steps.

The procedure just illustrated may be regarded as the basic procedure. Many others are used in various machines, employing straight numbers, complements of various kinds, and mixtures of the two. Those interested in reading further will find a much more complete treatment in Chu.*

Floating-Point Arithmetic

Of increasing importance in computer calculations is the system known as "floating-point" operation. Even in ordinary decimal computation, such as with a slide rule, it is often desirable to express each number as a given sequence of significant digits, and an appropriate power of ten—6.29×10^3. Borrowing (imprecisely) from logarithm terminology, the exponent is frequently called the "mantissa" and the significant figures, the "characteristic." Standard practice for expressing decimal numbers in "floating" form is to write the decimal point immediately to the right of the most significant digit; in machines, however, it

```
                         1101
                         1011   —
        1.              +0010
                         0101   1    —
        .0              −0011   1
                         0010   11   +
        .00             −0000   11
                         0001   011  +
        .001            +0000   101
                         0000   1011 —
        .0000           −0000   0001
                         0000   01011 +
        .00001          +0000   01001
        ‾‾‾‾‾‾
        1.00101
```

Figure 8.3-6   Nonrestoring binary division.

* Yaohan Chu, *Digital Computer Design Fundamentals,* McGraw-Hill, New York, 1962, (pp. 35–43).

is frequently simpler to assume the binary point at the extreme left. In this notation all numbers will range in absolute value between $\frac{1}{2}$ and 1 (except zero); for example, 629 becomes

$$.629 \times 10^3 = .1100010010 \times 2^{13}$$

or expressing the exponent in binary

$$= .1100010010 \times 2^{1101}.$$

Floating-Point Addition

If exponents agree, addition is simple.

$$
\begin{array}{rl}
1101 = & .1101 \times 2^{100} \\
(+) \quad 1011 = & .1011 \times 2^{100} \\
\hline
& 1.1000 \times 2^{100}
\end{array}
\qquad
\begin{array}{rl}
1.3 \times 10^1 = & 13 \\
(+) \quad 1.1 \times 10^1 = & 11 \\
\hline
\end{array}
$$

$$
\text{or} \quad 11000 = \quad .1100 \times 2^{101}
\qquad\qquad
2.4 \times 10^1 = 24
$$

If exponents do not agree, the number with the algebraically smaller mantissa (exponent) must have its characteristic (significant figures) shifted to the right. The number of places shifted is equal to the difference between exponents. Not until the numbers have been brought in line as a result of shifting can addition actually be performed.

$$
\begin{array}{rl}
& .10001111 \times 2^{1000=8} \\
(+) \quad & .10101000 \times 2^{0101=5}
\end{array}
\qquad
\begin{array}{l}
1.43 \times 10^2 \\
2.1 \quad \times 10^1
\end{array}
$$

$$
\begin{array}{rl}
& .10001111 \times 2^{1000} \\
(+) \quad & .00010101 \times 2^{1000} \\
\hline
& .10100100 \times 2^{1000}
\end{array}
\qquad
\begin{array}{l}
1.43 \times 10^2 \\
.21 \times 10^2 \\
\hline
1.64 \times 10^2
\end{array}
$$

$$
= \quad .64 \times 256 = 164
$$

Floating-Point Multiplication

Multiplication poses no problem. The 2 sets of significant figures are multiplied together, and the new exponent is the algebraic sum of the two original exponents.

$$
\begin{array}{rl}
& .1101 \times 2^{0100} = \\
(\times) \quad & .1011 \times 2^{0100} = \\
\hline
& 1101 \qquad 1000 \\
& 1101 \\
& 0000 \\
& 1101 \\
\hline
& .10001111 \times 2^{1000} =
\end{array}
\qquad
\begin{array}{l}
1.3 \times 10^1 \\
1.1 \times 10^1 \\
\hline
13 \qquad 2 \\
1\,3 \\
\hline
1.43 \times 10^2
\end{array}
$$

$$.10001111 \times 2^{1000} = 1.43 \times 10^2$$
$$\underline{(\times) \quad .10101000 \times 2^{0101} = 2.1 \ \times 10^1}$$

10001111	1101	143	3
10001111		2 86	
10001111			

$$.0101110111011000 \times 2^{1101}$$

$$.10111011 \qquad \times 2^{1100} \doteq 3.003 \times 10^3$$
$$(\text{check: } .73 \times 4096 \doteq 3000)$$

Mechanizing the Operations

If these arithmetic operations are going to be mechanized (performed by a machine), several modifications should be made.

(1) We should minimize the number of different operations to be performed, so that, for instance, multiplication by an n-bit number requires, ideally, only the repetition of a basic set of operation n times.

(2) Instead of accumulating long lists of numbers to be added (as in manual multiplication), we should restrict the number of operands to be added at any one time to 2, by scheduling an addition as soon as a pair of numbers is ready to be added.

(3) Each number must be held in a register, usually of fixed length,

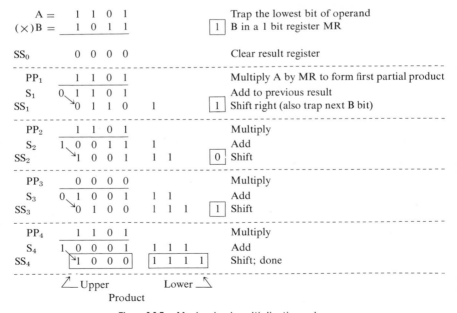

Figure 8.3-7   Mechanized multiplication scheme.

so we should design operations and intermediate results in terms of filling these registers exactly. When working with n-bit numbers, we should use n-bit registers, although they can usually detect and temporarily store an overflow or underflow bit. If more than n bits are needed, for example, to store the $2n$-bit product of 2 n-bit numbers, two registers will be needed.

(4) These registers, however, have the capability of shifting their contents, usually one bit at a time, in either direction. This, it turns out, is needed in all four of the basic arithmetic operations.

To see how these principles influence the design of arithmetic operations, we present in Figure 8.3-7 a revised scheme for multiplying two 4-bit numbers in a fashion which lends itself excellently to mechanization, since we can accomplish the multiplication shown earlier by a four-fold repetition of the basic set of three operations: multiply, add to previous sum, and shift right.

8.4   VARIABLE MANIPULATION IN BINARY (BOOLEAN ALGEBRA)

It would not be at all difficult to design circuitry to process binary numbers, if these numbers were all constants—that is, if the numbers were always fixed and the same, and therefore known in advance. However, problems of far greater interest in real life can be handled in any mathematics as the mathematics progresses from the fixed to the variable. This, of course, is the difference between *arithmetic* and *algebra;* in the former, symbols stand for fixed numbers, each symbol always representing the same number; in the latter, the symbol represents a variable, which may take one or another of many different values.

As long ago as 1854, in England, George Boole published *An Investigation of the Laws of Thought**, in which he developed a two-valued algebra for application to statements considered to be either "true" or "false." This approach was found both interesting and successful in certain restricted mathematical areas, and came to be called "symbolic logic." Not until 1938, apparently, did anyone try applying this to electric circuits. For his master's thesis at MIT, Claude Shannon showed the usefulness of this symbolic approach, and the paper he subsequently published, "A Symbolic Analysis of Relay and Switching Circuits,"† has become a modern scientific classic.

Many good presentations of the logical foundations and development of Boolean algebra now exist (see, for instance, Phister‡). For the pur-

---

* Reissued by Dover Publications, New York, 1954.
† *Trans. AIEE*, Vol. 57, pp. 713–723 (1938).
‡ Montgomery Phister, Jr., *Logical Design of Digital Computers*, John Wiley and Sons, New York, 1958.

pose of gaining a familiarity or even a facility with this algebra merely as a tool for the analysis and synthesis of what are called "switching" circuits, however, a much less rigorous approach will suffice.

Fundamental Concepts

We begin by choosing our two fundamental concepts:

(1) *A class of variables,* which we will here take to be the class of all 2-valued variables. The 2 values will be symbolized 0 and 1.

These variables can be made real by devices such as a manual switch, an electromagnetically operated switch (relay), or an electronically operated switch (flip-flop). Not only is observation simplified, but cascading and other interconnecting is made possible by connecting a source of potential to the device, so that the state of the variable is reflected in the voltage appearing at the output.

(2) *Three rules of combination* (besides the principles of logical procedure, significance of $=$, etc., which are taken for granted).

Note: In the following, certain references are made to diodes. A diode is a device which permits current to flow in one direction but not in the other (see Figure 8.4-2).

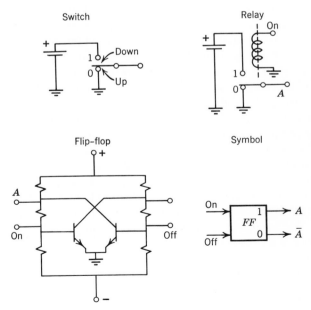

Figure 8.4-1 Two-state devices (storage of 1 bit).

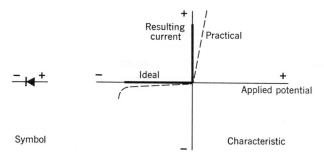

Figure 8.4-2   Diode.

(a) ⊕ Here, the operation OR, meaning the combination in such fashion that EITHER (or any one) of the inputs will yield an output. If $C = A + B$, as is shown in Figure 8.4-3, C will have the value 1 if A is 1 OR if B is 1 (or both—this is the *inclusive* OR). This operation can be realized by switches in parallel, diodes with common cathodes, etc.

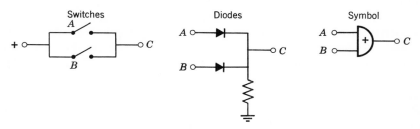

Figure 8.4-3   "OR" gates.

(b) ⊙ Here, the operation AND, meaning the combination in such fashion as to require BOTH (or all) of the inputs to yield an output. If $C = A \cdot B$, then C will have the value 1 if A is 1 AND if B is 1. The AND operation is realized by switches in series, diodes with common anodes, etc.

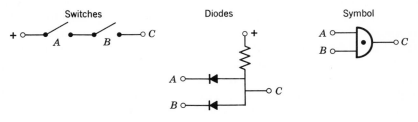

Figure 8.4-4   "AND" gates.

(c) $\ominus$ Here, the operation NOT, or negation, meaning the opposite value (in the Boolean sense, where only two possibilities are permitted) of that taken by the variable (or function) being negated. If $C = \overline{A}$, then C will have the value 1 if A is 0, and vice versa. This operation cannot be performed by diodes or other passive devices alone, but requires an active element (one which taps energy from an external source, such as a battery or other voltage supply).

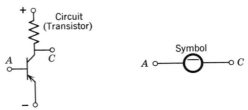

Figure 8.4-5   Negators.

It should be remarked, in passing, that a rigorous logical development will show one of these three to be dependent, in the sense that whichever two are chosen to be the fundamental concepts, the third can be derived from combinations of the other two. In practical circuitry, it is easy to show that, given devices which will generate the functions AND and NOT, combinations can be found which will generate the function OR; and, conversely, given devices which will generate the functions OR and NOT, combinations of these can be made to generate the function AND. As noted above, however, it is not possible with purely passive AND and OR gates to generate a NOT function.

Useful Relations

The operations of AND, OR, and NOT have been symbolized in many ways, some symbols being preferred by mathematicians to describe relationships in an important area called set theory, which has recently received much attention; others by those who specialize in symbolic logic; and still others by engineers interested in telephone and communication networks and in electronic computers. Since our primary interest is this last approach, we have chosen to make use of the symbols most commonly used in "switching theory": $\cdot$, $+$, and $^{\overline{}}$.

If a little care is observed to ensure that the Boolean significance of these symbols is not confused with their more common meanings, the convenience of their use and the nearly complete correspondence with the conventional rules of operation combine to make this the most useful and certainly the most widespread convention.

Let us see how well some of the common operations of continuous variable algebra carry over to the restricted operations of binary, discrete variable algebra. For one thing, what about the relationships between constants and variables?

In Boolean algebra, dealing as it does with variables which take on only a discrete set of values, and only two such values at that, there are only 2 constants, 0 and 1. Three of the four possible combinations of the constants and a variable shown in Figure 8.4-6 seem perfectly orthodox; the fourth will take a little explaining.

Think of each of these rules as descriptions of a set of electric switches. A switch having the value 1 is always closed—a short circuit; a switch having the value 0 is never closed—an open circuit. A switch having the value A is closed when the value of A is 1, and open when the value of A is 0.

Let us draw the circuit that corresponds to each of the 4 equations in Figure 8.4-6.

As was established in the definition of the OR operation, two switches in parallel perform the OR. In this case, it should be obvious that nothing is going to change the condition of the always open switch marked zero, so that the condition at C is dependent solely on the state of the switch A. In other words, A or NOTHING is A (Figure 8.4-7a).

It was similarly shown in defining the AND operation that two switches in series perform the AND. Since the short-circuited switch marked 1 is always closed, the condition at C, just as in the preceding case, is dependent solely upon the state of A. The requirements that both A be satisfied, and something which is always satisfied be satisfied, reduce merely to the condition of A (Figure 8.4-7b).

If C will be 1 only when it is simultaneously true both that A is a 1, and that a never satisfied condition is satisfied, it will be rare that the total condition is ever satisfied, regardless of what A may do (Figure 8.4-7c).

Here, for the first time, the conventional rules of algebraic combination do not carry over to Boolean algebra. It should not be hard, however, to figure out why. In the circuit shown here, there is little point in worrying whether switch A is closed or not, since there is always a

$$P_2$$
$$\text{(a)} \quad | \quad A + 0 = A$$
$$\text{(b)} \quad | \quad A \cdot 1 = A$$

$$T_3$$
$$\text{(a)} \quad | \quad A \cdot 0 = 0$$
$$\text{(b)} \quad | \quad A + 1 = 1$$

Figure 8.4-6   Operations with constants (using the notation of Figure 8.4-13).

(a)

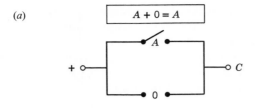

(b)

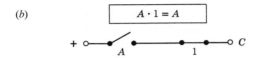

(c)

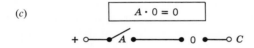

(d)

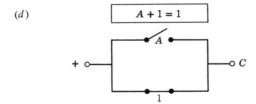

Figure 8.4-7   Circuits with constants.

closed path between the voltage source and the output terminal C along the bottom path, marked 1. In other words, if C is to be 1 whenever either A is a 1 or 1 is a 1, C will frequently be found to be 1. To paraphrase it still further, a gamble in which the uncertain alternative is always covered by a sure thing is not much of a gamble (Figure 8.4-7d).

In much the same way as we verified the rules for operations with constants, it should not be hard to convince ourselves that multiple switches that all operate together are no different from a single switch (in theory, at least), whether they are wired together in series or in parallel.

Drawing such series and parallel circuits will frequently help us visualize the significance of a statement in Boolean algebra, and enable

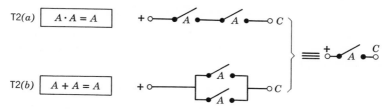

Figure 8.4-8 Multiple appearance of the same variable.

us to see the validity of a relationship that is not quite so obvious without the picture. For instance, if we symbolize the realization of T4(a) in Figure 8.4-13 by series and parallel switches, as in Figure 8.4-9, it is then easy to see that the only time the lower path can be effective in conducting current to C is when both A and B are closed (1). But if A is 1, then the upper path is closed, too. In fact, C is connected to the voltage source whenever A is 1, and B neither adds to nor subtracts from the effect of the rest of the circuit. The entire lower branch is superfluous, and the whole circuit produces exactly the same effect as the single switch A.

There are a few other conventional rules of operation in ordinary algebra, that it would be well to examine in Boolean algebra. To be specific, do the commutative and distributive laws apply? That is, is it true in Boolean algebra, as it is in ordinary, that we can interchange the sequence of the operands without changing the result?

$$A + B \stackrel{?}{=} B + A$$
$$A \cdot B \stackrel{?}{=} B \cdot A$$

Once again, consideration of the switching circuits such statements represent, should make the truth of these statements obvious, for, since the circuits are symmetric, a switch certainly does not care which input lead is applied to which terminal.

How about the distributive law? Can an OR operation, applied to a function consisting of the AND of two variables, be distributed to apply separately to the two variables?

T4(a) $\boxed{\quad A + A \cdot B = A \quad}$

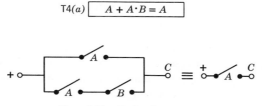

Figure 8.4-9 Redundant terms.

$$\text{P4}(a)\colon \quad A + (B \cdot C) \overset{?}{=} (A + B) \cdot (A + C)$$

or its counterpart: can an AND, applied to a function consisting of the OR of two variables, be distributed across the OR to apply separately to the two variables?

$$\text{P4}(b)\colon \quad A \cdot (B + C) \overset{?}{=} A \cdot B + A \cdot C$$

To prove that both of these are legitimate operations, we will employ two new techniques. We will first prove the second, P4(b), by means of what is called a "truth table," and then use that postulate in a strictly algebraic proof of P4(a).

One of the most satisfying proofs of any hypothesis, but one which is a luxury we can rarely afford, is to "consider all possible cases." Fortunately in Boolean algebra that possibility is much simpler to achieve. Remember that each variable can take only one or the other of two possible values. If a function contains two variables, A and B, there are only two possible numbers which A might represent, and, for each of these, two possible numbers for B, so that there are but four possible sets of circumstances in real life which the function could ever describe. With only four possible cases, it now is a relatively simple matter to examine the behavior of, say, one side of an equation for all four sets of conditions, and see whether it does or does not agree with the other side of the same equation for the same sets of conditions.

This is truly an empirical test, but it is a precise test, because it is a "test of exhaustion."

To familiarize ourselves with some of these techniques, let us look at the truth table for a few of the simple Boolean functions. As inputs we list the possible values that each variable can take on, in a systematic manner which treats the last-named variable as the lowest-order digit, and the first named variable as the highest:

Inputs A	0	0	1	1		Inputs A	0	0	1	1		Inputs A	0	1
B	0	1	0	1		B	0	1	0	1				
$A + B$	0	1	1	1		$A \cdot B$	0	0	0	1		$\overline{A}$	1	0

(a) OR	(b) AND	(c) NOT

Figure 8.4-10   Truth tables for fundamental concepts.

Now let us prepare a table in which we write down separately the behavior of the left- and right-hand sides of equation P4(b), with intermediate lines to insert the intermediate steps as an assistance in arriving at the final value. (See Figure 8.4-11.)

Two conventions that are common in ordinary algebra might well be

P4(*b*): $$\boxed{A \cdot (B + C) \stackrel{?}{=} (A \cdot B) + (A \cdot C)}$$

Inputs	A	0	0	0	0	1	1	1	1
	B	0	0	1	1	0	0	1	1
	C	0	1	0	1	0	1	0	1

$B + C$		1	1	1		1	1	1
Ⓛ $= A \cdot (B + C)$						1	1	1

$A \cdot B$							1	1
$A \cdot C$						1		1
Ⓡ $= (A \cdot B) + (A \cdot C)$						1	1	1

Same!   Q.E.D.

Figure 8.4-11   Truth table for distributive law of AND.

introduced at this point, since they will be convenient in the following algebraic manipulations. First, to cut down on the number of parentheses introduced solely to indicate order of calculation, we will adopt the usual convention that multiplication ($\cdot$), or more properly the AND operation, takes precedence over addition ($+$), which is actually the operation OR. In other words, the expression

$$A + B \cdot C \quad \text{means} \quad A + (B \cdot C) \quad \text{not} \quad (A + B) \cdot C$$

Second, so long as we are dealing with single literal names, we will usually omit the AND sign between two variables, so that

$$AB \quad \text{means} \quad A \cdot B$$

Now for P4(*a*) which says

$$A + (B \cdot C) \stackrel{?}{=} (A + B) \cdot (A + C)$$

Let us operate on the right-hand side first. We will introduce a new variable named W which is defined as $W = A + B$. The equation now reads

$$= W \cdot (A + C)$$

This is now in the form of the left-hand side of P4(*b*) which we have just proven. We can therefore employ P4(*b*) to get (using our new convention)

$$= WA + WC$$

Now replacing W by its original equivalent in both appearances we obtain

$$= (A + B) \cdot A + (A + B) \cdot C$$

Applying P4(b) twice more we find

$$= AA + AB + AC + BC$$

We have previously shown [T2(a)] that $A \cdot A = A$, so

$$= A + AB + AC + BC$$

Now applying T4(a) to the first two terms, we can drop out the second term, AB,

$$= A \quad + AC \quad + BC$$

and by repeating the process, AC.

$$= A \qquad\qquad + BC \qquad \text{Q.E.D.}$$

Such a proof by algebraic manipulation is best arranged in the same form in which one would organize a similar derivation or proof in conventional algebra, mathematics, or science. A recommended form is shown in Figure 8.4-12, in which on the same line with each step in the derivation, is the suporting documentation giving the operation performed, or citing the (previously proven) postulate or theorem permitting you to make that statement.

We have now seen that there are at least three ways in which any equation in Boolean algebra might be tested or proven

(1) By inspection or analysis of the equivalent switching circuit.
(2) By truth table.
(3) By algebraic manipulation (properly documented).

If the relationships are complicated, sometimes a combination of (1) and (2) may be used—having drawn the equivalent switching circuit, consider its behavior exhaustively.

Some of the more useful basic relationships in Boolean algebra are

P4(a): To prove:

Step	$A + BC = (A + B) \cdot (A + C)$	Justification
1.	$= (A + B)A + (A + B)C$	P4(b)
2.	$= AA + AB + AC + BC$	P4(b)
3.	$= A + AB + AC + BC$	T2(b)
4.	$= A \quad\quad + AC + BC$	T4(a)
5.	$= A \quad\quad\quad\quad + BC$	T4(a) Q.E.D.

Figure 8.4-12   Algebraic proof for distributive law of OR.

summarized in Figure 8.4-13. The terminology and numbering scheme of postulates and theorems are those of Phister, for while we are not proceeding on so formal a basis as he does, it is convenient to have a framework to set them in, and a terminology and set of labels by which to refer to them.

Only one additional feature of Figure 8.4-13 is worth commenting on, and that is the pair of relationships T7, which are also well known

Postulates

P1 (a)	$A + B$	(means OR)
(b)	$A \cdot B$	(means AND)
P2 (a)	$A + 0 = A$	
(b)	$A \cdot 1 = A$	
P3 (a)	$A + B = B + A$	Commutative
(b)	$A \cdot B = B \cdot A$	
P4 (a)	$A + BC = (A + B) \cdot (A + C)$	Distributive
(b)	$A(B + C) = AB + AC$	
P5 (a)	$A \cdot \overline{A} = 0$	(means NOT)
(b)	$A + \overline{A} = 1$	(means NOT)

Theorems

T1	Uniqueness	
T2 (a)	$A + A = A$	
(b)	$A \cdot A = A$	
T3 (a)	$A + 1 = 1$	
(b)	$A \cdot 0 = 0$	
T4 (a)	$A + AB = A$	
(b)	$A(A + B) = A$	
T5	$\overline{A} =$ unique	
T6	$\overline{\overline{A}} = A$	
T7 (a)	$\overline{A + B} = \overline{A} \cdot \overline{B}$	De Morgan's laws
(b)	$\overline{AB} = \overline{A} + \overline{B}$	
T8 (a)	$(A + B) + C = A + (B + C)$	
(b)	$(AB)C = A(BC)$	
T9 (a)	$A + \overline{A}B = A + B$	
(b)	$A(\overline{A} + B) = AB$	
T10	$(A + B)(\overline{A} + C) = AC + \overline{A}B$	

Figure 8.4-13   Laws of Boolean algebra.

under the name of de Morgan's laws. These are the rules for finding the negative of a function, and, by repeated application of these two, any function, no matter how complicated, may be negated. What de Morgan's laws say, in words, is:

To negate any function involving AND and OR operations, interchange all AND and OR operations, and negate each appearance of each variable. Parentheses, both expressed and implied, must be strictly preserved.

Whether this is carried out in several operations, one step at a time, or all in one step, is immaterial, provided it is done carefully and correctly. To illustrate:

$$\overline{(A + B\overline{C}) \cdot (\overline{B} + C)} = \text{in one step:} \quad [\overline{A} \cdot (\overline{B} + C)] + [B\overline{C}]$$

$$= \text{in 3 steps:} \quad \overline{A + B\overline{C}} + \overline{\overline{B} + C}$$

$$= \quad [\overline{A} \cdot \overline{B\overline{C}}] \quad + [B\overline{C}]$$

$$= \quad [\overline{A} \cdot (\overline{B} + C)] + [B\overline{C}]$$

8.5 APPLICATIONS OF BOOLEAN ALGEBRA

The principal value of Boolean algebra is in its application to the analysis (and, indirectly, synthesis) of switching circuits. By switching circuits is meant electrical circuits which operate in an all-or-nothing fashion, insensitive to any intermediate variations in level. Designers of telephone switching systems, digital computers, and automatic control devices have all found the algebra extremely useful in representing the circuits involved. The similarity between these apparently diverse devices lies in the fact that in all cases each output must be one or the other of two, and only two, states, and each output is a logical function of the input (the connections to the outputs can be determined by performing a series of deductive logical operations on the inputs).

Suppose the logical process that we wish to study is that of arithmetic: i.e., of performing the sequences of operations upon the inputs which will give us their sum, their difference, their product, etc. And suppose further that in order to increase the reliability of the circuits involved, these numbers are to appear in binary radix, so that the signals the circuits will have to operate on will be binary variables. If we wish to design circuits to perform such binary arithmetic, we can make use of Boolean algebra in either of two ways: we can, through intuition, trial and error, or otherwise, come up with circuits, and then use Boolean algebra to analyze the behavior of each in terms of the desired output; or we can try to develop techniques in which we can use the algebra directly to synthesize circuits, preferably optimum circuits, to perform the given function. In practice, of course, various in-between paths and combinations of the two methods are used.

Let us look step-by-step at some of the most fundamental of these binary arithmetic operations in algebraic terms.

Arithmetic Operations with Two Bits

Addition. The addition table in binary arithmetic, as we have seen, is particularly simple, since there are only four entries. Once we recognize that the sum of two bits a and b involves not only a sum digit d but also a possible carry digit c, we can diagram the operation as shown in Figure 8.5-1.

From the truth table, Figure 8.5-1b, only 2 of the 4 possible input combinations give rise to a 1 for d, and only 1 input combination yields a carry. The rules for generation of these 2 digits are apparently:

$$d = \bar{a}b + a\bar{b}$$
$$c = ab$$

This function $d = \bar{a}b + a\bar{b}$ is sufficiently important to be given a name, the *exclusive OR,* and a special symbol $\oplus$. The equation can be written, then,

$$d = a \oplus b$$

With this equation we can fill in the symbolic operator box of Figure 8.5-1a, and get Figure 8.5-2. Note, however, that considerable simplification can be achieved in this circuit by using one of the alternate forms of the expression for d. It is not hard to prove (see Problem 8.4-3) that

$$\bar{a}b + a\bar{b} = (a + b)\overline{ab}$$

Let us realize the expression in the form shown in Figure 8.5-3. Assuming, for example, the use of diode-input passive gates and active-

		a	0	0	1	1
Inputs		b	0	1	0	1
Outputs		d	0	1	1	0
		c	0	0	0	1

(a) Symbol   (b) Truth table

Figure 8.5-1   Two-bit addition.

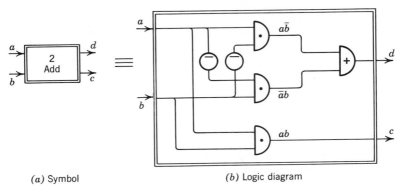

(a) Symbol   (b) Logic diagram

Figure 8.5-2   Half-adder (version a).

element (transistor) negators, we might reasonably describe the a circuit as requiring 8 diodes and 2 negators, while the b needs only $6 + 1$. In any practical situation, however, the components, packaged building blocks and the circumstances of use, pose their own unique conditions and determine their own "optimum" circuits.

Subtraction. It can easily be shown that the corresponding table for the difference digit d and the "borrow" e are given by Figure 8.5-4, from which the equations are apparently

$$d = \bar{a}b + a\bar{b}$$
$$e = \bar{a}b$$

Here e merely means a signal that a borrow from the next higher column must take place; we will postpone for a bit consideration of how this is to be handled. Note also that the row for d is identical with the corresponding row in the addition table.

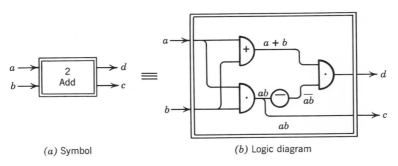

(a) Symbol   (b) Logic diagram

Figure 8.5-3   Half-adder (version b).

a	0	0	1	1
b	0	1	0	1
d	0	1	1	0
e	0	1	0	0

Figure 8.5-4 Two-bit subtraction.

a	0	0	1	1
b	0	1	0	1
p	0	0	0	1

Figure 8.5-5 Two-bit multiplication.

Multiplication. Two-bit multiplication is the easiest of all (Figure 8.5-5). Its realization is, therefore, a single AND gate

$$p = ab$$

Arithmetic Operations With Three Bits

Addition. Consider the addition of two binary numbers a and b, each consisting of a string of bits. Their addition produces a sum d. If a and b are each n bits long, then the sum can be formed by considering a pair at a time, as in Figure 8.5-6a, with any carries generated, added in with the next column to the left (next higher power of 2).

Note that the largest number of bits that ever needs to be handled at one time is 3: a_i, b_i, and the carry from the preceding column c_{i-1}; the result of adding these 3 is a sum digit d_i and a carry c_i, thus

$$a_i \text{ plus } b_i \text{ plus } c_{i-1} \text{ produces } d_i \text{ with } c_i$$

which is shown symbolically in Figure 8.5-6b.

Let us see if we can determine what logical circuitry must go inside this "3 Add" box.

The truth table for these 3 inputs is shown in Figure 8.5-6c, although the variation sequence of the inputs has been reversed from our former practice, to simplify what follows. The truth table does not look very promising; it leads to the expression

$$d_i = a_i\bar{b}_i\bar{c}_{i-1} + \bar{a}_ib_i\bar{c}_{i-1} + \bar{a}_i\bar{b}_ic_{i-1} + a_ib_ic_{i-1}$$

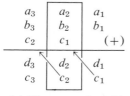

(a) The general problem

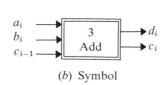

(b) Symbol

Figure 8.5-6 Three-bit addition.

a_i	0	1	0	1	0	1	0	1
b_i	0	0	1	1	0	0	1	1
c_{i-1}	0	0	0	0	1	1	1	1
d_i	0	1	1	0	1	0	0	1
c_i	0	0	0	1	0	1	1	1

(c) Truth table

a_i	0	1	0	1	0	1	0	1
b_i	0	0	1	1	0	0	1	1
h_i	0	1	1	0	0	1	1	0
c_{ab}				1				1

h_i	0	1	1	0	0	1	1	0
c_{i-1}	0	0	0	0	1	1	1	1
d_i	0	1	1	0	1	0	0	1
c_{hc}					1	1		

$c_i = c_{ab} + c_{hc}$	0	0	0	1	0	1	1	1

(d) Truth table in two steps

Figure 8.5-6 (cont.)

Now although this can be factored and reduced with a few steps of Boolean algebra, it is perhaps more helpful to consider the problem in two steps (Figure 8.5-6d). We will try forming h first, the sum of a_i and b_i, and then combine h and c_{i-1}. We will then show that exactly the same results are produced for d_i and c_i as in Figure 8.5-6c. Note that a carry may be produced at either stage of this process, but not both.

Although there are only 4 possible cases to consider for 2 inputs, a and b, both h_i and c_{ab} are shown in Figure 8.5-6d for all 8 of the cases laid out in Figure 8.5-6c. Having obtained the h_i row, we then add the

c_{i-1} row, exactly as it appeared in Figure 8.5-6c, and perform 2-bit addition to obtain the sum, d_i. It should be observed that this d_i row in Figure 8.5-6d *is* identical with the d_i row from Figure 8.5-6c.

How does this help us? Only by showing that d_i is the same function of h_i and c_{i-1} (exclusive OR) that h_i is of a_i and b_i, so that d_i may be written

$$d_i = h_i \oplus c_{i-1}$$

The new carry c_i occurs not only as a 2-bit carry does,

$$\text{carry}_2 = h_i \cdot c_{i-1}$$

but also whenever one did in the first stage:

$$\text{carry}_1 = a_i \cdot b_i$$

Therefore, a carry c_i occurs whenever either carry$_1$ or carry$_2$ does:

$$c_i = h_i c_{i-1} + a_i b_i$$

With these two equations we can now realize our full 3-bit adder (Figure 8.5-7).

Now that we have seen a full adder, or 3-bit adding circuit, we can appreciate the significance of the name "half-adder"—a full adder is made up of two of them.

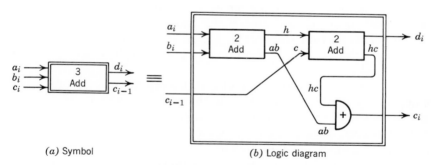

(a) Symbol   (b) Logic diagram

Figure 8.5-7   Full adder.

8.6   ORGANIZATION

So far we have seen several typical ways in which switching circuits —flip-flops, AND and OR gates, and inverters—can be used to implement some of the isolated operations associated with binary arithmetic. Now we are ready to put some of these separate operations together—

to see, for instance, how we might perform the electronic addition of two n-bit binary numbers, and even how we should organize the sections, communication paths, and control signals of the computer as a whole.

Serial and Parallel Data Transmission

One of the first concepts to grapple with is that there are two distinct ways in which the several bits that make up a "word" within a computer, be it an instruction word or a number, can be sent from one place to another: one bit after another, in serial; or all bits simultaneously, in parallel. If the bits go one after another, a single electrical conductor will suffice, but it will obviously take longer to transmit the whole message; if the bits go side by side, they can all get there at the same time, but it requires as many parallel conductors as there are bits to be transmitted.

In computers, as in almost all engineering projects, performance has to be balanced against cost, and the cost of building the additional circuits needs to be compared with the increase in speed of operation capable. A one-lane bridge is obviously cheaper to build, but a six-lane bridge will handle much more traffic.

Registers

Not only the transmission lines themselves, but the sending and receiving equipment, including the devices that hold the information at both ends, must be replicated if the transmission is to be done in parallel. This in turn leads us to the *register,* which is a device for receiving, storing, and transmitting a group of bits, as shown in Figure 8.6-1.

If the transmission is to be parallel, such a register consists of a set of independent flip-flops, side by side, but unconnected to each other except that they are activated by a common timing signal. They must each, however, have a complete set of input and output gates. On the other hand, if the information is to be received serially, stored temporarily, and then sent on again serially, the flip-flops need the capacity of shifting information from one stage to the next within the chain; but they do not, in general, need input and output facilities except for the first and last stages.

In some cases, where truly versatile performances are desired, a very general type of register can be employed which can combine the capability of handling both serial and parallel information, and even of converting from one to the other. Figure 8.6-2 illustrates by analogy some of the functions which such a general shift register can perform.

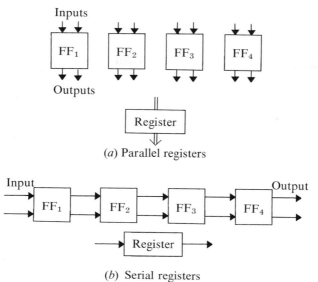

(*a*) Parallel registers

(*b*) Serial registers

Figure 8.6-1   Parallel and serial registers.

Serial and Parallel Operations

In addition to the distinction discussed above, as applied to the transmission of information, it is possible for the data processing operations themselves to be performed in either serial or parallel fashion. Figure 8.6-3 illustrates these two concepts as they might apply to the addition of two n-bit numbers (in the figure, $n = 4$).

To add 2 n-bit numbers serially, only 1 full adder is needed, but addition takes n-bit times. Three n-bit shift registers (serial registers) are needed. It is assumed that the circuits operate synchronously; that is, with each clock pulse, all information is advanced 1 bit. The adder is fast enough to complete the generation of both of its output digits before the appearance of the next pair of inputs.

To add 2 n-bit numbers in parallel, n full adders are needed, but addition takes only 1 bit time. Three sets of n flip-flops (parallel registers) are needed. Here synchronous operation is not quite so important, for it may take a small but measurable extra time for the carries which might be generated in the lower-order stages to propagate their effect to all the higher-order stages.

Even recognizing such side effects and minor complications, this parallel adder is about n times as fast as the serial one, but costs about n times as much to build. The choice between these two is one of

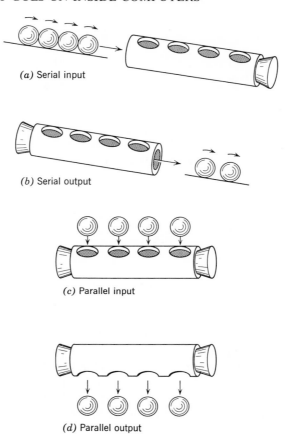

(a) Serial input

(b) Serial output

(c) Parallel input

(d) Parallel output

Figure 8.6-2 General shift register.

the earliest decisions in the computer-design process, and must be based upon a careful evaluation of the speed and performance desired, the cost, and the components and technology that will be employed.

Overall Organization

So far we have considered some of the processing operations that go on within the arithmetic unit, and have talked about data transmission, without specifying from where to where. It is about time that we made a thorough examination of the overall logical organization of a computer, and developed a better picture of the various paths of data flow. Recall at this point Figure 1.2-4, which in very general terms, purports to be a functional block diagram of any automatic digital computer. Look at the 5 different units shown in that figure, trace the paths of data flow as well as the control signals shown there, and keep them in mind as

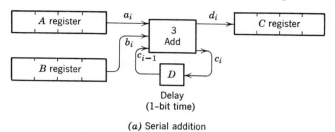

(*a*) Serial addition

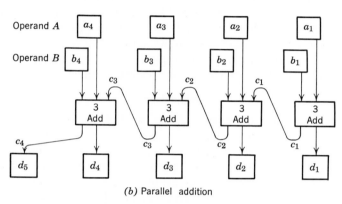

(*b*) Parallel addition

Figure 8.6-3   Serial and parallel arithmetic.

we turn our attention to Figure 8.6-4, which shows the same general configuration, but with more detail included in the data-flow paths and particularly in the control section.

This diagram has the same general layout as our earlier one, and shows at least 4 of the original 5 blocks, in the same relative position. It is the control unit which at first glance seems to have disappeared, but closer study will reveal that it has really been exploded to show several of its component parts.

Another point of difference which immediately catches our attention is the presence of many sets of parallel lines, some with small circles containing a symbol superimposed on them. A pair of parallel lines represent a group of parallel transfer paths, which constitute a cable or a buss in electrical terms, and the symbol in the circle tells how many lines this buss comprises. This in turn is the number of bits being transmitted in parallel along that channel. The symbol

for instance, means that all *w* bits of a *w*-bit word are transmitted in parallel along this path.

The solid double lines in Figure 8.6-4 represent the paths along which data actually flow, including both numerical *data,* as in the input and output to the arithmetic unit, and computer *instruction* words, as in the path which leads along the bottom of the diagram and into the instruction register. The broken parallel channels, on the other hand, represent the parallel transmission of control information only, which includes both the instruction *type* information to and from the decoder, and the *address* information which tells the reader what location in memory to read material from, and the writer what to write it into.

To see the significance of these different kinds of information, and how they effect the flow of data from point to point, we had better establish a few typical machine language instructions. As these are introduced, constant reference to Figure 8.6-4 will assist greatly in understanding the significance of their operating effect.

Instructions

An instruction to a computer will, in most cases, refer to data: move it, combine it, test it, do something with it. Since there are several kinds of things we want to do with the data, we will need several different kinds of instructions, or operation types. Also, since we need to tell the machine what data to operate on, an instruction must contain at least one data-reference or memory-reference, called an address. Hence, the simplest instruction format with enough versatility to be useful is of the form

OP   ADDRESS

where OP specifies one of an assortment of different kinds of operations (add, subtract, store), and ADDRESS identifies a piece of data to work with.

Information inside a computer is not identified by its nature, or any inherent characteristic it may possess, but solely by its address—where it is stored. In this respect, a computer is similar to the desk clerk at a large hotel, who has access to many mailboxes, each identified by a room number. You can ask this desk clerk: "Give me the mail for room 409," or tell him, "Please put this message in box 127." The desk clerk pays no attention to the contents of any of these messages (if he is properly trained), but acts solely as a file clerk, locating and retrieving or filing away information whose sole identification is its address.

In the same way, we may tell a computer: "Add to the current sum the contents of location 409," or, "deliver this result to memory location

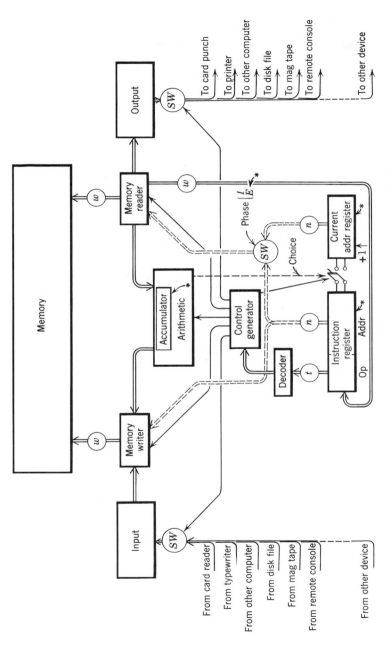

Figure 8.6-4 Overall computer organization (single address decimal).

321

127," and the computer, blind moron that it is, obeys exactly, with never a concern for significance or appropriateness of these actions with these pieces of data. It is up to the programmer to see that the operations make sense!

The observant reader may have detected that there is something lacking in this description: almost all such operations with data require *two* data references in order to be complete. If it is a combining type of operation, one must have 2 operands to combine—add A and B; multiply X by 2. If it is a data-transfer operation, the computer has to be told both source and destination—move the data from *here* to *there*. The instructions we have been talking about specify only a *single* address—that is, make only a single data-reference. How does the computer know what to take for the second?

The solution for this simple type of computer is the same as that used in the ordinary desk calculator that we referred to back in Chapter 1. In the computer, as in the calculator, there is a register that accumulates running totals and stores results of individual operations. In the desk calculator, the contents of this register are usually indicated by the lower dials; in the computer, we merely call this register the accumulator, often abbreviated AC. The number currently in the accumulator is the implied second operand in all data manipulating operations.

With this interpretation, therefore, the arithmetic instruction

ADD   409

means "add to the present contents of the accumulator the contents of memory location 409, leaving the result in the accumulator," and if the next instruction is

STO   127

it means, "store the present contents of the accumulator (the result of the last instruction) in memory location 127."

It should be mentioned that both of these are copying operations in the sense that they do not destroy the original contents of the source of the operation. That is, the ADD instruction above does not change the contents of 409, and the STO leaves the contents of the accumulator unchanged.

With this philosophy of using a different machine instruction to specify each tiny step of an operation, it becomes quickly apparent that to accomplish even some of the familiar basic mathematical operations we may have to write a great many machine instructions. For instance, to add 2 numbers and store the result would take a sequence of three separate instructions, thus:

CLA	409	clear AC and add contents of location	409
ADD	410	add to contents of AC contents of location	410
STO	127	store contents of AC into contents of location	127

As though this tedious detail were not sufficiently irritating, it is a further electronic fact that the circuits of most computers do not recognize commands couched in such nice groups of alphabetic symbols as CLA; they recognize and interpret only numerical information, and binary numerical information at that. A set of actual machine instructions for a computer like this is shown in Figure 8.6-5.

This describes the instruction set for a hypothetical computer having

Type		Address	Meaning
0	INP	n	Input 1 word into location n
1	STO	n	Store contents of AC into location n
2	STT	n	Store type portion of contents of AC into location n
3	STA	n	Store address portion of contents of AC into location n
4			
5			
6			
7			
8	SHL	n	Shift left n places
9	SHR	n	Shift right n places
10	TRA	n	Transfer to instruction in location n
11	TRN	n	Transfer to instruction in location n *if* contents of AC is −
12	TRZ	n	Transfer to instruction in location n *if* contents of AC is zero
13	HTR	n	Halt; when started, transfer to contents of location n
14	OUT	n	Output 1 word from location n
15	CLA	n	Clear AC; add the contents of location n
16	ADD	n	Add to contents of AC the contents of location n
17	SUB	n	Subtract from contents of AC the contents of location n
18	MPY	n	Multiply contents of AC by contents of location n
19	DIV	n	Divide contents of AC by contents of location n
20	LOD	n	Load n words into locations 1 to n

Explanation of address:

.000–996	standard core-memory
999	accumulator (AC)
998	upper accumulator (UAC)
997	current address register (CAR)

Figure 8.6-5 Structure of numbers and instructions.

one operation code and one data reference address in each instruction. We will ignore the additional problems of communicating in binary by further postulating that this computer uses BCD, or decimal coding. It is therefore a single-address decimal machine, and will consequently be known as the SAD computer. By reference to Figure 8.6-5 you can see that the trio above would have to be encoded as

$$
\begin{array}{cc}
15 & 409 \\
16 & 410 \\
01 & 127
\end{array}
$$

before they could be punched onto cards or tape and actually fed into such a computer. Such is the native language of computers.

Here, we have been assuming that the computer executes the instructions in the same sequence that they are written, one after another down the list. Normally, this is true, although we must realize that for instructions just as for data words, the only way the computer can identify and keep track of them is by their location. The programmer, therefore, must see to it that his instructions are loaded into sequentially numbered storage locations in the computer memory, in order for this to work. This is the significance of the $+1$ shown below the box marked current address register in Figure 8.6-4. Each time the computer has finished with one instruction, this circuit adds 1 to the address in the CAR, and takes the result to be the address of the next instruction.

Note the sequence of operations: first the instruction has to be located and read out of memory, after which it has to be executed, and the data manipulation it calls for carried out. Following this, the next instruction is located; then this instruction is executed. And so on down the line. There are two phases that make up the complete cycle associated with each instruction: first, the instruction location or I phase; second, the execution or E phase. The control generator generates signals appropriate to each of these phases, among them the signal controlling the address selection switch leading to the memory reader (right center).

We have by now enough of the picture of the makeup and effect of some of these simple instructions to try following them through Figure 8.6-4 to see their actual operation. We see that each instruction consists of an *operation* type portion, consisting of t digits (here $t = 2$), and an *address* portion of n digits (here $n = 3$). The total number of digits w in an instruction word is apparently $w = t + n$ (here $w = 5$).

Let us start by assuming that the simple instruction sequence shown in Figure 8.6-6 is actually stored in memory in the locations shown, and that the current address register CAR now reads 037. To initiate the

Location	Instruction	
	Op	Address
37	15	409
38	16	410
39	01	127

Figure 8.6-6 Simple instruction sequence.

activity, the phase switch is set to I, enabling the contents of the CAR to be sent to the memory reader. This, in turn, is told to find the memory location with that address, and to read out its contents. As it is still in the instruction phase, that word being read out of memory by the memory reader is sent by way of the long path across the bottom of the diagram into the instruction register IR. In one final action, the contents of the CAR are incremented by 1, yielding 038, and the instruction phase is complete.

During the execution or E phase, the contents of the IR are examined, decoded, and executed. Since the IR has just been loaded with the contents of memory location 037, we know that it now contains the number

$$15 \quad 409$$

The two t digits (15) are picked up first and sent to the decoder, which upon looking up this number in its built-in table, decides that this is a CLA or "clear and add" instruction. It so informs the control generator, which issues the following commands and timing signals, all in the proper sequence: first, it instructs the arithmetic unit to clear itself—meaning, set the contents of the accumulator to zero—and to be ready to accept and read into the accumulator the number which will be shortly supplied by the memory reader. Second, it tells the address portion of the IR to make its contents (currently 409) available to the memory reader, as the address of a piece of data to be used as an operand. Third, it causes the memory reader to locate memory address 409, read out its contents, and send those contents to the arithmetic unit. When all this has been accomplished, the control generator issues a signal marking the end of the execution phase, the phase switch flips to instruction phase, and the next instruction cycle starts.

In the instruction portion of the next cycle, the instruction in location 038 is located and read into the IR, and the CAR is incremented to 039. The new instruction turns out to be

$$16 \quad 410$$

During execution, this is decoded to be an ADD—"Add to the previous contents of the accumulator"—type of instruction; its data address 410 is supplied to the memory reader, which reads out the number currently stored in 410 and sends it to arithmetic. Here this number is added to the previous contents of the accumulator (the number from 409), and this instruction cycle is ended.

Lastly, in the third cycle the contents of 039 is found to be

01   127

This is decoded to be a STO or "store" instruction, which this time causes the data address 127 to be sent, not to the memory reader, but to the memory writer, and the contents of the accumulator (the sum of the numbers from 409 and 410) to be sent to the memory writer to be written into location 127.

This is typical of a normal sequence of instructions, which are executed in sequential order. There are times, however, when it is necessary to jump out of the normal sequence, either ahead—thereby skipping some instructions—or back—so that some may be repeated. This jumping out of sequence may be either unconditional, happening every time this point in the instruction sequence is reached, or it may be desirable to make the jump conditional upon the progress of the calculations, by making it dependent upon the present state of the accumulator.

The instruction set of Figure 8.6-5 shows examples of both types. Instruction 10—the TRA instruction—accomplishes the former; regardless of the state of anything, the next instruction following it will not be the one found in the next sequential location, but will be one found in the location specified by the data address of the TRA instruction. Here is how this works.

Suppose we have the pair of instructions shown below

Location	Instruction	
	Op	Address
42	10	016
43	17	412

and the CAR currently reads 042. During the I phase of the cycle the instruction from location 042 is found and read into the IR, and the CAR incremented to 043, as usual. But when the instruction in the IR is decoded and found to be a TRA, the switch between the IR and the CAR is closed, and the address portion of the current instruction, the 016, is transferred into the CAR, replacing its former contents 043. Now, when the I phase of the next cycle is initiated, it is the contents of 016, whatever that is, which is taken for the next instruction, and not 043 at all.

If the instruction from 042 were found to be a type 11 or type

12, rather than a 10, an additional test would be needed. In addition to being a transfer type of instruction, it is also necessary that the condition of the accumulator be that described in the definition of the instruction type before the contents of the CAR is replaced. If the instruction is a TRN or "transfer if negative" instruction, *and* if the number in the accumulator *is* currently negative, then the address portion of the IR is shifted into the CAR and becomes the address of the next instruction; if the instruction is a TRN but the number in the accumulator is *not* negative, then no transfer takes place, the E portion of the cycle is complete, and the next cycle proceeds using the original contents of the CAR—043. In the same way, if the instruction is a TRZ or "transfer if zero" instruction, *and* if the number in the accumulator *is* currently zero, then the transfer takes place; if it is *not* zero, no transfer takes place, and the normal sequence proceeds.

Only a couple of basically different types of operations remain to be discussed of the set shown in Figure 8.6-5. Operations 00 (INP) and 14 (OUT) are designed for the input and output of data numbers between the computer and the outside environment, through such devices as a card reader or punch, or paper tape equipment. In either case, execution of one instruction moves only 1 piece of data into the computer or out; it is possible, however, to specify arbitrarily the memory location it is to be put into or read out from. Instruction 20 (LOD), on the other hand, is needed to get started, by loading an entire set of words (such as a program) into a sequentially numbered set of storage locations. In the LOD instruction, the first word being loaded always goes into memory location 001, the next into 002, and so forth until the set is finished. The significance of the address portion N of the LOD instruction is, at the same time, the number of words to be loaded by the instruction, and the address into which the last of them is to go.

An example of a very simple, but complete, program which is executed in an in-line fashion is given in Problem 8.6-4(B); the same problem is rewritten to show looping and the use of conditional transfer operations in Problem 8.6-4(C). It is recommended that both of these programs be traced completely through, so that it is clearly understood what the actual contents of each register and each memory location are at all times.

PROBLEM 8.2-1   "Decimal-Binary Table"

Write a decimal-to-binary conversion table for the integers from

(A)   1   to   50
(B) 50   to   75

(C) 10100_2 to 110010_2
(D) 12_8 to 36_8

PROBLEM 8.2-2   "Decimal to Binary"

Express the following decimal numbers in binary:

(A)   100
(B)   7/4/1776
(C) 1620
(D) 7090
(E)   360
(F) 4096
(G) today's date

PROBLEM 8.2-3   "Radix Conversion"

Convert

(A) $476_8 =$ [   ] $_2$

(B) $23_5 =$ [   ] $_{10}$

(C) $2101_3 =$ [   ] $_4$

PROBLEM 8.2-4   "Mars"

The first expedition to Mars found only the ruins of a civilization. From the artifacts and pictures, the explorers found that the creatures who produced this civilization were four-legged beings with a tentacle that branched out at the end with a number of grasping "fingers" on it. After much study, the explorers were able to translate the Martian mathematics. They found the following equation:

$$5x^2 - 50x + 125 = 0$$

with the indicated solutions $x = 5$ and $x = 8$.

This was strange mathematics. The value $x = 5$ seemed legitimate enough, but $x = 8$ required some explanation. Then the explorers reflected on the way in which our number system developed and found evidence that the Martian system had a similar history. How many fingers would you say the Martians had?*

* From *The Bent* of Tau Beta Pi, February, 1956.

PROBLEM 8.2-5   "Mars-Venus"

One of the greatest scientific controversies of the 21st century, which owed its origin to premature publication of only part of a historic document separated from its context, was finally cleared up in 2058 by J. Langeweile von Ausgestrocknet. He published the translation of the *entire* inscription found by the first Terrestrial expedition to Mars in the tomb of Zsht-Susj. Herr von Ausgestrocknet's translation from the Martian M-script reads as follows:

Our first expedition to Venus has unmarsed a sample of Venusian mathematics which sheds a peculiar light on the appendage structure of the now extinct Llorr, once the dominant race of that planet. The sample reads:

$$5x^2 - 50 \times + 125 = 0$$

with the indicated solutions $x = 5, 8$

Now since 8 is obviously a solution, while 5 is not, in our Martian juz-based number system, the conclusion of Zsht-Susj, the beloved and googol-wise leader of that expedition, is that the Llorr, since they used a base shuu number system, undoubtedly had a total of shuu tentacles."

Translation: shuu ____ juz ____ .

PROBLEM 8.3-1   "Binary Arithmetic—1"

(A) Convert the numbers 29_{10} and 13_{10} to binary. Using binary arithmetic:
(B) add them
(C) subtract the smaller from the larger
(D) multiply them
(E) divide the larger by the smaller
(F) deconvert the answers to decimal and check.

PROBLEM 8.3-2   "Binary Arithmetic—2"

Repeat Problem 8.3-1 for the numbers 37_{10} and 19_{10}.

PROBLEM 8.3-3   "Binary Arithmetic—3"

Repeat Problem 8.3-1 for the numbers 38_{10} and 22_{10}.

PROBLEM 8.3-4   "Floating Binary Arithmetic"

Repeat Problem 8.3-1 for the numbers 1.13×10^2 and 2.7×10^1.

PROBLEM 8.3-5   "Mechanized Multiplication"

Produce a table like Figure 8.3-7 for the numbers $A = 11$, $B = 13$.

PROBLEM 8.4-1   "Truth Table"

Construct truth tables for the following Boolean functions

(A) $\overline{A + B}$ (called the NOR)
(B) $\overline{A \cdot B}$ (called the NAND)
(C) $\overline{A} \cdot \overline{B}$
(D) $A \cdot B + \overline{A} \cdot \overline{B}$

PROBLEM 8.4-2   "Switching Circuits"

Construct switching circuit diagrams for the following Boolean functions

(A) $A\overline{B} + \overline{A}B$
(B) $(A + B) \cdot (\overline{A} + \overline{B})$
(C) $(A + \overline{B}) \cdot (\overline{A} + B)$
(D) $AB + \overline{A} \cdot \overline{B}$

PROBLEM 8.4-3   "Truth Table Proof"

Prove by truth table the following identities

(A) $A\overline{B} + \overline{A}B = (A + B) \cdot (\overline{A \cdot B})$
(B) $A\overline{B} + \overline{A}B = (A + B) \cdot (\overline{A} + \overline{B})$
(C) $AB + \overline{A}\overline{B} = (A + \overline{B}) \cdot (\overline{A} + B)$
(D) $A + BC + \overline{A}B + A\overline{C} = A + B$

PROBLEM 8.4-4   "Algebraic Proof"

Prove the identities in Problem 8.4-3 by algebraic manipulation.

PROBLEM 8.4-5   "Simplification"

Simplify

$$(AB + \overline{A} \cdot \overline{B}) \cdot (A + \overline{A}B) + \overline{(\overline{A}B + A\overline{B}) \cdot (AB + B) \cdot (A\overline{B})}$$

PROBLEM 8.5-1   "3-bit Adder"

Eliminate h from the equations for the 3-bit sum d_i, and carry c_i. Express d_i and c_i as functions of the 3 primary inputs to the "3-add" box: a_i, b_i, and c_{i-1}.

PROBLEM 8.5-2   "3-bit Subtracter"

a is a 2-bit number: a_2 a_1
b is a 2 bit number: b_2 b_1 $(-)$

$$\frac{\qquad\quad c_2'\quad c_1'}{(c_2')\quad d_2\quad d_1}$$

d is the difference $a - b$:
c_2' is the borrow resulting from the last (highest order) subtraction.
(A) Set up truth tables and derive the Boolean equations for d_1, d_2, and c_2'. Note that d_2 will involve a_2, b_2, and c_1'.
(B) Derive a logic (symbolic) diagram showing an efficient way to generate these.

PROBLEM 8.5-3   "Adder-Subtracter"

Compare the results of Problems 8.5-1 and 8.5-2, and design an adder-subtracter unit which combines the features of the 3-bit adder and the 3-bit subtracter. The inputs are now

$$a_1, a_2, b_1, b_2, \text{ and } P,$$

where $P = 0$ means "form a plus b", $P = 1$ means "form a minus b."

PROBLEM 8.6-1   "SAD Instruction Categories"

Classify the instructions in the SAD instruction set shown in Figure 8.6-5 according to the following categories of significance of the *address* in each case:

(A) destination
(B) source of piece of data
(C) source (or possible source) of next instruction
(D) other (explain).

PROBLEM 8.6-2   "Decoder Logic Design"

Write the numerical op-code for all the instructions in the instruction set shown in Figure 8.6-5 in BCD notation (see section 8.2). Using the classification worked out in Problem 8.6-1, write the Boolean equations to enable the decoder and control generator to generate the following signals

(A) read from memory
(B) send from reader to arithmetic
(C) send from reader to output
(D) send from reader to "IR"
(E) write into memory
(F) write from input
(G) write from arithmetic

PROBLEM 8.6-3   "Internal Operations"

Using Figure 8.6-4, show the data-flow paths used, and list the command signals generated, to accomplish the execution of each of the instructions in Figure 8.6-5.

PROBLEM 8.6-4   "Tracing SAD Operations"

Using Figure 8.6-4, trace the sequence of instructions and the data flow carried out at each step, as the following programs are executed:

(A) Assume program and data already loaded as follows:

Loc	T	Addr
01	15	005
02	16	006
03	01	031
04	13	000
05	+00	041
06	+00	026

(B)

	T	Addr
	20	007
	00	031
	15	031
	00	031
	16	031
	01	032
	14	032
	10	001

(C)

	T	Addr
	20	017
	15	015
	01	062
	01	063
	00	061
	15	062
	16	061
	01	062
	15	063
	16	016
	01	063
	17	017
	11	004
	14	062
	10	001
	+00	000
	+00	001
	+00	002

CHAPTER 9.

Things Worth Computing:
[D] WHEN TIME IS IMPORTANT

9.1 PERSPECTIVE

Time is of prime importance in the applications of computers to many problems—it is involved in the operations of data input, processing, and output. We will see that it is desirable in many cases to reduce the time in performing these sequential operations, and will classify these systems as "open-loop" and "closed-loop." Finally, we shall describe the common requirements of both types of systems, and some of the computational methods used in the data-processing operations.

9.2 OPEN-LOOP SYSTEMS
Definition

For an open-loop system, data gathered from a physical process are not used to affect that process. Weather forecasting and reporting of returns of political elections are examples. They are open-loop in that we wish to know about the weather and the elections, but little, if anything, can be done to change or alter them; as Mark Twain once said, "Everyone talks about the weather, but no one ever does anything about it." The output from the data-processing operations may influence our actions or satisfy our curiosity, but they are never used to change the process that supplied the data.

The Analysis of Weather Forecasting as an Open-Loop System

We will use weather forecasting as an example of the operations of open-loop systems. Figure 9.2-1 shows the weather over the earth as an equivalent process P which cannot be controlled. Weather stations, as data sources, are geographically distributed where measurements of such conditions as temperature and barometric pressure are made. The data-input operations are (a) measuring and recording of data, (b) transmission of data to the processing center, and (c) data preparation for processing on the computer. When any, or all, of these serial operations are performed manually, the computer performing the data-processing operations is called "off-line." If the data from the sources enter the computer directly without human intervention, the computer is called "on-line."

The output operations are (a) preparation of computer output for transmission, (b) transmission of output and (c) preparation of output for application at the destinations—the homes of people who want the weather forecast. When any, or all, of these serial operations are performed manually, the computer producing the output is "indirectly connected" to the output destinations. If the output of the computer

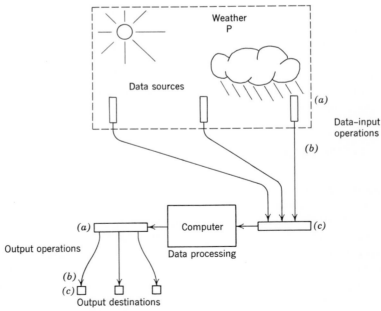

Figure 9.2-1   Weather forecasting—an open-loop system.

reaches the output destinations directly without human intervention, the computer is "directly connected" to the output destinations.

An important value to determine for this type of system is the interval of time, beginning when a value of a condition, such as wind velocity, is read, and the earliest time the calculated output, which requires that value, reaches the destinations. This interval of time is called *time delay*. The longest time delay is for the conditions of the computer operating *off-line* and *indirectly connected* to the output destinations, i.e., when all operations of input and output are manually performed. The shortest time delay is for the conditions of the computer operating *on-line* and *directly connected*. For these conditions, the time delay is so short that it is negligible, and the system is said to be a "real-time" system.

Comparison of the Effects of Large and Small Time Delays

We will now investigate and compare the effects of a large and a very small time delay on the data-processing operations of Figure 9.2-1, and the accuracy of the outputs. Figure 9.2-2a will aid in describing the analysis for the case of the large time delay. The velocity of a cold front, v, in miles per hour, is plotted against time in days, and is one of the many conditions of weather which may be analyzed individually before it enters into an overall forecast. Three consecutive and latest readings of velocity v_0, v_1, and v_2, occurring at 12:00 noon Sunday, Monday, and Tuesday are considered necessary in predicting a velocity required in a forecast. It is assumed that only one reading can be taken in a one-day period.

The large time delay t_d, equal to one day, as shown in the figure, is the sum of the time delays of the operations of input, processing, and output which, say, have the values of 11, 2, and 11 hours, respectively. The velocity v_2, occurring at 12:00 noon Tuesday, would be recorded, and the value would not enter the computer until 11:00 P.M. the same day. At 1:00 A.M., Wednesday, the processing would be completed, and at 12:00 noon Wednesday, the people would receive the two-day forecast for Thursday and Friday.

The sum of the time delay t_d of one day, and the period of forecast t_f of two days, equals the required prediction time of the velocity t_f' to make the forecast of weather for Friday. Thus, the velocity must be predicted as far as three days in advance of the actual occurance, and this predicted value of v_5 must be obtained from the three past values v_0, v_1, and v_2. The figure shows a curve passing through the three known velocity points, and extended by three days to obtain the velocities v_4 and v_5.

We will now assume our example of weather forecasting to be a real-

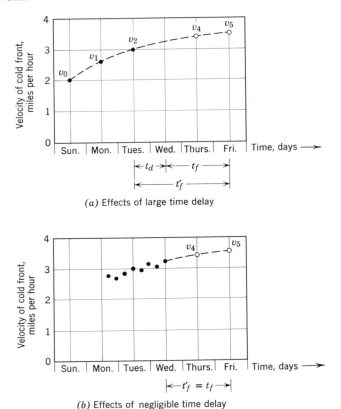

(a) Effects of large time delay

(b) Effects of negligible time delay

Figure 9.2-2   Analysis for open-loop operation.

time system, in order to study the effects of negligible time delay on the operations and the accuracy of the output. Figure 9.2-2b shows velocity of the cold front plotted against time as before. Because the input operations are performed very rapidly, measurements may be made more frequently at little additional cost. The figure shows the measurements of velocity to be made every 6 hours, instead of every 24 hours as before. And since the time delay t_d is considered negligible, the time of prediction t_f' equals the forecast time $t_f = 2$ days. The figure shows a sketch of a curve drawn approximately through the 8 points and extended to obtain predicted values of velocity v_4 and v_5.

Advantages of Real-Time Open-Loop Systems

There are two principal reasons why a real-time open-loop system is better than a system in which the computer operates off-line and indirectly connected. They are: (1) more accuracy in predicting because more values are obtained over a more recent past, and a shorter period of predicting is required; and (2) since measurements are made more frequently, predicted values may be updated more often. In Figure 9.2-2*b*, 8 points over a past period of 48 hours are used to predict over a period of two days, while in Figure 9.2-2*a*, 3 points over a past period of 72 hours are used to predict over a period of three days. For the case described by Figure 9.2-2*b*, predicted values may be updated every 6 hours, while updating for the other case cannot occur more frequently than every 24 hours.

Some open-loop systems, such as those of weather forecasting, operate continuously, i.e., repeated predictions are required. Other systems are established for a particular event, such as a system for predicting the outcome of elections, and not only is it desirable from the viewpoint of accuracy to reduce the time delay, but the time delay cannot be so large that the condition being predicted actually occurs before the prediction can be made. In the case of elections, if the time delay is too long, the election will be over and the votes counted before data can be prepared, processed, and the predicted outcome calculated.

Systems for data gathering in research, which is one of the principal applications of computers in this area, are sometimes open-loop systems, and it is often desirable that they perform as real-time systems. Predicting may be desirable to determine conditions of experimentation before they occur. Being able to make frequent measurements of conditions is also desirable in some cases in the investigations of rapidly changing events, and in determining accurate equations for curves which pass through the points of plotted data.

Types of Equipment Used in Open-Loop Systems

We see that it is always desirable to reduce the time delay in these open-loop systems. Usually the reduction occurs over a period of time, in discrete steps, as various types of equipment are installed. We will now describe some of these types of equipment. Figure 9.2-3 shows data-transmission equipment which may be installed between the data-processing center and each of the stations at the sources of data. The transmission terminals at the stations are connected to telephone lines, and a transmission circuit is established by dialing the number of the center. Data are transmitted by inserting prepunched cards, which contain, for example, the station's identification and the time, into the carriage of the terminal. Variable data, such as instrument readings, are inserted manually through the keyboard shown at the right of the terminal equipment. At the center, the line signals are converted into

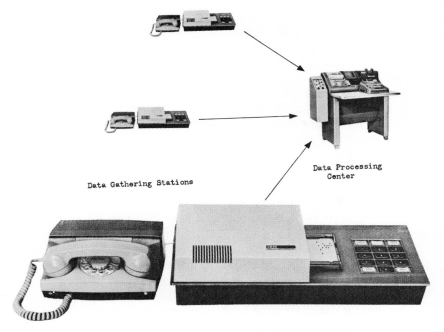

Figure 9.2-3   A data-transmission system (Courtesy of the IBM Corp.).

punched card code, and the information originating at the terminals is punched into cards for direct input to the computer.

Figure 9.2-4 shows a unit of equipment designed for on-line operations. It replaces the manual reading and recording of values from as many as 300 different instruments. Data are transmitted from each of these units to the central computer.

Figure 9.2-5 shows one of a number of available types of equipment for reducing time delay in output operations. The unit provides recorded voice response which is composed from a prerecorded voice on a magnetic-drum memory within the unit. A message from the computer selects the words from the vocabulary on the magnetic drum and transmits a verbal message. An example of a current use of this type of terminal is in the reporting of stock market prices.

Transmission of Data in Binary-Coded Decimal

Data, when handled by equipment in these input and output operations, are normally in the *binary-coded decimal* (BCD) form, and the handling is performed with very little chance of error. Conversions to the BCD form are made at the sources of data and at the computer

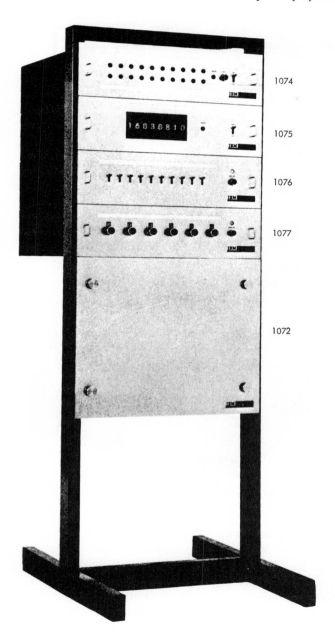

1074

1075

1076

1077

1072

Figure 9.2-4   Equipment for location at data sources for on-line operation (Courtesy of the IBM Corp.).

Figure 9.2-5 Equipment to reduce time delay in the output operations (Courtesy of the IBM Corp.).

before transmission of output. A set of 7 bits is required to represent a character set of 56 characters, and to provide the ability for error detecting. The 7-bit code is 1, 2, 4, 8, C, A, B, as shown in Figure 9.2-6. One bits appropriately placed in the 4 left-bit positions, as shown, represent the number symbols. The additional A- and B-bit positions, on the right, provide for the representation of the alphabetic characters and a number of special characters. The C-bit position provides for error checking. For example, in the input operations, when measurements are made at the sources of data and converted to the BCD form,

Sym.	BCD code						
	1	2	4	8	C	A	B
1.	1	0	0	0	1	0	0
2	0	1	0	0	1	0	0
3	1	1	0	0	0	0	0
4	0	0	1	0	1	0	0
5	1	0	1	0	0	0	0
6	0	1	1	0	0	0	0
7	1	1	1	0	1	0	0
8	0	0	0	1	1	0	0
9	1	0	0	1	0	0	0

Figure 9.2-6   Binary-coded decimal with check bit in position C.

a 1 bit is added in the C-bit position whenever it is required to make the total number of 1 bits in the 8-bit set equal an even number. After each character is transmitted, a check is made to see if the sum of the bits is still an even integer. If the sum is an odd integer, a bit has been lost or gained and an error is indicated.

Transmission of input and output over large distances is usually accomplished by common carrier lines, that is, by telephone and telegraph lines of utility companies. A transmission rate of 600 bits per second per channel can be achieved. Where many thousands of measurements of a rapidly changing condition are made each second, as in some research applications, other means of transmission of data must be used, such as microwave. In some cases, multiple lines may be used to transmit the 7-bit set, for example, 7 channels may be used—1 for each bit of the set. The bits are then transmitted in parallel or simultaneously, rather than 1 at a time through a single channel.

9.3   CLOSED-LOOP SYSTEMS

Definition

The three operations of data input, data processing, and output are also performed in closed-loop systems, but for this type of system the information of output is returned to the process where it may cause changes in those process operations. The process and the computer then form a closed loop through the communication channels as shown in Figure 9.3-1*a*. Note the difference between this diagram and that of the open-loop system of Figure 9.2-1. For this closed-loop system, the data output of the computer pertain to *action requests* and the data channels are shown by solid line arrows. Data input to the computer

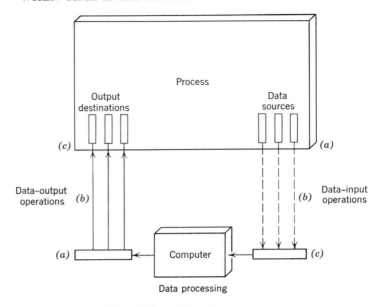

Figure 9.3-1a A closed-loop system.

pertain to the *results of actions,* and the channels are shown by dashed arrows.

The Principal Closed Loops in an Industrial System

We will expand on some of the material presented in Chapter 4 to establish where the closed loops exist. Figure 9.3-1b shows a diagram of an industrial system containing the process P and daily operations control C_1. To simplify the diagram, warehouses for product distribution have been omitted, and C_1 contains only the operations directly concerned with the process, namely, design and control of flow. The solid arrows associated with C_1 indicate communication channels that carry action requests, and the dashed arrows indicate those that carry results of the actions.

We have said in Chapters 4 and 7 that these operations of design and control of flow may be performed partially, or completely, by computers. To investigate how these computers operate within closed-loop systems, we will add the industrial systems of the supplier and the customer to Figure 9.3-1b, and the diagram of Figure 9.3-2a results. Purchase orders of our industry are customer orders for the supplier, and product output of the supplier is material input to our industry. Purchase orders of our customer are customer orders for our industry, and product output of our industry is material input of the customer.

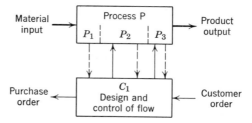

Figure 9.3-1b   Process P and the design and control of flow operations of C_1.

We may assume the control operations of our industry to be performed by four separate computers. A diagram showing these computers, and those of the supplier and customer which are directly involved in the closed loops of our industry, are shown in Figure 9.3-2b. The P_3 operations must be divided into those of product storage P_3' and shipping P_3'' to establish the loops for computers 3′ and 3″. Computer 1 of our industry, and computer 3″ of our supplier, are involved in the operations for controlling the flow of material into our industry. Computer 2 of our industry controls the proportioning and shaping of

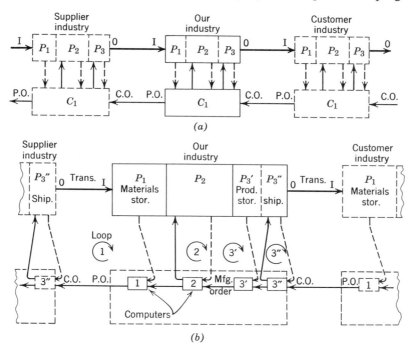

Figure 9.3-2   A system of three industries.

materials of the product, and the flow of the materials through the various material processing facilities. Computers 3′ and 2 of our industry are involved in the operations for controlling the product inventory. Computer 3″ of our industry controls product shipment, and is also involved in the operations of our customer in controlling the flow of materials into his industry.

The closed-loop systems which concern our industry are shown as loops 1, 2, 3′, and 3″, and each may be generally described by the diagram of Figure 9.3-3. The material-process operations of the diagram, are those of P_2 for loop 2, and those of $P_3″$ for loop 3″. The material-process operations for loop 1 are considered to be the combination of the operations of loop 3″ of the supplier, the transportation of materials, and P_1 of our industry. The process operations for loop 3′ of the general diagram are considered to be the combination of the operations of loop 2 and $P_3′$ of our industry. The input operations involve the measuring and recording of conditions related to the material-process operation, transmission of the data, and preparation of data for processing. The output operations involve the preparation of the output of the computer for transmission, transmission of output, and preparation of the output for application to the material-process operations which may now be caused to change. The output, then, pertains to *action requests* and the input operations pertain to the *results of those actions* which enter into the calculations in data processing to produce new action requests.

Classifications of Systems

Since closed-loop systems involve the same principal operations of input, processing, and output as open-loop systems, they may be classified in the same way as open-loop systems. Figure 9.3-4 summarizes this classification. There is a total of eight types listed. As examples, the type described by the first line is open-loop, off-line, and indirectly connected, and the last line describes a real-time closed-loop system.

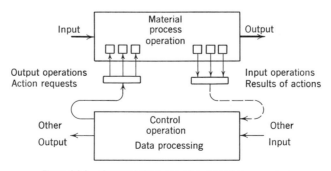

Figure 9.3-3   General diagram of a closed-loop system.

System	Computer operation	
Closed loop (1) Open loop (0)	On-line (1) Off-line (0)	Directly connected (1) Indirectly connected (0)
0	0	0
0	0	1
0	1	0
0*	1	1
1	0	0
1	0	1
1	1	0
1*	1	1

Figure 9.3-4   Classification of systems. The asterisks denote real-time systems.

The Advantages in Reducing Time Delays

Why do we strive for real-time closed-loop systems? The end result must be that they are more economical, or that profits are greater. This is accomplished through (1) a reduction in human error in the input and output operations, (2) improvement in predictions, and (3) frequent readjustments of conditions to maintain optimum results from the process operations. We have seen that parity checking in the handling of data by equipment reduces the chances of undetected errors. It is apparent that whenever manual effort is removed from the input-output operations, reliability of results is greatly improved.

We found that there were two principal advantages of real-time open-loop systems: (1) more accuracy in predicting, and (2) since measurements are made more frequently, predicted values may be updated frequently. There are also these two advantages of real-time closed-loop systems. Generally, whenever time delays exist in systems, there is a need to predict certain conditions. Two time delays exist in closed-loop operations. One of these also exists in open-loop systems and was identified as t_d. It pertains to the time required in performing the operations of input, data processing, and output, and may be made to approach zero in real-time operation. The other pertains to the material-process operations, and has the same effect in predicting as the time of a weather forecast (used as an example in describing open-loop systems). We will identify this delay by t_f, the forecast time.

Unless the input and output operations of data processing can be performed rapidly, frequent readjustments of conditions to maintain optimum results from the process operations cannot be realized. In Chapter 5 the subject of optimization was discussed, and Figure 5.5-21 and 5.5-22 showed that a high frequency of recalculations of problems of optimization may be required to achieve the best results. The large amounts of data required in solving many of these problems, and the large numbers of conditions that must be continually readjusted, require that the operations of input and output be performed at a low cost and very rapidly in order to achieve and maintain the highest possible net savings.

We will now investigate the effects of reducing the time delay t_d on the performance of each of the closed loops 1, 2, 3', and 3'', of our industrial system of Figure 9.3-2b. An important problem in the operations of loop 1 and loop 3', as we have already discovered, is predicting inventory. A plot of the number of units of inventory against time is shown in Figure 9.3-5, and is similar to that of Figure 4.2-5. The time delay $t_d = 1$ day is the time required to perform the operations of input, data processing, and output, where the time to perform the output operations pertains only to those for which the functions of inventory control are responsible. For loop 1, the time t_f is the sum of the times involved in performing the operations of loop 3'' of the supplier, transportation, and P_1 of our industry (see Figure 9.3-2b). For loop 3', t_f is the sum of the times involved in performing the operations of loop 2 and P_3'. The actual prediction time of inventory is $t_f' = t_d + t_f$. A curve is drawn through the plotted points of inventory and extends over the period of prediction t_f' to obtain I_f. The results for this example show that we need not issue a purchase order or an order to manufacture more units of product. If I_f is predicted to have a value near zero, an order is initiated and inventory is replenished before an outage occurs. When inventory records are frequently updated and the time delay t_d is made small by rapid performance of the input and output operations, the accuracy of predictions is improved and they are made more often.

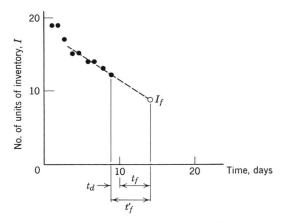

Figure 9.3-5   Inventory as a function of time.

Ordering decisions can then be made without the use of the minimum order-level quantity discussed in Chapter 4.

An important problem in the operation of loop 2 is achieving and maintaining optimum results from the material-process operations. The controlling operations pertain to design of products and control of flow of materials through the process facilities. Many conditions in proportioning and shaping of materials of products and in the use of the process facilities must be adjusted. Large amounts of data gathered from the process operations enter into such computational methods as linear programming and critical path, discussed in Chapter 5. Since a product requires a definite length of time to make, conditions prevailing during the various stages of material processing must be predicted when the planning and controlling instructions are established for the product, which is before any material processing begins. The total time of prediction is then $t_f' = t_d + t_f$, where t_f is measured from the time material processing for a product begins, to the time the predicted condition actually occurs. Rapid performance of the input and output operations permit frequent adjustment of conditions for achieving and maintaining maximum savings, and the predicted conditions that enter in the calculations can be determined accurately because of the increase in measured values and the decreased time delay t_d.

A decrease in t_d for loop 3″ reduces delivery time, and gives our industry a favored position with the customer for, as we have said, the operations of loop 3″ decrease t_f, which improves the accuracy of prediction of inventory in the customer's operations of loop 1.

Figure 9.3-2 shows data flow between computers 3″ and 3′, and between 2 and 1. The speed at which these input and output operations are performed are also important although the data may not enter directly in the closed-loop operations. Sales predictions calculated by computer 3″ may aid the operations of computer 3′ in predicting inventory. Data received by computer 1 from computer 2 may be beneficial to the loop 1 operations for the same reason, but more important, are the data giving the specifications of new materials for inventory.

A separate computer was shown for each of the 4 major loops in Figure 9.3-2, but to speed up the flow of data between the various data-processing operations, it is desirable to perform as many of these operations as is practical on a single computer. The data-processing operations of loops 3′ and 3″ are most frequently performed by a single computer.

Minor Closed Loops in an Industrial System

It must be remembered that there are many minor closed loops operating in P and C_1. The major ones are shown in Figure 9.3-2b, and are the only ones involving both data-processing operations for instruction generation in C_1, and material-processing operations in P. The minor loops occur totally, either in P, or in C_1. The operations of those in C_1 must involve only data processing, and are performed by the four computers of the major loops. Computermation then occurs in C_1 when the minor loop operations are performed by computers.

Many other minor loops operating totally within process P must involve the materials of process. Every machine engaged in a material process and its controller, forms a closed loop through communication channels. The controller watches the output of the machine and is able to initiate corrective measures when necessary, in executing the instructions generated by C_1. If an electro-mechanical controller replaces the human controller, the machine is *automated.*

There are many other closed loops in the operations of control and planning, but since only part of the data-processing operations of these loops are being performed by computers, they are not involved in our studies of real-time operation.

Types of Equipment Used

Where significant progress has been made in computermation, equipment has been installed to speed up the input and output operations. The type of equipment may be the same as that used in open-loop systems such as the type shown in Figure 9.2-3. When the sources of data are near the applications of the output, equipment for performing both the input and output may be integrated into single units, and the transmission lines shared. Examples of this type of equipment are shown in Figure 9.3-6a and b. The equipment of (a) consists of a printer keyboard, printer, paper-tape reader and punch, and a card reader. The equipment of (b) is frequently located in the area of material processing. The input unit on the right, and the output on the left, may share the same transmission facilities. The input unit accepts data punched in cards and entered by the keyboard, and the output unit presents instructions or requests for action in printed form. Figure 9.3-7 shows a terminal of this type installed in an automobile assembly plant for quality control.

Real-Time Operations in Discrete and Continuous Processes

We will now investigate real-time operations in the two principal types of material processing, *discrete* and *continuous.* The discrete type is concerned with materials and products that can be counted, such as automobiles, refrigerators, computers, and electric motors. Chapter 4 described some of the complexities of the material-processing operations for the discrete type. We found that in some cases machines have not

(*a*) IBM Model 1050; Equipment that transmits and receives.

(*b*) Equipment for location in the area of material processing.

Figure 9.3-6   Equipment for transmitting and receiving information (Courtesy of the IBM Corp.).

Figure 9.3-7   Equipment of the type shown in Figure 9.3-6*b* in an automobile assembly plant (Courtesy of the IBM Corp.).

yet been built to perform the highly complex motor skills of the human, and we are still dependent on his judgments and experiences in the operations. An example is the processing of electric motor-coils, described in Figure 4.3-2. Even though machines can be made to perform many of the discrete process-operations, and automation can be applied, manual efforts are still required in the handling of materials and products, and in the assembling of the parts with screws and bolts, as in the manufacture of automobiles. The control operations of C_1 for such systems are complex and progress in accomplishing computermation and automation is generally difficult.

Material-process systems of the continuous type may be completely automated, and made to approach real-time operation with less difficulty than the discrete type. The continuous type is concerned with continuous flows of materials and products, such as petroleum, cement, chemicals, and paper. Processing for many of the operations is natural, and has never required human motor skills. Since the human controller of the various operations generally required simple motor skills, as in the operating of valves and electrical switches, he can be replaced by electro-mechanical controllers. Also, the flows of materials and products between process operations do not require human handling—they flow continuously in pipes, or by conveyor belts.

Examples of Computer Applications to Process Control

Since many of these continuous process industries are fully automated, all the operations of input and output of the computers in the closed loops may also be performed without human intervention. Figure 9.3-8 describes a petroleum industry operating real-time for all 4 of the principal loops. Data are obtained directly from the material-process operations through such devices as flow meters and thermocouples. The computers are directly connected to the process operations through valves, switches, or other actuating devices. The equipment PCS performing in the input and output lines, is process-communication equipment of the type shown in Figure 9.2-4.

Figure 9.3-9 shows a cement kiln (upper right) which is on-line, with an IBM 1710 process-control computer (lower left). The kiln is over 400 feet in length and 13 feet in maximum diameter. Readings from 58 instruments are relayed directly to the computer where they are analyzed. The computer generates kiln operator instructions necessary to maintain optimum production.

Figure 9.3-10 shows the control operations room in another cement industry operating real-time. The plant is controlled from raw materials to finished product by a G.E. process-control computer (foreground of figure) operating on-line. Chemistry of incoming raw material is controlled to 0.1% accuracy. The burning of the product in the kiln is optimized on a continuous basis.

Other unique examples of closed-loop real-time systems are worth mentioning. One is the airline reservation system in which no material-process operation is performed in the closed loop, and a loop is in operation only when a reservation is being made. The system consists of a central computer and many remote input-output devices located at agents' offices throughout the country, and at the air terminals where flights of the airline are scheduled. Common carrier lines provide the two-way communication between the computer and the remote input-output terminals. Data on flight schedules, which are affected by unpredictable breakdowns of flight equipment and by weather, are entered into the computer through the input devices at the air terminals. The part of the system performing these operations is open loop, and the operations are performed with negligible delay.

A closed-loop system is established when a customer desiring reservations calls an agent. The agent, in effect, serves as an interpreter between the customer and computer through the use of the input-output device in the agent's office, and he establishes the computer-customer closed loop. Since all reservations are made through the system, the records in computer memory for the status of flight space are always

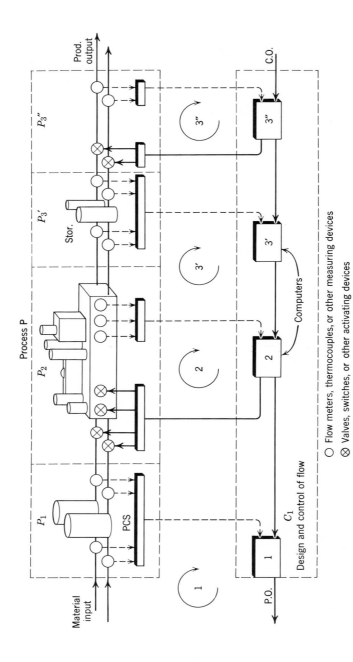

Figure 9.3-8 Diagram of petroleum industry operating real-time.

○ Flow meters, thermocouples, or other measuring devices

⊗ Valves, switches, or other activating devices

Figure 9.3-9   Cement kiln on-line to a computer (Courtesy of the IBM Corp.).

Figure 9.3-10   Control operations room of a cement industry (Courtesy of the General Electric Co.).

current. Delays are negligible in the closed loops, and predictions of conditions are not required.

The launching of a satellite is an excellent example of a real-time system, where events are happening so fast that only the great speed of the computer makes closed-loop control possible. In this situation, delicate instruments monitor the performance of all parts of the rocket system during those critical moments of blast-off. The information they gather is transmitted to a computer system, either onboard or ground-based processed by the computer; the trajectory is calculated, and the final orbit predicted. This orbit must be compared with the desired one whose characteristics have previously been fed into the computer and decisions made as to the corrections which must be applied to the rocket engines if the performance is not satisfactory. In spite of the complexity of the calculations involved, the control signals must be returned to the rocket with a total time delay measured in fractions of a second, or a few seconds at most.

In the worst case, the predicted path may deviate from the established course so greatly that the maximum correction which can be applied is insufficient, or it may be that the rocket does not respond to the correction signals, and the only recourse is to send a signal to the rocket which will trigger its destruction. Obviously, the time required to perform the operations of input, data processing, and output should not be so great that the rocket returns to earth and explodes before the output signal to accomplish the mid-air destruction reaches the rocket.

Still another interesting case in which a real-time system has been realized is in the electric utility industry. In this case, the computer generates the instructions for the complex operations of starting up and shutting down large turbine generators. Figure 9.3-11 shows the installation of a computer that operates on-line and is directly connected to 2 turbine generators with generating capacities of 42,000 and 44,000 kilowatts. This real-time system of the Gulf States Utilities Company was the first of its kind when completed in 1963, and was designed and implemented by the Allis-Chalmers Mfg. Co. One of the turbine generators is shown on the left of the upper photograph, and the control room where the computer is installed is shown on the right. The lower photograph shows the inside of the control room with an RCA 110 computer in the foreground. In the background are the many meters which had to be read manually, and the large number of switches which had to be operated before the implementation of the real-time system. Data from 350 different sources enter the computer, and 135 various actuating devices are operated directly from the computer's output.

Figure 9.3-11   Real-time operation during startup and shutdown of a turbine generator (Courtesy Allis-Chalmers Mfg. Co.).

Only one turbine generator can be started and synchronized on the power line at a time, but both can be shut down simultaneously. During the start-up period, 121 different sets of action-requests are generated by the computer, and during shut-down, there are 48. A total of 65 man-years of effort was required to convert the system to real-time operation over a period of three years. Personnel was reduced to approximately one-half.

9.4 PREDICTING

We found that predicting conditions is a common requirement of most open- and closed-loop systems, and arises from the fact that a time delay t_f' exists. This time delay was defined as the sum of the time delays t_d and t_f, where t_d was established to be the sum of the times to perform the operations of input, data processing, and output, which could be made negligible for real-time operation, and t_f was either a given value of time, or pertained to the time required to perform other operations of the system, which generally must be accepted as fixed. We showed values of a condition plotted against time in Figure 9.2-2 and drew a curve through the points as best we could. We then extended the curve over the time delay t_f' to obtain a predicted value.

Since predicting must be made a part of the operations performed by the computer, we see a great need for computational methods for calculating predicted values. In this section, we will present two such methods. The one can more often be applied to operations of off-line, indirectly connected computers in which the time delay t_d is large and values of conditions are obtained infrequently. Large changes occur in the values of the conditions among successive measurements. The other method is better suited for application to the operations of real-time systems where t_d is negligible, and values of conditions are obtained frequently, so that there are small differences in the values of conditions between successive measurements.

The problem of predicting for both methods is to find an equation whose curve best fits the points of plotted values described by Figure 9.2-2. We will use the algebraic polynomial equation which was discussed in Chapter 2:

$$Y = A(0) + A(1)X + A(2)X^2 + \ldots + A(N)X^N$$

Since the independent variable in our studies is time, we will rewrite the equation, replacing X with T, to obtain

$$Y = A(0) + A(1)T + A(2)T^2 + \ldots + A(N)T^N$$

In Chapter 2 the coefficients $A(I)$ were given, and we were required to calculate the value of Y for various values of the independent variable X. In our use of the equation, we must first obtain the coefficients from the given values of T and Y obtained by measurements. We can then predict Y by substituting the value of T for that desired value of Y in the resulting polynomial equation.

First Method

We choose to use as a first method "Newton's Divided-Difference Polynomial[1]" which can be applied more often to operations of off-line computers. This nth-degree difference polynomial is

$$Y(N) = Y_0 + (T - T_0)F_1 + (T - T_0)(T - T_1)F_2$$
$$+ \cdots + (T - T_0)(T - T_1)(T - T_2) \cdots (T - T_{N-1})F_N \quad (9.4\text{-}1)$$

The curve of this polynomial passes through all points of plotted values which are used to determine its coefficients, and the measured values of Y need not be equally spaced in time.

We will demonstrate the method with the use of a second-degree polynomial which requires three sets of measured values of Y and T. The equation may be written from equation 9.4-1 as

$$Y(2) = Y_0 + (T - T_0)F_1 + (T - T_0)(T - T_1)F_2$$
$$= A_0 + A_1 T + A_2 T^2 \quad (9.4\text{-}2)$$

where

$$A_0 = Y_0 - T_0 F_1 + T_1 T_0 F_2$$
$$A_1 = F_1 - F_2(T_0 + T_1)$$
$$A_2 = F_2 \quad (9.4\text{-}3)$$

The F quantities are called divided differences, and their values are calculated from the equations:

$$F_1 = \frac{Y_1 - Y_0}{T_1 - T_0}$$

$$F_2 = \frac{(Y_2 - Y_1)/(T_2 - T_1) - F_1}{T_2 - T_0} \quad (9.4\text{-}4)$$

where the subscripted Y and T quantities are measured in the order of the subscripts as shown in Figure 9.4-1.

A Demonstration of its use. We will now solve an example problem of predicting, using the first three sets of measured values in Figure 9.4-1a. These values, for $i = 0$, 1, and 2, are plotted in Figure 9.4-1b. The first task is to calculate the A_i coefficients of the difference-polynomial equation 9.4-2. From equations 9.4-4, the values of F are $F_1 = 2$, and $F_2 = -\frac{1}{2}$. With these values known, the coefficients A_i of equations 9.4-3 may be calculated, and equation 9.4-2 gives the second-order difference polynomial

$$Y = -2 + \tfrac{7}{2} T - \tfrac{1}{2} T^2 \quad (9.4\text{-}5)$$

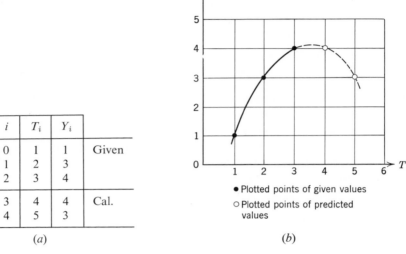

i	T_i	Y_i	
0	1	1	Given
1	2	3	
2	3	4	
3	4	4	Cal.
4	5	3	

(a)

- Plotted points of given values
- ○ Plotted points of predicted values

(b)

Figure 9.4-1 Application of 2nd order divided-difference polynomial to predicting.

The second part of the problem is to predict Y_3 and Y_4 by substituting each of the values of $T_3 = 4$ and $T_4 = 5$ in equation 9.4-5. The results $Y_3 = 4$ and $Y_4 = 3$, and the corresponding values of T, are shown as the last two sets of values in Figure 9.4-1a, and the values are shown plotted in Figure 9.4-1b.

A divided-difference table, Figure 9.4-2a, may also be used to find the values of F for the second-degree polynomial, and may be expanded and used to obtain the coefficients of a polynomial of any larger degree. It provides for an orderly sequence of calculations. The calculations of F_1 require the first two columns of given values of T and Y, and are performed first. The calculations of F_2 require the values of F_1 and T, and are performed next. F_1 and F_2 are generally defined as

$$F_1 = f_{i,i-1} = \frac{Y_i - Y_{i-1}}{T_i - T_{i-1}}$$

$$F_2 = f_{i,i-1,i-2} = \frac{f_{i,i-1} - f_{i-1,i-2}}{T_i - T_{i-2}} \tag{9.4-6}$$

We will now demonstrate the use of the divided-difference table by solving our example problem. The first three sets of values in Figure 9.4-1a are placed in the first two columns for T and Y of the difference table of Figure 9.4-2, and the calculations for F are performed to complete the table. The first values of the columns for F_1 and F_2

T_i Y_i F_1 F_2
T_0 Y_0

f_{10}

T_1 Y_1 $\qquad f_{210}$

f_{21}

T_2 Y_2

(*a*) General form of divided-difference table

T_i Y_i F_1 F_2
1   1

2

2   3 $\qquad -\tfrac{1}{2}$

1

3   4

(*b*) Divided-difference table for example problem of Figure 9.4-1

Figure 9.4-2   Divided-difference table for determining second-order polynomial.

are equal to those obtained from equations 9.4-4, and when substituted in equation 9.4-2, yield the equation 9.4-5.

Second Method

Chance variations, or experimental errors, occur in measured values even for systems in which computers operate on-line, and the values are measured and transmitted without human intervention. For example, if a given weight is weighed a number of times on the same scale, the indicator would likely be in a slightly different position for each weighing operation, perhaps, as a result of friction in the moving parts, or from temperature changes. The general appearance of plotted data is as shown in Figure 9.2-2*b*. When data can be obtained frequently, as is usually the case with on-line operations, an analysis may be performed to determine the best curve for predicting.

An Example Set of Measured Values. The second method of determining a curve requires a deviation analysis, and draws on our knowledge of probability obtained in Section 5.6. We will assume that we have the 40 measured values of Y shown in Figure 9.4-3*a*, which are obtained at 1-second intervals. We will analyze the data to determine the best curve for the plot. Three sets of values will be analyzed to obtain 3 points for the curve. The first 20, mid 20, and last 20 values constitute the 3 sets where the mid set has 10 values common to each of the other 2 sets. A frequency distribution, or histogram, for each of the 3 sets is shown in

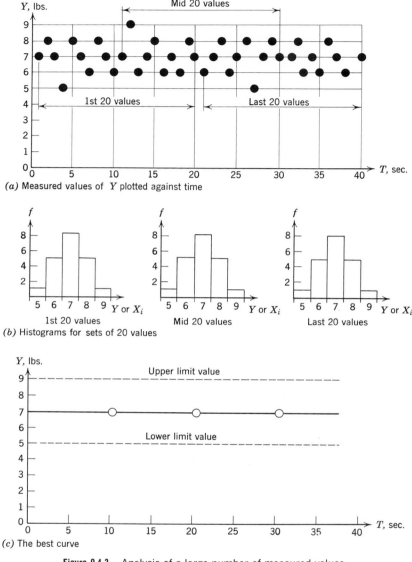

Figure 9.4-3 Analysis of a large number of measured values.

Figure 9.4-3*b* in which the frequency plotted against *Y* is the number of times a given value of *Y* appears within a set. We note the frequency distributions are the same, and the value of $Y = 7$ appears most frequently. Points for the best curve are established at $Y = 7$, and $T =$

the mid value of time for each set. The best curve is drawn through these 3 points as shown in Figure 9.4-3c, and the equation for the curve is $Y = 7$. All the measured values lie on and between the upper-limit value for $Y = 9$, and the lower-limit value of $Y = 5$.

From the material presented in Section 5.6, we can reason that if we placed 20 identical pieces of cardboard in a container, with the values of Y equals 5 through 9 assigned to the pieces of cardboard according to the frequency distribution of Figure 9.4-3b, the probabilities of with-drawing each of the numbers from the container are $\frac{1}{20}$ for values 5 and 9, $\frac{5}{20}$ for 6 and 8, and $\frac{8}{20}$ for 7. The first 6 columns of data in the table of Figure 9.4-4 demonstrate a procedure for performing these calcula-tions from measured data, and provide information for plotting the probability distribution curve of Figure 9.4-5a. The symbol Y_i is now replaced with X_i to maintain consistency with the nomenclature gener-ally used for this type of analysis. From the third column, the total number of measured values N is

$$N = \Sigma f_i \qquad (9.4\text{-}7)$$

where Σf_i is the sum of the number of times the individual values were measured, and equals 20 for our example. In the fourth column, the probabilities P_i' are calculated from the equation

$$P_i' = f_i/N \qquad (9.4\text{-}8)$$

and their sum, $\Sigma P_i'$, must equal 1. The arithmetic mean $\overline{X}$ may be determined from the calculated values in the fifth column. It is equal to 7 for our example, and is determined by the equation

$$\overline{X} = \Sigma f_i X_i/N \qquad (9.4\text{-}9)$$

Columns

1	2	3	4		5	6	7	8
i	X_i (Y_i)	f_i	P_i' f_i/N		$f_i X_i$	x_i $(X_i - \overline{X})$	x_i^2	$f_i x_i^2$
1	9	1	0.05		9	2	4	4
2	8	5	0.25		40	1	1	5
3	7	8	0.40		56	0	0	0
4	6	5	0.25		30	−1	1	5
5	5	1	0.05		5	−2	4	4
		$N = \Sigma f_i = 20$	$\Sigma P_i' = 1.00$		$\Sigma f_i X_i = 140$			$\Sigma f_i x_i^2 = 18$
					$\overline{X} = \Sigma f_i X_i/N = 7$			$s^2 = \Sigma f_i x_i^2/(N-1)$
								$= 18/19 = 0.946$
								$s = 0.97$

s^2 = Mean of squared deviation or variance
s = Root-mean-square deviation or standard deviation

Figure 9.4-4   Deviation analysis of data of Figure 9.4-3.

The measured deviations x_i in column 6 are determined by the equation

$$x_i = (X_i - \bar{X}) \tag{9.4-10}$$

The Gaussian Probability Distribution. Before discussing the remaining 2 columns, we will use the results of the calculations of the first 6 columns to plot the probability distribution, and will compare this distribution of our example with another important distribution curve. The probabilities P_i' of column 4 are plotted against the measured values X_i and against the measured deviations x_i of column 6 to obtain the probability distribution shown in Figure 9.4-5a. A continuous curve is drawn through the midpoint of the horizontal segments of the bar graph, i.e., through points established by assigning the 5 calculated probability values to integer values of X_i and x_i. When we compare this distribution with the probability distribution of Figure 9.4-5b, we find the curves very similar in shape. This second distribution curve is called a *Gaussian* or *normal* probability distribution and is often used as a standard for comparison. It is described by the equation

$$P = (1/\sqrt{2\pi})e^{-Z_i^2/2} \tag{9.4-11}$$

where e is the base of natural logarithms, 2.7183, and Z is a standard measured value. It has been found that in many cases the distributions obtained from a very large number of measured values are similar to this normal distribution. Values were chosen for our example problem which would give very nearly the same distribution. Five values of probabilities for values of $Z_i = x_i$ are given in the figures, and serve to show the close agreement.

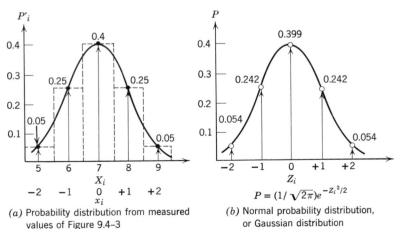

(a) Probability distribution from measured values of Figure 9.4-3

(b) Normal probability distribution, or Gaussian distribution

Figure 9.4-5   Actual and normal distributions for comparison.

The Standard Deviation s. We will now continue with the discussion of Figure 9.4-4 in order to discover other ways of comparing probability distributions with the normal distribution. From the results of the calculations of x_i^2 in column 7 and $f_i x_i^2$ in column 8, a mean of the squared deviation or *variance*, s^2, may be calculated by the equation

$$s^2 = \Sigma(f_i x_i^2)/(N - 1) \tag{9.4-12}$$

which for our example problem has the value of 0.946. The equation for the root-mean-square deviation or *standard deviation*, s, is then

$$s = \sqrt{\Sigma(f_i x_i^2)/(N - 1)} \tag{9.4-13}$$

and is equal to 0.97 for our example.

We will use this calculated standard deviation for comparing the distribution with the normal, but we must first investigate s for the normal distribution. Figure 9.4-6a shows areas under segments of the normal-distribution curve as determined by the ranges of Z, and the information is tabulated in the first 2 columns of Figure 9.4-6b. For example, in the range of Z from $Z = 0$ to $Z = +1$ and from $Z = -1$ to $Z = 0$, the area under the curve is 0.3413. The area from $Z = -1$ to $Z = +1$ is then $2 \times 0.3413 = 0.6826$. Since the normal-distribution curve approaches the Z axis asymptotically, i.e., approaches the Z axis but never crosses it, a range from $Z = +3$ to $Z = +$infinity and from $Z = -3$ to $Z = -$infinity, is shown in the table and the area is 0.0013 for each range.

The relationship between s and Z for the normal-distribution curve is shown by the scales for these 2 variables along the horizontal axis of the plot of Figure 9.4-6a and in Figure 9.4-6b. For $Z = 0$ to $Z = 1$, and $Z = -1$ to $Z = 0$, the area of 0.3413 is 1 standard deviation s on either side of the mean ($Z = 0$). For $Z = -1$ to $Z = +1$, the area of 0.6826 is within 1s of the mean; that is to say, of the total number of measured values giving the normal distribution, 0.6826 of the total will have values that lie within 1s of the mean. The relationships of the remaining areas and deviations given in the table should be apparent.

How can we use the calculated value of s of the given set of measured values of our example? From Figure 9.4-4, the mean value of Y was calculated equal to 7, and the value of s equal to 0.97. This means that the distance along the X axis for the plot of Figure 9.4-5a, from $X = 7$ to $X = 7.97$, is equal to 1 standard deviation and the value 7.97 is said to be 1s above the mean. 0.6826 of all measured values will be within 1s of the mean, or between $7 - 0.97 = 6.03$ and $7 + 0.97 = 7.97$. The plot of Figure 9.4-3c is redrawn in Figure 9.4-7 to show the distribution of the measured values around the mean for 1s, 2s, and 3s. If a

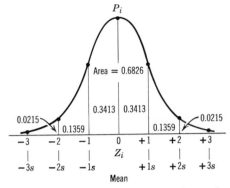

(a) Normal-distribution showing area under curve for various ranges of Z

1	2	3
Range of Z	Area under curve	Explanation in terms of the standard deviation s
0 to +1	0.3413	Area which is 1 standard deviation
−1 to 0	0.3413	on either side of the mean ($Z = 0$)
−1 to +1	0.6826	Area within $1s$ of the mean
+1 to +2	0.1359	
−2 to −1	0.1359	
−2 to +2	0.9544	Area within $2s$ of the mean
+2 to +3	0.0215	
−3 to −2	0.0215	
−3 to +3	0.9974	Area within $3s$ of the mean
+3 to Inf.	0.0013	
−Inf. to −3	0.0013	
−Inf. to +Inf.	1.000	Total area

(b) Ranges of Z, areas, and explanation of s

Figure 9.4-6.

very large number of measurements were taken, and it were assumed that the distribution for these measured values was normal, the points would lie scattered about the value of $Y = 7$ as indicated in the figure.

Analysis of a Set of Values Selected at Random. We said that values were chosen for the example problem of Figure 9.4-3 which would very nearly give the normal distribution. We also said that if 20 identical pieces of cardboard were placed in a container with the values of Y

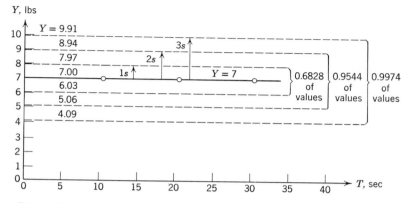

Figure 9.4-7 Application of standard deviation to example problem of Fig. 9.4-3.

equaling 5 through 9 assigned to the pieces of cardboard according to the frequency distribution of Figure 9.4-3b, the frequency curves for sampling numbers from the container and for the example problem would be similar, provided a very large number of samples were taken. What results would we obtain from a deviation analysis if instead of a nearly normal frequency-distribution, we took relatively few samples from the container and the frequency curve differed from the normal by a large amount? Since there is a limit to the number of values that can be obtained and analyzed over a practical period of time, even for on-line computer operations, the question is important. We will now proceed to determine the answer by analyzing our example problem for these conditions. We can make use of the random numbers in the table of Figure 5.6-1 by assigning a frequency value of 1 to each of the random numbers 5 and 9 in the table, a frequency value of 5 to each of the numbers 6 and 8, and a value of 8 to each of the numbers 7. All remaining numbers from 0 through 4 will be disregarded. The first 75 numbers of the table are considered, and we search for values 5 through 9 beginning at the top of the left column. The values of X_i and f_i are given in Figure 9.4-8. The 3 sets of values were established in the same manner as those in Figure 9.4-3. The total number of equivalent measured values is 115 with 58 in the first set and 57 in each of the other 2 sets. The calculations for the first and last sets are complete. The calculations for the mid set are to be completed as an exercise.

The calculated probability values P_i' of the first and last sets are plotted against X_i as shown by curve A in Figures 9.4-9a and b. Both distributions are "skewed" to the left, i.e., the curves are not symmetrical about the center value of $X_i = 7$, and the values of P' on the left of this value are in general larger than those on the right. If a very large num-

i	X_i	f_i	P_i' f_i/N	f_iX_i
1	9	$4 \times 1 = 4$	0.069	36
2	8	$2 \times 5 = 10$	0.172	80
3	7	$2 \times 8 = 16$	0.276	112
4	6	$5 \times 5 = 25$	0.431	150
5	5	$3 \times 1 = 3$	0.052	15
		$N = \Sigma f_i = 58$	$\Sigma P_i' = 1.000$	$\Sigma f_iX_i = 393$

$$\overline{X} = \Sigma f_iX_i/N = 6.78$$

x_i $(X_i - \overline{X})$	x_i^2	$f_ix_i^2$
2.22	4.928	19.71
1.22	1.488	14.88
0.22	0.048	.77
−0.78	0.608	15.20
−1.78	3.168	9.50
		$\Sigma f_ix_i^2 = 60.06$

$$s^2 = \Sigma f_ix_i^2/(N - 1) = 1.054$$
$$s = 1.026$$

(a) First set

i	X_i	f_i
1	9	$9 \times 1 = 9$
2	8	$1 \times 5 = 5$
3	7	$2 \times 8 = 16$
4	6	$4 \times 5 = 20$
5	5	$7 \times 1 = 7$
		$N = \Sigma f_i = 57$

(b) Mid set

i	X_i	f_i	P_i' f_i/N	f_iX_i
1	9	$5 \times 1 = 5$	0.088	45
2	8	$1 \times 5 = 5$	0.088	40
3	7	$2 \times 8 = 16$	0.281	112
4	6	$5 \times 5 = 25$	0.438	150
5	5	$6 \times 1 = 6$	0.105	30
		$N = \Sigma f_i = 57$	$\Sigma P_i' = 1.000$	$\Sigma f_iX_i = 377$

$$\overline{X} = \Sigma f_iX_i/N = 6.62$$

Figure 9.4-8 Deviation analyses for 115 sampled values.

$(X_i - \overline{X})$	x_i x_i^2	$f_i x_i^2$
2.38	5.664	28.32
1.38	1.904	9.52
.0.38	0.144	2.30
−0.62	0.384	9.60
−1.62	2.624	15.74

$$\Sigma f_i x_i^2 = 65.48$$
$$s^2 = \Sigma f_i X_i^2/(N-1) = 1.169$$
$$s = 1.08$$

(c) Last set

Figure 9.4-8   (*cont.*)

ber of samples is taken, the distributions would be the same as that shown in Figure 9.4-5a. The continuous curve for this distribution of Figure 9.4-5a is shown as curve B in Figures 9.4-9a and b.

The values of the standard deviation s are calculated in Figures 9.4-8a and b, from which a distribution can be calculated on the assumption that the distribution is normal for a very large number of sampled values. The values of X_i for integer values of deviation are calculated and shown along the horizontal axis. The normal-distribution curve C of the Figures 9.4-9a and b, which is the same curve in Figure 9.4-6a, is established by plotting known values of P_i for integer values of deviation $-1s, +1s$, etc.

The difference between curves B and C in the figures is the error resulting from the small number of samples. The mean $\overline{X}$ for a very large number of samples should equal 7, but with the number of samples taken, $\overline{X} = 6.78$ and 6.62 for the first and last set, respectively.

The equation for a best curve for a very large number of samples would be $Y = 7$, as was established from the previous analysis and shown by the plot of Figure 9.4-7, but with the small number of samples taken, the best curve for $Y = \overline{X}$ plotted against T for the 2 points is not parallel to the T axis. And, if we had completed the calculations for the mid set, we would have had three values of $\overline{X}$, and the best curve would not likely be a straight line.

If a very large number of samples had been taken, the value of s would be 0.97 as determined by the calculations of Figure 9.4-4, but with the number of samples actually taken, the value of s is 1.026 and 1.08 for the first and last set of values, respectively. The values of a large number of samples are calculated to be less concentrated near the mean than they would be if a large number were sampled.

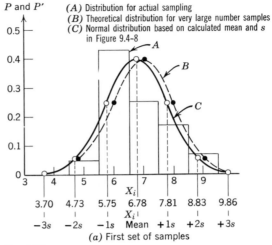

(a) First set of samples

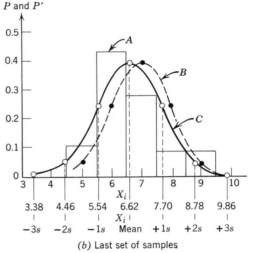

(b) Last set of samples

(*A*) Distribution for actual sampling
(*B*) Theoretical distribution for very large number samples
(*C*) Normal distribution based on calculated mean and *s* in Figure 9.4-8.

Figure 9.4-9   Plotted results of calculations of Figure 9.4-8.

We have established that if we can assume that a very large number of sampled values produce a normal distribution, it can be calculated from a relatively few values actually sampled. The meaning of the *calculated* normal distribution is that if a very large number of samples would be taken, they would produce that calculated distribution. We see that this becomes truer as more sampled values are obtained and included in the calculation of the normal distribution. Computers operating on-line make it possible to sample values frequently and to include a large number in the calculation.

A Demonstration of the Use of the Method of Least Squares. The analysis we have just completed is basic to the understanding of the second method, the "method of least squares,"[1,2] for establishing a best curve through a large number of plotted points. We will limit the method of analysis to a straight-line curve described by the equation

$$Y = a + bT$$

Basically, the method determines values for a and b such that the sum of the squares of the deviations of measured or sampled values from the line are mimimal. A numerical example will be used to describe the method.

Assume that the system which supplied the data for the 3 plotted points of Figure 9.4-1 becomes on-line to a computer and that values are sampled more frequently. Also, assume that the values of T as well as the values of Y are subject to deviations. The table of data is shown in Figure 9.4-10a and includes the data for the 3 plotted points of Figure 9.4-1. The data are plotted in Figure 9.4-10b.

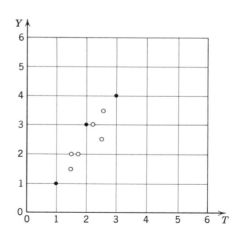

i	T_i	Y_i
1	1.0	1.0
2	1.5	1.5
3	1.5	2.0
4	1.75	2.0
5	2.0	3.0
6	2.25	3.0
7	2.5	2.5
8	2.5	3.5
9	3.0	4.0

$\Sigma T_i = 18.00$ $\Sigma Y_i = 22.75$

(a)

• Points of plotted values from figure 9.4-1
o Additional points of plotted values

(b)

Figure 9.4-10 Data to be analyzed by the method of least squares.

The equation of concern is

$$Y = a + bT \qquad (9.4\text{-}14)$$

where

$$b = \Sigma t_i y_i / \Sigma f_i t_i^2$$
$$a = \overline{Y} - b\overline{T} \qquad (9.4\text{-}15)$$

We are already familiar with the terms appearing in the equations, and calculations similar to those in the tables of Figures 9.4-4 and 9.4-8 must be performed. In this case, a variation analysis must be made on both Y and T as shown in Figures 9.4-11a and b. The second table for the analysis of the Y values contains an additional column of calculated values $t_i y_i$ and the sum $\Sigma t_i y_i$. Substituting the calculated values of the tables in equation 9.4-15 we have:

$$b = \Sigma t_i y_i / \Sigma f_i t_i^2 = 4.50/3.125 = 1.44$$
$$a = \overline{Y} - b\overline{T} = 2.5 - 1.44 \times 2.0 = -0.38$$

i	T_i	f_i	$f_i T_i$
1	1.0	1	1.0
2	1.5	1	1.5
3	1.5	1	1.5
4	1.75	1	1.75
5	2.0	1	2.0
6	2.25	1	2.25
7	2.5	1	2.5
8	2.5	1	2.5
9	3.0	1	3.0
		$N = \Sigma f_i = 9$	$\Sigma f_i T_i = 18.00$

$$\overline{T} = \Sigma f_i T_i / N = 2.0$$

t_i $(T_i - \overline{T})$	t_i^2	$f_i t_i^2$
-1.0	1.00	1.00
-0.5	0.25	0.25
-0.5	0.25	0.25
-0.25	0.0625	0.0625
0.0	0.00	0.00
$+0.25$	0.0625	0.0625
$+0.50$	0.25	0.25
$+0.50$	0.25	0.25
$+1.00$	1.00	1.00
	$\Sigma t_i^2 = 3.125$	$\Sigma f_i t_i^2 = 3.125$

(a) Analysis of T values

Figure 9.4-11   Analysis of measured values of the table of Figure 9.4-10.

i	Y_i	f_i	$f_i Y_i$
1	1.0	1	1.0
2	1.5	1	1.5
3	2.0	1	2.0
4	2.0	1	2.0
5	3.0	1	3.0
6	3.0	1	3.0
7	2.75	1	2.5
8	3.5	1	3.5
9	4.0	1	4.0
		$N = \Sigma f_i = 9$	$\Sigma f_i Y_i = 22.50$
			$\overline{Y} = \Sigma f_i Y_i / N = 2.5$

y_i $(Y_i - \overline{Y})$	y_i^2	$f_i y_i^2$	$t_i y_i$
-1.5	2.25	2.25	1.5
-1.0	1.00	1.00	0.5
-0.5	0.25	0.25	0.25
-0.5	0.25	0.25	0.125
$+0.5$	0.25	0.25	0.0
$+0.5$	0.25	0.25	0.125
$+0.0$	0.00	0.00	0.0
$+1.0$	1.00	1.00	0.5
$+1.5$	2.25	2.25	1.5
	$\Sigma y_i^2 = 7.50$	$\Sigma f_i y_i^2 = 7.50$	$\Sigma t_i y_i = 4.50$

(*b*) Analysis of *Y* values

Figure 9.4-11   (*cont.*)

and the best straight-line curve that can be drawn through the plotted points is

$$Y = a + bT = -0.38 + 1.44T \tag{9.4-16}$$

Comparison of the Two Methods

The measured values of Figure 9.4-10 are plotted in Figure 9.4-12, and the straight-line curve described by equation 9.4-16 is shown as curve *A*. Curve *B* is the curve of Figure 9.4-1 obtained by the first method, and passes through the same 3 points. The predicted values of *Y* for $T = 4$ and 5, using the equation of curve *A*, are 5.38 and 6.82 as compared to 4.0 and 3.0 for the equation of curve *B*.

The deviations for our example problem have been exaggerated but caution must always be exercised in fitting a curve through just a few points when they are plotted from values which are subject to deviations.

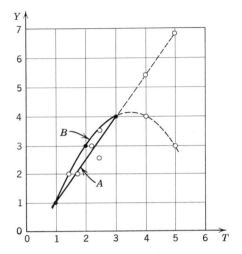

Figure 9.4-12   Comparison of results of the first and second methods.

The equation of curve B, determined by the first method, would have given greater accuracy in the predicted values if it had been an equation of a straight-line curve passing through the 2 latest points.

PROBLEM 9.2-1   "Data Transmission"

(A) How many 4-digit numbers can be transmitted in BCD per second over a channel of a common carrier line with a maximum capacity of 600 bits per second?

(B) How many of these channels are required for transmission of 70 4-digit numbers per second?

PROBLEM 9.3-1   "Out to Launch"

The altitude of a satellite being launched is monitored every tenth of a second. Write a program to use each new piece of data *as it is received* (do not read in all the data at the beginning), to form successive estimates of what the altitude of the satellite will be 2.5 seconds after launching. Compare the estimated altitude at 2.5 seconds with the desired altitude of 470 feet.

(A) If any estimate differs from the required altitude by more than 1%, issue a warning.

(B) If three successive estimates differ from the required altitude by more than 1%, issue a warning.

(C) If three successive estimates differ from the required altitude by more than 1% in the same direction (all higher or all lower), issue a warning.

In any case, discontinue the calculation after the warning condition has been met.

INPUT

T	D	T	D
0.0	0.0000000	1.3	1.2724575E + 02
.1	7.5000000E − 01	1.4	1.4754859E + 02
.2	3.0086620	1.5	1.6933524E + 02
.3	6.7744214	1.6	1.9261119E + 02
.4	1.2046340E + 01	1.7	2.1739475E + 02
.5	1.8824530E + 01	1.8	2.4370391E + 02
.6	2.7128614E + 01	1.9	2.7168805E + 02
.7	3.6912778E + 01	2.0	3.0135626E + 02
.8	4.8211852E + 01	2.1	3.3279715E + 02
.9	6.1023955E + 01	2.2	3.6411648E + 02
1.0	7.5318956E + 01	2.3	3.9795033E + 02
1.1	9.1222195E + 01	2.4	4.3317739E + 02
1.2	1.0843712E + 02	2.5	4.7000661E + 02

HOW TO CALCULATE

Since velocity is defined as rate of change of position, the average velocity over any time period can be calculated from 2 successive measurements of position, thus:

$$V_n = \frac{D_n - D_{n-1}}{\Delta t}$$

Similarly, acceleration is defined as rate of change of velocity, so the average acceleration over any 2-interval period can be calculated from 2 successive velocity figures:

$$A_n = \frac{V_n - V_{n-1}}{\Delta t}$$

In this problem, nothing can be calculated after receipt of the first observation only. After receiving the second observation, 1 velocity calculation can be made, but no acceleration. Not until 3 observations have been received can the first acceleration be calculated, and the first projection of estimated altitude be made.

For each new reading after the third one, the record should be updated so that only the current reading and the two immediately preceding ones are retained. With these three most recent readings, a new projection ahead should be made each time.

This rocket engine is supposed to produce a constant acceleration. For our approach, we will proceed as follows: as soon as any acceleration has been calculated, it will be assumed that that acceleration will hold constant for the remainder of the 2.5-second test period. Using it, and the most recently measured value of distance, we will calculate future values of velocity and position until we reach the 2.5-second mark.

By way of illustration, consider the following sample data points (not identical with those values given above as input).

T	D
0.	0.
.1	.75
.2	2.99
.3	6.73
.4	11.98
.5	18.73

When the first 2 points have been read in, a calculation of velocity can be made:

N	T	D	V
1	0.	0.	
2	.1	.75	7.5

$$\left(V_2 = \frac{D_2 - D_1}{T_2 - T_1} = \frac{0.75 - 0.}{0.1 - 0.} \right)$$

When the third point has been read in, another calculation of velocity and a first calculation of acceleration can be made:

N	T	D	V	A
1	0.	0.		
2	.1	.75	7.5	
3	.2	2.99	22.4	149.0

$$\left(A_3 = \frac{V_3 - V_2}{\Delta t} = \frac{22.4 - 7.5}{0.1} \right)$$

Now, if we assume that the value of A will be the same for each successive interval, we can work backwards across each row, and calculate for each row a new V and a new D. If this is repeated for each row, always using the same A, we eventually arrive at D corresponding to 2.5 seconds.

N	T	D	V	A
1	0.	0.		
2	.1	.75	7.5	
3	.2	2.99	22.4	149.0
4	.3	6.72 ← 37.3 ← 149.0		
5	.4	11.94 ← 52.2 ← 149.0		
.	.	.		
.	.	.		
. etc.	.			
2.5	467.00			

Now compare this⌐ with 470.

For the second calculation, use:

2	.1	.75		
3	.2	2.99	22.4	
4	.3	6.73	37.4	150.0
	.4	11.97 ← 52.4 ← 150.0		
	.5	18.71 ← 67.4 ← 150.0		
	.	.		
	.	.		
	. etc.	.		
2.5	469.			

PROBLEM 9.4-1   "Predicting with a Small Amount of Data"

Write a program for predicting, using the second-order divided-difference polynomial. Determine the coefficients from Equations 9.4-3 and use the information supplied in Chapter 3 for evaluating the polynomial equation. Assume the first three sets of data in the table of Figure 9.4-1a as given, and check the program by calculating Y for values of T in increments of 1 unit from 1 through 5.

PROBLEM 9.4-2   "Deviation Analysis"

(A) Complete the table of Figure 9.4-8 for the mid set of values by manual calculations. Compare $\bar{X}$ and s with the values shown in the figure for the first and last sets. Is the best curve, which passes through the three values of $Y = \bar{X}$, a straight line?

(B) Write a program to perform the deviation analysis and check the results with those obtained by manual calculations of part (A). Obtain as output N, $\bar{X}$, s^2, and s.

PROBLEM 9.4-3   "Predicting with a Large Amount of Data"

(A) Write a program for predicting using the method of least squares.

GIVEN

Measured values Y_i and T_i punched 1 pair per card, and time values T_{p1} and T_{p2} for calculating predicted values Y_{p1} and Y_{p2}.

WANTED

$$\bar{Y},\ \bar{T},\ \Sigma f_i t_i{}^2,\ \Sigma t_i y_i,\ b,\ a,\ (T_{p1},\ Y_{p1}),\ \text{and}\ (T_{p2},\ Y_{p2})$$

(B) Prepare as input the measured values in Figure 9.4-10a. Also, prepare as input $T_{p1} = 4$, and $T_{p2} = 5$. Compare the values of the coefficients a and b calculated by the program against those in Equation 9.4-16.

(C) Repeat (B) with the following modification: Assume that values were measured at a slower rate by preparing as input the first pair listed in Figure 9.4-10a and every other pair in the list.

REFERENCES

1. Carnahan, Brice, H. A. Luther, and James O. Wilkes. *Applied Numerical Methods*, John Wiley & Sons, Inc., in press.

CHAPTER 10.

The Language of the Machine

10.1 PERSPECTIVE

In Chapter 8 we developed a picture of what goes on inside computers to the point where we could draw a fairly detailed diagram of the overall computer organization. On it we could trace the internal operations of decoding, control signal generation, and data flow that accomplish the execution of certain typical machine language instructions. We described a limited set of such instructions, and worked out the operations of the logical units that would be necessary to successfully execute each of these.

While we presented these instructions from the point of view of the computer designer, it is clear that programming considerations enter here too. Picking a vocabulary for a new computer—that is, choosing a set of native or machine language instructions—is always a compromise between what is desirable for flexibility and usefulness, and what is simple to implement.

The SAD set presented in Chapter 8 is near the bottom end of that scale. This set was chosen, however, with a third requirement in mind, that it be not only reasonably complete and simple to implement, but that it also be particularly easy to understand and to learn to work with. We are now about to put it to the test; we shall address ourselves to the task of learning to write a few simple programs in the SAD machine language. We shall find that it is indeed quite simple.

10.2   MACHINE LANGUAGE PROGRAMMING

Details of the Instruction Set Available

Let us take a closer look at SAD itself, our hypothetical single address decimal computer. By putting together Figure 8.6-4 on computer organization and Figure 8.6-5 which shows the SAD Instruction Set, we can see that the instruction word is 5 digits long, and always plus. Of these, 2 digits determine the operation type, and 3 constitute the address. Data words, therefore, can also be up to 5 digits long, with a sign, and accordingly, correspond closely with integer constants in FORTRAN. Floating point is not wired into SAD.

With 3 decimal digits available for the address, it follows that the memory has a maximum of 1000 words. In practice, three of these 1000 address possibilities are reserved, as shown in Figure 8.6-5, since both halves of the AC and the CAR are addressable as 999, 998, and 997 respectively, leaving for the main memory a capacity of 997 words. By addressing the accumulator, for instance, we can write such things as

$$\text{SUB} \quad 999$$

which will always clear the AC to zero, and, to raise the number in 247 to the fourth power,

$$\text{CLA} \quad 247$$
$$\text{MPY} \quad 247$$
$$\text{MPY} \quad 999$$

The accumulator in SAD, as in most computers, is double length, to store the product of 2 single-length numbers. For instance, if locations 201 and 202 contain 12345 and 67890, respectively, then the product formed by

$$\text{CLA} \quad 201$$
$$\text{MPY} \quad 202$$

would appear in the double accumulator thus:

+	08381	02050

To store this in memory requires two separate store instructions, with a shift in between:

STO 252
SHR 005
STO 251

Similar additional programming steps will be necessary when we wish to make subsequent use of such extended (commonly called double-precision) numbers.

A complete description of the operation of each of the instructions can be found in Appendix 10A.

Constructing a Sample Program

Let us simultaneously address two problems—learning how to put these instructions together to make a program, and improving our understanding of how SAD operates—by working an example. Before going further, read Problem 10.2-1 at the end of this chapter, and we shall proceed to work it out.

No matter what programming language is being employed, it is almost always desirable to draw a flow chart first, even though at this stage many of the operations will be described in very general terms. Drawing a flow chart is not much more than making an organized list of the steps in carrying out the solution of the problem, to make sure we have included everything that will need to be done.

Steps 4, 5, and 8 of Figure 10.2-1 are certainly obvious; it is also realized quite early that, since there is a prescribed number of pieces of data to be added, we will somehow have to count these and test for completion. Not having anything comparable to a DO statement in machine language, we shall have to include the programming steps which will set up a counter, increment it each time through, test for satisfaction of the completion criterion, and either return or go on. Blocks 2, 6, and 7 indicate that we will somehow accomplish these steps. Block 3 recognizes the necessity of an initialization step just as with FORTRAN programming: if a variable (meaning a location) is to be used for accumulating a running sum, we had better be sure that the value of this variable is set to zero before we start.

Now that we have accounted for all the steps we can think of which will be necessary to obtain the desired answer, are we ready to start writing machine language instructions? Possibly, but an intermediate step is recommended first. We shall probably get there faster, and certainly with less likelihood of confusion or error, if we always start our machine language programming by making a memory-assignment table (Figure 10.2-2).

Because of the way the clearing and loading operations work (which

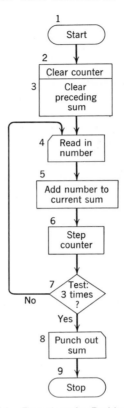

Figure 10.2-1 Flow chart for Problem 10.2-1.

we shall describe in detail later), location 000 should always be kept clear for loading operations, and the program itself is always loaded into the first *m* sequential locations commencing with 001. We do not yet know how many instructions it will take, but 100 positions will be left vacant for it.

What other quantities must have addresses reserved for them in our memory-allocation table? There are two more types of quantities we must assign addresses to: constants, which will be loaded at the start of our program, and variables, which will be assigned values during the running of our program. We have indicated 2 bands of memory locations for these 2 in Figure 10.2-2.

For variable storage we will need 1 location for reading in the numbers 1 at a time, since the input instruction allows transmission only from the outside directly to a specified memory location; another

	Location	Contents
Program	0	LOD instruction
	1	Program
	.	
	.	
	.	
	?	
Variables	101	_____ reserved for data as read in
	102	_____ reserved for the running sum
	103	_____ reserved for counter
Constants	121	the constant 1
	122	the constant 3

Figure 10.2-2 Tentative memory assignments for Problem 10.2-1.

separate location must be used to accumulate the sum; and a third will be needed to store a constantly increasing number which acts as our counter. We will assign locations 101, 102, and 103 for these purposes.

Consideration of blocks 6 and 7 in the flow chart should lead us to realize that we are going to need 2 constants: a 1 to increase our count by, and a 3 to test against. We shall tentatively assign addresses 121 and 122 to these 2 numbers.

Now we are ready to start transcribing our program from an English-language flow chart description into a machine-language coded program. Let us take each block in the flow chart, one at a time, and write the instructions necessary to accomplish that step (Figure 10.2-3).

When we have written out all these instructions, we are at last in a position to say how long the program is, and able to write the LOD instruction that gets it started. Since there are 14 instructions in the list in Figure 10.2-3, we could get all these loaded at once by writing as our very first instruction

Loc	T	Addr
0	20	014

This would cause the set of instructions in Figure 10.2-3 to be loaded into locations 1–14 inclusive, and the control then to be transferred to the instruction in location 1 for the next operation. There is just one thing wrong with this, however. How, and when, do our constants 1 and 3 get loaded? There are two ways we can handle this.

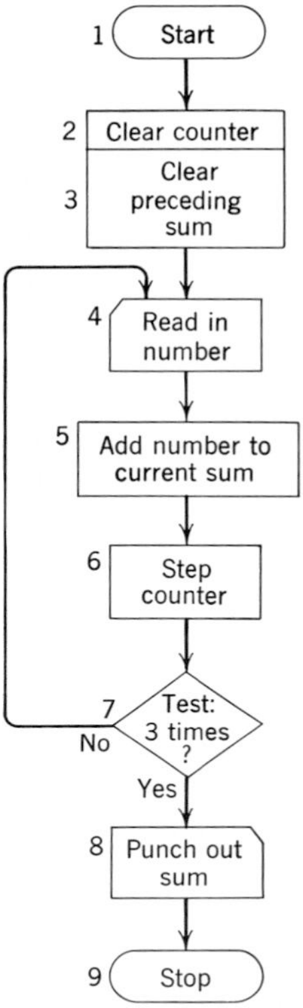

	Loc	T	Addr	Meaning
	1	17	999	SUB AC from itself, forming zero
	2	01	103	STO zero in 103, setting counter to zero
	3	01	102	STO zero in 102, clearing preceding sum
	4	00	101	INP one number to 101
	5	15	102	CLA preceding sum
	6	16	101	ADD new number
	7	01	102	STO new sum
	8	15	103	CLA counter
	9	16	121	ADD 1
	10	01	103	STO new value of counter
	11	17	122	SUB 3
	12	11	004	TRN to instr No. 4, to input next number
	13	14	102	OUT sum
	14	13	001	HTR halt

Figure 10.2-3 Translating blocks into instructions.

After loading the program of instructions, we could use a pair of input instructions to load our 2 constants. It would be a nuisance to have to stop the machine and manually execute the clear and load operations two more times, so the simplest way to accomplish this would be to make the 2 *input instructions* the first two words of our program, ahead of all the others. Execution of the load instruction would then cause these 2 input instructions to be loaded into locations 001 and 002, and the rest of the program into location 003 to 016. Then, when the load instruction is completed, the 2 input instructions would be executed before going further, causing the 2 constants to be read into 121 and 122, after which the program would continue to the instruction found in 003, and the program proper would commence. Such a program would look like

Loc	T	Addr
0	20	016
1	00	121
2	00	122
3	17	999
.		
.		
.		
16	13	003

One precaution would have to be observed here: when the program is moved down 2 locations in the memory listing, the location of the "INP one number to 101" instruction is also increased by 2. Therefore, the address portion of the TRN instruction would have to be changed to say

14 | 11 006

Another approach, however, is more commonly employed to get our constants loaded. If we assign the program itself and the constants that need to be loaded *adjacent* sets of locations, we can read them all in with a single LOD instruction. In this example, reverting to the program shown in Figure 10.2-3, once we find that the program is 14 instructions long, we can re-assign our constants to occupy locations 015 and 016, and with suitable changes in the address portion of 2 of the instructions (which ones?), the program now takes the form shown in Figure 10.2-4, the final version.

It is perhaps worth following through the starting procedure for loading this (or any other) program into SAD and starting execution. As is described in Appendix 10A, pressing the CLEAR button on SAD clears (sets to 0) the entire AC, the IR, and the CAR, and sets the phase switch to EXECUTION. With the program deck shown in Figure 10.2-4 in the read hopper, pressing START now causes the first word, the LOD instruction, to be read into location 000, whereupon execution is signaled as being complete. Since the CAR now reads 000, that word is picked up for the next instruction and read out of memory into the IR, where it is decoded and executed. Meanwhile, of course, the contents of the CAR are incremented by 1, so that it now contains the address 001. Since the word which was found in 000 says

LOD 016

it will cause the next 16 words found at the input station to be read into locations 001 to 016. Execution of this instruction will then be

Loc	T	Addr	Meaning
0	20	016	LOD program and constants
1	17	999	SUB AC from itself, forming zero
2	01	103	STO zero in 103, setting counter to zero
3	01	102	STO zero in 102, clearing preceding sum
4	00	101	INP one number to 101
5	15	102	CLA preceding sum
6	16	101	ADD new number
7	01	102	STO new sum
8	15	103	CLA counter
9	16	015	ADD 1
10	01	103	STO new value of counter
11	17	016	SUB 3
12	11	004	TRN to instr. No. 4, to input next number
13	14	102	OUT sum
14	13	001	HTR halt
15	+00	001	1
16	+00	003	3
	to be punched		
101			_____ reserved for input of data
102			_____ reserved for sum
103			_____ reserved for counter

Figure 10.2-4 Program for Problem 10.2-1.

completed. With the CAR now reading 001, the first word read in by the LOD instruction is located and executed, and the program is under way.

It is essential that this entire program be traced through in detail, in order to gain both a good understanding of how a computer operates internally, and a mastery of at least one simple example of programming in the language of the machine.

Additional features of SAD—the use of MPY and DIV instructions, the double length accumulator, shifting operations—are explained in Appendix 10A. It is interesting to contemplate that any operations for which FORTRAN instructions can be written can also be carried out using SAD machine-language instructions. In fact one could write a complete FORTRAN compiler and processor using nothing more than this instruction set. It would not, of course, fit into a mere 1000 words of memory, but we will assume that better machines than SAD are available if our goal is to run programs in FORTRAN.

Our goal in fact has been twofold: to use SAD to study some of the concepts and organizational structure of general-purpose digital computers, and to learn enough about the native language of the machine and how to speak to it, to make us aware of how great the contribution of FORTRAN is in making problem solving quicker and easier.

10.3   AN EASIER DIALECT—SYMBOLIC LANGUAGE

Drawbacks to Machine-Language Programming

If we look back at machine-language programming from the point of view of one familiar with FORTRAN programming, what are the most annoying aspects of the process? Let us analyze the disadvantages of this method of communicating with machines, listing those features which

(a) consume too much time,

(b) tend to cause mistakes, which in turn, leads to wrong answers or more time spent in correcting the program,

(c) irritate and frustrate, thereby tending to cause mistakes.

Undoubtedly the most frustrating difference is the necessity for writing the instructions in far greater detail. Algebraic and arithmetic operations that we are used to thinking of as single concepts, and represent by a single symbol or expression, must be broken down into an elaborate sequence of very elementary operations: add, store, shift, etc. This means not only that the programmer must be thoroughly familiar with the precise effect of each of the set of operations available to him for use on his particular machine, but that he must at the same time have readily at hand, and make constant reference to, a manual describing their operation quite exactly. Although he will quickly memorize the more common instructions, some of the more elaborate sets may run over 100 different instructions and the less frequently used ones will require constant checking and refreshing even after years of experience. Furthermore, bookkeeping operations such as counting and indexing have to be explicitly coded, and even the three-way branch of an IF test has to be coded as a sequence of two two-way tests.

The second restriction that requires a tremendous increase in time and attention to detail is the necessity for keeping track of the storage assignment for all quantities—constants, variables, data, and the instructions themselves—and for writing all instructions in terms of absolute memory addresses. Having to construct a storage allocation table such as in Figure 10.2-2, and even worse, having to refer to it at every step to be sure that the right address is used for the right quantity, and that two different quantities are not assigned the same address, are procedures that not only require painstaking (and pains giving) attention, but that greatly increase the probability that the finished program will have one or several mistakes in it. This is the type of bookkeeping operation that by its very nature the computer can do more efficiently and more accurately than can the human.

Third, this same exactness of reference to specific memory locations makes the process of correcting or modifying a program a major undertaking. If in Figure 10.2-4, for instance, it had been found that one instruction had been omitted, the insertion of that one instruction would move the location of all subsequent instructions down by 1, thus increasing their location address. This in turn would change the location of the constants 1 and 3, which would then require changing the address portion of all instructions that refer to those constants. It can be seen that such a seemingly simple change initiates a whole succession of further changes throughout the program—and every one of them must be caught and made correctly or the program is valueless.

A fourth source of annoyance and error is the necessity for converting the alphabetic names for all the instructions themselves into numeric codes before punching them out for the machine. Once again, although the regular user may quickly memorize the numeric equivalence for the most commonly used names, use of the others will require constant reference to a table. The only procedure worse than insistent unnecessary reference to a table to verify an op-code because there was some doubt, is *failing* to make a *necessary* reference to the table and writing an 11 when it should have been a 12.

Development of Symbolic Programming

This was the state of the art of computer programming at the beginning of the 1950's when the first of the stored-program computers were being built on university campuses, and forerunners of the modern generation were beginning to emerge from Univac, ERA, and, later, IBM. Small wonder that the average user of the computer preferred to explain his problem to a member of the computer laboratory staff, and let him prepare the program for the machine. This programmer was a highly trained expert, multi-lingual both in the various areas of the problems to be solved and in the coldly precise language of the machine. Most of these early programmers, grappling with the task of converting a problem statement into a program for the machine, found they could somewhat simplify their task by breaking it into two stages.

First, the general scheme for solution of the problem, as laid out in a very general flow chart, was converted into a detailed procedure, and a first draft of the program steps themselves was written using symbolic names for various quantities which would later be identified more precisely. The "meaning" column of a program might be filled in first, or a hybrid type of instruction code written which referred to the actual quantities being manipulated rather than the addresses of these quantities themselves. Particularly troublesome were complicated programs composed of many segments. Fitting the different segments into a sequentially numbered whole became quite tricky, and it was a problem to keep the names straight from one segment to another—both to maintain the identity of one variable if different names were assigned, and to maintain the distinction between different variables if the same name should be assigned. Allocating memory assignments to the different blocks of instructions themselves was particularly difficult when the segments were written by different people, or at different times. One technique used was to number instructions in a particular segment relative to the beginning of that segment, in such a way that the sequence could be readily indicated, yet insertions and corrections easily made. For example, the instructions to accomplish block 17 in the flow chart might be numbered

> 17.1
> 17.2
> 17.3
> etc.

so that if it were discovered that an omission had been made, it could easily be inserted as

> 17.1
> 17.2
> 17.21
> 17.3

In a similar way, individual instructions, or even whole groups, could be deleted without affecting the sequence numbering of the rest.

As another approach, when it was necessary to refer in one instruction to another in the program, a temporary name, called a label, could be assigned to that instruction.

Finally, when the programmer had completed a program in terms of these symbolic and temporary assignments, and felt reasonably confident that all the steps had been taken care of and no more additions or insertions were going to be needed, the second stage of writing a program could be carried out, by assigning actual machine addresses to every instruction and every data reference.

The entire set of instructions could now be serially numbered, and actual addresses corresponding to labelled instructions could be inserted wherever references to such had been made. Once the amount of storage needed for the program was determined, assignment of specific locations for the data could also be made. A symbol table was usually made up, both to make certain that all quantities were listed, and to insure no conflicting assignments had been made. From this table, as a final step in programming, the actual machine code could be written, using both the numeric op-code for each instruction, and the actual machine address that constituted each data reference. This last operation, that of converting a detailed set of instructions still written in human usable form—using alphabetic op-codes, statement labels, and symbolic names for addresses—into the corresponding coded form necessary to be usable by the machine, was commonly known as "coding." It was a dreary job, strictly mechanical in nature, and full of possibilities for mistakes, yet the overall speed and reliability of the programming process gained appreciably by being split in two.

To illustrate this technique, let us go back to the flow chart of Figure 10.2-1, and carry out the translating operation of Figure 10.2-3,

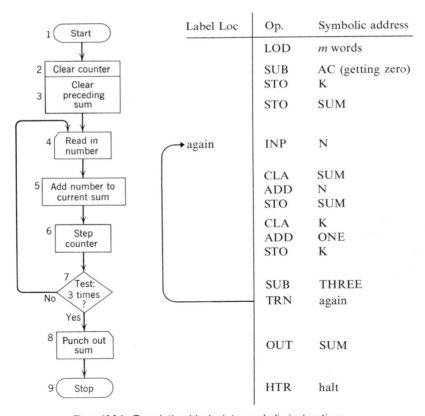

Label	Loc	Op.	Symbolic address
		LOD	m words
		SUB	AC (getting zero)
		STO	K
		STO	SUM
again		INP	N
		CLA	SUM
		ADD	N
		STO	SUM
		CLA	K
		ADD	ONE
		STO	K
		SUB	THREE
		TRN	again
		OUT	SUM
		HTR	halt

Figure 10.3-1 Translating blocks into symbolic instructions.

but this time introducing the intermediate stage of symbolic coding (Figure 10.3-1).

Note that in the process we found it necessary to refer to the INP instruction, so assigned a label to it—"again." In the next step we shall assign a numeric value to this as well as to our data names.

Now that we have determined how many instructions our program will take, we can fill out a memory assignment table like that of Figure 10.2-2, and proceed to complete the final program, as shown in Figure 10.3-2.

Further Symbolic Programming

To further illustrate how some of the iterative operations which are so nicely carried out for us by the IF's and DO's of FORTRAN are actually handled in machine language, let us consider one more example in symbolic programming. We will see how lists and arrays may be handled by the technique known as "address modification."

Consider Problem 10.3-1, "Out List," which is reproduced here for convenience:

GIVEN

An array of 10 numbers stored in SAD locations 301-310.

	Label	Loc	Op	Symbolic address	Code	
Load		0	LOD	*m*	20	016
		1	SUB	AC	17	999
		2	STO	K	01	103
		3	STO	SUM	01	102
	again	4	INP	N	00	101
		5	CLA	SUM	15	102
		6	ADD	N	16	101
Program		7	STO	SUM	01	102
		8	CLA	K	15	103
		9	ADD	ONE	16	015
		10	STO	K	01	103
		11	SUB	THREE	17	016
		12	TRN	again	11	004
		13	OUT	SUM	14	102
		14	HTR	—	13	001
Constants		15		ONE	+00	001
		16		THREE	+00	003
Variables		101		___ N	(to be	
		102		___ SUM	(punched)	
		103		___ K		

Figure 10.3-2   Final address assignment for symbolic program of Figure 10.3-1.

WANTED

An iterative program that will output the entire array, using address modification. The program should be self-contained, loading any constants needed, and should reset (or preset) itself so that it can repeat.

Before we can even flowchart the program, it is necessary to recognize the nature of the problem, and just how we can go about handling it.

Obviously, somewhere in the middle of our program will be an OUT instruction, which will output the contents of location 301, thus:

LOCATION	OPERATION	OPERAND	T	N
Output	OUT	A(1)	14	301

We do not yet know the location of this instruction, so we will hang a symbolic label on it, "Output."

Now one solution would be to write 9 more such instructions, one to output the contents of 302, one for 303, and so forth. By now we have learned that this is a very inefficient way of using a computer, so we will see how to do this using iteration.

What is the difference between this instruction: 14 301

and the instruction to output the second item in the list: 14 302

The difference is 1 in the least significant digit position of the instruction, is it not? And this is the clue to the technique whereby we can accomplish our iteration. We shall treat the instruction itself as an operand, as a number, and perform arithmetic on it. Specifically, we will add 1 to the instruction called "Output," thereby increasing its address portion by 1.

If we execute the following four instructions, what will the contents of "Output" look like when we are through?

LOCATION	OPERATION	OPERAND	T	N
Output	OUT	A(1)	14	301
	CLA	Output	15	· · ·
	ADD	One	16	· · ·
	STO	Output	01	· · ·

It will say:

Output	OUT	A(2)	14	302

will it not? So, if we execute a

	TRA	Output	10	· · ·

the next time "Output" is executed we would get the second item in our array put out.

This technique, known as "address modification," is the direct consequence of the philosophy advanced by the late John von Neuman, who was the first to point out the tremendous advantages that could follow from storing numbers and instructions interchangeably in the memory of the computer, and permitting arithmetic operations to be carried out on the instructions themselves. It makes stepping down a list almost look easy.

Now let us put together a complete flow chart (Figure 10.3-3a); a corresponding symbolic program to carry out those operations (b), and the corresponding final code with all addresses assigned and filled in (c). Note that 3 constants have to be available to the program: one (+00001), ten (+00010), and the address of the first element in the array (+00301). The following convention is used in the figure, and will prove to be handy if you are working out such a program for yourself: if the contents of location N are X, then we write [N] = X, and conversely]X[= N.

A philosophical point. In this simple program we could write the output instruction to be loaded into location 5 as 00 301, and assume everything is set to output the first number, but if any such address modification program is to be used more than once, provision must be made either for resetting it after each use, or presetting it before each use. The latter is always to be preferred as a much safer approach, and the presetting is indeed carried out here in instructions 1 and 2.

It is worth noting in conclusion that it is just such a program that FORTRAN sets up in machine language when it compiles for you your simple pair of statements:

$$DO\ 3\ I = 1,\ 10$$
$$3 \quad PRINT\ 40,\ A(I)$$

Assembler Programs

This, then, was the technique being developed in the early 1950's, and some very complex and effective programs were written in this way. Nevertheless, the highly mechanical nature of that second stage of the process—encoding every operation into its machine equivalent— eventually gave rise to what in retrospect seems the only logical answer —the machine was programmed to do it.

The late 1950's saw the rise of this first significant step in new programming techniques: the development of the assembler program. This program, provided the user would follow some very carefully laid out rules governing the assignment of symbolic names and statement labels,

Program

Label	Loc	Op	Symbolic address
		LOD	Program
Again		CLA	]A(1)[
		STA	Output
		SUB	AC
		STO	K (zero)
Output		OUT	A(I)
		CLA	Output
		ADD	One
		STO	Output
		CLA	K
		ADD	One
		STO	K
		SUB	Ten
		TRN	Output
		HTR	Again

Constants

			One
			Ten
			]A(1)[

Data

	301		K
	.		A(1)
	.		.
	310		A(10)

(b) Symbolic program

Final program

Label	Loc	Op	Symbolic address	Code
	0	LOD	Program	20 017
Again	1	CLA	]A(1)[	15 017
	2	STA	Output	03 005
	3	SUB	AC	17 999
	4	STO	K (zero)	01 101
Output	5	OUT	A(I)	14 000
	6	CLA	Output	15 005
	7	ADD	One	16 015
	8	STO	Output	01 005
	9	CLA	K	15 101
	10	ADD	One	16 015
	11	STO	K	01 101
	12	SUB	Ten	17 016
	13	TRN	Output	11 005
	14	HTR	Again	13 001
	15		One	+00 001
	16		Ten	+00 010
	17		]A(1)[	+00 301
	101		K	
	301		A(1)	
	310		A(10)	

(c) Final program

Figure 10.3-3 "Out List"

would perform the entire second-stage process for him. This concept in programming was a contribution of such significance that the assembly program still plays a very important role today. In use, the procedure works like this.

The programmer writes out his detailed flow chart and symbolic program, working through as many stages of problem analysis and flow chart as necessary, developing his detailed problem-solving procedure, and from it writing a complete symbolic program using mnemonic op-codes, symbolic data names for both constants and variables, and statement labels wherever necessary. When ready to run, he first loads into the computer the assembly program that exists for his particular computing system (SAP, CODAP, SPS, or whatever the name might be). Of course, if he is working under a monitor system, he merely writes the necessary job or control cards to call the assembler in from tape, disk, or drum. He then loads his symbolic program, which goes through the assembly process. By a simple dictionary type of table look-up, the mnemonic op-codes are replaced by their numeric equivalents. The various segments of the program are assigned computer-memory addresses, and the equivalent address corresponding to each statement label is substituted wherever a reference is made to that label. All symbols used for data reference are collected in a symbol table, and machine addresses assigned to each. Once they are all entered into the table, and it has been ascertained that all symbols used are properly defined somewhere in the program, the absolute machine address corresponding to each symbol can be substituted in the program everywhere that symbol appears, and the entire machine-language program can be made up. This object program is usually put out from the computer, either by punching it on cards or writing it on a tape or auxiliary storage device, and corresponds very closely to the object program punched by a compilation process from a FORTRAN source program. Then, when execution is wanted, the program is either reloaded or recalled, data added as appropriate, and the program is ready to run.

It might be noted from the above description that for at least two reasons the assembly operation is usually a 2- or even 3-pass process. By that, we mean that the assembler usually has to make 2 or 3 passes over the source program, building up first an outline, then a rough draft, and finally the complete program with all the details filled in. For one thing, it is often necessary to go all the way through the program once to determine how many instructions will be needed, before any actual addresses can be assigned. A symbol table somewhat like the one in Figure 10.3-2 is the most important product of the first pass. Furthermore, if one instruction contains a branch or transfer to another location which the assembler has not yet encountered, how can it insert a specific address in the instruction being assembled? Although there are techniques for getting around this, which involve indirect addressing either in the machine language instructions or in the assembly process, it is often possible to produce a more efficient object code—one which will run faster and/or take up less memory space—by taking a little longer in the assembly process and going back over it again.

This points up the fact that we have been familiar with on a small scale already—that desirable features in a program are often conflicting or incompatible, and that it is often therefore desirable to have several different assembler and compiler programs, depending on the nature of the program and how it is going to be used.

The second reason for breaking the assembly process into more than one stage is the limitation on memory space available to work with. It is easy to realize that a powerful assembler is itself quite an elaborate program, and when high-speed storage is limited, but intermediate storage is relatively plentiful (the usual situation because of storage costs), it is possible to break the assembler into two or three, more or less separate, portions, only one of which needs to be in high-speed memory at any one time, and work in shifts. When the first pass over the program is completed, for instance, the second portion of the assembler can be called in from intermediate storage, written on top of the first portion, and the partially completed object program passed through again to have the next set of operations performed on it. On small machines such as the 1620, this usually means that an object deck is punched out of the computer as the result of pass 1, and the deck which constitutes the second part of the assembler is then loaded along with that intermediate output for pass 2. On larger machines the input and output can be at much higher speed and the manual handling is eliminated by using tape, disk, or drum storage and monitor-type automatic control of the process.

10.4 ALGEBRAIC LANGUAGE

At this point it is worth looking back at the list of objectives we compiled at the beginning of Section 10.3. Does use of an assembler program overcome any of these difficulties?

This list is summarized in Figure 10.4-1.

It should be readily apparent that writing in an assembly language, and using an assembler program to carry out the coding stage, eliminates items 2, 3, and 4 from the list, and replaces them with the much

1. Number of steps necessary.
2. Assignment and use of absolute addresses for all data references.
3. Assignment and use of absolute addresses for all program references.
4. Use of numeric operation codes.

Figure 10.4-1   Undesirable aspects of programming in machine language.

simpler chore of using symbolic references. The programmer may use symbols made up of alphameric characters for all his data references— called "names." He may use symbols which are similarly made up of numeric or alphameric characters for all references to specific instructions in his program, whether these are needed as transfer points, as instructions requiring arithmetic, etc. Such symbolic program references are called "labels."

Objection Number 1, however, still remains: writing in assembly language, it is still necessary to spell out every individual step in moving and manipulating data, and every step in testing and branching from one segment of the program to the next. Why cannot something be done about this too?

In "conventional" algebraic notation, we have established certain conventions regarding the sequence in which arithmetic operations are supposed to take place. As we found in Chapters 1 and 2, there is a convention with respect to hierarchies in the operational sequence, the implication being that within an algebraic expression, operations are to be performed in the sequence

(1) exponentiation
(2) multiplication and division
(3) addition and subtraction

To indicate any departure from this implied sequence, one conventionally uses parentheses to denote that the operations within the parentheses are to be carried out first, and the expression within the parentheses is therefore to be treated as a single element in the remainder of the expression.

If this is true—if there exists already a convention sufficiently rigid to prescribe a unique calculating sequence for any algebraic expression— why should it not be possible to write a computer program which will accept such a statement in its conventional algebraic form, decode it into the appropriate sequence of arithmetic operations necessary to evaluate it or perform the indicated data manipulations on it, and cause an appropriate set of symbolic or even absolute instructions to be compiled that will accomplish this evaluation? All that is necessary is to add one additional rule not needed in ordinary (infinite-precision) calculation, but which sometimes is critical in finite-precision arithmetic—that among operations at the same level of the hierarchy, operations will be programmed to be executed in the sequence in which they are encountered in scanning the statement from left to right. With this addition, all the necessary conditions are met. The answer, therefore, is that it *is* possible to write a program to do this.

Such a program to accomplish the machine translation of algebraic formulas was first written in the period from 1954 to 1957, by a team of programmers made up primarily from IBM, with contributions from the University of California Radiation Laboratory and from United Aircraft. It was first made available to IBM users in 1957. Its immediate success is certainly a tribute to the care with which the writers had worked, but its acceptance and spread in the intervening years is merely a demonstration of the principle that has been emphasized throughout this book: to the extent that man can reduce any portion of the task he is engaged in to a precisely described sequence of step-by-step operations, with all eventualities considered and anticipated—to that extent, the computer can take over, and do the job better, faster, and more accurately than he can.

Machine translation of such a formula-like language is such a task, and the process is carried out so successfully, that not only have translators been written for just about every computer in use today, but this is the process by which the great bulk of computing the world over is currently being done.

This process, of course, and its formula-like language, are called FORTRAN.

10.5 OTHER INSTRUCTION FORMATS

We shall close this chapter, in which we have been examining the internal or machine language of computers, by a look at some of the variety of different types of instruction formats that have been used. We shall consider the nature of the instruction word and how it relates to two other areas: the design of the machine, and how it is programmed.

From the design point of view, three factors are intimately related: the length of the data word, the size of the memory, and the instruction format. Limiting our discussion to the fixed-word length type of machine —and we saw back in Section 8.2 that computers for scientific and engineering applications most often assign such a fixed length to their data words—we still have the question of what word length. The two most common solutions are those used by International Business

Machines Corporation and Control Data Corporation, which employ 36 and 48 bits respectively. As is shown in the top line of Figure 10.5-1, this enables an internal representation of real numbers to a precision of from 8 to 11 decimal digits, with an exponent which, as a power of 2, ranges from $2^{\pm 64}$ to $2^{\pm 1000}$, the equivalent of, from $10^{\pm 19}$ to $10^{\pm 300}$. Since the same fixed word length is also used for storage of instructions, let us see how the instruction word might take advantage of all these bits.

Offhand, it seems difficult to use all of the bits to advantage. Since we covered a minimum but fairly complete instruction set with less than 20 instructions in SAD, it would certainly seem that 6 bits for operation type ($2^6 = 64$) should suffice for even the most complicated set. In the same way, the size of memory determines the number of bits that must be left for the address portion. Although memories of 1000 words or less were quite common only a few years ago, modern computers need 4000, 8000, 32,000, or even more words of high-speed storage to operate efficiently. Combining these two requirements for the type portion and the address portion respectively, we see that the sum of these two parts together accounts for only 18–24 bits (Figure 10.5-1). What shall we do with the rest?

Several approaches are possible. In the 1604 and 3600, CDC limits the instruction word to exactly $\frac{1}{2}$ the length of a data word, and packs 2 instructions per memory location (or uses 2 memory locations to store 1 data word, depending on how you want to look at it). Another approach puts more than 1 data address in the instruction word itself, thereby achieving a better match in word length between the instruction word and the data word. Historically, many varieties of such schemes have been tried; a few are shown in Figure 10.5-2.

You will note that an accumulator is the implied address of a second operand and/or a destination in examples 1 and 3, where there is only one address that may be used for data; the accumulator may or may not be used with two data addresses; and the accumulator is not needed (at least in so far as the programmer needs to be aware of it) in the cases where three data addresses are available.

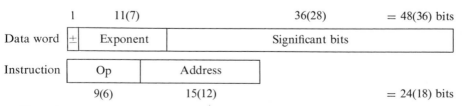

Figure 10.5-1   Structure of data words and instructions in the CDC 3600 (IBM 7094).

No. of addresses	Instruction format		Typical instructions	Used in computers
Type A	Op	Addresses		
1		| t | n |	ADD add $(AC) + (n) \rightarrow (AC)$: take next instr	Many machines of the 1950's
			STO store $(AC) \rightarrow (n)$; take next instr	
			TRZ next instr from n if $(AC) = 0$; otherwise next in sequence	
2		| t | p | q |	A add $(p) + (q) \rightarrow (p)$: take next instr	IBM 1620; UNIVAC 1101
			B next instr from p	
			BI next instr from p if indicator q is on	
1 + 1		| t | D | I |	AL add $(AC_L) + (D) \rightarrow (AC_L)$; go to I	IBM 650
			BRMIN next instr from D if $(AC) < 0$; otherwise go to I	
3		| t | A | B | C |	ADD add $(A) + (B) \rightarrow (C)$: take next instr	WISC; Bell Interpretive System
			TRN next instr from C if $(A) - (B) < 0$; otherwise take next instr	
3 + 1		| t | A | B | C | I |	ADD add $(A) + (B) \rightarrow (C)$: go to I	IBM 7090, 7094; CDC 1604, 3600; SDS 930, 9300; PDP 5, 6, 7, 8
				and many others
Type B				
Typical form	Op | Index | Address			
Sample special form	Op | Index | Address | Sub Op | 2nd Index | Jump Address			CDC 3600

Figure 10.5-2 Types of instruction formats.

This figure also shows the significance of the $+1$ in the names of some of the types. A $1 + 1$ address machine is not equivalent to a 2-address machine, because in the latter case, either address may be a data reference, but in a $1 + 1$ format, only one address may refer to data, and the other *always* acts as an instruction address. In conditional transfer or branching instructions, both addresses may be instruction references, but the reverse situation with both addresses serving as data references is not permitted.

Until just a few years ago there was still considerable controversy over whether type 1 or type 4 was to be preferred. It was fairly well agreed that the single-address design provided the greatest variety in number of instructions, and the greatest flexibility, permitting an experienced programmer to take maximum advantage of his experience and his craft, but it was also argued with some merit that 3-address instruction was simpler to learn to use, being closer to the way one normally thinks about operations that need to be done. The argument was settled finally by two new developments.

On the one hand, the widespread use of automatic programming techniques such as FORTRAN compilers had made it less and less important for the average user to have to learn to write in machine language, so that more weight can be given to the advantages available to expert programmers. Secondly, other types of information have been found that are very useful to incorporate into the instruction along with the operation type and a single data reference. Without going into detail, it has been found extremely valuable to build some of the features of a DO loop into the hardware of the machine itself. These devices, called *index registers,* greatly assist in the indexing operations of counting and stepping, and are valuable in even broader forms of address modification and relative address assignment. In order to refer to these registers and other devices, additional portions of the instruction word are marked off. One segment may indicate which of several index registers is to be used; another may be used to specify a counting increment or decrement, sometimes used like the m_3 of a DO loop, and sometimes merely to specify the necessary techniques of stepping through a 2- or 3-dimensional array. Instructions which make use of the index register features are usually listed as a separate class (Type B in Figure 10.5-2), and, as can be seen, easily make use of the entire complement of bits available if the instruction word is made the same length as the data word.

This last type of instruction—the single address with index register capabilities—is undoubtedly the commonest type encountered today.

One or two trends might be noted as affecting the direction of future development of machine languages and computer design itself. For one, automatic programming is coming into wider and wider use, and with the newest computers increasingly complex programming systems (software) are supplied to the customer, making it less and less necessary for him to have to program in machine language. A second trend, toward integrated networks of intercommunicating computers and terminal equipment, is less easy to categorize. Just what additional requirements this will impose on the structure of the instruction word is not at all clear, but the trend itself is unmistakable.

PROBLEM 10.2-1   "SAD Add"

Write a SAD machine-language program that will read in 3 numbers, 1 at a time, form their sum, and punch it out. Include loading instructions necessary to make the program complete and ready-to-run.

PROBLEM 10.2-2   "SAD Add N"

Modify the program of Problem 10.2-1 as follows:
(A) Find the sum of N numbers. N is punched on the first data card, followed by N data cards containing 1 number each.
(B) This is part (A) with repetition. The data are divided into several blocks. The first card of each block contains N, the number of data cards in that block. Find and put out the sum of the numbers in each block, then repeat for the next block. The last block contains just one card, punched 00000. The program should sense this card and stop.

PROBLEM 10.3-1   "Out List"

GIVEN
An array of 10 numbers stored in SAD locations 301–310.

WANTED
An iterative program that will output the entire array, using address modification. The program should be self-contained, loading any constants needed, and should reset (or preset) itself so that it can repeat.

PROBLEM 10.3-2   "In List"

GIVEN
An array of 8 numbers punched one to a card in SAD format.

WANTED

An iterative program that will input the 8 numbers into SAD locations 401–408, using address modification. The program should be self-contained, loading any constants needed, and should reset (or preset) itself so that it can repeat.

PROBLEM 10.3-3   "In Sets"

GIVEN

Several sets of data, each consisting of 1 card containing an integer N, followed by N cards each containing one of the N elements of an array.

WANTED

(A) An iterative SAD program that will input one set of data into N locations starting with 501, and then repeat until all sets have been read. (It is recognized that this will result in one set obliterating part or all of the preceding set, but tracing will make it possible to check the success of the program.)

(B) An iterative SAD program that will first input one set, then output that set, and then repeat until all sets have been read.

PROBLEM 10.3-4   "POLY SAD"

(A) Using address modification, write a SAD program equivalent to POLY (Figure 2.2-9).

(B) Using address modification, write a SAD program equivalent to POLY (Figure 2.2-9) for an nth degree polynomial.

(C) Using address modification, write a SAD program equivalent to POLYPLOT (Figure 3.4-2).

PROBLEM 10.3-5   "POLYPLOT SAD"

Use the program of Problem 10.3-4(C) above to solve problem 3.5-6( ).

CHAPTER 11.

Things Worth Computing

[E] SIMULATING THE REAL THING

11.1 WHAT IS SIMULATION?

Simulation is a word used with increasing frequency in describing applications of computers to certain types of problems. *Simulation may be defined as a study of the performance of a system through the use of a model in which the performance varies with time, or is a function of time.* The model, then, performs like the real system. When an electronic computer is used to perform a simulation, the model must be a computational model. In this chapter, we will investigate simulation as it applies to systems which are simulated on the digital computer. A number of problems presented in preceding chapters were simulation problems and will be referred to in our discussion of the subject. We will see in a later chapter that an electronic analog computer and the combination of analog and digital computers are also useful in performing certain types of simulations.

To better understand what is meant by simulation, we will consider the forward movement of an object. First, we shall assume the object to be an automobile traveling on an open highway. At intervals, the driver records the velocity and the time that each reading of velocity is taken. If the velocity is constant, say, at 30 miles per hour (0.5 mile per minute) over a period of interest, the curve of velocity versus time will be a straight line as shown by curve (*v*) of Figure 11.1-1*a*. The driver

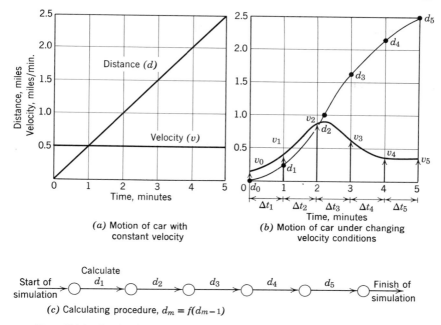

(a) Motion of car with
constant velocity

(b) Motion of car under changing
velocity conditions

(c) Calculating procedure, $d_m = f(d_{m-1})$

Figure 11.1-1 Study of the distance traveled by a moving object by simulation.

could also obtain values of distance traveled at intervals during the
5-minute period by reading the odometer. If these values are obtained
and plotted, curve (d) of Figure 11.1-1a results.

If the driver failed to read the odometer, he could easily construct
curve (d) from the velocity curve, making use of the simple fact that the
distance traveled by an object in going from one point to another at
constant velocity is equal to the product of the velocity and the time:

$$d = v \times t \tag{11.1-1}$$

This simple equation is, then, the simulation model for this special case.
The performance of the automobile in terms of the distance it traveled
is a simple function of time, and the simulation is readily performed.

But what if the velocity did not remain constant over an interval of
time as shown by the curve of Figure 11.1-1b? In that case, we ought to
use the average velocity over the period:

$$\Delta d = v_{ave} \times \Delta t \tag{11.1-2}$$

If t is a very short period of time, then a good approximation to the
average velocity can be obtained from the velocity at the beginning and
end of that interval:

$$v_{avg} = \frac{v_{beg} + v_{end}}{2}$$

$$= \frac{v_0 + v_1}{2}$$

then

$$\Delta d = \frac{v_0 + v_1}{2} \Delta t_1 \qquad (11.1\text{-}3)$$

In Figure 11.1-1b, the time elapsed is not a very short period, and equation 11.1-3 would not give a very accurate approximation. In such a case, the time period may be divided into many small intervals. The number depends on the number of points we want on our curve, and the accuracy we desire in determining a value of the total distance traveled. If we divide the given time period into n intervals, we obtain distance values as a function of time from the following equations:

$$d_1 = d_0 + \frac{v_0 + v_1}{2} \Delta t_1$$

$$d_2 = d_1 + \frac{v_1 + v_2}{2} \Delta t_2$$

$$d_3 = d_2 + \frac{v_2 + v_3}{2} \Delta t_3$$

$$d_n = d_{n-1} + \frac{v_{n-1} + v_n}{2} \Delta t_n \qquad (11.1\text{-}4)$$

If the time period of Figure 11.1-1b is divided into five equal intervals, the distance values d_1 through d_5 would be plotted as indicated in the figure.

Equations 11.1-4 are calculated in the sequence listed beginning with the first. The job of calculating any value d_m has as a prerequisite job the job of calculating d_{m-1}, i.e.,

$$d_m = f(d_{m-1})$$

Drawing on the knowledge we have gained from Section 5.5, the task of performing the simulation can be described by the graph of Figure 11.1-1c.

The general model for simulating the distance an automobile moves in the forward direction is described by equations 11.1-4. The moving object could just as well be a satellite during launching, or during travel in space. The velocity and time values may be measured and transmitted to ground stations where the simulation of the travel is performed.

Performances measured in other terms may be described by equations similar to those that calculate distance. We know from experience, for example, that the amount of heat we obtain from an automobile heater for a period after we first start out on a cold day, depends on the velocity of the car or the speed of the engine and the time. Is it not reasonable to expect that performance can also be expressed in terms of temperature, and that a similar set of equations might be used to perform the simulation?

We know too, that heat is generated by air friction when an object such as a satellite or meteor moves through an atmosphere. Can we not expect that the performance of the moving object expressed in terms of temperature may also be described by similar equations for these conditions?

Thus, we see that performance may be expressed in a variety of terms and that equations 11.1-4 may be representative of the type required to perform the simulations.

11.2   VARIATIONS IN SIMULATION

Now that we have a general idea of the meaning of simulation, we will explore a number of important variations. The variations are related to

(1) simulated time period
(2) amount of data available
(3) speed of performance of the simulator relative to that of the real system
(4) statement of time of real system

The Simulated Time Period

The first variation we shall study is related to the simulated time period. The period may be in the past or in the future.

Past Time Period. In simulating over a past period of time, all values of v and t of equations 11.1-4 should be available as input to the simulation program. They are obtained by measurement from the moving automobile or from any forward moving object. The measured values are then observed data and the input is largely these data. For simulations in general, the data are the values of the coefficients and the variables of the simulation equations.

In certain cases, all the values may not be available as observed data, and an attempt must be made to obtain the missing values by theoretical calculations of additional equations. Since performance will more nearly represent the true performance when calculated directly from data obtained from the actual system, observed data will always be made as complete as possible, i.e., these data will be a maximum, and the data to be obtained by theoretical calculations will be a minimum.

We will now go through the numerical calculations of a past period simulation. The simulation equations 11.1-4 will be used to calculate the performances, and the observed data will be those used to plot the v versus t curve of Figure 11.1-1b. The measured values are

m	t_m	v_m
0	0	0.2
1	1.0	0.4
2	2.0	0.8
3	3.0	0.6
4	4.0	0.4
5	5.0	0.4

After substituting the measured values in equations 11.1-4 for $n = 5$, we have for the performances

$$d_0 = 0, \qquad\qquad\qquad\qquad\qquad\qquad t_0 = 0$$

$$d_1 = 0 + \frac{0.2 + 0.4}{2} \times 1 = 0.3, \qquad t_1 = 1$$

$$d_2 = 0.3 + \frac{0.4 + 0.8}{2} \times 1 = 0.9, \qquad t_2 = 2$$

$$d_3 = 0.9 + \frac{0.8 + 0.6}{2} \times 1 = 1.6, \qquad t_3 = 3$$

$$d_4 = 1.6 + \frac{0.6 + 0.4}{2} \times 1 = 2.1, \qquad t_4 = 4$$

$$d_5 = 2.1 + \frac{0.4 + 0.4}{2} \times 1 = 2.5, \qquad t_5 = 5$$

These results, when plotted, give the d versus t curve of Figure 11.1-1b.

Figure 11.2-1a shows a general flow chart of a program for performing simulations over past periods of time. A maximum of observed data is read as input to the computer in block 1, and a minimum of theoretical data is calculated in block 2.

The calculations required to obtain the performances P(M) from the total data available are performed in the simulation block (block 3). A value is calculated for each increment of time T(M) from M = 1, N.

After the simulation over the time period is completed, times T(M) and performances P(M) for M = 1, N are produced as output (block 4).

For the example problem, all values of V(M) and T(M) for M = 1, 6 are obtained as observed data and no theoretical calculations are

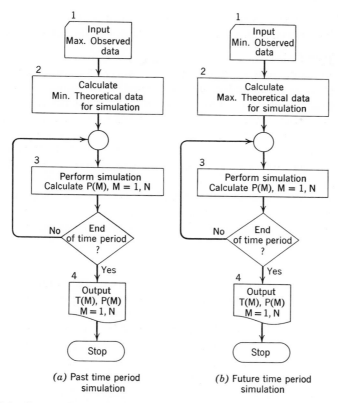

Figure 11.2-1   General flow charts for performing the variation of simulation related to time period.

required in block 2. The performances are $d(M)$, and are calculated by equations 11.1-4 in block 3, which is the simulation block.

The inventory problem 4.2-1 of Chapter 4 is another example of a simulation problem over a past period, and the program flow chart takes the form of that in Figure 11.2-1a. It requires the derivation of the simulation equations and the writing of the program. The input to the simulation block is totally observed data.

There are two principal reasons for performing simulations over past periods:

(1) When failures or malfunctions occur in existing systems, simulation studies are often made to determine the causes of failures or the improvements that can be made.

(2) When simulation equations such as equations 11.1-4 are first

established for the purpose of designing new systems, they are best verified by applying them to simulations of similar existing systems.

Future Time Period. In simulating over a future time period, the values of the coefficients and variables, such as v and t of equations 11.1-4, are not available as measured values, and must be obtained by theoretical calculations. Observed data are then a minimum for the future periods and the theoretical values obtained by calculations are a maximum.

What do we mean by theoretical values? Since they are particularly important to simulations over future periods, we shall determine the meaning by investigating the origin of the equations used for calculating the values.

If the moving object is free falling, with negligible air resistance, and the values v_m and Δt_m of the simulation equations 11.1-4 are not available as observed data, the values may be calculated from the basic equation of physics

$$v_m = g \times t_m \qquad (11.2\text{-}1)$$

in which g is the acceleration of gravity and equals 32 feet per second per second, and time is measured from the beginning of the fall.

We can extend the above example to a more practical case of the simulation of the launching of a satellite. When a new rocket is to be built for launching, its performances as a function of time must be determined from calculated data. The basic equation 11.2-1 is still important but so are others. They are required in describing the net acceleration provided by the thrust of the burning fuel, the reduction in mass as the fuel is burned, and the air resistance of the rocket-satellite system.

For the example problem of simulating inventory control over a future period, the number of items removed from stock each day must be calculated from an analysis of the future needs of the customer, or by predicting the values from observed data by the methods discussed in Section 9.4.

The general flow chart of a program for simulating over a future time period is shown in Figure 11.2-1b, where the number of blocks and the connections are the same as the flow chart of the past period. The difference is in the amount of data supplied to simulation block 3 by blocks 1 and 2. For simulations over future periods, the input to the computer provided by block 1, may now be said to consist of a minimum of observed data instead of a maximum and, instead of obtaining a minimum of data for the simulation by theoretical calculations, a maximum is calculated in block 2.

Simulations over future periods are made to study the performances of new or modified physical systems before they are built and, in some cases, to determine how existing systems will perform in the future under unusual circumstances.

Amount of Data Available

The second variation for study is related to the amount of data available for performing a simulation. The available data may be either complete or incomplete.

Complete Data. When the data are complete, all values of the coefficients and variables of the simulation equations for calculating P(M), such as v_m and Δt_m of equations 11.1-4, are available as measured and theoretical values. In general, the flow charts of Figure 11.2-1*a* and *b* also apply here. The data entering block 3 are complete for calculating P(M) from the simulation equations.

Incomplete Data. The data are incomplete when certain values of the coefficients and variables of the simulation equations for calculating P(M) have not been measured and cannot be obtained as theoretical values. We are not helpless in this situation. The missing values may be determined from the known data entering block 3 by any one or a combination of the methods of

(*a*) curve fitting
(*b*) direct solution
(*c*) iterative solution

Curve fitting methods may be used to approximate the missing values from known data for the same quantity. Known values are used to establish a polynomial equation that best describes one of the measured quantities as a function of another. Unknown values of the dependent quantity can then be approximated by substituting corresponding known values of the independent quantity in the established equation. Newton's divided-difference polynomial, or the method of least squares described in Section 9.4, may be used to establish the polynomial.

For the example problem, if we assume that the missing values are v_m, the polynomial equation of degree n would express v as a function of t:

$$v = a_0 + a_1 t + a_2 t^2 + \cdots + a_n t^n \qquad (11.2\text{-}2)$$

It requires a minimum of $n + 1$ known sets of values of v and t to calculate the $n + 1$ coefficients a. Unknown values of v can then be approximated by substituting corresponding known values of t in the equation.

We will go through a numerical calculation to better understand the procedure. Newton's divided-difference polynomial of the second degree will be used to approximate a missing value v_2 of the observed data used to plot the v versus t curve of Figure 11.1-1b. We shall then proceed to calculate performances from equations 11.1-4.

The measured values from Figure 11.1-1b are

m	t_m	v_m
0	0.0	0.2
1	1.0	0.4
2	2.0	—
3	3.0	0.6
4	4.0	0.4
5	5.0	0.4

Equations 9.4-2, 9.4-3, and 9.4-4 describe the divided-difference polynomial of the second degree. When Y is replaced with V in these equations, we have

$$V = A_0 + A_1 T + a_2 T^2 \qquad (11.2\text{-}3)$$

where

$$A_0 = V_0 - T_0 F_1 + T_1 T_0 F_2$$
$$A_1 = F_1 - F_2(T_0 + T_1)$$
$$A_2 = F_2 \qquad (11.2\text{-}4)$$

and

$$F_1 = \frac{V_1 - V_0}{T_1 - T_0}$$

$$F_2 = \frac{(V_2 - V_1)/(T_2 - T_1) - F_1}{T_2 - T_0} \qquad (11.2\text{-}5)$$

We shall use the first three sets of known values to establish the polynomial which will then describe a curve passing through the plotted points of these values in Figure 11.1-1b. The values are

$$\begin{array}{ll} T_0 = 0.0 & V_0 = 0.2 \\ T_1 = 1.0 & V_1 = 0.4 \\ T_2 = 3.0 & V_2 = 0.6 \end{array}$$

When they are substituted in equations 11.2-5, we have

$$F_1 = \frac{0.4 - 0.2}{1.0 - 0.0} = 0.2$$

$$F_2 = \frac{(0.6 - 0.4)/(3.0 - 1.0) - 0.2}{3.0 - 0.0} = -\frac{1}{30}$$

With these values of F_1 and F_2 known, we can calculate the coefficients of the polynomial from equations 11.2-4:

$$A_0 = 0.2$$
$$A_1 = 0.2 + (1/30) = 0.233$$
$$A_2 = -0.033$$

From equation 11.2-3, the second-degree polynomial becomes

$$V = 0.2 + 0.233T - 0.033T^2 \qquad (11.2\text{-}6)$$

When $T = t_2 = 2.0$ for the time of the missing value of v_2, the equation calculates

$$v_2 = 0.2 + 0.466 - 0.133 = 0.533$$

We note that this approximated value of 0.533 compares with the measured value of 0.8 for v_2, in Figure 11.1-1b, which we considered to be missing. Let us see how this approximated value of v_2 affects the results of the simulation.

After substituting the measured values and the approximated value of v_2 in equations 11.1-4 for $n = 5$, we have for the performances

$$d_0 = 0 \qquad\qquad\qquad\qquad\qquad\qquad t_0 = 0$$

$$d_1 = 0 + \frac{0.2 + 0.4}{2} \times 1 = 0.3, \qquad t_1 = 1$$

$$d_2 = 0.3 + \frac{0.4 + 0.533}{2} \times 1 = 0.767, \qquad t_2 = 2$$

$$d_3 = 0.767 + \frac{0.533 + 0.6}{2} \times 1 = 1.334, \qquad t_3 = 3$$

$$d_4 = 1.334 + \frac{0.6 + 0.4}{2} \times 1 = 1.834, \qquad t_4 = 4$$

$$d_5 = 1.834 + \frac{0.4 + 0.4}{2} \times 1 = 2.234, \qquad t_5 = 5$$

The last value of 2.234 compares with the value 2.5 for d_5 when all the values are measured. In actual practice, the error resulting from the approximation would not be known.

The flow chart that describes this first method is shown in Figure 11.2-2a. Block 3, the simulation block, now contains a subprogram for approximating missing data. This requires establishing a polynomial from known data obtained by measurement and theoretical calculations, using either Newton's divided-difference polynomial, or the method of least squares.

The direct solution method of obtaining missing data may be applied

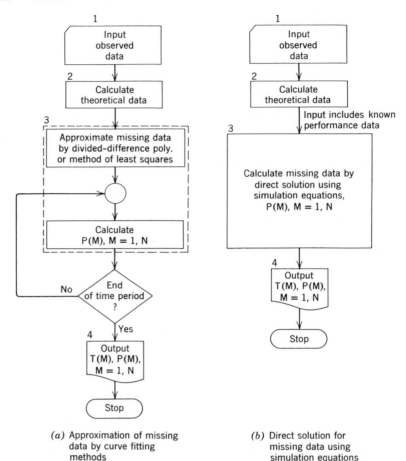

(a) Approximation of missing
data by curve fitting
methods

(b) Direct solution for
missing data using
simulation equations

Figure 11.2-2   General flow charts for performing the variation of simulation related to amount of data available—incomplete data.

if certain performance data are also known. The method requires the use of the simulation equations.

Suppose, for example, that the value of v_2 of Figure 11.1-1b is missing, but that the value of d_5 is also known by measurement to be 2.5 miles. We can proceed to perform the simulation, as before, using equations 11.1-4 up to the point where the missing value prevents us from continuing. The simulation is performed by the equation

$$d_0 = 0$$
$$d_1 = d_0 + \frac{v_0 + v_1}{2} \times \Delta t_1 \qquad (11.2\text{-}7)$$

Since the initial definition of the problem establishes that $d_0 = 0$ at the beginning of the time period, all values involved in the calculations on the right of the equation are known, and there is no problem in calculating d_1. However, the next equation for calculating d_2 requires the value v_2.

Since we know d_5 at the end of the time period which is frequently called a boundary condition at time $t = t_n$, we may proceed to calculate the distances in the reverse order up to the point where we again require v_2. After rearranging the d variables of equations 11.1-4 and starting with the last equation for $n = 5$, we have

$$d_5 = 2.5$$

$$d_4 = -\frac{v_4 + v_5}{2} \times \Delta t_5 + d_5$$

$$d_3 = -\frac{v_3 + v_4}{2} \times \Delta t_4 + d_4 \qquad (11.2\text{-}8)$$

The equations that remain for consideration are

$$d_2 = d_1 + \frac{v_1 + v_2}{2} \times \Delta t_2$$

$$d_3 = d_2 + \frac{v_2 + v_3}{2} \times \Delta t_3$$

Since we have calculated d_1 and d_3, the only unknowns are v_2 and d_2.

Solutions can now be obtained for the two unknowns from these two equations. After substituting the value of d_2, defined by the first equation into the second, we have

$$d_3 = d_1 + \frac{v_1 + v_2}{2} \times \Delta t_2 + \frac{v_2 + v_3}{2} \times \Delta t_3$$

The solution of this equation for v_2 gives

$$v_2 = (d_3 - d_1 - \frac{v_1}{2} \times \Delta t_2 - \frac{v_3}{2} \times \Delta t_3) \times \frac{2}{\Delta t_2 + \Delta t_3} \qquad (11.2\text{-}9)$$

and d_2 can then be calculated from the first equation:

$$d_2 = d_1 + \frac{v_1 + v_2}{2} \times \Delta t_2 \qquad (11.2\text{-}10)$$

Let us now proceed with a numerical solution using the sequence of calculations just established. The data available from Figure 11.1-1*b* for the simulation are

m	t_m	v_m	d_m
0	0.0	0.2	0
1	1.0	0.4	—
2	2.0	—	—
3	3.0	0.6	—
4	4.0	0.4	—
5	5.0	0.4	2.5

The first step is to perform the simulation in the usual way to the point in time where the missing value appears. From equation 11.2-7

$$d_0 = 0, \qquad\qquad\qquad t_0 = 0$$

$$d_1 = 0 + \frac{0.2 + 0.4}{2} \times 1 = 0.3, \qquad t_1 = 1$$

The second step is to begin the calculations at the end of the time period, solving the equations in reverse order back to the point in time where the missing value appears. From equations 11.2-8

$$d_5 = 2.5, \qquad\qquad\qquad t_5 = 5$$

$$d_4 = -\frac{0.4 + 0.4}{2} \times 1 + 2.5 = 2.1, \qquad t_4 = 4$$

$$d_3 = -\frac{0.6 + 0.4}{2} \times 1 + 2.1 = 1.6, \qquad t_5 = 5$$

The third step is to calculate the missing value v, making use of the values of performance calculated in the forward and reverse order of the simulation equations. From equation 11.2-9

$$v_2 = (1.6 - 0.3 - \frac{0.4}{2} \times 1 - \frac{0.6}{2} \times 1) \times \frac{2}{1 + 1} = 0.8$$

Finally, with the missing value of v calculated, the performance calculations can be completed. From equation 11.2-10

$$d_2 = 0.3 + \frac{0.4 + 0.8}{2} \times 1 = 0.9, \qquad t_2 = 2$$

We see that the assumed missing value v_2, obtained as a direct solution of equation 11.2-9, is equal to the measured value, which in actual practice may not be the case. This comes about as a result of taking a value of d_5 equal to 2.5, which was the value obtained from a previous simulation when v_2 had the value 0.8. If the missing value can be obtained by a direct solution, the values are likely to be more accurate than those approximated by curve fitting methods.

The general flow chart for obtaining missing data by direct solution is shown in Figure 11.2-2*b*. The input data to the simulation block include performance data when the simulation equations are used to obtain solutions for the missing data.

The *iterative solution method* for obtaining missing data must be used when the first two methods cannot be applied. It requires information on performance, and repetitive use of the simulation equations.

For a case study, we shall choose the simulation model

$$i = \frac{V}{R}[1 - e^{-(R/L)t}] \tag{11.2-11}$$

The equation describes the performance *i* as a function of time of the simple electrical circuit shown in Figure 11.2-3*a*. An inductor *L* is connected in series with a resistor *R* and a battery of voltage *V* through a switch. The time period of the simulation is to begin when the switch is closed and the current *i* is allowed to flow.

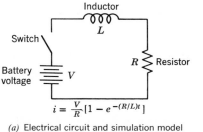

(a) Electrical circuit and simulation model

m	t_m	L_m	V_m	R_m	i_m
0	0.0	1.0	1.0	—	0
1	0.1	1.0	1.0	—	—
2	0.2	1.0	1.0	—	—
3	0.3	1.0	1.0	—	—
4	0.4	1.0	1.0	—	—
5	0.5	1.0	1.0	—	—
6	0.6	1.0	1.0	—	—
7	0.7	1.0	1.0	—	0.5

$e = 2.718$, a mathematical constant

(b) Input data for simulation equation of (a)

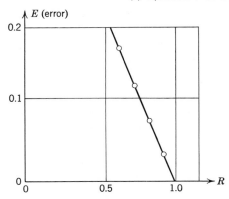

(c) Plot for finding value of R by iterative solution

Figure 11.2-3   Analysis for performing the variation of simulation related to amount of data available—missing data obtained by iterative solution.

The availability of data for the simulation equation is described in Figure 11.2-3b. The value of R_m is missing, and is to be obtained by making use of the available performance data $i_7 = 0.5$. L_m and V_m have constant values over the time period t_m, $m = 0, 7$.

This is a problem in design. We wish to modify a given circuit by changing the resistor R. The performance specifications are that the current i is to have a value of 0.5 ampere 0.7 second after the switch is closed. A timing relay is operated by this particular value of current. Our simulation is to provide values of i as a function of time every tenth of a second after the switch is closed.

Since R is associated with both a coefficient and an exponent, we cannot calculate a direct solution, and an iterative solution must be obtained. We begin by assigning an initial value to R which we know must be greater than zero to be realistic. We will say $R = 0.4$ for all values of t, and perform a simulation. A value of i will be obtained at the end of the period of simulation which will not likely agree with the specified value of 0.5. We shall call this value i_7', and the error is

$$E = 0.5 - i_7'$$

Our next step is to increment the value of R, say, by 0.1 to obtain a new value

$$R = R + 0.1$$

The simulation is repeated, giving a second calculated value of i_7' and a second error value. If this error is greater than the preceding error, we must change the sign of the increment.

If we continue the procedure, we can plot a curve of error E versus R as shown in Figure 11.2-3c. The correct value of R is the value at the intersection of the curve and the R axis. This suggests that the program for solving the simulation problem will be very similar to the programs for finding the roots of polynomials discussed in Sections 3.5 and 5.2.

Speed of Performance of the Simulator
Relative to that of the Real System

If we have a set of observed data obtained from a real system over a period of time T_R, and if the time to calculate the performances over the simulated time period T_R is T_S, the speed of performance of the simulator relative to the speed of performance of the real system is

$$R_{SR} = T_R/T_S \qquad (11.2\text{-}12)$$

For the example problem described by Figure 11.1-1*b*, the given set of observed values is $t_m, v_m, m = 0, 5$. The velocity values were obtained from the moving object, and the time values were obtained simultaneously from a clock which measured time in the standard units and which was synchronized with the 24-hour daily cycle. This real system may then be said to have performed in real time over a period

$$T_R = t_n - t_0 \qquad (11.2\text{-}13)$$

which equals 5 minutes. If the time to calculate the performances $d_m, m = 0, 5$ over the simulated time period is $T_S = 1$ minute, which is also measured by a clock, the speed of performance of the simulator relative to that of the real system is

$$R_{SR} = T_R/T_S = 5/1 = 5,$$

that is, the values of d_m are obtained from the simulator 5 times faster than they would be obtained from the real system.

When values cannot be observed from an existing system, but must be obtained by theoretical calculations, how do we determine the time period of performance T_R? To answer the question, we will suppose that an object is free falling and that the theoretical values of velocity may be calculated from equation 11.2-1

$$v_m = g \times t_m$$

where g is the gravitational constant, 32 feet per second per second. When the values of time t_m, say, for $m = 0, 5$ are substituted in the equation, we have the set of data

Velocity, feet per second		Time, seconds
$v_0 = 32. \times 0. = 0.$		$t_0 = 0$ (beginning of fall)
$v_1 = 32. \times 1. = 32$		$t_1 = 1.$
	etc.	
$v_5 = 32. \times 5. = 160$		$t_5 = 5.$

Since the gravitational constant g involves the second as a unit of measure of time, the time values substituted in the equations must also be in seconds, and the values of velocity in feet per second are calculated over a time period $T_C = t_n - t_0 = 5$ seconds. The resulting set of calculated data for the time period $T_C = 5$ seconds corresponds to the set that would be obtained by observation of the actual system performing real time over a period $T_R = 5$ seconds.

In general, the basic physical constants of the equations for calculating theoretical values establish the units of measure of the time period of performance, and T_R and T_C are identical quantities. The speed of performance of the simulator relative to that of the real system is also determined by equation 11.2-12

$$R_{SR} = T_R/T_S$$

in which T_R is now obtained from the range of values of time from t_0 to t_n, used in the equations to calculate the theoretical values, and its value is calculated from equation 11.2-13

$$T_R = t_n - t_0$$

We have established how the values of T_R are determined for both conditions of observed and calculated data. But before we can be sure of calculating R_{SR} correctly, we must also clearly define the period of performance T_S of the simulator. Figure 11.2-4 will aid in the examination of a simulation study for T_S.

The simulation study is of a moving object described by Figure 11.1-1b. The operations required in accomplishing the simulation are timed by observing a clock synchronized with the 24-hour daily cycle, and are recorded along a horizontal time scale shown at the bottom of Figure 11.2-4. At the beginning of the series of operations, the value of v_0 is observed on the system, and simultaneously t_0 is observed on the clock. These observations are made at 1-minute intervals until 6 of these subsets of data are obtained. The time T_1 for the system to output the complete set of data is measured from t_0 to t_5, and the simulation of the system is to be over this period. Then

$$T_1 = T_R = t_n - t_0 = 5 \text{ minutes.}$$

The second operation shown in the figure is the transmission of the output data of the real system to the location of the computer, and is assumed to begin at time T_{02}. A short time later, the first data subset t_0, v_0 is received at the computer location. The time T_2 for the transmission system to output the complete set of data is measured from the time the first subset is received to the time the last t_5, v_5 is received. This time is 1 minute, as determined by the real-time scale of the figure. We can say that the speed of performance of the transmission system relative to that of the real system in outputting the complete data is

$$R_{2R} = T_R/T_2 = 5/1 = 5$$

Data input to the computer as a third operation is assumed to be accomplished with a card reader as shown in the figure. The data subsets t_m, v_m are produced as output from the card reader, and are stored in computer memory. This input operation begins at time T_{03}, and the

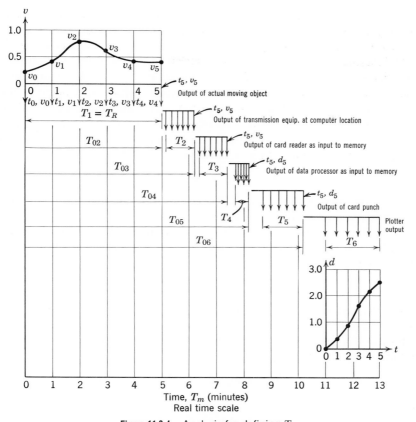

Figure 11.2-4   Analysis for defining T_S.

time for the reader to output the complete set of data is $T_3 = 1$ minute as determined by the real-time scale. The speed of performance of the card reader relative to that of the real system in outputting the complete data is then

$$R_{3R} = T_R/T_3 = 5/1 = 5$$

The data-processing operation is the fourth operation shown, and begins at time T_{04}. A short time later, the first subset of performance data t_0, d_0 is calculated from the simulation equations as output for storage in computer memory. If the data for the equations had not been observed from the real system, but had to be calculated as theoretical data, the time beginning at T_{04} to the time of the output of the first performance data would have been increased in order to perform these theoretical calculations.

The time T_4 for the data-processing operation to output the complete set of performance data into memory is measured from the time the first subset is calculated as output to the time the last subset t_5, d_5 is calculated, and is equal to $\frac{1}{2}$ minute. The time between the outputs of adjacent data subsets need not be equal, as shown in the figure, and they need not be calculated in the sequence in which they occur in the system. For example, d_3 need not be calculated following the calculation of d_2. The speed of performance of the data-processing operation in outputting the performance data relative to the speed of performance of the real system in outputting the observed data is then

$$R_{4R} = T_R/T_4 = 5/\tfrac{1}{2} = 10$$

The fifth operation shown, is the output operation of the computer which is assumed to be performed by a card punch. The operations begin at time T_{05}, and the time to output the complete data set is $T_5 = 1.5$ minutes. The speed, or performance, of the card punch in outputting the data relative to that of the real system is calculated to be

$$R_{5R} = T_R/T_5 = 5/1.5 = 3.33$$

Finally, the sixth operation is the plotting operation, which begins at time T_{06}, and plots the data from the cards at a speed of $2\frac{1}{2}$ points per minute. The speed of performance of the plotter in outputting the complete data set relative to that of the real system is

$$R_{6R} = T_R/T_6 = 5/2 = 2.5$$

Now that we have analyzed the set of operations that may be involved in a simulation, what operation or operations are to be considered in calculating T_S? Do the operations of the simulator include data input, processing, and output? Since T_R is the time period beginning with the time of the output of the first data subset to the time of output of the last subset from the real system, we would also expect T_S to be related to the time of output of a single operation. The time to perform the output operation of a computer is sometimes used as a value of T_S. However, since the performances are calculated from the simulation equations, it is the data processor that performs like the real system, and its speed should determine the simulation speed. Therefore, *we choose to define T_S to be the time period beginning when the first subset of performance data is calculated as output by the data processor, and ending when the last data subset has been calculated.* For the example problem of Figure 11.2-4, T_S is then equal to T_4.

For the problems presented, the speed of performance of the simulator relative to that of the real system, was calculated to be greater than one as calculated by the equation

$$R_{SR} = T_R/T_S$$

that is, the simulator performed faster than the real system for these problems. We would expect that the speed of performance of the simulator may be *faster* or *slower* than, or *equal* to the speed of the real system.

The speed of performance of the simulator may be slower when the performance of the real system changes very rapidly with time. Two examples are simulations for particle tracing in high-energy accelerators, and for current flow in high-voltage circuit breakers. For such systems, the human sensory mechanisms are incapable of obtaining performance information directly, but through simulations, we are able to "slow the systems down" to observe their performance at our leisure.

For many problems, it is desirable that the simulator perform faster than the real system. Systems that change slowly over long periods of time, such as economic and industrial systems, are speeded up through simulations. Trial changes can be made in the simulation models, and their effects on the performances determined in a relatively short time.

Statement of Time of the Real System

The fourth variation of simulation is related to the time of the real system. The time of the real system in a simulation study may be either explicit or implied.

Explicit. *The time is explicit when performance is expressed as a function of time,* i.e., when it enters into the calculations of the model, and is included in the computer output. The simulation problems already discussed are examples.

Implied. *When a simulation study does not have performance expressed as a function-time, the time is said to be implied.* This is sometimes the case in applications of computers to design. As the performance of each member or part of a product is calculated, and the dimensions established, the actual manufacture and testing of that part is being simulated, even though time is not expressed. The design of the roof truss of Figure 4.2-3 is an example. Since time does not appear in the model equations, and is not included in the results, a study of this type is generally overlooked as a simulation study.

These four principal variations of simulation are summarized in Figure 11.2-5. Each arrow represents a single variation. Any simula-

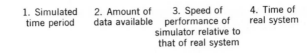

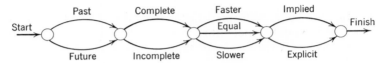

Figure 11.2-5 Variations of simulation.

tion can be classified by taking the proper path through the entire system, and a path between any 2 nodes is independent of the path between any other 2. An example classification of a simulation may be the following: (1) simulated time period—past; (2) amount of data available—incomplete; (3) speed of performance of simulator relative to that of real system—faster; (4) statement of time of real system—implied.

PROBLEM 11.2-1   "Missing Values Obtained by Iteration"

Program the simulation problem described in Figure 11.2-3. Obtain the missing value of R by an iterative solution.

Output: R and performance i as a function of t.

PROBLEM 11.2-2   "Missing Values Obtained by Curve Fitting"

GIVEN

Observed data over a past period:

m	t_m, minutes	v_m, miles/minute
0	0.0	0.2
1	1.0	0.3
2	2.0	—
3	3.0	0.4
4	4.0	0.4
5	5.0	0.3
$d_o = 0$		

REQUIRED

(A) Write a program for making a simulation study. Use Newton's divided-difference polynomial to obtain the missing value of v_2. Fit the polynomial through the points for $m = 1, 3,$ and 4. Produce as output t_m and d_m for $m = 0, 1, \ldots, 5$.

(B) Classify the simulation. If the time of performance of the simulator is $1\frac{1}{2}$ minutes, what is the speed of performance of the simulator relative to that of the real system?

CHAPTER 12.

Other Kinds of Computers

12.1 PERSPECTIVE

In Chapter 1 we contrasted the desk calculator with an automatic computer, calling the former a manual computer in that manual intervention, in the form of pushing a button, is necessary to carry out each successive arithmetic operation, whereas the high-speed computer is automatically sequenced from one operation to the next, according to a prearranged program.

There are, however, other ways of breaking computers into two or more types, as, for instance, the distinction between mechanical, electromechanical, and electronic. In the first, information is transferred, stored, and operated upon by the movement of mechanical parts—sliding of rods, rotation of shafts, or turning of wheels. In the second, of which relay computers are an important example, mechanical linkages from one element to the next are replaced by electric current, although the actual data storage and logical operation is carried by the mechanical moving of contact arms in switches or relays. In the third, the purely electronic computer, a still more tremendous gain in speed is realized by replacing even these light-weight contact arms by the lightest known particle—the electron. In a vacuum tube or transistor, the change of state that signifies storage or logical control is effected by the establishment of current, or the building up of charge on a tiny circuit or interface. The gain in speed over the operating time of a relay runs from 1000–1 to 1,000,000–1.

Still another major classification of computers occurs when we sort them according to whether they are analog, digital, or a combination of analog and digital—the principal subject of this chapter. An analog computer essentially does not solve the specific problem we want solved, but it does solve an analogous one. When set up to solve a problem, there is a physical correspondence or similarity; mathematically, the computer is the analog of the system under study.

12.2 ANALOG COMPUTERS

What They Are

Analog computers have a long and varied history, including hydraulic systems, mechanical contraptions, and electronic devices. One of the most successful early analog computers was, and still is, the slide rule, invented many years ago after an earlier and cruder arrangement called "Napier's Bones." The electronics of analog computers begins, however, at just about the same time as it did for digital computers—the late 1940's, under the stimulus of World War II.

The electronic analog computer, usually called a differential analyzer, is the general-purpose computer of this type, and is the most common in use today. Like the general-purpose digital computer, it relies on vacuum tube and transister circuits to achieve a very high speed of operation. Unlike its digital counterpart, however, the analog computer deals not with just two voltage levels, but with a whole continuous range of values.

We saw in Chapter 8 that the circuits of a digital computer carry time varying voltage pulses like those shown in Figure 12.2-1*a*. The upper and lower levels of these pulses are interpreted as ones and zeros. Their exact values are not important in the interpretation; to be able to distinguish between two discrete levels is all that is required.

In comparison, the analog computer circuits carry continuous time-varying voltages (Figure 12.2-1*b*). These voltages, which are the actual solutions to the problem being solved, could be measured by voltmeters, but more frequently they are displayed and plotted against time by cathode ray oscilloscopes or automatic plotters. The values read or plotted are analog values.

In everyday life we read analog quantities. The speedometer reading of an automobile is an analog quantity, as is the reading of a bathroom scale. The accuracy of these measured quantities (including those of the

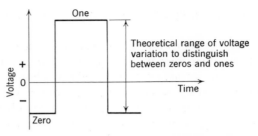

(*a*) Representative voltage in a digital computer circuit

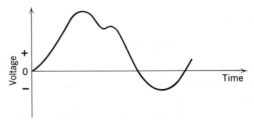

(*b*) Representative voltage in an analog computer circuit

Figure 12.2-1   Comparison of voltage signals in digital and analog computer circuits.

analog computer) seldom exceeds 3 decimal digits, but in most cases this is sufficient. For example, the purchase price by weight of a fruit or vegetable in a supermarket may be $2.45 as read from the weight scale, and the accuracy is within the accuracy of our money system. If an analog computer is applied to the proper type of problems, the solutions have sufficient accuracy.

Uses of the Analog Computer. In Chapter 4, mention was made that analog computers as well as digital computers are used in the planning operations of an industrial system. They are used in the planning of new and special products, and in research. The products may be consumer or capital goods. An example of consumer goods is the automobile; the analog computer is very useful in the development of the spring system for the next year's automobile. The computer also plays a very important role in automation in the development of automatic machines that are capital goods used to perform the processing operations, such as automatic machine tools and automatic steel rolling mills. The automatic controls used in space vehicles and in the launching equipment are also developed with the aid of the analog computer.

One of the areas of research in which the analog computer has had important application is medical research. Here, for example, the computer is used to study the heart and blood circulatory system.

The Analog Computer as a Simulator. Most of the problems solved on the analog computer are simulation problems. The discussion and classification of simulation in Chapter 11 apply also to those problems solved on the analog computer. We shall have an opportunity to become better acquainted with the uses of the analog computer as a simulator after we learn how it operates.

Basic Types of Components

From the point of view of their logical functions, there are three basic types of components that make up an analog computer, each performing a particular function: adders, multipliers, and integrators. However, in an analog computer, unlike the digital, we do not perform these functions one at a time, but all at once. This means that there must be a separate component for each mathematical operation to be performed. To solve the problem, we must connect these components together so that they are all acting simultaneously. Because the components are all working simultaneously, the analog computer is a parallel processor, and this fact accounts largely for its great speed advantage over the digital computer, which must perform all its operations in serial fashion, one after the other. On the other hand, this does mean that we must have many components of each type, and the size of computer and, hence, the size of a problem we can handle is specified by the number of these component packages it contains.

Adder Component. The "adder" adds a number of time-varying voltages simultaneously and continuously. A practical maximum number of voltages that can be added by a single adder may be as high as 10. Figure 12.2-2a shows, for example, two voltages v_1 and v_2 as inputs to an adder

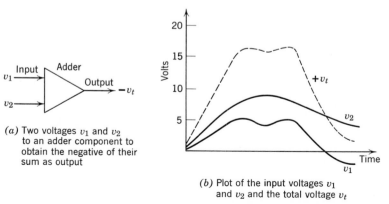

(*a*) Two voltages v_1 and v_2 to an adder component to obtain the negative of their sum as output

(*b*) Plot of the input voltages v_1 and v_2 and the total voltage v_t

Figure 12.2-2 Addition—one of the important functions performed by an analog computer.

component which obtains their negative algebraic sum $-v_t$ as the output voltage. The function performed is then

$$v_1 + v_2$$

Figure 12.2-2b shows representative plots of these voltages in which time is plotted along the horizontal axis. The total time along the axis may be anywhere within the range of a fraction of a second to a few minutes, depending on the design of the adder and the plotting equipment.

Multiplier Components. "Multipliers" are also frequently used in analog computers. There are two types of multiplications to perform

$$c \times v$$

and

$$v_1 \times v_2$$

where c is a constant coefficient and the v's are variables. The first type, $c \times v$, is used much more frequently than the second. Figure 12.2-3a shows the first type of multiplication in which a time-varying voltage v is input to the analog component, and the output voltage is $-(c \times v)$. When a constant coefficient is less than 1, a very simple component called a potentiometer may be used as a multiplier, and no sign change appears in the output, i.e., the output is $+(c \times v)$. Figure 12.2-3b shows the second type, in which 2 time-varying voltages v_1 and v_2 are inputs to the component, and the product voltage $-(v_1 \times v_2)$ is the output. The multiplying functions of both types are performed continuously; i.e., the output voltages when plotted are continuous curves as were the curves produced by the adder component.

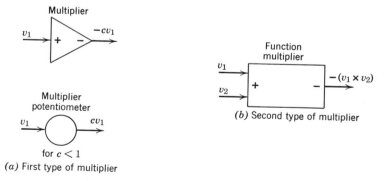

(a) First type of multiplier

(b) Second type of multiplier

Figure 12.2-3   Multiplication—a second important function performed by an analog computer.

Integrator Component. The third important function of an analog computer is integration. This is a new word to those who have not had the mathematics of calculus, but integration, as performed by the analog computer, is easily understood. The example problem of Figure 11.1-1*a* is also described in Figure 12.2-4*a*, and can be used to demonstrate the function of the integrator. The observed values of velocity are plotted as a function of time to obtain curve *v*. The curve of distance *d* is easily calculated from this simple velocity curve, making use of the equation

$$d = v \times t \qquad (12.2\text{-}1)$$

We found in Chapter 11 that when curve *v* is not a straight line, the following simulation model for the digital computer must be used:

$$d_1 = d_0 + \frac{v_0 + v_1}{2} \Delta t_1$$

$$d_2 = d_1 + \frac{v_1 + v_2}{2} \Delta t_2$$

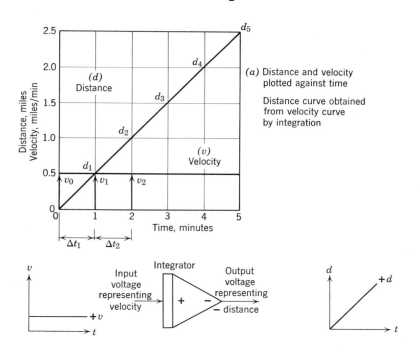

(a) Distance and velocity plotted against time

Distance curve obtained from velocity curve by integration

(b) Voltage representing velocity as input to an analog integrator to produce a voltage output representing distance

Figure 12.2-4   Integration—third important function of an analog computer.

$$d_3 = d_2 + \frac{v_2 + v_3}{2} \Delta t_3$$

etc.

$$d_n = d_{n-1} \frac{v_{n-1} + v_n}{2} \Delta t_n \qquad (12.2\text{-}2)$$

where

$$\Delta t_n = t_n - t_{n-1} \qquad (12.2\text{-}3)$$

These equations represent a simple numerical method of integration. Numerical methods must always be used when integration is performed on a digital computer.

A component called the "integrator" performs integration in the analog computer. A sign change is produced in computing the output. If we let voltage represent velocity, and let this voltage be the input to an integrator component (Figure 12.2-4b), we will obtain a voltage output representing distance. Since the input and output voltages of the integrator component are continuous over the given time interval, integration is performed continuously. This means that the intervals of time, Δt, of equations 12.2-2 are very, very small, and that the number within a given period is infinite.

The integration process may also be used to find a velocity-time curve from an acceleration-time curve. Figure 12.2-5a shows acceleration plotted against time (curve a). The values for the curve may have been obtained from acceleration tests of an automobile. It is required to obtain velocity-time and distance-time curves, shown as curves v and d in the figure. Since the integration process is also required to obtain velocity curves from acceleration curves, we can easily write the equations for the simple numerical method of integration from equations 12.2-2. These equations are

$$v_1 = v_0 + \frac{a_0 + a_1}{2} \Delta t_1$$

$$v_2 = v_1 + \frac{a_1 + a_2}{2} \Delta t_2$$

etc.

$$v_n = v_{n-1} + \frac{a_{n-1} + a_n}{2} \Delta t_n \qquad (12.2\text{-}4)$$

The equations of 12.2-2 can be used as before, to calculate distance curves from velocity curves.

If the acceleration data are in the form of a voltage, we can easily obtain velocity and distance using 2 integrator components connected in

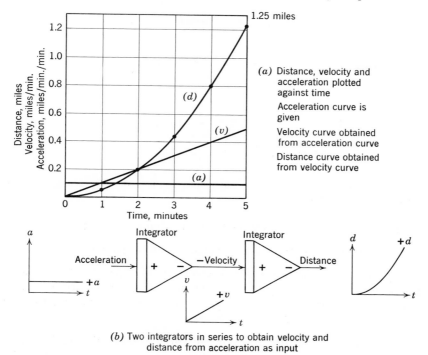

(a) Distance, velocity and acceleration plotted against time

Acceleration curve is given

Velocity curve obtained from acceleration curve

Distance curve obtained from velocity curve

(b) Two integrators in series to obtain velocity and distance from acceleration as input

Figure 12.2-5   Double integration for obtaining distance from acceleration.

series. Figure 12.2-5*b* shows voltage representing acceleration as given input to an integrator. The output voltage representing velocity is input to a second integrator whose output is a voltage representing distance. The velocity and distance voltages may then be plotted against time, using mechanical plotters.

Simulating an Automobile Spring System on the Analog Computer

Description of the Problem. We have been discussing the horizontal movement of an automobile. Vertical motion is also present, involving acceleration, velocity, and distance. We shall establish how we might study this vertical action with an analog computer.

To simplify the problem, we shall neglect such factors as the spring action of the tires and consider only the body of the car and the springs and shock absorbers connecting the body to the wheel axles. We can combine the four springs and shock absorbers and treat them as single units supporting the mass of the car. A sketch of the equivalent system is shown in Figure 12.2-6.

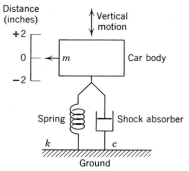

Figure 12.2-6   A representation of an automobile spring system for analog computer study.

The system is described by the following dynamic equation:

$$m \times \text{acceleration} + c \times \text{velocity} + k \times \text{distance} = 0$$

m, c, and k are constants for a given automobile; m is related to the weight of the car, c to the characteristics of the shock absorber, and k to the characteristics of the spring. Acceleration, velocity, and distance pertain to motion of the body of the car.

Programming the Problem. To facilitate programming the analog computer, it is desirable to make the coefficient of acceleration equal to 1 by dividing the equation by m, and to equate acceleration to the sum of the other terms. Then

$$\text{acceleration} = -c/m \times \text{velocity} - k/m \times \text{distance} \qquad (12.2\text{-}5)$$

If acceleration does not appear in dynamic equations to be programmed, velocity is equated to the sum of the other terms.

The steps required to program equation 12.2-5 for the analog computer are shown in Figure 12.2-7. The resulting program serves as a wiring diagram for connecting the analog computer components.

The objective of the first two steps of programming is to obtain the function variables; acceleration, velocity, and distance. The components required will be integrators. For the first step, we assume the variable on the left of the equal sign, acceleration, is available as input to our first integrator. The output will then give negative velocity.

In the second step, we add another integrator to our program. The input is the negative velocity obtained as output from the first integrator, and the output is distance.

We now have all three variables available in our program. The next objective of the programming is to obtain the terms of the equation, or

Integrator *(I)*

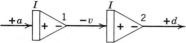

Step 1. Assume acceleration input to first integrator and obtain negative velocity

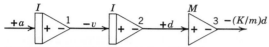

Step 2. Connect second integrator to obtain distance

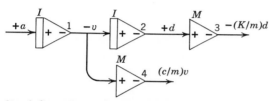

Step 3. Connect multiplier to obtain $-(K/m)d$

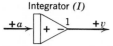

Step 4. Connect second multiplier to obtain $(c/m)v$

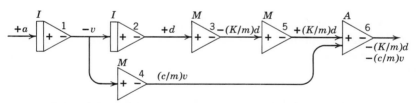

Step 5. Connect multiplier to effect sign change and obtain sum of terms with adder

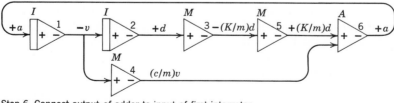

Step 6. Connect output of adder to input of first integrator

Figure 12.2-7 Steps required in programming the analog computer for solving the problem of the auto spring system.

the products of the variables and their coefficients. Type 1 multipliers are required in the third and fourth steps to obtain $-k/m \times$ distance, and $+ c/m \times$ velocity. The coefficient of acceleration is 1, and no multiplier is required.

Our next programming objective is to sum all the terms appearing on the right of the equal sign of the equation. This is accomplished in the fifth step by adding an adder component to the program. First, we must insert a multiplier between component 3 and the adder, and multiply by a constant coefficient of -1 to effect a change of sign of $(k/m) \times$ distance. Since the adder input includes all the terms on the right of the equal sign of the equation, the output must be plus acceleration, allowing for a sign change through the adder.

In our first step, we assumed we had positive acceleration as input to our first integrator. It has now been made available as output from the adder component. The sixth step is to connect the output of the adder to the input of the first integrator, and the computer circuit is then complete.

Exciting the Analog Circuit to Obtain a Solution. We have not as yet completed our preparatory work for a dynamic analysis of the automobile spring system. Just as the automobile parked by the curb is in the static state, so would an analog computer be if programmed as shown in Figure 12.2-7. Just as we must apply an outside disturbance to the automobile spring system to put it in a dynamic state, so must we apply an external voltage disturbance to the analog circuit to put it in a dynamic state. We must establish the type of dynamic analysis we wish to make and the manner in which we wish to disturb the physical system. We must then determine the disturbance of the analog computer circuit which will simulate that of the system.

To put the physical system in a dynamic state, we will proceed to displace the mass a distance d_0 by applying a constant external force. Several people standing on the bumpers of the automobile can produce the desired force. After the system has again reached the static state with the external force applied, the force is suddenly removed at a time $t = 0$. From similar experiences with dynamic systems, we expect the mass to oscillate and the oscillations to decay to zero with time.

We can now specify mathematically these conditions of the system at time $t = 0$, and when $t = t_{\text{large}}$

$$\text{at } t = 0 \tag{12.2-8}$$
$$\begin{aligned} \text{acceleration} &= 0 \\ \text{velocity} &= 0 \\ \text{distance} &= d_0 \end{aligned}$$

when $t = t_{large}$ (static state conditions)

acceleration = 0
velocity   = 0
distance   = 0

We are interested in how the system behaves during the period of time from $t = 0$ to t_{large}. Equation 12.2-5,

$$\text{acceleration} = -c/m \times \text{velocity} - k/m \times \text{distance},$$

describes this period when the above initial conditions at $t = 0$ are applied.

Our next task is to determine the disturbance of the analog computer circuit that will simulate the disturbance of the actual system. The integrators are the components of interest in effecting disturbances, and their general circuit structure must be investigated.

The three basic building blocks of the integrator are amplifier, resistor, and capacitor. Two switches and a variable voltage source are also required in the operation. Figure 12.2-8 shows the structure of the integrator.

Figure 12.2-9*a, b,* and *c* shows how the switches of the integrator accomplish the simulated disturbance of the system.

The output of the integrator is assumed to be distance. Figure 12.2-9*a* shows the storing of voltage e_0 on the capacitor. The closed switch T_{01} places the voltage across the capacitor, and the open switch T_{c2} isolates the capacitor from the rest of the circuit. This operation corresponds to the displacement of mass of the physical system.

In Figure 12.2-9*b*, the capacitor has stored the voltage e_0, and the switch T_{c1} is opened. The switch T_{c2} remains open to hold the voltage on the capacitor. This operation corresponds to holding the mass of our physical system at a distance d_0.

In Figure 12.2-9*c*, switch T_{c1} remains open, and switch T_{c2} closes at time $t = 0$ to complete the computer circuit. This operation corresponds to suddenly removing the external force applied to the mass of our physical system.

These same switching operations are carried out on the integrator

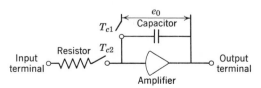

Figure 12.2-8   Basic structure of integrator.

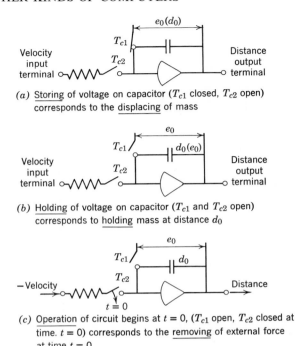

(a) Storing of voltage on capacitor (T_{c1} closed, T_{c2} open)
corresponds to the displacing of mass

(b) Holding of voltage on capacitor (T_{c1} and T_{c2} open)
corresponds to holding mass at distance d_0

(c) Operation of circuit begins at $t = 0$, (T_{c1} open, T_{c2} closed at
time. $t = 0$) corresponds to the removing of external force
at time $t = 0$

Figure 12.2-9   Operation of switches of integrator to accomplish simulated disturbance of system.

with velocity as output. Since we have established that at time $t = 0$ the velocity $= 0$, the voltage e_0 for this integrator must be made equal to zero.

With the disturbance of the physical system simulated on the analog computer, we can now study the characteristics of the system, using the computer. We change the values of m, c, and k as we choose, to obtain the best automobile spring system. Each time we make a change in any of these parameters the disturbance is reinitiated.

Since the analog computer operates in parallel, we may simultaneously plot voltages corresponding to acceleration, velocity, and distance. Figure 12.2-10a and b shows what we might expect as plotted output for our example problem when distance is plotted against time. Plot (a) might be considered to be for a system with normal operating shock absorbers and Plot (b) for one with defective shock absorbers.

There are many special components of the analog computer that enable one to handle very difficult problems, called nonlinear problems. For example, with the use of "limiters," one can study the automobile

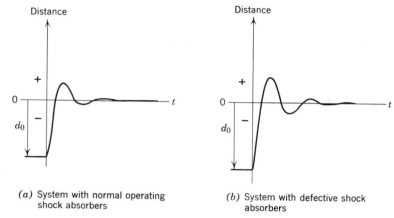

(*a*) System with normal operating shock absorbers

(*b*) System with defective shock absorbers

Figure 12.2-10 Representative output from computer for automobile spring system.

spring problem when, under certain disturbing conditions, the oscillations are so great the body strikes the axles.

Classifying the Simulation. Just as we have classified simulations performed on the digital computer, we can classify simulations performed on the analog computer. If the spring system is for next year's automobile, the simulation is performed as a planning operation in the automobile industry, and the simulated time period is then the *future*.

Let us now examine the amount of data available for the simulation. The spring system design follows the design of the body and engine so that the value of the mass of the automobile is known. The vertical motion of the mass that will give the best riding comfort is also known. However, the spring constant k and the damping constant c are unknown. The amount of data available is then *incomplete*, which is the case for most analog simulations. Trial selection of values must be made, and a number of simulations performed to find the values of k and c that will give the known performance for the best riding comfort. This method is the *iterative* method of finding values of missing data. These values are changed by manually turning the knobs on the multiplier components.

For this example problem, the speed of performance of the simulator relative to that of the real system is likely to be *faster*. The speed of the analog simulator is easily determined by observing the time it takes the plotter to plot the results. The speed can be varied by changing the size of the capacitors of the integrators, and this is frequently done. For a given size digital computer, the speed of the simulator is fixed.

Finally, since performance is expressed as a function of time, the time of the real system is *explicit*.

Description of Analog Equipment

Figure 12.2-11*a* shows a 1965 model of a small size transistorized analog computer used to solve smaller problems and for teaching purposes. The complement of components includes 16 integrators, 24 coefficient multipliers ($c < 1$), 8 function multipliers, and 20 adders and coefficient multipliers ($c \geq 1$). They are distributed throughout the cabinet, and their input and output leads are terminated behind the upper panel. This panel is removable, and is called a plugboard or patchboard. It is used to connect the components into a circuit to solve a problem, and is similar to a telephone switchboard. The connection from one component terminal to another is made by plugging the ends of a wire into the proper holes or receptacles of the plugboard where they make contact with the terminals of the components. A plugboard wired for a particular problem can be removed from the computer without disturbing the plugged wires, and stored to obtain solutions of future problems requiring the same circuit but different problem data. Another plugboard may then be mounted and a different problem solved. The storing of a problem plugboard for an analog computer is equivalent to the storing of a problem deck for a digital computer.

Output equipment for plotting the results of an analog computer is shown in Figure 12.2-11*b*. With the use of the plugboard, voltages in any part of the problem circuit can be plotted as output. For the example problem, the voltages that would be plotted represent distance, velocity, and acceleration, as functions of time.

12.3 HYBRID COMPUTERS

What They Are

Hybrid computer systems contain the computing features of both the analog and digital computers, and have utility for solving certain types of scientific problems. When the merits of the analog and digital computers are combined in a hybrid computer system, many problems can be solved better on the hybrid system than on either the analog or digital computers, and in some cases solutions cannot be obtained without the hybrid system. The merits of both types of computers were mentioned in the preceding section and will be reviewed here for the discussion of the hybrid computer systems.

The principal advantage of the analog computer over the digital computer is speed of problem solving, because:

(a) It performs calculations in parallel, while the digital computer performs calculations in series. The number of calculations performed

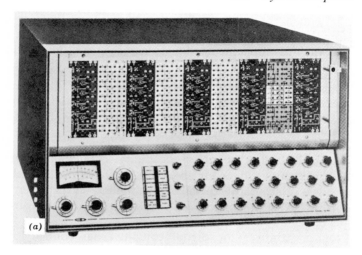

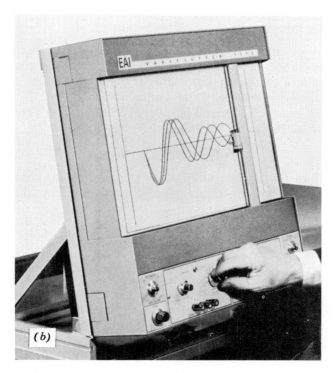

Figure 12.2-11 Analog computer equipment. (*a*) Portable Analog Computer. Courtesy of the Systron Donner Corp. (*b*) Plotter for Plotting the Output of the Analog Computer. Courtesy of Electronic Associates, Inc.

in parallel equals the number of analog components that are used to solve a problem.

(b) The analog computer calculates functions as continuous functions, while the digital computer calculates functions in discrete steps. A very large number of steps are required for many problems involving numerical integration.

The digital computer has two principal advantages over the analog computer. They are:

(a) High calculating accuracy—the digital computer performs the arithmetic operations by counting, and produces numerical results of many digits of accuracy. The analog computer, on the other hand, is a measuring device, and produces results which are measured to a few digits of accuracy.

(b) Program control—the digital computer has control logic and addressable memory for altering courses of action during a problem solution. The standard analog computer has very limited control and memory for this purpose.

The two principal classes of hybrid computer systems are distinguishable by the number of these digital capabilities that are incorporated with the capabilities of the analog computer. The two classes are (1) the iterative analog computer, which contains a minimum of the digital capabilities, and (2) the general-purpose hybrid computer which contains a maximum of the digital capabilities.

The Iterative Analog Computer

We shall review the operation of the standard analog computer in a problem solving experience, and improve its operation by adding digital capabilities.

Review of the Problem of the Automobile Spring System. In the preceding section, the example problem of an automobile spring system was presented for solution on the analog computer (Figure 12.2-6) in which the values of the spring stiffness k and damping c were to be determined to give the best riding comfort. This is an optimizing problem, and is representative of those frequently solved on the analog computer. The values of the parameters which work best cannot be determined by the linear programming method discussed in Section 5.5, and an iterative method must be used.

Before the iterative process begins, a criterion for best performance is established. Variations of parameter values are then made from solution to solution, using the criterion for best performance and calculated performance of one solution to influence the choice of parameter values to be used in the next solution. For our example problem, we shall assume that the criterion for the best riding comfort of the automobile has been established, and is described qualitatively by the curve of distance versus time shown in Figure 12.3-1a. The values of the parameters k and c

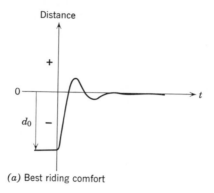

(a) Best riding comfort

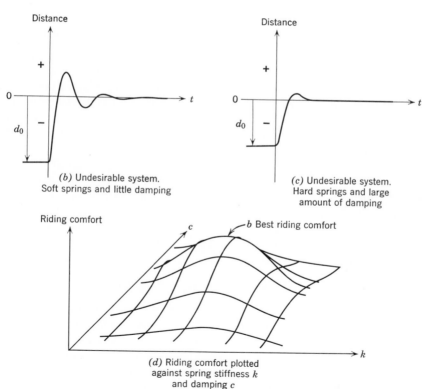

(b) Undesirable system.
Soft springs and little damping

(c) Undesirable system.
Hard springs and large
amount of damping

(d) Riding comfort plotted
against spring stiffness k
and damping c

Figure 12.3-1   Effects of spring stiffness and damping on riding comfort of an automobile.

required to give this performance are unknown. Values which are too small give an undesirable, bouncing ride as shown in Figure 12.3-1b, while values which are too large give an undesirable, rough ride as shown in (c) and the system approaches that of one with no springs. The three-dimensional curve of riding comfort versus k and c must then take the general form shown in Figure 12.3-1d, and is the same as the curve of Figure 5.5-3. The objective of an iterative method of solution is to find the peak shown as point b.

Program Control Performed by Man. When this problem is solved on the standard analog computer, variations of parameters are made manually by adjusting knobs on the coefficient multipliers for the parameters k and c. The human, then, provides program control in finding the peak of the three-dimensional curve. Man is a natural optimizer, and the iterative method he uses is a natural one. It is no different from the one he uses in obtaining maximum clarity on a television set, or in obtaining the best performance of a boat motor, discussed in Section 5.5. The computer results that he uses to influence his choices of parameter values to obtain subsequent results are stored by plotting them on graph paper, by recording them as observed values, or by storing them mentally.

Program Control Performed by Digital Circuits. When the iterative analog computer is used to solve these optimizing problems, digital logic circuits, not man, performs program control. The computer contains the full compliment of analog components and basic digital components consisting of a variety of flip-flops, gates, and counters discussed in Section 8.4. Circuits containing the digital components are designed and incorporated with the circuits of the analog components to provide control in the solving of a problem. A number of basic digital circuits may perform in parallel and at different times during the problem solving operation, in order to control the selection of parameter values. The iterative method must be well defined in order to design the digital circuits. If the circuits have been properly established, the computer operates with a minimum of human intervention from one solution to the next, until it finds parameter values that give the best performance.

The General-Purpose Hybrid Computer

The general-purpose hybrid computer contains the full complement of components of the iterative analog computer and, in addition, a general-purpose digital computer. The limitations in the capabilities of the digital circuits that can be constructed from the digital components are overcome by incorporating a general-purpose digital computer in the problem solving system. The digital computer equipment includes the input and output equipment for communicating with the iterative analog computer, and is the same as the equipment used in the real-time operation of computers in the control of continuous processes. The input equipment is capable of measuring a large number of quantities from the iterative analog circuits, converting analog values to digital values when required, and transmitting the data as input to the digital data processor. The output equipment is capable of converting digital values to analog values, and transmitting the data to the analog circuits to produce the desired effects.

The digital computer of the hybrid computer system can be used in two principal ways in a problem solving experience:

(1) As a control computer to aid the digital part of the iterative analog computer in performing the control operations.

(2) As a problem solver to aid the analog part of the iterative analog computer in the model computations.

The Digital Computer as a Control Computer. The digital computer is used as a control computer when the capabilities of the digital part of the iterative computer are exceeded in controlling the analog computer during problem solutions. This condition may arise when the criterion for a best performance involves complex arithmetic calculations, and requires large amounts of data storage. For example, if the criterion for a best spring system for an automobile involves the cost of the system as well as riding comfort, data on prices of materials and labor would require large amounts of memory, which must be provided by a digital computer. The cost that affects the selection of each new set of parameter values would require lengthly calculations, and must be performed by a digital computer.

A very important application of the hybrid computer where the digital computer performs as a control computer is the design of real-time systems for the control of continuous processes. A simulation of the complete system is performed. The simulation of the process is performed best on the analog computer. Since a digital computer is to be used to control the actual process, it is used in the same manner to control the analog simulator.

The Digital Computer as a Problem Solver. The digital computer of a hybrid system is used as a problem solver when it aids the iterative analog computer in the model computations. The models of certain types of complex problems have a wide variation in requirements of speed, accuracy, and memory, and require the merits of both the analog and digital computers to obtain solutions. Both computers operating together in a hybrid system, each performing the parts of the model calculations for which it is best suited, can produce results not obtainable with either computer by itself.

An example of a very important application is the simulation of a space vehicle (Figure 12.3-2). The part of the model describing the rotation or tumbling action of the vehicle in space requires high speed relative to the remaining part, but accuracy is not important. This part is best solved by the iterative analog computer. The part of the model that describes the trajectory of the vehicle, i.e., its forward direction through space, requires great accuracy, but the speed of calculation is not important. The digital computer meets these computational requirements and is used to solve this second part.

Description of Hybrid Computer Equipment

Figure 12.3-3a shows a 1965 model of a large iterative analog computer made by Applied Dynamics, Inc., installed in the Electrical Engineering Department, University of Wisconsin. It is totally transistorized. The analog components are contained in the right wing, and the digital components in the left wing of the unit.

The analog section contains 150 potentiometers; 30 function multipliers; 192 integrators, adders, and coefficient multipliers ($c > 1$); and a number of other special components for solving complex nonlinear problems.

The digital section contains 56 logic gates and flip-flops, 3 counters, and other basic components, such as electronic switches.

An 8-channel plotter is shown on the extreme left of the figure. Each channel can plot values of a function, and 8 different functions may be plotted simultaneously.

Figure 12.3-3b shows an enlarged view of the plugboards. The digital

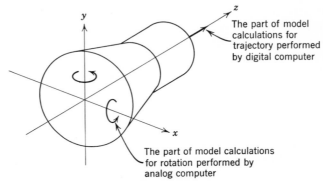

Figure 12.3-2 Space vehicle simulation performed by general-purpose hybrid computer.

Figure 12.3-3 Hybrid computing equipment of the iterative analog class. (*a*) A large iterative analog computer with analog components contained in the right wing and the digital components in the left wing. (*b*) Enlarged view of the digital plugboard (left) and the analog plugboard (right).

plugboard is on the left, and the analog plugboard on the right. The input and output leads of the components are terminated behind the boards. Connections are made between components when wires are inserted in the holes on the front of the plugboards. Both boards may be removed and the program circuits stored for subsequent usage.

A general-purpose digital computer is installed in the same room (not shown in the figure), which makes the installation a general-purpose hybrid system. The digital computer contains the analog-to-digital, and digital-to-analog converting equipment, which provides for communication between the iterative analog and the digital computer.

PROBLEM 12.2-1   "How Smooth the Ride"

(A) The wheel and axle system of an automobile can be represented as a mass and spring system as shown in Figure P12.2-1a. The air in the tires has the same effect as a spring with a stiffness constant K_2, and m_2 represents the mass of the wheels and axles. The dynamic equation is

$$m_2 a_2 + K_2 d_2 = 0$$

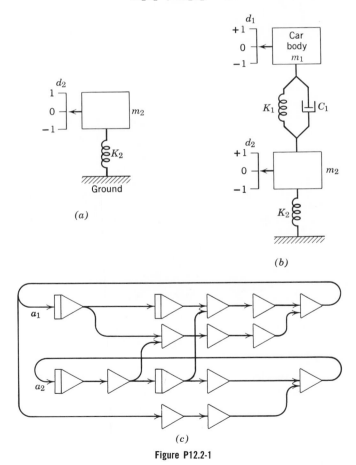

(a)

(b)

(c)

Figure P12.2-1

Draw the flow chart for the equation. Identify the analog computer components and their inputs and outputs.

(B) To more accurately represent the automobile spring system, the system for part (A) is combined with that of Figure 12.2-6 as shown in Figure P12.2-1*b*. The equations that describe the system are:

$$m_1 a_1 = -C_1(v_1 - v_2) - K_2(d_1 - d_2)$$
$$m_2 a_2 = -m_1 a_1 - K_2 d_2$$

The flow chart for the equations is shown in Figure P12.2-1*c*. Identify the analog computer components and their inputs and outputs.

(C) Classify the simulation. Assume that the system is being planned for next year's automobile, and the values for the parameters k_1 and c_1 are to be determined. A time of one minute required in plotting a variable represents one-half minute of real time. What is the numerical value of R_{SR} of equation 11.2-12?

What principal industrial operation performs this simulation study?

PROBLEM 12.2-2   "What Equation Are We Solving"

The spring system of Figure 12.2-6 is assumed to describe the landing gear system of an airplane. A force caused by air friction acts on the mass and is included in the analysis. The analog flow chart for simulating the system to include the effect of this force is shown in Figure P12.2-2.

(A) Identify the output of each component, and write the simulation equation from the flow chart.

(B) Classify the simulation. The data necessary to perform the simulation are observed data. A time of one minute required in plotting a variable represents two minutes of real time. What is the numerical value of R_{SR} of equation 11.2-12?

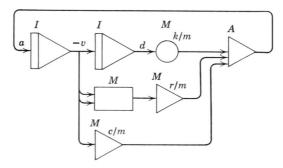

Figure P12.2-2

PROBLEM 12.3-1   "Which Computer to Use"

Why would a hybrid computer have an advantage over the standard analog computer in solving Problem 12.2-1, and which class (or classes) could be used if

(1) only values k_1 and c_1 determine directly the best spring system?
(2) the criterion for the best spring system also considers the costs?

Explain the function they perform in the problem solving operation.

CHAPTER 13.

Things Worth Computing

[F] MAKING INFORMATION AVAILABLE

13.1 PERSPECTIVE

Thus far we have studied the use of computers in scientific, business, real-time, and simulation applications. Computers are also widely used to solve problems of information retrieval.

Before considering some specific examples that will show the effectiveness of the computer in information retrieval, let us first define what is meant by "information retrieval." Information may be defined as communicated fact which enlarges one's knowledge. Thus if a Russian said to you, "У меня только одна мать" very possibly you would not have received any information. The Russian sentence contains a fact, but the fact probably was not communicated. Now the Russian says the same sentence in English: "I have only one mother." Again, you would not receive any information since (presumably) this *communicated* fact does not increase your knowledge. Trying hard to gain your interest, the Russian says that his mother likes apple pie. Although this is probably something you did not know before, and hence qualifies as information, it is quite possible that this fact does not hold a great deal of interest for you, and it may therefore be received but not stored; it "goes in one ear and out the other."

A statement by our Russian conversationalist, however, that "Today I witnessed the signing of a pact between your President and our

Premier," is much more likely to be classified as information of interest, and hence filed away for almost certain retrieval and use.

In the last two examples, the communicated fact contained information (something you did not know before); whether or not this information gets *stored* is (apparently) dependent upon conscious and unconscious associations with the fact at the time it is received.

Retrieval means simply the recovering upon demand of something which has been previously stored away. *We are now in a position to define information retrieval as the process of communicating to man previously stored facts which serve to increase his knowledge.*

In addition to fact storage on the medium of paper containing written words and photographs, facts can be stored in the form of recordings of the spoken word, or stored as objects, such as Egyptian pottery and statues.

With the current rapid expansion of known facts, there is an urgent need for efficient information retrieval systems. Zip-codes, telephone numbers, social-security numbers, and license plate numbers are a few such facts. All such facts must be appropriately cataloged for easy, efficient retrieval. For the above examples, this cataloging is relatively easy. The numbers are listed in order, or the names of the associated people are listed in alphabetical order, as in a telephone directory. The cataloging process is much more complex when abstract, nonnumeric facts are being stored. For example, in 1959, 1,200,000 articles were written in scientific journals on the physical and life sciences alone. Consider the problem of consolidating, reading, abstracting, and cataloging all these articles so that titles and brief descriptions of all the articles in any given field may be made readily available—an enormous task. As we shall see, computers can greatly help in creating such an information retrieval system.

There are many fascinating applications of computers to information retrieval. A computer could search through thousands of legal cases to find a legal precedent for a lawyer. A computer could scan through millions of patents to determine the originality of an invention. A computer could scan the characteristics of millions of fingerprints to find the fingerprint that matches one found at the scene of the crime. There are many other such possible applications, but let us now examine in detail how computers might be used to create effective information retrieval systems in three completely different areas.

In all three applications, there are three basic steps in the information retrieval process:

(1) The cataloging and indexing of new facts.

(2) The storage of facts.

(3) The retrieval of desired facts from storage.

These three steps must be present in *any* information retrieval system.

13.2 LIBRARIES

Description of the Library Functions

A library constitutes an information retrieval system. The computer can be beneficial both to the library and to the library customer (Figure 13.2-1).

New literature is submitted to the cataloging department. The cataloging department must read (in sufficient detail to determine the subject material covered), classify, catalog, and then store the new literature on the appropriate shelf in the library stacks. Cataloging usually consists of assigning a catalog number, as specified in a classification system such as the Dewey decimal system, to each new volume, according to its principal subject. Since the catalog number does not usually impart enough information, a catalog card is additionally made for each book, containing catalog number, title, author, and a brief description of the book.

When a library customer inquires about books on a given topic, there is a problem in fact location. Fact location usually involves looking through various drawers in a card catalog and writing down books which may contain desired content. This can be a tedious task if there are many books on the desired topic, or a frustrating task if the topic is somewhat unusual and the librarian cannot decide which subject to look under in the card catalog. When the customer has finally obtained a collection of titles and corresponding abstracts on the books and articles about his subject, he may select those which will be most helpful. The librarian obtains the books from storage and checks them out to the customer. If the material is not in the form desired by the customer, the librarian may possibly have the material processed for the customer. For example, a large library will probably have facilities for magnifying microfilmed documents and reproducing the material on printed pages. A large library might even be able to process foreign papers for the customer by translation.

An alternative path through Figure 13.2-1 can be followed when the customer requests a specific book. In this case, steps 2 and 3 can be eliminated. The librarian must still go to the card catalog to ascertain the

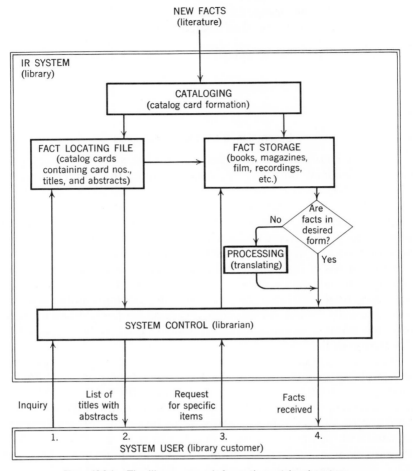

Figure 13.2-1 The library as an information retrieval system.

call number, but can then go directly to the library stacks and return with the book to the customer.

Figure 13.2-1 shows the librarian executing all four operations between the library and the library customer, but often some operations, such as 1, 2, and 3, may be performed by the customer and only the checking out of books at step 4 done by the librarian.

Let us examine how computers might assist the library in the above process.

Cataloging and Indexing of New Facts

Keyword Frequency Method. The computer can be programmed to "read" the new literature and catalog it correctly. This time saving process can be accomplished by the method of keywords. In this method, an article is read into the computer (either on cards, magnetic tape, or some such medium) along with a general topic number. For each general topic, a committee of experts has compiled a list of keywords in that field, and this list is stored in the computer. Suppose the topic number denotes that the article is generally about cigarettes. Inside the computer, the keywords for this topic might be as shown in Figure 13.2-2. A frequency count is made by checking each word in the article against the keywords. A record is kept of the number of times each keyword appears in the publication. Suppose the library is to catalog the following (fictitious) article on cigarettes, using the keyword table of Figure 13.2-2.

"Smoking and Health" by Sharon Brickson

"Our research this past year has centered upon the effect smoking has on one's health. It is well known that smoking is on the increase, as is also the rate of lung cancer, especially among men. For this reason we have undertaken this controversial research.

"Our research has demonstrated that nicotine and tar induce cancer in rats. We therefore began by determining which types of filters reduce the tar and nicotine content inhaled. Charcoal filter and paper filter cigarettes were examined. We suspected the charcoal filter would be superior because of the high absorptive properties of charcoal. The charcoal filter allowed less nicotine and tar than the paper filter.

"Mentholated cigarettes are also very popular today, especially those of regular size. The results on this type of cigarette are still inconclusive, however."

The article has the keyword frequency shown in Figure 13.2-3.

From the bar graph of Figure 13.2-3 we would like to assign a catalog number to the article which would indicate, for example, that it contained many facts about cigarettes and charcoal filters, but not many about kingsize cigarettes. The computer could assign the appropriate catalog

Size	Menthol
1. kingsize	8. mentholated
2. regular	9. unmentholated
Tip	Health
3. cardboard	10. cancer
4. cork	11. nicotine
5. plain	12. tar
Filter	13. research
6. charcoal	Advertising
7. paper	14. federal regulation

Figure 13.2-2   Keywords for the topic cigarettes.

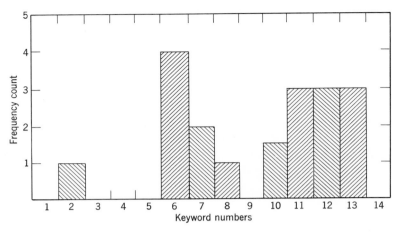

Figure 13.2-3   Keyword frequencies for "Smoking and Health."

number by determining the prime keywords for the material. The prime keywords for any material are those that occur most frequently in the material and are of prime importance to the content of the material. One method would be to assign a number like 396-00000110011110 to indicate that the article is generally about cigarettes (topic number 396) and that keywords 6, 7, 10, 11, 12, and 13 are prime keywords. The rule might be to designate a keyword as prime if it occurred at least half as often as the most popular keyword in the material. The computer then forms the appropriate catalog number by assigning a "1" to a prime keyword position and a "0" otherwise. In our example, the keyword, charcoal, occurs 4 times, hence all keywords occurring at least 2 times are prime keywords and are assigned the value 1. This method will indeed give catalog number 396-00000110011110. The titles of all articles are stored in the computer according to their catalog numbers.

In addition to cataloging new material, the computer can greatly assist the library by rapidly producing brief abstracts of each new book or article. Again, keywords are essential to this operation. The computer obtains the prime keywords for a book or article from the catalog number for the material. Thus the prime keywords for "Smoking and Health" are charcoal, paper, cancer, nicotine, tar, and research. According to one method, each sentence in the material is then assigned a significance factor, which is the density of prime keywords for that sentence. The density is the number of prime keywords in the sentence divided by the total number of words in the sentence. The significance factor for each sentence in "Smoking and Health" is given in Figure 13.2-4.

Sentence number	Number of prime keywords	Total number of words	Significance factor
1	1	15	.07
2	1	21	.05
3	1	9	.11
4	4	12	.33
5	2	16	.13
6	2	8	.25
7	2	15	.13
8	4	12	.33
9	0	12	.00
10	0	11	.00

Figure 13.2-4   Significance factors for sentences in "Smoking and Health."

Depending upon the length of abstract desired, a specified number of sentences with the highest significance factors are printed out. The significant sentences are of course printed out in the order they appear in the material. If we wanted three sentences for each abstract, the computer would produce the following abstract for the article "Smoking and Health."

"Our research has demonstrated that nicotine and tar induce cancer in rats. Charcoal filter and paper filter cigarettes were examined. The charcoal filter allowed less nicotine and tar than the paper filter."

Indexing. Indexing is a problem closely related to cataloging and abstracting. The library wishes to index its books in such a way that the library customer will have the greatest chance for finding relevant information. Such indexing usually involves placing the catalog card for the material in several strategic locations within the subject catalog.

In about 1960, IBM developed a computerized indexing scheme called keyword-in-context (KWIC) indexing. For this method, the titles and names of authors for many different articles are read into the computer. The computer then produces a KWIC index for all the material—each article is indexed under each keyword occurring in its title. For these purposes, keywords are all words except common prepositions, conjunctions, and articles, such as the, but, and, if, which.

As a specific example in the use of a KWIC index, let us suppose we wish to obtain information on computerized business games for accountants. A logical first step would be to scan various issues of the journal *Computer Reviews,* hoping to find a review on some material describing computerized business games for accountants. The first four years (1960-63) of *Computer Reviews* contain reviews on nearly 5000 different entries, so it would be a formidable task to scan through all the reviews. Using the "Permuted (KWIC) Index to Computing Reviews" published by the Association for Computing Machinery, the task becomes much simpler. Like most KWIC indexes, this one is divided into three sections: Bibliography, Author Index, and Keyword Index. As shown in Figure 13.2-5, we can locate information on the review of "A Business Game for Accountants" by looking in the keyword index under any one of the three keywords: business, game, or accountants. The code number 6235 2780 found to the right of the title informs us that the review is found in the 1962 issues of *Computing Reviews*, volume 3, issue 5, review number 2780. By looking in the bibliography under number 6235 2780, we see that the original article was written (in English) by M. Kennedy. The review can now be quickly located and read.

Computers can also help libraries keep their information storage areas (bookshelves) "clean"—that is, up-to-date and relevant to the needs of the communities they serve. Many libraries experience a "trash" problem. Books are placed on the shelves only to remain there year after year collecting dust. A computer can solve this problem by tabulating how often each book is checked out of the library. Each month a list of books which have been inactive for, say, ten years is produced. The inactive books can then be transferred to less accessible storage, thus making room for more popular material. For example, historical books could be condensed onto microfilm.

The Retrieval of Desired Facts

Use of the Keyword Catalog in Retrieval. Now let us examine some of the ways in which the computer assists the library customer. In a computerized library, the computer scans through the card catalog and frees the library customer or librarian from this time-consuming, frustrating, and sometimes unproductive task. Suppose a library customer wants some titles and brief descriptions on books and articles which contain facts about the effectiveness of charcoal filters in reducing lung cancer. The customer simply submits the catalog number 396-00000100010000 to the computer. The 396 indicates that he is generally interested in cigarettes, and the 1's indicate that he is specifically interested in articles with many facts on both charcoal filters and cancer. The computer then prints out a list of all books and articles in storage which have topic number 396 and a 1 in the sixth and tenth positions. There may be 1's elsewhere also, but that is immaterial so long as there is a 1 at least in the sixth and tenth position. For each relevant source, the catalog number, title, author, and computer-produced abstract are produced for the customer.

From Bibliography

(a)

6235	2778	STUDIES IN APPLIED PROBABILITY AND MANAGEMENT SCIENCE (MATHPROG) * K. J. ARROW(ED), S. KARLIN(ED), H. SCARF(ED)
6235	2779	AN OPERATING MODEL AS A HELP IN MANAGEMENT OF ENTERPRISES (MATHPROG, FOREIGN-GERMAN) * W. HEINEKEN
6235	2780	A BUSINESS GAME FOR ACCOUNTANTS (MATHPROG) * M. KENNEDY
6235	2781	THE PROBLEM OF DYNAMIC PROGRAMMING AND AUTOMATA (MATHPROG, FOREIGN-RUSSIAN) * YU. A. SHREIDER
6235	2782	THE POSSIBILITY OF AUTOMATIZATION OF CONTROL OF THE NATIONAL ECONOMY (MATHPROG, FOREIGN-RUSSIAN) * A. I. BENG, A. I. KITOV, A. A. LIAPUNOV

From Keyword Index

(b)

LPROG, FOREIGN-FRENCH =	ACCOUNT OF DEVICES FOR INPUT, OUTPUT	6236	3143
THE COST	ACCOUNTANT (MGNTDP) =	6124	0900
A BUSINESS GAME FOR	ACCOUNTANTS (MATHPROG) =	6235	2780
CRISIS IN MACHINE	ACCOUNTING (MGNTDP) =	6231	1348
THE JOURNAL OF MACHINE	ACCOUNTING (MGNTDP) =	6236	2982

(c)

LANNING =	BUSINESS FORECASTING AND LONG TERM P	6124	0900
INTOP, AN INTERNATIONAL	BUSINESS GAME (MATHPROG) =	6232	1754
ROG) = A	BUSINESS GAME FOR ACCOUNTANTS (MATH	6235	2780
DON'T BET ON	BUSINESS GAMES (MATHPROG) =	6126	1267
TOWARDS A COMMON	BUSINESS LANGUAGE =	6016	0290

(d)

SCIENCE (SOCLSCI) = THE	GAME AND MYTH AS TWO LANGUAGES OF SO	6345	4521
DESIGNING A SIMPLE	GAME COMPUTER (ARTINT) =	6125	0978
A BUSINESS	GAME FOR ACCOUNTANTS (MATHPROG) =	6235	2780
ROG) = A MANAGERIAL	GAME FOR AN INSURANCE COMPANY (MATHP	6015	0236
THE	GAME MONOPOLOGS (MATHPROG) =	6233	1989

Figure 13.2-5 Examples of KWIC indexing.

457

There are many other advantages to the customer in the above system. For example, a given book might have a whole chapter on the relation between charcoal filters and cancer, and yet the information in the card catalog would probably make no mention of the chapter. Thus the customer would skip over a valuable source of facts if he relied on thumbing through the card catalog. The computer, having used the keyword method, would sense the desired chapter, and would alert the customer to this valuable source of facts.

Other Uses in Retrieval. There are many ways in which the computer can be of additional service in information retrieval operations at a library. As shown in Figure 13.2-1, the computer can be used to convert stored facts into meaningful information by translating foreign articles for the customer.

The computer can also keep a mailing list of the appropriate people whom it will notify if new literature in the field of interest to each is added to the library. International Business Machines Corporation has used such a system since 1960 to inform its employees of recent scientific literature. The IBM system is abbreviated SDI—selective dissemination of information. Under this system, an IBM scientist submits to the computer a list of up to 60 keywords designating areas of special interest to him. The scientist is notified whenever an article arrives containing a sufficient number of these keywords. As of 1964, the IBM SDI system was using abstracts on roughly 11,000 articles, and the "average" SDI user received notices on five new articles daily. The system appears highly successful since the "average" user replied that two-thirds of the notices were "of interest."*

A notification list, such as the one described above, can be updated by deleting from the list the names of those people who have not ordered an article for a considerable period. With such a system as SDI, the library becomes an active organization. We do not have to go to the library and reread the catalog cards every several days to find new literature; rather the library comes to us daily and keeps us informed of literature in our field of interest.

Computer Requirements

Information retrieval systems require vast amounts of memory. In addition to core storage for working purposes, a useful system must also

---

* Donald H. Kraft, "Application of IBM Equipment to Library Mechanization, Keyword-in-Context (KWIC) Indexing and the Selective Dissemination of Information," a paper presented at a clinic on library applications of data processing at the University of Illinois on May 1, 1963.

contain large amounts of less expensive bulk storage such as tapes, disks, and drums (Figure 13.2-6). All information about the library material is stored on the cheap bulk storage media. These are shown as magnetic tape reels A, B, C, and the disk file. Information is brought into the central core memory only when the information is to be actively involved in either matching keywords or in matching index numbers. The memory space available in core storage is much less than the memory space available on a reel of magnetic tape or on a disk file. Thus only a small part of the total information stored on a tape unit or disk file is brought into the main computer memory at one time. If an article entering from tape reel A is about cigarettes, then only the keywords for cigarettes will be transferred from tape reel B to core storage for the matching of keywords.

Note that tape reel C contains the records of individuals who wish to be informed of new publications of interest without special request. Also note the similarity in structure of Figure 13.2-1 and Figure 13.2-6.

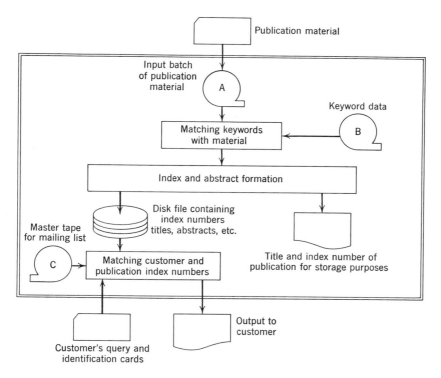

Figure 13.2-6   Use of disk file and magnetic tapes in library information retrieval system.

13.3 MEDICAL DIAGNOSIS AND TREATMENT

When a doctor makes a decision concerning a patient, it is primarily a result of two factors: material the doctor has read in medical textbooks and journals; and his personal experience with previous patients. But should a human life depend upon the small amount a single man has read, or upon the relatively few experiences of a single man or of several men? Why not store the facts from *all* medical articles and the experiences of *all* doctors in a central computer where these facts will be readily available to any physician? The case histories of millions of patients would be cataloged according to symptom and disease. In this way, all the world's knowledge and experience would be working for the patient, rather than just a small part of that knowledge and experience. Such a system would have all the characteristics of a true information retrieval system: many facts gathered, cataloged, and stored. At the request from a physician, the appropriate facts are located and rapidly relayed to him as information. Let us suppose such a system exists and analyze how it functions.

The model for our system has the following ingredients:

$$
\begin{aligned}
&\text{Diseases:} & &D_1, D_2, \ldots, D_\alpha \\
&\text{Symptoms} & &S_1, S_2, \ldots, S_\beta \\
&\text{Diagnostic tests:} & &TE_1, TE_2, \ldots, TE_\gamma \\
&\text{Treatments:} & &T_1, T_2, \ldots, T_\delta
\end{aligned}
$$

Thus, we might have the following:

$$
\begin{aligned}
D_{46} &= \text{Asian flu} \\
S_3 &= \text{Sore throat} \\
TE_5 &= \text{Take patient's temperature} \\
T_{19} &= \text{Rest, drink liquids, take aspirin}
\end{aligned}
$$

We assume at the outset that all patients have some symptoms, $S_1, \ldots, S_\beta$, and some disease, D_1. If the patient has no physical disease, he is assumed to be suffering from the emotional disorder hypochondria, over-anxiety about one's health.

The operation of such a system begins with the patient presenting the doctor with certain symptoms, say S_3 and S_6. Usually, however, a patient is aware of only a partial list of symptoms, and is unaware of those remaining. Thus, a patient with mononucleosis may be aware of a sore throat and a general lack of energy, but he is unaware of a swollen spleen. The doctor thus submits this partial list of symptoms S_3 and S_6 to the computer. The computer scans the case histories of all other patients who complained of symptoms S_3 and S_6 and then prints out what hidden symptoms usually occurred in such cases. The computer also prints out the diagnostic tests that have been most successful in discovering the hidden symptoms, and which also minimize cost and pain to the patient.

The doctor then conducts the tests and gains a more complete list of symptoms, say S_3, S_6, and S_8 which he presents to the computer. The computer again scans its case histories to find the different diseases had by all patients with symptoms S_3, S_6, and S_8. Suppose 1000 previous patients throughout the world were known to have had symptoms S_3, S_6, and S_8; by one method or another, it was discovered that 800 patients had disease D_1, 150 patients had D_2, and 50 had D_4. The computer then prints out for the doctor the following disease probabilities:

$$\text{Probability } (D_1) = \frac{800}{1000} = 80\%$$

$$\text{Probability } (D_2) = \frac{150}{1000} = 15\%$$

$$\text{Probability } (D_4) = \frac{50}{1000} = 5\%$$

The computer then scans the case histories of all patients with diseases D_1, D_2, and D_4 to find all the treatments which have cured each disease. Let the facts found by the computer as to the success of the various treatments be represented in Figure 13.3-1.

To find which treatment will probably cure this patient, the computer is programmed to calculate that which would have cured the greatest number of the 1000 previous patients with symptoms S_3, S_6, and S_8. We recall that

800 patients had D_1, 150 patients D_2, and 50 patients D_4

Hence, T_3 cures

$$0.50(800) + 0.10(150) + 0.90(50) = 460 \text{ patients}$$

and T_5 cures

$$0.10(800) + 0.80(150) + 0.60(50) = 230 \text{ patients}$$

Treatment	Disease		
	D_1	D_2	D_4
T_3	50%	10%	90%
T_5	10%	80%	60%

Figure 13.3-1   Cure percentages for possible treatments.

Based on these past facts, the computer is then able to print out the following cure probabilities:

$$\text{Cure probability } (T_3) = \frac{460}{1000} = 46\%$$

$$\text{Cure probability } (T_5) = \frac{230}{1000} = 23\%$$

The doctor naturally tries treatment T_3. The usefulness of the computerized system does not stop here, however. At regular intervals the doctor makes checks on the patient's progress. If he feels the patient is not making adequate progress, he may consult the computer and ask it to compare this patient's recovery history with those of other patients. If the patient is not responding properly, the computer may recommend another treatment.

The usefulness of such a system can constantly increase as thousands of new case histories are cataloged and stored daily within the computer's memory.

This information retrieval system can also be used effectively in preventive medicine. Suppose all people annually file a brief form giving their weight, height, pulse, number of colds that year, and so forth. The computer can then find various characteristics which suggest that people with these characteristics are more susceptible to a given disease. People with these characteristics are then alerted and are watched more closely by their doctor. It may turn out that some characteristics found have no known causal connection with the disease they seem to forewarn. Thus, the computer may find that people whose hair growth slows down have a tendency to contract polio. This might seem ridiculous to the medical profession, but it is very possible that medical knowledge has not advanced enough to understand the relationship.

One final advantage of a computer used in medicine, is the computer's complete objectivity and lack of pride. An older doctor who has been treating patients in a given way for forty years may be slow to change his methods even though evidence indicates much more effective treatments have been developed. The computer has no such pride, and will prescribe the most effective treatment known, as based on recent case histories.

13.4 THE HUMANITIES

Unfortunately, the computer revolution has not yet made the large impact on the humanities that it has made on scientific and business

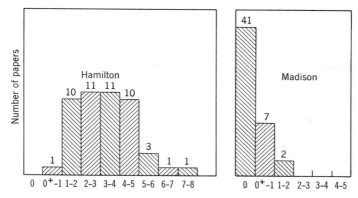

Figure 13.4-1   Frequency of the word "upon" per thousand words in works by Alexander Hamilton and James Madison.

applications. Computerized information retrieval systems, however, are beginning to be applied to the humanities, and are thus forming the foundation for new and important dimensions in computer application.

In an application to literary scholarship, the facts stored in such a system are all the works by several authors. Information retrieved from the fact storage is the frequency at which certain keywords appear in a given author's works. By analyzing which words each author uses most frequently and most infrequently, one can gain valuable insight into how much one author's works have influenced another author. An efficient computer system might even be able to discover cases of plagiarism.

One fascinating extension of this technique is the use of keyword analysis to help determine the authorship of papers or books. Professor Frederick Mosteller of Harvard and Professor David L. Wallace of the University of Chicago used computers to establish Madison's authorship of disputed essays in the Federalist Papers.*

The bar graph of Figure 13.4-1 shows the frequency of the word "upon" per thousand words in works by Hamilton and Madison. The keyword analysis makes it apparent that Madison's works are characterized by a very infrequent use of the word "upon." Such analyses strongly suggest that Madison, rather than Hamilton, wrote the disputed essays in the Federalist Papers.

It is interesting to speculate upon what role computers will play in art forms such as music, painting, and architecture.

* "Horizons," *Think,* Nov.–Dec., 1964, p. 30.

13.5 THE FUTURE

A recent development that holds great potential for information retrieval systems is the time-sharing computer system. Under this system, many different input-output stations, scattered about a university campus, an industrial plant, or even about the country, can share the services of a centrally located computer. With national time-sharing computer systems, a professor doing scientific research would not be handicapped by a small science library on campus. He would simply request information from a nearby input-output station which is directly connected to a master computer maybe hundreds of miles away. Stored within the master computer system are most of the recent science books, journals, theses, and special papers. The computer rapidly finds the desired information and sends it back to the professor. In Section 13.3 we also read how doctors could use a time-sharing system. Each doctor, possibly from his own office, could obtain case histories and cure percentages from a centrally located medical center. Clearly, time-sharing systems allow large masses of information to be distributed to many, widely scattered individuals, without requiring the construction of many large libraries.

The storage of more and more facts in information retrieval systems would seem to create problems of access time. For these purposes, access time is the time required to locate the desired information in bulk storage, and then transfer it to core storage for processing. Fortunately, computer hardware has been steadily improved so as to minimize the problem of access time. A very common form of bulk storage has been magnetic tape. Tape units which pack the information more and more densely on the tape, and revolve the tape reels more rapidly, are continually being produced. This reduces the access time for the desired information. New bulk storage devices such as disk files, drum units, and the recently introduced data cells have reduced this access time even further. With such promising developments occurring in bulk storage devices, it seems that the access-time problem will not be a major obstacle to huge information retrieval systems of the future.

At present, a major obstacle to computerized information retrieval systems is the amount of labor and time required to get many facts stored in the computer's memory system. For example, an Italian Jesuit has spent years working with a staff of sixty people on a computer system to complete a fifteen-million word inventory of the works of St. Thomas Aquinas.

Great improvements, however, are now being developed in input-output machinery for computers. The computer manufacturers are making good progress on character-reading input devices. With such a device, facts may be fed into the machine, printed on paper, and no time is spent on converting the printed material to punched cards. When such devices are perfected, a major obstacle to information retrieval systems will have been overcome.

Certainly computers will play an increasingly important role in information retrieval. The fact explosion will create the necessity for accurate, high-speed information retrieval; and new computer hardware, such as character-reading devices, will enable the computer to fulfill this need.

PROBLEM 13.3-1   "To Bed or Not to Bed"

When one is taking a trip, sometimes it is difficult to find a lodging for the night which has all the characteristics one desires. Thus, if the traveler wants a motel in the Chicago area that has a cocktail bar, airconditioned rooms, and does not allow pets (the traveler is allergic to dog hair), he may have to spend precious time thumbing through the yellow pages of the phone book before discovering the ideal motel for him. How much simpler if he could simply slip a data card into a computer on which were punched the desired characteristics. In the vast memory of the computer have been stored the characteristics of thousands of lodgings across the country. The computer rapidly locates and prints out the names of all the lodgings with the desired characteristics. This problem involves writing and running a program to accomplish this information retrieval operation.

The data base to be used consists of facts on 26 lodgings, and is shown in Figure P13.3-1. On each card are punched the following facts:

(1) From 1 to 8 integers, each of which designates the lodging possessing a certain characteristic. These integers are punched in columns 1-24, three columns per integer.

(2) In columns 25–72 is punched the name of the lodging.

This system considers 14 characteristics significant. The numeric codes for these characteristics are:

1. Lodging in Madison
2. Lodging in Milwaukee
3. Lodging in Chicago
4. Hotel
5. Motel
6. T.V. in rooms
7. Cocktail room at lodging
8. Pets allowed
9. Rooms airconditioned
10. Swimming pool available
11. Dining facilities available
12. Telephone in rooms
13. Coffee shop at lodging
14. Cost does not exceed $12 for couple

```
3    4    6    9   13  14              ALLERTON HOTEL
3    4    6    9   11   8              AMBASSADOR HOTELS
3    5    6   12    9   7  11  10ASCOT MOTEL
3    5    9   12    6   7  11   8AVENUE MOTEL
3    4    9    6   11  13   7   BISMARK HOTEL
3    4    9    6   11  13   7   CONRAD HILTON HOTEL
3    4    9    6   11   7       DRAKE HOTEL
3    4   12   11   13   7  10   8ESSEX INN
3    4    9    6    7  11       EXECUTIVE HOUSE
1    5   12    6    9  13   7  10HOLIDAY INN
1    5   12    6    9   7  11  14IVY INN MOTOR HOTEL
1    5   12    6    9  14       MOTEL MADISON
1    5   12    6    9  14       MOTEL MAYFLOWER
1    5    6    9   10  14       MID VIEW MOTEL
1    5    6   14               SIMON MOTEL
1    5   12    6    9  14       STERLING MOTEL
1    5   12    6    9  13  14   TOWN CAMPUS MOTEL
1    5   12    6    9   8  14   TRAILS END MOTEL
2    4    6    9    8   7  11  14PLANKINTON HOUSE
2    4    6   11   13   7   8  14SCHROEDER HOTEL
2    5   12    6    9   8  14   BLINKIN N NOD MOTEL
2    5    6    9    7  11   8  14BLUE CREST MOTEL
2    5   12    6   14           BLUE AND WHITE MOTEL
2    5   12    6    9  13   8  14BRAVES MOTEL
2    5   12    6    9  13   8  14CHALET MOTEL
2    5   12    6    9  14       EDGE O TOWN MOTEL
0
```

Figure P13.3-1   Data for Problem P13.3-1.

A typical fact card will be punched as

`··1··6·11··7·14··4·······BELMONT·HOTEL···`

This card specifies that the Belmont is a hotel located in Madison with dining facilities and a cocktail bar. The rates are inexpensive and the rooms contain television sets.

The first step in executing any of the three options to this problem is to read in the supplied facts on lodgings. The last card in the deck is to have a zero punched for the first characteristic number. The data should be read in using the following format:*

FORMAT(8I3, 9A5, A3)

(A) Write a program that will read in a single characteristic number, and will output all lodgings with that characteristic. All the characteristics of the lodgings should also be output with the name of the lodging, so that you may use the same FORMAT statement for output as you used on input.

(B) The same as (A), but this time read in several characteristic numbers (not more than 8) and output all lodgings (and their characteristics) which have the desired characteristics. Your output should identify which

* See Appendix 13A for a discussion of the use of the A specification.

characteristics you desire, and should also indicate if there are no lodgings with all the desired characteristics.

(C) Same as (B) but also read in several characteristic numbers for characteristics you do not want the lodging to have. (If you're traveling to Alaska, you probably do not want characteristic 9.)

CHAPTER 14.

Things Worth Computing:
[G] DOES IT HAVE TO BE A MORON?

14.1 PERSPECTIVE

So far we have considered a wide variety of situations in which the digital computer has made itself useful in the technical, commercial, political, and social pattern of life around us. In this chapter we are going to look at some challenging problems to which the power of the computer has been turned, in areas where the rewards are less tangible, and the economic payoff much less certain and immediate.

Payoff or not, man's inquisitive and competitive nature has always led him to invent games and pose puzzles. His reward is merely the intellectual satisfaction of winning, or of achieving a correct solution. But what a "merely" that is. Some of the keenest minds the human race has produced have found that challenge irresistible, and have devoted much time and energy to the pursuit of fruitless and frustrating, but fascinating and entrancing intellectual pastimes.

It is only in recent years that the direct economic payoff of the study of how to play games has been clearly pointed out. This study was first brought to a sharp focus in the early days of World War II by the now famous examination of Game Theory by von Neumann and Morganstern. The subsequent application of the theory to the open conflict of war and the only slightly more subdued competition of the market place has shown the deadly earnest with which this game is now played.

In addition to the tangible benefits of such applications, and sometimes it seems in spite of them, man has consistently found the challenge of the game, the proof, the problem itself to be self-rewarding. Small wonder, then, that he very early began to find ways to apply this marvelous new toy—the information machine—to such pursuits.

14.2 PLAYING GAMES

One of the first things almost any new computer installation does when it first gets its new machine working, and this probably applies all the way back to the first working computers, is to program the machine to imitate such obviously human behavior as game playing. Tic-tac-toe, nim, blackjack, checkers, chess, and many more, have all been more or less successfully played by a computer.

Why Play Games?

What justification can be given for the expenditure of large amounts of time, money, and energy devoted to playing games? There are several answers:

(1) Games are frequently modeled after real-life problems, but with the essential characteristics reduced to manageable proportions, and many of the worrisome complications eliminated. Analysis, understanding, and solution are frequently much simpler.

(2) Games, particularly the better known ones, represent complex conflict situations in which the *rules* (the restrictions determining permissible moves) and the *goal* (the end toward which both sides are striving) are usually well known and clear cut.

(3) On the other hand, *strategy* (methods of choosing the most desirable move) is usually not completely known, and often not at all.

(4) Particularly since the mid 1950's there has been very serious interest in the use of the computer to simulate some of the thinking processes that go on in the central nervous system of some of the higher animals. The execution of proofs, the finding of proofs, recognition of patterns, learning procedures, and problem solving in general have recently become an object of interest to psychologists, neurophysiologists, and computer engineers. The next section, "Artificial Intelligence," will discuss this in more detail.

(5) Games are fun!

Ways of Playing

Any serious attempt at game playing can be classified under one or more of the following approaches:

(1) *Algorithm.* An algorithm is a precisely described procedure, a set of steps, for arriving at a specified goal. For some games (e.g., nim) an algorithm can be found which will guarantee to lead to a win if one is possible.

(2) *Exhaustion.* Look all the way ahead. Consider each possible move, and each possible consequence, until all possibilities have been examined. This procedure is possible even for humans for a few games, such as tic-tac-toe. Games that lend themselves to this kind of attack are (in principle) so easily solved that mathematicians call them trivial. It turns out that very few games have endured the historical test are, even with a computer, "trivial."

(3) *Dictionary.* Store the results of past look-ahead operations or past actual games. The dictionary entry is not necessarily dependent upon the past history of the game; regardless of the process of arriving at a given situation, in that situation *this* is the move to make (or *not* to make). Chess players learn many standard openings and end games by this technique.

(4) *Rote Learning*—dictionary by trial and error. (a) positive: when games are won, store good plays. (b) negative: store all possible plays at each position, select at random. If games are lost, eliminate losing moves, working backward. This is an easy technique to implement for simple games on a computer (see Figure 14.2-1).

(5) *Known Principle.* Particularly in games of chance, calculate probabilities. Although one cannot guarantee results for any one trial, accurate predictions can be made as to what the results will be "in the long run." Betting guides in poker are based upon the calculation of probabilities of drawing the needed cards.

(6) *Minimax.* If it is not possible to produce a complete analysis, either by developing an algorithm or by looking all the way ahead, it is at least desirable to determine in which direction to proceed so as to move closer to the goal and not further away. This means both setting some intermediate goals, and finding some criteria for evaluation in terms of those goals. Then, even though it is possible to look only so far ahead, at least the strength of one's position or score can be evaluated at each step so that each step is hopefully in the right direction. The problem is now: given a situation, which choice of moves leads to the best "value" at the end of the look-ahead path?

Exhaustion. Theoretically any "finite" game—a game which can be ended in a finite number of moves—can be completely analyzed by exhaustion. Although it may well be beyond the scope of a mere human, surely it should be within the capability of the computer, with its almost

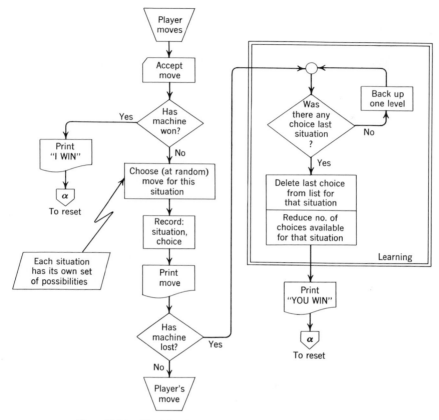

Figure 14.2-1 Machine learning (game playing method 4(b)).

infinite speed, to complete in a reasonable time the necessary analysis for any known game—particularly, a game situation in chess or checkers.

Oh? Let us try some figures. It is estimated that there are some 30 possible legal moves for a typical situation in a game of chess, and that, on the average, a chess game may be 40 rounds (where a round consists of one move by each player) long.* This poses something like 10^{120} continuations to be explored ($30^{80} = 1.5 \times 10^{118}$). Assuming that a super computer were available which could consider each variation in 1 picosecond ($= 1$ micromicrosecond $= 10^{-12}$ seconds), it would still take over 10^{98} years to compute the first move!

At this point it should be apparent that the exhaustive approach has

---

* Claude E. Shannon, "Programming a Computer for Playing Chess," *Phil. Mag.*, Vol. 41, No. 256, March, 1950.

some severe limitations. Let us see what can be done with some of the other methods.

Rote Learning. To illustrate how effective the straightforward procedure of negative rote learning can be, let us apply it to a simple game. We will take the very elementary one pile version of nim, which is also known as "Last One Loses" as an example.*

The only equipment necessary for this game is a pile to count with, which may be a pile of chips, matches, stones, or dead fish; marks on a piece of paper or a blackboard; or keys on a desk calculator or even on a computer. Let us talk about a pile of matches.

To start the game, a variable number of matches is set out in an initial pile; we will simplify things here by making it a constant number —10. Each player, when it is his turn, may take from 1 to 3 matches from the pile, but must take at least 1. The person who takes the last one loses.

Using the stupidest possible approach, one could chose blindly at each move among the three possibilities: take 1, 2, or 3 matches. This would, of course, almost always lead to a loss against any form of intelligent play. If, however, one could merely remember all wrong moves and follow the principle of "never making the same mistake twice," it would not be long before most of the poor moves were eliminated, and the number of wins would begin to increase. In fact, such a system could be made completely mechanical, and the modifications that should be made each time to the list of possible choices for next time could be done according to a very simple rule. If such a mechanistic scheme for chosing a move is set up, with a similarly mechanistic method for modification after each loss, the result is a procedure that simulates to a surprising degree what is commonly called "learning."

Block describes in considerable detail a method for putting together a "machine" for demonstrating this learning process, using in his case twelve drinking glasses, thirty-three numbered pieces of paper or cardboard, pencil and paper with which to keep the tally, and a person to do the manipulating. Figure 14.2-2 shows this machine in the act of deciding a move against a human opponent.

Although such a "machine" of glasses, cardboard, and discard boxes

---

* Several interesting discussions of such applications have appeared recently, three of the most interesting by Donald Michie, Martin Gardner, and H. D. Block. Deciding that Michie's "Educable Engine" used to play tic-tac-toe with 300 match boxes was slightly complicated for home experimentation, Martin Gardner, in his *Scientific American* column on Mathematical Games, recounts how he devised a simplified game called hexapawn which requires a machine of only 24 match boxes. Block uses a similar approach to the nim game we are describing here.

Figure 14.2-2   A "machine" which learns (from H. D. Block, Ref. 1).

demonstrates quite vividly the mechanical nature of the procedure, it is hardly an efficient device for conducting experiments involving long sequences of games. As might be suspected, such a completely deterministic procedure lends itself perfectly to programming for a digital computer, and Appendix 14A describes a FORTRAN program called NOPE (nim one-pile educator)* that plays almost the same game, according to the same rules for choosing a move, and makes the same modifications after losing games. This program even on a 1620 will play against a human opponent as fast as the human can act and react, and automatically makes the specified modifications at the conclusion of each game it loses with only a second or two delay. It is programmed to produce, as a by-product, a complete record not only of the playing sequence of each game, but, more importantly, a complete record of the modifications made to its own strategy at every step. A typical game conversation, as carried on through the console typewriter, is displayed in Figure 14.2-3; the record which is produced for later printing is shown in Figure 14.2-4.

Going one step further, the program has now been modified to simulate not only the learning novice, but also the completely educated expert. Now the computer can be set to play games against itself, one program always making the best possible move, and the other

* Written by G. T. Kroncke of the Engineering Computing Laboratory, University of Wisconsin.

```
I AM THE 1620 NOPE, A LEARNING PROGRAM.  THE GAME
IS PLAYED WITH A PILE OF 10 MATCHES.  EACH PLAYER
MAY DECREASE THE PILE BY 1, 2, OR 3.   THE ONE WHO
TAKES THE LAST ONE LOSES.  YOU MAY TAKE ZERO ON
THE FIRST TURN WHENEVER YOU WANT ME TO GO FIRST.


     I HAVE WON  0 OUT OF  0 GAMES.


     THERE ARE NOW 10 MATCHES.   YOU TAKE...
  1
     THERE ARE NOW  9 MATCHES.
     I TAKE 3 WHICH LEAVES 6 .  YOU TAKE...
  1
     THERE ARE NOW  5 MATCHES.
     I TAKE 2 WHICH LEAVES 3 .  YOU TAKE...
  2
     THERE ARE NOW  1 MATCHES.
     I TAKE 1 WHICH LEAVES 0 .  YOU WIN.

     I HAVE WON  0 OUT OF  1 GAMES.


     THERE ARE NOW 10 MATCHES.  YOU TAKE...
```

Figure 14.2-3   NOPE versus human opponent.

making initially random choices but gradually improving its play as bad choices are eliminated. The learning program, called player *B*, was always permitted to play first, so that with proper play it should always win. The record of the first 36 such games played is shown in Figure 14.2-5, and it forms a curve clearly demonstrating the improvement in

```
PLAYER        1   1   2        M      = 10 9 8 7 6 5 4 3 2 1
  1620          3  [2]  1      MANY(M) =  3 3 3 3 3 2 3 3 2 1
PILE = 10      96  53  10      NCH       - - - - - - - - - -
                               1         1 1 1 1 1 1 1 1 1 1
1620 HAS WON   0               2         2 2 2 2 2 3 2 2 2 0
     OUT OF   1 GAMES.         3         3 3 3 3 3 Ⓞ 3 3 0 0


PLAYER        1   1   3        M      = 10 9 8 7 6 5 4 3 2 1
  1620          3  [1]  1      MANY(M) =  3 3 3 3 3 1 3 3 2 1
PILE = 10      96  54  10      NCH       - - - - - - - - - -
                               1         1 1 1 1 1 3 1 1 1 1
1620 HAS WON   0               2         2 2 2 2 Ⓞ 2 2 2 2 0
     OUT OF   2 GAMES.         3         3 3 3 3 3 0 3 3 0 0


PLAYER        1   2   1        M      = 10 9 8 7 6 5 4 3 2 1
  1620         [2] [3]  1      MANY(M) =  3 2 3 3 3 1 3 3 2 1
PILE = 10      97  52  10      NCH       - - - - - - - - - -
                               1         1 1 1 1 1 Ⓞ 1 1 1 1
1620 HAS WON   0               2         2 3 2 2 2 0 2 2 2 0
     OUT OF   3 GAMES.         3         3 Ⓞ 3 3 3 0 3 3 0 0
```

Figure 14.2-4   Internal modifications in NOPE's array of available moves.

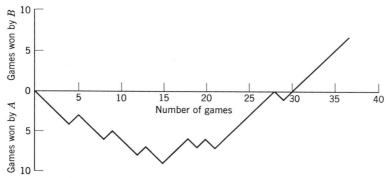

Figure 14.2-5   Record of first 36 games played.

performance of *B*. In fact, *B*'s record corresponds almost exactly to the response of humans or other biological organisms to "learning" situations.

Figure 14.2-5 shows that the stupid, blindly obedient moron, doing nothing but what it is told, has seemingly "figured out" the best strategy for playing one-pile nim. This strategy can be summarized by the following definitions and rules:

Basic Fix. If your move leaves your opponent 1 match in the pile, you have won. This is the basic winning situation, called the basic fix.

Basic Loss. If your move leaves your opponent a situation reducible to the basic fix in one move, he will win (we assume an intelligent opponent). This is a basic losing situation, called a basic loss. There are three of them: 2, 3, and 4 matches left, since he may take 1, 2, or 3.

Next Fix. If your move leaves your opponent more than 4 matches in the pile, he cannot leave you with the basic fix. If your move leaves him less than 6 matches, then whatever he takes you can leave him the basic fix. Therefore, a pile of 5 matches is safe to leave, for it cannot be reduced to the basic fix in one move, but it can be in two moves. Five, then, is also a fix.

Other Fixes. By the same reasoning, nine is also a fix, and so (if the starting pile were big enough) would be thirteen, seventeen, etc.

Fix. In general, if the maximum number that can be taken by one player at a move is *n*, a fix is a pile containing

$$1 + k(n + 1)   \qquad k = 1, 2, 3, \ldots$$

Rule. (a) If the situation facing you is not a fix, make it so. This can always be done in one move.

  (b) If the situation facing you is a fix:
    (1) move at random, hoping your opponent will make a mistake when faced with a new situation.
    (2) Stall, making the minimum legal move (1 match).
    (3) Resign.

Note: The expert program follows plan (b1), making sure the learning program eventually learns to handle all possible situations.

  This is how a human would analyze the game of one-pile nim, extracting from the various specific situations the general rule cited above. The human mind is very good at such problems, using inductive reasoning to infer the general rule from the specific, and deductive reasoning to determine from the general the specific move to make in any given situation.

  Is this, however, what the "learning" program actually does? No, it is not. There is never in this program, nor in the drinking-glass machine version of the game, anything approaching a general rule. Faced with a situation it has not encountered before (a larger-size pile, or a change in the rules to permit a different number of matches to be taken in one move), the program would have to start all over again, learning each situation by trial and error. The program has learned only in the sense that it has, by elimination, found the winning move *for each situation it has encountered.*

  This same difference in philosophy shows up whenever we consider how to write a program to have a computer play any game. Do we use the generalized approach and build the winning strategy in the program, using it to deduce the best move in any given situation? Or do we consider each specific situation separately, building the proper choice for that situation into the program?

  Although the self-modifying technique we have been describing is of the latter type, either can be designed to incorporate "learning." Method 2—the specific approach—is useful only if the number of possible situations is small enough so that all can be considered in a reasonable period of time. Nim is such a game, and therefore lends itself well to such demonstration programs; however, the principle for general strategy of nim is so simple that a program can be built around it even more easily than around the specific approach (see Problem 14.2-3). Block (1, p. 69) even suggests that in some more complex but still finite games the machine may be able to ferret out winning moves more rapidly than a human, and hence be of possible assistance to him in discovering the strategies themselves.

  Although the NOPE program is a very rapid learner, and indeed "never makes the same mistake twice," the drastic nature of its modification scheme is potentially dangerous. If anything goes wrong or is changed (a mistake in the handling of the numbers, in the drinking-glass version of the machine, or a change in the rules such as the maximum number that may be taken), this simple machine will never recover. Gardner and Block, however, both describe variations in the modification procedure which act to reinforce desirable responses, and suppress undesirable ones, in a probabilistic rather than in a completely deterministic way. Such programs are somewhat slower in achieving the same degree of proficiency, but are far more adaptable to changing environments, and hence a bit higher on the evolutionary scale.

Minimax Strategy. Number 6 in the list above—the minimax approach—will now be considered in more detail. The game situation considered will be that of the conventional two-player, alternate move, win-lose-draw (zero-sum) game—such as checkers and chess. Checkers is an excellent example for exposition purposes for several reasons: the rules are simple with very few different kinds of moves; playing situations are easy to visualize; the game is well known by many; and it has been the subject of a now classic study and experiment by Arthur L. Samuel of IBM, from whose work much of the following has been taken.*

There are three elements to this approach to game playing:

(1) Finding a valid evaluation scheme by which to determine whether one board situation is better than another;

(2) Setting limits for the tree of moves as to:

    (a) the number of branches (possible sequence of moves) to explore,

    (b) the depth to which explore each;

(3) At the end of each branch, applying the evaluation rules to evaluate the strength of the resulting board position on the assumptions that:

    (a) whenever there is a choice, the player represented by the machine will always try to maximize his strength

    (b) his opponent will always move so as to minimize it.

This is the process called "Minimaxing."

Two examples of evaluation schemes will be cited:

(1) In chess, it is often said that a bishop or a knight is worth about three and a half pawns, a rook five, and a queen ten. This equivalence scale is often offered as a guide in determining whether to accept a proffered exchange. Obviously, other factors such as board position and

---

* References 5 and 6.

strength of attack must be taken into account to modify this precise arithmetic scale.

(2) In checkers, the total number of pieces, as well as the number of kings, plays a similar role; in addition, in an attempt to reduce the less tangible factors of board position to numerical values, such factors as control of the center squares, control of the diagonal lanes, and general mobility are sometimes defined by mathematical formulas which can be evaluated in connection with any given board position.

The concept of branches in the tree of possible moves can be illustrated first by drawing one for the game of one-pile nim. Figure 14.2-6 is adapted from one of the figures of Block.* This displays (starting from the bottom) the possible choices available to player *B* when there are 6 matches left in the pile, the possible responses of player *A* to each of these, player *B*'s next possible moves in each of these cases, and so on up the tree until each branch is terminated at the twig representing the taking of the last match. In this figure, the numbers in the circles represent the number of matches remaining in the pile at each situation, the number beside each line shows the number of matches taken in that move, a square represents the termination of the game, and the letter in the square identifies the winning player. Player *B*'s moves are shown against a clear background; player *A*'s are shaded. It is easy, from Figure 14.2-6, to see why each move by one player or another is often called a "ply."

One-pile nim is not only a finite game, its tree has a sufficiently small number of branches so that all its possibilities can be conveniently explored. In this case, every twig at the end of the branches can have a definite win or loss associated with it. We will denote a win for player *B* as a + and a loss as a −. Let us work backward, from the top down, and hang a tag on each and every move in Figure 14.2-6; the result will be Figure 14.2-7. Let us see how those tags are determined.

At ply six it is *A*'s move. He has no choice, but must take the 1 match remaining. Since this constitutes a win for *B*, this branch representing *A*'s move is marked + as shown in Figure 14.2-7*a*. This is the only branch at ply six.

At ply five *B* has apparently six moves, but a closer look reveals four of them to be identical. There are thus three possibilities to consider. Faced with a 1, he has little choice. He takes the 1 and loses; therefore each of these four plays should be tagged as −. If, when faced with a 2, he takes both he also loses; this move also rates a −. Only if he takes 1

* "Learning in Some Simple Non-Biological Systems," Figure 17, page 77.

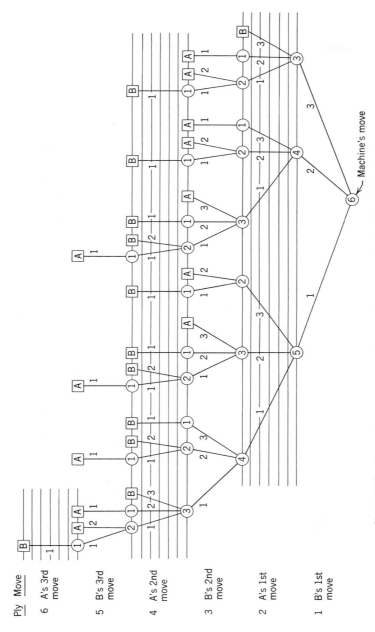

Figure 14.2-6 Tree of moves for one-pile nim, 6 remaining in pile (after H. D. Block).

479

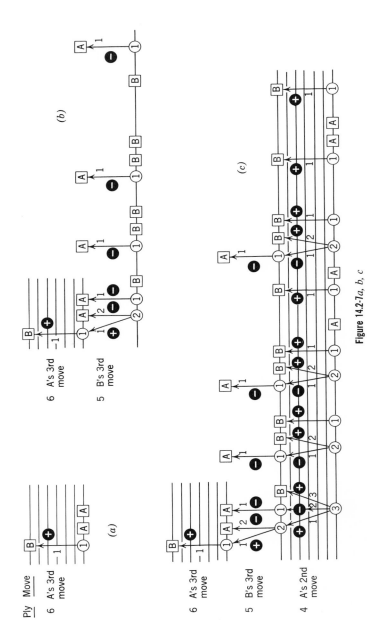

Figure 14.2-7 a, b, c

480

of the 2 does this path lead inevitably to a win; therefore this path and this alone on the fifth ply is marked + in Figure 14.2-7*b*.

Most of the fourth ply is equally obvious, but one of the moves (taking 1 from a pile of 3) leaves *A*'s opponent *B* with an option at ply five. One of these alternate branches is already marked + and the other − . Which determines the tag at ply four? To determine this, we recall the concept of minimaxing presented earlier in this section. Each player always moves so as to maximize his chances for success, and he assumes that his opponent always moves so as to maximize his own, which is the equivalent of saying, to minimize the first player's chances. Player *A* (whose turn it is at ply four) can therefore assume that at ply five player *B* will act to maximize his own score. Player *B* can therefore be assumed to choose the + branch at ply five; therefore the value of this branch at ply four would also be +, as indeed it is shown to be in Figure 14.2-7*c*. If player *A* makes this choice it leads to a win for *B*.

At ply three, however, the situation is somewhat different. For player *B* to choose 1 match from a pile of 4 would be quite foolish, even though there are two + branches leading out of the next node at ply four. To travel along either of these two + branches would require the cooperation of the opponent, since at ply four it is the opponent's move. Since there is a move possible for him out of this 3 pile with a − tag, it has to be assumed he will take this move at ply four; therefore the tag of the branch corresponding to removing 1 match from the pile of 4 at ply three will have to be − . Similar application of the minimax principle results in the assignment of the remaining tags in Figure 14.2-7*d*.

Similar ziz-zag reasoning results in a + tag on each of the branches out of the pile 5 node at ply two, for out of each of the subsequent nodes at ply five there is a + move available for *B* to take. Out of the pile 4 node at ply two, however, there is a − move, a way for *A* to guarantee a win for himself, and the same situation exists at the pile 3 node of ply two (see Figure 14.2-7*e*).

The reasoning for ply one should be familiar by now. *B* can mark the move that converts a 6 pile into a 5 pile as a + move, for *all* the possible *A* moves out of this node at ply two are +; no move *A* can make, can force a win. For the other two possible moves at ply one, however, such is not the case. Out of both the pile 4 and the pile 3 node at ply two there exists a − path, whereby *A* *can* win. Both of these two other possible moves for *B* at ply one must be marked − , therefore, as shown in the final version in Figure 14.2-7*f*.

At last we are in a position to see what the results of our analysis say about the move to make at ply one, where we are faced with a pile of 6. Of the three paths leading from the pile six node, one is + and the other

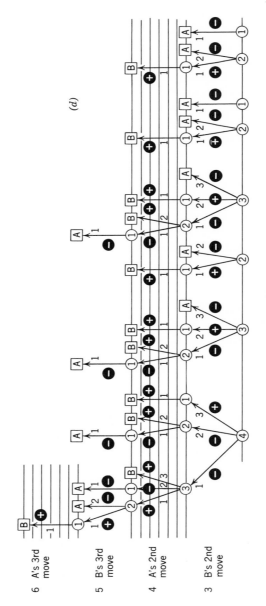

Figure 14.2-7*d*

6 A's 3rd
move

5 B's 3rd
move

4 A's 2nd
move

3 B's 2nd
move

(d)

482

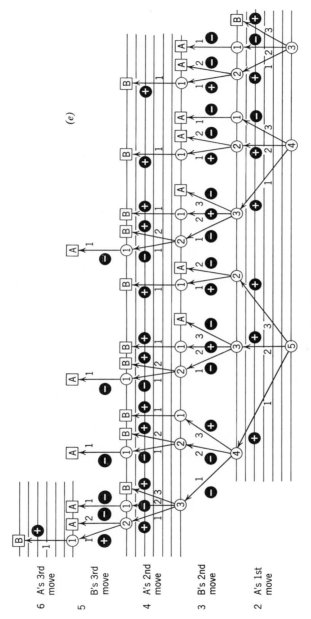

Figure 14.2-7*e*

(e)

6 A's 3rd
move

5 B's 3rd
move

4 A's 2nd
move

3 B's 2nd
move

2 A's 1st
move

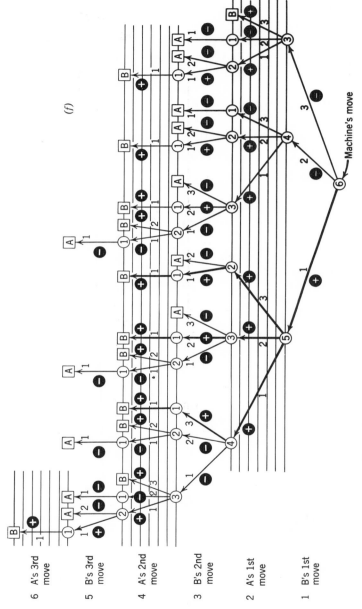

Figure 14.2-1f Evaluation of tree of moves (carried to end of game).

6 A's 3rd move

5 B's 3rd move

4 A's 2nd move

3 B's 2nd move

2 A's 1st move

1 B's 1st move

(f)

484

two −. If *B* makes the move tagged + (takes 1), the tree says he can force a win. If he takes either of the other two, *A* can win. His possible winning paths through the tree, then, depending on the response of his opponent, are shown by the heavy lines in Figure 14.2-7*f*.

Having completed this analysis of the tree of moves for this situation, we should be quick to say that a game in which the analysis is carried ahead to the end is not a useful field for application of this technique. We used the situation in one-pile nim to illustrate how the tree is growing, and how the various tags were determined, working from the top down. But it should be recalled, as stated above, that the area in which the minimaxing technique is valuable is the one where it is *not* possible (or at least not feasible) to look all the way ahead, and that it is necessary to work with some intermediate set of goals and evaluation schemes. Now what becomes of our plus and minus signs?

Let us illustrate, with a tree of moves, a situation from the game of checkers. We shall not try to develop here any practical evaluation scheme, but shall assume that one has been proposed and worked out. In the same way, the problem of deciding how many moves to explore, and the depth to which each will be followed before applying the evaluation scheme, can become very complicated. For instance, Arthur Samuel (9, p. 214) found that an initial procedure of following all possible moves a depth of three plies was considerably inferior to a scheme which explored to a variable depth, tracing some of the moves (those involving an exchange, for instance) to a considerably greater depth. Let us once again assume that some such scheme has been devised, and that the tree of Figure 14.2-8 represents, for a given board situation in checkers, only those possible moves that have been selected to merit study, each one traced only so far as our method (whatever it is) decrees. Even with such restrictions, it is still quite a formidable task.

The significant difference between Figure 14.2-8 and Figure 14.2-6 is that in none of these paths is the end of the game reached. In all cases we shall have to apply our formula (whatever it is) to evaluate the resulting board situation at the specified terminal point on each branch, and come up with a number, a score. Hopefully, a high score signifies a high probability of winning, and vice versa. But even after the evaluation formula has been applied, we must be careful to back down through the tree using minimaxing, before deciding on our best next move.

In Figure 14.2-9 we have filled in at the terminal of each path a typical set of scores as they might have been determined by our evaluation formula. Furthermore, we have carried these numerical values back down through the tree, applying the minimax principle at every stage. The resulting tags on all the branches, and the best move path to

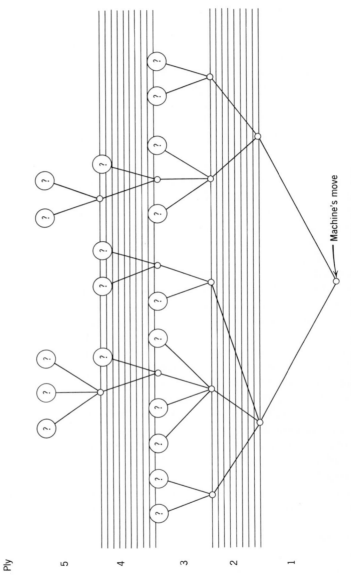

Figure 14.2-8 Tree of moves for situation in checkers.

Ply

5

4

3

2

1

Machine's move

486

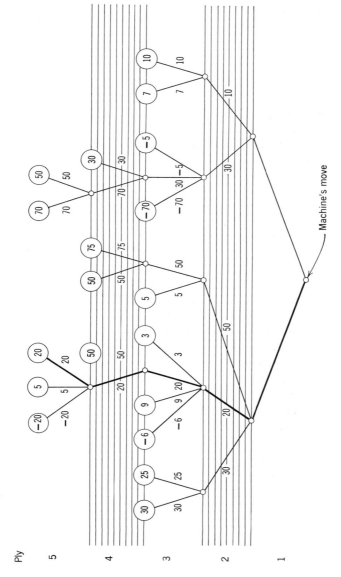

Figure 14.2-9 Evaluation of tree of moves (at intermediate level).

487

be followed, are also indicated. It is even more evident now that the chosen path does not lead to the highest possible score, but that only an unseemly solicitude on the part of our opponent could ever get us there. The indicated path, rather, leads to the highest possible score we can be *sure* of getting. And that is the best that minimax can do.

This principle, first formulated by the late John von Neumann, underlies all game programs that have been evolved in recent years to tackle the traditional games of great complexity, such as checkers and chess. Noticeable progress has been achieved, but a completely successful chess-playing program seems yet a considerable distance off. The root of the problem is our inability to write a precise description of the process to be used in carrying out the analysis. Here again, two or more different approaches are possible.

The first, as we have been describing it, consists in spelling out as intelligent a set of evaluation formulas and branch limitation criteria as we can devise. For instance, we will get a chess expert and try to tap his vast experience and proven analytic ability. We will ask him to try to analyze and describe his own thinking processes as he considers a situation: how is he able, without a second thought, to reject immediately perhaps 27 of a possible 30 alternate moves, and to pick out 3 that want further consideration. How far ahead does he look in his consideration of these? When does he determine that a path, or further consideration of it, is unprofitable? How does he decide that the situation which would result if he made *this* play is better than the resulting situation if he made *that* one? Having obtained, with considerable difficulty and many remaining blank spaces, the best answers we can, we shall proceed to incorporate these principles, methods, and criteria into a program that makes all these decisions. The answer for every situation, or at least the precise procedure for finding the answer, is built into the program. The program itself is an algorithm, and even though the goal embodied in the program may be a limited and imperfect goal, the program does guarantee to reach that goal.

A second approach seeks to substitute for the experience of the human expert the ability of the computer to store experiences and draw upon them to guide future actions. An outstanding series of experiments embodying this technique was carried out by Arthur Samuel of IBM, using the then available IBM 704 in his own time to test this method. He deliberately chose checkers rather than chess because he knew he could more easily develop a successful checker playing program, and could then concentrate more of his effort on ways of getting the machine to improve its own play. He accordingly first wrote a program which could record game situations and moves for checkers. It contained the rules whereby it could select all legal moves possible, and could also test for achievement of the goal, that is, a complete denial of mobility to either player. He then tackled the problem of determining *which* move should be made.

Samuel used the algorithmic approach to select branches and determine branch-path lengths, although his formulas frequently became quite elaborate. For instance, one program (9, p. 214) always looks ahead a minimum distance, usually set at three plies. At this point the program stops exploring and evaluates the board positions unless one or more of the following conditions exist:

(1) The next move is a jump,
(2) The last move was a jump, or
(3) An exchange offer is possible.

If any of these conditions exist, the program continues looking ahead up those branches. At the next ply—ply four—condition (2) (last move a jump) is not enough to keep the program from stopping and evaluating the resulting board positions; a new jump or exchange offer must be possible. At ply five exchange offers are dropped from further consideration, and only active jump sequences are pursued. At ply eleven or greater, the program will terminate the look-ahead even if the next move is to be a jump, should one side be ahead by more than two kings (to prevent the needless exploration of obviously winning or losing sequences). The program stops at a ply of twenty, regardless of conditions, since the memory space allotted is used up.

For his evaluation formula, however, he did not prescribe everything completely in advance; instead, he prescribed ways of letting the experience of the program modify the evaluation formula to produce the best results. He started by listing all the factors anybody could suggest that might have an effect on the outcome of the game: numerical superiority in pieces is an obvious one, but others include such things as mobility (number of moves possible), control of the center squares, support (protection of one piece by another), advance, and attack. Each of these had to be describable by a formula that would permit it to be measured in a given situation, but the influence it had in the general evaluation formula was controlled by a multiplying coefficient the magnitude of which was variable and under control of the program itself.

Then, when the program was put into operation against a human opponent, it would periodically review the success of its evaluation formula, comparing its predicted scores with scores which actually developed, and predictions of wins against actual game wins and losses. Depending on the success of this formula, it would alter the magnitude of the coefficients, increasing or decreasing them as experience indicated, rejecting those factors which seemed to have little effect, and giving the largest coefficient magnitudes to those factors that seemed to be the most significant. The result of this modification was that at the end of a hundred games this checker-playing program, which was initially playing as stupidly random a game as our NOPE, had progressed to the point where it could not only beat occasional or average players, it could give an expert a run for his money. Its most impressive accomplishment was that it could even beat the man who wrote the program!

In a biological organism, we call this "learning." Does the fact that we can describe the exact mathematical procedure by which the modification with experience takes place make this "nonlearning"? We will not press the point, for we are getting very close to arguing over the meaning of the word according to preconceived and personal biases.

Samuel's program, although it achieves levels of competence surpassing those which its author could explicitly build into it, still satisfies one of the principal characteristics of an algorithm. The precise criteria for analysis and determination of the need for modification, and the procedure for modification itself, are all explicitly written into the program. It is true, however, that its performance, and hence the goal achieved at the end of its sequence of operations, cannot be precisely predicted, and hence it departs from the accepted definition of an algorithm on this count.

One additional field of programming investigation will be mentioned, and that is the research in more general problem solving capability as typified by the general problem solver (GPS) of Newell, Shaw, and Simon.* In this type of program the contribution of the human programmer is removed one stage further from the final operation. Not only does the program contain segments that determine its next move, and segments that modify the criteria and formulas by which it determines its next move in terms of progress toward a built-in goal, the program now has spelled out only a general set of goals and principles, and one segment of the program uses these to determine what the specific goals should be. The abstraction is now pushed one level further back.

It is extremely difficult now to predict the course of execution through a given program, since choices are made in accordance with criteria set by goals that are themselves determined by operations within the program. It certainly cannot be claimed that execution of such a program can be guaranteed to lead to any predetermined goal, but only that,

---

* See Newell, Alan, and H. A. Simon, "A Program That Simulates Human Thought," and also Newell, Alan, J. C. Shaw, and H. A. Simon, "A Case Study in Heuristics," both in Reference 2.

hopefully, if it is well designed, sufficient experience of the trial and error sort will gradually lead either to convergence on the ultimate goal, or at least progress in that general direction. Such a process is frequently called a "heuristic" one. A heuristic program is generally distinguished from an algorithmic one by two factors:

(1) The algorithm consists of a complete set of operating steps precisely spelled out in advance, whereas the heuristic process bases its decisions on what to do next upon its past experience.

(2) An algorithm is guaranteed to lead to a precise goal, while the heuristic process only hopes that progress will be made toward it.

Heuristic programming has been able to achieve some encouraging, sometimes startling, results, and the interested reader will find quite a few discussed in the excellent anthology by Feigenbaum and Feldman.* Not the least of the results of these investigations, however, and in the minds of some, the most valuable, is the additional insight that such research brings to the processes that go on in the human mind itself.

14.3 ARTIFICIAL INTELLIGENCE

The observant reader may well be bothered at this time by an uneasy feeling that we have been somewhat contradicting ourselves. He is certainly aware of the general attitude that this book has worked so hard to build up—that the computer is nothing but a giant moron, and incapable of anything approaching intelligent activity on its own. Suddenly, in this chapter, we find ourselves treating the computer with a great deal more respect, and talking about not only programming the computer to tackle problems of a much higher level of sophistication, but actually getting it to perform functions previously reserved for living intelligent beings: learning, abstracting, generalizing. Now that we have learned a great deal more about what computers are, how they function, and how they are applied, let us try to make a much more careful comparison, and see what we know about the similarities and differences between electronic computers and biological computers, or human brains.

Electronic Computers

In Chapter 1 (Figure 1.2-4) we saw that we could represent the functional organization of a digital computer with just five types of units: at the heart, a logical or arithmetic unit, communicating with a high-speed memory, and buffered from the outside world by input-

* Reference 2.

output units; to regulate, integrate, and synchronize the operation of all of these, there must be control units to interpret instructions and send control voltages and timing signals to all the rest.

The fundamental building blocks of all of these units were seen in Section 8.4 to be two: the logical gate, and the bit-storage element, or flip-flop—both dealing with binary or two-level signals. Physically these devices employ increasingly compact and reliable solid-state technology, using semi-conductor diodes and transistors, integrally embedded with their associated circuits on tiny encapsulated wafers which can plug into larger units for quick assembly and replacement. (See Figure 14.3-1.) The back panels of these frames may resemble mazes to the uninitiated, but they represent carefully designed and laid out point-to-point interconnections that will guarantee the desired information processing by the whole machine.

For storage of information, almost all commercially available computers today use magnetic cores—tiny electromagnetic devices which, threaded together in assemblies of several thousand (Figure 14.3-2), give current computers memories of from ten thousand to several million bits of information, with an ability to retrieve selected items in times ranging from a few microseconds down to fractions of one microsecond.

For auxiliary or bulk storage, computers use related techniques of recording information magnetically on a moving surface, giving rise to extensive use of magnetic tapes, drums, and disks. Figure 14.3-3 shows a few such devices.

In use, these contraptions have been built to respond to a rather small and limited set of command signals, each of which causes a specific and completely predictable action or set of actions. These actions can be programmed, as we saw in Chapter 10, so as to carry out very elaborate tasks within their domain of information handling, by presenting the computer with an elaborate and meticulously detailed set of instructions consisting of sequences of these command signals. Not only will the computer not undertake any action requiring initiative, it will not in general even accept information from the outside world unless specifically programmed to do so.

Neurophysiological Computers

The fundamental constituent of living information-processing systems is a highly specialized type of cell found only in nervous systems tissue, called the neuron. Although neurons from different parts of the nervous system vary widely in structure, and apparently in many other respects as well, they all seem to possess at least three basic parts (see Figure 14.3-4): a central body, frequently called, in the more esoteric

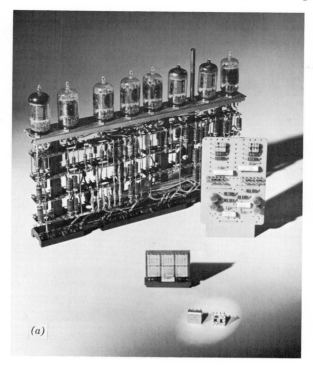

(a)

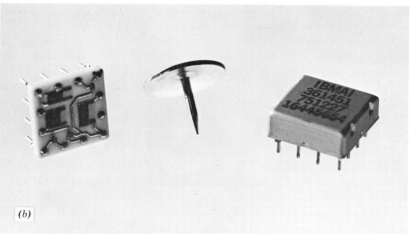

(b)

Figure 14.3-1   Computer components and solid-state circuits (Courtesy IBM Corporation). (a) Three generations of computer circuits: vacuum tube plug-in strip (1951), transistor printed circuit card (1959), solid logic chip transistor module (1964). (b) Solid logic technology: circuit module before and after encapsulation.

Figure 14.3-1   (c) Solid logic technology: six-module card being plugged into computer frame.

literature, the soma or perikarion; a diffuse input structure, frequently consisting of many branched extensions or appendices, called dendrites; and an output device, usually much more concentrated in a single fibre called the axon. The axon has some rather peculiar electrochemical properties that permit it, once an electrical discharge is started at one end, to transmit this impulse at a fairly rapid rate, virtually undiminished, from one end to the other, drawing energy from the chemistry of the surrounding medium to maintain the discharge as it goes. This "spike" potential, as it is called, has a very sharp and remarkably regular time course.

Left to themselves, the chemical processes build up and maintain a resting potential difference between the inside of the cell and the fluid outside the surrounding membrane of about -50 mv (1 millivolt $= 0.001$ volt), as shown in Figure 14.3-5. This condition is relatively stable against fluctuations of a few millivolts, but if, as the result of some disturbance, the potential is forced up about 10 mv to -40 mv, an irreversible discharge sets in, and the cell "fires." When this occurs, the potential jumps some 80 to 100 mv, becoming perhaps 40 mv positive with respect to the outside of the cell, and then, somewhat more slowly,

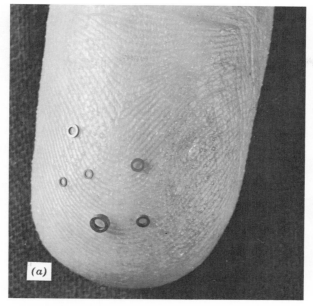

Figure 14.3-2 Magnetic-core memory components.

decays toward its original value. The rise time of the leading edge of the pulse is as short as 0.1 millisecond, and the duration of the discharge runs about 1 to 1.5 milliseconds.

A spike discharge, once initiated, will propagate down the axon with a velocity of from 2 to 200 meters/sec (about 4 to 400 miles/hour).

Figure 14.3-3   Auxiliary memory devices—magnetic tape drives, magnetic disk storage.

Over most of its length, the axon merely acts like a transmission line, conducting the impulse to its destination without in any way altering its information content. As it nears its destination, however, the axon splits and branches many times, ending up with thousands of tiny "fingers" which may make contact upon the dendrite walls, or even upon the bodies of other neurons. Although the axon does not actually penetrate the membrane walls of a dendrite, it does form definite tiny contacts, called "synapses," across which the impulses of one neuron must be transmitted in order to reach the next. One neuron may transmit information to thousands of other neurons, and each of these in turn is receiving information from many others. A schematic representation of such a neuron chain is shown in Figure 14.3-6.

Looking at these impulses from the point of view of the neuron on the receiving end, we see that any one neuron may be receiving impulses from tens or even thousands of other neurons in an irregular but almost continuous fashion. These impulses are, in general, received at various positions along the dendritic arms, from which they are thought to propagate with time delay and decaying amplitude down the dendrites toward the body of the cell. Along the way, they are mixed with impulses being received at other synapses so that the resulting potential at the body of the cell is a very complex pattern indeed. Most impulses would appear to be excitatory in nature—that is, tending to fire the receiving

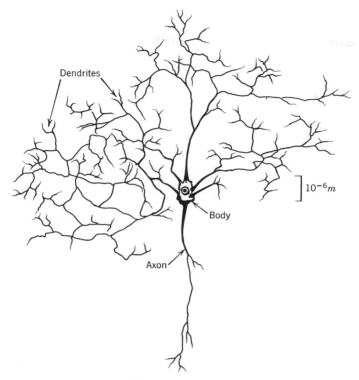

Figure 14.3-4   A neuron.

neuron—but some also appear to be inhibitory. The process by which these effects are mixed, and the logical operation upon the inputs which the output represents, is very imperfectly understood.

Nevertheless, the outstanding characteristic of the body of the cell is that it has a threshold: potential fluctuations less than this threshold cause no activity; a potential rise equal to or greater than this threshold causes the cell to discharge, which in turn causes a single potential impulse to be transmitted along its axon to subsequent neurons in the chain. It should be noted that the cell fires in what is called an all-or-none fashion: the magnitude of the spike is essentially constant and independent of firing conditions; the information content of the signal lies in its presence or absence, and in the frequency with which the discharge takes place.

In computer terms, the neuron is a complex information-processing unit; receiving more or less simultaneous inputs on thousands of lines, combining these inputs in a continuous or analog fashion, in some way

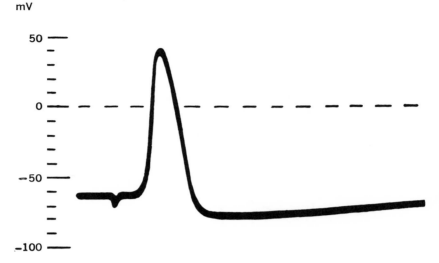

Figure 14.3-5   Spike discharge of neuron. (Credit: A. L. Hodgkin, Courtesy of the Royal Society.)

determining a single logical function of these inputs which triggers a pulse, and transmitting that pulse as a piece of binary-digital information to many other locations for further processing. Unfortunately, the nature of these processes, and most of the details of the organization of the system as a whole, are as yet beyond our threshold of knowledge,

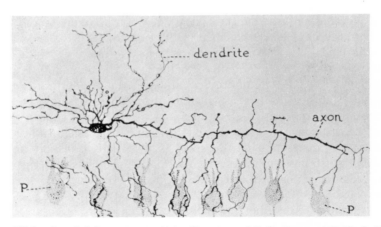

Figure 14.3-6   One link in a neuron chain. (Courtesy of E. G. Gray and R. W. Guillery, *International Review of Cytology*, Academic Press. Redrawn from Ramon y Cajal, 1954.)

and the first clues to understanding the nature of the information processing going on there are just beginning to emerge.

Unfortunately, even this attempt to reduce the information-processing functions of the neuron to engineering terminology is quite drastically oversimplified, on at least two counts.

First, the desire of the engineer to standardize on a very few types of elements is apparently not shared by nature. Not only are no two neurons ever exactly alike, but there is a wide variation in general types and characteristics, which is all the more complicated by the realization that there are all stages of variation in between (Figure 14.3-7). Some seem to be all input and no output; some are double ended; and some seem to have no organization or form to them at all.

Second, complicated though the back panel wiring plan of an electronic computer may look to the uninitiated, to the trained eye there is form and organization. Cabling collects individual wires into bundles, and conducts them along essentially parallel paths through common junctions to common destinations. The wiring diagram of a biological

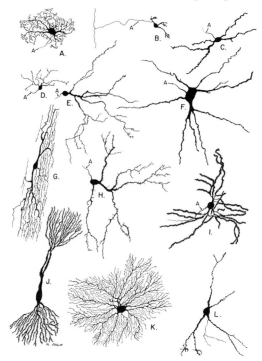

Figure 14.3-7   Variety of neuron types (From Strong and Elwyn, *Human Anatomy,* Williams and Wilkins Company, Courtesy of Dr. Clement Fox.)

computer, on the other hand, defies tracing. Figure 14.3-8 conveys a sense of the confusion one faces. It is true that there appears to be a measure of large-scale order: near the top, the surface of the cerebral cortex, transmission fibres have many horizontal branches, constituting an intercommunicating network with other information processors handling supposedly different aspects of the data; farther down, the neurons have long vertical fibres, extending many times the size of the body itself, corresponding to trunk lines which transmit the information after collecting and associating to other centers in the brain. But at the local level, on the fine scale, the mass of connections seems to be beyond the capability of complete description. This impression is further heightened by the realization that the staining technique used to prepare the specimen for this photograph is estimated to make not more than about 10% of the neurons visible!

In spite of this apparent lack of organization, however, these living nervous systems have evolved, as we are aware, into highly complex information-processing systems. They receive information from a variety

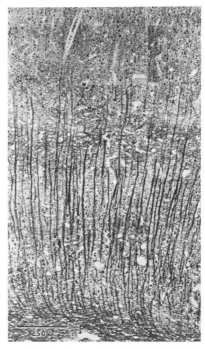

Figure 14.3-8 Neural tissue showing communication fibers. (D. A. Scholl, *The Organization of the Cerebral Cortex*, by permission of Methuen and Co., Ltd., London.)

of input sensing devices; they can carry out quite elaborate pre-programmed sequences (instincts); they are capable of being programmed to perform automatically a host of other functions (reflexes); and, most remarkable of all, they possess the capacity to learn, modify, associate, abstract, generalize, and create, in a fashion that puts their intellectual capacities many levels beyond the most sophisticated learning yet shown to be possible with electronic computing devices. There is still a very real meaning to the term "thinking" that differentiates living from nonliving systems.

Similarities

Let us take a closer look at some of the similarities and differences between the electronic and the biological computers.

On the similar side, we can certainly cite at least two reasons why the comparison should have found such acceptance. For one, compare Figure 1.2-4 on the organization of the electronic computer with Figure 14.3-9, which shows in a very general way some of the information processing that is going on in its biological counterpart. Certainly, both kinds of systems have the capacity to store information—to receive it at one time and deliver it upon request at a later time. The widespread use of the term "computer memory" points up the strong similarity in function between the two systems in this regard. In the biological system information is received from the outside world via sensory receptors such as eyes, ears, and fingers; the output of the system in the form of information to, and sometimes control of, the outside world is by means of motor effectors—essentially muscles. Receiving, manipu-

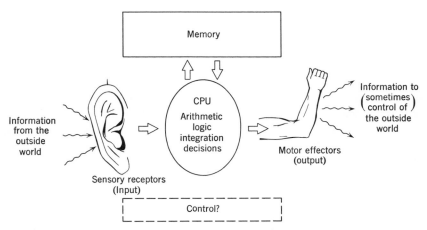

Figure 14.3-9 Organization of a biological computer.

lating, and disgorging this information is a central processing unit (or units) which is constantly comparing, associating, abstracting, and filing away. These processes, in turn, though in large measure automatic, are themselves under the control of some high-level control which directs attention, initiates activity, and adjusts the priority of control according to the purposes of the job at hand.

A second factor inviting the comparison is the similarity in results accomplished by the two systems. To the average mind, the fact that our electric computer can do arithmetic, perform deductive logic, make decisions, and solve problems, is ample proof that it is "thinking," for is not that what thinking consists of? Furthermore, since it can do almost all these operations both faster and more reliably than living brains, it must also be a better brain, must it not?

Differences

Small wonder then that the "giant brain" epithet reflects the most popular concept of the role of the automatic computer even in today's world. To show that it is hasty and misguided, let us now look at some of the differences between the two types of systems.

Memory Capacity. Let us consider first the storage device we have already talked about—the memory of the system. First, from the standpoint of memory capacity alone, the living organism has an advantage in size and capacity that is so great it constitutes virtually a difference in *kind* of function possible. Estimates of the storage capacity of the human brain vary from 10^{10} to 10^{20} bits of information carried in immediately accessible storage.* For comparison purposes, let us take a number in the middle of that range, say 10^{15} bits. If we add to that the auxiliary files of information to which the living system has access at various slower rates, we will have to include the entire amount of man's recorded knowledge. By contrast, although great strides are being made in increasing the capacity of the electronic computing system, the largest such systems we can talk about as commercially available today may have a capacity of 50–100 million (10^8) bits (one to two million words at less than 50 bits per word) of high-speed random access storage. Auxiliary memories of read-only data cells, laser-written disk files, etc., may expand the accessible memory to 10^{12} bits, but with an appreciably slower access time and by a much less directly accessible route.

Memory Access. Second is the memory-access method used by the two different systems. As we have learned, storage of information in the elec-

---

* Dean E. Wooldridge, *The Machinery of the Brain,* McGraw-Hill, New York, 1963, p. 189.

tronic computer is always accompanied by saving the address of the information—either in the program itself or in a table to which the program has access. Retrieval is accomplished by knowing *where* the information wanted is, and telling the computer to go and get it. The nervous system, on the other hand, seems to use an entirely different approach, best portrayed by an example. If someone says to you, "Santa Claus," what comes to mind? Perhaps it is an image of a portly figure in a fur trimmed suit, with associated details of pipe and smoke wreaths, reindeer, and bag of toys; perhaps it is the memory of wide-eyed excited children and all the joy that Christmas morning brings; perhaps it is the indirect or second-level associations with the symbol, such as bell-tolling, cadaverous Santas on the downtown streets beside makeshift chimneys, or gilt-wrapped hollow shells of milk chocolate, poured into a Santa mould. The images evoked may not even be visual: added to the sights remembered may be the smell of balsam or pine, the sound of children's shrill laughter and Santa's deeper "ho's," and the tinkle of sleighbells against the glistening whiteness of the snow.

Just where in your brain was all this set of concepts stored? How did you know where to address it? You do not know? Then how did that ordinary two-word cue trigger off their recall? Just what was the mechanism by which the brain responded to this (implied) request for information? We have to admit that we do not know.

We observe that the brain seems to store and retrieve information by *associating* certain facts with others; sometimes because they occurred simultaneously in the original impression, but more often because a conscious or unconscious act of will determined that fact *A* had an association with fact *B*, and maybe with fact *C* as well. Subsequent presentation of any one of these stored facts, together with a request to "read from memory," results in a virtual stream of these facts being sent from the storage banks back to the centers of consciousness, presumably until one of them passes certain comparison tests and is accepted as "the one wanted."

We call the electronic computer memory system "addressable" storage, and the brain's method "associative" storage. But giving it a name puts us no closer to understanding either the method or the mechanism. We have only faint glimmerings of some crude rudimentary ways of implementing an associative memory. We are trying very hard to learn more.

In addition to memory capacities and memory access methods, what other differences exist between the two classes of computers? Let us say a brief word about just a few.

Reliability. In spite of early pessimists who predicted that computers would never be able to rack up enough consecutive hours between failures to tackle successfully any really long problems, computers have been developed into fantastically reliable devices. It is taken for granted nowadays that computers will perform from ten billion to many trillion operations between errors, yet the overall dependence of the system on the proper functioning of every part is such that a single failure may be catastrophic. If one flip-flop fails, the result may be an occasional wrong bit in the 36th place, or the computer may put out pure garbage. The components of living tissue, on the other hand, have much higher error rates and fluctuations, but the nervous system itself possesses an incredible degree of overall reliability. Furthermore, it can often repair its own damage, and either grow new connections or learn to use other paths.

Deterministic Structure. This is the key to much of the rest of the difference. There is evidence both from neurophysiology and from genetics and heredity that brains are not completely "pre-wired" according to a precise blueprint, but that only the overall system features and some of the larger aspects of the organization are built in. Much of the rest of the structure, especially at the fine detail level, may be initially randomly connected and disorganized, but can modify itself to develop the needed organization, so that reliable behavior patterns develop as the organism grows, is trained, and learns. This field of research is often referred to as the study of "self-organizing systems."

Learning. Computer circuits do not learn. Programs, as we have seen in the preceding section, can be made to modify themselves on the basis of experience, but in most cases only along pre-determined lines. Research is going on in both directions: "heuristic" programming, and components that adjust to their environment.

Language. The limited language-handling capability of a computer is in large measure a consequence of the lack of learning ability discussed above. No natural language turns out to be so logical that it can be reduced to a completely pre-determined and specified set of rules. After all, humans take years to learn it. It seems to take as long to develop the ability to communicate accurately and fluently as to reach physical maturity in our own species—and some college teachers would say much longer.

Creativity. Philosophically speaking, true creativity is incompatible with determinism, exact structure, and, therefore, exactly predictable behavior. Even "pseudo-random" number generators, while capable of causing varying behavior, cannot bring forth one suggestion or new idea. One of the difficulties, of course, is that we have not the faintest idea how man himself performs generalizations, creates hypotheses, or carries out inductive reasoning or creative thinking. As was mentioned when discussing the study of heuristic programming, one of the fascinating aspects of this branch of computer engineering is the degree to which it is causing attention to be directed toward the study of the human mind itself.

Synthesis of Intelligence

Two general approaches have been followed by the modern practitioners of the robotic art, the creation of artificial intelligence.

Upgrading Present Machines. On the one hand are those who take the most complicated and highly organized device yet constructed by man, the electronic computer, and use it to push further into the realm of intellectual achievement. Here the approach is to upgrade the intelligence level of existing computers by learning how to get it to perform more and more complex tasks of a type previously considered to require higher and higher degrees of intellectual capacity. In this category would be put all the improvements in computer language and communication, including new developments in the medium itself, such as optical-character recognition devices. We have already seen many of the achievements of this approach: programs to do deductive logic, such as those which not only check the proofs of logic theorems and geometry theorems, but actually search for and carry out the proofs; programs which solve puzzles and play games (particularly those that improve their own ability); and even programs which tackle the problem of "how does man go about thinking in the first place?"

Unfortunately, say some, the very deficiencies inherent in the computer itself, as discussed in the last few pages, doom this approach to certain ceilings of achievements. Certainly, they say, if our goal is to simulate not only the intellectual performances of the brain, but the methods which the brain uses to perform them, we need to back up and start with components, structure, and an organization that is much closer to that of the living brain.

Neural Net Approach. The type of component hypothesized here is the *threshold device* (Figure 14.3-10). Though often called neurons or artificial neurons, the term "neuromime" as proposed by Leon Harmon* is undoubtedly to be preferred, since they mimic the behavior of living neurons to a greater or less degree of accuracy. As shown here, the

---

* W. A. van Bergeijk and L. D. Harmon, "What Good Are Artificial Neurons?" *Proceedings of First Bionics Symposium,* WADD Technical Report 60–600, Office of Technical Services, Washington, 1960, p. 396.

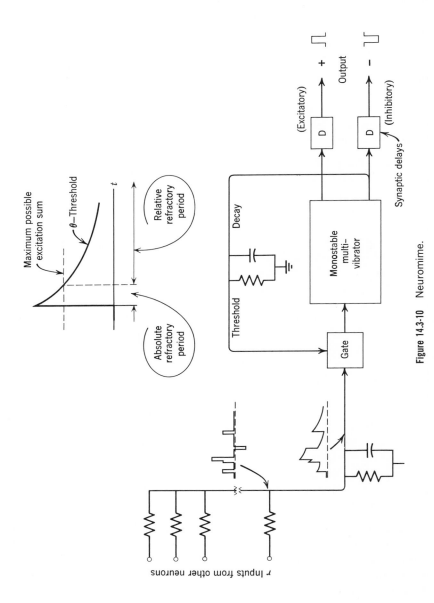

Figure 14.3-10 Neuromime.

neuromime can receive inputs from many different sources, sum them both spatially and temporarily, and present the resulting input to a threshold-controlled gate. If the input is equal to or greater than the threshold, the element fires, emitting a single pulse of either positive or negative polarity that can be transmitted to other elements. Furthermore, the element incorporates what the physiologists call "refractory behavior"; upon firing, a fraction of the output is fed back to the gate and acts to raise the threshold appreciably above its former level. In most cases the value of the threshold immediately after firing is so great that no combination of available inputs would suffice to fire it again. In this condition it is said to be "absolutely refractory." The threshold, however, immediately begins to decay toward its equilibrium value, so that for a period it is possible for the device to be fired, but only with an input greater than that necessary when it has attained its equilibrium condition; this is its "relatively refractory" period. After a brief period (in the living cell, from 10 to several hundred milliseconds) the threshold has returned to the resting potential at which it started, and the cycle is ready to start all over again.

Such a device incorporates much of the behavior that is known to be associated with biological neurons, and the study of artificial systems built up out of such components can lend considerable insight into their corresponding living counterparts. Here is an example of the use of simulation, not to improve performance, but just to try to find a model. If a model can be constructed whose performance, as observed either by computer simulation or by experimentation with an actual physical model, can be made to duplicate that of the living prototype, then the model can give some valuable clues as to what *may* be the internal structure of the original.

For instance, it was hypothesized by D. O. Hebb in 1949[*] that one method by which the learning-from-experience process, discussed a few pages back, might take place could be a modification of the synapse, with use, to make it easier for an impulse to be transmitted across it. This process he called "facilitation," and its existence, effect, and mechanism have been argued ever since. Although no such change has ever been conclusively demonstrated, such a process, or something like it which would have the same effect, has seemed to be a necessary ingredient of just about every successful simulation model. Note that there are three ingredients to this process: an axon which is attempting to transmit an impulse across a synapse to a succeeding neuron; a control which determines that this is a desirable transmission path, and that such

---

[*] D. O. Hebb, *The Organization of Behavior,* John Wiley and Sons, New York, 1949.

transmission ought indeed to be facilitated next time; and a feedback mechanism which makes a corresponding change in the mechanical, chemical, or electrical property of the path.

We shall describe one such simulation, which incorporates threshold elements, random initial structure, and feedback controlled facilitation. The model, which is designed to learn to recognize patterns and perceive relationships, is called the Perceptron.*

We shall begin with an idealized, simplified picture of the set of pathways and elements comprising one functional set of circuits in the human nervous system, as shown in Figure 14.3-11:

A sensory receptor (let us use the eye as an example) which forms a two-dimensional representation on the retina of the three-dimensional scene in front of it.

A "projection" region in the cortex itself onto which is mapped with reasonable accuracy the image formed on the retina of our sensory device.

A network of adaptable threshold units into which the projection layer feeds its impulses on a randomly-connected, many-sources-to-one-input, and one-source-to-many-inputs basis. This associates, compares, and integrates the information from these many sources, and is known as the association layer; its components are called "association" units or just *A* units.

Deeper layers of *A* units to coordinate the conclusions formed by the first *A* layers.

Output devices, driven by the last stage of the *A* unit layers, being in general motor effectors.

Lastly, feedback paths from the output back to the association layers. These feedback paths have the effect of reinforcing selected paths so that a similar stimulus will find it easier to generate the same response next time. We will see shortly how this reinforcement might be carried out.

Grossly oversimplified though this picture of the nervous system might be, let us simplify it still further for the purpose of attempting to build a model that might perform in some similar ways. Figure 14.3-12 shows the organization of what is called a three-layer Perceptron, having reduced the diagram of Figure 14.3-11 to three units:

A retina which is a gridwork of many small receptor cells, upon which is superimposed a two-dimensional spacial pattern set up by the outside world.

* Frank Rosenblatt, "The Perceptron: A Probabilistic Model for Information Storage and Organization in the Brain," *Psych. Rev.,* vol. 65, No. 6, November, 1958.

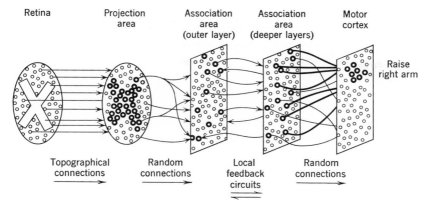

Figure 14.3-11   Organization of one set of circuits in the brain.

A set of *A* units fed by the units of the retina on a random-connection basis.

Two output units, themselves threshold devices, representing the simplest possible decision—a binary choice.

Feedback connections from the output units to the *A* units. These connections allow a feedback impulse from one output to cause all those *A* units, which are in the process of trying to fire that output unit, to have their output strength or value increased, and those trying to fire the other unit to have their value decreased.

Now let us see how such a device might be caused to modify itself on the basis of experience.

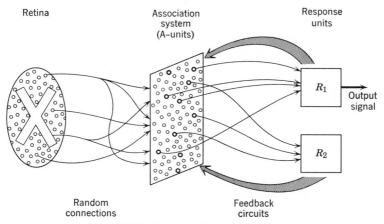

Figure 14.3-12   Organization of a Perceptron.

We shall select two classes of patterns to present to the retina of our Perceptron—squares and circles. We shall present these one at a time. When one of the patterns—say a square—is presented to the retina, certain of the elements in the retina will be stimulated to send signals to a randomly selected set of A units, some of which will fire. Some of these A units, in turn, will send their output signals to output unit 1 and some to output unit 2. These are so constructed that the output unit receiving the larger stimulus will always fire.

When we wish to "train" the Perceptron, we will, simultaneously with the presentation of an input pattern, force the response unit that we wish to have associated with that input to fire. When it does, it will feed back a reinforcement only to those A units which are themselves firing, and whose firing would contribute to the firing of the selected response unit. This reinforcement could take any of several forms: it could lower the threshold, increase the rate of firing, or increase the magnitude of the output pulse when it does fire. In the simplest version of the Perceptron, the last of these three is actually done.

What effect does this have? It means that even if the effect of a given stimulus had been initially to try to fire response unit B, after sufficient training and forced firing of output unit A, that same stimulus would eventually produce a sufficiently strong set of impulses to succeed in firing unit A without any external forcing. Similarly, the device can be conditioned to respond to patterns of the other class by producing an output from unit B.

Figure 14.3-13 shows the result of one set of simulated experiments, plotting the probability of successful response as a function of the length of training sequence. Let us look at the point on the abscissa corresponding to a training sequence consisting of exposure to 100 squares and 100 circles, each accompanied by a forced firing of the desired response unit. Then let us show the Perceptron a square and not tell it what the pattern is—let it select its own response. Even for a Perceptron containing as few as 100 A units, the curve of P_r shows that the probability of a correct response is 0.92; it has a 92% chance of correctly identifying this as a square.

Consider one further test. P_g is the probability of correct generalization, the probability of giving the correct response to a pattern which the Perceptron has never seen before. Choose a pattern that is a member of one of the two classes, but which was not included in the training sequence—a square of different size, or different tilt, or different position in the field of view. This chart tells us that, after a similar training sequence of 100 samples of each class, when shown a new pattern of a square the Perceptron still has an 85% probability of correctly identify-

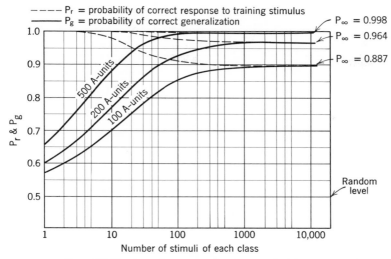

Figure 14.3-13 Learning curves for three typical Perceptrons.

ing it as a square! In other words, it has abstracted from its experience the property we call "squareness," and can correctly apply it.

This is but one of many intriguing experiments in bionics or artificial intelligence which are aimed at improving both the ability to synthesize intelligent behavior, and our understanding of the greatest challenge to man, the mechanism by which understanding itself is achieved—the human mind.

It is not only in the realm of the nervous system that this new alliance of biological and engineering scientists is forming. The developing field of bio-engineering brings physiologists, biologists, and medical researchers together with electronic technicians, mechanical and chemical engineers, and experts in feedback control in a similar collaboration: to apply engineering techniques and devices to assist in the solution of specific problems in the life sciences, and to join in seeking a better understanding of the life processes themselves.

In all this, of course, the computer plays an important role, but nowhere is it so significant as in the study of artificial intelligence, where. the computer, in the simulation of mental processes, is both the principal tool and the subject of the research itself.

PROBLEM 14.2-1   "Tree Evaluation"

Fill in a score evaluation for player *B* at the unlabeled nodes. Mark the best path for *B*.

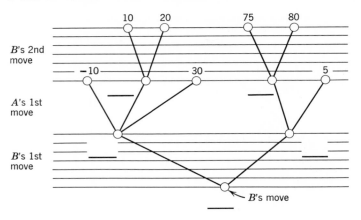

Figure P14.2-1

PROBLEM 14.2-2   "Last One Wins"

Modify the flow chart of Figure 14.2-1 to have the computer learn one-pile nim if the rules were changed to "last one *wins*".

PROBLEM 14.2-3   "Strategy Nim"

Write a program using the "fix" principle of Section 14.2 to play one-pile nim against a human opponent. You may wish to refer to the NOPE program in Appendix 14A for input-output techniques.

REFERENCES

1. Block, H. D., "Learning in Some Simple Non-Biological Systems," *American Scientist,* Vol. 53, No. 1 (March, 1965).
2. Feigenbaum, Edward, and Julian Feldman, eds., *Computers and Thought,* McGraw-Hill, New York, 1964.
3. Gardner, Martin, "Mathematical Games," *Scientific American,* Vol. 206, No. 3 (March, 1962).
4. Harmon, Leon D., "Natural and Artificial Synapses," *Self-Organizing Systems 1962,* M. C. Yovits, G. T. Jacobi, and G. D. Goldstein, eds., Spartan Books, New York, 1962.
5. Hebb, D. O., *The Organization of Behavior,* John Wiley and Sons, New York, 1949.
6. Kraitchik, Maurice, *Mathematical Recreations,* Dover, T-163, New York, 1953.
7. Rosenblatt, Frank, "The Perceptron: a Probabilistic Model for Information

Storage and Organization in the Brain," *Psych. Rev.,* Vol. 65, No. 6 (November, 1958).

8. Samuel, Arthur L., "Programming Computers to Play Games," *Advances in Computers,* Vol. 1, Franz Alt, ed., Academic Press, New York, 1960.
9. Samuel, Arthur L., "Some Studies in Machine Learning Using the Game of Checkers," *IBM Journal of Research and Development,* Vol. 3, No. 3 (July, 1959).
10. Van Bergeijk, W. A., and L. D. Harmon, "What Good are Artificial Neurons?", *Proceedings of First Bionics Symposium,* WADD Technical Report 60-600, Office of Technical Services, Washington, 1960.
11. Von Neumann, J., and O. Morganstern, *Theory of Games and Economic Behavior,* Princeton Univ. Press, Princeton (Third Edition) 1963.
12. Wooldridge, Dean E., *The Machinery of the Brain,* McGraw-Hill, New York, 1963.

CHAPTER 15.

Computers and the Future

15.1 COMMUNICATING WITH COMPUTERS

Our survey of computers and their use has taught us that there is very little in the information-processing realm they cannot do, provided that first, we are able to organize the processing we wish to have carried out into an algorithm, and second, that we are able to describe that algorithm to the computer. In fact, even that first requirement is starting to be relaxed, in that we are beginning to find techniques (heuristic programming) for giving the computer not a complete prescription, but a set of guides and principles whereby it can determine for itself what to do next.

But whatever the degree of organization and detail planning, the second step is an indispensible part of the process—describing the procedure to the computer. It is often such a tedious and painful process, and so fraught with error, that it becomes the principal bottleneck to the use of computers at all.

A great deal of effort has gone into the development of a great many computer languages, each intended to simplify the process of communicating with the computer in some way. Let us take a small survey to see what some of these languages are.

Symbolic or Assembly Languages

We learned in Chapter 10 that for every type of computer there are at least two levels of language that are closely tied to the actual structure of that particular machine. There is first, a machine language, consisting of the instructions and addressing procedures actually wired into the machine itself. At the second level there is a symbolic or assembly language, consisting basically of the same set of machine instructions, but with some simplifications and extensions: simpler mnemonic codes; an augmented set of instructions usually dealing with function or input-output operations, called macro instructions; a symbolic representation for instruction labels and data names; and a set of instructions to the assembler itself like BEGIN or DORG (Define ORiGin), define constant, and END or DEND (Define END), called pseudo instructions. Since this basic set of instructions has a one-for-one correspondence with the machine instruction set for that computer, these languages are strongly *machine-dependent,* which means that programs written in these languages, while quite efficient in that they take advantage of the particular instruction codes for that machine, do not lend themselves to easy conversion to run on other types of machines. They usually have to be completely rewritten.

General-Purpose Languages

At the next higher level of language construction a host of different languages appear. These languages are usually designed to describe a broad class of problems in some area, and to make it easier for the programmer to formulate his algorithm in a language closer to that in which he thinks about the problem and its solution, and one less dependent on the hardware features peculiar to a particular machine. These "higher-level languages" are, therefore, to a greater degree, *machine-independent,* which leads to more freedom of exchange of programming effort among different groups of users, and greater continuity with past effort when a particular installation changes machines.

Algebraic Languages. The language with which we have the greatest familiarity is, of course, FORTRAN. FORTRAN was designed for those problems whose solution is naturally expressed as a formula, and it is in these areas—science, engineering, the more mathematical aspects of business computations—that FORTRAN has been widely adopted. Particularly in America, FORTRAN accounts for an overwhelming majority of programming being done today.

FORTRAN is not of course the only algebraic language. Its most serious rival, ALGOL, is the outcome of an attempt on the part of a committee of American and European experts to design a more useful and practical ALGorithmic Oriented Language that would be flexible, yet precise and unambiguous. ALGOL has much the same structure as

FORTRAN, in having data words (but more classes); operations, called assignment statements; functions; input-output operations; and control statements. It is in the control statements that the most noticeable differences occur. ALGOL includes several types of relational operators, such as greater than, less than or equal to, in addition to simple arithmetic operators, and a broad class of control statements similar to the DO which give even greater flexibility in controlling the range and conditions of the iteration. For instance, one can say

for $x := 1, 2, 5$ **step** 5 **until** $50,$ **step** 10 **until** 100 **while** $y \leq 6$ **do**
begin

> RANGE OF DO

end

An equivalent FORTRAN program to accomplish the same thing is shown in Figure 15.1-1.

ALGOL has some other advantages that are particularly useful for larger-problem operation, where it becomes both more important and more difficult to keep separate the variables and operations that belong in one part or block from those in another, and yet maintain continuity across block lines where necessary.

Although ALGOL has some very real advantages over FORTRAN, the increased power of the language is nothing like the power that FORTRAN has over assembly language. The result is that, in the United States at least, where FORTRAN had become fairly widely entrenched by the time ALGOL was announced in 1958, ALGOL did not offer enough advantages over FORTRAN to cause many users to switch over. Too many companies and people had too much invested in their FORTRAN programs to be able to afford the great effort that re-programming would constitute. Only one major manufacturer really pushed ALGOL, the rest offering their own version of FORTRAN. The use of ALGOL in this country today centers around the installations of that manufacturer and certain university programming groups.

In other parts of the world, particularly in Europe, FORTRAN had a much smaller head start. Several European and British computer manu-facturers provided ALGOL rather than FORTRAN compilers with their machines, and many users were able to compare the two languages under working conditions. The result is that in Europe ALGOL has been adopted much more widely than in America, and both languages are in fairly common use there.

Even in this country, ALGOL exercised considerable influence in the design of other languages. In fact, the later versions of FORTRAN (FORTRAN IV, FORTRAN 63) have adopted outright so many of the

for $x := 1, 2, 5$ **step** 5 **until** 50, **step** 10 **until** 100 **while** $y \leq 6$ **do**
begin

> | RANGE OF DO |

end

(*a*) An ALGOL **for** statement


```
        X = 1.
        IF (Y − 6.) 1, 1, 500
   1    CALL RANGE ( )
        X = 2.
        IF (Y − 6.) 2, 2, 500
   2    CALL RANGE ( )
        DO 201 L = 5, 45, 5
        IF (Y − 6.) 200, 200, 500
 200    X = L
        CALL RANGE ( )
 201    CONTINUE
        DO 301 L = 50, 100, 10
        IF (Y − 6.) 300, 300, 500
 300    X = L
        CALL RANGE ( )
 301    CONTINUE
 500    NEXT = ...
```

(*b*) An equivalent FORTRAN program fragment

Figure 15.1-1   Sample comparison of ALGOL and FORTRAN control statements.

features that ALGOL had shown to be valuable, that it can be said that ALGOL, while losing most of the battles, has just about won the war.

Commercial Languages. We have seen in Chapter 7 that a somewhat different type of language is used for commercial and business data processing. COBOL (COmmon Business Oriented Language) has a structure somewhat similar to that of FORTRAN and ALGOL, but differs from them in two main aspects:

(1) In business data processing (at least in the era that generated COBOL), handling large masses of data is more often a problem than it is in scientific computing, so a business data-processing language must be richer in techniques for dealing with this kind of information.

(2) More people with a greater variety of background and technical training need to know what the procedure is, and what a program does. COBOL is therefore more verbose, using more full words and phrases

instead of symbols, with the goal that a COBOL program might be directly readable and self-explanatory.

COBOL, developed out of a Conference on Data Systems Languages (CODASYL) sponsored in 1959 by the U.S. Department of Defense, has achieved a near monopoly of the business language field. The advantages of conformity, whether voluntary or coerced, have resulted in the almost complete disappearance of all other languages in this area.

Combination Languages. Although there are certain areas where either FORTRAN or COBOL is better adapted to handling the problem, there are, as we saw in Chapter 7, many classes of applications having both sets of characteristics. Since a single language did not exist with both sets of characteristics, many computing installations were forced into mounting major programming efforts in both languages, with all the multiplicity of effort that this implies in terms of writing programs, developing and maintaining processors, building libraries, training staff, complicating the operating procedures, etc.

For these reasons, there have been several attempts at the development of a single all-purpose language, having the characteristics necessary for scientific computing and business data processing. Sometimes these attempts take the form of extensions to one of the languages in the direction of the other, and sometimes of completely new languages.

In the middle 1960's appeared the most ambitious of these undertakings, called modestly "Programming Language One," and abbreviated, not quite accurately, PL/I. PL/I was originally developed by a committee composed of members of SHARE (the users group for large IBM machines) and IBM. It was first announced as a language for the IBM System/360 series of computers. Other manufacturers cautiously declared their intentions of implementing PL/I, too, and in 1965 the Business Equipment Manufacturers Association (BEMA) joined the development effort. It is currently (1967) being investigated by a subcommittee of the U.S.A. Standards Institute as to its suitability as a candidate for standardization.

Only time will show whether PL/I will achieve its goal of replacing both FORTRAN and ALGOL and of becoming a universal programming language, or whether it will compound the situation by becoming merely a third programming language.

Progress toward standardization. In addition to the problems caused by the existence of such obviously different languages as FORTRAN, ALGOL, and COBOL, we have frequently had to comment on the differences between one FORTRAN and another. Not only are there at least as many FORTRANs as there are computers having FORTRAN compilers, even for the same computer there may be a variety of different FORTRAN compilers, each having slightly different features and ways of implementing them.

The biggest disadvantage in this situation is the barrier to free exchange of programs between users. Although the modifications to one FOR-TRAN program to permit it to run on another system might be small, the job of determining what the differences are and what changes need to be made is often very great indeed.

For this reason, the U.S.A. Standards Institute, under the sponsorship of BEMA, began in 1962 a major standardization effort in all phases of computers and data processing. This project tackled such diverse subjects as the binary coding of numeric and alphabetic information, vocabulary and terminology, standardization of hardware characteristics, and, of most immediate bearing on our subject, the standardization of programming languages. Enormous though the task of reconciling differences was, this project was supported by all the major manufacturers, users and user groups, and the interested professional groups and societies.

The most significant output of this effort to date has been the adoption, in 1966, of a U.S.A. Standard FORTRAN on two levels: full FORTRAN, corresponding approximately to FORTRAN IV, and Basic FORTRAN, approximately on the level of FORTRAN II, the FORTRAN we have been using throughout this book. Although there is nothing compulsory about such a standard, many of the computer manufacturers have indicated their intention to go along with U.S.A. Standard FORTRAN, and to make it an "internal standard" for their own company. Just how much processors will be changed to conform to the standard is not clear, but, in any event, two advantages should ensue:

(1) To the extent that the manufacturers and other compiler writers do follow the guide lines set out in the standard, the degree of compatibility between programs written in different FORTRANs for different machines will be increased, improving communication between users and decreasing present redundant effort.

(2) Even where the compilers are not equivalent, the one compulsory aspect about the U.S.A. Standards Institute is the control of the right to use its name. A manufacturer may not advertise that its product conforms to the U.S.A. Standard unless in fact it does, or unless he lists the areas in which it falls short. Since he must specify all such *negative* differences (features described in the standard but not available in his version) and since we can surely expect him to make a point of advertising all

positive differences (features found in his version but not described in the standard), we should have for the first time a precise list of the differences between one FORTRAN and another. This in turn will greatly facilitate the interchangeability of FORTRAN programs.

List Processing Languages

Although the so-called general-purpose languages discussed above have developed into extremely powerful tools for a great many kinds of computation, there are certain other areas for which they are not well adapted. They are particularly inadequate when it comes to working with information organized into lists, arrays, strings, or trees—situations where an important part of the problem is the structural relationship between different elements of the data.

To illustrate, recall a problem that was encountered in Chapter 5 in the section on sorting. In working out the program of Figure 5.3-4, "Sorting with plenty of room," you may recall that we found ourselves in the following quandary. At the end of one pass through the data, we had found one element A(L) to be the largest, we had copied it into the proper position in list B( ), and were faced with the job of eliminating that one from the original list.

We said at the time that there was no convenient way in FORTRAN to do this directly, and instead resorted to the subterfuge of making it a large negative number. We still say so, but now invite your detailed consideration of just how it could be done. A loop would have to be set up causing every element beyond A(L) in the list to be copied one place higher in the list, and the length of the list changed. Although the loop itself is fairly simple, the various tests and special considerations end up making it quite complicated. In fact, although the old approach accomplished the effective elimination in one statement (statement 8), to do a true elimination requires a collection of about seven statements—almost doubling the length of the processing portion of the program.

FORTRAN arrays, organized on the principle of sequential storage locations for an immutably ordered list, are painful things to alter.

Now let us consider a completely different way of keeping track of the ordered relationships among the elements in a list. Since sequential ordering in a set of machine addresses is so extremely hard to break out of, let us not use it at all, and set up our own means of keeping track of the list.

First, what do we mean by "ordering a list"? In the most basic sense, do we not mean which one follows which? That is, which one comes first, which next, and so on?

Whether we are talking about books on a shelf, a deck of playing cards, or an alphabetic file of names, we are used to indicating this implied order by physically arranging the elements of the list in a row or column. Then, when we wish to do something with the entire list, all we have to do is to start at the top for the first one, and iterate, using an implied or explicit instruction of the type "move to the adjacent position for the next."

This is not, of course, the only way to keep track of the order. Another way of indicating the proper sequence is somewhat analogous to going on a treasure hunt, or following a trail of arrows. At each location let us store two things: the piece of data that belongs there, and the address of the next location in the list. If the location is a computer-memory location, for instance, the information stored there might consist of the following:

LOCATION	DATUM	LINK
Symbolic address of location	List element	Address of next list element

Use of the array name A, for instance, would send control to the location called A(1); at this location would be found two things: the datum a_1, and the address A(2). Similarly, at location A(2) would be found a_2 and the address A(3).

In the case we talked about above, to eliminate, say, a_4 from the list, all that would have to be done would be to change the address stored in the link portion of A(3) so that it pointed not to the location of a_4 but to the location of a_5. From then on, element a_4 would have disappeared from the list. In the same way, additional elements can be inserted or removed at will, expanding or contracting the size of the list without the necessity for moving any data item at all. All that is necessary is to modify the links that chain the list together.

This method has several advantages, even for this simple situation. For one thing, if we truly eliminate each item from the original list after entering it into the new one, the list remaining to be processed becomes progressively shorter, thus cutting down on the processing time. Even forming the new list of assorted elements does not actually require any moving of data; if we merely modify the links between the data so that they build up a new chain in the new desired sequence, we will end with the sorted ordering we set out to achieve.

This same way of showing relationships can be even more useful when the information is structured in more than one dimension. Cross references may be necessary, as in a dictionary for language translation, or there may be a tree-like, branching structure to the relationships, as in studying the endings of a root word.

Although it would be awkward to do this sort of linking within the FORTRAN language, it is quite possible to design a language in which this is the natural way of expressing relationships, and to build a compiler that executes programs written in this language. Several such languages have indeed been written, including a series of Information Processing Languages (of which the most widely used is IPL-V), LISP, SLIP, and SNOBOL. These languages are particularly valuable for the processing of nonnumerical information, and are widely used in studies of natural language translation, pattern recognition, and artificial intelligence research.

Special-Purpose Languages

In addition to the broad general-purpose languages so far discussed, the 1960's have seen a varied collection of languages designed to make it easier for people in various special application fields to get the assistance of the computer in performing tasks in their special area of interest. The common characteristic of most of these is that they do not require the user to tell the computer what sequence of arithmetic or information processing steps to go through to get the desired result; he needs only to say what the characteristics or configuration of his particular system are, supply the data, and specify what particular output he would like.

Such special-purpose applications include dynamic analysis (DYANA), graphics and design (DAC-I and CAD), coordinate geometry (COGO), machine tool control (APT), simulation (SIMSCRIPT, GPSS), block diagram formulation (BLODI), higher mathematics (FORMAC), and accounting (WISAL).

On the Use of Natural Language

Are these languages enough? Is it enough to improve the power of programming languages? What more could we want than languages that make it possible to specify more of the details, and easier to specify them? Primarily, languages that do not require details!

As machines grow faster, more complex, and more powerful there is great danger that the communication gulf between man and machine will widen and deepen at the same time. As computers grow into systems, networks, and utilities they are going to have to learn to communicate on an everyday interchange basis with the man in the street, in the factory, warehouse, and office, in the library—with the people whose lives they both enrich and control. Communication has to be brought to their level.

To this end there would be a great deal of merit in the use of "natural language" for communication with computers. The rules for such a programming language would not have to be learned anew, but borrowed from the large, already existing body of knowledge possessed by the user. Natural language contains much more flexibility and freedom from syntax rigidity than any programming language yet proposed. Few experiences are so frustrating when working in an existing programming language as the collapse of an entire program for lack of a comma. Beginning programmers find the lack of permissible variation one of the best evidences of the extremely low intelligence of the computer—and with good reason. Fewer rules, fewer restrictions, and a general relaxation of syntax rigidity would permit not only more option in punctuation, but some option in the use of elements at all, and particularly much greater freedom in the sequence in which elements are required to appear.

The coming revolution in communicating with computers will mean richer vocabularies, a wider variety of symbols, graphics, and sounds, and an escape from the tyranny of the keypunch. Nowhere will the contrast be more startling than in the transition from monologue to dialogue that time sharing will bring. Working with a computer in the conversational mode will make it unnecessary to specify all the details in advance, to anticipate every eventuality. In the two-way interactive aspect of tomorrow's communication, the computer will have to recognize the completeness or incompleteness of information given, and ask for more when needed. As Douglas Ross put it, "We should not expect the machine to understand what we mean the first time."*

It will not be easy. No natural language, probably English least of all, is sufficiently logical that it can be completely deterministically described. Humans take years to learn it, and still more years to learn to use it effectively. Can we honestly expect to be able to write an algorithm that contains the English language? It is quite probable that heuristic procedures will prove a necessity in developing such processors, and that, further, we will probably not really succeed until we develop in the machine itself the ability to learn. Particularly when we include the requirement of dynamic responsiveness to changing human communications, the goals we are setting for our computer-processor combination are going to tax all the research in artificial intelligence we have so far dreamed of, and then some.

Does this mean, then, that the programming language characteristics

* Panel discussion, "The Next Step in Programming Languages," Association for Computing Machinery 20th National Conference, Cleveland, August, 1965.

we should like to see are so far fetched that they are impossible to achieve? Not at all. This movement toward natural language communication with computers is essential and inevitable. Many of the steps toward this goal are within our grasp in the late 1960's, and are already being taken.

15.2 COMPUTER SYSTEMS

We have discussed the systems concept in Chapters 4 and 7, and real-time closed-loop systems in Chapter 9. For the closed-loop system, the computer performs the functions of daily operations control as an instruction generator, and is a component in the loop with a physical process.

There are also closed-loop systems in the applications of computers to problem solving and information retrieval where man and the computer are the components. In these cases, man generates instructions or action requests for the computer, asks the computer to execute them as a processor, and then receives the results of the action taken by the computer.

For still other applications, the computer functions in the loop alternately as an instruction generator and as a processor in executing received instructions.

Many of these systems are becoming real time and will account for a large percentage of computer usage in the future. We shall discuss the computer component of these systems from the operational aspect. Such words and phrases as time sharing, multiprocessing, and multiprogramming are becoming important in describing the operations, and must be defined and included in our vocabulary. The computer component in a loop will not be identified as a single piece of hardware, but will be referred to as a computer system consisting of the remote input and output devices, communication channels, and auxiliary equipment. The computer system may also include more than one single computer.

Computer Systems as Instruction Generators

The computer system performs as an instruction generator when applied to controlled experiments in research, and to daily operations control in an industrial system for one or all of the principal loops shown in Figure 9.3-2. These closed-loop systems are becoming real time for a large number of controlled research experiments and industrial processes—particularly for continuous processes. Progress in the implementation of real-time systems in discrete processes on a full scale will depend largely on the advances in automation. Automatic machines require disciplined and well defined instruction that can be provided by computer systems. Assembly operations for most discrete processes currently require the manipulative skills of the human. For example, workers employed in an automobile assembly plant repeat assigned assembly operations with each automobile passing through the assembly line at the rate of one every few minutes, day after day. These assembly operations will eventually be performed by robot-like machines executing instructions provided by a computer system, just as automatic machine tools of today, such as lathes and drilling machines, execute instructions generated by computer systems.

Figure 15.2-1*a* shows a real-time closed-loop system containing a physical process and a computer system. This closed-loop system may be one of the four principal loops of an industry illustrated in Figure 9.3-2, or may be a composite of two or more of these single loops. Instructions generated by the computer system are sent to the remote output devices RO_1, RO_2, and RO_3 at the location of the physical process where they are received and executed. The observed data from the process enter the remote input devices RI_1, RI_2, and RI_3 at the location of the process and are received by the computer where they enter into the calculations of the next set of instructions. These data communication lines are generally *simplex,* that is, they carry data in one direction only.

An electronic stepping switch, here shown to have three positions, connects the remote terminals with the computer in sequence as it scans the three lines. The data are transmitted during the time the circuits are completed.

The computer system operates as an instruction generator when viewed as a closed loop with the process. How it operates as a system itself is the subject we now wish to discuss.

How a Computer System Operates as a Generator of Instructions. Figure 15.2-1*b* shows the computer system of Figure 15.2-1*a* consisting of two or more computers, a control processor CP and data processors DP_1, DP_2, ..., DP_n. Part of the memory storage is identified for the storage of input data DI_1, DI_2, and DI_3, and for the storage of output data DO_1, DO_2, and DO_3. Note that the diagram of the computer system is very similar to that of an industrial system which contains a computer system, when only the process P and daily operations control C_1 are considered, and when process flow is from right to left. The processing and control functions are, therefore, similar, and are described in Figure 15.2-2.

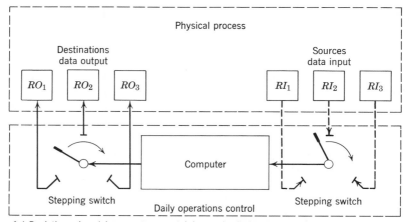

(*a*) Real–time closed–loop system containing a physical process and a compter system for generating instructions

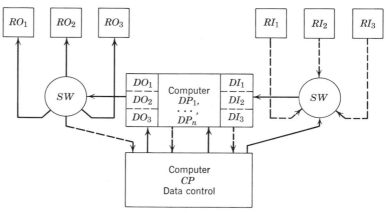

(*b*) Computer system of (*a*) consisting of two or more computers, *CP* and $DP_1, \cdots, DP_n$

Figure 15.2-1   Analysis of computer system for generating instructions.

Complex physical processes require complex computer systems for daily operations control when implemented as a real-time system. These complex computer systems require a *CP* computer and one or more *DP* computers. For the simpler physical processes, or when fewer than the four principal loops are to operate real time, the functions of data processing and control may be performed by a single computer in the computer system.

Figure 15.2-3*a* illustrates the division of time between data processing

Computers $DP_1, DP_2, \ldots, DP_n$ —— Processors

1. Perform the functions of data processing. If the computer system contains more than one processor, it can be controlled to operate as a multiprocessing system. *Definition:* A *multiprocessing system* is one that is capable of processing parts of a single program or related programs concurrently on two or more processors with common-memory storage.

Computer CP —— Control Processor

1. Data input control. Identifies and controls incoming data from remote terminals; performs editing and auditing, and stacks data in memory storage.
2. Process control. Schedules all work to be performed, giving consideration to priorities; monitors entire operation; takes appropriate action when undesirable or unusual circumstances arise.
3. Data output control. Identifies, edits, and stacks program results, dispatches outgoing data to the remote terminals, giving consideration to priorities.

Figure 15.2-2   General description of data processing and control functions.

and control for a single computer in a computer system. Data processing begins at time t_0 and continues until time t_1, when it is interrupted so that the computer can perform a function of control. The interrupt may have originated either externally or internally to the computer, and there are a number of each type.

An important external interrupt is one that is initiated at a remote input typewriter when new data are to be entered into the system. We may think of this interrupt as being similar to one we might experience when performing a manual calculation. If someone knocks at our door to announce that he has brought new data, we must stop calculating to accept these data for use in our later calculations.

An internal interrupt important in the application to continuous processes is one that is initiated by a time clock internal to the computer, signaling that it is time to stop data processing and start reading such quantities as temperature and process flows. This interrupt may also be similar to one we might experience when performing a manual calculation. In this case, an alarm clock rings to tell us we must stop calculating in order to take a new set of readings, which becomes new data.

If we do not wish the computer to reperform calculations, it must be capable of continuing the calculations at the point where it left off when the interrupt occurred. This is a requirement of any kind of interrupt when the computer must leave a data-processing program and switch to a control program, or to another program. To mark the place in the program, the interrupt causes the number in the program counter

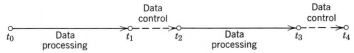

(a) Operations of data processing and control performed by a single computer in a computer system

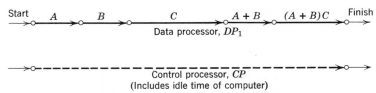

(b) Operations performed by a data processor in calculating the function $(A + B)C$ and the operations of control performed by a separate computer

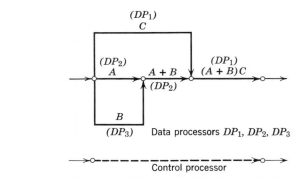

(c) Multiprocessing operations for calculating the function $(A + B)C$ using three data processors and a control processor

Figure 15.2-3   Diagrams for illustrating the operations of computer systems containing different numbers of computers.

(similar to the current address register of Figure 8.6-4) to be stored after the current program instruction is completed. When the control program has completed the servicing of the interrupt, the stored value is returned to the program counter and data processing is resumed at the place of interrupt.

When a separate control processor is used to perform the control functions, processing proceeds more smoothly. Figure 15.2-3*b* illustrates the operation of a *CP* computer and a single *DP* computer for calculating the function $(A + B)C$ where A, B, and C may each involve a number of program steps and may require data input from the remote terminals. Since data processing and control are performed on separate computers, data processing may proceed uninterrupted during the calculation of a function.

When two or more data processors are contained in the computer system, the scheduling operations of the control processor are more involved. For example, when three data processors DP_1, DP_2, and DP_3 are contained in the computer system, the multiprocessing feature can be used in calculating the function $(A + B)C$ as illustrated by Figure 15.2-3c. It is the job of the control processor to assign and schedule the jobs to be performed on each data processor with consideration given to their speeds and capabilities. Included may be a critical path analysis discussed in Chapter 5.

Computer Systems as Executors of Instructions

When a computer system functions as an executor of instructions, the instructions received as input are generated by man. There are two general applications of this type system: (1) problem solving, and (2) information retrieval. Both involve a closed-loop system, but now man is a part of the loop in that he supplies a set of instructions, and, on the basis of the response by the computer after executing those instructions, he initiates more instructions.

Time delays in this closed loop are often annoying, frustrating, and grossly inefficient—for the user and for the machine. We shall look briefly at three techniques that have been employed for coupling man into the system.

For small computers, the simplest connection is to give the man *direct access* to the machine (Figure 15.2-4a). Here, the man has two interfaces with the machine, one for input and one for receiving output. As compared with Figure 15.2-1, the data flow is reversed, for now instructions, represented by solid lines, are *to* the computer, and the results, shown by dashed lines, are returned *from* the computer.

Although this method of connection is highly efficient for the user, as the computer gets faster and more expensive, it becomes prohibitively costly to make the computer wait for the response of the human, and particularly for one user to replace another. As we saw in Chapter 6, the solution which was developed in the late 1950's for this problem was to interpose an additional buffer between the user and the machine, called an input-output stack, and let the computer operate on batched jobs under control of a monitor. As shown in Figure 15.2-4b, operating in the *batch processing* mode has the effect of greatly increasing the time delay in the loop between submission of instructions and return of

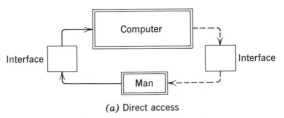

(a) Direct access

Each user preempts machine for duration of his job;
user efficiency high, machine efficiency low

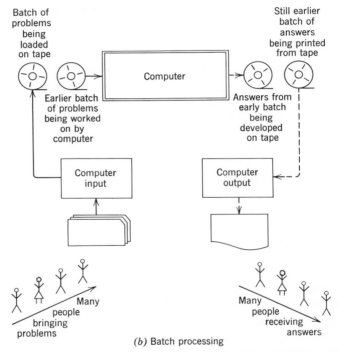

(b) Batch processing

Users wait while jobs are batched for input, processing, and output;
user efficiency low, machine efficiency high

Figure 15.2-4*a, b*   Analysis of man-machine systems where computers are executors
of instructions.

the results. It does, of course, enable the computer system itself to
be operated at a relatively high efficiency, since it is rarely allowed
to squeak to a stop and wait to be told what to do next.

The dissatisfaction with the overall delays presented to the human
user in this closed loop perpetuated the arguments between the small

direct-access machine and the large batch processing shop for nearly a decade, until, in the middle 1960's, a third approach became technically feasible. With the increase in speed of processing units, the lowering of cost for large mass-storage devices, and the development of multi-processing techniques and equipment, it became possible to share a large computer system simultaneously among many different users. This mode of operation is called *time sharing*. A time-sharing system may be defined as one that serves more than one user concurrently through separate input-output interfaces by alternating its attention from one to another. If this is done rapidly enough, the computer returns to each user with such negligible delay that the user is unaware of the use of the computer by others. He receives the impression that he has the entire computer to himself. In this case the computer system is indeed operating in real time.

Since the user receives such rapid and frequent response, and since he is not kicked off the machine each time he receives a response, it now becomes feasible to decrease the size of the information unit involved in each communication. For example, in developing a FOR-TRAN program, it is no longer necessary to compile an entire program before getting back diagnostic comments from the processor; it is now possible to treat each statement as a unit and have the processor return diagnostic comments line by line as the user enters it. Indeed, since the user stays coupled to machine and the machine can accumulate and retain his input until instructed to output it, file it, or destroy it, the user can make corrections as he goes, receiving comments on the internal completeness and correctness of each statement, on the consistency of this statement in the light of the preceding portion of the program, and even on the result of trying to execute any selected portion of the program. This mode of operation, called the *conversational mode,* offers tremendous advantages to the user, as is obvious in comparison with the process of waiting hours or even days for the return of the computer response under the batch processing mode.

How the Time-Sharing System Operates. Figure 15.2-4*c* shows that time sharing can take sufficient advantage of the relatively small cost of human speed I/O terminals to scatter them widely at locations conven-ient to the users, and connect them by relatively inexpensive communi-cation lines, such as telephone connections, to the central computing system. Instructions generated by a user at one of the remote terminals may be in the form of new program instructions, new data together with a request that they be processed using a stored program, or a request to find and present information in storage.

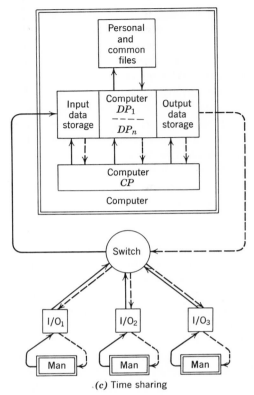

(c) Time sharing

Computer system divides attention among multiple users;
user efficiency very high, machine efficiency fair

Figure 15.2-4c   Analyses of man-machine systems where computers are executors of instructions.

Note that if a single communication line is used between the interface and the data switching unit, it must be capable of sending data in either direction, and such a line is called a *half-duplex line*. If the communication channel is capable of transmitting data in two directions simultaneously, a *full-duplex line* is used, usually composed of two simplex lines.

In a time-sharing system the data-processing and control functions are essentially the same as in an instruction generating system; observe the similarity between the computer portions of Figure 15.2-1 and Figure 15.2-4c. When the control and processing functions are performed by a single computer, computing time is shared between these two functions by interrupting the processing when a control function is to be performed (Figure 15.2-3a) for the instruction generating system. A system used to serve a large number of users through complex interface devices, such as light pens and graphical display units, requires complex control, particularly if it is to operate on a real-time basis, and it becomes practically essential to have a separate control processor. In either case, since the user is the instruction generator, he initiates the interrupts for reading data, which are external interrupts, and interrupt servicing is a control function.

Some timing problems may appear. Once a program has been entered, compiled, and accepted, and enters the execution phase, it may call for fairly extended periods of computation. If the processing of such a program is allowed to continue until finished without interruption, other users may have to wait a long time for responses, and the delay becomes highly objectionable. One of these other users, for instance, may have entered an instruction calling for an extremely simple action, and he naturally expects a fairly quick response. To avoid this frustration, and to accomplish its objective of providing real-time service to the largest number of users, the control processor is given the authority to interrupt the processing of any of the data processors DP_1 after a specified length of time.

Figure 15.2-5 demonstrates the division of processing among three users with an interruption in processing occurring if it is not completed in a period of 0.5 second. The system is programmed to process data in the sequence DI_1, DI_2, DI_3. Processing for data DI_1 from user 1 is completed in 0.2 second, and processing of data DI_2 from user 2 is started. It is not completed, however, by the end of 0.5 second, so an interrupt occurs in order to process data DI_3 of waiting user 3. When this is completed in only 0.3 second, the control processor checks user 1, but since it finds no request waiting, it resumes work on the processing for user 2, and this time completes it in 0.2 second.

Note that any processor of the system must be capable of interrupting execution of any program before completion, turning to another or many other programs, and at a later time returning to the execution of

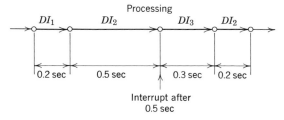

Figure 15.2-5   Division of processing between three users showing interruption of processing to service a waiting user.

the original program. A system with this operating feature is called a *multiprogramming* system.

Since there are competing demands of both time and memory space, very sophisticated control programs are necessary to handle this "time slicing." When a processor is forced to interrupt a program, it may leave that program in core memory and return to it when its time comes next, or, if the room is needed, it may be necessary to return that interrupted program to disk or drum auxiliary memory. When it is next brought into core memory for processing, it will very likely have to be assigned a different section of memory, so that all addresses will be different. Programs must be compiled and loaded in "relocatable" form, and the whole problem of "re-entrant" coding is extremely complex.

It is not hard to see why the software enabling a time-sharing computing system to operate efficiently is at least as complicated and expensive as the hardware, and in fact is rapidly becoming the largest part of the cost of a modern computing system.

Computer Systems as Combined Generators and Executors of Instructions

A computer system performing either as an executor or generator of instructions may also have a minimum of the features of the other type. An example is in the application of a computer system to daily operations control. The system is predominantly an instruction generator, but the application requires that information be retrieved from the system, i.e., that it also executes instructions. These real-time systems must always have human monitors who need information from the system. Also, managers like to be able to obtain certain business information, such as the amount of inventory of a product, and may desire to have remote terminals in their offices for entering requests and receiving results.

In the application of computer systems to problem solving, the system is predominantly an executor of instructions, but, with a minimum of the features for generating instructions, it can perform its predominating role more effectively. For example, a system that generates diagnostics for correcting programming errors is very helpful in this first stage of problem solving, as you may have found. These are, in effect, instructions generated by the computer, requesting the user to correct his program.

For both examples, the added features are easily incorporated in the controls of a system relative to an application we are about to discuss.

Knowledge Transfer Systems. There is an important application of computer systems of the future where these systems perform dual roles as generators and executors of instructions, and where the requirements are very demanding. The application is multiple closed-loop systems, containing as components computer systems and people, and, in some cases, man's contrivances, and plant and animal organisms. "Synnoetics"* is the science dealing with the intelligent properties of these composite systems. A composite system whose principal function is to transfer knowledge, as in teaching, will be called a "knowledge transfer system."

Unless knowledge can be transferred from one generation to the next more effectively and efficiently, it would appear that acquisition of new knowledge would ultimately come to a halt, and increasing the degree of specialization to delay the situation can have undesirable effects. If the total lifetime of an individual must be spent in learning an established body of facts, no time is left to explore and add new facts. Increased specialization can reduce the learning time required of an individual, but research requiring the association and relationships of facts from so many areas of specialization may be seriously hampered. Also, lack of common knowledge and mutual interest among very specialized groups of people does not foster a compatible and unified society.

We shall study a knowledge transfer system whose components are the computer system and one or more learning subjects, and may also include laboratory equipment such as that used in chemistry and physics. First, however, it is desirable to analyze the operations and limitations of the conventional method of teaching.

Figure 15.2-6a shows a teacher and a group of students in a classroom-type learning process. For the closed loop a, information for the students is generated by the teacher, and includes class instructions, problem assignments, and examination questions. This information flow is identified by the solid arrow. The dashed arrow describes the flow of information from the students to the teacher. This information consists of the student's responses and answers to the teacher's questions.

The second closed loop b also provides for communication between the class and teacher, and is necessary for a good teaching system. In this case, questions are asked by the students and are received by the teacher over the channel identified by the solid arrow. Replies to these questions are received by the students over the channel identified by the dashed arrow.

Communications for the closed loop b for the conventional method of teaching are especially limited, and information flow for the system as a whole has many interruptions and delays. The tutor-student method is generally considered desirable for improving conditions, but education

---

* "Synnoetics" was coined and defined by Dr. L. Fein, 1962.

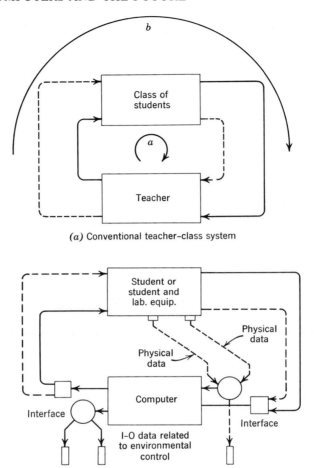

(a) Conventional teacher–class system

(b) Knowledge transfer system with computer system as tutor

Figure 15.2-6   Analysis of computer systems as combined generators and executors of instructions.

becomes much too costly, and, even assuming qualified tutors could be trained, the drain of human effort from the economy would reduce the standard of living below an acceptable level.

A computer system performing the functions of a tutor in the teaching of standard courses can overcome some of the limitations of the conventional teaching system, and may even be superior to a human tutor. It can get to "know" the student better, and can gather and analyze a great deal of data, not only on the factual knowledge he possesses, but on his mistakes, his difficulties, and his methods of approaching a problem. In application to medicine, the computer operating on-line with a patient has often been found to be more capable than the human in obtaining data and establishing a diagnosis. Also, in application to psychology, a computer monitoring a human subject can very rapidly evaluate reactions and responses. Thus, as our understanding in these fields increases, the employment of a computer system as a tutor can make possible the observation and analysis of more physiological and psychological data for helping a student in a learning experience than can be obtained with a human tutor, and the help can be given at the time it is needed.

With the advancing technology in man-machine interfaces, conversation between the student and the computer can be in a natural manner. Conversation can be in the form of spoken language and visual arts (written language, drawings, and photographs).

For teaching involving laboratory experiments, the laboratory equipment can contain devices for reading experimental data into the computer, and the student can be guided by the computer to a successful conclusion of the experiment. For example, in a chemistry laboratory course, thermocouples may be attached to the test tubes and temperatures of chemical reactions read directly into the computer. From these and other observed data, the actions taken by the student can be determined by the computer, which can then direct the student in the next step of the experimental learning experience, and at the same time can present theoretical explanations.

Environmental conditions such as room temperature, humidity, and lighting can be controlled on an individual basis if these variables are significant. This part of the operation is identical to that of process control, and introduces still a third loop in which the computer system is a component.

In addition, learning is much more convenient for the individual, not requiring fixed schedules at single established locations. An ultimate knowledge transfer system, involving an interconnected network of many individual systems, would permit a student to continue his education as he traveled across the country, having access to terminals at many locations en route. Complete records of his progress would be maintained at all times.

How the Computer System Operates. From the discussion, we see that this third type of computer system, as a component of a knowledge transfer system, has the combined requirements of the first two types. Figure 15.2-6*b* shows the block diagram of a knowledge transfer system where the teacher in the conventional system of Figure 15.2-6*a* is replaced with a computer system performing as a tutor. A second block represents a single student, or a student and laboratory equipment which he may be using during the learning experience. The knowledge transfer system also shows the two loops indicating the dual functions of generation and execution performed by the computer system. Communication channels are also shown for the transmission of physical data which are obtained from the laboratory equipment and/or from the student, such as pulse rate and skin resistance. Finally, at the bottom of the figure are shown the communication lines and terminals related to the control of environment.

In actual practice, a computer system serves more than one student at a time in a time-sharing mode of operation, which can not only greatly improve the economy of the operation, but may also be capable of providing competition between two or more students in a learning experience.

The computer system is shown to contain a single computer performing both the data processing and control functions. Because of the complexity of controls, a separate control computer will be desirable as these systems are more fully developed and more of the desirable operating features are incorporated. Since multiprocessing increases the complexity of controls, it is not likely that more than one data processor will be used in a system. However, multiprogramming is a desirable feature.

Summary of Operating Features of Each of the Three Types of Systems

Figure 15.2-2 lists the data-processing and control functions common to all three types of computer systems. From the discussions of the three systems and from what we have learned in other chapters, we may summarize the operating features for each of the three types. They make a difference in the way the control and processing functions are accomplished.

Computer Systems as Generators of Instructions. Applied to controlled experimental research and to process control, in which a physical process is a component in the closed loop.

(1) The programs executed are stored programs, located in common addressable memory, and executed repeatedly.

(2) The stored programs are related; i.e., a program for producing a given output may require data from a number of input terminals, and may require the results calculated by other stored programs.

(3) The input terminals may not be at the same physical locations as the output terminals, and the communication lines are usually simplex.

Definition: A *simplex* line is a single line that transmits data in one direction.

(4) Interrupts for entering data into the computer may be internal or external to the computer.

Computer Systems as Executors of Instructions. Applied to problem solving and to information retrieval systems in which man is a component of the closed loop.

(1) Time sharing promises to combine many of the advantages of the 2 older methods of coupling man to the machine, direct access and batch processing.

> (a) *Direct Access:* Each user preempts the machine for the duration of his job.
> User efficiency high
> Machine efficiency low
> (b) *Batch Processing:* Users wait while jobs are batched for processing and output.
> User efficiency low
> Machine efficiency high
> (c) *Time Sharing:* Computer system divides attention among multiple users.
> User efficiency high
> Machine efficiency fairly high

Definition: A *time-sharing system* is one that serves more than one user concurrently through separate I/O interfaces by alternating its attention from one to another.

(2) Some programs (called utility programs) and some files are stored in common addressable storage and can be used by any user in the processing of his own requests and data.

(3) New problem programs and requests are entered at various times at various terminals. They are generally unrelated, and a program being executed for a user usually requires only the data entered at that user's terminal, and returns responses only to that terminal. Users at different terminals can communicate, however, and share data and programs.

(4) To provide real-time services to the largest number of users, the computer system is made a multiprogramming system.

Definition: A *multiprogramming system* is one that is capable of terminating the execution of a program before completion for the purpose of executing a different program and, at a later time, can be made to resume the execution of that program.

(5) An input and an output terminal exist at the same location; the two functions may be combined in an integrated device such as a tele-typewriter. The communication lines are either half-duplex or full-duplex.

Definition: A *half-duplex* line is a single line that transmits data in either direction.

Definition: A *full-duplex* line consists of two simplex lines, and permits transmission of data in both directions concurrently.

(6) Interrupts for reading data into the system are initiated at the terminals.

Computer Systems as Combined Generators and Executors of Instructions. Applied to knowledge transfer systems with a student as a component of the closed loop.

(1) To reduce the complexity of controls, a single data processor is used; i.e., multiprocessing is not employed.

(2) The programs executed are stored programs, and are used repeatedly. (An exception is the teaching of programming.)

(3) Programs require data from a single student terminal for execution.

(4) The systems are time-sharing systems.

(5) The systems are multiprogramming systems.

(6) Input and output terminals of a wide variety exist in the immediate area of the student, and the communication lines may be of all three types.

(7) Only the student at a terminal sending data receives the results, i.e., teaching is on an individual basis. (Exceptions involve the interaction between two or more students in a cooperative or competitive learning situation.)

(8) Interrupts are either internal or external.

Large Networks of Computer Systems

It is likely that in the future more and more data processing will be done by terminals connected into computer systems, and computer systems will be interconnected to form networks stretching over cities, states, and regions, even spanning continents and oceans. The types of information interchange handled by these networks include at least three classes of operations: (1) solving problems in the multiprocessing mode of operation, (2) information exchange for business and military operations and for library type information retrieval, and (3) instructional activities such as knowledge transfer systems.

Schools and universities will be important centers for all three types of information handling. Not only can the use of prepared learning materials under control of the computer-tutor augment traditional educational techniques (some see the computer virtually replacing the teacher in the classroom situation), but in the information retrieval usage new scientific information may be entered at any location and be instantly available to other workers at other locations. Libraries need not duplicate one another; a single reference collection can serve all.

Use of networks of computer systems offers many advantages. To name four: (1) economies of scale in computing power and capacity, (2) access by any user to the largest computer in the system, (3) greater reliability and uninterrupted service, (4) greater utilization of computing equipment.

On the first point, it has been shown to be roughly true over the past fifteen years that the computing power (speed, capacity, and throughput) of computing equipment goes up approximately as the square of the price. In other words, if you traded in a computer which rented for $2000 a month for one costing $20,000, the new computer would be about one hundred times as fast. The number of computations per dollar would go up by a factor of about ten.

Along with the decreased cost to each user is the increased capacity that comes with a larger computing system: the capability of handling larger programs, with larger data sets; the availability of a greater variety of programming languages and packaged programs; and the accessibility of large data files and records.

On the national scale, a properly established network can enable the computer systems in one area where the demand is low at a given time to supply capacity for solving problems to another area of peak demand. The three hour time difference across the United States, for instance, results in continuous shifting of the areas of high demand for electric power to the west as the daily activities wax and wane. The establishment of regional and national networks by the electric power utilities may serve to point the way towards similar establishment of regional and even global networks of computer systems in the future.

15.3 COMPUTERS AND YOU

Computers as a Utility

The growth in sophistication and power of computers, and the improvements in techniques for coupling them into systems and networks, seem to point toward the emergence of a new concept. The computer is becoming a public utility. Like transportation, water, and electric power, the provision of computing power is a job for a large complex supplier, and his customers represent large segments of the public as a whole. For the great majority of users it makes much more sense for the individual or group needing electricity or computing to tap into the supply, and consume what they need, rather than maintain expensive and less adequate independent generators of either type. Computing for many years has been a commodity to be sold, but now it is simpler to supply it to the doors and desks of people who need it, rather than make them come to the computer.

Consider the growth of several of the smaller information systems we have studied in this book. The airline reservation system, the stock exchange reporting service, the bank teller, the catalog order desk, and the shipping department have all seen these systems grow through three phases: (1) to keep records, for subsequent reports and analysis, (2) to answer inquiries in real time as to the current status, and (3) to change the status by entering transactions in real time as well. It does not take much imagination to picture this expansion beyond the confines of one company, one industry, or one nation. Travelers commonly need more than one carrier for different legs of a trip, and often in more than one country; the transactions of many brokers touch the stock exchange and its quotations; checks cashed at one bank alter the balance accounts at many others, and so on. There are those who predict the emergence of a vast computer-based national credit system, in which neither cash nor checks are needed, but each purchase is accomplished by instantaneous transfer of funds from one account to another. Others hold that the loss of privacy in such a system is too frightening to be tolerated; government access to all financial transactions for tax purposes (or for other reasons) is more than they would like to see.

To a school or university the concept of a local computer utility has a great deal to offer. Not only does it offer the services of high-speed data processing for the administrative operations of the school—payrolls, attendance, grades, and records; not only does it bring instantaneous access and powerful search techniques to the assistance of would-be gleaners from the library; not only does it make available the powerful tutoring capabilities of the knowledge transfer systems for instructional purposes; but it very specifically makes information processing so cheap and so readily available that every student can and should be given training in it and access to it. In the school with the computer utility, computing service will be supplied to the entire student body and faculty on just as free a basis as the library or electric power is today.

Not only on the campus. In the market place, in the political arena, in government operations and economic enterprises, in the daily life of every man, we see the increasing impact of the computer. The fantastic growth of information processing, the breadth of its power, and the scope of its application point to its emergence as a true public utility in the society of tomorrow.

Computers and Individuality

Many people have become increasingly concerned about the dehumanizing effects computers will have in our society. An analysis will be made to establish that these fears are unfounded and that, if computers are applied with the proper objectives in mind, they can have a humanizing influence, and much of the individuality we lost before computers came to the scene can be restored.

The Loss of Individuality in Our Civilization through Standardization. We have sacrificed individuality and have concerned ourselves with the interest of the human average in order to have the high social development we have today. The social system operates on the principle that many more commodities and services can be made available if they are standardized, and if groups with specialized training devote large portions of their time toward the system. Any individual must contribute to the providing of commodities and services in the interest of the average if he is to benefit from this civilization.

In a competitive economy, standards are established to satisfy the largest number of people who might be involved, and never with the intent of satisfying any one individual. These standards are in reference to costs, dimensions, styles, colors, composition, performance, quality, and reliability and are fixed over a period of time. Automobiles, prepared foods, clothing, and consumer goods in general, almost without exception, are standardized by business and also by government, when necessary in the public interest. There are standard educational courses and degrees, insurance policies, retirement care and banking—all established for the average person and made available to anyone who satisfies the specified conditions. Even television and radio programs, musical compositions, and novels are written to please the largest number of people in particular groups.

Our highly developed society requires a complex governing system which functions in the interest of the average. Rules, laws, and policies are designed by our government and by any group with which we may be associated. They are designed for some well-defined set of conditions, and seldom can exceptions be made or all contributing factors be considered in a given case.

Effect of Standardization on the Individual as a Recipient of the Benefits of Society. The fact is that not a single person is average or is subject to average conditions, so that of all the commodities and services available in our society and of all the rules of conduct, there are not likely to be many that are exactly as we would like them to be or that satisfy our exact requirements. An individual may like to be considered average or to be like other people in some cases, but in other cases he likes to be respected as an individual and to have some identity apart from the masses in those things that society provides.

If an individual is different from the average and tries to satisfy his own tastes and conditions, and to express his talents, he is severely handicapped. Commodities of special design, such as automobiles and custom-made clothes, are costly, and these can be acquired only at the sacrifice of other things. A student with an intelligence quotient below 70 or above 130 may find the standard school system rather trying, and to attend a special school or to hire a tutor may be out of the question. For other individuals, unusual circumstances and conditions may make it impossible to purchase insurance. Red lights and traffic regulations do not permit individual consideration based on weather or traffic conditions.

The Effect of Standardization on the Individual as a Contributor to Society. When an individual functions as a contributor to the system, his success depends largely on how well he has adapted to the average in his performance and in his thinking. He must concern himself with the average person and conditions in providing standard commodities and services, and in forming policies and rules. He must be concerned with the average in designing automobiles, insurance policies, educational courses, and policies. He must make the standard product on standard machines, teach the standard educational course to the average student in the class, learn to sell the standard product to the average customer, and enforce the standard rules based on fixed conditions. In general, the individual as a contributor is primarily concerned with the interest of the average, and this concern must be very great if he is to achieve success.

A Return of Individuality through the Use of Computers. We shall now investigate the various ways computers can help to restore much of the individuality we have lost, and to increase our concern for the individual.

Computermation, when integrated with automation, can be an important factor in regaining individuality through a reduction in standardization and an increase in custom commodities and services. To determine how this can be accomplished, we shall consider an example of automation and computermation applied to the manufacture of ladies' dresses.

There are two manufacturers of ladies' dresses. The one called manufacturer S makes dresses in large quantities in standard sizes, styles, and materials. The other, manufacturer C, specializes in custom-made dresses of dimensions, style, and materials to suit the individual. Manufacturer S has implemented the methods of automation and computermation to meet the requirements for large quantity production. He sells directly to the customer and keeps a product inventory so that he can give immediate delivery. The average dress costs $40 to make, and he has been able to hold this cost constant for the several years since the new methods were implemented.

Manufacturer C begins a program to implement the methods of automation and computermation about the same time as S does, but to meet his more demanding requirements for a job-type production, the time of implementation takes longer and is completed after a number of phases in, say, two years. After completion, his computer system accepts as input data the dimensions, style, and type material which are provided by the customer. Since a custom-made dress is for a particular person, the number of given dimensions is much larger than the number specified by a customer when purchasing a standard dress from S. Furthermore, the selection of styles and materials is greater.

The computer system generates the process instructions for making the dress, and they are sent directly to the shop by wire transmission. The instructions include those for adjusting the machines for cutting cloth according to the dimensions specified by the customer.

Before the beginning of the implementation period, the cost of making an average custom dress might have been $80 as compared to $40 for the standard dress made by manufacturer S. The $40 difference is mainly in labor costs required in the making of new dress patterns or drawings for each dress, and in the special set-up work in the processing operations.

At the end of the period of implementation, we would expect that the cost to make the custom dress would decrease to an amount approaching that of the standard dress as shown by the plots of cost versus time in Figure 15.3-1. If we assume that the need for manual drawings and manual effort in special set-up work is eliminated after implementation of the new methods, the cost of making a dress in a job-type operation should nearly equal that cost for a mass-production type operation. The additional cost that results in data processing for the design of each custom dress might be offset by the cost of inventory and control required in the manufacture of the standard dress.

Delivery time of the custom dress might have been reduced from perhaps a week to less than a day, while delivery of the standard dress is immediate if the customer selects a dress from stock. In this respect, Manufacturer S can still give better service than can C. But the advan-

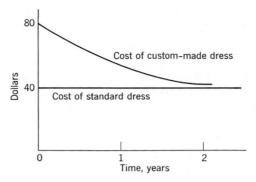

Figure 15.3-1   Difference in costs of custom and standard commodity reduced through computermation and automation.

tages to the customer in obtaining custom fit, as well as complete choice of style and color combinations, will more than outweigh this advantage.

We would expect that before the difference in cost and delivery of the standard and custom dresses reached a minimum, S would begin losing business to C. We would also expect that S would begin modifying his operations so that he too could make custom dresses.

By the mid 1960's, technological advances appeared in man-computer interfaces which may be used to further the advances of custom-type operations from the manner just described. Figure 15.3-2 shows an interface for communicating information in the form of drawings. Designs, such as dress designs, made by an individual with the aid of a computer, may be drawn on the face of a scope or screen using a special pen. This graphic interface permits the individual to work on all views of a design just as if he worked with a physical model and had access to all sides. What is drawn in one view is incorporated into other views by the computer. The computer may also check the theoretical performance with each step of the design when required. After the design is finished to the satisfaction of the individual, it is read by the computer which may then generate instructions for making the commodity.

There is also a method for transmitting information through the telephone system, over any distance, in the form of written words, drawings, and photographs. The time of transmission of information on a sheet $8\frac{1}{2} \times 11$ inches is several minutes, and an exact duplicate of the original is received.

The time may come when interfaces similar to these just described are in many homes, or are in immediately accessible locations. With the dial-

Figure 15.3-2   Interface for communicating information in the forms of drawings. (Courtesy of the IBM Corp.)

ing of a telephone number, an individual can be interfaced with many different computer systems—each serving a different purpose. Space satellites and lasers will play an important role in providing the expanded and advanced requirements in communications. Shopping for commodities for which there is a wide selection of standard designs may be done in the home through the use of these interfaces in such a way that seeing the actual commodity offers no advantage.

The change to custom-type operations through the use of computer-mation applies to commodities and services in general. It is possible to design custom life and health insurance and retirement systems if a computer program is established that considers as variables the many conditions that affect a design. Computer systems operating as generators and executors of instructions can bring about custom teaching thus enabling the human teacher to spend his time working with students on an individual basis on creative projects. Computer systems applied to traffic control can treat the many driving conditions as variables, and can set the rules for speed and the timing of lights to meet current conditions.

Future Outlook for Custom Commodities and Services through Computermation

We have established that the implementation of the methods of computermation and automation can decrease standardization and increase custom commodities and services, but we do not know if the number of implementations will be large enough to have a significant effect. The number will depend on the economic factors which we shall now explore.

The cost of providing a commodity or service using the new methods may currently be much greater than the cost using the old, which involves relatively large amounts of labor. The difference in these two costs decreases with time, until a point is reached when the new methods can be justified and the rising cost of the commodity or service resulting from rising salaries and wages is halted. Consider for analysis a particular commodity, where the difference in costs between the old and new methods is large at the present time. The commodity is currently produced by the old methods at a cost, say, of $40. The change in cost is assumed to have been $+3\%$ per year due, mainly, to the regular increases in salaries and wages. If the per cent change is constant, future costs may be calculated and plotted as shown by curve (*a*) of Figure 15.3-3, where the projections are made over the next twenty years.

An analysis is made to determine the current cost of producing the commodity using the latest equipment and methods of computermation and automation, and the cost is found to be, say, $80, which is twice the cost of the old method. Therefore, it would be very unreasonable to implement the new methods at this time, but let us investigate the possibility for the future.

Further analysis shows that over the past several years the cost to produce the commodity with new equipment and methods available at the time has been changing -4% per year due, mainly, to the decreasing

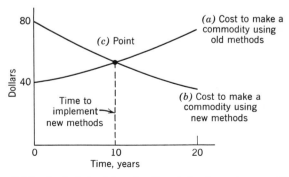

Figure 15.3-3   Analysis to determine time to implement new methods.

costs and improvements in equipment and methods. If this percentage change in costs is assumed to remain constant, future costs may be calculated and plotted as shown by curve (*b*) of Figure 15.3-3. The point of intersection of curves (*a*) and (*b*) then establishes the time the methods of computermation and automation should be implemented, which is ten years from the current date. If implementation occurs, the cost of the commodity rises along curve (*a*) to point (*c*) and then decreases with time, following curve (*b*).

These conditions of changing costs, and also the cost difference at any given time, will vary with the commodity and service. In our example, these $+3$ and -4% changes in costs for the old and new methods may be considered typical values for many commodities and services for the period 1960 to 1965. For any commodity or service under consideration, we can say that implementation of the methods will probably take place in the future, if at any given time

$$c_o - c_n \text{ is positive}$$

where c_o and c_n, respectively, are the per cent changes in costs for providing a commodity or service by the old and new methods. For our rising standard of living, wages have been increasing faster than the prices of commodities and services, and this condition favors a positive value of $c_o - c_n$. Also, since it is the use of new methods that produces a rising standard of living, any one implementation reflects changes of conditions throughout the total social system which make other implementations of the new methods more favorable.

We conclude that a large number of implementations of computermation and automation are likely to occur, over a long period, making it possible to provide many custom commodities and services.

Computers to Personalize Domestic Services. Computers can play a much greater part in our personal lives in the future than has already been demonstrated. They can appear as distinct devices in the home separate from any utility or business system with which we may choose to communicate. They may be integrated into consumer commodities, performing as instruction generators in these miniature process loops. They may also appear as small separate devices performing the data-processing operations related to business matters of the home. What are the indicators that lead one to believe this might take place, and how might miniature computer systems perform to personalize domestic services?

Perhaps the history of energy conversion has significance as an indicator of what will happen in computing. Beginning, say, in 1900, there was a very limited range of sizes of energy conversion equipment. The sizes were intermediate compared to those of today, and the equipment was installed in industry. As time went by, the range of available sizes increased. The largest sizes became larger with time, and the smallest sizes became smaller. The large sizes of electric generators have been interconnected by power lines to form larger and larger power networks, as was previously discussed in relationship to networks of computer systems.

A time was reached when the smallest of energy conversion equipment became integrated with consumer commodities and entered our homes. Today we have a 300-horsepower gasoline motor in the automobile, and a 2-horsepower motor in the lawnmower; we have a 1 horsepower electric motor in the workshop, and a very small fraction of a horsepower motor in the electric razor and the toothbrush.

For the short time that computers have been with us, they have exhibited the same range of available sizes as energy conversion equipment did in the early years of its existence. In view of the most recent trends in technology and research, there is every indication that this parallel will continue to exist, and that the computer, too, will appear as a distinct device in the home, and will be integrated into consumer commodities.

How can a computer system perform as an integral part of a consumer product to personalize domestic operations? A number of consumer commodities, such as washing machines and stoves, can be considered miniature processors, and the housewife performs the dual role of instruction generator and executor of instructions in the operation of these devices. If the methods of computermation and automation can be implemented in large industrial processes, there is no reason why they cannot be implemented in these relatively simple processes. A small computer system integrated into the product can be programmed to treat many more conditions as variables than the housewife, and can alter control instructions more frequently to produce an output of the exact specifications of the housewife.

There are several ways in which the computer program may be established for these miniature systems. The housewife may choose to write her own, or the manufacturer may supply the program. In the latter case, the data specifying the output would be established by the housewife and entered into the computer. Still another interesting way is for the computer to "learn" how to perform the operations the human performs and to then take over the task. Consider, for example, a power lawnmower that contains a computer system. The supplier of the mower also supplies a built-in learning program. While the individual mows the lawn for the first time in the conventional way, the computer system measures and stores the values of the conditions necessary to mow the lawn and takes over the operations for all subsequent mowings. It uses the stored values of conditions as reference, and adjusts the steering and speed so that the new values match as nearly as they can the stored values.

We conclude that not only is it likely that we will have custom commodities, but that some of these will probably be able to condition themselves on a continuous basis to perform personalized domestic services.

15.4   PERSPECTIVE

It is time to sit back, shut our eyes, and reflect. What, if anything, have we learned about computers in the past fifteen chapters? For one thing, we have learned to mistrust the popular accounts in the newspaper headlines about computers. Encouraged by sensational stories about giant brains and machines that think, the general public has come to regard the computer as twentieth-century magic—all for want of a few simple facts.

If you have studied the text, programmed a number of problems, and experienced the frustrations and satisfactions of actually working with a computer, you are no longer to be identified with the uninformed audience when subjects such as information processing, artificial intelligence, information retrieval, data communications, and automated factories are mentioned. You have learned that a computer has extremely low intelligence, but extremely fast, accurate, and complex powers for getting things done when instructed in the right fashion. Properly applied, and intelligently controlled, the computer can be a slave whose usefulness to society surpasses anything yet seen on this earth. It is bringing about a veritable second industrial revolution.

You should have a keen feeling for the difficulties and dangers in putting computers to work. If you have been through the process of checking out programs for obscure logical errors in the many possible paths the computer may take in executing a program, you will understand some of the potential dangers that lie ahead when a highly developed society relies on computers controlled by enormously large networks of interrelated programs. This danger can be demonstrated by the easily overlooked error in the program of Figure 3.5-1, for the condition of "branch if $F = 0$," treated in Problems 3.5-3 to 3.5-5. A completely automated and computermated factory might make enough tin cans to fill the oceans, or turn out cans with neither tops nor bottoms, if a similar error condition were overlooked and we assumed 100% reliability of the factory. A nation highly dependent on computers in decisions of war might face a probability of complete accidental annihilation unless proper measures were taken in program design to prevent these unlikely situations.

There is no question that computers will bring about tremendous social changes, making more goods available to more people, cheaper, and at the same time restoring individuality and producing a humanizing effect. The automated and computermated factories will provide us with vast amounts and varieties of commodities and services to satisfy our individual wants and conditions. Computers will do this not by running our lives, but by spreading underneath the structure of society, supporting, strengthening, and pushing it onward. They will take the individual out of social isolation, where he performs monotonous, mundane tasks, and put him in personal contact and communion with vast numbers of individuals all over the world (or the universe), and in an environment full of rewarding sensory experiences. They will free man to use his conscious, creative brain to enrich his own life and that of all society.

Who can say where it will end?

PROBLEM 15.2-1   "Multiprocessing"

A function $A(B + C)/D$ is to be calculated by a computer system containing three data processors I, II, and III, and a control computer. The function was calculated on processor I and the following values of time were required to perform the calculating jobs.

Calculating Job	Time, Minutes
A	1
B	1
C	$\frac{1}{2}$
$B + C$	$\frac{1}{2}$
$A(B + C)$	1
D	2
$(A(B + C))/D$	$\frac{1}{2}$

WANTED

(A) Draw a graph for calculating the function.

(B) If processors II and III have the same speed as I, determine the critical path and the time to calculate the function.

(C) If processor II is two times faster than processor I, and III is three times faster than I, determine the assignment of calculating jobs to be given to the control computer to give the shortest time to calculate the function. What is the value of this shortest time?

PROBLEM 15.3-1   "An Interesting Effect of Computers"

An analysis was made in Section 15.3 to determine if implementations of the methods of computermation and automation in providing commodities and services would be likely to occur. Using the same type of analysis, demonstrate how repair of commodities will be affected when the commodities are produced using these new methods. Consider some commodity, such as a pair of shoes. Assume:

(1) the purchase price remains constant with time, and is $20.00

(2) the current cost of repair is $10.00, and because of increasing labor costs will change +4% per year.

WANTED

(A) Discuss why, in general, these assumptions are reasonable.

(B) Show a plot similar to that of Figure 15.3-3 and determine how long it will be before repairs will no longer be made.

Input-Output with Free Format

Unquestionably, the single most complicated statement in FOR-TRAN is the FORMAT statement. That is why in Chapter 2 we reduce format to the barest minimum necessary to get data into and out of the computer, and postpone any more elaborate discussion until Chapter 6, Further FORTRAN.

A few FORTRAN and FORTRAN-like systems have recognized the desirability of a still simpler procedure, and provide a "free format" option as well. Designed primarily to ease the burden for the beginning programmer, these systems often seem to have much to offer the experienced programmer too. If you have access to such a system, what you have to learn right now can be drastically cut down. Even though there is some variation in the form of the input-output statement used in different systems, in any of them the amount of detail and complexity that the programmer has to specify is greatly reduced.

FORGO for the IBM 1620 is based on FORTRAN II, which is the FORTRAN described in this book. In Fortran II, an input statement has the form

$$READ \ n, \quad List*$$

As is described in Section 2.2, the n is the statement number associated with a FORMAT statement, and such a FORMAT statement must also

*Or READ TAPE, or READ MAGNETIC TAPE, or FETCH DISK, or various other commands describing input from a particular device.

be included to describe in complete detail the location and nature of the data being read. In FORGO free format, this statement is simplified to the form

READ, List

No *n* is necessary, nor is any FORMAT statement either.

DITRAN for the CDC 1604, on the other hand, is based on U.S.A. Standard Basic FORTRAN, which is defined to be a subset of full FORTRAN or FORTRAN IV. It is, therefore, committed to the FORTRAN IV type of generalized I-O statement. Here an input statement has the general form

READ (*m, n*) List

where *n* is the number of a FORMAT statement as described in Section 2.2, and *m* is the label of a device from which data is read. Different values of *m*, for example, might specify the card reader, a paper-tape reader, any of several magnetic-tape drives, or the console typewriter. This a lot of information to specify, and a lot more than the beginning programmer wants to be bothered with. So in DITRAN all he has to write is

READ (—, —) List

whereupon the standard input device (usually a designated card reader) is activated, and the data can again be read in free format.

In either system the rules and restrictions on placement, arrangement, and form of the data are considerably relaxed. The numbers giving the values of the quantities named in the READ list may be punched in any columns whatsoever on the card,* and the numbers representing the different items on the list may be separated by one or more blank columns, a comma, or a comma followed by one or more blanks. Not only does this mean data can be punched without worrying about which columns they get into, but there is also a great deal of freedom as to how many items may be punched on one card. The input statement at the bottom of page 36, for instance, could be written simply

READ, N, A, B

It could then read in the three items called for from three different cards, or all from one card, or any combination thereof. For example, the data could appear as

*In FORGO, stay between columns 1 and 72. In any system, mind the warning on page 234 about column 1!

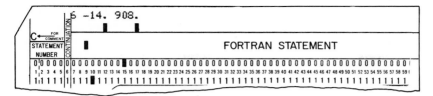

or as

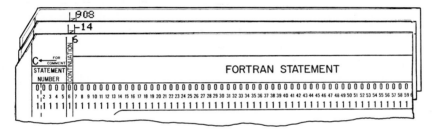

even as

Note that although blanks may be freely used between items to position them anywhere on the card, and even entire blank cards can be inserted, blank spaces may not be used within any datum itself. This is contrary to the freedom existing within the FORTRAN statements in the program proper. Furthermore, the sign is considered part of the datum, too, so that the arrangement + 2.3 will not work.

In mode, the presence of a decimal point establishes the number as a real datum, and it can therefore be read in only as a value for a real-variable name in the READ list. The converse is not true, however. Not only can a number without a decimal point be used as an integer, it can be read in as the value for a real-variable name too. If the processor, looking for a datum to be read in as a real value, encounters an integer, it will affix a decimal point at the right end of the number and store it away as the value of the real variable named in the READ list. It is best, however, to follow the same rule in data as in constants within the arithmetic statements of the program itself—if the variable name is real, include a decimal point with the digits being punched; if integer, do not use a decimal point.

At output time, what a free format system supplies is a standard format. The same two distinctions are made, between integer and real quantities, but the type of output is completely specified by the name appearing in the output list, and no further information needs to be supplied. All the output statement has to say is

PRINT, N, X, Y

For real variables, the most general and flexible way to write them is in floating-point notation, as described on page 25. Hence, when an instruction calls for the output of a real variable in free format, the number will appear in scientific notation consisting of the sign (if minus), a digit, a decimal point, four more significant digits (rounded), followed by the exponent in E notation. Since this is eleven characters of information, and since we would always want at least one space between items, such numbers are always put out right-justified in a 12-column field.

To keep spacing on the page uniform regardless of the type of variable, integers are also put out in 12-column fields. Again the sign is printed only if it is minus, and leading zeros are suppressed to make a natural appearing number.

The effect of the PRINT statement above, then, in outputting the quantities just read in, would be to produce the following line:

6 -1.4000E+01   9.0800E+02

The number of quantities which can appear on one line is limited primarily by the output device. Up to six can be punched on one card, but ten can appear on one line of a 120-character/line printer. If ten items are called for when output is being punched for subsequent printing, the contents of the second card, items 7–10, are usually shifted to the right and caused to appear on the same line as the first six, so that the programmer effectively gets 120-character lines whether he is working with PUNCH or PRINT.

In summary, if free format is available on your computer, use it. Get yourself a healthy bit of experience in successful program running. By the time you get to Chapter 6 you will have a much better feeling for when and how you would like to use FORMAT to dress up your output. It is the authors' experience, however, after six years of working with such systems, that you get so spoiled you will never want to bother with input FORMAT.

Over 300 Areas of Application of Computers*

One of the indications of the tremendous growth of the Second Industrial Revolution is the large number of areas of applications for automatic computers. Following is a list of slightly over 310 types of applications—only 15 years after the first automatic digital computer started working, the Harvard IBM Automatic Sequence Controlled Calculator.

The list will undoubtedly lengthen rapidly. We invite additions, clarifications, and corrections from our readers.

4A.1 BUSINESS

BANKING
Check processing accounting
Corporate trust accounting
Demand deposit accounting
Factoring accounts processing
Fund accounting
Installment loan accounting
Interoffice record transmission, filing, and recall

Loan accounting, records, and analysis
Mortgage loan accounting
Payroll accounting
Personal trust accounting
Real estate loan accounting
Savings and loan postings
Savings Club deposit accounting
Signatures verification
Stockholder records

*From *Computers and Automation,* January, 1960.

BUSINESS
  File maintenance
  Filing operations, single and
    multiple
  Mailing list operations
  Management games
  Management reports using the
    exception principle, and others
  Management statistics analysis
  Management strategy analysis
    and simulation
  Overhead cost allocation
  Payroll determination and issuing
  Production scheduling
  Vending machine programming
  Warehousing and stocking
    records and analysis

FINANCE
  Bond evaluation
  Dividend calculation
  Equipment trust accounting
  Fund analysis
  Portfolio evaluation
  Stock analysis
  Stock price index computed
    hourly, etc.
  Stock transfers

GOVERNMENT
  Census analysis
  Election return analysis
  Mail sorting and routing
  Planning
  Simulation of sections of the
    economy
  Statistical analysis
  Supplies: inventory and control

INSURANCE
  Agency accounting
  Agents' commission calculations
  Automobile coding
  Dividend formula analysis
  Dividend scale calculations
  Gross premiums calculation
  Group annuity calculations
  Group insurance commissions

  Mortality tables
  Net premiums calculation
  Policy reserves calculation
  Renewal rating calculations

LAW
  Crime analysis and prediction
  Laws: analysis and consistency
    studies
  Traffic violations: recording
    accounting, analysis

LIBRARIES
  Abstracting from scientific
    materials
  Information retrieval
  Records and control

MAGAZINE PUBLISHING
  Renewal analysis
  Subscription fulfillment

MANUFACTURING
  Budgeting and forecasting
  Inventory control
  Labor allocation and distribution
  Materials and parts: require-
    ments, allocation, scheduling,
    and control
  Machine tools: control for auto-
    matic reproduction of complete
    parts, etc.
  Machine utilization analysis
  Overhead costs: allocation and
    control
  Process control
  Production load scheduling, fore-
    casting, and control
  Quality control studies
  Repair and maintenance records,
    scheduling, and control
  Vacation scheduling
  Wage and salary analysis

OIL INDUSTRY
  Aerial surveys and exploration:
    analyses
  Bulk stations: wholesale sales,
    billing, accounting

Credit card accounting
Crude oil: analysis of properties, evaluation
Depletion accounting
Economic factors: studies, analysis
Flow: control
Fuel deliveries: degree-day accounting
Gasoline blending
Heat and material balances
Inventory: control, forecasts
Lease and well expenses and investments: records and analysis
Map construction
Market research: studies, applications of operations research
Off-shore installations: studies of design variations
Oil and gas production: accounting
Oil field analysis: correlation of data from different drill holes; correlation of data from seismic tests; estimated amount and direction of flow of fluids through porous rocks
Oil purchase accounting
Quality control
Refinery and gas plant components: design, operation
Refinery shutdown and maintenance: scheduling calculations
Refinery simulation
Royalty calculations
Secondary recovery: analysis
Seismic data reduction
Well logs: corrections
Wells and fields: prorating analysis

PUBLIC UTILITIES
Billing
Circuits and lines: mileage analysis

Demand forecasting
Electric distribution networks
Equipment: attrition and life expectance
Gas distribution networks
Natural gas measurement
Pipe line design
Power distribution calculations
Power plants: stability of control
Power production scheduling
Rate determination
Repair calls: dispatching, scheduling
Sag-tension studies
Steam turbine output
Transmission line design and losses
Water reservoir management

SALES
Accounts receivable, posting and rebilling
Advertising effectiveness analysis
Billing and invoicing
Mailing list updating and addressing
Market research: analysis, simulation of consumer decisions, etc.
Price analysis
Sales analysis
Sales area distribution
Transportation optimization

TRANSPORTATION
Aircraft maintenance scheduling
Air traffic control
Collision warning systems
Elevators: automatic control
Navigating systems
Railroad freight cars: accounting allocation, distribution, control
Rail traffic control centralized
Subways: automatic control
Trains: automatic control
Travel reservations

4A.2 SCIENCE AND ENGINEERING

AERONAUTICAL ENGINEERING
Aerodynamical formulas:
  evaluation
Airframe stress analysis
Critical speed problems
Curve fitting
Factor analysis
Flight simulation
Flight test data reduction
Flight training devices
Flutter analysis
Ground controlled approach:
  programming
Gyroscopic calculations
Heat transfer analysis
Helicopter piloting studies
Navigation training devices
Satellite tracking
Systems evaluation
Theodolite data reduction
Vibration analysis
Wind tunnel data reduction

BIOLOGY
Animals: behavior models
Hybrid optimization
Livestock-feed ingredient-mix:
  optimization
Species characteristics:
  correlation analysis
Species varieties: automatic
  classification

CHEMICAL ENGINEERING
Chemical compounds: structure
  studies
Distillation processes: determina-
  tion of starting times, etc.
Equilibrium equations: studies
Hydrocarbons: structure analysis
Ion exchange column: perform-
  ance appraisal
Mass spectrometer analysis
Organic compounds: file searching
Process control

Process simulation
Reaction analysis

CHEMISTRY
Organic compounds: classifica-
  tion
Spectrum analysis

CIVIL ENGINEERING
Highway engineering
Cut and fill calculations
Photogrammetric data reduction
Route optimization
Traffic density: pictorial
  simulation
Traffic simulation
Transformation of coordinates
Traverse adjustment
Traverse closure

SOILS ENGINEERING
Freezing and thawing of soils
Pressure distribution in layered
  media

ELECTRICAL ENGINEERING
Antenna design
Cathode tube design
Circuit analysis and design
Component design
Electromagnetic wave propagation
  in various media
Filter analysis
Generator calculations
Logical networks: design
Motor calculations
Radar echos
Radio interference
Systems evaluation
Transformer design
Transient performance
Traveling wave tube calculations
Triode design

HYDRAULIC ENGINEERING
Backwater profiles
Compressible and incompres-
  sible flow analysis

Flood and flow forecasting
Flood control
Flood frequency analysis
Flood routing
Ground water, flow of
Hydraulic circuits and components: design
Hydraulic network analysis
Hydroelectric dam design
Multi-purpose water reservoir system: management
Pipe stresses
Reservoir aggradation
Shock-wave effect analysis
Surge-tank analysis
Turbine speed regulation
Unit hydrographs: determination
Water hammer analysis
Wave motion analysis
Wind-wave analysis

LINGUISTICS
Concordances: construction
Syntax pattern analysis
Translation from one language to another
Word frequency analysis

MARINE ENGINEERING
Compartment pressures in emergency situations
Compartment ventilation calculations
Force analysis of space structures
Form calculations
Fuel rate analysis
Gyroscopic-compasses sea-test: data reduction
Hydrostatic functions
Large ship maneuvering
Plate and angle combinations: calculations
Ship displacement calculations
Ship models: extrapolation of observations
Ship waterline characteristics
Shock isolators

Turbine reduction gear systems: vibration analysis
Ullage tables

MATHEMATICS
Boolean algebra calculations
Calculus of variations
Constants, important: evaluation
Curve fitting
Difference equations solution
Differential equations solution
Differentiating symbolically
Eigenvalues and eigenvectors: calculations
Function tables: computation
Integration of functions
Linear programming
Matrix inversion and other calculations
Maximum likelihood functions
Numerical base conversion
Polynomial roots
Simulation of mathematical equations and solutions
Simultaneous linear equations
Stochastic difference equations
Table computation (evaluation of functions)

MECHANICAL ENGINEERING
Air conditioning calculations
Arch analysis and design
Building frames for reinforced concrete construction: Hardy Cross analysis
Cam design
Critical speeds
Foundation settling: effects
Heat flows
Machine vibration analysis
Moments of inertia
Pipe-stress analysis
Reinforced concrete: bending, stress, etc.
Rigid frames: moment distribution analysis

Shell analysis stress distribution

Temperature stresses

Truss analysis: stress and deflections

MEDICINE

Anaesthesia control

Diagnosis of disease

METALLURGY

Alloy calculations

Crystal structure computations

METEOROLOGY

Weather forecasting

MILITARY ENGINEERING

Ballistic trajectories

Bomb impact analysis

Fire control

Missiles: calculations re launching, directing, intercepting, and recovery

Pursuit and combat control

Rocket trajectories

Strategy analysis and optimization

NAVAL ENGINEERING

Cavitation studies

Component attrition rate analysis

Decompression tables

Submerged flow: potential patterns

NUCLEAR ENGINEERING

Neutron diffraction

Radioactive fallout analysis and prediction

Radioactive level calculations

Reactor design and evaluation

Reactor simulators

PHOTOGRAPHY

Color separation negatives: scanner for automatic production

PHYSICS

Cosmic radiation: statistical analysis

Crystallography analysis

Electron distributions

Electron trajectories

Lens coating calculations

Optical ray tracing and optical system design

Thermodynamic equations

STATISTICS

Analysis of variance

Correlation

Factor analysis

Forecasting

Least square polynomial fitting

Moments

Multiple regression

Time series analysis and adjustment

SADSIM: A Single-Address Decimal Computer Simulator

A FORTRAN program to simulate operation of the SAD computer on the 1620 has been developed by the authors. The program, called SADSIM, is written in FORTRAN II, and requires a 40K digit memory 1620 or comparable computer.*

SADSIM has been added to the program library of COMMON, the users group for small IBM computers, as Program 10.2.013. Complete copies of the documentation and/or card decks may be obtained from Program Information Department, IBM Corporation, 40 Saw Mill River Road, Hawthorne, N.Y. 10532, through any IBM customer or IBM branch office.

10A.1 SYSTEM DESCRIPTION

The SAD Computer is a hypothetical single-address decimal stored program computer simulated on the IBM 1620 Computer. Execution is in the interpretive mode, with both normal I–O and extensive tracing options available on an on-line printer. SADSIM is written in FOR-TRAN II and is executable either alone or as a job under MONITOR I.

*A limited version of SADISM, written in 1620 FORTRAN with FORMAT, which will operate on a 1620 with 20K storage, has been written by Russell Johnson, University of Wisconsin—Fox Valley Center, Menasha, Wisconsin.

It should be noted that the integer word length must be set to 5 before compiling SADSIM. Since the source language description is available, it can easily be adapted to other output configurations.

System Characteristics

Address logic	Single address
Instruction word length	5 decimal digits
Number word length	5 decimal digits + sign
	(integer arithmetic, modulo 10^5)
Memory size	1000 words
I–O	1622 card reader/console typewriter or printer
Instruction set	26 types
Registers	10-Digit accumulator
	Instruction register
	Current address register
Register display	By console typewriter or printer

A logical block diagram of the system is shown in Figure 8.6-4.

10A.2 WORD FORMATS AND ADDRESSING

Word Format

A SAD word consists of 5 decimal digits and an associated sign.

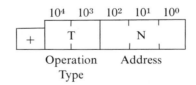

Each word is either a data word of 5 decimal digits and an associated sign, or an instruction with the 2 high-order digits as the OP code (T) and the 3 low-order digits as the address (N). Some instructions also require use of the sign.

Storage Addressing

Each location is directly addressable by a SAD instruction, with addresses ranging from 0 to 996. The ACcumulator (AC), the Product-Remainder register (PR), and the Current Address Register (CAR) are directly addressable as storage locations 999, 998, and 997 respectively.

TYPE	ADDR	MEANING
00 INP	n	Input 1 word into location n
01 STO	n	Store the contents of the AC into location n
02 STT	n	Store type portion of the AC into location n
03 STN	n	Store the address portion of AC into location n
04 CLM	n	Clear AC, and add the number n
05 ADM	n	To AC add the number n
06 RAP		Replace AC by the contents of PR (the address portion is ignored)
07 RPA		Replace PR by the contents of AC (the address portion is ignored)
08 SHL	n	Shift left n places
09 SHR	n	Shift right n places
10 TRA	n	Transfer to location n
11 TRN	n	Transfer to location n if contents of AC is negative
12 TRZ	n	Transfer to location n if contents of AC is zero (0)
13 HTR	n	Halt; when started, transfer to contents of location n
14 OUT	n	Output 1 word from location n
15 CLA	n	Clear AC, and add the contents of location n
16 ADD	n	To AC add the contents of location n
17 SUB	n	From AC subtract the contents of location n
18 MPY	n	Multiply contents of AC by contents of location n
19 DIV	n	Divide the contents of AC by the contents of location n
20 LOD	n	Load n words into locations 1 to n
26 XCH		Exchange the contents of AC and PR (the address portion is ignored)
30 TRP	n	Transfer to location n if AC is positive
36 AAB	n	To AC add the absolute value of the contents of location n
37 SAB	n	From AC subtract the absolute value of the contents of location n
38 ACT	n	Accept from typewriter 1 word into location n

Explanation of address:

000–996	Standard core memory
999	Accumulator (AC)
998	Upper accumulator (UAC)
997	Current address register (CAR)

Figure 10A.3-1 SAD Instruction Set.

10A.3 INSTRUCTION REPERTOIRE

The complete instruction set is shown in Figure 10A.3-1. It is perfectly feasible to work with subsets of the complete instruction set for beginning classes. For example, Figure 8.6-5 illustrates the set used in this text. It has the advantage that the sign of an instruction has no effect, so all instructions can be taken as $+$. The accumulator AC normally refers to the low-order 5 digits, where arithmetic usually takes place.

Arithmetic operations are therefore very similar to integer operations in FORTRAN. The product-remainder register PR contains the high order 5 digits of an arithmetic sum or a product, or the remainder after a division.

INPUT/OUTPUT

INP N (00)   INPut to N. Data input to SAD is normally only from cards read by a FORTRAN format of (6X, I6).

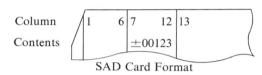

SAD Card Format

The INP N instruction reads 1 card from the card reader, stores the digits from columns 8 to 12 into location N, and sets the sign of N to be the same as the sign of the input word in column 7 of the card (+ or blank is positive, − is negative).

Note: On end of file (last card), an INP N instruction will give the error message:

NO INPUT DATA

and the 1620 will hang up with the Reader No Feed light on the 1620 console. Operator intervention may be required if this occurs.

OUT N (14)   OUTput from N. Output on the console typewriter or printer, using the SAD card format, 1 word from location N (i.e., print the sign in column 7, and the number in columns 8 to 12).

LOD N (20)   LOaD N words. Load the next N cards from the card-read hopper, assumed to be punched in the SAD card format, into locations 1 through N of the SAD memory. This instruction is especially useful to load a program into the SAD computer. A master clear will clear the SAD registers including CAR to 000 and the instruction register to INP 00 000. An INP 00 000 instruction reads 1 word into location 000 and, with CAR 000, then executes it. If this 1 word is a LOD N, an N-word program can be loaded into the SAD memory, and the first instruction following the LOD instruction will be executed. See Figure 10A.4-1 for sample SAD program.

Note: On an End-of-File (last card), a LOD N instruction will give the error message:

NO INPUT DATA

and the 1620 will hang up with the Reader No Feed light on the 1620 console. Operator intervention may be required if this occurs.

ACT N (38) ACcepT N words. Accept 1 word from the typewriter according to the SAD card format and store in location N. This instruction is very difficult to use because both correction of errors in typing and the selection of automatic or manual mode of the SAD computer make use of console switch 4. To be used efficiently it is necessary to leave SAD in the manual mode.

Register Transmission

STO N (01) STOre AC into N. Store the contents of the accumulator AC into location N of the SAD memory. The contents of AC are unchanged.

	BEFORE			AFTER	
	T	N		T	N
IR	0 1	3 5 9		0 1	3 5 9
AC	+ 2 2	2 2 2		+ 2 2	2 2 2
Loc. 359	+ 0 0	7 0 6		+ 2 2	2 2 2

STT N (02) STore the Type portion of AC into N. Store the type portion (high-order 2 digits) of the accumulator AC into location N of the SAD memory. The contents of AC, and the sign of the word in memory, are unchanged.

	BEFORE		AFTER	
IR	0 2 0 0 6		0 2 0 0 6	
AC	− 1 7 6 5 8		− 1 7 6 5 8	
Loc. 006	+ 0 0 0 0 9		+ 1 7 0 0 9	

STN N (03) STore address portion (N) of N. Store the address portion of the accumulator AC into the address portion of location N. After a STN instruction, the sign of the word in memory is the same as the sign of the accumulator.

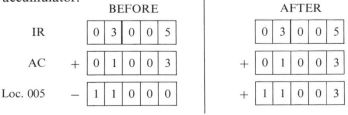

	BEFORE		AFTER	
IR	0 3 0 0 5		0 3 0 0 5	
AC	+ 0 1 0 0 3		+ 0 1 0 0 3	
Loc. 005	− 1 1 0 0 0		+ 1 1 0 0 3	

CLA N (15) CLear AC and Add contents of N. Clear the accumulator to +000000 and add the contents of location N. The instruction CLA 999 will guarantee that the accumulator will be set to 0.

		BEFORE					AFTER				
IR		1	5	0	1	6	1	5	0	1	6
AC	−	8	7	6	5	4	+	0	0	0	0	1
Loc. 016	+	0	0	0	0	1	+	0	0	0	0	1

IR		1	5	9	9	9	1	5	9	9	9
AC	−	9	9	8	9	9	+	0	0	0	0	0
Loc. 999 = AC	−	9	9	8	9	9	+	0	0	0	0	0

Immediate Operations

CLM N (04) CLear AC and add iMmediate N. Clear the accumulator AC to +00000 and add the number N itself. The sign left in the accumulator is the same as that of the CLM instruction itself.

		BEFORE					AFTER				
IR	+	0	4	8	8	8	+	0	4	8	8	8
AC	+	7	7	8	5	9	+	0	0	8	8	8

IR	−	0	4	0	0	1	−	0	4	0	0	1
AC	+	1	2	3	4	5	−	0	0	0	0	1

ADM N (05) ADd iMmediate N. Add to the contents of the accumulator AC the number N itself. Addition is performed algebraically, taking into account the signs of both AC and the ADM instruction itself. Overflow or underflow can occur with this instruction.

	BEFORE	AFTER
IR	+ 0 5 0 0 3	+ 0 5 0 0 3
AC	+ 0 0 0 0 1	+ 0 0 0 0 4
IR	− 0 5 0 0 3	− 0 5 0 0 3
AC	+ 0 0 0 0 1	− 0 0 0 0 2

Register Operations

These instructions are useful to detect overflow and underflow, and to determine the value of the remainder in division and the high-order digits in multiplication.

RAP—(06) Replace AC by PR. Replace the contents of the accumulator AC by the contents of the product-remainder register. The contents of PR are unchanged. After execution of this instruction the contents of AC and the contents of PR are exactly equal. The address portion of the instruction is not used.

	BEFORE	AFTER
IR	0 6 X X X	0 6 X X X
AC	4 3 2 1 0	− 9 8 7 6 5
PR	− 9 8 7 6 5	− 9 8 7 6 5

RPA—(07) Replace PR by AC. Replace the contents of the product-remainder register by the contents of the accumulator. After execution of this instruction the contents of the accumulator remain unchanged. The address portion of the instruction is not used.

	BEFORE	AFTER
IR	0 7 X X X	0 7 X X X
AC	+ 1 2 3 4 5	+ 1 2 3 4 5
PR	− 0 0 0 0 1	+ 1 2 3 4 5

XCH—(26)   eXCHange AC and PR. Exchange the contents of the accumulator and the product-remainder register. The address portion of the instruction is not used.

	BEFORE	AFTER
IR	2 6 X X X	2 6 X X X
AC	+ 1 2 3 4 5	− 6 7 8 9 0
PR	− 6 7 8 9 0	+ 1 2 3 4 5

Shifting

The shift instructions can be used to clear AC and PR in one instruction in the least amount of time.

SHL N (08)   SHift Left N places. Shift the contents of the combined accumulator and product-remainder register left N places. N zeroes are brought in from the right (low-order) end of AC. Shifting 10 or more places clears both registers to 00000.

	BEFORE	AFTER
IR	0 8 0 0 3	0 8 0 0 3
AC	4 3 2 1 0	1 0 0 0 0
PR	9 8 7 6 5	6 5 4 3 2
IR	0 8 0 1 1	0 8 0 1 1
AC	4 3 2 1 0	0 0 0 0 0
PR	9 8 7 6 5	0 0 0 0 0

SHR N (09)   SHift Right N places. Shift the combined accumulator and product-remainder register right N places. N zeroes are brought in from the left (high-order) end of PR. Shifting 10 or more places clears both registers to 00000.

	BEFORE	AFTER
IR	0 9 0 0 2	0 9 0 0 2
AC	4 3 2 1 0	6 5 4 3 2
PR	9 8 7 6 5	0 0 9 8 7

Transfer of Control

TRA N (10) TRAnsfer to N. Replace the contents of the CAR by N, and continue. The SAD computer takes the next instruction from SAD location N and then normally continues to location N + 1.

	BEFORE	AFTER
IR	1 0 0 0 8	1 0 0 0 8
CAR	3 2 1	0 0 8

TRN N (11) TRansfer to N if AC is Negative. Execute a transfer to location N if the sign of the accumulator AC is negative; otherwise go on to the next instruction.

	BEFORE	AFTER
IR	1 1 0 1 5	1 1 0 1 5
AC	+ 0 0 0 0 1	+ 0 0 0 0 1
CAR	0 2 0	0 2 0
IR	1 1 0 1 5	1 1 0 1 5
AC	− 0 1 6 2 0	− 0 1 6 2 0
CAR	0 2 0	0 1 5

TRZ N (12) TRansfer to N if AC is Zero. Execute a transfer to location N if the contents of the accumulator AC are 00000; otherwise go on to the next instruction.

	BEFORE	AFTER
IR	1 2 1 1 5	1 2 1 1 5
AC	0 0 0 0 3	0 0 0 0 3
CAR	0 7 2	0 7 2
IR	1 2 1 1 5	1 2 1 1 5
AC	0 0 0 0 0	0 0 0 0 0
CAR	0 7 2	1 1 5

TRP N (30) TRansfer to N if AC is Positive. Execute a transfer to location N if the sign of the accumulator AC is positive.

	BEFORE	AFTER
IR	3 0 8 2 0	3 0 8 2 0
AC	− 3 6 0 2 0	− 3 6 0 2 0
CAR	6 1 5	6 1 5
IR	3 0 8 2 0	3 0 8 2 0
AC	+ 1 6 0 4 0	+ 1 6 0 4 0
CAR	6 1 5	8 2 0

HTR N (13)   Halt and TRansfer to N on start. Halt the SAD computer and IBM 1620. When start is pushed on the 1620 console, transfer to SAD location N.

	BEFORE	AFTER (After pushing start)
IR	1 3 0 0 7	1 3 0 0 7
CAR	0 1 7	0 0 7

The 1620 then halts with a 48 in the instruction register. Pushing start continues operation.

Arithmetic Instructions

ADD N (16)   ADD N to AC. Add algebraically the contents of location N to the accumulator. If an overflow from AC develops it will cause a carry up to PR. Overflows from PR are lost.

	BEFORE		AFTER
IR	1 6 0 1 5	IR	1 6 0 1 5
AC +	0 1 1 0 3	+	0 1 6 0 4
015 +	0 0 5 0 1	+	0 0 5 0 1

	BEFORE		AFTER
IR	1 6 0 7 3	IR	1 6 0 7 3
PR	0 0 0 0 0	PR	0 0 0 0 1
AC +	9 9 9 9 9	+	0 0 0 0 2
073 +	0 0 0 0 3	+	0 0 0 0 3

SUB N (17)   SUBtract N from AC. Subtract algebraically the contents of location N from the accumulator. Overflow is treated as in the ADD N instruction.

	BEFORE		AFTER
IR	1 7 0 3 5	IR	1 7 0 3 5
AC +	0 0 0 0 7	+	0 0 0 0 4
035 +	0 0 0 0 3	+	0 0 0 0 3

	BEFORE		AFTER
IR	1 7 0 4 6	IR	1 7 0 4 6
AC +	0 0 0 0 7	+	0 0 0 1 5
046 −	0 0 0 0 8	−	0 0 0 0 8

MPY N (18)   MultiPlY AC by N. Multiply the contents of the accumulator (multiplicand) by the contents of N (multiplier). The product is formed in the combined registers AC and PR, with the high-order portion of the product in PR and the low-order portion in AC. The previous contents of PR are lost.

		BEFORE						AFTER				
IR	MPY	1	8	0	2	5	MPY	1	8	0	2	5
PR	−	0	8	3	4	5	+	0	0	0	0	0
AC	+	0	0	0	0	6	−	0	0	1	0	8
025	−	0	0	0	1	8	−	0	0	0	1	8
IR	MPY	1	8	0	7	3	MPY	1	8	0	7	3
PR	+	1	2	3	4	5	+	9	9	9	9	8
AC	+	9	9	9	9	9	+	0	0	0	0	1
073	+	9	9	9	9	9	+	9	9	9	9	9

DIV N (19)   DIVide AC by N. Divide the contents of location N (divisor) into the contents of the accumulator (dividend). The quotient is formed in AC and the remainder is formed in PR. The resulting sign of the AC is the proper algebraic sign of the quotient. The sign of the remainder is the sign of the dividend.

		BEFORE						AFTER				
IR		1	9	1	2	5		1	9	1	2	5
PR	−	8	7	6	5	4	+	0	0	0	0	1
AC	+	0	0	0	0	4	−	0	0	0	0	1
125	−	0	0	0	0	3	−	0	0	0	0	3

$$\frac{\text{DIVIDEND (AC)}}{\text{DIVISOR (MEMORY)}} = \text{QUOTIENT (AC)} + \frac{\text{REMAINDER (PR)}}{\text{DIVISOR (MEMORY)}}$$

AAB N (36)   Add ABsolute value of N to AC. Add the absolute value of the contents of location N into the accumulator. Overflow is treated as in the ADD N instruction.

	BEFORE		AFTER	
IR	3 6 0 1 2		3 6 0 1 2	
AC	+ 0 0 0 0 5		+ 0 0 0 0 8	
012	+ 0 0 0 0 3		+ 0 0 0 0 3	
IR	3 6 0 1 2		3 6 0 1 2	
AC	+ 0 0 0 0 5		+ 0 0 0 0 8	
012	− 0 0 0 0 3		− 0 0 0 0 3	

SAB N (37)   Subtract the ABsolute value of N from AC. Subtract the absolute value of the contents of location N from the number in the accumulator. Overflow is treated as in the ADD N instruction.

	BEFORE		AFTER	
IR	3 7 0 6 3		3 7 0 6 3	
AC	+ 0 0 2 4 6		+ 0 0 2 4 5	
063	+ 0 0 0 0 1		+ 0 0 0 0 1	
IR	3 7 0 7 5		3 7 0 7 5	
AC	+ 0 0 2 4 6		+ 0 0 2 4 5	
075	− 0 0 0 0 1		− 0 0 0 0 1	

10A.4 OPERATION AND THE SAD CONSOLE

Starting SAD

The SAD computer is simulated in the 1620 computer using the FORTRAN program SADSIM. In order to use the SAD computer, the SADSIM program must have previously been compiled and be available for execution. Once this has been done, to run a SAD program put the deck consisting of the SAD program (see Figure 4.1-1 for a sample) into the 1622 card read hopper and push Reader Start. Turn all the console switches on the 1620 off, and push START on the 1620. The computer will commence execution, type the following message, and halt.

```
TO  CLEAR,  TURN  SWITCH   3   ON
AND  PRESS  START.
```

If console switch 3 is turned on at this point and start is pushed, the AC, IR, and CAR will be set to 0 and the following will be typed:

```
TURN  SWITCH   3   OFF,
SET  OTHER  SWITCHES  AS  DESIRED,
AND  PRESS  START.
```

When start is pushed, SAD will have an INP 00000 instruction in the instruction register, which will read in the first card in the read hopper and execute it as an instruction. Normally this will be a LOD N instruction, which will LOD the N cards of the program. This feature may also be used to change an instruction of a program in the SAD memory or to LOD N data words.

A sample SAD program to add 3 numbers, taken from Problem 8.6-4, is shown in Figure 10A.4-1.

```
20017
15015
01051
01052
00053
15051
16053
01051
15052
16016
01052
17017
11004
14051
13001
00000
00001
00003
+00142
+00087
+02365
```

Sad Control

The start and stop button on SAD are the 1620 START and the STOP/SIE keys respectively. The 1620 program switches have the effect on the SAD computer shown in Figure 10A.4-2.

SWITCH	ON		OFF
1	Flow trace =	DISPLAY CAR AND OP	SUPPRESS DISPLAY
2	Full trace =	DISPLAY CAR, OP T, N, AC, AND MEMORY	SUPPRESS DISPLAY
3	Clear	= IN MANUAL MODE CLEAR REGISTERS	Nothing
4	Auto	= AUTOMATIC MODE	MANUAL MODE

Figure 10A.4-2   Program switch control

Full Trace. Figure 10A.4-3, a partial trace of the program shown in Figure 10A.4-1, illustrates the "full trace" feature of SADSIM.

LOCATION	INSTRUCTION			ACCUMULATOR	MEMORY
CAR	OP	T	N		
0	INP	0	0		20017
1	LOD	20	17		
2	CLA	15	15	0	
3	STO	1	51	0	
4	STO	1	52	0	
5	INP	0	53		142
6	CLA	15	51	0	
7	ADD	16	53	142	142
8	STO	1	51	142	
9	CLA	15	52	0	
10	ADD	16	16	1	1
11	STO	1	52	1	
12	SUB	17	17	-2	3
4	TRN	11	4	-2	

Figure 10A.4-3   Full trace of part of the SAD program of Figure 10A.4-1.

It should be noted that the values shown for the accumulator and the memory are the numbers stored in these registers *after* completion of the instruction shown in the instruction register. Since the current address register is assumed to be stepped by one immediately following the locating of a new instruction, and *before* that instruction is executed, it follows that the value displayed in the CAR is the address of the *next* instruction. In the ordinary sequence, this is merely one more than the memory location of the instruction shown; in the case of a transfer instruction, the address replacement (if the transfer condition is satisfied) has already taken place. In all cases, the instruction displayed in the IR is the contents of the CAR location shown in the *preceding* line.

The contents of the referenced memory location are shown only if they represent a different quantity from the contents of AC.

Flow Trace. Using flow trace (console switch 1 on and 2 off), only the CAR location and mnemonic OP code are shown for each instruction executed, as shown in Figure 10A.4-4. This reduced output allows much faster execution, yet still permits looping and branching in the program

LOCATION	INSTRUCTION			ACCUMULATOR	MEMORY
CAR	OP	T	N		
0	INP				
1	LOD				
2	CLA				
3	STO				
4	STO				
5	INP				
6	CLA				
7	ADD				
8	STO				
9	CLA				
10	ADD				
11	STO				
12	SUB				
4	TRN				

Figure 10A.4-4   Flow trace of part of the program of Figure 10A.4-1.

to be followed. It should be noted again that the CAR location shown is that of the *next* instruction.

Dump. If neither trace option suffices to locate and clarify all problems in the program, it is possible to dump the contents of the SAD memory by inserting and executing a DN $y5000$ ($35y50000x00$) where y is 3 or 5 for a 40K or 60K memory, and where x is 1, 4, or 9 for typewriter, card punch, or printer, respectively. Each SAD word in the dump begins with a flag and is a total of 5 digits long.

Terminating SADSIM. The 1620 will remain under control of SADSIM until the system is reset, or, if operating under MONITOR, the FORtran I–O routines read an

‡‡‡‡END OF JOB

Therefore, as many SAD programs can be run in sequence as necessary. The operator can end SAD operation at any time by a reset and next job or a COLD START.

10A.5   OPERATING SADSIM UNDER MONITOR

If a disk file and 40K or more of core are available, one need only place the cards as supplied by the library in the 1622 as a standard FORTRAN II-D job under Monitor I control. The disk must have 397 contiguous available sectors to store the compiled program. After compilation, the DUP routine DREPL is executed which converts the SADSIM program to absolute code. Using this the actual storage required is 239 sectors on the disk. In order to use the DREPL routine a DIM number must be specified, so arbitrarily 0800 is used in the example. As long as the *LDISK and the *LDREPL cards are changed appropriately, any available DIM number may be used.

Once SADSIM has been compiled and loaded on disk, a SAD program can be run merely by executing (XEQS) SADSIM as a job under MONITOR.

Figure 10A.5-1 displays a listing of the control cards used to load SADSIM onto disk, and Figure 10A.5-2 shows the program of Figure 10A.4-1 arranged as a job under MONITOR.

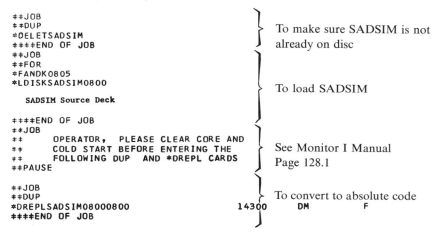

```
‡‡JOB
‡‡DUP                                       To make sure SADSIM is not
*DELETSADSIM                                already on disc
‡‡‡‡END OF JOB
‡‡JOB
‡‡FOR
*FANDK0805
*LDISKSADSIM0800                            To load SADSIM

    SADSIM Source Deck

‡‡‡‡END OF JOB
‡‡JOB
‡‡      OPERATOR,   PLEASE  CLEAR  CORE  AND
‡‡      COLD  START  BEFORE  ENTERING  THE   See Monitor I Manual
‡‡      FOLLOWING  DUP  AND  *DREPL  CARDS   Page 128.1
‡‡PAUSE

‡‡JOB
‡‡DUP                                       To convert to absolute code
*DREPLSADSIM08000800              14300    DM            F
‡‡‡‡END OF JOB
```

Figure 10A.5-1   Monitor I control information when loading SADSIM.

```
            ‡‡JOB
            ‡‡XEQSSADSIM
                    20017
                    15015
                    01051
                    01052
                    00053
                    15051
                    16053
                    01051
                    15052
                    16016
                    01052
                    17017
                    11004
                    14051
                    13001
                    00000
                    00001
                    00003
                    00142
                    00087
                    02365
            ‡‡‡‡END OF JOB
```

Figure 10A.5-2   SAD program as a Monitor job.

10A.6 PROGRAM

The flow chart of SADSIM shown in Figure 10A.6-1 illustrates the simple, straightforward nature of the simulator, and the ease with which other OP codes maybe added if the user desires.

A complete source listing of SADSIM is supplied with the documentation available from the Program Information Department.

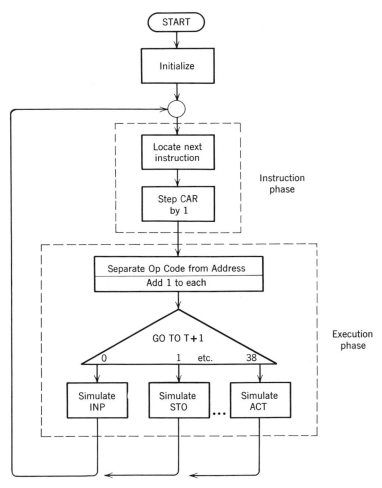

Figure 10A.6-1   Flow chart of SADSIM.

Getting Nonnumeric Facts into the Computer: A Format

So far we have learned only how to read numeric data into the computer. In Chapter 6, we used FORMAT statements containing combinations of I, F, and E specifications for numeric data, and H specifications for alphameric *constants.* For alphameric *variables,* however—alphameric information to be read into the computer at run time as *data,* and later perhaps punched out in the same or changed form— we must learn to use another type of FORMAT specification, the "A" specification.

Example.

Suppose we wish to read into the computer a list of baseball players, the times at bat for each player, and the hits for each player (Figure 13A-1). We want the program to punch out the player's name and his batting average. We note that all the alphameric material (i.e., players' names) has been stored in the two-dimensional floating-point array PLYER(I,J). It is instructive to observe exactly which data are contained by each array element:

$$PLYER(1,1) = (C\ L\ EM\ E) \qquad PLYER(1,2) = (NT\ E\ \cdot\ \cdot)$$
$$PLYER(2,1) = (C\ AR\ T\ Y) \qquad PLYER(2,2) = (\cdot\ \cdot\ \cdot\ \cdot\ \cdot)$$
$$PLYER(3,1) = (R\ OB\ I\ N) \qquad PLYER(3,2) = (S\ ON\ \cdot\ \cdot)$$
$$PLYER(4,1) = (M\ AZ\ E\ R) \qquad PLYER(4,2) = (OS\ K\ I\ \cdot)$$

Dots have been used to help indicate blank spaces where appropriate.

```
      DIMENSION PLYER(100,2), KABS(100), KHITS(100), BAVE(100)
      READ 40,  N
   40 FORMAT (I12)
      DO 10 I = 1, N
      READ 5, (PLYER(I,J), J = 1, 2), KABS(I), KHITS(I)
    5 FORMAT (6X2A5,2I5)
      IF(KABS(I)) 20, 25, 6
   20 PRINT 12, (PLYER(I,J) , J = 1, 2)
   12 FORMAT (6X19HINCORRECT DATA FOR 2A5)
      GO TO 10
   25 BAVE(I) = 0.
      GO TO 14
    6 HITS = KHITS(I)
      ATBAT = KABS(I)
      BAVE(I) = HITS/ATBAT
   14 PRINT 15, (PLYER(I,J), J = 1, 2), BAVE(I)
   15 FORMAT (6X2A5,F5.3)
   10 CONTINUE
      STOP
      END
            4
      CLEMENTE      622   211
      CARTY         455   150
      ROBINSON      568   174
      MAZEROSKI     601   161


ANSWERS


      CLEMENTE     .339
      CARTY        .330
      ROBINSON     .306
      MAZEROSKI    .268
```

Figure 13A-1   Program illustrating use of the "A" specification.

The following two rules must be observed when handling alphameric data using A Format.

(1) The A field may have width from 1 to 5.

(2) Format statements are necessary.

NOPE:
Nim One-Pile Educator

14A.1 PROGRAM DESCRIPTION

NOPE is a program written in FORTRAN II which is designed to demonstrate computer learning by the elimination of wrong moves in a game. The program requires NMRAN or an equivalent pseudo-random number-generating function.

The computer plays a version of NIM which uses only 1 pile of 10 "matches." The name NOPE is an acronym for Nim One-Pile Educator. The original account of this learning process applied to a hand-operated mechanism appears in Block (see list of references, Chapter 14).

The operator and computer alternate, each removing any desired number of "matches" from the pile, up to the move limit, which in this case is 3. The one who is forced to take the last match loses. When it is the computer's turn it makes a random choice from a set of all the possible moves. It also keeps a record of the sequence of moves.

If the machine loses, it backtracks to its last move. If it has a choice of two or three moves, it eliminates the chosen play from the set of possible plays. If the computer has no choice then this is a "lost" position. The machine initiates a stalling game at this point by inserting a 1 as the proper move in this position, but it then repeatedly backtracks to higher levels until it reaches a position where it had a choice, or the beginning of the game. As wrong answers are eliminated, the machine plays a better and better game, until it has only the best solution for each situation.

When the computer wins it makes no change in the set of possible moves.

Note: The pseudo-random number generator degenerates to zeroes after approximately 500 cycles. However, this situation will rarely be reached, since only 30–50 games are needed to eliminate the 17 wrong choices initially in the set.

14A.2 OUTPUT FORMAT

At the conclusion of each game two outputs are produced on punched cards: a record of the game played, and the new set of choices that still exist for each situation. The left half of the output is a record of the game that was just played, plus a cumulative score of games played and games won. The right-hand portion is the set of choices remaining for each situation after the learning process has been applied. Zeroes replace incorrect choices so that they may be easily seen. In this table M is the number of matches when it is the machine's play, MANY(M) is the number of choices which still exist for the machine when there are M matches; NCH is the choice number which will be selected by NMRAN, ranging from one through MANY(M); and the table then presents the move corresponding to that choice number.

A typical game conservation, as carried on through the console typewriter, is displayed in Figure 14.2-3; the record which is produced for later printing is shown in Figure 14.2-4.

14A.3 OPERATING INSTRUCTIONS

NOPE and NMRAN should be executed like any FORTRAN II job consisting of a mainline program and a function subprogram.

After the computer has typed out the instructions on how to play the game, the player is asked for his play. To type in his move he must shift the carriage to NUM and type a single-digit number according to the rules. He then presses release-start, and the machine will play. If the player neglects to upshift the carriage before typing in his number, the machine will read the move as zero.

To terminate the program the operator should turn on Switch 3 and play to the completion of the present game.

14A.4 IMPORTANT VARIABLE NAMES

NPLAY—total number of games played

IWON—number of games won by the computer

M—number of matches which exist at any situation

MANY(M)—number of choices which exist when there are M
matches

NCH—random number chosen by NMRAN

MYCH(M,NCH)—machine's choice when there are M matches, and
random number NCH chosen

MOVE—player's move

L—turn. Player always starts, so odd numbers correspond to player's
turn, and even to machine's turn

LM(L)—record of how many matches existed when L turn

NMRAN—a single-digit random number

NX, K, I, NY, JA, MANYD, MYCHD—dummy variables

14A.5 PROGRAM AVAILABILITY

NOPE was written for the IBM 1620 by Tom Kroncke of the Engineering Computing Laboratory of the University of Wisconsin. It exists
as Program No. 11.055 in the Program Library of COMMON (the users
group for small IBM machines). Documentation and a copy of the
FORTRAN source deck may be obtained from:

International Business Machines Corporation
DP Program Information Department
40 Saw Mill River Road
Hawthorne, N.Y. 10532

For those who prefer to punch their own, or who need to adapt it to
other FORTRANs for other machines, a complete FORTRAN source
listing is given as Figure 14A-1.

```
C       ***** NOPE  (NIM ONE PILE EDUCATOR)  *****                        00001
C       THIS SECTION SETS UP THE GAME                                     00002
        DIMENSIONMYCH(10,3),MANY(10),NWPLC(10,3),LM(11),LCH(11),LEARN(11) 00003
        DIMENSION MANYD(10),MYCHD(10,3)                                   00004
        READ 136,((NWPLC(M,NCH),NCH=1,3),M=1,10)                          00005
        K=0                                                               00006
        TYPE 101                                                          00007
        READ 137,(MANY(M),M=1,10)                                         00008
        TYPE 102                                                          00009
        NPLAY=0                                                           00010
        TYPE 103                                                          00011
        NCH = NMRAN(0)                                                    00012
        TYPE 104                                                          00013
```

```
      IWON=0                                                      00014
      TYPE 105                                                    00015
      DO 1   NCH = 1,3                                            00016
      DO 1   M = 1,10                                             00017
    1 MYCH(M,NCH)=NWPLC(M,NCH)                                    00018
    2 TYPE 106,IWON,NPLAY                                         00019
      IF(SENSE SWITCH 3) 138,3                                    00020
    3 L=1                                                         00021
      M=10                                                        00022
      LM(L)=10                                                    00023
    4 IF(M-10) 6,5,6                                              00024
    5 TYPE 107,M                                                  00025
    6 ACCEPT 108,MOVE                                             00026
C        THIS SECTION CHECKS FOR LEGAL MOVES                     00027
      IF(M-10) 7,8,7                                             00028
    7 IF(MOVE) 11,9,11                                            00029
    8 IF(MOVE) 11,13,11                                           00030
    9 TYPE 109                                                    00031
   10 IF(M) 42,42,5                                               00032
   11 IF(MOVE-3) 12,13,9                                          00033
   12 IF(MOVE-1) 9,13,13                                          00034
   13 M=M-MOVE                                                    00035
   14 IF(M) 9,15,17                                               00036
   15 TYPE 111,M                                                  00037
C        THIS SECTION RECORDS THE LEGAL MOVE FOR THE LEARNING    00038
      LEARN(L)=MOVE                                               00039
      LM(L+1)=0                                                   00040
   16 GO TO 42                                                    00041
   17 LEARN(L)=MOVE                                               00042
   18 L=L+1                                                       00043
      NX=K                                                        00044
   19 K=L                                                         00045
   20 TYPE 110,M                                                  00046
   21 LM(L)=M                                                     00047
   22 I=LM(L)                                                     00048
   23 IF(M) 9,42,24                                               00049
C        THIS SECTION PICKS AND RECORDS THE MACHINES MOVE        00050
   24 IF(MANY(M)-2) 25,27,34                                      00051
   25 NCH=1                                                       00052
   26 GO TO 28                                                    00053
   27 NCH = NMRAN(L)/5 + 1                                        00054
   28 M=M-MYCH(M,NCH)                                             00055
   29 IF(M) 41,30,32                                              00056
   30 TYPE 115,MYCH(I,NCH),M                                      00057
   31 GO TO 36                                                    00058
   32 TYPE 112,MYCH(I,NCH),M                                      00059
   33 GO TO 36                                                    00060
   34 NCH = NMRAN(L)/3 + 1                                        00061
   35 IF(NCH-3) 28,28,34                                          00062
   36 LEARN(L)=MYCH(I,NCH)                                        00063
   37 LCH(L)=NCH                                                  00064
   38 L=L+1                                                       00065
      NX=K                                                        00066
      K=L                                                         00067
   39 LM(L)=M                                                     00068
   40 IF(M) 41,79,6                                               00069
   41 TYPE 113                                                    00070
   42 IWON=IWON+1                                                 00071
      N=K-3                                                       00072
      K=K+1                                                       00073
      NY=NX+1                                                     00074
      IF(NPLAY) 46,44,46                                          00075
   43 N=K-4                                                       00076
      NY=NX                                                       00077
C        THIS SECTION IS THE OUTPUT                              00078
   44 DO 45   J1 = 1,10                                           00079
      I1 = 11 - J1                                                00080
      MANYD(I1) = MANY(J1)                                        00081
      DO 45   J2 = 1,3                                            00082
   45 MYCHD(I1,J2)=MYCH(J1,J2)                                    00083
   46 GO TO (47,51,55,59,63,67,71,75),N                           00084
   47 PUNCH 120,(LEARN(J),J=1,NY,2)                               00085
   48 PUNCH 124,(LEARN(J),J=2,NX,2),(MANYD(N),N=1,10)             00086
   49 PUNCH 131,(LM(L),L=1,K)                                     00087
   50 GO TO 78                                                    00088
   51 PUNCH 119,(LEARN(J),J=1,NY,2)                               00089
   52 PUNCH 124,(LEARN(J),J=2,NX,2),(MANYD(N),N=1,10)             00090
   53 PUNCH 130,(LM(L),L=1,K)                                     00091
   54 GO TO 78                                                    00092
```

```
   55 PUNCH 119,(LEARN(J),J=1,NY,2)                                     00093
   56 PUNCH 123,(LEARN(J),J=2,NX,2),(MANYD(N),N=1,10)                   00094
   57 PUNCH 129,(LM(L),L=1,K)                                           00095
   58 GO TO 78                                                          00096
   59 PUNCH 118,(LEARN(J),J=1,NY,2)                                     00097
   60 PUNCH 123,(LEARN(J),J=2,NX,2),(MANYD(N),N=1,10)                   00098
   61 PUNCH 128,(LM(L),L=1,K)                                           00099
   62 GO TO 78                                                          00100
   63 PUNCH 118,(LEARN(J),J=1,NY,2)                                     00101
   64 PUNCH 122,(LEARN(J),J=2,NX,2),(MANYD(N),N=1,10)                   00102
   65 PUNCH 127,(LM(L),L=1,K)                                           00103
   66 GO TO 78                                                          00104
   67 PUNCH 117,(LEARN(J),J=1,NY,2)                                     00105
   68 PUNCH 122,(LEARN(J),J=2,NX,2),(MANYD(N),N=1,10)                   00106
   69 PUNCH 126,(LM(L),L=1,K)                                           00107
   70 GO TO 78                                                          00108
   71 PUNCH 117,(LEARN(J),J=1,NY,2)                                     00109
   72 PUNCH 121,(LEARN(J),J=2,NX,2),(MANYD(N),N=1,10)                   00110
   73 PUNCH 125,(LM(L),L=1,K)                                           00111
   74 GO TO 78                                                          00112
   75 PUNCH 116,(LEARN(J),J=1,NY,2)                                     00113
   76 PUNCH 121,(LEARN(J),J=2,NX,2),(MANYD(N),N=1,10)                   00114
   77 PUNCH 114,(LM(L),L=1,K)                                           00115
   78 NPLAY=NPLAY+1                                                     00116
      PUNCH 133,(MYCHD(N,1),N=1,10)                                     00117
      PUNCH 134,IWON,(MYCHD(N,2),N=1,10)                                00118
      PUNCH 135,NPLAY,(MYCHD(N,3),N=1,10)                               00119
      GO TO 2                                                           00120
C     THIS SECTION CHANGES THE ANSWER SET                              00121
   79 L=L-1                                                             00122
   80 I=LM(L)                                                           00123
   81 J=LCH(L)                                                          00124
   82 IF(MANY(I)-2) 83,86,92                                            00125
   83 L=L-2                                                             00126
   84 MYCH(I,1)=1                                                       00127
   85 IF(L) 96,96,80                                                    00128
   86 IF(LCH(L)-1) 87,87,88                                             00129
   87 MYCH(I,1)=MYCH(I,2)                                               00130
   88 MYCH(I,2)=0                                                       00131
   89 MANY(I)=MANY(I)-1                                                 00132
   90 MYCH(I,3)=0                                                       00133
   91 GO TO 43                                                          00134
   92 IF(LCH(L)-2) 93,94,89                                            00135
   93 MYCH(I,1)=MYCH(I,2)                                               00136
   94 MYCH(I,2)=MYCH(I,3)                                               00137
   95 GO TO 89                                                          00138
   96 DO 99  J = 2,NX,2                                                 00139
   97 I=LM(J)                                                           00140
   98 JA=LCH(J)                                                         00141
   99 MYCH(I,JA)=1                                                      00142
  100 GO TO 43                                                          00143
  101 FORMAT(49HI AM THE 1620 NOPE, A LEARNING PROGRAM.  THE GAME)      00144
  102 FORMAT(42HIS PLAYED WITH A PILE OF 10 MATCHES.  EACH,9H PLAYER  ) 00145
  103 FORMAT(49HMAY DECREASE THE PILE BY 1, 2, OR 3.  THE ONE WHO)      00146
  104 FORMAT(49HTAKES THE LAST ONE LOSES.  YOU MAY TAKE ZERO ON     )   00147
  105 FORMAT(48HTHE FIRST TURN WHENEVER YOU WANT ME TO GO FIRST.// )    00148
  106 FORMAT(11H I HAVE WON, I3, 7H OUT OF, I3,7H GAMES.//)             00149
  107 FORMAT(15H THERE ARE NOW ,I2,22H MATCHES.  YOU TAKE...)           00150
  108 FORMAT (I1)                                                       00151
  109 FORMAT(45HLA GLOIRE NE PEUT ETRE OU LA VERTU N EST PAS. )         00152
  110 FORMAT(15H THERE ARE NOW ,I2, 9H MATCHES.)                        00153
  111 FORMAT(15H THERE ARE NOW ,I1, 18H MATCHES.  I WIN. //)            00154
  112 FORMAT (8H I TAKE ,I1,14H WHICH LEAVES ,I1,15H .  YOU TAKE...)    00155
  113 FORMAT (7HERROR 1)                                                00156
  114 FORMAT(7H PILE =,2I3,5(I1,I2),    5X,3HNCH,8X,9(1H-,1X),1H-)      00157
  115 FORMAT (8H I TAKE ,I1,14H WHICH LEAVES ,I1,15H .  YOU WIN. //)    00158
  116 FORMAT(7H PLAYER,5X,6(I1,2X), 1X,29HM    = 10 9 8 7 6 5 4 3 2 1)00159
  117 FORMAT(7H PLAYER,5X,5(I1,2X), 4X,29HM    = 10 9 8 7 6 5 4 3 2 1)00160
  118 FORMAT(7H PLAYER,5X,4(I1,2X), 7X,29HM    = 10 9 8 7 6 5 4 3 2 1)00161
  119 FORMAT(7H PLAYER,5X,3(I1,2X),10X,29HM    = 10 9 8 7 6 5 4 3 2 1)00162
  120 FORMAT(7H PLAYER,5X,2(I1,2X),13X,29HM    = 10 9 8 7 6 5 4 3 2 1)00163
  121 FORMAT(7H    1620,6X,5(I1,2X), 2X,11HMANY(M) =  ,9(I1,1X),I1)     00164
  122 FORMAT(7H    1620,6X,4(I1,2X), 5X,11HMANY(M) =  ,9(I1,1X),I1)     00165
  123 FORMAT(7H    1620,6X,3(I1,2X), 8X,11HMANY(M) =  ,9(I1,1X),I1)     00166
  124 FORMAT(7H    1620,6X,2(I1,2X),11X,11HMANY(M) =  ,9(I1,1X),I1)     00167
  125 FORMAT(7H PILE =,2I3,4(I1,I2),I1,4X,3HNCH,8X,9(1H-,1X),1H-)       00168
  126 FORMAT(7H PILE =,2I3,4(I1,I2),    5X,3HNCH,8X,9(1H-,1X),1H-)      00169
  127 FORMAT(7H PILE =,2I3,3(I1,I2),I1,7X,3HNCH,8X,9(1H-,1X),1H-)       00170
  128 FORMAT(7H PILE =,2I3,3(I1,I2),    8X,3HNCH,8X,9(1H-,1X),1H-)      00171
```

```
129 FORMAT(7H PILE =,2I3,2(I1,I2),I1,10X,3HNCH,8X,9(1H-,1X),1H-)        00172
130 FORMAT(7H PILE =,2I3,2(I1,I2),   11X,3HNCH,8X,9(1H-,1X),1H-)        00173
131 FORMAT(7H PILE =,2I3,1(I1,I2),I1,13X,3HNCH,8X,9(1H-,1X),1H-)        00174
132 FORMAT(7H PILE =,2I3,1(I1,I2),   14X,3HNCH,8X,9(1H-,1X),1H-)        00175
133 FORMAT(31X,1H1,9X,9(I1,1X),I1)                                      00176
134 FORMAT(14H 1620 HAS WON ,I3,14X,1H2,9X,9(I1,1X),I1)                 00177
135 FORMAT(14H        OUT OF ,I3,7H GAMES.,7X,1H3,9X,9(I1,1X),I1///)    00178
136 FORMAT (30(1X,I1))                                                  00179
137 FORMAT (10(1X,I1))                                                  00180
138 STOP                                                                00181
    END                                                                 00182
```

```
      FUNCTION NMRAN(L)                                                 S 01
C     THIS FUNCTION GENERATES A SINGLE DIGIT FIXED POINT RANDOM NUMBER  S 02
      IF(L) 3,2,3                                                       S 03
    2 DUM = 7955.                                                       S 04
    3 DSQ = DUM**2 /100.                                                S 05
      ISQ = DSQ / 1.E4                                                  S 06
      OSQ = ISQ                                                         S 07
      DUM = (DSQ/1.E4 - OSQ)*1.E4                                       S 08
      IDUM = DUM/10.                                                    S 09
      EUM = IDUM*10                                                     S 10
      NMRAN = DUM - EUM                                                 S 11
      RETURN                                                            S 12
      END                                                              S 13
```

Figure 14A-1   FORTRAN source listing of NOPE.

Index

Index to Problems